Objects, Components, and Frameworks with UML

The Catalysis^SM Approach

ID608357

The Addison-Wesley Object Technology Series

Grady Booch, Ivar Jacobson, and James Rumbaugh, Series Editors

For more information check out the series web site [http://www.awl.com /cseng/otseries/] as well as the pages on each book [http://www.awl.com/cseng/I-S-B-N/] (I-S-B-N represents the actual ISBN, including dashes).

David Bellin and Susan Suchman Simone,
The CRC Card Book
ISBN 0-201-89535-8

Grady Booch, *Object Solutions: Managing the Object-Oriented Project*
ISBN 0-8053-0594-7

Grady Booch, *Object-Oriented Analysis and Design with Applications, Second Edition*
ISBN 0-8053-5340-2

Grady Booch, James Rumbaugh, and Ivar Jacobson,
The Unified Modeling Language User Guide
ISBN 0-201-57168-4

Don Box, *Essential COM*
ISBN 0-201-63446-5

Don Box, Keith Brown, Tim Ewald, and Chris Sells, *Effective COM: 50 Ways to Improve Your COM and MTS-based Applications*
ISBN 0-201-37968-6

Alistair Cockburn, *Surviving Object-Oriented Projects: A Manager's Guide*
ISBN 0-201-49834-0

Dave Collins, *Designing Object-Oriented User Interfaces*
ISBN 0-8053-5350-X

Bruce Powel Douglass, *Real-Time UML: Developing Efficient Objects for Embedded Systems*
ISBN 0-201-32579-9

Desmond F. D'Souza and Alan Cameron Wills,
Objects, Components, and Frameworks with UML: The Catalysis Approach
ISBN 0-201-31012-0

Martin Fowler, *Analysis Patterns: Reusable Object Models*
ISBN 0-201-89542-0

Martin Fowler with Kendall Scott, *UML Distilled: Applying the Standard Object Modeling Language*
ISBN 0-201-32563-2

Peter Heinckiens, *Building Scalable Database Applications: Object-Oriented Design, Architectures, and Implementations*
ISBN 0-201-31013-9

Ivar Jacobson, Grady Booch, and James Rumbaugh,
The Unified Software Development Process
ISBN 0-201-57169-2

Ivar Jacobson, Magnus Christerson, Patrik Jonsson, and Gunnar Overgaard, *Object-Oriented Software Engineering: A Use Case Driven Approach*
ISBN 0-201-54435-0

Ivar Jacobson, Maria Ericsson, and Agneta Jacobson,
The Object Advantage: Business Process Reengineering with Object Technology
ISBN 0-201-42289-1

Ivar Jacobson, Martin Griss, and Patrik Jonsson,
Software Reuse: Architecture, Process and Organization for Business Success
ISBN 0-201-92476-5

David Jordan, *C++ Object Databases: Programming with the ODMG Standard*
ISBN 0-201-63488-0

Philippe Kruchten, *The Rational Unified Process: An Introduction*
ISBN 0-201-60459-0

Wilf LaLonde, *Discovering Smalltalk*
ISBN 0-8053-2720-7

Lockheed Martin Advanced Concepts Center and Rational Software Corporation, *Succeeding with the Booch and OMT Methods: A Practical Approach*
ISBN 0-8053-2279-5

Thomas Mowbray and William Ruh, *Inside CORBA: Distributed Object Standards and Applications*
ISBN 0-201-89540-4

Ira Pohl, *Object-Oriented Programming Using C++, Second Edition*
ISBN 0-201-89550-1

Terry Quatrani, *Visual Modeling with Rational Rose and UML*
ISBN 0-201-31016-3

Walker Royce, *Software Project Management: A Unified Framework*
ISBN 0-201-30958-0

James Rumbaugh, Ivar Jacobson, and Grady Booch,
The Unified Modeling Language Reference Manual
ISBN 0-201-30998-X

Geri Schneider and Jason P. Winters, *Applying Use Cases: A Practical Guide*
ISBN 0-201-30981-5

Yen-Ping Shan and Ralph H. Earle, *Enterprise Computing with Objects: From Client/Server Environments to the Internet*
ISBN 0-201-32566-7

David N. Smith, *IBM Smalltalk: The Language*
ISBN 0-8053-0908-X

Daniel Tkach, Walter Fang, and Andrew So, *Visual Modeling Technique: Object Technology Using Visual Programming*
ISBN 0-8053-2574-3

Daniel Tkach and Richard Puttick, *Object Technology in Application Development, Second Edition*
ISBN 0-201-49833-2

Jos Warmer and Anneke Kleppe, *The Object Constraint Language: Precise Modeling with UML*
ISBN 0-201-37940-6

Objects, Components, and Frameworks with UML

The Catalysis^{SM} Approach

Desmond Francis D'Souza

Alan Cameron Wills

ADDISON-WESLEY

An imprint of Addison Wesley Longman, Inc.

Reading, Massachusetts • *Harlow, England* • *Menlo Park, California*
Berkeley, California • *Don Mills, Ontario* • *Sydney*
Bonn • *Amsterdam* • *Tokyo* • *Mexico City*

Many of the designations used by manufacturers and sellers to distinguish their products are claimed as trademarks. Where those designations appear in this book and Addison-Wesley was aware of a trademark claim, the designations have been printed in initial caps or all caps.

The authors and publisher have taken care in the preparation of this book, but make no expressed or implied warranty of any kind and assume no responsibility for errors or omissions. No liability is assumed for incidental or consequential damages in connection with or arising out of the use of the information or programs contained herein.

The publisher offers discounts on this book when ordered in quantity for special sales. For more information, please contact:

Corporate, Government, and Special Sales Group
Addison Wesley Longman, Inc.
One Jacob Way
Reading, Massachusetts 01867

Library of Congress Cataloging-in-Publication Data

D'Souza, Desmond Francis
    Objects, components, and frameworks with UML : the Catalysis℠
approach / Desmond Francis D'Souza, Alan Cameron Wills.
        p.   cm. — (The Addison-Wesley object technology series)
    Includes bibliographical references and index.
    ISBN 0-201-31012-0 (alk. paper)
    1. Object-oriented methods (Computer science)   2. UML (Computer
science)   I. Wills, Alan Cameron.   II. Title.   III. Series.
QA76.9.035D76   1998
005.1'17--dc21   98-31109
                                                                      CIP

ISBN 0-201-31012-0

Text printed on recycled and acid-free paper.

1 2 3 4 5 6 7 8 9 10 – MA– 02 01 00 99 98
First printing, October 1998

Contents

Preface

Businesses, and the worlds in which they operate, are always changing. Nearly all businesses use software to support the work they do, and many of them have software embedded in the products they make. Our software systems must meet those business needs, work properly, be effectively developed by teams, and be flexible to change.

First Requirement of Software: Integrity

The first two points are old news; since 1968, the software community has been inventing methods to help understand and meet the business requirements. The average piece of desktop software may work properly in some average sense; perhaps the occasional bug is better than waiting until developers get it perfect. On the other hand, these days so much more software is embedded—in everything from vehicle brakes, aircraft, and smart cards to toasters and dental fillings.[1] Sometimes we should care deeply about the integrity of that software. The techniques described in this book will help you get the requirements right and implement them properly.

Second Requirement of Software: Team Development

To enable development by distributed teams, work units must be separated and partitioned with clear dependencies, architectural conventions and rules must be explicit, and interfaces must be specified unambiguously. Components will get assembled by persons different from the developers, potentially long after they are built; the relationships between the implementations, interface specifications, and eventual user requirements must be testable in a systematic way.

---

1. Teeth have historically been a central part of a user's interface.

This book's techniques will help you build work packages and components with these properties.

Third Requirement of Software: Flexibility

To stay competitive, businesses must continually provide new products and services; thus, business operations must change in concert. Banks, for example, often introduce new deals to lure customers away from the competition; today, they offer more new services via the phone and the Internet than through branch offices. Flexible software, which changes with the business, is essential to competitiveness.

Flexibility means the ability not only to change quickly but also to provide several variants at the same time. A bank may deploy the same basic business system globally but needs to be able to adapt it to many localized rules and practices. A software product vendor cannot impose the same solution on every customer nor develop a solution from scratch each time. Instead, software developers prefer to have a configurable family of products.

This book's techniques will help you partition and decouple software parts in a systematic way.

Flexible Software

The key to making a large variety of software products in a short time is to make one piece of development effort serve for many products. Reuse does not mean that you can cut-and-paste code: The proliferation that results, with countless local edits, rapidly becomes an expensive maintenance nightmare.

The more effective strategy is to make generic designs that are built to be used in a variety of software products. Such reusable assets include code as well as models, design patterns, specifications, and even project plans.

The following are two key rules for building a repertoire of reusable parts.

- They should not be modified by the designers who use them. You want only one version of each part to maintain; it must be adaptable enough to meet many needs, perhaps with customization but without modification.
- They should form a coherent kit. Building things with a favorite construction toy, such as Legos, is much easier and faster than gluing together disparate junk you found in the back of the garage. The latter may be parts, but they weren't designed to fit together.

Reusable parts that can be adapted, but not modified, are called *components*; they range from compiled code without program source to parts of models and designs.

Families of Products from Kits of Components

Hardware designers have been building with standardized components for years. You don't design one new automobile; rather, you design a family of them. Variations are made by combining a basic set of components into different configurations. Only a few components are made specifically for one product. Some are made for the family of products, others are shared with previous families, and still others are made by third parties and shared with other makes of cars.

We can do the same thing with software, but we need technologies for building them, and assembling them, into products as well as methods for designing them.

Component Technology

For a component to be generic, you must provide ways that your clients' designers can specialize it to their needs. The techniques include parameters passed when a function is called; tables read by the component; configuration or deployment options on the component; *plug-points*—a place where the component can be plugged into a variety of other components; and frameworks, such as a workflow system, into which a variety of components can be plugged.

Object-oriented (OO) programming underscores the importance of pluggability, or *polymorphism*: the art and technology of making one piece of software that can be coupled with many others. People have always divided programs into modules; but the original reasons were meant to divide work across a team and to reduce recompilation. With pluggable software, the idea is that you can combine components in different ways to make different software products—in the same way that hardware designers can make many products from a kit of chips and boards—and can do so with a range of delayed binding times (see Figure P.1).

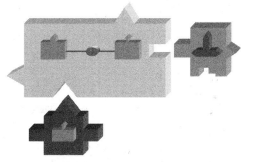

Figure P.1　Component-based assembly, any binding time.

The other great idea reemphasized in OO programming is the separation of concerns. The idea is that each object or component, or reusable part, should have one responsibility and that its design should be as decoupled (independent) as possible from designs and even the existence of other components.

Both these ideas work whether or not you use an OO programming language and whether you are talking about objects in programming, large distributed systems, or departments in a business.

Where Do We See Components?

On a small scale, pluggable user-interface widgets form components. Several such kits come with visual builders, such as Visual Basic, which help you plug the components together. Kits also may extend to small parts outside the user interface domain (for example, VisualAge and JavaBeans). These components all work within one executable program.

On a larger scale, self-contained application programs can be driven by each other; object linking and embedding/Component Object Model (OLE/COM), UNIX pipes and signals, and Apple events allow this to happen. Communicating components can be written in different languages, and each can execute in its own space.

On a still larger scale, components can be distributed between different machines. Distributed COM (DCOM) and Common Object Request Broker Architecture (CORBA) are the latest technologies; various layers underneath them, such as TCP/IP, provide for more primitive connections. When you deploy components on this scale, you must worry about new kinds of distributed failures and about economies of object location. Workflow, replication, and client-server, or n-tier architectures, provide frameworks into which this scale of component can fit. Again, there are tools and specialized languages that can be used to build such systems. Enterprise JavaBeans and COM+ are newer technologies that relieve the component developer of many of the worries of working with large-grained server-side shared components.

A component, on the larger scale, often supports a particular business role played by an individual or department with responsibility for a particular function. Businesses talk increasingly of open federated architectures, in which the structure of distributed components mirrors the organizational structure of the business. When reorganizing a business, we need to be able to rewire software in the same way.

Challenges of Component-Based Development

The technology of component-based systems is becoming fairly well established; not so the methods to develop them. To be successful, serious enterprise-level development needs clear, repeatable procedures and techniques for development, well-defined and standard architectures, and unambiguous notations whereby colleagues can communicate about their designs.

A key technique for building a kit of components is that you must define the interfaces between the components very clearly. This brings us back to integrity. If we are to plug together parts from different designers who don't know one another, we must be very clear about what the contract across the connection is: what each party should provide to and expect of the other.

In component technologies, such as COM, CORBA, and JavaBeans, the emphasis is on defining interfaces. (The idea has a long history, however, stretching back to experimental languages such as CLU in the 1970s.) The same thing is true no matter what the technology: UNIX pipes, workflow, RPC, common access to a database, and the like. Whenever a part can fit into many others, you must define how the connection works and what is expected of the components that can be plugged in.

In Java or CORBA, though, *interface* means a list of function calls. This definition is inadequate for good design on two counts. First, to couple enterprise-scale components, we need to talk in bigger terms: A connection might be a file transfer or a database transaction involving a complex dialog. So we need a design notation that doesn't always have to get down to the individual function calls; and it should be able to talk about the messages that come out of a component as well as those that go in. JavaBeans (and Enterprise JavaBeans) go some of the way in this direction. In Catalysis, we talk about *connectors* to distinguish higher-level interfaces from basic function calls.

Second, function calls that are described only by their parameter signatures do not tell enough about the expected behavior. Programming languages do not provide this facility because they are not intended to represent designs; but we need to write precise interface descriptions. The need for precision is especially acute because each component may interface with unknown others. In the days of modular programming, designers of coupled modules could resolve questions around the coffee machine; in a component-based design, the components may have been put together by two people and assembled independently by a third.

To develop a coherent kit of components, we must begin by defining a common set of connectors and common models of what the components talk to one another about. In a bank, for example, there is no hope of making the components reconfigurable unless all of them use the same definition of basic concepts such as customer, account, and money (at their connectors, if not internally).

Once a common set of interfaces and a common architectural framework are laid down, many designers can contribute components to the kit. Products can then be assembled from the components (see Figure P.2).

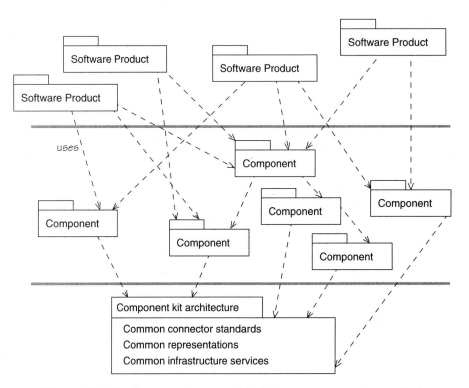

Figure P.2 Products can be assembled from components supplied
by many sources.

What Does Catalysis Provide?

If this component-based scenario seems far-fetched, recall the fate of Babbage's
Analytical Engine. He couldn't make it work because it had so many parts and
they didn't have the machining techniques to make the parts fit together well
enough. Today's machining has enabled working versions to be made. As our
software industry improves its skills and consistency in making matching parts,
we will also make products from components.

This book gathers together some of the techniques we see as necessary for that
movement into a coherent kit. To make component-based development work, we
need our best skills as software designers, and we need to reorganize the ways in
which software is produced.

The techniques and method in Catalysis provide the following:

- *For component-based development*: How to precisely define interfaces independent of implementation, how to construct the component kit architecture and
the component connectors, and how to ensure that a component conforms to
the connectors.

- *For high-integrity design*: Precise abstract specifications and unambiguous traceability from business goals to program code.
- *For object-oriented design*: Clear, use case driven techniques for transforming from a business model to OO code, with an interface-centric approach and high quality assurance.
- *For reengineering*: Techniques for understanding existing software and designing new software from it.

Catalysis and Standards

Catalysis uses notation based on the industry standard Unified Modeling Language (UML) now standardized by the Object Modeling Group (OMG). Both authors have been involved in the OMG standards submissions for object modeling; Desmond's company helped define and cosubmit UML 1.0 and 1.1.

Catalysis has been central to the component-specification standards defined by Texas Instruments and Microsoft, the CBD-96 standards from TI/Sterling, and services and products from Platinum Technology; it has been adopted by several companies as their standard approach for UML-based development. It fits the needs of Java, JavaBeans, COM+, and CORBA development and supports the approach of RM-ODP. It also supports systematic development based on use cases.

Where Does Catalysis Come From?

Catalysis is based on, and has helped shape, standards in the object modeling world. It is the result of the authors' work in development, consulting, and training and is based on experience with clients from finance, telecommunications, aerospace, GIS, government, and many other fields.

Many ideas in Catalysis are borrowed from elsewhere. The Bibliography section lists many of the specific references. We can identify and gratefully acknowledge general sources of the principal features of Catalysis.

- We began applying rigorous methods to object analysis with OMT [Rumbaugh 91]. Integrating snapshots, transactions, state models, treating system operations and analysis models separately from design classes, and the basic ideas of refinement of time granularity date from Desmond's work at this time.
- The rigorous aspects (specifications, refinement, and the influence of VDM and Z) were seen particularly in some previous OO development methods: Fusion [Coleman93], Syntropy [Cook 94], and Bon [Meyer88]. Our interest in applying rigorous methods, such as VDM and Z to objects goes back to Alan's Ph.D. thesis [Wills91].
- Collaborations as first-class design units were first introduced in Helm, Holland, and Gangopadhyay's "contracts" and developed in Trygve Reenskaug's [Reenskaug95] method and tool OORAM.

- Abstract joint actions come from Disco [Kurki-Suonio90], the OBJ tradition [Goguen90], and database transactions as well as from the general notion of the Objectory use case.
- Component connectors have been mentioned in a variety of patterns in recent years. They date back to Wong's *Plug and Play Programming* work [Wong90], previous work (mostly in the Smalltalk arena) on code frameworks, and architecture work on components and connectors [Shaw96b].
- Process patterns are a corruption of work by several of the contributors to the Pattern Languages of Programming conferences.

During the development of Catalysis, we have also had a great deal of input and feedback from many clients and fellow consultants, teachers, and researchers (see Thank You section of this Preface).

How to Read This Book

Don't read it all in one night. If you think this is a bit long for a Preface, wait until you see the rest of the book. What background will you need? Some basic knowledge of UML, OMT, Booch, or Fusion modeling will help; the succinct UML summary by Martin Fowler is quite readable [Fowler98]. If you already know UML, take an early look at the UML perspective in the Appendixes.

Begin with Chapter 1—a tour that leads you through the essence of a design job. Along the way it bumps into all the main Catalysis techniques and ends with a summary of our approach and its benefits. Then read the introduction to each subsequent part (I–V) to get a feel for the book's structure. Most of the subsequent chapters are designed so that you can read the first sections and the summary at the end and then skip to the next chapter. After you've gone through the book this way, go back and dig down into the interesting stuff.

There are places in the book where we discuss some of the darker corners of modeling, and it's safe to skip these sections. We have marked most of these sections with this icon. There are also places where we illustrate implementations using Java; if this is new to you, you can usually skip these bits as well.

Chapters 2, 3, and 4 are groundwork: They tell you how to make behavioral models and what they mean and don't mean. Chapter 5 is essential: how to document a design. Chapter 6, Abstraction, Refinement, and Testing, is about how to construct a precise relationship between a business model and the program code. Chapters 7 through 9 (Using Packages, Composing Models and Specifications, and Model Frameworks and Template Packages) deal with breaking models into reusable parts and composing them into specifications and designs. Chapters 10, 11, and 12 (Components and Connectors, Reuse and Pluggable Design: Frameworks in Code, and Architecture) are about building enterprise-scale software from reusable components. Chapters 13 through 16 are about the process of applying Catalysis, exploring a case study in considerable detail. Depending on your role, here are some suggested routes.

• *Analysts*: Mainstream OO analysis is difficult if you are used to structured methods. In some ways our approach is simpler: You explore system-level scenarios, describe the system operations, capture terms you use in a static model of the system, and then formalize operations using this model. In other ways, our approach is more difficult; we do not like fuzzy and ambiguous analysis documents, so some of the precision we recommend may be a bit unfamiliar for early requirements' activities. Read Chapters 1 through 7, 9, and 13 through 15.

• *Designers*: Object-oriented design is as novel as OO analysis. Again, in some ways our approach is simpler. You start with a much clearer description of the required behaviors, and there is a default path to basic OO design that you can follow (see Pattern 16.8, Basic Design). For doing component-based design, you will use the techniques of an analyst, except at the level of your design components.

If you are already an OO designer, be prepared for a different focus. First, you understand the behavior of a large-grained object (system, component) as a single entity. Then you build an implementation-independent model of its state, and then design its internal parts and the way they interact. You strictly distinguish type/interface from class and always write an implementation class against other interfaces. Read Chapters 1 through 6 (omit sections that go into specification details), 7, 9, 10 through 12, and 16.

• *Implementors*: OO implementation should become easier when the task of satisfying functional requirements has been moved into the design phase. Implementation decisions can then concentrate on exploiting the features of a chosen configuration and language needed to realize all the remaining requirements.

• *Testers*: Testing is about trying to show that an implementation does not meet its specification by running test data and observing responses. Specifications describe things that range from what a function call should do to which user tasks the system must support; the way to derive tests varies accordingly. Read Chapters 1 through 6. Also, read about QA (see Section 13.1, Model, Design, Implement, and Test—Recursively; and Section 13.2, General Notes on the Process), and insist that it be followed well before testing.

• *Project managers*: Consider your goals for using components or objects carefully and the justifications for building flexible and pluggable parts (Chapter 10). Watch out for the project risks, often centered on requirements and infrastructure (Chapter 13). Together with the architect, design and follow the evolution of the package structure (Chapter 7) and how it gets populated; if there is such a thing as development architecture, that is it. Recognize the importance of a precise vocabulary shared by the team (Chapters 2 and 3). Read Chapters 1 through 5, and (optionally) Chapters 6, 7, 12, and 13. Consider starting with "Catalysis lite" (www.catalysis.org).

- *Tool builders*: Catalysis opens new opportunities for automated tool support in modeling, consistency checking, traceability, pattern-based reuse, and project management. Read the book.

- *Methods and process specialists*: Some of what we say is new; the parts fit together, and the core is small, so look closely. Read the book.

- *Students and teachers*: There is material in this book for several semester-long courses and several research projects, and perhaps even for course-specific books. Few courses are based on a rigorous model-based approach to software engineering. We have successfully used the material in this book in several one-week courses and workshops and know of several universities that are adopting it. If you want to use some of the illustrations in this book in your presentations, you need to have permission. Please contact Addison Wesley Longman, Inc. at the address listed on the copyright page.

- *Others*: The activities and techniques in this book apply to both large and small projects, with different emphases and explicit deliverables, and to business modeling, bidding on software projects, out-tasking, and straightforward software development, even though the rigor in our current description might intimidate some. See www.catlysis.org.

Where to Find More

When you've finished the book and are eager for more, there is a Catalysis Web site—www. catalysis.org—that will provide additional information and shared resources, potentially including the following:

- Example models, specification, documentation, and frameworks
- Discussion of problems this book has not yet fully addressed: concurrency, distribution, business process models, and so on
- Web-based discussion forums and mailing lists for users, teachers, consultants, researchers, tire-kickers, and lost souls to share experiences and resources
- Free as well as commercial tools that support the Catalysis development and modeling techniques
- On-line versions of the book and development process patterns
- Modeling exercises and solutions for university use
- Resources to help others use and promote Catalysis, including short presentations to educate fellow modelers, designers, and managers; summary white papers that can be handed out on Catalysis; and so on.

In addition, there are Web sites for each author's company. Each contains a great deal of interesting material, which will continue to be updated:

- http://www.iconcomp.com/catalysis—ICON Computing, a Platinum Technology company (www.platinum.com)
- http://www.trireme.com/catalysis—TriReme International Limited

Thank You

Thanks to our editors—Mike Hendrickson and Debbie Lafferty—for their patience and encouragement; and to our production coordinator, Marilyn Rash, and her team—Betsy Hardinger, copyeditor; Maine Proofreading Services; and Publisher's Design and Production Services for expert, speedy art rendering and typesetting.

Our book reviewers bravely hacked through initial drafts and greatly helped improve this book. To Joseph Kiniry (a heroic last-ditch effort), Doug Lea, Jennie Beckley, Ted Velkoff, Jay Dunning, and Gerard Meszaros—many thanks.

Several others provided comments and ideas: John McGehee, Stuart Kent, Mike Mills, Richard Mitchell, Keith Short, Bill Gibson, Richard Veryard, Ian Maung, Dale Campbell, Carol Kasmiski, Markus Roësch, Larry Wall, Petter Graff, and John Dodd. Aamod Sane and Kevin Shank helped sort out issues with nested packages. We would also like to thank, for useful technical discussions and support: Balbir Barn, Grady Booch, John Cameron, John Cheesman, Steve Cook, John Daniels, Chris Dollin, John Fitzgerald, Ian Graham, Brian Henderson-Sellars, Benedict Heal, John Hogg, Trevor Hopkins, Iain Houston, Cliff Jones, Kevin Lano, Doug Lea, Clive Mabey, Tobias Nipkow, David Redmond-Pyle, Howard Ricketts, John Robinson, Jim Rumbaugh, Susan Stepney, Charles Weir, Anthony Willoughby, and Jim Woods.

We are very grateful to many others for their feedback and suggestions. For their encouragement and support, thanks to Clive Menhinick at TriReme and the team at ICON; and, from Desmond, a very special thanks to Mama, Tootsie and Clifford, and to Tina's parents. Alan would like to thank his remaining friends.

Should these good folks deny any responsibility for the final product, we will gladly take the blame for all inconsistencies and omissions; we know there are some lurking in these pages, and hope you find this work useful despite them.

Desmond Francis D'Souza   *Alan Cameron Wills*

Objects, Components, and Frameworks with UML

The Catalysis[SM] *Approach*

Part I   Overview

Software development continues to be, as always, a difficult and fascinating mixture of art, science, black magic, engineering, and hype. Major advancements have been proposed in the past, and not all of them have delivered what was promised. Object technology, open distributed systems, component technology, and rapid iterative development are all current approaches. Catalysis defines an approach that covers all of them.

Chapter 1, A Tour of Catalysis, provides an abbreviated tour of the method, touching on all of its key points. If you read anything in this book, read this chapter. It explains the basic modeling constructs, the scope of problems to which they apply, and the method's underlying principles. It also walks through an example of applying the method.

Subsequent sections discuss in detail the individual modeling constructs, techniques for factoring and composing models and designs, and process guidelines.

Chapter 1 A Tour of Catalysis

As a software professional you have just been charged with the following task:

> Build an application for a seminar company. Clients call and request courses, and the company says yes or no based on the availability of qualified instructors. Instructor qualification is based on exams instructors take and results from the courses they teach. Your solution must integrate with the existing calendar package (which is currently used for vacation planning) and the database of clients.

Where do you begin attacking this problem? What objects should you have? How should you use the ready-made components? When are you finished?

This chapter takes you through the principal stages of a Catalysis development, covering the main features. We recommend that if you read a single chapter of this book, this should be the one. For a greatly abbreviated sound-bite version of the tour, see Section 1.15, Summary.

The rest of the book deepens and generalizes the ideas developed in this chapter so that they are applicable to a wide variety of problems. In reading the rest of the book, if you feel lost you can reorient yourself by coming back to this chapter.

1.1 *Objects and Actions*

Object-oriented development (OOD) bases the software structure on a model of the users' world within which the software will work. One benefit is that when the users talk in their own vocabulary about changes in their requirements, it is easier to see which parts of the software are relevant. The mirroring is not always exact—because of the constraints of platform, performance, and generalization—but if the differences are localized and clearly documented, the benefits of OOD are not lost.

Object-oriented analysis and design therefore use the same basic concepts to describe both the users' domain and the software. In Catalysis, these basic concepts are the *object*, representing a cluster of information and functionality; and the *action*, representing anything that happens: an event, task, job, message, change of state, interaction, or activity (see Figure 1.1). Catalysis places the action on an equal footing with the object, because good decoupled design requires careful thought about what actions occur and what they achieve.

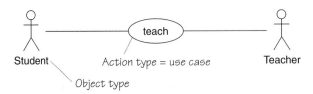

Figure 1.1   Objects participate in actions.

This analysis is done separately from focus on any one object. (Diagrams such as this one help make clear the principal relationships in a description but are insufficient in themselves. They should always be accompanied by an explanation, in a separate dictionary or embedded in narrative, of what the elements represent.)

Unlike some object-oriented design methods, Catalysis does not always begin by assigning responsibility for actions to specific objects. We believe in not taking decisions all at once. We first state what happens; then we state which object is responsible for doing it and which one is responsible for initiating it; and finally we state how it is done.[1]

1.1.1   Actions Affect Objects

Not only do objects participate in actions, but they are also used to describe the actions' effects on the participants.[2] Actions are characterized primarily by what they achieve and only secondarily by how they achieve it; there might be many different ways. For example, we might say

<u>action</u> (student, teacher) :: teach (skill)
<u>post</u>   -- this skill has been added to the student's accomplishments

This description uses new terms to describe the effect, or *postcondition*. It implies that every Student has a set of Skills called her accomplishments. We can draw this relationship or can write it textually as an attribute of Student (see Figure 1.2).

The stars indicate that every Student can have any number of accomplishments, and every Skill can be the accomplishment of any number of Students. The stick figure and the box represent types of objects; the use of the stick figure instead of a box is optional and highlights the expectation that Student may be one of many roles played by any one object.

To visualize an occurrence of an action, we can use a *snapshot*.[3] Figure 1.3 shows sample instances of objects in two states: immediately before and after an

---

1. Details on refinement are in Chapter 6.

2. Defining actions is covered in Chapter 4 and specifying actions in Chapter 3 and Chapter 4.

3. Snapshots are described in detail in Section 2.2.

Figure 1.2   Participants have associations.

example occurrence of the action. In this book, the alterations in the "after" state are shown in bold; you might prefer to draw them in two colors.

The associations may represent real-world relationships: if we asked Jo some deep question about lettuce curling, she should now know the answer. Or associations can represent software: there is now a row in a database table saying that Jo has completed the lettuce-curling course, or Jo's name is in a record somewhere. The useful aspect of associations is that we don't have to say exactly how they are realized, but we can still make meaningful statements about how actions affect them.

This use of the associations, or a *static model*, to provide a vocabulary for the actions, or a *dynamic model*, gives a clear guide as to what objects you need: those that are required to describe the actions.

1.1.2   Precise Specifications

Associations provide a vocabulary in which it is possible to describe the effects of actions as precisely as in programming language:

<u>action</u> (student, teacher) :: teach (skill)
<u>post</u>   -- this skill has been added to the student's accomplishments
            student.accomplishments = student.accomplishments@pre + skill

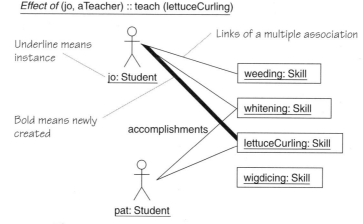

Figure 1.3   Action occurrence and snapshots.

A *postcondition* is a relationship between the before and after states; @pre refers to the before state.

Postconditions allow us to make precise statements about what happens in a business or what is required of a piece of software even though we are working at an abstract level. Unlike natural-language requirements documents, these specifications are abstract and yet precise. Experience shows that the effort of writing them exposes inconsistencies that would be glossed over in natural language. Although there is extra effort involved, it saves work further down the line and focuses attention on the important issues.

1.2   *Refinement: Objects and Actions at Different Scales*

Figure 1.4 shows a picture of some interacting . . . let's just call them "things" for a moment. Each one has a set of tasks it can perform, and each one performs its tasks in part by making requests to others. You can look at the picture in different ways and at different scales.[4] The picture might represent the seminar business, the boxes representing departments interacting to achieve the corporate goals. We could look inside any department and find the same sort of picture, with different people sending one another memos and documents and exchanging phone calls. Some of the actors in the picture might be pieces of software such as the scheduling system; we could zoom in on one of these boxes and find the same kind of picture again, showing major components such as the vacation planner.

Looking inside any component, we can identify the same kind of structure again: if it's an object-oriented program, the units will be (we hope) neatly encapsulated objects. Each object has a set of tasks it performs and data that it uses to

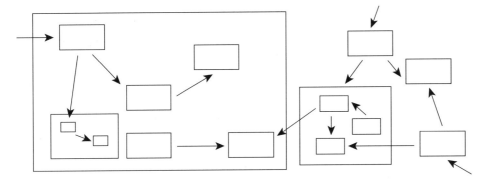

Figure 1.4   Objects at all scales interact.

---

4. For more than you ever wanted to know about refinement, see Chapter 6.

perform these tasks—just as, at the larger scale, the people have their jobs to perform, and their filing cabinets and Internet browser shortcuts are full of (we hope) relevant information.

We consider the essential issues in design to be the same at all scales, with some differences only in detail. To this fractal[5] picture, we apply a fractal method. In this book, we call all these units *objects:* business departments, machines, running software components, programming language objects. The interactions between them are called *actions,* a term that encompasses big business deals, phone calls, bike rides, file transfers, electronic signals, taps on the shoulder, function calls, and message sends in an object-oriented programming language. Like objects, actions contain smaller actions and are parts of bigger ones.

1.2.1   Actions at Different Scales

The seminar system is part of a larger organization, some aspects of which we must understand before we can design it. The company teaches courses to clients. We show the interaction as an ellipse (see Figure 1.5). We can *zoom in* on the action to show a more detailed picture, as in Figure 1.6. We can draw another diagram to relate together the two levels of description, stating that the teach action is a composition made up of the smaller ones. Or we can overlap them on the same diagram (see Figure 1.7).

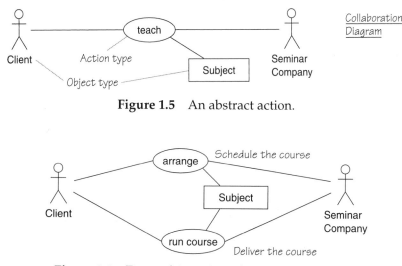

Figure 1.5   An abstract action.

Figure 1.6   Zoomed-in actions that constitute teach.

---

5. A fractal picture has the same appearance at all scales.

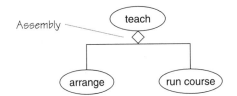

Figure 1.7   Showing action constituents.

We haven't detailed here how the composition works. The smaller actions might happen in parallel or in sequence, or they might be repeated: we give that detail separately. One way to do that is with a *sequence diagram*. This is used to illustrate a typical occurrence of an action (see Figure 1.8). The horizontal bars in these diagrams are occurrences of actions; the vertical bars are instances of objects.

By contrast, the ellipses in the previous diagrams are *action types* representing definitions of all the interactions that can take place. The actors they link are *types* of object: each type describes a role that specific instances can play. (We don't always put arrows on the actions at this stage, because each action may represent a sequence of smaller interactions between the participants; there may be several alternative sequences, each of which has a different initiator. We'll see shortly how we distinguish who does the teaching and who gets taught.)

Notice that the different levels of detail correspond to the way we normally account for things in everyday life. You might say, "I had a Java course last week from SeminoMax" to a friend who doesn't care when or whether you arranged it in advance, or whether they grabbed you off the street. But such detail is appropriate when you work out exactly how to become taught.

Of course, the arrange or the run_course can be further detailed into finer and finer actions, some of which might involve or be inside computer software.

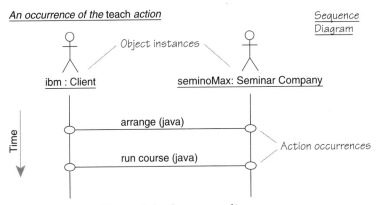

Figure 1.8   Sequence diagram.

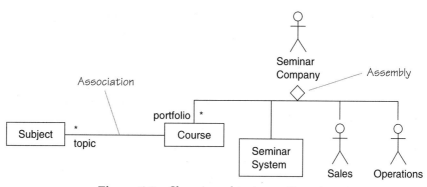

Figure 1.9   Showing object constituents.

1.2.2   Objects at Different Scales

The objects can also be detailed or abstracted. A seminar company has a Sales department and an Operations department; a Seminar System, which helps coordinate activities; and a portfolio of courses, each of which deals with a number of Subjects (see Figure 1.9). As before, boxes are the default representation of object types. We can use stick figures instead to highlight roles; several roles can be played by one object. There is no implication that the stick figures represent individual people, although there is usually some human element involved.

The line from Course to Subject is an association; it represents the fact that you can ask about a Course, "What topics does it cover?" and the answer will be a set of Subjects. By implication, you can ask which Courses have any one Subject as their topic. The association says nothing about how the information is represented or how easy it is to obtain. Like objects and actions, associations can be refined, going into more detail about the information they represent.

At this level of refinement, we can show that the arrangement of courses is dealt with not only by the Seminar Company as a whole but more particularly by Sales, assisted by the Seminar System; and Operations run courses, also with the help of the Seminar System (see Figure 1.10).

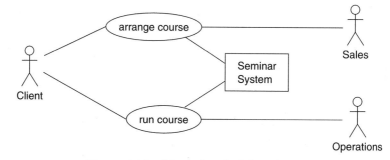

Figure 1.10   More-detailed description.

Normally we zoom actions and objects at the same time. Notice that at the coarser scale, you are not compromising the truth but only telling less of it. Everything you say in the big picture is still true when you look at the finer scale.

This technique of zooming in and out is useful when you're seeking to understand what a business does and why it does it. It is also useful for understanding the requirements on a software component separately from the internal design and for understanding the overall design separately from the fine detail. The ability to see not only the big picture but also how it relates to the fine detail is essential to coherent, traceable, maintainable design.

1.3 *Development Layers*

Abstraction is the most useful technique a developer can apply: being able to state the important aspects of a problem uncluttered by less-important detail.[6] It's equally important to be able to trace how the more-detailed picture relates to the abstraction. We've already seen some of the main abstraction techniques in *Catalysis*—the ability to treat a complex system as one object and to treat complex interactions as one action and yet state the outcome precisely. This approach contrasts with more-traditional design techniques in which *abstract* also tends to mean *fuzzy,* so you can't see whether a statement is right or wrong because it might have many different interpretations.

Different projects will use these abstraction techniques differently. Some project teams may work with a simple design that needs little transformation from concepts to code. Others, starting with an existing system and existing procedures for using it, may need to abstract its essentials before devising an updated solution.

A "vanilla" development from scratch is typically treated in two to five layers of abstraction:[7] bigger projects have more abstraction layers, each one separately maintained. Typical layers are as follows.

- *Business model (sometimes called domain or essential model):* Describes the users' world separately from any notion of the target software. This model is useful if you are building a range of software all in the same world or as a draft to transform into a requirements spec.
- *Requirements specification:* Describes what is required of software without reference to how it is implemented. This spec is mandatory for a major component or complete system. It may be approached differently when the complete system is created by rapidly plugging kit components together.[8]

---

6. For an overview of the development process, see Chapter 13.

7. There are many "routes" through the method—see Section 13.2.1.

8. Heterogenous components: see Section 10.11. Homogenous component kits: see Section 10.6.

- *Component design:* Describes on a high level how the major components collaborate, with references to a requirements specification for each one. It is needed if there are distinct major components.

- *Object design:* Describes how a component or system works, down to programming language classes or some other level that can be coded (or turned into code by a generator). It is mandatory.

- *Component kit architecture:* Describes the common elements of the way a collection of components work together, such as standard interaction protocols. It is needed to allow a variety of developers to build interoperable components that can be assembled into families of products.

1.4 *Business Modeling*

The examples we have looked at so far are typically part of a business model.[9] The main objective is for the model to represent how the users think of the world with which they work. A great many of the questions that arise during a project can be uncovered by good business modeling.

The construction of a business model is a subject for a book in itself. Typically, there is a cycle of reading existing material and interviewing domain experts.

- The starting questions are "What do you do?" and "Whom do you deal with?"
- Every time a verb is mentioned, draw an action and add to your list of questions "Who and what else participates in that? What is its effect on their state?" The answers to these questions lead you to draw object types and to write postconditions; these in turn lead to associations and attributes with which to illustrate the effects.
- Every time you introduce a new object type, add to the list of questions "What actions affect that? What actions does it affect?" Or ask it individually about the type's associations and attributes.
- Go up and down the abstraction tree. Ask, "What are the steps in that action?" "What are the parts of that object?" "What does that form part of?" "Why is this done?"

Here's an example.

> ANALYST THINKS: *What is the postcondition of* (Client, SeminarCo) :: arrange (Subject)?
> ANALYST SAYS: *What is the result when a client arranges a course with you?*
>
> CLIENT: *We find a course that suits the subject they're interested in. Then we must find an instructor qualified to teach that course. We assign him or her to do a run of the course for the client on a date the client is available. An instructor is available when not on vacation or doing another course.*

---

9. A more detailed discussion of business modeling is in Chapter 14.

ANALYST: *Presumably it's a rule of the business that instructors can teach only courses they're qualified for; and an instructor can't be on more than one holiday or assignment on the same day.*

ANALYST THINKS: *So we need to refer to instructor qualifications and their schedules, including vacations and assignments to course runs along with the dates, courses, and clients for any assignment (among other things).*

1.4.1   Static Models and Invariants

This interview yields the static relationships and attributes[10] shown in Figure 1.11. (The analyst decided that CourseRun and Vacation are both kinds of Instructor-Outage—that is, situations when that instructor is not available.)

These business rules can be written as *invariants:*

> inv -- for every CourseRun, its instructor's qualifications must include the course
> CourseRun :: instructor.qualifications -> includes (course)

> inv -- for any Instructor, and for any date you can think of, the number of the
>   instructor's outages on that date is never more than 1
> Instructor :: d:Date :: outage[when=d] <= 1

An invariant, like a postcondition, is written by following the links from a given starting point. The invariants are described informally and are written in a simple language of Boolean conditions and set relationships. Again, their power lies in the ability they give you to write unambiguous statements about abstract descriptions.

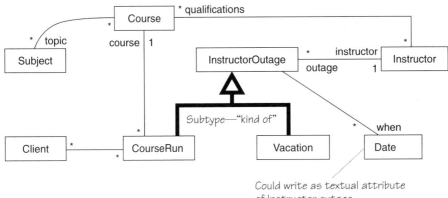

Figure 1.11   Static type model.

---

10. Static invariants are detailed in Section 2.5; precise action specification is discussed in Section 3.4.

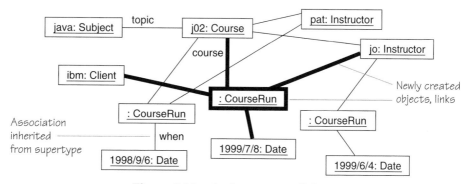

Figure 1.12   Action postconditions.

The action's postcondition can be written in terms of these static relationships. We can draw snapshots to help visualize the effect (see Figure 1.12). This might lead to some follow-up questions—"What actions affect the Instructor's qualifications? What other actions create an outage?"—and so on.

<u>action</u> (c: Client, s: SeminarCompany) :: arrange (t: Course, d: Date)
<u>post</u>   -- a new CourseRun is created with date, client, course
          r : CourseRun.new [date=d, client=c, course=t,
               -- assigned instructor who was free on date d and qualified
                 for the course
             instructor.outage@pre[when=d] = 0 &
             instructor.qualifications -> includes (t)]

1.5 *Model Frameworks as Templates*

Some of the same patterns of relationships and constraints crop up frequently in modeling and design. In a package separate from our project-specific models, we can define a generic modeling framework for resource allocation; it acts as a macro-like template that can be applied in many places. A template can contain any of the modeling constructs in the form of both diagrams and text. Additionally, any name can be written as a <placeholder>, which will be substituted when it is applied to a model.[11]

The resource allocation constraints of the seminar company are quite common. They can be generalized as shown in Figure 1.13. Now we can re-create the original model by using the generic model for resource allocations. We can easily add allocation of, say, rooms (see Figure 1.14).

The framework is applied twice, with placeholder names substituted as indicated. Each substitution for <Resource> defines a derived type <Resource>_Use.

---

11. Such frameworks can be used in a great many ways; see Chapter 9.

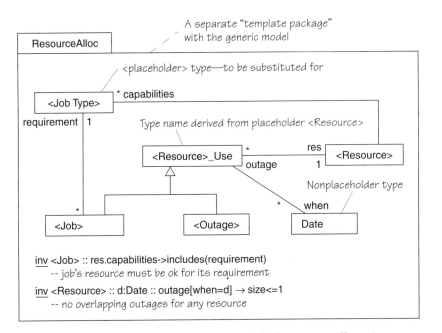

Figure 1.13   Generic framework model of resource allocation.

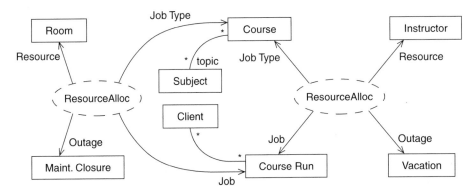

Figure 1.14   Applying the resource allocation framework.

The framework applications can be *unfolded* to reveal the complete model. The benefits of frameworks are that they simplify a picture, and, having been tried and tested, they often deal with matters you might not have thought of (such as the possibility of a Room being closed). The details and precise specifications have already been worked out for you.

Templates can also contain actions and can be used to generalize interaction protocols between components.

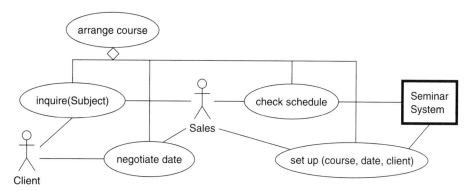

Figure 1.15   Zooming in to the software system boundary.

1.6 *Zooming In on the Software: System Context*

The seminar company uses a software system[12] to run its courses. If we proceed with our successive refinement, we will get down to interactions between people and the Seminar System, which we initially treat as one object (see Figure 1.15). Once again, we can draw a sequence diagram to illustrate how the refinement works (see Figure 1.16).

What other roles does the Seminar System play? The Operations department uses it to schedule the various tasks involved in running a course and to record the qualifications and availability of instructors. Also, the administrators perform various systems management and peformance tuning tasks on it (see Figure 1.17).

We can show separately how these objects and actions are part of what we've already seen. Some objects and actions, such as those associated with the system management tasks, may not be relevant to what we've seen at the abstract level (see Figure 1.18).

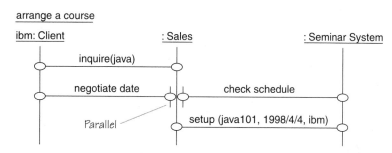

Figure 1.16   Sequence diagram, including the role of the software system.

---

12. For information about describing a system's context and proceeding to specify it, see Chapter 15.

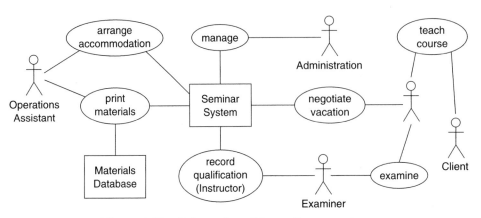

Figure 1.17   Other roles of the software system.

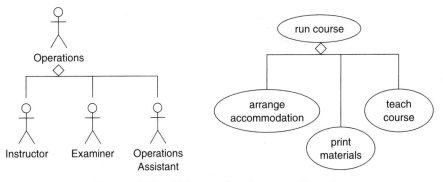

Figure 1.18   Object and action constituents.

So we can now see the actions in which a Seminar System takes part from the viewpoints of several different users. (Notice that even when we focus on the system we're proposing to design, we don't limit ourselves to the actions that the system is immediately involved with. We also show, for example, teach course, to emphasize that this is not among the responsibilities of this particular object but is something that will be taken care of by someone else.)

We can also trace the software requirements back through the assembly (or refinement) links up to the business goals: print materials is part of run course, which is part of teach. Presumably, we could go further up and see that teach is part of make_money or maybe satisfy_ego—who knows what motivates pedagogues?

1.7 *Requirements Specification Models*

Now that we know which actions we want our software to take part in, we have the option of making the descriptions more precise. We can describe the effect of each action on this system.

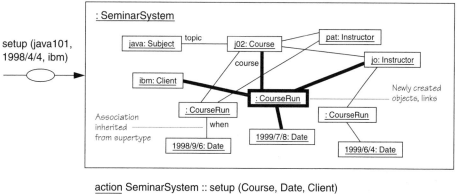

action SeminarSystem :: setup (Course, Date, Client)

post   A new CourseRun has been created, linked to the client,
        the date, the course, and any Instructor available on that
        date qualified to teach that course

Figure 1.19 Snapshots of software system state.

As in the business model, we can illustrate an effect of an action with a snapshot; but in this case, the objects in the diagram denote not the real objects but rather the system's own representation of them (see Figure 1.19). For that reason, we draw the objects inside the system boundary, whereas the actions themselves are still actions on the whole system. This reflects the fact that we are not yet designing the internals of the system.

A system requirement spec often reflects the business model closely, as in this case. Differences occur where the business model is general to several systems or where there are special mechanisms of interaction with the user apart from any domain concepts (for example, a word processor's clipboard has nothing to do with the basic model of the documents it manipulates).

Gathering all the specs for the actions the system is required to take part in and the static models needed to draw snapshots for those specs, we compile a formal functional requirements model. Notionally it looks like the drawing in Figure 1.20.

The static model is a hypothetical picture created for the purpose of explaining the system's externally visible behavior to its users. There is no absolute mandate on the designer to implement it exactly with classes and variables that directly mirror the types and associations in the spec. For one thing, there are usually complications such as managing a database, and there may be performance and decoupling issues. Also, there may be a layer of partitioning between different components. Nevertheless, it is preferred to keep to this model as much as possible to minimize the conceptual gap between the users and the implementation.

The principal difference between the requirements spec and the implementation is therefore that the latter defines how the objects inside the design collaborate to achieve the effects specified by the former.

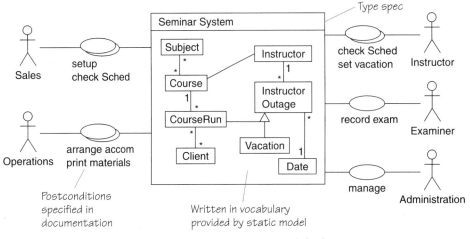

Figure 1.20 Requirements model—basis.

1.7.1 Packaging

A *package* is a container for development artifacts; it is roughly like a section in a document or a directory in a file system.[13] A package contains some quantity of information, whether models, software, refinement relationships, or information about the structure of other groups of packages. Development work should be separated into packages. Typical packages might contain a component specification; a component implementation; a reusable collaboration framework; and a single type specification. Documentation is part of a package; document structure parallels the package structure.

A real requirements document[14] will be spread over many pages, covering action specifications, narrative, rationale, and so on. Different external views of the system might be partitioned across multiple packages, separated from packages that will reflect internal design decisions (see Figure 1.21). One package can import another: if one set of terms refers to another, in code or in models, you should import its package; if you want to say something to relate two other descriptions, use a package that imports them both.

It is often useful to manage dependencies on the package level, checking that the number of dependencies from and to any one package is not too large.

1.8 *Components*

The actions we've so far documented at the Seminar System boundary are abstract in two dimensions. First, they show us nothing of how they are implemented

---

13. Chapter 7 says more about packaging.

14. For guidelines on how to structure documentation, see Chapter 5.

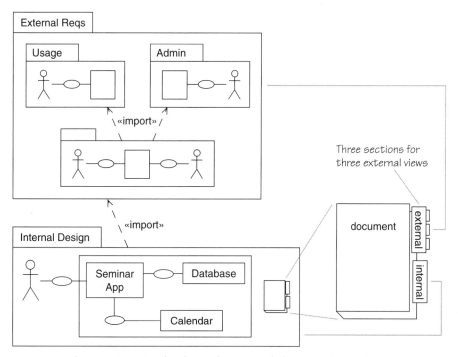

Figure 1.21   Multiple packages and document structure.

inside any of their participants, and in particular our system. Second, each of them still represents what will turn out to be a more detailed dialog; by refining in this dimension, we ultimately get down to menus, keystrokes, and mouse clicks. But let's take the implementation track and peer inside the system.

Our sample system consists of several major components.[15] They could be modules within a single program, or they could be running on different machines. There is a seminar scheduler and a separate vacation planner (and that is just the way we use a more general calendar program).

1.8.1   Two Versions of the System Design

Actually, there are two designs for this system. In version 1, the vacation calendar, the qualifications database, and the seminar planner are not significantly coupled in software: it's up to the Sales people to make sure that they don't schedule a course for an unsuitable or recuperating Instructor (see Figure 1.22).

Version 2 of the system does some of this work: it compiles a list of the available instructors within a range of dates (see Figure 1.23). We introduce a role

---

15. More discussion of component-based design is in Section 10.11 and Section 16.3. A broader discussion of component technology is in Chapter 10.

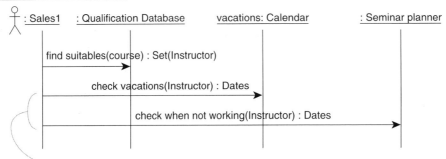

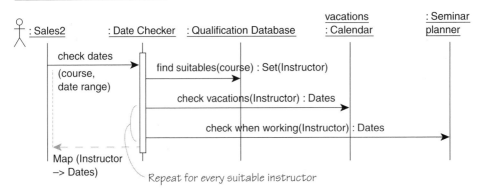

Figure 1.22   Sequence diagram including internal software components.

Figure 1.23   Alternative sequence diagram, design version 2.

called Date Checker, which might be combined with others in some object not yet decided, such as a Schedule; it may be useful to create such a role explicitly. Again, we can summarize the breakdown of actions and objects, as shown in Figure 1.24.

Not only are the two variants of the system different, but so are the users. Although the effects achieved by the overall action are equivalent, the details of using the two systems are different—human salespeople would need retraining, and mechanical ones would need reprogramming—so we give them different type names. Nevertheless, many of the System components are the same (that is, different instances of the same designs).

(For the sake of the illustration, we've cut a corner here. The different system variants imply different operating procedures throughout, so we should strictly go up to the topmost level of analysis at which the system was introduced and break it all down separately.)

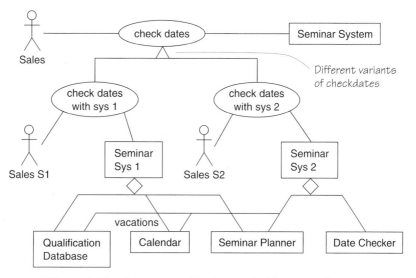

Figure 1.24   Summary of action and object constituents.

1.8.2   Roles

We have begun to put arrows on the actions because they have definite initiators. At this stage we can also identify roles[16] that should be played by the same component—because they access the same information or their functions are closely related. The Date Checker, for example, might turn out to be a role of the same component that helps Sales staff set up courses[17] (see Figure 1.25).

The façade symbol denotes an object type that we could draw with a plain box. The symbol highlights the nature of this object's role as an interface between the central components of the system and the users.

1.8.3   Partitioning the Model between Components

Each of the components[18] performs only some of the system's functions and includes only part of its state, which we can see by drawing the static models (see Figure 1.26).

Each component has its own model. Because some of them are more general than required for this system—for example, the Calendar associates any Strings with dates and is not specific to Instructors and CourseRuns—not all of them use the same vocabulary. But we can *retrieve* or map the separate components' models back to the system model. For example, each SeminarSystem::Instructor is primarily

---

16. Façades and other interface issues are discussed in Section 6.6.4.

17. Chapter 8 explains composition of roles (and other descriptions).

18. A full discussion of such partitioning from business to code is in Section 10.11.

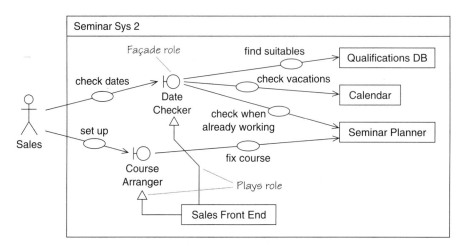

Figure 1.25   Combining roles in the design into Sales FrontEnd.

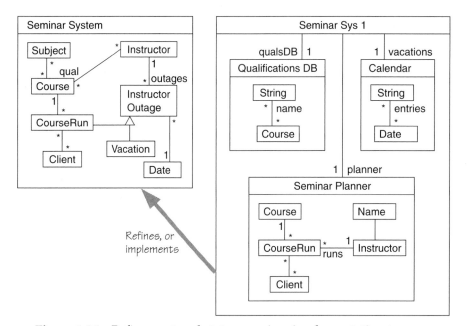

Figure 1.26   Refinement and state mapping: implementation to spec.

represented in Seminar Sys 1 components by a String, which is the Instructor's name. To obtain the associations of a SeminarSystem::Instructor given a String n, use these definitions:

```
qual = qualsDB.courses [name=n]
     -- all the courses in the qualsDB linked to name n
outages = vacations.dates [n:entries]
```

-- all the dates in the vacations component whose entries contain the name n
+ planner.instructors [name=n].runs
-- all runs associated with those instructors in the planner that have name n

In this manner, we can reconstruct all the attributes and associations we used in the requirements model from the component design.

1.8.4   Collaborations

Now let's compare the functional requirements summaries for the spec and implementation 1 (see Figure 1.27). The dashed boxes are collaborations.[19] A *collaboration* is a collection of actions and the types of objects that participate in them. Note that it is the collaboration that is being refined rather than only the software systems, because the different versions require different user behaviors to achieve the requirements. The same thing generally applies to collaborations between components or objects at any scale.

Catalysis treats collaborations as first-class units of design work. This is because we take seriously the maxim that decisions about the interactions between objects are the key to good decoupled design. Collaborations can be generalized and applied in many contexts.

1.8.5   Postcondition Retrieval

Each action can be documented with a postcondition in the terms of its participating component. We can check that, given the mappings between the components' models and the overall specification, the various operations in Seminar Sys 1 achieve what was set out for them in the requirements spec for Seminar System.

For example, Calendar::make_entry is supposed to implement SeminarSystem:: set_vacation. Let's presume that the postcondition of make_entry is to associate a String to a Date. In the preceding section, we said that what the spec calls Outages include the dates in which the instructor's name appears in the vacations diary. So make_entry of the Instructor's name will indeed add an outage, as required by the spec's set_vacation. With a bit more work, we can document how some sequence of find suitables, check vacation, and check working together constitute a correct implementation of the abstract action check schedule.

A practical advantage of postconditions is that they can be executed as part of a test harness. As we've just seen, this is true even when they are written in terms of an abstract model: the retrievals can be used to translate from the implementation to the specification's terms.

---

19. The refinement of collaborations is covered in Chapter 6.

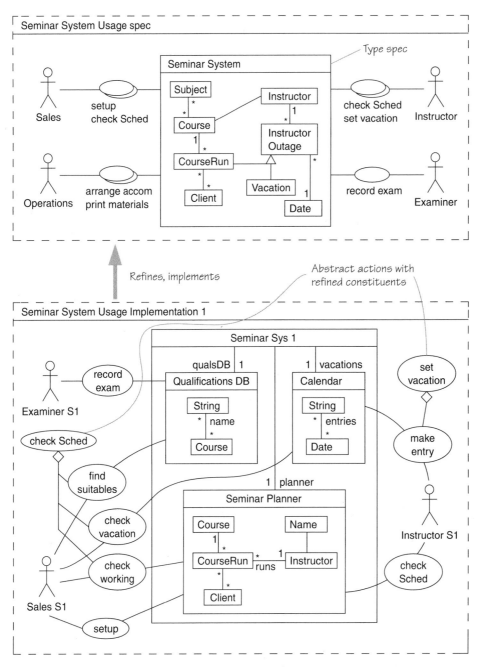

Figure 1.27   Action refinement.

1.9 *Assigning Responsibilities*

Until now we have used actions to represent something that happens between a set of participants. We can write exactly what the outcome is but still abstract away from the exact dialog: who takes responsibility for what and how the outcome is achieved. So we could draw, for example, Figure 1.28.

This is part of the Catalysis philosophy of being able to write down the important decisions separately from the detail. At some stage in a completed design, we must have rendered all actions down to a dialog, in which each action is a message with a definite sender (with responsibility for initiating the action), a receiver (with responsibility for achieving the required outcome), and parameters (that do what the receiver asks of them). These are called *directed* actions; when viewed strictly from the side of the receiver, they are called *localized* actions.

Directed actions may be implemented in CORBA, in COM, as method calls in an OO programming language, or as a set of calling conventions in some other style; the directed actions are mapped based on technical architecture choices.[20] There is still a dialog at some level (such as call and return), but this is set by the architecture and local conventions rather than being specific to the participants.

A general strategy for assigning responsibilities is to begin with the holder of the responsibility as a separate role, such as VacationScheduler (see Figure 1.29). Then you decide whether and how to combine the roles (see Figure 1.30).

So when you describe roles in a collaboration using types, you can still defer decisions about how those roles are packaged into objects or components. Appropriate combinations are those that place responsibilities together whose nature and implementation may be changed together.

1.9.1   Flexibility and Decoupling

As a designer, you have a number of concerns. Your job is to put together some objects and make a bigger one that meets a requirement. You must be clear what

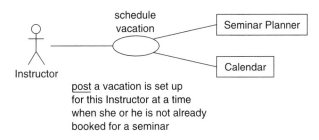

Figure 1.28   An action postcondition can abstract a detailed dialog.

---

20. Technical architecture is discussed in Section 10.7 and Section 12.6.

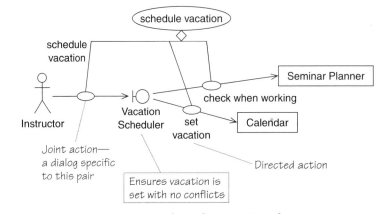

Figure 1.29   Role and interaction design.

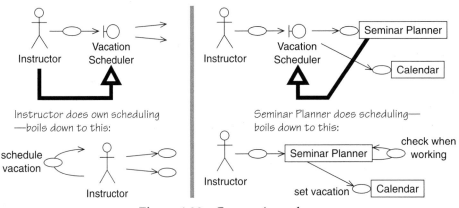

Figure 1.30   Composing roles.

that requirement is; you must ensure that the design meets the requirement (perhaps renegotiating the requirement after the design!), and you must bring in the finished result on time with the available resources. You need considerable skill to balance these constraints.

A further constraint, traditionally not so high on the list, is the primary thrust of object-oriented and component-based design. This is to ensure that the finished system not only works but also can be changed easily to meet changing business requirements.

We do this (on any scale) by *decoupling:* separating concerns.[21] The object that deals with vacations need not be the same as the one that deals with exams. The

---

21. Section 7.4 discusses package-level decoupling. Design patterns (such as Pattern 16.15, Role Decoupling, or Pattern 16.17, Observer) provide specific techniques for decoupling.

two concerns should be separated so that (1) it is easy to change the way that vacations are scheduled without disturbing how exams are set and (2) it would be possible to create a different configuration of the same kit of objects in which there were vacations but no exams or vice versa.

The design may also have to provide for a family of related products rather than only one end product. For example, our seminar company's branches in various countries may have to comply with various local regulations. One solution is to make several copies of the code and make small modifications to the code wherever the differences apply. As other modifications are made through time, the national versions will become separate and will need separate teams of programmers to maintain them. A better solution is to move all the national differences into one object so that we need substitute only that one to set up for a different country.

This skill of decoupling, or separation of concerns, distinguishes good designs from those that merely work. Decoupling (at any scale) means a careful distribution of responsibilities among the objects and careful design of how they collaborate to achieve the overall goals of the larger object of which they form a part.

Because this skill is crucial, in Catalysis we provide the means to separate different layers of design decisions:

- The behavior that is required (postconditions)
- Assignment of responsibilities (roles and collaborations)
- The way each object and action is implemented (successive refinement)

1.9.2   Component Frameworks

Let's look at an overall view of the second implementation of the Seminar System, the one with the front end. Indeed it could have different front ends for the different user roles. This view (see Figure 1.31) combines the various façade roles we've discussed previously.

The Seminar System Implementations may be complete in the sense that every required action is dealt with, but what we see in the diagram are specifications of the components. We can't really take our money and go home until we've procured or made an implementation for each one.

In fact, there may be several implementations for each component, but the functional success of the overall scheme is dependent only on their specifications. The choice of implementation to *plug in* to each component socket is independent of the others (at least from a functional point of view—there may be performance or other couplings).

In general, a component framework is a collaboration in which all the components are specified with type models; some of them may come with their own implementations.[22] To use the framework, you plug in components that fulfill the

---

22. Chapter 11 discusses such framework techniques. Specific techniques for "plugging in" to a larger implementation are discussed in Section 11.5.

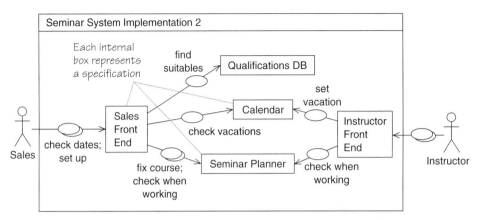

Figure 1.31   A specification of the design.

specifications. The plug-in implementations may do far more than the spec requires; that doesn't matter, provided that we can retrieve the models and post-conditions as we illustrated before. For illustration, let's draw implemented objects in bold (see Figure 1.32).

Preferably, the relationship between the sockets in the framework and the components that plug in to them is a pure implementation relationship not involving inheritance of program code. Inheritance in that sense tends to introduce coupling between the superclasses and the subclasses. It restricts the plugs and sockets to being written in the same language, and it means that the framework designers must provide some source code, which they may not want to give away.

1.9.3   Component Kits

Car designers don't usually design a car entirely from scratch. At least the nuts and bolts are usually borrowed from previous designs. Designers usually design a whole family of products, which are built from a kit of components.[23] The components are built to a common architecture—that is, a set of design conventions that allow interoperability between components in many different configurations. Steering wheels might have different shapes, but all of them have the same attachment to the central shaft. Components from different kits are hard to couple together, because they don't share architecture.

Our seminar system might one day be expanded to support scheduling equipment, invoicing the clients (as soon as possible) and paying the instructors (as late as possible). Several such systems may be federated in the different branches of the company worldwide (so that they can borrow resources from one another). Different branches may want different configurations of the system to support

---

23. The need for standardization across components is discussed in Section 10.2.2.

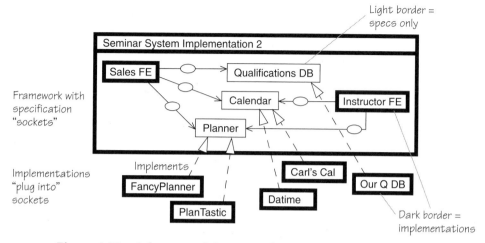

Figure 1.32   A framework is a partial implementation with specs of missing parts.

their own working practices (as determined by analysts and written down as a business model).

This family of software systems is best built with pluggable components. Some of this partitioning will allow behavior to be changed easily by plugging in alternative components; other partitioning will reflect the fact that operations and accounting departments are distributed to different rooms and use different computers.

The component architecture covers three principal areas:

- The choice of technology (CORBA, function calls, and so on) for connecting components.
- The interchange models—how Clients, Instructors, and so on are represented. This is done with static models.
- Definition of abstract *connectors*[24] between components and their realization down to localized actions (see Figure 1.33). This is done with template collaborations, showing a scheme of interaction that can be mapped into specific types for any pair of components.

---

24. See Section 10.8.3 for specifics on how to define abstract connectors.

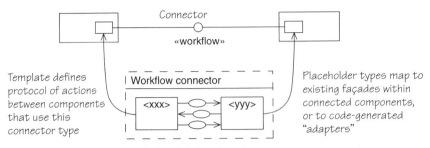

Figure 1.33 Defining higher-level component connectors.

1.10 *Object-Oriented Design*

Components can be treated as robustly packaged objects.[25] This might mean that a component comes with a test kit, that it is designed to be fairly defensive against its interlocutors that do not observe the documented preconditions, that it executes in its own space, and that it can cope with intermittent failure of its neighbors. All the principles we have discussed hitherto are therefore just as applicable within a single programming space as they are between objects that are distributed all over the planet.

Nevertheless, it is often useful to make a distinction between a component layer of design and an object layer. There are factors that in practice impose differences in style. One is that there may be significant replication of information between the components in a distributed system, for both performance and reliability reasons. A component generally works with others (including people) to support a particular business-level action (or *use case*); an object generally represents a business concept. These two process-biased and object-biased views give rise to separate tiers in many designs.

The vanilla process of object-oriented design begins with the types used for a component model and turns many of them into classes (see Figure 1.34). Hence, Instructor, Course Run, and Course now become classes. Collaborations are worked out and roles are assigned to the classes, as we did for components in Section 1.8. The actions at this level are finally standard OO messages. The associations become pointers, decisions are made about their directionality, and object cleanup is designed (if garbage collection is not built into the language).

Design patterns are used to guide these decisions (as they can be used throughout the development process). The end result of OO design is a collection of

- Classes that encapsulate program variables and code.

---

25. More-detailed discussion of object-oriented design can be found in Chapter 16. Classes and types in OO languages are discussed in Section 3.13.

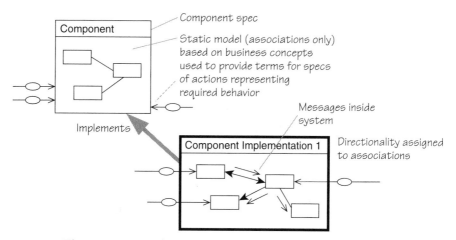

Figure 1.34   Package imports and structured documents.

- Types that define the behavior expected at the interfaces to classes. Classes implement types. In some design styles, all parameters and variables are declared with types; classes are referred to in the code only to instantiate new objects, and even that is encapsulated within *factory* objects.

1.11 *The Development Process*

There is no single process[26] that fits every project: each one has different starting points, goals, and constraints. For this reason, we provide *process patterns* that help you plan a project appropriately to your situation. However, there are some general features.

- *Component-based development:* The main emphasis of component-based development (CBD) is on building families of products from kits of interoperable components. CBD separates design into three major areas:
  - *Kit architecture:* The definition of common interconnection standards, in which great skill and care are required
  - *Component development:* Careful specification and design and subsequent enhancement of reusable assets
  - *Product assembly:* Rapid development of end products from components
- *Short cycles:* The principles of rapid application development (RAD) are recommended. In particular, short development cycles with a well-defined goal at the end of each cycle are good for morale and for moving a project forward. Also, we follow the maxim "Don't wait until it's 100% done" for any one phase.

---

26. For a process overview, see Chapter 13. The entire process is detailed in Part V.

- *Phased development:* This approach is sometimes known as the Empire State Building: take a small vertical slice as far as you can as early as possible in order to get early feedback. Build the rest gradually around it. Phased development is possible if the design is well decoupled.

- *Variable degree of rigor:* The extent to which postconditions are written in a formal style or in natural language is optional. We prefer more rather than less rigor because we have found it helps find problems early.

The same variability applies to the number of separate layers of design you maintain. Clearly, more layers require more maintenance work as well as suitable support tools.

- *Robust analysis phase:* The construction of Catalysis business and requirements models covers more than in the more conventional style. In Catalysis, more of the important decisions are pinned down. As a result, there is less work later in the design stage and less work over the maintenance part of the life cycle, the part that accounts for most of a software system's cost. (To cope with any uncomfortable feeling of risk that this approach may generate, see the remarks in Sections 1.11.2 and 1.11.3.)

- *Organizational maturity:* Depending on where your team is in its organizational maturity, there are different ways to approach and adopt Catalysis. If your team is used to a repeatable process with defined deliverables and time scales, fuller adoption would be advised; otherwise, start with a "Catalysis lite" process. The team should be prepared to learn the same notations and techniques so as to be able to communicate effectively, and management should sign up to invest in component design and to provide resources for migration.

1.12 *Three Constructs Plus Frameworks*

Catalysis is based on three modeling concepts—type, collaboration, and refinement—and frameworks are used to describe recurring patterns of these three (see Figure 1.35). With these concepts we build a great variety of patterns of models and designs. Types and refinement are familiar to people who are accustomed to precise modeling. Collaborations and frameworks are perhaps more novel, and they add an important degree of expressive power.

1.12.1   Collaboration: Interactions among a Group of Objects

The most interesting aspects of design involve partial descriptions of a group of objects and their interactions. For example, a trading system might involve a buyer, a seller, and a broker. Their behavior can be described in terms of their detailed interaction protocols or, more abstractly, in terms of a single high-level action, trade.

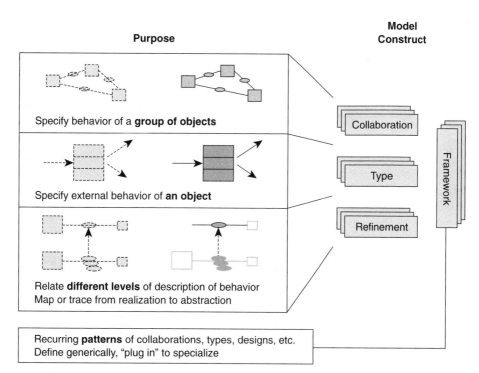

Figure 1.35   Three modeling constructs, with patterns as frameworks.

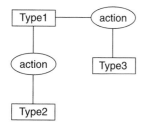

A collaboration defines a set of actions between objects playing roles relative to others in the collaboration. It provides a unit of scoping—constraints and rules that apply within versus outside the group of collaborators—and of refinement: more-detailed realizations of joint behavior. Each action abstracts details of multiparty interactions and of detailed dialogs between participants.

Chapter 4, Interaction Models: Use Cases, Actions, and Collaborations, describes modeling of interactions among a group of objects.

1.12.2   Type: External Behavior of One Object

A type defines an object by specifying its externally visible behavior. Whereas a class describes one implementation of an object, a type does not prescribe implementation; you can have many implementations of the same type specification.

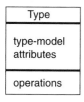

Precise description of behavior needs an abstract model of the state of any correct implementation and of input or output parameters. Catalysis uses a *type model* for this. Types specify behavior in terms of the effect of operations on conceptual attributes. For a simple type, these attributes and their types are listed textually; more-complex types may have a type model drawn graphically and even factored into separate drawings.

Chapter 2, Static Models: Object Attributes and Invariants, describes how attributes abstract variations in the implementation of object state. Chapter 3, Behavior Models: Object Types and Operations, describes how operation specifications describe externally visible behavior of an object, independently of algorithmic and representation decisions.

1.12.3   Refinement: Layers of Abstraction

A *refinement* is a relationship between two descriptions of the same thing at two levels of detail, wherein one—the *realization*—*conforms* to the other—the *abstraction*. A refinement is accompanied by a mapping that justifies this claim and shows how the abstraction is met by the realization.

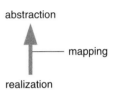

There are several kinds of refinement. A component design—a realization—refines the component specification—its abstraction. A class implements its behaviors in terms of a particular representation that conforms to a type spec. A particular sequence of fine-grained actions may realize a single, more abstract action. Refinement in Catalysis is more general than the standard ideas of subclassing and subtyping.

A significant part of a Catalysis development process consists of refining or abstracting a description, creating a series of refactorings, extensions, and transformations that ultimately shows the implementing code to conform to the highest-level requirements abstraction (although not necessarily produced in top-down order!). Reengineering, whether business or code, consists of abstracting the existing design to a more general requirement and then refining it to a new design having better performance and so on. In Catalysis, a *design review* is largely concerned with refinement: what did you set out to build, and how did you build it?

Catalysis uses *packages* to separate design units that will be managed separately, such as different levels of abstraction, permitting reuse of abstract models by multiple independent realizations. A package groups a set of definitions—including types, actions, and collaborations—that can then be *imported* into other packages, making its definitions visible in the importing package.

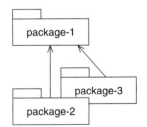

Chapter 6, Abstraction, Refinement, and Testing, discusses refinement in detail; basic forms of refinement are introduced in Part II, Modeling with Objects.

1.12.4   Frameworks: Generic, Reusable Models and Designs

Specifications, models, and designs built with the three preceding constructs all show recurring patterns. The collaborations for processing an order for a book at an on-line bookstore and for accepting a request to schedule a seminar are also similar in structure—a generic collaboration.

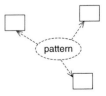

The key to such patterns is the relationships between elements, as opposed to individual types or classes. An application of such a pattern specializes all the elements in parallel and mutually compatible ways. Catalysis provides a fourth construct to capture the essence of such patterns: frameworks. A *framework* is described as a generic package; it is applied by importing its package and substituting problem-specific elements for the generic model elements as appropriate.

Chapter 9, Model Frameworks and Template Packages, describes how frameworks are defined in Catalysis and shows how frameworks provide an enormous degree of extensibility to a modeling language.

1.13   *Three Levels of Modeling*

As shown in Figure 1.36, Catalysis addresses three levels of modeling: the problem domain or business, the component or system specification (externally visible behavior), and the internal design of the component or system (internal structure and behavior).

1.13.1   Problem Domain or Business: The "Outside"

The term *domain* or *business* covers all concepts of relevance to your clients and their problems—that is, the environment in which any target software will be deployed. If you are designing a multiplexor in a telecommunication system, your users are the designers of the other switching components, and the business

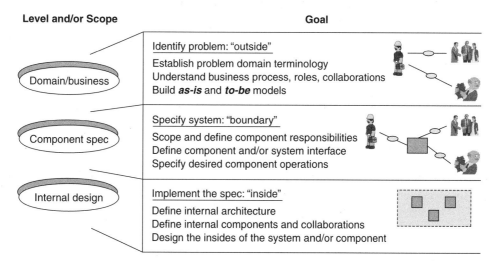

Figure 1.36   Three recursive levels of description.

model will be about things such as packets, addresses, and so on. If you are redesigning the ordering process of a company, the business model is about orders, suppliers, people's roles, and so on.

There may be many views of a business. The concerns of the marketing director may overlap those of the personnel manager. Even when they share some concepts, one may have a more complex view of one of them than the other. The modeling constructs support separating and joining of such views. Chapter 14, How to Build a Business Model, describes how to go about building a business model.

1.13.2 Component Specification: The "Boundary"

A component specification describes the external behavior required of the component. Catalysis uses a type specification to describe behavior that is visible at the boundary between the component and its environment. A type specification defines the actions in its environment that a component or object participates in.

Chapter 10, Components and Connectors, discusses more-general component models, in which the kinds of the *connectors* between components can themselves be extended to include new forms of component interaction, such as *properties* and *events*. Chapter 15, How to Specify a Component, describes how to go about writing a component specification.

1.13.3 Component Implementation: The "Insides"

The internal design of a component describes how it is assembled from smaller parts that interact to provide the required overall behavior. The design is described as a collaboration, and it must conform to the specification of the component. Note that the "outside" for this design is the type model in the component specification.

At some point during internal design, you must consider the implementation technology and make trade-offs on performance, maintainability, reliability, and so on. Hardware choices (solitary or distributed) and software choices (database, user interface, programming language, tiered architectures) affect how the system is implemented.

Chapter 16, How to Implement a Component, describes how to do the internal design of a component. Chapter 10, Components and Connectors, discusses how to define component designs abstractly and precisely; and Chapter 11, Reuse and Pluggable Design: Frameworks in Code, discusses the design of pluggable class and component frameworks.

1.14 *Three Principles*

Catalysis is founded on three principles: abstraction, precision, and pluggable parts (see Figure 1.37).

1.14.1   Abstraction

To *abstract* means to describe only those issues that are important for a purpose, deferring details that are not relevant.

The word *abstract* often has connotations such as esoteric, academic, and even impractical. In our context, however, it means to separate the most important aspects of a problem from the details, enabling us to tackle first things first. Abstraction is essential in dealing with complexity.

▶ *abstraction*   A process of hiding details that provides the following benefits:
   – The ability to deal with far-reaching requirements and architecture decisions uncluttered by detail
   – Layered models—from business rules and processes to code
   – Methodical refinement and composition of components

Think of a software development project as a stream of decisions. Some of them depend on others. There would be no point in trying to design database tables before you establish what the system is going to do. In other words, some decisions are more important than others; making them is a prerequisite to getting the others right.

The important abstractions include the following.

• *Business model and rules:* The context our design is operating in
• *Requirements:* What must be done, as opposed to how it is to be achieved

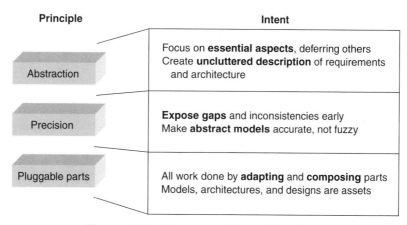

Figure 1.37   Three principles of Catalysis.

- *Overall schemes of interaction:* General descriptions without detailed protocols
- *Architecture:* The big decisions about major patterns and components
- *Concurrency:* Which functions can be performed simultaneously and how they will avoid interference while working in coordination

The important choices often don't get made, or even noticed, until way down the line, often in coding. And almost as often, people worry about trivial problems to avoid tackling the big issues.

We need a language to describe the important decisions separately from the clutter of performance and platform issues involved in full implementations. Typical programming languages are better suited for expressing solutions than problems. For this reason, requirements and other high-level descriptions are usually written in a mixture of prose and ad hoc diagrams.

1.14.2   Precision

Whereas code is precise, natural language and ad hoc diagrams are not. How often do groups of analysts or designers discuss requirements around a whiteboard and leave with different interpretations of the problem to be solved? or produce reams of documents ridden with latent bugs and inconsistencies? Documentation that is concise and accurate is far more likely to be useful.

▶ *precision* A characteristic of accuracy that allows you to do the following:
   - Expose gaps and inconsistencies early by being precise enough to be refutable
   - Trace requirements explicitly through models
   - Support tools at a semantic level well beyond diagrams and databases

During implementation, the unforgiving precision of the programming language forces any gaps and inconsistencies to the surface. For this reason, many of us feel confident about a design only when the code has been written. Unfortunately, code also makes us deal with many detailed language and platform-specific issues.

Abstract descriptions are not necessarily ambiguous. If I say "I am quite old, really," that's ambiguous. You might think I am geriatric or perhaps that I am a teenager pleased at nearing the age of 18. But if I say "I'm over the age of 21," that is abstract but perfectly precise. There is no question about what I am prepared to tell you, nor about what I am not prepared to give away.

Abstract high-level descriptions that are not clearly defined are often impossible either to refute or to defend convincingly. Although being precise takes effort, when appropriately used it enhances testability and confidence at all levels. We place a high value on refutable abstractions.

Given a precise notation for abstractions, you can determine whether a given design conforms to the abstraction and can trace how each piece of an implementation realizes each requirement. Tools can help keep track of the propagation of changes in either requirements or implementations.

1.14.3   Pluggable Parts

Building adaptable software is about designing components and plugging them together. Each component is a cohesive piece of design or implementation.

▶ *pluggable parts*   The portions of a software effort that are designed to let you do the following:
  – Get the most from each piece of design work
  – Gain fast, reliable development through reuse
  – Reuse not only classes but also frameworks, patterns, and specifications

Software built without using well-defined components will be inflexible: difficult to change in response to changes in requirements. If you don't use previously built components in your designs, you're doomed to repeatedly cover the same ground and make many of the same mistakes. And changes will be much more difficult to incorporate.

A good component is one that can be made to work with a wide variety of others, and that is the key idea behind polymorphism. Such a design makes sense only if you can express accurately what you expect of the other components to which it may be coupled. Plug-in compatibility relies on unambiguously specified interfaces.

This idea of adapting and using components to produce other components should apply at all levels of development, from business models to components that encapsulate generic problem specifications to assembling binary components to produce a running system.

1.15   *Summary*

The three sections that follow briefly recap this chapter's overview of the Catalysis method.

1.15.1   Process Overview

We have seen an example taken through various stages in design:

• Business process modeling
• System context design and requirements specification
• Component design and component specification
• Object-oriented design and implementation of components

The rest of the book elaborates these techniques.

1.15.2   Features Overview

The tour has taken us through a number of features of Catalysis.

- The most important decisions can be separated from the more-detailed ones. What happens, who does it, and how it is done are all separable issues (see Section 1.9.1).
- The states of objects are modeled with associations and attributes (see Section 1.4.1).
- Actions are described in terms of their effects on objects. They can be defined with postconditions (or state charts, as we'll see later) and illustrated with snapshots (see Section 1.1.1).
- Abstract specifications can be made very precise, avoiding ambiguities (see Section 1.1.2).
- Actions and objects can be abstracted and refined—that is, described at different levels of detail. The relationship can be traced, or retrieved, all the way from business goals to program code (see Section 1.2).
- Development is separated into a number of layers, dealing with business analysis, requirements specification, components, and object design (see Section 1.3).
- Templates abstract similar models. We have seen them used to simplify a static model and to define component connectors (see Section 1.5).
- Collaborations—schemes of interaction—are first-class units of design (see Section 1.8.4).
- Components and objects are designed similarly, although with different emphasis on the way they are chosen and responsibilities assigned (see Sections 1.8 and 1.9).
- Components with different views and representations of a business concept can be related to the common business model with retrievals (see Sections 1.8.3 and 1.8.5).
- Components can be designed to plug in to each other and in to frameworks. The plug-points are defined with action specifications (see Sections 1.9.2 and 1.9.3).
- A component architecture defines a kit by establishing the conventions of interoperation, which are represented by connectors (see Section 1.9.3).

1.15.3   Benefits Overview

- *Enterprise-level design:* The separability of different layers of decision makes Catalysis particularly suitable for design in very substantial projects.
- *High-integrity design:* The precision of Catalysis specifications makes them suitable for the design of mission-critical systems and embedded software, where reliable design is an important issue. The rigor can be used in a variable manner.

- *Traceability:* Catalysis refinement lets you separate abstract models from many possible realizations. The abstract models are still precise enough to be traced to, and even refuted or defended against, concrete realizations; the refinement also enables change propagation management.

- *Pattern reuse and full extensibility:* Catalysis frameworks can be used to define domain-specific patterns of models, collaboration protocols, and component/connector architectures. In fact, primitive types and even the modeling constructs themselves are defined in Catalysis.

- *Component-based development:* Components can be specified by one party, implemented by a second, and used by a third. All these parties must understand the specifications they are working to. To be truly configurable, the components in a kit must work with a wide variety of other members of the kit. Therefore, each designer cannot know exactly what other components he or she is dealing with. For this approach to work, component kit architecture and component development must be seen as a high-integrity design. Catalysis extends clear component specification with the connector abstraction, simplifying the design of component-based products.

- *A behavior-centric and data-centric approach:* Previous methods, such as OMT, have been criticized by "behaviorists" for what is perceived as a data-centric approach. In Catalysis the two views support each other simply. You describe the behavior of a component in terms of attributes that relate to the clients' concerns rather than any implementation.

- *Tool support:* Catalysis enables a high level of tool support far beyond drawings on a database with some document generation. The standard notations and the clear relationship between artifacts also mean that you can use popular object-modeling UML tools on a Catalysis process by following simple usage guidelines.

Part II   Modeling with Objects

Modeling is the central skill of analysis and design. It is how we describe the structure and behavior of things either as they exist or as we intend to build them. The important feature of a model is that it is a simplified description, showing just enough detail for the purpose at hand.

Models can be divided into three parts: static, dynamic, and interactive.

- The static part deals with the information we have about the state of an object at any given moment. At a given level of time granularity, we describe static attributes, relationships, and constraints between objects. Chapter 2, Static Models: Object Attributes and Invariants, is about modeling static aspects using abstract attributes.

- The dynamic part deals with the changes that happen to the state as events occur. It shows how actions affect objects, using the objects and attributes defined in the model of the object state. Chapter 3, Behavior Models: Object Types and Operations, is about describing these dynamic aspects of an object by specifying its operations in terms of effects on its attributes and information exchanged.

- The interactive part deals with interactions between objects. It shows how the responsibility for achieving a goal is divided among collaborating objects and how object interactions can be abstractly described. Chapter 4, Interaction Models: Use Cases, Actions, and Collaborations, is about describing and abstracting object interactions using use cases, joint actions, and collaborations.

Chapter 5, Effective Documentation, provides guidelines for documenting using these modeling techniques to aid in structuring the documentation and accompanying models.

If there's one thing that distinguishes object-oriented (OO) design methods from their predecessors, it is the Golden Rule that an object-oriented design is based on a model of the domain in which it works. Clearly, an early step in doing an OO design must therefore be to establish the objects that exist in the domain. Moreover, the language we use to describe the domain (the concepts and entities in the business with which the software is concerned) must be the same as the language for describing software designs. And we must have systematic ways of carrying this principle through to our designs and code. This is part of the power of an object technique: it allows hardware, software, and users, at all levels from business to code, to be seen as part of the same continuum of interacting objects.

Part II is mainly about techniques and notations, the language for modeling using objects. These techniques are used to describe how an individual object behaves externally (its specification as a type) and how it is designed internally as a group of interacting objects (a collaboration).

Objects that have similar behaviors are members of the same type; they satisfy the specification of that type. Behaviors are specified in terms of attributes that are a valid abstract model, called a *type model*, of many possible implementations. Each action is described in terms of its effect on the attributes of the participating objects and the outputs it produces. The most interesting aspects of a design are the interactions between objects. You can abstract away detailed interaction protocols between objects by using joint actions and collaborations; and you can describe specific interactions as refinements of a more abstract description.

These techniques apply at the level of a business process, problem domain description, software component specification, design, or implementation. Part V describes how to apply these techniques at different levels in a systematic process. It says more about the process of discovering objects and of achieving continuity and traceability from problem domain to code.

Chapter 2   Static Models
Object Attributes
and Invariants

Models can be divided into static, dynamic, and interactive parts dealing with, respectively, what is known about an object at any one moment, how this information changes dynamically with events, and how objects interact with one another. This chapter discusses the static part of a model, in which you characterize the state of an object by describing the information known about it at any point in time. It uses the type model diagram to capture the static model and snapshot diagrams to show instantaneous configurations of object state.

The first section is an overview of what a static model is about. Section 2.2 introduces objects, their attributes, and snapshots and distinguishes the concept of object identity from object equality. The attributes that model an object's state can be implemented in very different ways. Section 2.3 outlines some implementation variations using Java, a relational database, and a real-world implementation.

Section 2.4 abstracts from individual objects and snapshots of their attribute values to a *type model*, which characterizes all objects having these attributes. Here, we introduce parameterized attributes; graphical associations between objects, collections of objects, and type constants; and type combination operators.

Not all combinations of attributes values are legal. Section 2.5 introduces static invariants as a way of describing integrity constraints on the values of attributes, shows some common uses of such invariants, and outlines how these invariants appear in the business domain as well as in code.

The same model of object types and attributes could describe situations in the real world, for a software specification, or even of code. Section 2.6 introduces the dictionary as a mechanism for documenting the relationship between model elements and what they represent.

2.1 *What Is a Static Model?*

Much of how an object responds to any
interaction with its surroundings depends
on what has happened to it up to now.
Your success in checking into a hotel, for
example, depends on whether you have
previously called to arrange your stay. The
hotel with which you've successfully gone
through this preliminary courtesy will wel-
come you with open arms, whereas others
on the same night might well turn you out
into the cold. The response to your arrival
depends on the previous history of your
interactions. So it is with many other
encounters in life: the beverage machine
that will not yield a drink until you have
inserted sufficient money; the car that will
not respond to the gas pedal unless you
have previously turned the starter key and

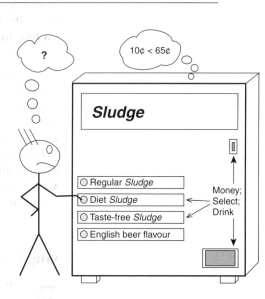

provided that you have not since switched it off; the file that yields a different
character every time you apply the read operation. The response to each interaction you have with any of these objects depends on what interactions it has
already had.

To simplify our understanding of this potentially bewildering behavior, we invent the
mental notion of *state*. The hotel has a reservation for me, the machine is registering 20¢, the
car's engine is running, the file is open and
positioned at byte 42. The idea of state makes it
easier to describe the outcome of any interaction because instead of talking about all the
previous interactions it might have had, we
merely say (a) how the outcome depends on
the current state and (b) what the new state
will be.

It doesn't matter much whether the user can
observe the state directly through a display on a
machine, by an inquiry with a person, or by
calling a software function. To provide such a facility is often useful, but even if it
isn't there the model still fulfills its main purpose: to help the client understand
the object's behavior. If you take away the numeric display in the cartoon but
leave the instructions and the crucial state attribute Amount, the machine is still
more usable than with no such model.

Nor does it matter how the state is realized. The hotel reservation might be a record in a computer, a piece of paper, or a knot in the manager's tie. The same principle applies inside software; the client objects should not care how an object implements its state. State is a technique that helps document the behavior of an object as seen by the outside world.

In fact, it is important that a client not depend on how the state is implemented. Back in the olden days of programming when a team would write a software system from scratch, every part of the system was accessible to every other part. You just had to stick your head above the partition to shout across at whoever was designing the bit whose state you wanted to change. But in recent times, software has joined the real business world of components that are brought together from many sources, and you shouldn't interfere with another object's internal works any more than you should write directly on the hotel's reservation book (or the manager's tie). It would be wrong and inflexible to make assumptions about how they work.

2.1.1 Snapshots: Drawing Pictures of States

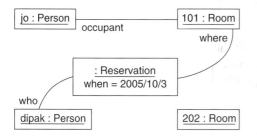

To illustrate a given state, we use *snapshots* (see Section 2.2.2). The objects represent things or concepts; the links represent what we know about them at a particular time. In this example, we can see that Jo is currently occupying Room 101 and Dipak is currently scheduled to occupy Room 101 next week.

Actions can be illustrated by showing how the attributes (drawn as lines or written in the objects) are affected by the action. Here, the rescheduling operation has been applied to shift Dipak to Room 202 next week. (Although we say that a snapshot illustrates a particular moment in time, it can include current information about something planned or scheduled for the future and also a current record of relevant things that have happened previously.)

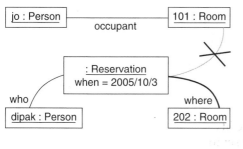

These drawings first and foremost represent states. The same kind of drawing can be used to represent specific implementations of a state. For example, we could decide that each link represents a row in a relation in a relational database; or they might be pointers in main memory; or they might be rows in a chart at the hotel's front desk. But at the start of a design the most useful way is to say that we don't care yet: we're interested in describing the states and not the detail of how they're implemented. We will make the less important representation decisions in due course as the design proceeds.

2.1.2   Static Models: Which Snapshots Are Allowed

Whereas snapshots illustrate specific sample situations, what we need to document are the interesting and allowed states: the objects, links, and labels that will be used in the snapshots. This documentation is the purpose of a static model, which comprises a set of type diagrams and surrounding documentation. Notice the difference in the appearance of type boxes and

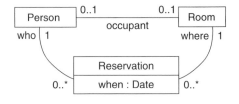

object-instance boxes: the headers of instances are underlined and contain a colon (:). This example summarizes the ways in which rooms and people can be related.

Most analysts and designers are familiar with the idea of establishing a project glossary at an early stage as a way to get everyone using the same words for the same things. In Catalysis, the type diagrams are the central part of the glossary: they represent a vocabulary of terms and make plain the important relationships between them. That vocabulary can then be used in all the documents surrounding the project and in the program code itself.

2.1.3   Using Static Models

Static models have different uses in different parts of the development life cycle. If we decided to start from scratch in providing software support for a hotel's booking system, our analyst's first deliverable would be a description of how the hotel business works, and a type model would be an essential part of it, formalizing the vocabulary. Later in the life cycle, the objects in the software can be described in the same notation.

When applied to analyzing the real world, modeling is never complete. There's more to say about a Person than which room he or she is in; every type diagram can always be extended with more detail. This is just as true within software. We saw earlier that as a client of an object, you are interested in a model that helps explain the behavior you expect of it—but you don't care how it is actually implemented. The model can omit implementation detail and have a completely different structure from that of the implementation as long as the client gets an understanding to which the actual behavior conforms.

Some tools and authors use the term *class diagram*. We reserve *class* for the most detailed level of design, representing what's actually in the code. A class box (marked «class») shows all the directly stored attributes and links of its instances. A *type* is more general: Its attributes and associations represent information that can be known about any of its members, without stating how. We use types much more than classes in analysis, and both during design.

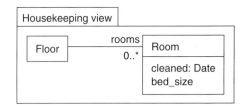

A model may focus on one view among many possible views. For example, the housekeeping staff may be interested in recording when a room was last cleaned. When we come to implement the software, we will need it to cope with all these different views, so we must combine them at some stage. Conversely, part of our overall implementation might be to divide the system into components that deal with different aspects, in which case we must do the reverse. (We'll discuss both operations in Part III.)

It's important to realize that the simplified model is still a true statement about the complex implementation. The attributes and associations tell us about what information is there; they do not tell us how it is represented. Different models can be written at different levels of detail, and we can then relate them together to ensure consistency; you'll find more about this in Chapter 6, Abstraction, Refinement, and Testing.

A model of object state is used to define a vocabulary of precise terms on which to base an analysis, specification, or design. A well-written document should contain plenty of narrative text in natural language along with illustrative diagrams of all kinds, but the type models are used to make sure that there are no gaps or misunderstandings. More on this in Chapter 5, Effective Documentation.

2.2   *Object State: Objects and Attributes*

In this section we introduce the basics of objects and their attributes. Before going any further, we'll introduce an example that will run through the rest of the chapter. IndoctriSoft Inc. is a seminar company that develops and delivers courses and consulting services. The company has a repertoire of courses and a payroll of instructors. Each session (that is, a particular presentation of a course) is delivered by a suitably qualified instructor using the standard materials for that course, usually at a client company's site. Instructors qualify to teach a course initially by taking an exam and subsequently by maintaining a good score in the evaluations completed by session participants.

2.2.1   Objects

Anything that can be identified as an individual thing, physical or conceptual, can be modeled as an object; if you can count it, distinguish it from another, or tell when it is created, it is an object. All the things in Figure 2.1 are valid objects, drawn as boxes with underlined names for each object. Of course, not all valid objects are interesting. As we will see, the behaviors that we wish to describe determine which objects and properties are relevant.

▶ *object* Any identifiable individual or thing. It may be a concrete, touchable thing, such as a car; an abstract concept, such as a meeting; or a relationship, a number, or a computer system. Objects have individual identity, characteristic behavior, and a (perhaps mutable) state. In software, an object can be represented by a combination of stored state and executable code.

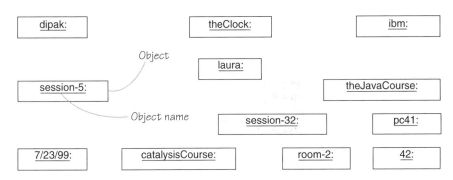

Figure 2.1 Some objects.

2.2.2 Attributes and Snapshots

The state of an object, the information that is encapsulated in it, is modeled by choosing suitable *attributes*. Each attribute has a label and a value; the value may change as actions are performed. In constructing a model, we choose all the attributes that we need to say everything we need to say about the object.

▶ *attribute* A named property of an object whose value describes information about the object. An attribute's value is itself the identity of an object. In software, an attribute may represent stored or computable information. An attribute is part of a model used to help describe its object's behavior and need not be implemented directly by a designer.

For example, session-5 (in Figure 2.2) has the attributes startDate, instructor, course, and client. The value of an attribute is the identity of another object, whether a big, changeable object such as IBM or a simple thing such as 1999/7/23. The attributes of an object link it to other objects. Some attributes are mutable (that is, they can be altered to refer to other objects); others are unchanging, defining lifetime properties of the object. For session-5, the value of its startDate and instructor attributes will change as scheduling needs change; but its client attribute will remain unchanged for the lifetime of session-5. These snapshots, or instance diagrams, are useful for illustrating a given situation, and we will use them for showing the effects of actions.

▶ *snapshot* A depiction (usually as a drawing) of a set of objects and the values of some of their attributes at a particular point in time.

The predefined name *null* or ∅ refers to a special object; the value of any unconnected attribute or link is *null*. In Figure 2.2, the catalysisCourse does not currently have an owner.

2.2.3 Alternative Ways of Drawing a Snapshot

The links drawn between the objects and the attributes written inside the objects are different ways of drawing the same thing. We tend to draw links where the

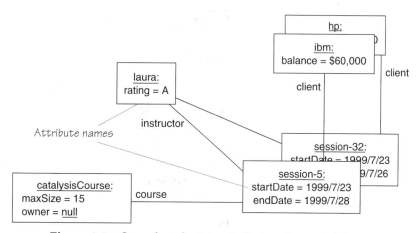

Figure 2.2   Snapshot depicts attribute values of objects.

target objects are an interesting part of our own model and draw attributes where the value is a type of object imported from elsewhere, such as numbers and other primitives. To emphasize this point, let's look at some alternative ways of drawing Figure 2.2.

It's worth remembering, especially if you are designing support tools, that a diagram is a convenient way of showing a set of statements. There is always an equivalent text representation:

session-32 . instructor = laura
session-32 . startDate = 1999/7/23
session-32 . endDate = 1999/7/26
session-32 . client = hp
session-5 . instructor = laura
session-5 . course = catalysisCourse

session-5 . client = ibm
session-5 . startDate = 1999/7/23
laura . rating = A
catalysisCourse . maxSize = 15
catalysisCourse . owner = null
ibm . balance = $60,000

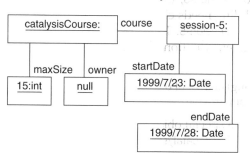

Alternatively, we could draw the boxes but write all links as attributes (see Figure 2.3). Notice that every link has an implied reverse attribute: if the instructor for session-5 is Laura, then by implication Laura has an attribute (by default called ~instructor) modeling the sessions for which Laura is the instructor, which must include session-5. Attributes in a model are about the relationships between things; whether we choose to implement them directly in the software is another question.

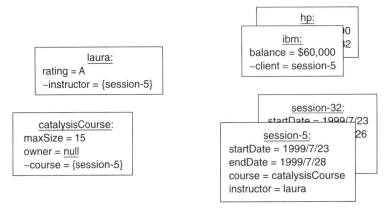

Figure 2.3   Snapshots with links written as attributes.

Now let's go to the other extreme and draw all the attributes as links. Picking out part of Figure 2.2, we could have just as well have shown Dates, and even the most primitive numbers, as separate objects. An attribute is generally written inside the box when we've nothing interesting to say about the structure of the object it refers to. Everyone knows what numbers and dates are, so we have no need to show them in detail.

We regard as objects primitive concepts such as dates, numbers, and the two Boolean values. You can alter an attribute (such as maxSize) to refer to a different number, but the number itself does not change. Useful basic and immutable attributes of numbers include "next" and "previous," so that, for example, 5.next = 6. (Many tools and languages like to separate primitives from objects in some fundamental way. The separation is useful for the practicalities of databases and the like, but for most modeling there is no point in this extra complication.)

2.2.4   Navigation

Given any object(s), you can refer to other related objects by a *navigation* expression using a dot ("."") followed by an attribute name. The value of a navigation expression is another object, so you can further navigate to its attributes:

    session-5 . course = catalysisCourse
    session-5 . course . maxSize = 15
    session-5 . client . balance = $60,000

In the preceding and the earlier expressions, session-5, ibm, and 1999/7/23 are names that refer to specific objects—only names of objects can start off navigation expressions; startDate, instructor, course, and client are attributes—they occur to the right of the dot. Usually the "names" that refer to objects are variable names, such as formally named parameters to actions or local variables, and constants, such as 1999/7/23, A, and 15. We build navigation expressions from names and attributes.

2.2.5   Object Identity

Every object has an *identity:* a means of identification that allows it to be distinguished from others. An identity might be realized in all sorts of ways: a memory pointer, a database key, a reference number or name of some sort, or a physical location. Once again, the point about making a model is to defer such questions until we get down to the appropriate level of detail.

If you've done any database design, you'll be familiar with the idea that every entity must have a unique key, which it is up to you to assign. The key is an explicit combination of the entity's attributes, and any two entities with the same attribute values are actually the same one. But in object-oriented design, we always assume an implicit unique key. If you implement in an OO language or on an OO database, it provides the key for you; otherwise, you make it explicit when you get to coding.

An object identity can be assigned to a suitable attribute or program variable. Changing an attribute value to refer to a different object—for example, the session's instructor is changed from dipak to laura—is different from having an attribute refer to the same object whose state has changed; for example. The maxSize for the session's course may change, but that session is still of the same course, and the number 15 itself has not changed.

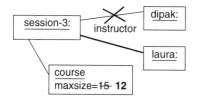

Two different navigation paths may refer to the same object; for example, the object referred to as "my boss" may be the same object as that referred to as "my friend's wife." In Figure 2.2, session-5.instructor and session-32.instructor both refer to the same object, laura. If both names refer to the same object, they both see the same attribute values and changes to those values. "x = y" means x and y refer to *same* object; "x <> y" means that x and y refer to different objects. These symbols are based on the Object Constraint Language (OCL) in UML; in C++ and Java we'd use == and !=.

But we must be careful about what relationships such as "equal" mean. session-5 and session-32 may be the same course, for the same client, starting on the same day, and yet they are two different sessions. The seminar company might choose to call two courses equal if their courses, dates, and clients are the same. But we know that they're different objects because operations applied to one don't affect the other: if session-5 is rescheduled, session-32's date remains unchanged.

Similarity or equality relationships must be defined separately for each type depending on the concerns of the business. We can attach a definition to each type in the model we build, picking out the attributes of interest:

```
Session::                              -- For any individual Session-instance 'self', we
    equal (another:Session) =       -- define "equal to another Session" to mean ...
        (          self.startDate = another.startDate
        and        self.endDate = another.endDate
        and        self.course = another.course
        and        self.client = another.client      )
```

The meaning of identity for an object type is defined, to a great extent, by constraints on whether two distinct objects can have the same attribute values. For example, in a navigation application we may deal with a type Location consisting of a latitude and longitude. If part of the definition of this type includes a constraint that no two distinct location objects can have identical latitudes and longitudes, then an identity check would suffice to determine same locations; otherwise, we would need to define Location::equal (another: Location): Boolean, an equality check that would compare the two attributes.

So in some cases "equal" might be defined to mean "identical," but this is by no means general. Suppose you're dining at a restaurant. When your waiter comes up to take your order, you point at the next table and say, "I'll have what she is having." If the waiter interprets your request in terms of object identity rather than your intended "equality" or "similarity," he need not expect a tip from either of you![1]

So even though the concept of object identity is fundamental to the object-oriented world view, there are usually also separate business-defined concepts of similarity or equality that depend on the values of particular attributes. Section 9.7, Templates for Equality and Copying, discusses these concepts in detail and provides templates for their use.

2.3   *Implementations of Object State*

Snapshots describe the information in a system. It might be about a business or a piece of hardware or a software component; we might be analyzing an existing situation or designing a new one. Whatever the case, we'll call the description a *model* and the concrete realization an *implementation*. Notice that this includes both program code and human organization: the implementation of a company model is in the staff's understanding of one anothers' roles. We could do an analysis, abstracting a model of the business by questioning the staff, and then do a software implementation, coding some support tools by implementing the model in C++.

An implementation must somehow represent information pertaining to the attributes of each object to describe its properties, status, and links to other objects. To represent the links between objects, the implementation must also provide a scheme to implement object identity.

2.3.1   Java Implementation

In a Java implementation, every object is an instance of a class. The class defines a set of *instance variables*, and each instance of that class stores its own value for that instance variable, as shown here:

---

1. Anecdote heard from Ken Auer of KSC.

```
class Session {                              class Client {
    // each session contains this data          String name;
    Date startDate;                             int balance;
    Date endDate;                           }
    // a client, instructor, and course     class Instructor {
    Client client;                              String name;
    Instructor instructor;                      char rating;
    Course course;                          }
    // and some status information          class Course {
    boolean confirmed;                          String name;
    boolean delivered;                          int maxSize;
}                                           }
```

According to this code, every session (an instance of the class Session) has its own instance variable values for startDate, endDate, client, instructor, and course along with some additional status attributes. A similar approach is taken for the other objects.

Object identity is directly supported by the language and is not otherwise visible to the programmer. Thus, the link from a session to its instructor is represented as a direct reference to the corresponding instructor via the instance variable instructor, implemented under the covers by some form of memory address.

The methods provided by the object will use, and possibly modify, these instance variables. Thus, if Session provides a confirm() method, it may set the confirmed flag and seek an appropriate instructor to assign to itself. The keyword this represents the current session instance that is being confirmed.

```
class Session {
    ....
    confirm () {
        this.confirmed = true;
        this.instructor = findAppropriateInstructor ();
    }
}
```

2.3.2   Relational Database Implementation

In a relational database, we might have separate tables, Session, Instructor, and Client. Each object is one row in its corresponding table (see Figure 2.4).

Object attributes are represented by columns in the table. Each session, instructor, and client is assigned a unique identification tag, ID, which is used to implement links between the objects. Links between objects are represented by columns that contain the ID of the corresponding linked object.

Object behaviors have no clear counterpart in this world of relational databases, which are concerned primarily with storing the attributes and links between objects. The database can be driven with something such as SQL, but the queries and commands are not encapsulated with specific relations.

Client

ID	name	balance
3	"acme"	$60,000
7	"micro"	$45,000

Instructor

ID	name	rating
9	"laura"	A
11	"paulo"	B

Session

ID	start	end	clientID	instructorID	courseID
5	2001/17/23	2001/7/28	3	9	2
32	2001/7/23	2001/7/28	3	11	2

Figure 2.4   Object state in a relational database.

2.3.3   Business World Implementation

In a noncomputerized seminar business, all the objects we have discussed still exist but not in a computer system. We might keep a large calendar on a wall, with the sessions drawn as bars and positions on the calendar determining the date attributes. Handwritten client, course, and instructor names would serve as "links"; clients and instructors would be recorded in an address book.

If we get two instructors having the same name, we could add their middle initials to remove ambiguity—a scheme for object identity. The balance owed by each client could be written into a ledger or totaled from the client's unpaid purchase orders. Actions would be procedures followed by the active objects—mostly human roles, in this case—in carrying out their jobs.

2.3.4   Other Implementations

The objects and their attributes are common to all implementations even though the specific representation mechanisms may differ. Even within a specific implementation technology, such as Java, there are many different ways to represent objects and their attributes. For those times when the implementation is as yet unknown or is irrelevant to the level of modeling at hand, we need a way to describe our objects and attributes independent of implementation.

2.4   *Modeling Object State: Types, Attributes, and Associations*

This section explains how to describe objects and their attributes independent of any particular implementation.

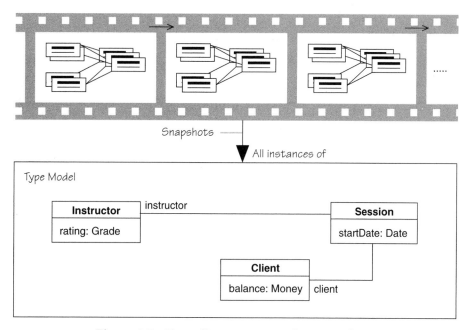

Figure 2.5   Type diagrams generalize snapshots.

2.4.1   Types Describe Objects

Objects and snapshots are concrete depictions, and we will make good use of them in the chapters ahead, but each one shows only a particular situation at a given moment in time. To document a model properly, we need a way of saying what all the possible snapshots are. This is what type diagrams are for (see Figure 2.5).

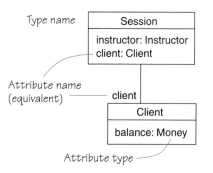

The boxes in these diagrams are object types (there is no colon or underlining in the header). A type is a set of objects that share some characteristics—their attributes and behavior—although we'll focus only on attributes for now. The diagram tells us that every Session has a startDate, an attribute that always refers to a Date; and an instructor attribute, which—a piece of imaginative naming, this—always refers to an object belonging to the type Instructor.

Attributes drawn as links on a type diagram are usually called *associations*. In these examples the association labels might seem a bit redundant, but associations are not always named for the type of the target object. We might decide, for example, to have two instructors associated with each session and call them leader and helper.

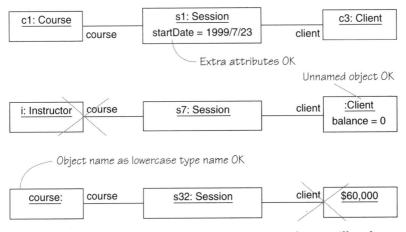

Figure 2.6   Attribute types define some snapshots as illegal.

The attributes in a type model define which snapshots are legal. As shown in Figure 2.6, the course attribute of a session must link to a valid Course. A given snapshot need not depict all attributes of an object, so if you omit an attribute from a snapshot you have said nothing about its value. If you want the attribute to be unconnected, it must be marked with a null value.

2.4.2   Attributes: Model and Reality

We've already said that an attribute *need* not correspond directly to stored data in an implementation.[2] A client is described as having a balance, but its implementation could be anything from a number tallied by hand in a ledger to a macro that summed selected purchase orders in a database.

But a model should surely tell us something about the business or design: if we're allowed to do things any old way, what's the difference between a system that conforms to the model and one that doesn't? The practical answer is that the information represented by each attribute should be in there somewhere. It should be possible to write a read-only function or procedure that retrieves the information from whatever weird format the designer has represented it. These *abstraction* or *retrieval* functions are a valuable aid to both documentation and debugging. (You'll find more about this in Chapter 6, Abstraction, Refinement, and Testing.)

The strict answer is that the static model, without actions, does not tell us enough. The only real test is whether the system we're modeling behaves (responds to actions) as a client would expect from reading the whole model, actions and all; the static part merely sets a vocabulary for the rest. This strict view allows some implementations to conform that might not otherwise. For example,

2. Unless you marked the boxes as «classes» when you are documenting your code.

suppose we never specified any actions that used the balance. By the retrieval function rule, we would still have to implement that attribute even though it would make no perceptible difference to clients whether or not it was implemented.

The power of seeing attributes as abstractions is that you can simplify a great many aspects of a system, deferring detail but not losing accuracy. The idea corresponds to the way we think of things in everyday life: whether you can buy a new carpet depends, in detail, on the history of your income and your expenditure. But it can all be boiled down to the single number of the bank balance: that number determines your decision irrespective of whether your bank chooses to store it as such. The attribute pictures we draw in Catalysis focus on the concepts, which are useful, and not just their implementations, which may be easier done in code.

2.4.3   Parameterized Attributes

Once you realize that attributes do not directly represent stored information, the unconventional concept of a parameterized attribute is a natural extension. A *parameterized attribute* is one that has a defined value for each of many different possible values of its parameter(s). Like attributes generally, it is best thought of as a *query,* or read-only, function that has been hypothesized for some purpose; it need not be directly implemented.

▶ *parameterized attribute* An attribute with parameters such as priceOf(Product). Its value is a function from a list of parameters to an object identity. Unlike an operation, a parameterized attribute is used only as an ancillary part of a state description and need not be implemented directly.

client-3 has a balance due, with amounts due on different dates. Figure 2.7 shows an attribute parameterized by the due date: balanceDueOn (Date): Money; the snapshot explicitly shows attribute values for specific interesting parameter values. Similary, client-3 had a favorite course last year and a (possibly different) one previously; it is modeled by a second parameterized attribute (depicted as a link). Parameterized attributes abstract many implementations,[3] and an implementation must be capable of determining the balance due on any applicable date.

Assuming that objects such as 1997/7/23 and $60,000 have appropriate attribute definitions for isLessThan, you can use this notion of parameterized attributes to write useful statements such as this one:

    session-5.startDate.isLessThan (today)
    session-5.client.balanceDueOn (1998/3/31).isLessThan (someLimit)

---

3. Traditional data modeling would use data normalization to define a relationship between Client and Date and describe balanceDue as a relationship attribute; parameterized attributes avoid the need for such data normalization and result in simpler models and more-natural specifications.

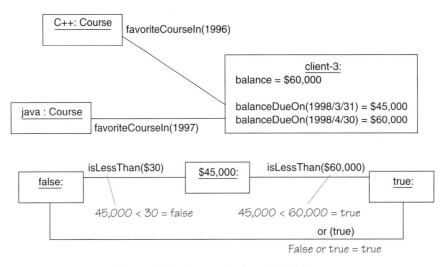

Figure 2.7   Parameterized attributes.

Here is the same thing in a more conventional syntax:

session-5.startDate < today
session-5.client.balanceDueOn(1998/3/31) < someLimit

These constraints simply navigate parameterized attributes; we could use the more conventional syntax a < b instead of a.isLessThan(b). Thus, a predefined type Date has a parameterized attribute < (Date): Boolean, which yields true or false for any given compared date.

The primitive types of numbers, sets, and so on can be defined axiomatically—that is, by a set of key assertions about the relationships between them—as outlined in Appendix A. Thus, 1 + 3 could be specified by a parameterized attribute, Number:: + (other: Number): Number, with the appropriate definitions constraining this navigation. These definitions can be taken for granted by most users. Other immutable types, such as dates, can be modeled using primitive attributes and operations. The read-only operations of immutable types should not be confused with attributes: the former are publicly accessible in any implementation.

It is easy to envisage both immutable and mutable versions of many types: a Date object whose attributes you can change, or a set you can move things in and out of (see Figure 2.8). Often a reasonable model could be built with either type. However, models of a mutable Date object often should instead use a mutable object, such as Clock, whose today attribute refers to different date objects as time passes.[4] Most interesting domain or business objects are naturally mutable—for example, Customer, Machine, Clock.

---

4. It's much more plausible to say, "The clock stopped" than "Time stopped."

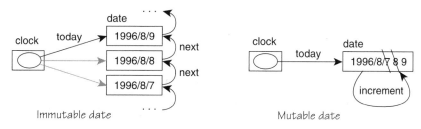

Figure 2.8   Immutable or mutable models of a Date type.

For objects such as dates, we can determine whether d1 < d2 without explicitly storing all the dates that are less than d1 by using a clever representation of dates, such as a single number representing the time elapsed since some reference date. The values of these numbers effectively encode the information about all dates that are less than d1; we simply compare the numbers for the two dates. This technique is often used for a value-type object whose links to other value-type objects are fixed. The 2's complement bit string "0110" in your running program is a clever encoding of a *reference* to the number 6 and, implicitly, to its links to the numbers 5 and 7; the numbers 6, 5, and 7 themselves existed before the bit strings appeared in your program.

2.4.4   Associations

An association is a pair of attributes that are inverses of each other, drawn as a line joining the two types on a type model. For example, each Session has a corresponding Evaluation on completion (not before); each Evaluation is for precisely one Session. This arrangement eliminates certain snapshots, as shown in Figure 2.9.

Drawing an association says more than simply defining two attributes. If defined by two independent attributes, the snapshot in Figure 2.9(c) would be legal. With an association, the attributes must be inverses of each other: s.eval = e if (and only if) e.session = s.

If an association is named only in one direction—for example, eval—then by default the attribute in the opposite direction is named ~eval. If no name is written on the association in either direction, you can use the name of the type at the other end (but with a lowercase letter); the default name for s1.eval would be s1.evaluation. Because two associations can connect the same pair of types, this practice can lead to ambiguity. It is good to name the attributes explicitly in both directions if you intend to refer to them.

▶ *association* A pair of attributes that are inverses of each other, usually drawn as a line connecting two types.

There are several other adornments available for any association (see Figure 2.10).

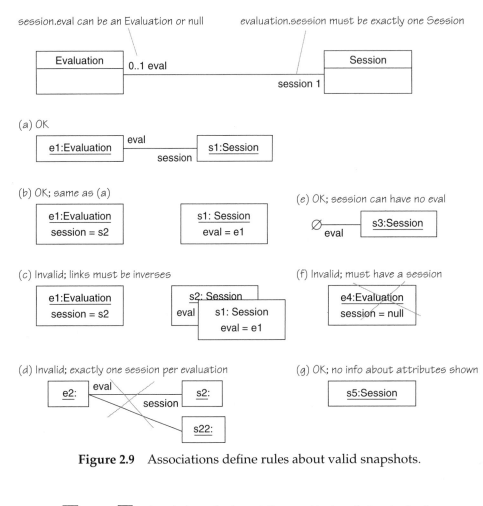

Figure 2.9   Associations define rules about valid snapshots.

 In a design or implementation, used to show that navigation in this direction is much easier than in the other. Further explicit annotation can mark it as a stored field.

 No defined navigation toward the x; equivalent to an attribute from the right to the left but not left to right.

A derived or redundant association; can be expressed as a function of others.

 If a:A, then a.b refers to the same object throughout the life of a.

Figure 2.10   Options for associations.

2.4.5   Collections

Many attributes have values that are collections of other objects. By default, the meaning of the * cardinality is that the attribute is a set, but we can be more explicit about the kind of collection we want, including the following:[5]

- **Set**: a collection of objects without any duplicates
- **Bag**: a collection with duplicates of elements
- **Seq**: a sequence—a bag with an ordering of its elements

For example, each client has some number of sessions, each with one instructor. Each instructor teaches many sessions in a date-ordered sequence. The rating of an instructor is the average of the rating in his or her last five sessions. The type model is illustrated in Figure 2.11.

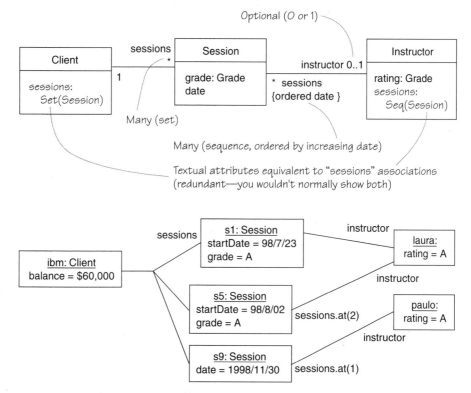

Figure 2.11   Collections: type model and snapshot.

---

5. Based on the Object Constraint Language (OCL) part of UML 1.1.

Here are some examples of useful navigations on this snapshot.[6] Try reading them as ways to *refer to* particular objects rather than as operations that are executed on software objects; they are precise, implementation-free definitions of terms. The operators are summarized later.

- The set of sessions for client3, written Set {element1, element2, ...}

  client3.sessions = Set { s1, s5, s9 }

- The instructors who have taught client3.

  client3.sessions.instructor = Set { laura, paulo } -- *Sets have no duplicates*

- The number of sessions for client3.

  client3.sessions->count = 3

- Sessions for client3 starting after 1998/8/1; in the following two equivalent forms, the second form does an implicit select from the set.

  client3.sessions->select (sess | sess.startDate > 1998/8/1) = Set { s5, s9 }
  client3.sessions [startDate > 1998/8/1] = Set { s5, s9 }

- Has laura taught courses to ibm (does the set of clients associated with the set of sessions that Laura has taught include IBM)?

  laura.sessions.client -> includes (ibm) -- *long version*
  ibm : laura.sessions.client -- *short version* "ibm belongs to laura's sessions' clients"

  Equivalently, has ibm been taught any courses by laura?

  ibm.sessions.instructor -> includes (laura)

  (ibm.sessions is a set of sessions; following the instructor links from all of them gives a set of instructors; is one of them Laura?)

- Every one of laura's session grades is better than pass.

  laura.sessions.grade -> forAll (g | g.betterThan(Grade.pass))

- At least one of laura's session grades is a Grade.A.

  laura.sessions.grade -> exists (g | g = Grade.A)

Mathematicians use special symbols to combine sets, but we keep to what's on your keyboard.

- The courses taught by either Laura or Marty:

  laura.sessions.course + marty.sessions.course

- The courses taught by both Laura and Marty:

  laura.sessions.course * marty.sessions.course

- The courses taught by Laura that are not taught by Marty:

  laura.sessions.course – marty.sessions.course

(+, *, and – can also be written -> union(...), -> intersection(...), and -> difference(...).)

---

6. These are also based on the UML's Object Constraint Language.

A dot (".") operator used on a collection evaluates an attribute on every element of the collection and returns another collection. So laura.sessions is a set of Sessions; evaluating the grade attribute takes us to a set of Grades. If the resulting collection is a single value, it can be treated as a single object rather than a set.

The –> operator used on a collection evaluates an attribute on the collection itself rather than on each of its elements. Several operations on collections—select, forAll—take a *block* argument representing a single argument function evaluated on each element of the collection. Some operators, such as sum and average, are specifically defined to apply to collections of numbers.

Collections are so widely used in modeling that there is a standard package of generic types, extensible by an experienced modeler, as detailed in Appendix A. In Catalysis, collections themselves are immutable objects, although they are not usually explicitly shown on type models. As usual, collection attributes do not dictate an implementation but are used simply to make terms precise; they are an abstraction of any implementation.

2.4.6   Type Constants

It is often convenient to define a fixed object or value and associate it with a particular type.[7] Often, we want to associate the constant with the type of which the constant is a member. For example, the Number type has a constant 0, a number; our Grade type has constants pass, A, B, and so on, each of which is a grade.

A type constant is still an attribute of type members so that all the members share the same constant value; so myGrade.pass = yourGrade.pass. An implementation would store this constant only once rather than in each member of that type.

If you want to refer to a type constant you can use the name of the type without any specific member of that type. Grade is the set of all objects that conform to the Grade type specification; Grade.pass takes you to the single object they're all linked to with that attribute.

Defining a type constant is one of the ways in which it is permissible to mix object instances (usually seen in snapshots) and types. Figure 2.12(a) indicates that following the A link from any Grade always takes you to a specific object, which itself happens to be a Grade. It has an attribute successor, which takes you to the next grade in the list, which happens to be the type constant Grade.B. Instead of drawing the links between the type and the objects, you can write an attribute in the type box with the modifier global, as in Figure 2.12(b).

▶ *type constant* A named member of the type—for example, "7" is a type constant of integer. Type constants can be globally referred to by type_name.member_name.

Type constants can be used to describe what are traditionally treated as enumerated types. To introduce a type Color whose legal values are red, blue, and yellow,

---

7. Corresponding to final static class variables in Java (const static pointers in C++).

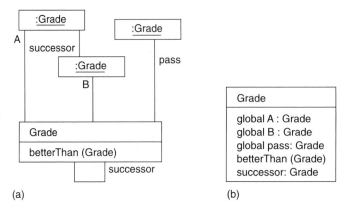

Figure 2.12   Mixing object instances and types.

use three type constants and an invariant specifying that there are no other colors (we permit a syntactic shortcut, <u>enum</u>).

Color
global red, blue, yellow: Color   <u>inv</u> self : { red, blue, yellow }

Be careful not to use type constants when a regular attribute of a higher-level object is needed. For example, rather than use Course::catalog as a global type constant to model the catalog of courses, it is much better to build an explicit object for the seminar company itself and use Company::catalog as a normal attribute on the company.

Use type constants sparingly for mutable types. A type constant says that there is only one object of this name across every implementation in which the type is used. If the shared object itself is immutable, it can be copied permanently in every implementation. For example, the relationship of Grade.A to Grade.B is always fixed, just as with Integer.0 and Integer.1 and Color.red and Color.blue; these shared objects can safely be replicated along with their (immutable) relationships to others. With mutable types you should be prepared to organize worldwide access to the shared object or replicate the object but have a fancy scheme to update the cache.

The global attribute is constant in that it always refers to one object even if the attributes of the target object can change. For example, URL.register could model the unique and mutable worldwide registry of Internet addresses.

2.5 *Static Invariants*

Not all combinations of attribute values are legal. We have already seen how the type diagram constrains the snapshots that are allowed (Figure 2.6 and Figure 2.9 showed some examples). Those constraints were all about the type of object an individual attribute referred to.

But sometimes we need to disallow certain combinations of attribute values. To do this we can write an invariant: a Boolean (true/false) expression that must be true for every permitted snapshot. (We will scope the snapshots by the set of actions to which this applies in Section 3.5.5, Context and Control of an Invariant.)

▶ *static invariant* A predicate, forming part of a type model, that should hold true on every permitted snapshot—specifically, before and after every action in the model. Some static invariants are written in text; other common ones, such as attribute types and associations as inverse attributes, have built-in notations.

2.5.1   Writing an Invariant

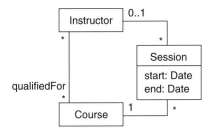

A graphical notation cannot cover all possible constraints and rules. For example, we have several rules about which instructor can be assigned to a particular session: An instructor must be qualified to teach any session he or she is assigned to.

First, we must model the set of courses an instructor is qualified to teach; that has been missing from the model so far. It is easily modeled with a many-many association between instructors and courses.

Based on this model, Figure 2.13 shows a snapshot that we would not want to admit. The problem is that session-25, a Catalysis course, is scheduled to be taught by Lee, who is not qualified to teach it. To ensure that an instructor is never assigned to a session unless qualified to teach it, qualifiedFor—the set of courses you get to by following the qualifiedFor link—includes all the courses of its sessions. Here is how to put it more formally.

<u>inv</u> Instructor::   qualifiedFor -> includesAll (sessions.course)

Or you can write it the other way.

<u>inv</u> Instructor ::   sessions.course <= qualifiedFor

--the courses I teach are a subset of the ones I'm qualified for

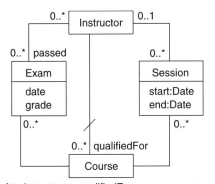

inv Instructor :: qualifiedFor = exams.course

Notice that we have deferred details of the rules that determine whether an instructor is qualified for a course. These details will have to be captured somewhere, but we might defer it for now if we are not yet considering concepts such as qualification exams and course evaluations.

To add some of these details later, we would enrich the model. Then we can define the less detailed attribute in terms of the new details by using an invariant. Now it's clear that being qualified for a course means having passed an exam for it.

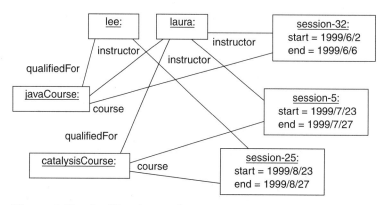

Figure 2.13   An illegal snapshot requiring an explicit invariant.

2.5.2   Boolean Operators

An invariant is a Boolean expression. The usual Boolean operators (as used in programming languages) are available; there are different ways of writing them depending on your preferences. Tables 2.1, 2.2, and 2.3 display them.

Some expressions may have undefined values—for example, attributes of null, daft arithmetic expressions such as 0/0, or parameterized attributes whose pre-condition is false. Generally, an expression is undefined if any of its subexpressions is undefined. However, some operators do not depend on one of their inputs under certain circumstances: 0 * n is well defined even if you don't know n; so is n * 0. The same applies to (true | b) and (false & b), again no matter what the order of the operands. (This works no matter which way you write the operands—we're not writing a program.)

2.5.3   About Being Formal

We said in the introductory chapters that Catalysis provides for a variable degree of precision, and it is good to repeat it here, among the high-precision stuff. The

Table 2.1   Boolean Operators

Long	Short	Explanation
and	&	False if either operand is false.
or	I	True if either operand is true.
a implies b	a ==> b	True if whenever a is true, so is b.
not a	! a	
aSet -> forall (x I P(x))	x: aSet :: P(x)	For every member (call it x) of aSet, the Boolean expression P(x) is true.
aSet -> exists (x I P(x))	exist x: aSet, P(x)	There is at least one member (call it x) of aSet for which P(x) is true.

Table 2.2　Collection Operators

Long	Short	Explanation
s1->size		The number of elements in s1.
s1->intersection(s2)	s1 * s2	The set containing only those items in both sets (math s1 ∩ s2).
s1->union(s2)	s1 + s2	The set of all items in both (s1 ∪ s2).
s1 − s2	s1 − s2	Those items of s1 that are not in s2.
s1->symmetricDifference(s2)		Those items only in one or the other.
s1->includes(item)	item : s1	Item is a member of s1.
s1->includesAll(s2)	s2 <= s1	Every item in s2 is also in s1 (s2 ⊆ s1).
s1->select(x|bool_expr)	s1[x | bool_expr]	Filter: the subset of s1 for which bool_expr is true. Within bool_expr, each member of s1 is referred to as x.
s1->select(bool_expr)	s1[bool_expr]	Same as s1[self | bool_expr]. Less general — gets self mixed up with self in the context.
s1.aFunction		The set obtained by applying aFunction to every member of s1.
s1->iterate (x, a= initial value | function_using(x,a)) E.g., scores: Set(integer); -- some attribute; Set(integer) :: average = (self->iterate (x, a= 0 | x+a)) / self->size; scores->average -- meaning now defined		The closure of the function. It is applied to every member x of s1. The result of each application becomes the a argument to the next. The final value is the overall result. Write the function so that order of evaluation does not matter.

Table 2.3　General Expressions in Assertions

Expression	Explanation
<u>let</u> x = expr1 <u>in</u> expression	In expression, x represents expr1's value
Type	The set of existing members of Type
x = y	x is the same object as y

notation gives you a way of being as precise as you like about a domain, a system, or a component without going into all the detail of program code. But you also have the option to use only informal descriptions or to freely intermix the two. However, it is the experience of many designers who've tried it that writing precise descriptions at an early stage of development tends to bring questions to the fore that would not have been noticed otherwise. Granted, the specification part of the process goes into a bit more depth and takes longer than it takes to prepare a purely text document. But it gets more of the work done and tends to bring the important decisions to the earlier stages of development, leaving the less important detail until later. The extra effort early pays off later in a more coherent and less bug-prone design.

The formal parts are not necessarily readable on their own by the end users of a software product. But the purpose of formal description is not necessarily to be a contract between you and the end users; rather, it is to give a clear understanding between your client, you, and your colleagues of what you are intending to provide. It is a statement of your overall vision of the software, and writing it down prolongs the life of that vision, making it less prone to disfigurement by quick-fix maintainers.

2.5.4 The Context Operator

Some of our examples have attached an evaluation to a session, but this makes sense only after the session has taken place. This rule can be expressed in informal prose; let's make it more precise and testable.

> -- A session has an evaluation exactly when it is completed.
> <u>inv</u> Session:: self.completed = (self.eval <> null)   --'self' is optional

The context operator (::) is short for an explicit forall. It says "the following is true for any member of this type (or set), which we'll call self":

> <u>inv</u> Session -> forall (self | self.completed = (self.eval <> null))

To capture this invariant we must define the term completed; we do so by simply adding a Boolean attribute to Session—and, of course, defining its real-world meaning in the dictionary.

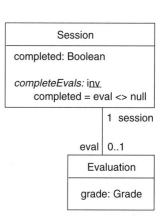

Writing the invariant within the type box is equivalent to writing it separately after a context operator. The predefined notation directly captures certain common invariants. Declaring the course attribute of a Session to be of type Course in Figure 2.5 is equivalent to

> <u>inv</u> Session:: -- for every session, its course must be an
>   object of type Course
>   self.course : Course -- ":" is set-membership; Course ->
>   includes (self.course)

Similarly, the association shown in Figure 2.9 implicitly defines attribute types and an inverse invariant that is equivalent to this text version:

> <u>inv</u> Evaluation:: -- for every evaluation
>   self.session : Session -- its session must be a Session
>   & self.session.eval = self -- whose 'eval' attribute refers back to me

2.5.5 Invariants: Code versus Business

An invariant captures a consistency rule about a required relationship between attributes. For example, at the business level, an instructor should never be assigned to a course unless qualified. For a given implementation, this means that certain combinations of stored data should never occur. An invariant representing a business rule, such as *assignQualified*, could look a lot more complex when expressed against an optimized implementation. For example, to efficiently find replacement instructors as availability changes, the assignment of instructors to courses may be represented by a complex data structure indexed by both date and course.

Laura's diplomatically explained position boils down to this: The bottom line when doing type modeling is this: What does a client need to say about a design or requirement? State this using terms natural to the client. Make sure that all the underlying terms are well defined in a glossary. Then make the glossary precise using attributes and invariants in a type model. Restate what you wanted to say more precisely in terms of this type model. Then make sure that your implementation has a consistent mapping to these abstract attributes and invariants.

2.5.6   Invariants in Code

Although an implementation can choose any suitable representation, every attribute in a type model must have a mapping from that representation. Hence, all invariants in a type model will have a corresponding constraint on the implemented state.

Consider the invariant *assignQualified* in Section 2.5.1. Suppose that we choose to represent the qualifiedFor(Course) attribute by storing in each instructor a list of the qualified courses and to represent the sessions attribute by storing a list of sessions:

```
class Instructor {
    Vector qualifiedForCourses;
    Vector sessions;
```

Then the *assignQualified* invariant corresponds to the following Boolean function, which should evaluate to true upon completion of any external operation invocation. Note that the code form is the same as that of the type model invariant, with each reference to an attribute in the type model expanded to its corresponding representation in the implementation.

```
boolean assignQualified () {
    -- for every session that I am assigned to
    for (Enumeration e = session.elements(); e.hasMoreElements;) {
        Course course = ((Session) e.nextElement()). course();
        -- if I am not qualified to teach that course
        if (! qualifiedForCourses.contains (course))
            return false; -- then something is wrong!
    }
    return true;
}
```

The combination of all invariants for a class can be used in a single ok() function, which should evaluate to true after any external invocation of an operation on the object. Such a function provides a valuable sanity check on the state of a running application. Together with operation specifications, it provides the basis for both testing and debugging.

```
boolean ok () {
    assignQualified() = true
    & notDoubleBooked() = true
    & ......
}
```

2.5.7   Common Uses of Invariants

There are several common uses of invariants in a type model.

• *Derived attributes:* the value of one attribute can be fully determined by other attributes—for example, the completed attribute in Section 2.5.1. Because an attribute merely introduces a term for describing information about an object and does not impose any implementation decision, we are free to introduce redundant attributes to make our descriptions more clear and concise. However, we define such attributes in terms of others and optionally use a forward slash (/) to indicate that they can be derived from others.

Suppose we need to refer to the clients taught by a given instructor in the past and to the instructors who are qualified candidates for a session. We introduce simple derived attributes on Instructor and Session, defined by an invariant:

inv Instructor:: -- *clients taught = clients of past sessions I have taught*
    clientsTaught = sessions[date < today].client
inv Session:: -- *my candidate instructors are those qualified for my course*
    candidates = Instructor[qualifiedFor (self.course)]

We can now directly use these attributes to write clearer expressions:

instructor.clientsTaught... or session.candidates....

• *Derived parameterized attributes:* these can also be defined by invariants. If the balance attributes in Figure 2.7 were defined in terms of some session history, we might have the following:

inv Client:: -- *for every client*
    -- *the balance due for that client on any date is...*
    balanceDueOn (d: Date)
        -- *the sum of the fees for all sessions in the preceding 30 days*
        = sessions [date < d and d > d - 30] . fees ->sum

• *Subset constraints:* the object(s) linked via one attribute must be in the set of those linked via another attribute. For example, the instructor assigned to a session must be one of the candidates qualified to teach that session. This form of invariant is quite common and has a special graphical symbol shown in Figure 2.14. It could have been written explicitly instead:

inv Session:: -- *my assigned instructor must be one of my qualified candidates*
    candidates->includes (instructor)

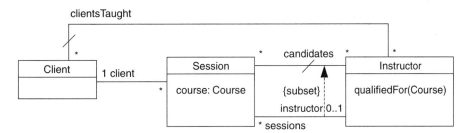

Figure 2.14 Derived attributes and subset constraints.

- *Subtype constraints:* a supertype can introduce attributes that apply to several subtypes; each subtype imposes specific constraints on the attributes. An example is illustrated in Section 3.7, Subtypes and Type Extension.

- *State-specific constraints:* being in a specific state may imply constraints on some other attributes of an object. From Section 2.5.1:

<u>inv</u> Session:: -- any confirmed session must have an Instructor
  confirmed implies instructor <> null

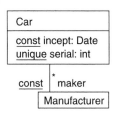

Other forms of invariants are common enough to merit special symbols:

The const attribute refers to the same object throughout the life of the "owner."

The unique attribute means that no other object of this owner type has the same attribute value. unique can apply to a tuple of attributes.

Association constraints (between the ends of two or more associations) are shown in Figure 2.15.

▶ *static model* A set of attributes, together with an invariant, constitutes the static part of a type model. The invariant says which combinations of attribute values make sense at any one time and includes constraints on the existence, ranges, types, and combinations of individual attributes.

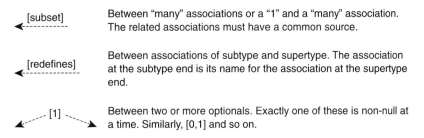

[subset]	Between "many" associations or a "1" and a "many" association. The related associations must have a common source.
[redefines]	Between associations of subtype and supertype. The association at the subtype end is its name for the association at the supertype end.
[1]	Between two or more optionals. Exactly one of these is non-null at a time. Similarly, [0,1] and so on.

Figure 2.15 Association constraints.

2.6 *The Dictionary*

When a link is drawn in a snapshot from a course to a session, does it mean that the session has happened, that it will happen, or that it is happening? Or does it mean that it might happen if we get enough customers? Does it mean that this session is an occurrence of that course or that it is some other event, intended for people who have previously attended the course? What is a course, anyway? Does it include courses that are being prepared or only those ready to run?

It's important to realize that the diagrams mean nothing without definitions of the intended meanings of the objects and attributes.

The rather precise notation in this chapter gives you a way of making unambiguous statements about whatever you want to model or design: you can be just as precise with requirements as you can with a programming language in code but without most of the complications. But the notation allows you to make precise relationships only between *symbols*. fris > bee is fearlessly uncompromising and precise in what it states about these two things, provided that someone will please tell us what fris and bee are supposed to represent. We can neither support or refute the statement unless we have an interpretation of the symbols.

Figure 2.16 could just as well be a model of a seminar business, a database, or a Java application. When we describe the *assignQualified* invariant, are we saying that an unqualified instructor never teaches in the business or that some piece of software should never schedule such a thing?

The *dictionary* relates symbolic names to the real world. So if I told you that fris is the name I use for my age and bee is how the age of the current British Prime Minister is referred to in my household, then you could find out whether fris > bee is true or false. If the model in Figure 2.16 were of a database, the dictionary would relate the model elements to tables, columns, and so on.

Suggestive names help, but they can also be misleading because readers readily make silent assumptions about familiar names. Should you be dealing with aileronAngle or fuelRodHeight you might want to be a little more careful than usual about definitions![8]

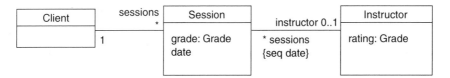

Figure 2.16   Is this a model of a business? a database? an application?

---

8. Safety-critical systems place much more stringent demands on precise definitions.

Type	Description (narrative, with optional formal expressions)		Created by (actions)
	Attr, Inv...	Description (narrative, with optional formal expressions)	written by (actions)
Instructor	The person assigned to a scheduled event		hireInstructor
	rating	*Attribute:* a summary of recent instructor results	deliverCourse, passExam
	sessions	*Attribute:* The sessions assigned this instructor	scheduleCourse
	assign-Qualified	*Invariant:* Only qualified instructors are assigned to a session **sessions->forall (s I self.qualifiedFor (s.course))**	
Session	One scheduled delivery of a course		scheduleCourse
	date	Start date of the session	rescheduleCourse

Figure 2.17   A typical dictionary.

To use a precise language properly, you must first define your terms; once that's done, you can use the definition to avoid any further misunderstandings. There's no avoiding the possibility of mistakes with our dictionary definitions, but we can hope to make them as simple as possible and then get into the precise notation to deal with the complex relationships between the named things.

Our dictionary contains named definitions for object types, attributes (including associations), invariants, action types and parameters, and other elements (which we'll discuss later). A typical dictionary is shown in Figure 2.17. Some of its contents are automatically derived from the models themselves.

▶ *dictionary* The collected set of definitions of modeling constructs. The definitions must include not only the formal modeling and specification bits (relating the formal names and symbols to each other) but also the (usually informal) descriptions that relate the symbols and names to things in the problem domain. Dictionary definitions are scoped according to package scope rules.

2.7 *Models of Business; Models of Components*

So far, we have used static modeling to describe the objects that exist in some world, but we can also use a static model to describe the state of a complete system. We said at the beginning of this chapter that this was the ulterior motive for making a static model. Figure 2.18 shows a model of a simple type.

This is the type of a system or component. The amount represents the money stored inside the machine and credited toward the current sale. We don't know how it is represented inside. Maybe it keeps the coins in a separate container, or maybe it counts the coins as they go into its takings pool. So Money isn't a type representing real coins; rather, it's the type of this component's internal state.

To represent the type of a more complex component, we could just add attributes. It may be easier to do it pictorially. For example, a system that helps

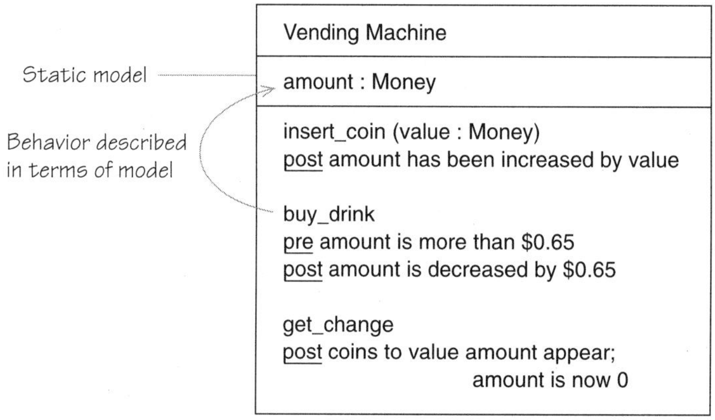

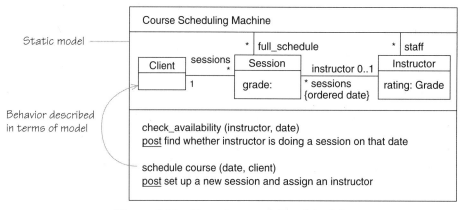

Figure 2.18   Simple type model with one attribute.

Figure 2.19   Complex model—pictorial.

schedule instructors for courses would clearly need to know all the concepts we have been discussing in the training business. That knowledge will form the model of the component's state, and we can then define the actions in those terms (see Figure 2.19).

2.8 *Summary*

A static model describes the state of the business or the component(s) we are interested in. Each concept is described with a type, and its state is described with attributes and associations; these lead in turn to other types. The formally defined types are related to the users' world in a dictionary.

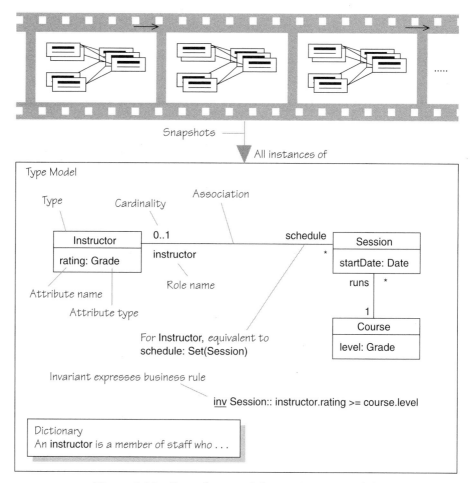

Figure 2.20   Snapshots and the static type model.

Invariants express constraints on the state: combinations of values that should always be observed. They can represent some categories of business rules.

The main purpose of a static model is to provide a vocabulary in which to describe actions, which include interactions in a business, between users and software, or between objects inside the software. We use snapshots to represent specific situations, and that helps to develop the static model (see Figure 2.20). Snapshots are an important thinking tool, but they are not fully general descriptions and therefore play only an explanatory role in documentation.

Chapter 3   Behavior Models
Object Types
and Operations

In component-based development you must separate the external behavior of a component from its internal implementation. You describe behavior by specifying the component's type: a list of actions it can take part in and the way it responds to them. The kinds of actions we focus on here are the *operations* that the object may be requested to perform. The type specification in turn has two parts:

- The static model of an object's internal state and of information exchanged in the operation requests, using attributes, associations, and invariants
- Specifications of the effects of the actions on the component, using the vocabulary provided by the static model

This chapter describes how to derive and write a type specification.

We dealt with the static model in Chapter 2; we next want to specify actions in a way that abstracts from the model's many possible implementations. An action is specified by its effect on the state of the object and any information exchanged in the course of that action. This state is described as a type model of the object and of its in/out parameters; the effect is specified as a precondition/postcondition pair. Effects can either be written textually or depicted as transitions on a state chart.

At this stage, the objective is only to specify the actions and not to implement them (although we will look at some program code as examples). The latter part of this chapter also briefly discusses programming language classes and explains how they relate to the specifications.

The key to designing an implementation is to choose how the objects inside the component collaborate to provide the specified effects. Such collaborations are the subject of Chapter 4.

3.1 *Object Behavior: Objects and Actions*

In component-based development, you must construct software from components whose insides you can't see; you must treat them as black boxes. When you construct your own components, you m ust build them so that they will work with a wide variety of others even as their internal implementations change or are upgraded. Components that aren't interoperable have little value. For that reason, we are interested in separating external specification of behavior from the internal works. (This has been the situation in hardware for years; that it's novel to our profession should perhaps be an issue of some embarrassment for us.)

▶ *object behavior*   The effects of an object on the outcomes of the actions it takes part in along with the effects of the actions on the object.

3.1.1   Snapshot Pairs Illustrate Actions

Object state changes as a result of actions. Given the object snapshot in Figure 3.1(a), if a client requested a session of the javaCourse, we end up with Figure 3.1(b). The new session is assigned to paulo, because he is qualified to teach that course. A scheduleCourse action occurs between the two snapshots. These before-and-after snapshots sometimes provide a useful way to envisage what each action does. Looking at the diagram, can you see what cancel(session-32), reschedule(session-5, 2000/1/5), or qualify(paulo, catalysisCourse) would do?

This is the primary reason for making a static model: we choose objects and attributes, whether written inside the types or drawn as links, that will help us define the effects of the actions. It would be difficult to describe the effect of schedule course without the model attributes depicted on the snapshots.

▶ *action occurrence*   A related set of changes of states in a group of objects that occurs between two specific points in time. An action occurrence may abstract an entire series of interactions and smaller changes.

3.1.2   Pre- and Postconditions Specify Actions

The limitation of snapshots is that they show particular sample situations; we want to describe the effect an action has in all possible situations. We can do that by writing postconditions—informal statements or formal expressions that define the effect of an action, using—the same navigation style as invariants in Section 2.5, Static Invariants. For example:

action schedule_course (reqCourse: Course, reqStart: Date)
pre: Provided there is an instructor qualified for this course
            who is free on this date, for the length of the course.
post: A new confirmed session has been created, with course = reqCourse,
            startDate = reqStart, and endDate – startDate = reqCourse.length.

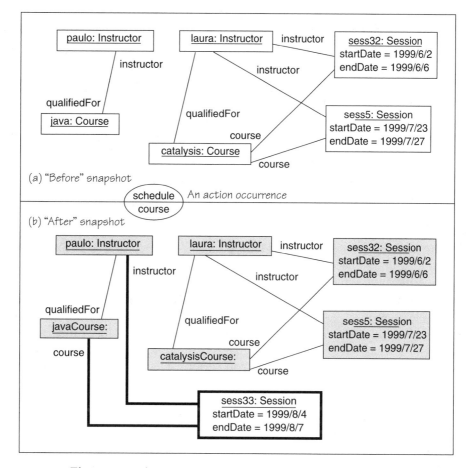

Figure 3.1 An action occurrence causes a change in state.

Notice that we have stated only some parts of what this action does. In fact, this is one of the nice things about specifying actions rather than designing them: you can stipulate only those characteristics that you need the outcome to have, and leave the rest unsaid, with no spurious constraints. This is exactly what's required for component-based development: we need to be able to say "A plug-in component must achieve this" but should not say how it achieves it or what additional things it might do, permitting many realizations. It is easy to combine requirements expressed in this way. Different needs can be anded together, something you can't do with chunks of program code. Moreover, different versions, expressed in different subtypes, can add their own constraints to the basic requirement (see Section 8.3.5, Joining Type Specifications Is Not Subtyping).

▶ *action type* The set of action occurrences that conform to a given action spec. A particular action occurrence may belong to many action types.

▶ *action spec*   A specification of an action type. An action spec characterizes the effects of the occurrences on the states of the participating objects (for example, using a postcondition).

Actions can be joint (use cases): They abstract multiple interactions and specific protocols for information exchange, and describe the net effect on all participants and the summary of information exchanged.

Actions can also be localized, in which case they are also called operations. An operation is a one-sided specification of an action. It is focused entirely on a single object and how it responds to a request, without regard to the initiator of the request.

3.1.3   Types

Different objects react in different ways to the same action. But rather than describe each object separately, we group objects into types: sets of objects that have some (but not necessarily all) behavior in common. A type is described by a type specification, which tells how some actions affect the internal state of the object and, conversely, how the state affects the outcome of actions.

Usually, types are partial descriptions. They say, "If you do X to one of my members, the resulting response will have this property and that property." But they don't always tell you everything there is to know about the outcome, and they don't tell you what will happen if you perform actions that aren't mentioned. This incompleteness is important, because it means that type specs can be easily combined or extended, essentially by anding them together. A type is quite different from a class in a programming language, which is a prescription telling the object *how* to do what it does.

A client defines the type it expects of any other object it will use: the minimal set of actions it must exhibit. An implementor of an object defines the type(s) she provides: that set of actions she guarantees to meet now and through subsequent releases. This implementation can be used by the client if the provided type can be shown to conform to the expected one.[1]

Types often correspond to real-world descriptions. An Employee is something that does work when you give it money; a Parent is something that does work and gives you money; a Shopkeeper gives you things when you give it money. All these descriptions are partial, focusing on the behavior that interests certain other objects that interact with them. In object design, we build systems from interacting objects, so these partial perspectives are crucial. Each object could play several roles, so we need to easily talk about Employee * Parent: someone who does work when paid (by the appropriate other person) and also provides money (ditto).

---

1. Even if the implemented type was not declared a priori as implementing the expected one, specific programming languages may impose stronger restrictions. See Chapter 6, Abstraction, Refinement, and Testing.

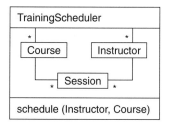

Because these descriptions are "black box" ("I don't care how my parent gets the money as long as she or he provides it"), it would be nice if we could describe the actions entirely without reference to anything inside the object. That is possible for simple behaviors but not for complex ones. "Why will my employees not work when I ask them to?" "Because their pockets are empty." "How can their pockets be filled?" "You pay them." In this conversation, it is implicit that an Employee can have a pocket representing an amount of money. It doesn't really matter to the Employer how or where employees keep their money; it is just a model, a device to explain the relationship between the actions of payment and request to work.[2]

In a complex model, we find a few attributes, such as pocket, insufficient, and we tend to use pictorial attributes instead. But the idea is the same: the model is principally there to explain the effects of the actions. We can use the same principle to describe small, simple objects and large, complex systems. Of course, the large complex systems will need a few more tools for managing complexity and structuring a specification, but the underlying ideas will be the same.

▶ *type*   A set of objects that conform to a given type spec throughout their lives.

▶ *type spec*   A description of object behavior. It typically consists of a collection of action specs and a static model of attributes that help describe the effects of the actions. A type spec makes no statement about implementation.

3.1.4   Objects and Actions Model Business and Software

In Section 2.7, Models of Business; Models of Components, we remarked that a type model can deal with things in the real world, or it can model the internal state of a larger object such as a computer system or component. We showed this graphically by drawing the type of the component containing the types of the objects it "knew" about.

The techniques in this chapter can be used to specify either changes in the real world or changes inside a component (see Figure 3.2); but what both situations have in common is that we are specifying only the outcome, or *effects*, of the actions rather than what goes on inside. We close our eyes between the start and end of every change and describe only the comparison between the two snapshots of the business or system state.

---

2. Legal contracts have the same structure (and are far more muddled): title, terms and definitions, actual contractual conditions using those terms

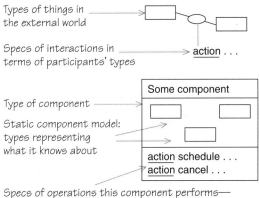

Types of things in the external world

Specs of interactions in terms of participants' types

Type of component

Static component model: types representing what it knows about

Specs of operations this component performs— use static component model as vocabulary

Figure 3.2 Real world through software.

Our terms *object* and *action* cover a broad range:

- *Object* includes not only individual programming-language objects but also software components, programs, networks, relations, and records as well as hardware, people, and organizations—anything that presents a definable encapsulated behavior to the world around it or can be usefully thought of as such.

- *Action* includes not only individual programming-language messages or proce- dure calls but also complete dialogs between objects of all kinds. We can always talk about the effects of an action even without knowing exactly who initiates it or how it works in detail, as in this schedule_course example.

The diagram in Figure 3.1 can be seen in two ways. First, it can be a picture of the real world. The objects represent human instructors, scheduled sessions, and so on. The attributes represent who is really scheduled to do what, as written on the office wall planner and the instructors' diaries. An action is an event that has happened in the real world, and, invariably, it can be looked at in more detail whenever we wish. Scheduling a course involves several interactions between participants and resources.

Alternatively, the diagram may be about what a particular object knows about the world outside it (which may be different from some other object's view). In particular, it can be a model of the state of a software component.

The occurrence of the schedule_course action could represent a dialog between players in the real world. A representative from the client's company contacts the course scheduler in the seminar company, negotiates the dates and fees for a new session of the course, and updates the office wall planner.

Equally, the action could be an abstraction of a dialog with a software system. In that case, because of the Golden Rule of OO design (that we base the design on

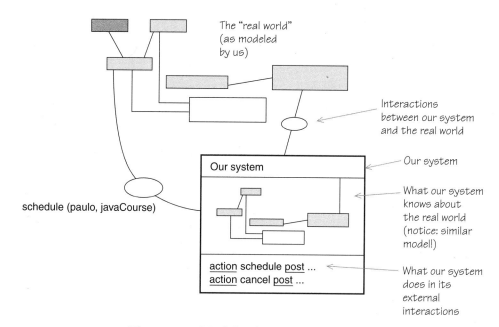

The "real world"
(as modeled
by us)

Interactions
between our system
and the real world

Our system

What our system
knows about
the real world
(notice: similar
model!)

schedule (paulo, javaCourse)

action schedule <u>post</u> ...
action cancel <u>post</u> ...

What our system
does in its
external
interactions

Figure 3.3   Models of domain and system.

a domain model), we can use the same picture to denote objects (whether in a database or main memory) that the system uses to represent the real world. The interesting actions are then the interactions between the system and the rest of the world: They update the system's knowledge of what is going on in the world, as represented in the attributes.

Now schedule (paulo, javaCourse) can refer to whatever dialog someone must have with our system to get it to arrange the session, and we can use snapshots of the system state to describe the effect the action has on the system (see Figure 3.3). In turn, the system's state (as described by the snapshots) will have an effect on the outcome of future actions, including the outputs to the external objects (including people!) who interact with it.

3.1.5   Two Kinds of Action

There are two main kinds of actions we are concerned with in this book. They correspond to individual and collective behaviors of objects.

The first kind, a *localized* action (often called an *operation* in code), is an action which a single object is requested to perform; it is specified without consideration of the initiator of the action. You can recognize localized actions by their focus on a single distinguished object type:

<u>action</u> Type::actionName (...) ...

In program code, one object requests that another object per- 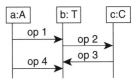 form an operation; the result is a state change, and some outputs. The interactions are illustrated with a sequence diagram: Objects are vertical lines, and each operation request is an arrow. This also applies outside of code; objects a,b, and c could be real-world objects such as client, company, and instructor; or they could be instances of software classes, such as session, calendar, and event. This is the subject of the current chapter.

The second kind of action is a *joint* action To describe behavior and interactions of a group of objects, we focus on the net effect of interactions between multiple objects, and we specify that effect as a higher-level action with all objects involved. A joint action is written

    <u>action</u> (party1: Type1, party2: Type2, ...) :: actionName (...)

Notice that the joint action is not centered on a single distinguished object type. There are *directed* variations of joint actions in which a sender and a receiver are designated, but the action effect is still described in terms of all participants.

At the business level, it takes a sequence of interactions 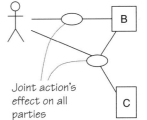 between client and seminar company, including enquire, schedule, deliver, follow-up, and pay, to together constitute an abstract purchaseCourse action. This sequence has a net effect on both client and seminar company: not only has the seminar company delivered a service and gained some revenue, but also the client has paid some fees and gained knowledge. In software, it may take a sequence of low-level operations via the user interfaces (UIs) of multiple applications and databases to complete a scheduleCourse operation. Such a joint action, also called a use case, is the subject of Chapter 4.

Each occurrence of such a joint action is shown as a horizontal bar with ellipses in a sequence diagram, whereas the 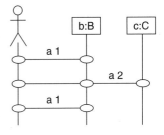 finer-grained operations were depicted as simple arrows. Note that each action occurrence could be realized by many different finer-grained interactions, eventually reducing to a sequence of operations.

3.2 *More-Precise Action Specifications*

Well-written postconditions can be used as the basis for verification and testing. For this purpose, we should write the postconditions in a more precise style: as test (Boolean) functions. You can use the Boolean expression part of your favorite programming language; we will use a general syntax from UML called Object Constraint Language (OCL). It translates readily to most programming languages but is more convenient for specification.

The other benefit of writing the postconditions more formally is that doing so tends to make you think harder about the requirements. The effort is not wasted. You would have had to make these decisions anyway; you're just focusing on the most important ones and getting a better end result.

The rest of this section deals with key features of the more precise style. It is applicable to both business and component modeling. Later sections differentiate the two and discuss action specification in greater detail.

3.2.1   Using Snapshots to Guide Postconditions

A postcondition states what we want an end result to be. For example, let's suppose one instructor can be the mentor of one other instructor; perhaps some of them get too outrageous in class from time to time. The action of assigning a mentor is, informally, as follows:

<u>action</u>   assign_mentor (subject: Instructor, watchdog: Instructor)
<u>post</u>:   The watchdog is now the mentor of the subject.

This can be shown in a pair of snapshots (Figure 3.4).

There wasn't any mention of mentors in the model we drew earlier, so we needed to invent a way of describing them. Every instructor might or might not have a mentor, so this fragment of static model seems appropriate.

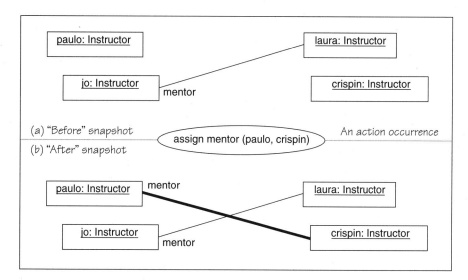

Figure 3.4   Assigning a mentor.

Now we can write the action in terms of this association:

<u>action</u>   assign_mentor (subject: Instructor, watchdog : Instructor)
<u>post</u>   *-- the watchdog is now the mentor of the subject*
            subject.mentor = watchdog

Notice the following points.

- The postcondition states what we need; it doesn't say anything about aspects we don't care about (although we might want to be more explicit about what happens to any existing mentee of the watchdog). Looking at the snapshot, you can see how the example we illustrated corresponds to the change.
- Associations are by default bidirectional, so it isn't necessary also to write watchdog.mentee = subject. However, that would be an alternative to what we wrote.
- Navigation expressions in an action spec should generally start from the parameters. (So mentor=watchdog would be wrong—whose mentor?) Other starting points are self (in actions performed by a particular object) and variables you have declared locally, in, for example, forAll and let clauses (see Section 2.5.2).

Informal → snapshot → formal. This basic procedure is the general way to formalize a postcondition. However, you must be careful of alternative cases: a snapshot illustrates only one case, and so you may need to draw several to get a feel for the gamut of possibilities. It's the action postconditions you're really trying to determine; the snapshots are mainly thinking tools.

3.2.2   Comparing Before and After

A postcondition makes an assertion about the states immediately before and after the action has happened. For every object there are therefore two snapshots and two complete sets of attribute values to refer to. By default, every mention of an attribute in a postcondition refers to the newer version; but you can refer to its prior value by suffixing it with @pre.

- subject.mentor@pre refers to subject's old mentor.
- subject.mentor.mentee@pre refers to subject's new mentor's old mentee.
- subject.mentor@pre.mentee@pre refers to subject's old mentor's old mentee.
- subject.(mentor.mentee)@pre refers to same as previous.
- subject.mentor@pre.mentee refers to subject's previous mentor's *new* mentee.

Each navigation expression is a way of getting from one object to another. By default, the navigation is within a single snapshot; @pre can be applied to an expression to evaluate it in the preceding snapshot. But what you get from an expression is the (constant) identity of an object; and unless you keep applying @pre, further expressions will always evaluate in the newer time. Figure 3.5 shows a before-and-after snapshot and the object referred to by subject.mentor.mentee@pre.

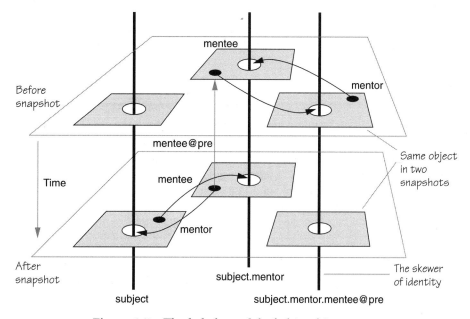

Figure 3.5 The kebab model of object history.

The before-and-after times are immediately before and after an action occurred. Here is an example:

<u>action</u>   assign_mentor (subject: Instructor, watchdog : Instructor)
<u>post</u>   subject.mentor = watchdog and   *-- watchdog is now subject's mentor,*
         -- and if watchdog had a previous mentee, they now have none
         <u>let</u> ex_mentee = watchdog.mentee@pre <u>in</u>
             ex_mentee <> null ==> ex_mentee.mentor = null

Here are some points to note.

- null is used to represent "no object" when an association permits it.
- ==>, also written implies, is used to mean: if ... then ... .
- @pre takes you back to the previous value of a changeable attribute; parameters refer to the same object, so there is no point in writing subject@pre.
- An action spec deals with just two states, so x@pre@pre is undefined.

Precise abstraction raises pertinent questions. The level of detail here is enough to draw out debate. When this example is discussed in groups, this is often a point when discussion arises about what should happen to the ex-mentee (dreadful expression! I hope never to be one). For example, should the static model be revised to allow more than one mentee per mentor?

Whatever the answer, this is a business question; but it might not have arisen at this early stage if we hadn't tried being more precise. And yet we have done so without waiting until we are wading in reams of program code.

3.2.3   Newly Created Objects

As a consequence of an action, new objects can be created. The set of these objects has the special name <u>new</u> in a postcondition,[3] and there are some special idioms for using it. After drawing the snapshot in Figure 3.1, we can write

<u>action</u>   schedule_course (reqCourse: Course, reqStart: Date)
<u>post</u>:   <u>let</u> ns: Session.<u>new</u> [course = reqCourse and startDate = reqStart
                             and endDate − startDate = reqCourse.length]
              <u>in</u>   ns.instructor.available@pre(startDate, endDate)
          -- there is a new Session—call it ns—with the attributes specified; and
          -- its instructor was initially available for the requested period

Notice the following points.

- The power of the postcondition is that it lets you avoid unnecessary detail. We have not said which instructor should be assigned nor how one should be chosen from the available ones. We have limited our statement to only the requirements we need: that the person chosen should have no prior commitment.
- We have deferred some complexity by assuming a parameterized attribute available defined with instructors. We can define its value later.

3.2.4   Variables an Action Spec Can Use

An action spec tells about the outcome of a named action happening to a set of parameter objects and (for localized actions) a receiver. The spec of an action can use the following:

- self, referring to the receiver object whose type is written
- The parameter names referring to those objects
- A <u>result</u> object
- The attributes of the type of self written or drawn as associations
- The attributes of the parameters and the result
- Local names bound in let, forAll, exists, and so on.

3.2.5   Collections

In the superposed pair of snapshots in Figure 3.6, the new state is shown in bold. Many of the associations in a model are of multiple cardinality and by default rep-

---

3. Postconditions have no sequencing, solving an age-old problem:
<u>action</u> which_came_first?() <u>post</u>: Chicken.new <> 0 & Egg.new <> 0

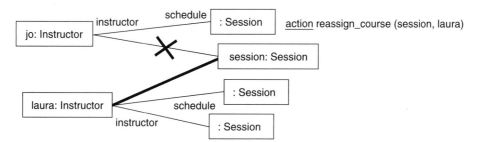

Figure 3.6   Snapshot for action reassign_course.

resent sets (without nested sets—we call these *flat* sets). We can use the collection operators (see Section 2.5.2):

<u>action</u>   reassign_course (session : Session, new_inst: Instructor)
<u>post</u>:   -- *An existing Session is taken off one instructor's schedule and placed*
              onto this new one
           <u>let</u> ex_instructor = session.instructor@pre
           <u>in</u>
                  ex_instructor.schedule = ex_instructor.schedule@pre – session
      and   new_inst.schedule = new_inst.schedule + session

Notice the use of + and – with collections—only the set union and difference. (The construct collectionAttribute= collectionAttribute@pre + x is so common that some of us have taken to writing collectionAttribute += x. But if you do this, please remember that this is not an assignment but is merely a comparison between two states. Also, a few extra keystrokes are usually better than the overloading of +, +=, and so on.)

We could perhaps more simply have asserted

           session.instructor = new_inst

Because the static model tells us a session has only one instructor, this might have been adequate. However, a designer might mistake the meaning of this and make this session the only one the new instructor is assigned to, deleting all the instructor's other commitments. So we choose to be more explicit.[4]

3.2.6   Preconditions

Many of the action postconditions we define make sense only under certain starting conditions, which can be characterized by a precondition. The precondition deals only with one state, so it doesn't have @pre or <u>new</u>. For example:

---

4. There is a deeper issue concerning "framing." In a fully formal spec such as for safety-critical systems, you would be more explicit about which objects are left untouched.

<u>action</u>   assign_mentor (subject : Instructor, watchdog : Instructor)
<u>pre</u>   *-- happens only if the subject doesn't already have one*
          subject.mentor = null
<u>post</u>   *...as before ...*

The precondition is also a purely Boolean expression and has no side effects; it can refer only to inputs and initial values of attributes. The corresponding postcondition is not guaranteed by the implementor if the precondition did not hold.

Precise preconditions are essential for system safety properties—the things to guard against to avoid undefined behaviors. The postconditions are primarily used to document the state changes and outputs guaranteed by the implementation.

3.2.7 More-Precise Postconditions: Summary

This section has looked at the basics of writing action specifications precisely enough to form the basis for testing a component and to make the model explicit enough to uncover business issues.

The techniques we have seen can be used to describe the interactions that occur within a business; or they can describe the actions performed by a software system or component; or—the simplest case—they can describe the operations performed by an individual object within a software design. That is what we will look at next.

(The syntax of action specs and postconditions is shown later in Exhibits 3.1 and 3.2. Specifying requirements for a complete software system, with a user interface and so on is the topic of Chapter 15, How to Specify a Component. Specifying the interface to a substantial component is covered in Chapter 10, Components and Connectors.)

3.3 *Two Java Implementations of a Calendar*

This chapter is about specifying types: what a component does as seen from the outside and ignoring what goes on inside. But "brains work bottom up," so it will be easier to understand what the specification means if we can see the kinds of implementation that it can have. Let's start the time-honored way: we'll hack the code first and write up the spec afterward.[5]

Our seminar scheduling application will have many classes in its implementation. One likely class is a calendar that tracks various scheduled events for various instructors. We start with two different Java implementations of the calendar.

---

5. If this offends your sense of decency, please skip to the next section. You may wish to avert your eyes from the naked code on display.

Then we show how the external behaviors can be specified independent of implementation choices and even of implementation language and technology. We will ignore any UI aspects.

Both implementations support just four external operations on a calendar; they may introduce other internal operations and objects as needed.

- addEvent adds a new event to the current calendar schedule.
- isFree determines whether an instructor is free on given dates.
- removeEvent deletes an existing event from the schedule.
- calendarFor returns the scheduled events for a particular instructor. It is returned as an Enumeration—that is, a small object that has operations to step through the collection until the end.

3.3.1   Calendar A Implementation

The implementation of calendar A keeps a separate unordered vector of events for each instructor in a hashtable, keyed by the instructor. The calendar's internal interactions are described in the sequence diagram in Figure 3.7, with each arrow indicating an operation request. Upon receiving an addEvent request, the calendar first creates a new event object. It then looks up the event vector for the current instructor in its hashtable, creating a new vector if none exists. The new event is added to this vector, and the hashtable is updated. The Java code for this design is shown on the next two pages.

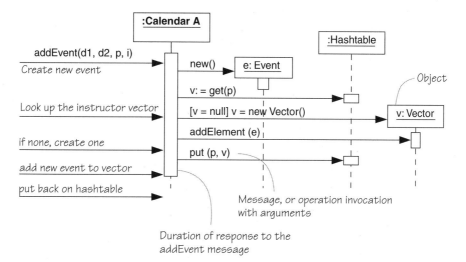

Figure 3.7   Internal design interactions of calendar A.

```java
import java.util.*;

// This calendar organizes events by instructor in a hashtable keyed by instructor
class Calendar_A {
    private Hashtable instructorSchedule = new Hashtable();

    // provided no schedule conflict, this creates and records new event
    public Event addEvent (Date d1,Date d2, Instructor p, Object info){
        if (! isFree (p, d1, d2)) return null;

        Event e= new Event (d1, d2, p,info);
        Vector v = (Vector) instructorSchedule.get (p);
        if (v == null) v = new Vector ();
        v.addElement (e);
        instructorSchedule.put (p,v);
        return e;
    }

    // Answer if the instructor free between these dates
    // do any of the instructor's events overlap d1-d2?
    public boolean isFree (Instructor p, Date d1, Date d2) {
        Vector events =(Vector) instructorSchedule.get (p);
        for   (Enumeration e = events.elements(); e.hasMoreElements (); ) {
            Event ev = (Event) e.nextElement ();
            if (ev.overlaps (d1,d2)) return false;
        }
        return true;
    }

    // remove this event from the calendar
    public void removeEvent (Event e) {
        Vector v = (Vector) instructorSchedule.get (e.who);
        v.removeElement (e);
    }

    // return the events for the instructor (as an enumeration)
    public Enumeration calendarFor (Instructor i) {
        return ((Vector) instructorSchedule.get(i)).elements();
    }
}

// internal details irrelevant here
class Instructor { }

// represents one session
// Just two public operations: delete() and overlaps()
class Event {
    Date from;
    Date to;
```

```
Instructor who;
Object info; //additional info, e.g. Session
Calendar_A container; // for correct deletion
Event (Date d1,Date d2, Instructor w, Object i) {
      from = d1;
      to = d2;
      who = w;
      info = i;
}

// does this event overlap the given dates?
boolean overlaps (Date d1, Date d2){
      return false;
}

public void delete() { /* details not shown*/ }
}
```

3.3.2   Calendar B Implementation

This version uses a more complex representation, not detailed here, to maintain the events so that they are indexed directly by their date ranges. This data structure is encapsulated behind an interface called EventContainer that does all the real work.

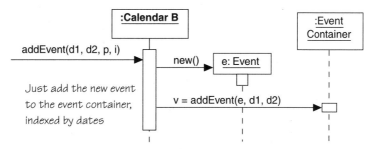

Figure 3.8   Internal design interactions of calendar B.

The internal interactions for this calendar implementation are shown in Figure 3.8, and the Java code starts below and continues on the next two pages.

```
import java.util.*;

// Organizes events by their dates using a fancy event container
class Calendar_B {
      privateEventContainer schedule;

      // create the event and add to schedule
      public Event addEvent (Date d1, Date d2, Instructor p, Object info) {
```

```
                Event e= new Event (p,info, schedule);
                schedule.addEvent (e, d1, d2);
                return e;
        }


        // is instructor free between those dates?
        // are any of the events between d1-d2 for this instructor
        public boolean isFree (Instructor p, Date d1, Date d2) {
            for   (Enumeration e = schedule.eventsBetween (d1, d2);
                        e.hasMoreElements (); )
                    if (((Event) e.nextElement()).who ==p) return false;
                return true;
        }


        // remove the event from the schedule
        public voidremoveEvent (Event e) {
                schedule.removeEvent(e);
        }


        // return the events for the instructor (as an enumeration)
        public Enumeration calendarFor (Instructor i) {
                // implementation not shown
                // presumably less efficient, since tuned for date-based lookup
                // e.g. get all eventsBetween (-INF, +INF)
                // select only those for instructor i
                return null;
        }

    }


    // internal details of instructor irrelevant here
    class Instructor { }


    // Just one public operation: delete() shown
    // dates not explicitly recorded; container maintains date index
    class Event{
        Instructor who;
        Object info;
        EventContainer container; // for correct deletion
        Event (Instructor w, Object i, EventContainer c) {
            who = w;
            info = i;
        }

        public void delete() { /* details not shown*/ }
    }
```

```
// event container: a fancy range-indexed structure
interface EventContainer {
        // return the events that overlap with the d1-d2 range
        Enumeration eventsBetween (Date d1, Date d2);
        // add, remove an event
        void addEvent (Event e, Date d1, Date d2);
        void removeEvent (Event e);
}
```

3.4 *Type Specification of Calendar*

A client could use either implementation of the calendar; both of them implement the same type. We must describe this type so that a client can use either implementation based solely on the type specification (this example is small enough to illustrate the details).

Figure 3.7 and Figure 3.8 show that the internal representation and interactions differ widely between the implementations. Our behavior specification must abstract these irrelevant "internal" interactions and include only interactions with objects that *the client should be aware of.*[6] What we really want to specify is the calendar together with some abstraction of its (hidden) event container, hashtable, vector, and so on (see Figure 3.9).

Our type specification must be precise enough that the client understands what assumptions the implementations can make and what guarantees they provide in return. For example, are the events returned by calendarFor ordered by increasing dates? When you delete() an event, is a separate call to removeEvent on the calendar required? If it is, which one should be done first? What happens if the dates d1,d2 are not in the right order on a call to isFree?

4. What outputs does it produce? To whom?

1. What operations does the object support?

2. What is required of the inputs?

3a. What state change does the object undergo . . .   3b. . . . ignoring "internal" interactions?

Figure 3.9 External object behavior abstractions internal details.

---

6. Try understanding a bureaucratic government office in terms of its internal interactions.

3.4.1 From Attributes to Operation Specification

Following is a sequence of steps to arrive at a precise type specification of the calendar.[7] We assume that the calendar can return output values to the client and that all other interactions are internal details that should not be known to the client. We omit discussion of error conditions and exceptions for now; they are covered in more detail in Section 3.6.3, Multiple Action Specs: Two Styles, and Section 8.4, Action Exceptions and Composing Specs.

1. List the operations: addEvent, isFree, removeEvent, and calendarFor.

2. Write informal operation descriptions of each one.

- addEvent creates a new event with the properties provided and adds it to the calendar schedule.
- isFree returns true if the instructor is free in the date range provided.
- removeEvent removes the event from the calendar.
- calendarFor returns the set of events scheduled for the instructor.

At this stage, it's usual to start sketching a static type diagram (see Figure 3.10), even though completing it is the focus of a later step. Draw a diagram that includes the nouns mentioned in the action specs and their associations and attributes.

3. Identify the inputs and outputs. At the level of individual operations in code, these are usually straightforward, perhaps already known.

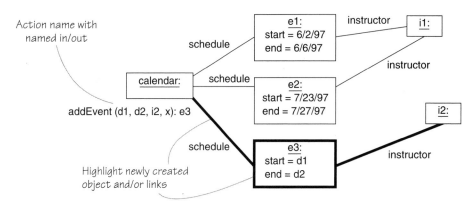

Figure 3.10 A snapshot pair for an action occurrence.

---

7. Thanks to Larry Wall for pulling apart the steps involved.

addEvent	(date1, date2, instructor, info): Event
isFree	(instructor): Boolean
removeEvent	(event)
calendarFor	(instructor): Enumeration

4. Working from your initial type diagram, sketch a pair of snapshots before and after each operation. Draw them on one diagram, using highlights to show newly created objects and links and X and for objects or links that do not exist in the "after" snapshot. Name the input and output parameters to the action occurrence consistently with the snapshots.

After an addEvent, the highlighted objects and links are created; the output is e3. On the same snapshot, after a calendarFor (i1), the snapshot is not changed, and the output enumeration will list {e1, e2}. For read-only functions such as isFree, check whether there is some way the information could be extracted from every snapshot.

5. Draw a static type diagram of the object being specified, generalizing all snapshots (see Figure 3.11).[8] Here are the attributes mentioned by each operation.

- addEvent: Calendar schedule represents events currently in the calendar. Each event has attributes instructor and start and end dates. The overlaps attribute will be convenient.
- isFree: Instructor has an attribute free on a given date, constrained by the events scheduled for that instructor as described by the instructor's schedule.
- removeEvent: No new attributes are needed; schedule on calendar suffices.

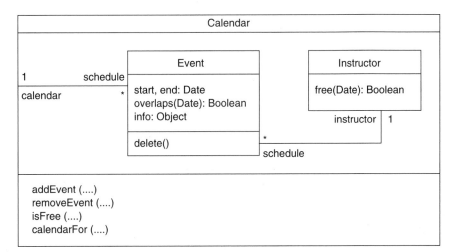

Figure 3.11   Type model attributes are used to specify operations.

8. Not all tools can draw one type inside another. An alternative is given in Section 3.11.

– calendarFor: Use a schedule attribute on instructor; note that the externally provided operation is not the same as the attribute that models the required state information.

6. Document the invariants that the model should satisfy.

-- the start of any event must be before (or at) its end
inv Event:: start <= end

-- instructor free on any date means "no event on his schedule overlaps that date"
inv Instructor:: free(d: Date) = (self.schedule [overlaps(d)] ->isEmpty)

-- event overlaps (d) means same as "d between start and end, inclusive"
inv Event:: overlaps(d: Date) = (start <= d & end >= d)

7. Specify operations. Make the operation specs more precise.

-- the addEvent operation on a calendar
action Calendar::addEvent (d1: Date, d2: Date, i: Instructor, o: Object): Event
      pre: -- provided dates are ordered, and instructor is free for the range
                      of dates
                      d1 < d2 & {d1..d2}->forAll (d | i.free (d))
      post: -- a new event is on the calendar schedule for those dates and
                      that instructor
                      result: Event.new [info = o &
                                start = d1 & end = d2 & instructor = i & calendar = self]

A function is an operation that may return a result and causes no other state change.

-- is a given instructor free for a certain range of dates?
function Calendar::isFree (i: Instructor, d1: Date, d2: Date) : Boolean
      pre: -- provided the dates are ordered
                      d1 < d2
      post: -- the result is true if that instructor is free for all dates between
                      d1 and d2
                      result = {d1..d2}->forAll (d | i.free (d))

-- remove the given event
action Calendar::removeEvent (e: Event)
      pre: -- provided the event is on this calendar
                      schedule->includes (e)
      post: -- that event has been removed from the calendar and instructor
                      schedules
                      not schedule->includes (e) and
                      not e.instructor.schedule@pre->includes (e)

-- return the calendar for the instructor; also a function or side-effect-free
   operation
function Calendar::calendarFor (i: Instructor): Enumeration
      pre: -- none; returns an empty enumeration if no scheduled events
                      true
      post: -- returns a new enumeration on the events on that instructor's
                      schedule
                      result: Enumeration.new [unvisited = i.schedule]

8. Create parameter models. Describe (by a type model) any input and output parameter types and their attributes and operations to the extent that the client and the implementor need to understand and agree on them.

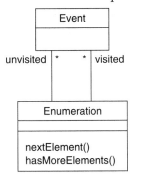

The Enumeration returned by calendarFor could also be modeled explicitly. It provides two operations, informally specified next. These operations could be made more precise by using the two attributes on the enumeration.

<u>action</u> Enumeration::nextElement() : Event
<u>pre:</u> -- provided the enumeration is not empty
<u>post:</u> -- returns (and visits) an unvisited event, in no particular order

<u>function</u> Enumeration::hasMoreElements() : Boolean
<u>post:</u> -- true if all events have been visited

Event has a delete() operation that is visible to the client. Clearly, the client needs to know the effects of this operation—for example, does delete also remove it from the calendar? They can be specified directly using the same type model:

```
-- deletion of an event
action Event::delete ()
      pre:      true
      post:     -- the event is no longer on the calendar's or instructor's schedule
                not (calendar.schedule)@pre->includes (e) and
                not (instructor.schedule)@pre->includes (e)
```

Or, more concisely (as discussed in Section 3.8.5):

```
-- deletion of an event
action Event::delete ()
      pre:      true
      post:     -- the same effect as removing the event from the calendar
                -- (though not necessarily by calling the removeEvent method)
                [[ calendar.removeEvent (self) ]]
```

Note that an adequate specification of Calendar requires a specification of other object types that are client-accessible, such as Event and Enumeration.

9. Write a dictionary of terms and improve your informal specifications.

instructor	the person assigned to a scheduled event
schedule	the set of events instructor is currently scheduled for
free	if an instructor is free on a date, it means that no event on his schedule overlaps with that date
Calendar	the collection of scheduled events
schedule	the set of events currently "on" the calendar
Event	a scheduled commitment (meeting, session, etc.)
when	the range of dates for this event
instructor	the instructor assigned to this event
overlaps	if an event overlaps a date, it means that date lies within the range (inclusive) of dates of the event

Even if invariants and operation specifications will not be formalized, you can concisely define the terminology of types and attributes and consequently of operation requirements. Contrast the following updated informal operation specifications with the ones we started with. (Which is worse: reams of ambiguous narrative, or tomes of formal or pseudoformal syntax with no explanatory prose?)

> *-- add an event to a calendar*
> <u>action</u> Calendar::addEvent (d1: Date, d2: Date, i: Instructor, o: Object)
>   <u>pre:</u>   *-- provided dates are ordered, and instructor is free for range of dates*
>   <u>post:</u>   *-- a new event is on calendar for those dates and that instructor*
>
> *-- is a given instructor free for a certain range of dates?*
> <u>function</u> Calendar::isFree (i: Instructor, d1: Date, d2: Date) : Boolean
>   <u>pre:</u>   *-- provided the dates are ordered*
>   <u>post:</u>   *-- return is true if instructor is free for all dates between d1 and d2*
>
> *-- return the calendar for the instructor*
> <u>function</u> Calendar::calendarFor (i: Instructor): Enumeration
>   <u>pre:</u>   *-- no assumptions; could return an empty set enumeration if no*
>   *scheduled events*
>   <u>post:</u>   *-- returns an enumeration on the events on that instructor's*
>   *schedule*
>
> *-- deletion of an event*
> <u>action</u> Event::delete ()
>   <u>pre:</u>   *-- no assumptions*
>   <u>post:</u>   *-- the same effect as removing the event from the calendar*
>   *-- (though not necessarily by calling the removeEvent method)*

10. Improve the model or design by some refactoring. For example, we can remove the repeated constraint d1<d2 by introducing a DateRange type, with attributes start,end dates and overlaps(date), and an invariant on these attributes.

3.4.2   The Resulting Object Type Specification

Calendar requirements have been specified in such a way that they can be fulfilled by either implementation—or indeed by any other that behaves suitably. The actions have been listed, and we have described the effect of each action on our model of the calendar state. Figure 3.12 shows the specification task's main products.

3.5 *Actions with Invariants*

Actions cause changes in attributes. Invariants are rules about relations that must hold between attributes. How are actions and invariants related?

3.5.1   Actions Need Not Duplicate Invariants

Operation specifications can be simplified by taking advantage of constraints in the type model. Consider the type model of Scheduler in Figure 3.13 with these invariants:

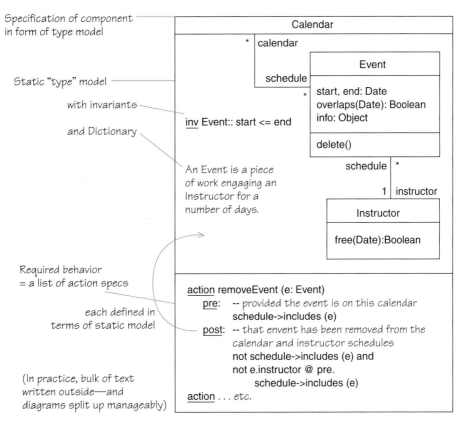

Specification of component
in form of type model

Static "type" model

with invariants

and Dictionary

An Event is a piece
of work engaging an
Instructor for a
number of days.

Required behavior
= a list of action specs

each defined in
terms of static model

(In practice, bulk of text
written outside—and
diagrams split up manageably)

Figure 3.12   The product of behavior modeling is an object type spec.

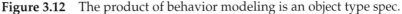

inv Instructor::   -- only assigned to sessions I am qualified to teach
    qualifiedFor -> includesAll (sessions.course)
            -- never double-booked; no 2 assigned sessions that overlap
    sessions ->forAll (s1, s2 | s <> s1 implies not s1.overlaps(s2))
inv Session::   -- only confirmed with assigned instructor
    confirmed ==> instructor <> null and
    -- session dates cover course duration
    end = start + course.duration -- assume suitable "Date+Duration: Date"

Let us try to define an operation against this model.

-- change the dates of a session
action Scheduler::change_dates (s: Session, d: Date)
    pre: s.start > now and   -- (1) not from the past
             s.course <> nil and   -- (2) has a valid course
             s.course.duration : Days   -- (3) course has a valid duration
    post: s.start = d and   -- (4) start date updated
             s.end = d + course.duration -- (5) end date updated

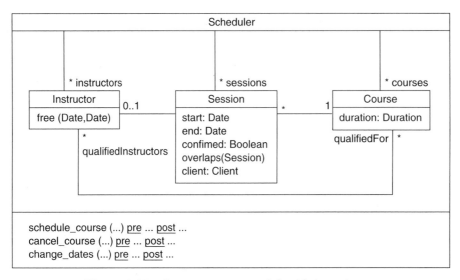

Figure 3.13   Scheduler type model with invariants.

Which parts of the specification are necessary, and which are unnecessary?

1. *Necessary*: One cannot change the dates of a session from the past.

2. *Unnecessary:* It would not make sense to change the dates of a session that did not have a course. However, the type model already uses a multiplicity of 1 to state that any session object must have a corresponding course. The operation parameter already requires s to be of type session, so we do not need to repeat (2); using the type name Session implies all required properties of session objects.

3. *Unnecessary:* The postcondition refers to start + course.duration, which makes sense only if duration was a valid Duration. Once again, the type model already stipulates that every course has a duration attribute that is a valid Duration.

4. *Necessary:* This is the essential part of the postcondition.

5. *Unnecessary:* It seems reasonable that the end date of the course is also changed. However, the relationship between the start and end dates and the course duration is not unique to this operation, so it has been captured in the type model as an invariant. It is sufficient to state that the start date has changed; the invariant implies that the end date is also changed.

The unnecessary parts would not be incorrect, only redundant. Removing them leaves a much simpler operation specification:

```
action Scheduler::change_dates (s: Session, d: Date)
    pre:    s.start > now        -- not from the past
    post:   s.start = d          -- start date updated
```

A more interesting example is schedule_course.

-- this spec deals with scheduling a confirmed course
action Scheduler::schedule_course (who: Client, c: Course, d: Date)
    <u>pre</u>:   -- Provided there is an instructor qualified and free for these dates
          c.qualifiedInstructors ->includes (i | i.free (d, d+c.duration))
    <u>post</u>:   -- A new confirmed Session has been created for that course, client,
          dates
          s:Session.new [*confirmed* & client = who & course = c & date = d]
          -- assigned one of the course qualified instructors who was free
          instructor : c.qualifiedInstructors [free(d, d+c.duration)@pre]

It is already an invariant that any confirmed course must have a qualified instructor and that instructors cannot be double-booked. Hence, the italicized parts of the postcondition are redundant, and the last line in this specification can be omitted. Implementations may choose among the available qualified instructors in different ways.

3.5.2   Redundant Specifications Can Be Useful

We have seen how certain elements of an operation specification are implied by the invariants. Writing them would not be incorrect, only redundant. It can still be useful to write them down; note the change_dates example earlier. However, it is worth distinguishing those parts of the specification the designer should explicitly pay attention to—the invariants and necessary parts of operation specs—from those parts that would automatically be satisfied as a result.

Just as we can introduce *derived attributes*—those marked with a / that could be omitted because they are defined entirely in terms of other attributes—we can also introduce *derived specifications:* properties we claim would automatically be true of any correct implementation of the nonderived specifications. Using /pre: / post:, we can more explicitly define the change_dates operation:

action Scheduler::change_dates (s: Session, d: Date)
    <u>pre</u>:   s.start > now   -- necessary
      <u>/pre</u>:   s.course <> nil and   -- derived: multiplicity 1
           s.course.duration : Days   -- derived: attribute definition
    <u>post</u>:   s.start = d   -- necessary
      <u>/post</u>: s.end = d + course.duration   -- derived: session invariant

The same holds for derived invariants. Of course, we would write only those claims we consider important to explicitly point out.

    <u>inv</u> Session::   end = start + course.duration
    <u>/inv</u> Session:: start = end – course.duration -- derived: definition of +, –

▶ *redundant specs*   A specification (including invariants and pre- and postconditions) that is implied by other parts of the model but is included for emphasis or clarity. Such specs are prefixed with a /.

3.5.3   Static Invariants

A static invariant is implicitly anded to the precondition and the postcondition of every action within a defined range of actions. In the simplest case, the range of an invariant means all operations on members of the type it is defined for (see Figure 3.14). Consider this code:

```
action Scheduler::change_dates (s: Session, d: Date)
      pre:      s.start > now            -- not from the past
      post:     s.start = d              -- start date updated
```

It combines with the invariant that every confirmed session has an assigned instructor; and an instructor is assigned only to a course she is qualified for; and she is never double-booked, to effectively yield

```
action Scheduler::change_dates (s: Session, d: Date)
      pre:      s.start > now               -- not from the past
         &      provided other invariants hold at start of action
      post:     s.start = d                 -- start date updated
         &      s.confirmed ==>             -- if still confirmed
                    (s.instructor <> null -- will have an assigned instructor
                    & s.instructor : s.title.qualifiedInstructors -- who is qualified
                    & s.instructor is not double-booked )
```

However, the private operations of any implementation may see situations in which the invariant is "untrue." For example, suppose the user assigns an instructor to a session whose dates overlap an existing assigned session. One acceptable implementation would be to deassign the existing session, but in the actual code, this might happen after assigning the new one. Thus, the invariant is temporarily broken between *internal* actions in the code, making it even more important to have the invariants properly scoped to a given set of externally available operations.

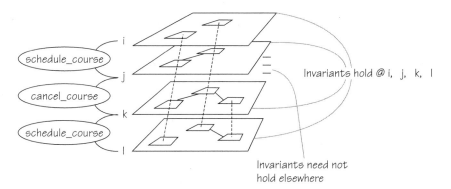

Figure 3.14   Invariants hold before and after a range of actions.

3.5.4 Effect Invariants

A static invariant is expected to hold before and after the actions in its range. Sometimes, an effect is required to be true of all the actions in its range. For example, suppose we want to count every operation invocation on our calendar. An *effect invariant* defines an effect that is invariant across all actions in its range and is implicitly anded to the postconditions of those actions. Unlike a static invariant, it can refer to before and after states. An invariant effect does not need to be named and cannot use parameters.

> inv effect Calendar::count_invocations post: count += 1

An effect invariant is anded to the postcondition of all actions in its range; it implicitly adds the last clause to this spec:

```
-- remove the given event
action Calendar::removeEvent (e: Event)
        pre:        -- provided the event is on this calendar
                    schedule->includes (e)
        post:       -- that event has been removed from the calendar and instructor
                        schedules
                    not schedule->includes (e) and
                    not e.instructor@pre.schedule->includes (e)
                    -- and the effect invariant is implicitly applied
                    and count += 1
```

By using effect invariant conditions in the postconditions, we can describe effects that apply selectively to any action that meets the condition. For example, here's how to keep a count of all actions that create or remove an event on the schedule:

```
inv effect count_event_creations_and_deletions
        post:       -- if the set of Events before and after differ, count this action
                        occurrence
                    schedule@pre <> schedule ==> count += 1
```

▶ *invariant effect* A transition rule that applies to the postcondition of every action in the range of the invariant; by writing a conditional (eff1 ==> eff2) you can impose the rule selectively on those actions that have effect eff1.—for example, "all operations that alter **x** must also notify **y**."

3.5.5 Context and Control of an Invariant

The type in which an invariant is written is called its context. It applies only to the operations of that type. (In Chapter 4 we will also see contexts of actions between groups of collaborating objects.)

Any object claimed to conform to the type should make it look to clients as if the invariant were always true. While the client is waiting for an operation to complete, the invariant can be broken behind the interface that the type describes; but it must be restored when the operation is complete. Behind that interface are components of the design that have their own nested contexts and invariants that govern them (see Figure 3.15).

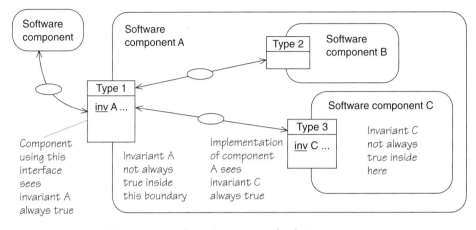

Figure 3.15   Invariants outside their contexts.

As with any specification, it is possible to write invariants that cannot be satisfied by an implementor. In your spec of a Sludge vending machine, you can write an invariant that the weather is always sunny in northern England; but I cannot deliver such a device.[9] But if you write an effect invariant that the machine's cashbox will always fill as the can stack decreases, I believe I can do that.

To achieve it, you must employ certain techniques in your design. For example, if you forget to include a stout metal case around the outside, your assets will monotonically decrease: people can get directly at the cans (and any cash that others may have been foolish enough to insert). Similarly, the developer of an alphabetically sorted list of customers cannot guarantee that the list will remain sorted if other designers' code can directly update customers' names. You can guarantee only what you have control over.

In designing to meet an invariant, then, you must think not only of your own immediate object but also of all the objects it uses; and you must be aware of any behavior they have that might affect the specs you are trying to meet. Fundamentally, objects must be designed in collaborating groups—the subject of Chapter 4.

3.6   *Interpreting an Action Specification*

An action specification generalizes all occurrences of the action; in other words, it should hold true for every snapshot pair (Figure 3.16), much as a type model generalizes all snapshots in Figure 3.11. Given a type T with operation M whose oper-

---

9. Although, come to think of it, with the right concoctions in the cans ...

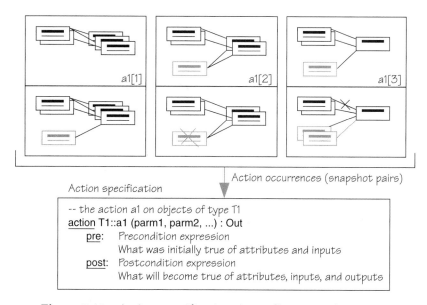

Figure 3.16   Action specification generalizes snapshot pairs.

ation spec has a precondition P and postcondition Q, we interpret this operation spec as follows:

> *If you examine the history of any object that correctly implements* T *and find in that history any occurrence of the operation* M, *then if* P *was true of the invocation parameters and attribute values immediately before that invocation occurred,* Q *should have become true immediately after that invocation completed.*

3.6.1   An Action Spec Is Not an Implementation

Writing a specification for an operation is very different from writing an implementation. The spec is simply a Boolean expression: a relation between the inputs, initial state, final state, and outputs. An implementation would choose a particular algorithmic sequence of steps, select a data representation or specific internal access functions, and work through iterations, branches, and many intermediate states before achieving the "final" state. Consider the specifications of these operations in contrast to their possible implementations:

<u>function</u> Calculator::squareRoot (in x: Real, out y: Real)
    <u>pre</u>:   not (x < 0)
    <u>post</u>:   y > 0 and y * y = x -- more realistically, allow rounding errors

<u>action</u> Scheduler::schedule_course (reqCourse: Course, reqStart: Date)
    <u>pre</u>:   Provided there is an instructor qualified for this course
              who is free on this date, for the length of the course.
    <u>post</u>:   A new Session has been created, with course = reqCourse,
              startDate = reqStart, and endDate − startDate = reqCourse.length,
              and with one of the qualified free instructors assigned

<u>action</u> FlightRouter::takeShortestPath (f: Flight)
<dl>
<dt><u>pre:</u></dt>
</dl>

pre: *provided there is some path between the source and destination of f*

post: *f has been assigned a path from its source to its destination*
          there is no other path between f.source and f.destination shorter than
          f.path
          (needs a supporting definition of path and its length)

These operations, and their corresponding type model attributes, have many possible implementations. Instructor qualification and schedules can be represented and calculated in many ways, as can flight paths and square roots. No matter how we implement these operations, they must conform to this specification. If we were to run any test data, which met the preconditions of the specification, through an implementation, we would expect the postcondition to be satisfied; if it is not, we have found a bug in either the implementation or the specification.

Some specifications fully determine the outcome of an operation. Our specification of squareRoot allows many implementations and even more than one result: 2* 2 are 4, but so are –2 * –2. If we want to exclude the latter, we would add y>0. Similarly, schedule_course constrains the new session to be assigned a qualified, available instructor but does not specify which one be assigned. And takeShortestPath does not say which path should be selected in the event there were multiple paths with the same length; it says only that there is no path with a shorter length.

What should squareRoot do in the case of a negative input? or schedule_course in the case when a qualified instructor is not available? Our specs, as written, do not cover these other conditions but rather leave these behaviors unspecified. If we said nothing further about these operations, the implementations could ignore these other conditions. However, we can have multiple specs for an action (see Section 3.6.3, Multiple Action Specs: Two Styles).

A good operation specification is much like a test specification. With a little infrastructure support—such as query functions to map from concrete data representations to the abstract attributes used in the specifications and some means to capture initial values of attributes—these operation specifications can be mapped to test code that is executable at runtime, at least during testing or debugging.

The operation specs often map directly to tests. Thus, the spec for squareRoot easily translates into test code; so does schedule_course, after we write query functions to determine attributes related to instructor qualification and availability in terms of the concrete implementation. Some specifications may need to be refactored a bit to be tested effectively. A literal usage of takeShortestPath as a test specification would require generating all possible paths to show that the computed path is the shortest, but that's not a very practical test strategy.[10]

---

10. You can reformulate the spec to solve this; or you could design it in steps, specify each step, show that the specified steps yield the shortest path, and test only the steps.

3.6.2   Parameter Types

Parameter types are an implicit part of pre- and postconditions. Our spec of squareRoot could be rewritten so as to make this explicit, although this is not the normal style:

```
action squareRoot (in x, out y)
      pre:      x: Real & not (x < 0)
      post:     y: Real & y*y = x
```

We permit a shorthand for parameter types. A parameter that is not explicitly typed has a name that is a lowercase version of its type name. The following spec implicitly types all three parameters:

```
action Scheduler::schedule_course (course, client, date)
```

3.6.3   Multiple Action Specs: Two Styles

The effect of an operation can be specified with an explicit pre/post pair of conditions or with a single postcondition and no explicit precondition. The main difference is that within the explicit precondition (starting with pre:) all references are implicitly to the initial values of attributes; within a single postcondition clause we must explicitly indicate initial values using x@pre. These two are[11] equivalent:

```
action Scheduler::schedule_course (reqCourse: Course, reqStart: Date)
      pre:      a qualified instructor available for those dates
      post:     a new confirmed session with ....
```

```
action Scheduler::schedule_course (reqCourse: Course, reqStart: Date)
      post:     (qualified instructor available for those dates)@pre
                ==> (a new confirmed session with ....)
```

Notice the ==>, also written implies or if...then.... If the precondition is not met, we have said nothing about the outcome.

If you have just one specification of the action, both forms are equivalent. The main difference arises when you have multiple specifications of the same action,[12] such as for different views of an action. (For details, see Section 8.1, Sticking Pieces Together.) Following are the guidelines for choosing.

• To write a single complete spec for the action—for example, to define in one contract what the implementor must code, and the caller must be careful of before invocation—both forms are equivalent. The explicit pre/post form makes the client responsibility a bit more visible. The caller is responsible for invoking this

---

11. Different specification languages have used different approaches, including entirely implicit preconditions.

12. As we all know, your write_the_code action must (a) meet the specs, (b) run fast, (c) have wonderful documentation, (d) be completed tomorrow.

operation only when the precondition is true; the implementor can assume the precondition is satisfied and must then guarantee the postcondition.

- To write a partial spec, which will be automatically composed with others for the same action,[13] things are a bit more complicated.

  - To define an outcome that must be guaranteed if your precondition holds, regardless of other partial specs, use a ==> b.

    Given another partial spec:—c==>d—the combined result is obtained by anding each one, so a client can fully rely on each partial spec:

    (a==>b) and (c==>d)

  - To define a precondition that can restrict (and be restricted by) the precondition of other partial specs, use <u>pre</u> a <u>post</u> b.

    Given another partial spec—<u>pre</u> c <u>post</u> d—the combined result strengthens the precondition and postconditions of both specs:

    pre a and b post c and d

Thus, here's how to write two specs for sqrt: one for a valid call and the other for the exception behavior required for negative numbers. (Specifying exceptions is described in more detail in Section 8.4, Action Exceptions and Composing Specs.)

<u>action</u> squareRoot (<u>in</u> x:Real, <u>out</u> y: Real)
    <u>post</u>:   not (x < 0) ==> y*y = x

<u>action</u> squareRoot (<u>in</u> x:Real, <u>out</u> y: Real)
    <u>post</u>:   x < 0 ==> (y = NAN)

An operation can be constrained by multiple specifications. Alternatively, the multiple specs can be combined into a single, more complex specification. Here, first, is an operation constrained by multiple partial specifications:

-- this spec deals with scheduling a confirmed course
<u>action</u> Scheduler::schedule_course (client, course, date)
    <u>post</u>:   *(there is an instructor qualified for this course*
            who is free on this date, for the length of the course.) **@pre**
            ==> A single new Session has been created for that course, client,
            dates and confirmed with one of the qualified free instructors
            assigned to it

-- this spec deals with a "loyalty program" for frequent course schedulers
<u>action</u> Scheduler::schedule_course (client, course, date)
    <u>post</u>:   *(the client is above some volume threshold)* **@pre**
            ==> The client has received a certificate for a free course

---

13. If the distinction between an explicit pre/post and a single post seems too subtle, use pre/post with explicit keyword restrictive.

Any reasonable tool should relate multiple specifications for an operation and be able to present some combined form. Here is the same operation written with a single specification.

```
-- this spec deals with combined aspects of a request to schedule a course
action Scheduler::schedule_course (client, course, date)
    post:    (instructor available)@pre ==> single new session for that course, ...
             and (client above threshold)@pre ==> client has received free
             certificate
```

3.7 *Subtypes and Type Extension*

Because a type spec is just a description of behavior, an object can be a member of many types. In other words, it can play several roles. (In fact, an object is a member of every type whose specification it conforms to even if the type specification was written after the object was created.) And one type can be a subset, or *subtype,* of another even if they were defined separately. To say that all sheep are animals is the same as saying Sheep is a subtype of Animal. You expect of Sheep everything expected of Animals in general; but there is more to say about Sheep. Some objects that are Animals—that is, they conform to the behavior specification for that type—may exhibit the additional properties of Sheep.

Putting more into a specification, raising the expectations, reduces the set of objects that satisfy it. It's often useful to define one type specification by extending another, adding new actions, or extending the specifications of existing ones; subject to certain restrictions, this will result in the definition of a subtype.

▶ *subtype*   A type whose members form a subset of its supertype; all the specifications of the supertype are true of the subtype, which may add further specifications. (Note that we use *subclass* to mean inheritance of implementation.)

3.7.1   Attributes and Invariants

A type defines a set of objects by specifying certain aspects of those objects; every object that conforms to that specification, regardless of its implementation, is a member of that type, and vice versa. For example, a ServiceEngagement type could define any object that constitutes a service engagement with a client. Any object with a suitable definition of the five attributes is a ServiceEngagement.

A subtype extends the specification of its supertype. It *inherits* all properties (attributes and invariants) of the supertype and adds its own specifics. Because all supertype properties still apply to it and because its members must conform to all properties, every member of a subtype is also a member of its supertype; a subtype's members are a subset of its supertype members.

```
Subtype->forAll (x | x.isTypeOf (Supertype))
```

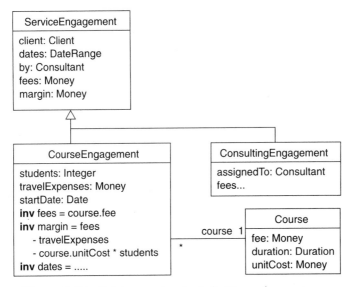

Figure 3.17   Subtype extends definition of supertype.

The types CourseEngagement and ConsultingEngagement could both be subtypes of ServiceEngagement (see Figure 3.17). Objects of the CourseEngagement type have a total of six attributes defined on them; these objects may have different implementations of these attributes as long as they map correctly to the specified attributes and are related consistent with all invariants. Their fees are determined by the fees set for the course; the margin must factor in travel expenses and production costs for student notes. Engagement dates are fixed by the startDate and the standard course duration.

Clearly, attributes students and course do not apply to consultingEngagements. The rules that constrain dates, fees, and margins could be quite different. Still, all five common attributes can be defined for any consultingEngagement.

We could well discover further commonality between the subtypes: both of them follow the same basic rule for their margin.

    margin = fees - travelExpenses - additionalCosts

Parts of this invariant are defined differently for each subtype. Consulting fees are determined by the expertise of the consultant and the length of the engagement. Additional costs for a course reflect the per-student production costs; additional costs for consulting may reflect the preparation time required for the engagement and the actual cost for the assigned consultant. Despite these differences, the broad structure of the invariant is the same and can be defined only once in the supertype.

A type is not a class. A class is an object-oriented programming (OOP) construct for defining the common implementation—stored data and executed methods—of some objects, whereas a type is a specification of a set of objects independent of their implementation. Any number of classes can independently implement a type; and one class can implement many types. Some programming languages distinguish type from class. In some languages, writing a definition of a class also defines a corresponding type.[14]

A subtype is not a subclass. Specifically, a subtype in a model does not imply that an OOP class that implements the subtype should subclass from another OOP class that implements the supertype. Subclassing is one particular mechanism for inheriting implementation with certain forms of overriding of *implementation*; however, with subtyping there is no overriding of *specifications*, only extension.

As with objects and attributes, there are many ways of partitioning subtypes. ServiceEngagements could be viewed based on their geographic location (domestic versus international), taxation status (taxable or not), nature of service provided (consulting versus training), and so on. Which of these are relevant is determined primarily by the actions that we need to characterize and the extent to which the subtyping helps describe these actions in a well-factored way.

3.7.2   No Overriding Behavior Specifications

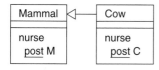

When one type is defined as an extension of another type, the subtype cannot *override* any behavioral guarantees of the supertype. The postcondition written for nurse on Cow does not override the corresponding specification for all Mammals; rather, it is an additional description about how cows nurse their young. In contrast, in an implementation class, a superclass can provide an implementation of some method that a subclass then overrides.

3.7.3   Common Pictorial Type Expressions

There are several commonly used combinations and variations of subtyping in models. This section outlines them and the corresponding notations.

3.7.3.1   Subtype

Cow extends Mammal and it inherits all Mammal attributes and action specs. Cow may add more action specs for the same or different actions. Here it is viewed as sets of objects:

Cow ⊆ Mammal

---

14. Java distinguishes interface (type) from class (type and class). A C++ class is also a type. In Smalltalk, type corresponds to a message protocol; class is independent of type.

3.7.3.2   Multiple Supertypes

Bat has all the properties specified on the supertypes. Any action with specifications in more than one supertype must conform to them all. Viewed as sets of objects:

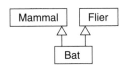

Bat $\subseteq$ Mammal * Flier

The subtype conforms to all the expectations that any client could have based solely on the guarantees of both supertypes. Further requirements particular to this subtype may be added. It's perfectly possible to combine two types that have conflicting requirements so that it would not be possible to implement the result.

3.7.3.3   Type Exclusion

The two types are mutually exclusive—that is, no object is a member of both.

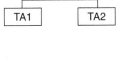

TA1 * TA2 = $\varnothing$

3.7.3.4   Type Partitioning

Every member of TA is a member either of TA1 or TA2 but not both. There may be more than one partitioning of a type, each drawn with a separate black triangle.

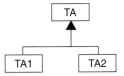

TA = TA1+TA2

Figure 3.18 shows an example.

3.7.3.5   State Types

TA1 and TA2 are sets (not true types) to which members of TA belong when in a given state defined by a predicate on TA (usually in terms of attributes of TA, but see Section 3.11). If the determining attributes are not const, then objects can migrate across the state types; otherwise, the classification of an object is fixed by the determining attributes at the time of its creation: *a TA is also a TA1 if it has property* x<a, *in which case it also has these other properties (*z *etc.).*

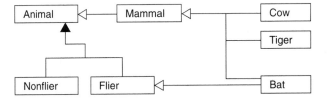

Figure 3.18   Type partitioning.

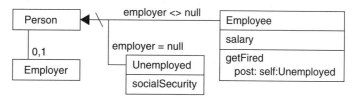

Figure 3.19   State types.

For example, suppose an employee is a person with an employer; employees have a salary (see Figure 3.19) and can get fired. This lets us *classify* objects based on a condition and define resultant properties they will have. For example, we could define two state types of Person: Teenager (age in the range 13 to 19) and Baby (appropriate baby predicate), ascribing each with appropriate attributes to define:

```
RockConcert::admit (t: Teenager)
    post:      t.stipend.depleted

RockConcert::admit (b: Baby)
    pre:       b.accompanyingAdult <> null-- only if accompanied
    post:      b.isBawling
```

▶ *state type*   A set of objects defined by a predicate: unlike a true type, objects may move into and out of it during their lives. The predicate is defined within a parent true type; for example, "caterpillar" is a state within "lepidopter."

3.7.4   General Type Expressions

Because types define sets of objects, we can use set operations to combine types and to define new types without drawing new boxes every time (see Table 3.1).

▶ *type expression*   An expression denoting a type using set-like operators—for example, Women + Men.

3.8   *Factoring Action Specifications*

As behavior specs become complex, we need ways to factor them so that they are still understandable and maintainable.

3.8.1   Invariants

We saw in Section 3.5, Actions with Invariants, that invariants are implicitly conjoined with action specifications. Static invariants factor those constraints that apply to every state, and effect invariants capture rules about every state change. Both of them simplify action specs by making them less redundant.

Table 3.1   Type Expressions

Type	Explanation
jo : Student	Object jo is a member of the type **Student** and conforms to the behavioral requirements set by **Student**; this notation is the same as the (short form) notation for set membership.
Tutor * Student	The type whose members are in both these types.
Tutor + Student	The type whose members are in either or both types. We might define a type **CollegeMember = Professor + Student**.
Person − Pilot	The type whose members behave according to the first type's definition but not according to the seconds.
Object	The type to which all objects belong; all other types are its subtypes.
Impossible	The empty type to which no object belongs, characterized by any type definition that is inconsistent.
NULL	Has only one member, null (or ∅), the value of an unconnected link.
Seq(Phone)	Application of a generic type **Seq(X)** to a specific type **Phone**. Other standard generic types include **Set** and **Bag**.
[T]	The same as **T + NULL**; all "optional" attributes, including 0..1 associations, are of this form: their value could be either null or a valid member of **T**.
enum {on, off}	An enumerated type whose only members are the two listed. You can name this type **Status = enum {on, off}**.

3.8.2   Convenience Attributes Simplify Specs

Because invariants can simplify action specifications and because attributes themselves simply represent a precise terminology for use in action specs, we can often simplify specs by introducing suitable attributes and invariants.

```
        -- cancellation of a session: might need to reassign the instructor to something else
        action Scheduler::cancelCourse (s: Session)
        pre:    -- if s was confirmed
                s.confirmed
                -- and if there was a tentative session within those dates
                and sessions->exist ( s1 | s1.tentative s1.datesWithin (s)
                    -- for which the instructor who was assigned is qualified
                    and s.instructor.qualifiedFor (s1.course) )
        post:   -- then the instructor is assigned to one such session
```

To simplify this specification, we introduce a new term. The precondition refers to a set of sessions that need an instructor for a particular range of dates—in this case, the dates of the session being canceled. Why not introduce a parameterized attribute alternateSessions(dates) and simplify the operation spec?

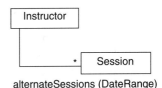

alternateSessions (DateRange)

```
        inv Instructor:: alternateSessions (d: DateRange) =
            -- all tentative sessions within that date range (assuming necessary
                attributes!)
```

sessions->select (s | s.tentative & s.dates.within (d)
    -- and that the instructor would be qualified to teach
    & self.qualifiedFor (s.course))

<u>action</u> Scheduler::cancelCourse (s: Session)
<u>pre</u>:   *-- if s confirmed and any alternate sessions for that instructor on those*
             dates
          s.confirmed and s.instructor.alternateSessions (s.dates)->notEmpty
<u>post</u>:   *-- then the instructor is assigned to one such session*

Judiciously chosen auxiliary attributes like this one can be quite effective in simplifying actions and invariants by introducing precisely defined terms that express the requirement in a natural way that's close to what a client might use (despite the formal syntax).

▶ *convenience attribute*   A redundant attribute (possibly parameterized) that is introduced to simplify the specification of actions or invariants—for example, age defined as well as birthday.

3.8.2.1   Parameterized Attributes versus Read-Only Operations

A parameterized attribute, such as alternateSessions(dates), is an abstraction of state. When it is implemented, there will be a way to determine the value of that attribute for each applicable value of the parameter in its range. In this sense, it can be easily confused with a read-only operation: a query that can be invoked as a service returns a value and has no side effect. We choose to distinguish clearly between state abstractions (attributes) and invocable operations.

Specifically, parameterized attributes are constrained by static invariants. In contrast, any operation is defined by its pre- and postcondition (see Section 3.1.2, Pre- and Postconditions Specify Actions); a read-only operation would have a postcondition that defined the returned value in terms of the inputs and current state.

Parameterized attributes can sometimes be modeled using a Map collection type:

Instructor::   *-- alternate sessions maps a daterange to a set of sessions*
        alternateSessions: Map(DateRange, Set(Session))

You can conveniently refer to the domain and range as attributes of this map type:

alternateSession ->domain : Set(DateRange)
alternateSession ->range : Set (Set(Session))

3.8.3   Effects Factor Common Postconditions

Another kind of convenience construct is called an *effect*. This function can use @pre and so can be used to factor out the parts that are common among some of the action specs. For example, schedule_course is an action; we have decided there will be some interaction for a client to schedule a course. Two possible outcomes of this action are schedule_confirmed_course and schedule_unconfirmed_course. We define these as *named* effects with a single postcondition; referring to them by name is exactly equivalent to writing their specifications directly. Effects can be listed on the type box, marked with a stereotype <<effect>>, along with the actions.

> -- saying that a schedule_confirmed_course has happened is exactly the same
>   as saying...
> effect Scheduler::schedule_confirmed_course (course, date)
>   -- that there was some available instructor initially
> post   instructorAvailable @ pre (course, date)
>   -- and a confirmed session is created
> **and**   Session.new [confirmed] → size = 1
>
> -- saying that a schedule_unconfirmed_course has happened is exactly the same
>   as saying...
> effect Scheduler:: schedule_unconfirmed_course (course, date)
>   -- that there was no available instructor initially
> post   not (instructorAvailable @ pre (course, date))
>   -- and an unconfirmed session is created
> **and**   Session.new [unconfirmed] → size = 1

We can now simply use these two effects to specify the action schedule_course. The resulting spec means exactly the same as though we had written the full specifications of the two effects.

> -- when a scheduler schedules a course
> action Scheduler::schedule_course (course, date)
>   pre: true -- no precondition, because the postcondition covers all cases
>   post: -- either a confirmed course has been scheduled
>   schedule_confirmed_course (course, date)
>   -- or an unconfirmed course has been scheduled
>   or   schedule_unconfirmed_course (course, date)

▶ *effect* A convenience postcondition introduced (and named) to factor parts of post-conditions that are common across more than one action. Unlike ordinary predicates, an effect can contain the special postcondition operator @pre.

3.8.4   Pre ==> post versus pre & post

In the preceding example, the two alternative situations and the associated outcomes are represented in two different effects. Within the effect, the @pre part is anded with the post. This means that when we bring the two effects together in the eventual action spec, we can say, "Either this happens or that."

An alternative style is to write the effects so each of them is a self-contained specification: "In this case ==> always do this" and "In that case ==> always do that." This style means that the two specifications are anded, because they are both instructions that we want the implementor always to observe:

-- *If an instructor is available, the course must be confirmed*
<u>effect</u> Scheduler::when_instructor_available_confirm (course, date)
         -- *if the instructor is available:*
<u>post</u>   instructorAvailable@pre (course, date)
         -- *then a confirmed session is created*
         ==> Session.new [confirmed]

-- *If an instructor is not available, the course must be unconfirmed:*
<u>effect</u> Scheduler:: when_no_instructor_reject (course, date)
         -- *if there was no available instructor initially ...*
<u>post</u>   not (instructorAvailable@pre (course, date))
         -- *then an unconfirmed session is created*
         ==> Session.new [unconfirmed]

And we then explicitly compose these two effects differently:

-- *You must always confirm or unconfirm a course depending on instructor
   availability:*
<u>action</u> Scheduler::schedule_course (course, date)
     <u>pre</u>:   true -- *no precondition, because the postcondition covers all cases*
     <u>post</u>:   -- *either a confirmed course has been scheduled*
            when_instructor_available_confirm (course, date)
            -- *or an unconfirmed course has been scheduled*
   and   when_no_instructor_reject (course, date)

Which style should you choose? Nice examples can be found to support either style; they have different meaning, and the choice also influences the composition of specs, errors and exceptions, and so on.[15] Experience suggests the following guidelines.

- Write the effect postcondition in a (pre ==> post) style when you wish to ensure that there is no getting out of the contract and that if the precondition is true, then the postcondition will be met. Then combine them into actions using and. This approach is generally better when you're combining several separately defined requirements—for example, when you're building a component that conforms to the interfaces expected by several different clients.

- Write the effect postcondition in a (pre & post) style when you wish each to describe one of many possible outcomes. Then combine them into actions using or. This style is generally better when you're building a specification model from different parts within the same document. You must combine these effects with your eyes open: none of them makes any guarantees that the outcome it describes will be met, because they may restrict each other.

---

15. This was a major difference between the specification languages Z and VDM.

3.8.5   Referring to Other Actions in a Postcondition

Whenever any action is specified, it implicitly defines an effect. That effect can be referred to from another action. Sometimes you want to say, "This operation does the same as that, but also ..."—in other words, to reuse the specification of another action. Specifications can be quoted within others' postconditions (this is analogous to calling subroutines in code). However, you need not do this too eagerly. Specifications must be clearly understandable, and abstract attributes and effects can be used quite freely; it is the implementations that must use careful encapsulation and hiding.[16]

Suppose there were an operation by which an assigned instructor could be explicitly unassigned:

```
action Scheduler:: unassign_instructor (s: Session)
       -- s was previously confirmed, and its instructor is no longer assigned to s
post: s.confirmed@pre ==> s.instructor <> s.instructor@pre
       -- and various other "unassign" things take place
```

You may find that the action of canceling a session might also need to accomplish all the effects of unassigning. You can *quote* the spec of another action in [[...]]:

```
action Scheduler:: cancel_session (s: Session)
post:     s.confirmed ==> [[ unassign_instructor (s) ]]
```

The quoting syntax [[...]] is a predicate, possibly involving initial and final states, that says, "This action achieves whatever unassign_instructor would have achieved, with these parameters," but not necessarily by invoking that action. It doesn't say how this must be achieved; the designer might know another way to achieve the same effect. If you want to go into the semantics a little more, the quotation is the same as rewriting [[...]] with all the ((pre)@pre ⇒ post) of the quoted operation, with appropriate parameter and self substitutions.

If you decide that a part of what this action must do is to actually invoke a specific operation, you can record that decision by inserting an arrow in front of the operation:

```
[[ -> self.cancel_session (s) ]]
```

This technique alters the postcondition to mean "The cancel_session operation has been invoked on self." The end result is no different, but we're now pinning down how to achieve it. You can quote operations on objects other than self with or without the ->.

▶ *quoted action*   A postcondition can refer to another action by naming it within brackets: [[action(...)]]; this is called *quoting*, and it means that the effect specified for that action is a part of this postcondition. If written as [[->action(...)]], then the action must actually be invoked as part of the postcondition; if further prefixed with <u>sent</u>, it indicates that an asynchronous invocation must be made.

---

16. Try telling a client, "I won't tell you what that operation does; it is encapsulated."

3.8.6   Specification Types versus Design Types

Specifications describe how a client can use a component. What we really want to say about a component is *what it does*: its behavior, or the actions it takes part in. We have seen how to specify the externally visible behavior of a type by specifying actions in terms of a type model of attributes. Because the component doesn't necessarily have to be implemented along the same lines as its model, the implementation need not explicitly represent distinct objects that belong to the types used within that model. Those types are used to structure the static model and relate it to the business.

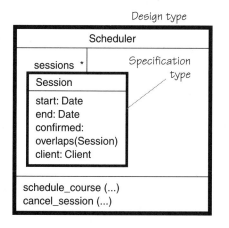

Design type

Specification type

It is possible to implement the Scheduler without a Session class and without unique and distinct objects for each session; such an approach would be quite common when you're assembling existing implementation components or legacy systems, such as a calendar (with events) and an employee database (with employees). When designing, some people like to distinguish those types they have decided to implement—*design* types—from those that are used simply to help write a specification—*spec* types. Design types can be drawn with a heavier border.

Clients are not interested in how it works inside: only the designer is interested in that, and the designer should be in a considerable minority. But to describe the actions clearly, we must write a model of the component's state. Here is a typical dialog or thinking process involved.

> "This command creates a session." *What's a session?* "It's a thing with dates, courses, and instructors." *What can I do with it?* "Oh, you can't get hold of one directly, but you can list all the sessions there are and cancel any of your own." *So there is one big list of sessions in there?* "Yup." *Isn't that a bit inefficient, considering we would need to search the whole list to determine schedules? Wouldn't it be better to organize by date and instructor?* "Uh, well yes, that's how it's really done, of course; and actually, there's really no such thing as a session. We just append the course and instructor names to events in the calendar. And actually, there's this hashtable..." *But if I think of it as a list of sessions, I'll understand how to use the system?* "Yes." *Thanks, that's what I need.*

In this scenario, not only the attributes of the scheduler system—the list of sessions—but also the type of objects they contain (Session) amount to a convenient fiction hypothesized to describe its behavior aside from all the implementation complexities. Session is a specification, or model, type. It is there only for the purpose of modeling. Types that are "really" there (in the sense that they are separable and take part in actions and we intend to implement them) are design types.

Many types are used for both purposes. For example, Date is often used in specifications and also has many implementations, and a good design would often have direct implementation of the specification types. Also, in some situations the specification requires an implementation not only of a primary type but also of related types required for input and output parameters. An example is shown in Step 8 in Section 3.4.1.

Typically, a design type will be specified with a model drawn inside it using specification types. Only a design type can participate in an action, and every type that is specified as participating in an action is a design type. Specification types do not really have actions of their own, but partial specifications (effects) can be attached to them for convenience, as shown in Section 3.8.7.

However, there is nothing to stop you from using a type in a model even though the type happens to have an implementation somewhere. In fact, good implementations of domain objects will often have their specs reused in this way. The more important design decision hinges on how the types in an implementation will be used, and those decisions involve joint actions recorded in collaboration diagrams.

▶ *specification type versus design type* A specification type is one that is introduced as a part of the type model of another type to help structure its attributes and effects in terms closer to the problem domain. The behaviors of the spec type are not themselves of interest, and the type may never be implemented directly.

A design type, in contrast, is one that participates directly in actions; its behaviors are of primary importance, and it is not just a means to factor the specification of some other type.

3.8.7 Factoring to Specification Types

In many cases the outcome of an action depends on the type of object, or objects, to which it is applied; indeed, this is one of the mainstays of the object-oriented approach. If our seminar system dealt with training and consulting engagements, the rules for canceling an engagement might be different. The appropriate parts of the effect of cancellation should be localized on the engagements (see Figure 3.20).

The outcome is different for each type of engagement: training sessions have the course material production canceled and instructor reassigned; consulting jobs may be charged for, confidential materials must be returned, and the consultant must be reassigned. Although the spec is simplified by factoring it across the different types of engagements, the action is simply on the scheduler system; committing to more would be a matter of internal design.

Does this mean that we are doing some design—assigning responsibilities and deciding internal interactions to the modeling types? Not really. We're only distributing the action spec among the concepts on which it has an effect. If there happens to be an implementation of, say, ConsultingEngagement, we are not referring to that implementation and the particular properties of its code: we're referring only to the specification. That said, the most straightforward design approach would parallel this spec localization.

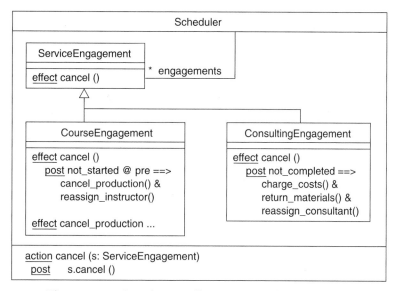

Figure 3.20   Localizing effects on specification types.

3.8.8   Factoring: Specify Effects Abstractly

The earlier example placed very different outcomes in each type. But where possible, it pays to look for something common among the supertypes. The cancel operation could be defined abstractly:

<u>effect</u> ServiceEngagement:: cancel ()
<u>post</u>:   can_be_cancelled@pre ==>
           reassign_resources() &
           cancel_preparations()
           ..etc.

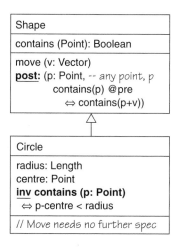

The subtypes would detail their own specs for can_be_cancelled and the other effects. This kind of factoring is the specification analog of the "template method" design pattern when you're implementing methods in superclasses. A straightforward design approach would parallel this factoring in the implementation, but alternative design choices would not invalidate the factored specification.

In some cases, we can even provide a complete spec in the supertype, with the subtypes simply defining the abstract attributes in more detail. For example, moving a Shape in a graphical editor is very different in terms of the attributes of each subtype; but we can express in common terms the required effect of what happens to the points contained within each Shape.

Although the most natural attribute models for circle, rectangle, and triangle would be quite different, we can abstract them into a single parameterized query, contains (Point); any shape is defined by the points it contains. We define move in terms of this abstract attribute and then simply relate the different shapes to this attribute.

3.9 *State Charts*

State charts, and their simpler cousins, "flat" state diagrams, can be useful modeling tools. In Catalysis, states and transitions that appear in a state chart are directly related to the attributes and actions in a type specification. The state chart merely provides an alternative view of the spec.

3.9.1   States as Attributes and Invariants

Sometimes it is easy to see distinct states that an object progresses through over its lifetime. A Session may go through tentative, confirmed, or delivered; if it is either confirmed or delivered it is considered sold. From another perspective, the session may be pendingInvoice, invoiced, or paid.

States are often drawn in a *state chart* showing the states and the relationships between them, as in Figure 3.21. Each state is a Boolean attribute[17]: an object either is or is not in that state at any time. The structure of states in the state chart defines invariants across these attributes.

- States in a simple state chart are mutually exclusive, with exactly one state true at a time, such as within sold; this is what the xor invariants mean.
- A state chart can be nested inside a state. While the containing state is false, none of the nested states is true; while it is true, the nested state chart is live, meaning that one of its states (or one from each of its concurrent sections) must be true. This is the or invariant defining sold.
- A state chart can be divided into concurrent sections by a dashed line. Each of these sections is a separate simple state chart. The object is simultaneously in one state from each of the sections. No explicit invariants are needed because the two sets of states are independent. There is no paradox in this, nor necessarily any concurrent processing in the usual sense: it's just that a state simply represents a Boolean expression, and there is no reason that two such statements should not be true at the same time.

To represent business rules, we can separately introduce invariants that eliminate certain combinations, For example:

---

17. We qualify the state name with superstate names to deal with nested states.

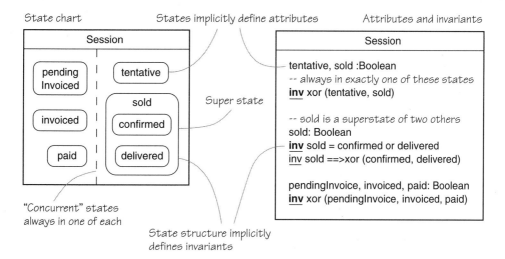

Figure 3.21 A state chart defines state attributes and invariants.

<u>inv</u> Session::   invoiced ==> sold
        -- A session can be invoiced only if it is sold

Because states simply define Boolean attributes, it is easy for states to be tied to the values of other attributes and associations via invariants. So for example, we can write

<u>inv</u> Session ::   -- an invoiced or paid Session always has an attached invoice
        (invoiced or paid) = (invoice <> null)

thereby tying the state to the existence of a link to another object.

▶ *state*   A Boolean attribute drawn on a state chart. The structure of the states defines invariants on those attributes (such as mutually exclusive states, inclusive states, or orthogonal states); additionally, you should write explicit invariants relating the state attributes to other attributes in the type model.

3.9.2   State Transitions as Actions

In addition to defining state attributes and their invariants, state charts depict transitions between states. An example state chart for Session is shown in Figure 3.22: A session can be confirmed, tentative, or delivered; changing the dates might switch between tentative and confirmed.

The change_dates action has multiple transitions, which translate into multiple partial action specifications. The transition from the confirmed state is translated next. For brevity, the state chart omitted the parameters used in the pre- and post-conditions, but we fill these in the textual action specs.

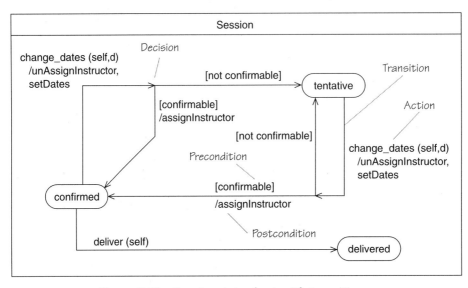

Figure 3.22   Session state chart with transitions.

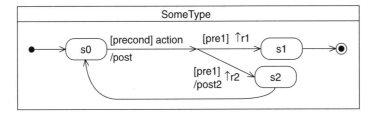

Figure 3.23   State chart notation.

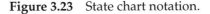

<u>action</u> change_dates (s: Session, d: date)
-- if s was confirmed, i.e., transition coming out of the confirmed state
<u>pre</u>:   s.confirmed
<u>post</u>:   unAssignInstructor(s) &   -- assuming an effect with that name
           setDates (s, d) &   -- assuming effect is defined
           (confirmable (d) @pre ==> s.confirmed & assignInstructor (s, d)) &
           (not confirmable (d) ==> s.tentative)

A state chart is part of the model of a type. The elements of state chart notation are
shown in Figure 3.23.

The arrows indicate the sequences of transitions that are possible. • indicates
the state that is first entered when the state predicates first become well defined.
This can mean when the object is first created or when this nested state chart is
entered. ◉ indicates where state predicates become undefined: when the nested
state chart is exited or the object is no longer of any interest. Until reaching the

"black hole," all the predicates for the states in the diagram should be well defined, either true or false.

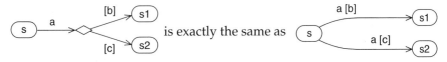

The decision point is not a branch point in the programming sense but instead says that there are two possible outcomes of this action: its postcondition includes (s1 or s2). Without the preconditions, either outcome would satisfy this spec. Decision points can sometimes simplify transitions: Figure 3.22 could be simplified to a single decision point, with creation and date change actions transitioning via that shared point.

State transitions share the machinery of action specs clauses, which are described in Section 3.6. State transitions can be used to specify actions as well as named effects; a transition labeled with the keyword <u>effect</u> represents a named effect (Section 3.8.3) rather than an action.

[pre] is a precondition: the transition is guaranteed to occur only if pre was true before the action commenced. Notice that this does not say that this transition definitely does not occur if the precondition is false; to say that, make sure you show transitions going elsewhere when it's false.

With /post, some effect is achieved as part of executing this transition.

↑action means that a (more abstract) action is completed as part of executing this transition. We'll have more to say about this in Chapter 6, Abstraction, Refinement, and Testing.

[[receiver.action]] means that part of the effect of this transition is the same as the documented effect of action on receiver (which is self, the state chart object, by default).

[[–>receiver.action]] means that part of the effect of this transition is that action is actually performed by an invocation on receiver.

3.9.3   Translating State Transitions to Actions

A transition illustrates part of the spec of an action.

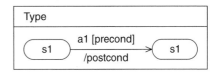

<u>action</u>   Type::a1
   <u>pre:</u>   s1 & precond
   <u>post:</u>   s2 & postcond

If there are several transitions involving one event, the effects are conjoined. State charts give a different way of factoring the description of an action, and a good tool would move readily between two views: state chart and textual action specification. Each state must be defined in terms of other attributes.

When you're using superstates, being in any substate implies being in the superstate. So any arrow leaving the superstate means that it is effective for any of the substates.

Transitions indicate the *completion* of the actions with which they are labeled. Although accomplishing the actions may take time, the transitions themselves are instantaneous; this will become more significant in Chapter 6, Abstraction, Refinement, and Testing.

▶ *state transition*   A partial specification of an action, drawn as a directed edge on a state chart. The initial and final states are part of the pre/post condition in the spec, and additional pre/post specs are written textually on the transition.

▶ *state chart*   A graphical description of a set of states and transitions.

3.9.4   State Charts of Specification Types

When you're drawing state charts, be aware of the primary type that is being modeled. In simple cases the states and transitions are directly of the primary type being modeled. If we are trying to specify the behavior of a gas pump, the states and actions labeling the transitions are those of the pump itself. It translates directly into action specs such as these:

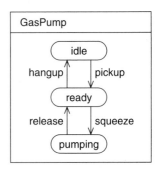

action Pump::hangup	pre: ready	post: idle
action Pump::pickup	pre: idle	post: ready

But when the primary type being modeled is complex, its states cannot necessarily be enumerated in the simple form required for representing it as a single state chart. The behavior of a Scheduler component such as the one in Figure 3.13 cannot be described on a single state chart (except with the most trivial states, exists, and all the interesting effects described in text on the transitions). This is because the state of the scheduler is defined by the states of its multiple sessions, instructors, and courses.

Instead, you should draw separate state charts for the specification types that constitute the type model of Scheduler. In reality, we are defining the states of the scheduler in terms of the states of its specification types. The transitions in the individual state charts show what happens to those objects for each of the scheduler's operations (see Figure 3.24).

Each individual state chart effectively specifies how every action on the primary type affects that one specification type. In contrast, a complete action specification defines how one action on the primary type affects any specification type member. The composition of all change_dates transitions, on any and all specification types, constitutes change_dates operation specification for the scheduler. Do not confuse this state chart view with internal design, when we will actually decide internal interactions between objects within the scheduler, the primary types whose behavior we describe will be these internal objects.

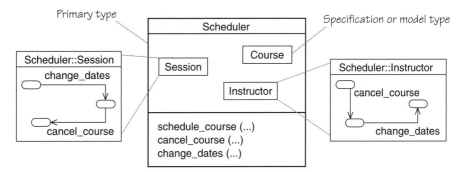

Figure 3.24   State charts of specification types.

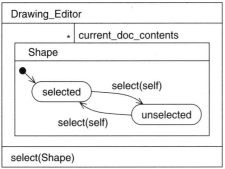

A useful technique in specifying a large component is to draw a state chart that focuses on all the elements of a particular type within a larger model—for example, showing what happens to the shapes in a drawing editor for each of the *editor's* operations. select(self) is a shorthand for select(s) [s=self]. It's important to realize that this is really a state chart for the editor, in which the states are defined in terms of the states of its shapes.

We can translate this to text form as follows. It is slightly more convenient to use a single postcondition clause than to separate the pre/post style.

<u>action</u>   Drawing_Editor::select (shape:Shape)

     <u>post:</u>   *-- every shape in the current document is affected as follows*
        current_doc_contents ->forAll (s |
           -- if it's the target and was selected, unselect it
           ((s.selected & s=shape)@pre ==> s.unselected)
           -- if it's the target and was not selected, select it
        &   ((s.unselected & s=shape)@pre ==> s.selected)
)

3.9.5   Underdetermined Transitions

Sometimes a state chart is deliberately vague about the outcome of an action. The reason is usually to allow subtypes to make different choices, within broad constaints given by the supertype, or simply to define a minimal partial constraint.

At any moment, a transition is said to be *feasible* if, before the current action began, the system was in the state at the arrow's source end and if any precondition it is labeled with was true. You are allowed to write a state chart for which there are several feasible transitions at any moment; this is called an *underdetermined* set of transitions. When this is the case, what state will you end up in?

The answer is that you will end up in one of them, but as a client you can't make any assumptions about which one it might be. This doesn't mean it's random, only that there are forces at work that you, based solely on the current spec, are unaware of. As a designer you might be able to choose whichever you like; but you will probably be constrained by the requirements from another view or a particular subtype.

For example, dialing a phone number—dial_number—has several possible outcomes. As users we are unaware of the factors that will influence the outcome (see Figure 3.25).

There is an engineer's view in which you can describe what the outcome will be in terms of the capacity of the lines and whether the other end is engaged on a call; but from the point of view of the phone user at one phone, these factors are unknown.

Isn't it a bit pedantic to insist on drawing the picture that doesn't show the preconditions on dial_number? After all, moderately educated phone users know what really causes these outcomes, and even when they don't, there is always a cause that we, the designers of the phone system, know about.

Perhaps that's true in this case. But indeterminate state charts will be important when we discuss components. This component may be combined with a wide variety of others, including ones not yet known of; so we actually don't know what the causes are, only what the possible outcomes can be. This situation might happen if we allowed our phone instrument to be connected to a new kind of switching system. As long as we have a way of reusing this underspecified model and adding to it in another context, it is worthwhile to make this separation.

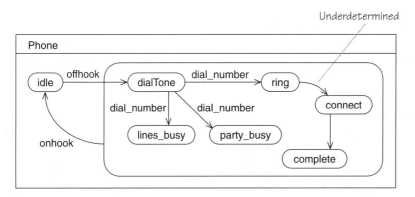

Figure 3.25   Underdetermined transitions.

3.9.6   Silent Transitions

The phone example shows one other way in which state charts can show nondeterminate behavior. It is possible for a system to change state without your knowing why or when and without your doing anything to it. Again, *silent* transition does not imply randomness. Instead, it means either that we don't know what might cause the change (as when we're waiting for public transport, which no mortal understands) or that, if we do know, we don't know whether or when that cause will happen (as when we're hanging on to see whether the phone will be answered).

Silent transitions also let us describe systems that are not purely reactive, because the partial descriptions permit transitions with unknown causes.

3.9.7   Ancillary Tables

State charts themselves provide a useful view of behavior that is different from the view provided by action specifications. State charts focus on how all actions affect one specification type, highlighting sequences of transitions, as opposed to focusing on the complete effect of one action on all affected types. Two related tables can be helpful in conjunction with state charts to check for completeness and consistency.

First, a state chart can be represented by a state transition matrix, as shown in Figure 3.26. In the matrix, X means shouldn't happen; | means nothing happens; and [ ] means determined in subtypes. Writing the matrix is a valuable cross-check to ensure that each action has been considered in each state. This matrix can be generated automatically from the state charts themselves; it better highlights combinations that may have been overlooked.

The second type of table is a state definition matrix. Each state should be defined in terms of attributes and associations in the model. Frequently, these boil down to simple conjunctions of assertions about them and so are easy to show in a table (see Figure 3.27). Even if this table is never written, it is always useful to define each state as a function of the existing attributes and associations.

State	e1	e2	e3
S1	[g1] S2	X	I
S2	X	S3 / pp	X
S3	S2	[ ]	S1

Figure 3.26   State transition matrix.

State	attr1	assn1	assn2	Full Definition of State
S1	>30	null	<> null	attr1>30 & assn1=null & assn2 <> null
S2	>2, < 3	null	<> null	2 < attr1 < 3 & assn1=null & assn2 <> null
S3	> 0	<> null		0 < attr1 & assn1 <> null

Figure 3.27   State definition matrix.

3.10 *Outputs of Actions*

Much of the focus of a typical postcondition is on the effect of an action on an object's internal state. But we also need to describe the information that results from an action and is returned to the invoker as well as any output signals or requests that are generated to other objects. There are several approaches to this.

3.10.1   Return Values

An action can have a return type whose return value is the identity of a new or pre-existing object used by the sender. Within the postcondition, **result** is the conventional name given to this value. Any actions can have a return value; those that have no other side effects are called *functions*.

```
function square_root (x:float)
    post: abs (result * result – x) < x/1e6
```

3.10.2   Out Parameters

Input parameters represent object references that are provided by the caller; return values represent object references returned to the caller to deal with as needed. Although out parameters can be broadly considered similar to return values, the details are somewhat different. The postcondition of the operation will determine the value of the out parameter and its attributes; however, the client will call this operation with these out parameters bound to an attribute selected by the client.

```
action Scheduler::schedule_course (course, dates, out contract)
    post: .... & contract: Contract.new [...]
action Client::order_course
    post: scheduler.schedule_course ( c1, 11/9, self.purchase_order.contract)
```

An ordinary parameter refers to an object; an out parameter refers to an attribute, which might be as simple as a local variable of the caller. An out parameter can therefore be used to specify that a different object is now referred to by the bound attribute; an ordinary parameter can only change the state of the object it refers to.

<u>out</u> is like a C++ reference parameter. Other programming languages, such as Java and Eiffel, do not have these features, showing that it is possible to do without them in an implementation language. However, the idea of having multiple return values is itself convenient in both specification and implementation.

3.10.3   Raised Actions

It is also possible to state as part of a postcondition that another action has been invoked either synchronously or asynchronously.

• *Synchronously:* The sent action will be completed as part of the sender. Its postcondition can be considered part of this one. It is written

    [[r := –> receiver.anAction(x,y)]]

r is a value returned from the message.

• *Asynchronously:* The request has been sent; the action will be scheduled for execution later, and its completion may be awaited separately.

    – Request sent to a specific receiver; action has been scheduled.

        [[<u>sent</u> m –> receiver.anAction(x,y)]]

    m is an event identifier that can be used elsewhere.

    – Request sent to an unspecified receiver; action has been scheduled.

        [[<u>sent</u> m –> anAction(x,y)]]

    – A previously sent action has been completed and returned r.

        [[m (...) = r]]

3.10.4   Specifying Sequences of Raised Actions

When you specify raised actions, it is sometimes necessary to specify that they happen in a particular sequence—to describe the protocol of a dialog. You might want an open_comms action to send certain messages to a modem object in a particular order. You might wish to specify this while retaining your basic premise of using only initial and final states in postconditions.

In effect, you are telling your designer something about the type of the intended receiver. Even if you tell me absolutely nothing else about it, I know that it can accept messages a, b, and c in a particular order and that at certain times you require me to have sent all three in that order.

This is equivalent to saying that I have been asked to get it into the state of "having received message c." I haven't been told what that state might signify as far as the receiver is concerned, only that I must get it there. But also, you tell me that I must first send message b: In other words, the modem has a state—as far as I am concerned—of "having received message b," which is a precondition of c.

So the simplest way to specify that a sequence of messages must be sent as part of the outcome of an action is to make a minimal local model of the state transitions for the receiver and specify that the final target state is reached:

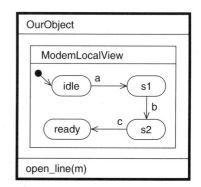

    action OurObject:: open_line(m:LocalViewOfModem)
        pre: m.idle
        post: m.ready
            &   *various effects on our own state*

By using the full apparatus of state charts, we can specify linear, branching, and concurrent sequences.

Used in this way, states shown as separate in this local view may turn out not to be separate in an implementation of the modem; they are, however, separate in our object's implementation, because it must generate them in sequence. OurObject would work if we provided a modem that ignored operations a and b but went straight from idle to ready on c. Provided that the intermediate states are purely specification attributes and that there are no operations for actually finding out its state, that's OK.

Sequential outputs are sometimes better dealt with as refinements, as described in Chapter 6, Abstraction, Refinement, and Testing. State charts are also used to describe a collaboration refinement (in which zooming in on an action shows it to be a dialog of smaller ones).

Occasionally it is useful to write a spec that refers to more than just the before-and-after moments in time—say, i, j and j, k. Putting the time indexes in [...] sets the scope within which the states are referred to.

    action [i, j, k] T::m (...)
        post: (x@j = x@i +3) &   *-- x@j means value of x at time "j"*
                   (x@k = x@j +2)
        ==>   (x@k = x@i + 5)

The main use for this would be in complex specs where you want to say, "The overall effect is the same as doing this followed by that" and in program proofs. Without explicit time indexes, you simply assume before and after and use @pre to distinguish them.

3.10.5 Sequence Expressions

Occasionally it is useful to write a sequencing constraint in text form, although it could usually be described using the preferred state chart technique from the preceding section. For example:

    action Scheduler:: cancel_session (s: Session)
        post:
            [[free_instructor (s.instructor@pre) ;
                reassign_instructor (s.instructor@pre) ;
            ]]

▶ *sequence expression*   A textual representation of a temporal composition of actions; some sequence expressions can be translated into an equivalent state chart.

Sequence-expression [[..; ..; ..]] shows the permitted sequence of more detailed actions—not a prescribed program. The elements of the syntax are as follows, where S1 and so on are usually expressions about actions:

- S1 ; S2   S1 always precedes S2
- S1 | S2   S1 or S2
- S1 *   Any number of repetitions of S1
- S1 || S2   S1 concurrent with S2

All such sequence expressions [[...]] are an abbreviation for a state model with the implication

(start ==> done)

The two states are defined by a state model as shown in Figure 3.28.

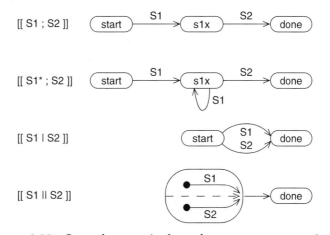

Figure 3.28   State chart equivalents for sequence expressions.

3.11 *Subjective Model: The Meaning of Containment*

When we specify a type, we often depict its attributes and specification types with a distinguished *root* type by using a form of visual containment, as shown in Figure 3.29(a). (An equivalent, alternative form distinguishes type nodes marked with «root» and selected associations marked with «cross<Root>» in (b).) This is more than a cosmetic choice; it has a specific semantic meaning. Both diagrams in Figure 3.29 are equivalent to the expanded model in Figure 3.30.

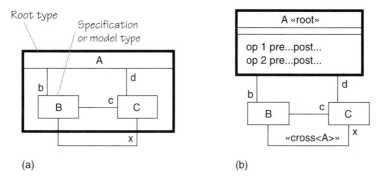

Figure 3.29   Type model: (a) with containment, (b) with root.

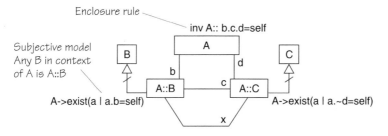

Figure 3.30   Interpretation of containment.

In the *enclosure rule*, all paths from A back to A that use only associations defined within the box (or that do not use any links marked «cross<A>») are guaranteed to get back to the same instance of A; that is, all links lie within the tree of objects that is rooted at self:A. By contrast, although a.b.**x**.d is certainly a member of type A, it need not be = a.

Thus, an engine is connected to a transmission, provided that they are within the same vehicle. This rule works as expected across multiple levels of nesting.

In the *subjective* model, the types locally named B and C, and their associations b, c, and d, all form part of a A's model; they are really *state types*. In other words, those members of B (or C) that happen to be contained within an A also satisfy any additional properties stated about B or C on this diagram. (Specifically, those additional properties do not universally apply to all B or C objects.) Brought outside the boundary of A, they have prefixes to their names.

In a different context, not every B will necessarily be linked to a C. For example, to the Invoicing department, customers are linked to products, whereas Warehousing knows only that products have parts; customers, universally, may not be required to have either association. Containment represents a localized view, which is a state type of the common usage.

In addition, local usages can also directly refer to attributes or operations on their container.[18] This makes it simple to write localized specifications of actions and effects, as discussed in Section 3.9.4.

As a matter of style, we use containment to depict specification types that have been introduced simply to describe operations on the primary type of interest. Sometimes we also need to describe operations on the input or output parameters of these operations, as shown in Figure 3.11.

Without such a mechanism, it becomes difficult to know whether the properties defined on B are intrinsic (that is, apply universally) to all Bs, or whether those properties are defined only on those Bs that happen to be within an A. When an engine runs, does it always turn the wheels of a car? How about when it is propelling a boat? Or when it is mounted on a test jig at the mechanic's?

3.12 *Type Specifications: Summary*

This chapter deals in detail with the business of specifying actions—what happens in some world or in some system—while deferring the implementation. Indeed, we have seen an example (Section 3.4) of how two different implementations can have the same behavioral specification. The action specifications use the terms defined in a static model (as in Chapter 2). The static and action models together make up the specification of a complete type (see Figure 3.31). In the chapters that follow, we will use these ideas to build specifications of complete software systems and interfaces to components.

- An object's behavior (or part of it) can be described with a type specification.
- A type specification is a set of action specifications; they share a static model that provides a vocabulary about the state of any member of the type.
- An action spec has a postcondition that defines a relationship between the states before and after any of its occurrences takes place.
- A precondition defines when the associated postcondition is applicable.

In Chapter 4 we deal with the interactions between objects—both inside the object we have specified (as part of its implementation) and between our object and others—to understand how it is used by our (software or human) clients.

Exhibits 3.1 and 3.2 show the syntax of action specs and postconditions.

---

18. In the manner of *inner classes* in JavaBeans and *closures* or *blocks* elsewhere.

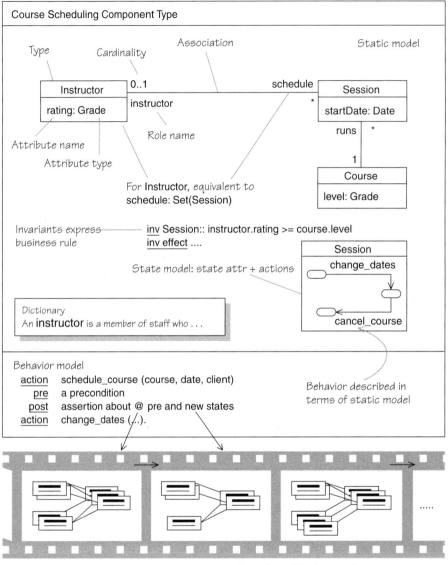

Figure 3.31 Type models and behavior specification.

Exhibit 3.1 Action Specifications

There are five constituents which may be part of an effect spec:

ReceiverType :: (parameter1 : Type1, parameter2 :Type2) : ResultType

Signature: a list of parameters—named values (references to objects) that may be different between different occurrences of the action(s) the spec governs.

- Some parameters may be marked <u>out</u>, denoting names bound only at the end of the operation.
- May also define a result type and a receiver type.

<u>pre</u>: *condition* **Precondition** is a read-only Boolean function that defines the situations in which this effects spec is applicable. If the precondition is not true when an action starts, this spec doesn't apply to it, so we can't tell from here what the outcome will be. There might be another applicable spec defined somewhere else.

The parameter type constraints are effectively terms in the precondition: d1>3 and d2:Date and d1<d2 ...

May refer to the parameters, to a receiver self, and to their attributes, but not <u>out</u> parameters or any <u>result</u>.

<u>post</u>: *postcond* **Postcondition** is a read-only Boolean function that specifies the outcome of the action (provided the precondition was true to begin with). The postcondition relates two states, before and after, so, the prior state of any attribute or subexpression can be referred to using @pre.

A postcondition may refer to self, all the parameters, any <u>result</u>, *and* their attributes.

<u>rely</u>: *condition* For concurrent or interleaved actions, if the rely clause ever becomes false during the execution of the action, the implemention is no longer guaranteed to meet the specification (Section 4.5).

<u>guarantee</u>: *cond* The implementor will maintain this true while executing the action concurrently with others, provided the pre and rely conditions hold (Section 4.5).

Pre, post, rely, and guarantee conditions are called *assertions*. Two further assertions appear in a type specification, outside any one action spec:

<u>inv</u> *condition* True before and after every action in the model. Effectively anded to each pre- and postcondition.

<u>inv effect</u> *effect* A "global" effects spec that applies to all actions conforming to its signature, pre, and rely conditions.

Exhibit 3.2 Special Terms in a Postconditions

A postcondition relates together two moments in time. By default, every expression denotes its value once the action is complete.

x@pre
The prior value of attribute x (there is no need to use them in a precondition). Here's an example of moving rooms:

jo.room@pre   -- jo's old room
jo.room@pre.isDirty@pre   -- prior state of jo's old room
jo.room@pre.isEmpty   -- current state of jo's old room
jo.room.isEmpty@pre   -- prior state of jo's new room

new
The set of all objects that exist in the after state that did not exist in the before, so T*new=(T − T@pre). Common usages with new in a postcondition:

Egg*new   -- all new Eggs from this action
Egg*new [size>5]   -- all new Eggs satisfying the filter
Egg.new   -- more familiar syntax for Egg*new
Egg.new [size>5]   -- new Eggs, with size>5
e : Egg.new[size>5]   -- e is a new Egg with size>5

This is most commonly used within a let; it implies that there is at least one new Egg.

[[an action]]
Action quoting, equivalent to copying its specification into the present postcondition. It does not imply a necessary actual invocation of the action — just that the same effect is achieved. If there are several effects-specs applying to the quoted action, they are all implied.

[[->an action]]
The quoted action will definitely be invoked in an implementation.

result
Reserved names for the value denoted by an operation that a programmer can invoke as an expression. Here's an example:

action square_root (x : int) post: x = result * result
... y = square_root (64); // y == 8

3.13 *Programming Language: Classes and Types*

Our focus in this chapter has been on specifying the behavior of objects using types and not on how to implement them with classes. This section briefly describes the link between modeling with types and implementing with classes.

▶ *class*   (a) A language-specific construct defining the implementation template for a set of objects, the types it implements, and the other classes or types it uses in its implementation (including by class inheritance).

(b) An implementation concept that defines the stored data and associated procedures for manipulating instances of that class; the implementation construct can be mapped to OO languages and to procedural and even assembly language.

A class is an implementation unit that prescribes the internal structure of any object that is created as an instance of it. Class is an OO programming concept but not necessarily an OO programming *language* concept. There are patterns for the systematic translation of OO designs to other data and execution models. You can employ these patterns if, for example, you need to write in a traditional language such as Fortran or assembler, perhaps for special control of performance. In that way, you still get the benefits of OO design (modularity, reuse, and so on). Of course, OO programming languages best support object design. OO-to-non-OO patterns must also be applied outside the scope of your programming language.

For example, C++ works with an OO model in main memory but leaves persistent data up to you; you can't send a message to an object in filestore. If you can secure a good OO database you're in luck; but otherwise, typically you're stuck with plain old files or a relational database and must to think how to encode the objects. Your class-layer design should initially defer the question of how objects are distributed between hosts and media.

So there is a *class layer* of design described entirely in terms of classes, with related types, which can be implemented directly in a language such as Java, Eiffel, or C++ or otherwise by judicious application of class-to-nonclass patterns (see Figure 3.32).

Not all OOP language (OOPLs) have classes. In Self, an object is created by cloning an existing one. Objects delegate dynamically to others rather than statically based on their class inheritance; and methods can be added dynamically. Nevertheless, Self designs certainly use the idea of Type. Contrary to many early popular writings, polymorphism is about types—multiple implementations of the same interface—and not about classes and implementation inheritance.

3.13.1 Messages and Operations

A class contains code for the operations the object "understands"—that is, the operations for which there are specifications, and hence clients could expect to send it.

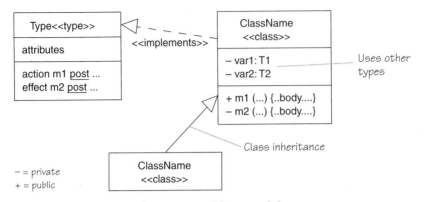

Figure 3.32 Class models.

• A *message* is an invocation of an operation. It consists of the name of the operation, the identity of the recipient, and a set of arguments. A message is like a procedure call except that it is a request *to* an object; the same message sent to different classes of object can have different outcomes. "Who performs this operation?" has an interesting answer in an OO program; in a conventional program, it's just the computer!

• An *operation* is a procedure, function, or subroutine. The traditional OO term is *method*, but we prefer to avoid confusion with the method you follow (hopefully) to develop a program. In analysis, and at a more abstract level of design, we talk about actions: an action occurrence may be one or more operation invocations.

• A *receiver* is the object distinguished as determining which operation will be invoked by a given message. It is usually thought of as executing the operation, which has access to the receiver's variables.

Not all OOPLs have a receiver. In CLOS, it is the combination of classes of all the parameters that determines what method will be called; methods are not specifically attached to classes.

3.13.2 Internal Variables and Messages

There are four primary kinds of variables in an object-oriented program.

• *Instance variables*: Data stored within fields in each object
• *Parameters*: Information passed into, and out of, methods
• *Local variables*: Variables used to refer to temporary values within a method
• *Class variables*: Data stored once per class and shared by all its instances.

Operations read and write variables local to each object. A variable refers to an object. It is important to distinguish variables from objects, inasmuch as one variable may be capable of containing at different times several types of object (for example, different kinds of Shape) that will respond to messages (such as draw) differently. In some cases, several variables may refer to one object.

Every variable has several key features.

• *Type*: The designer should know what types of object can be held in a variable—that is, the expected behavior of the object to which it refers. In Self and bare Smalltalk, this is left to the design documentation; in C++, Java, and Eiffel, it is explicit and some aspects are checked by the compiler. Explicit typing is allowed in some research variants of Smalltalk because it makes it possible to compile more-efficient code; other compilers try to deduce types by analyzing the code.

• *Access:* This refers to which methods can get at a variable. In Smalltalk, all variables are encapsulated per object: Methods cannot get at the variables of another object of any class. In Java, variable access can be controlled within a package (a group of classes designed together) or at a finer grain. This arrangement makes sense, because each package is the responsibility of one designer or team; any changes within the package can readily be accommodated elsewhere within the same package. Encapsulation is important only between different pieces of design effort. C++ has access control per class: an intermediate position, making an intermediate amount of sense.

• *Containment*: In Smalltalk, Eiffel, and Java, all variables contain references to other objects—implicit pointers that enable objects to be shared and allow the uses of an object to be decoupled from its size and the details of its internal declaration. In C++, some variables are explicit pointers, and others contain complete objects. The latter arrangement yields faster code but no polymorphism; that is, one class is tied to using one specific other. This is not a generic design. In general, we consider containment to be a special and less usual case.

Within this book, we assume that variables are typed, that access can be controlled at the package level, and that variables contain implicit references—in other words, the scheme followed by Java, Eiffel, and others.

3.13.3   Class Extension

Inheritance, derivation, or extension mean that the definition of one class is based on that of one or more others. The extended class has by default the variables and operations of the class(es) it extends augmented by some of its own. The extension can also override an inherited operation definition by having one of its own of the same name.

Various complications arise in inheritance from multiple classes. For example, both superclasses may define an operation for the same message, or both superclasses themselves inherit from a common parent, and each language will provide some consistent resolution convention. Java and standard Smalltalk prohibit multiple inheritance of implementations for this reason.

Inheritance was at one time widely hailed as the magic OO mechanism that led to rapid application development, reduced costs, and so on. "Programming by adaptation" was the buzzphrase: You program by adding to and overriding existing work, and you benefit from any improvements made to the base classes. In fact, this approach turned out to be useful to some extent but only under adherence to certain patterns connected with polymorphism.

In general, if you want to base your code on someone else's implementation, which happens to suit your need, it is best to use your favorite editor to copy and paste.[19] Unless you want the spec of the other person's code, it's quite unlikely you'd want to inherit any modifications he or she makes. In fact, the big benefit of OO design comes more from polymorphism—conformance of many classes to one spec. If, in some cases, this is achieved by sharing some code, then it's nice but not necessary. Arbitrary code-sharing only couples designs that should be independent.

3.13.4   Abstract Classes

So ideally, a class should be extended only if the extension's instances will be substitutable wherever the superclass is expected. For example, if a drawing builder is designed to accept a Shape in one of its operation's parameters, then a Triangle should be acceptable because, presumably, the latter does everything a Shape is expected to do.

That raises the question of what a Shape is expected to do, and that takes us into the next section on types (object specifications). In programming languages, it is common for a class to represent a type. The class may perhaps define no internal variables or operations itself but instead only list the messages it expects. The rest is defined by each subclass in its own way.

A class that stands for a type, and that may include partial implementation of some operations, is called an *abstract* class. It should be documented with the full spec of the type.

It is now widely accepted good practice that nearly every class should either be an abstract class (prohibited from having instances but possibly with a partial implementation) or a *final* class (prohibited from having extensions).

Types help *decouple* a design—that is, make it less dependent on others. Ideally, each class should depend only on other types and not specific classes. In that way, it can be used in conjunction with any implementors of the types it uses.

But there is one case in which this does not work well: When you want to create an object, you must say which class you want it to belong to. However, there are a number of patterns, such as Factory, that help localize the dependencies, so that adding a new Shape to the drawing editor (for example) causes only one or two alterations to be necessary to the existing code.

---

19. If the code is available.

3.13.5 Types

In a program, a type should be an implementation-free specification of behavior. Different languages provide different support for types:

A Java *interface* is a pure type—that is, client-visible behavior. You define interfaces for the major categories of clients you expect to have. You factor your services into different interfaces, and you can define some interfaces as extensions of other interfaces (subtypes) to offer suitable client views. This approach provides those clients with a pluggable type requirement, in which any object that provides that interface can be used.

```
interface GuestAtFrontDesk {
    void checkin();
    void checkout();
}

interface HotelGuest extends GuestAtFrontDesk, RoomServiceClient {
    ...
}
```

A class implements any number of interfaces and also implicitly defines a new type. Behavioral guarantees should be defined on interfaces but are not directly supported by the language itself. You cannot instantiate an interface, only a class.

```
class Traveler implements GuestAtFrontDesk, AirlinePassenger {
    ....
}
```

Now let's look at C++ A Java interface is very similar to a C++ *pure abstract* class, with only pure virtual functions and no data or function bodies.

```
class GuestAtFrontDesk {
    public:virtual checkin() = 0;
        virtual checkout() = 0;
};
```

Similarly, a Java extended interface is like an abstract subclass, still with all pure virtual functions.

```
class HotelGuest :public GuestAtFrontDesk, public RoomServiceClient {
    ....
};
```

You can use macros to make the distinction more visible in C++:

```
#define interface class
#define extends public
#define implements public
```

In Smalltalk, when a client Hotel receives a parameter x, that client's view of x can be defined by a set of messages HotelGuest={checkIn, checkOut, useRoomService} that the client intends to send to x. Hence, the type of x, as seen by that client, is the type HotelGuest. The language does not directly support, or check, types; but you can systematically use facilities such as *message categories* or *message protocols*.

- A client expects an object to support a certain protocol, HotelGuest.
- Any object with a (compatible) implementation of that protocol will work.
- It is often convenient to get that compatible implementation by subclassing from another class, but it never matters *to the client* whether or not we subclass; we could just as well cut and paste the methods, delegate, or code it all ourselves. In Smalltalk the only check is a runtime verification that each message sent is supported.
- The only time the client needs to know the class is to *instantiate* it.

The class of an object is not really important to that client as long as it supports the protocol. In Smalltalk this can be represented by systematically following programming conventions that use a message protocol or message category as a type.

3.13.6   Generic Types

A generic definition provides a family of specific definitions. For example, in C++, a template class SortedList<Item> could be defined in which everything common to the code for all linked lists is programmed in terms of the placeholder class Item. When the designer requires a SortedList<Phone>, the compiler creates and compiles a copy of the template, with Item replaced by Phone.

There are variants on the basic generic idea.

• *What is generic*: In C++ and Eiffel, classes and operations are the units of genericity. In Ada, in many well-thought-out experimental languages, and—with any luck—in a future version of Java, packages are generic. This means that you can define a generic set of relationships and collaborations between classes in the same style as the frameworks (Chapter 9, Model Frameworks and Template Packages). We argue that this is a very important feature of component-based design.

• *When validated*: C++ template classes are (and can be simulated by) macros, mere manipulations of the program text before it gets compiled. The template definition itself undergoes few compiler checks. This means that if the design of SortedList<Item> performs, say, a < comparison on some of its Items, the compiler remarks on this only if you try to get it to compile a SortedList<some class that doesn't have that comparison>. A big disadvantage of C++ template classes is that they cannot be precompiled: you must pass the source code around. By contrast, the generic parameters of FOOPS [Goguen] come with "parameter assumptions" about such properties. When first compiling the generic, the compiler will check that you have made all such assumptions explicit and can guarantee that it will work for all conforming argument classes.

Catalysis frameworks have parameter assumptions in the form of all the constraints placed on placeholder types and actions; these frameworks span single types and classes, to families of mutually related types and their relationships.

3.13.7   Class Objects

In Smalltalk, a class is an object just like everything else. A class object has operations for adding new attributes and operations that its instances will possess. Most commonly, only the compiler makes use of these facilities, but careful use of them can make a system that can be extended by its users or that can be upgraded while in operation. For example, an insurance firm might add a new kind of policy while the system is running. In this "reflexive" kind of system, there is no need to stop everything and reload data after compiling a new addition. Java offers comparable facilities.

Java also supports such a reflexive layer: Classes, interfaces, methods, and instance variables can all be manipulated as runtime entities, although in a more restricted form than in Smalltalk. The language still needs work in this area.

In open systems design, it is important that an object be able to engage in a dialog about its capabilities just as, for example, fax machines begin by agreeing on a commonly understood transmission protocol. This comes naturally to a reflexive language; others must have the facility stuck on. C++ has recently acquired a limited form of such a feature with runtime type identification (RTTI).

In C++, the static variables and operations of a class can be thought of as forming a class object but with limited features. There is no metaclass to which class-object classes belong and no dynamic definition of new classes.

3.13.8   Specifications in Classes

Classes are units of implementation, and they need clear links to specifications.

3.13.8.1   implements Assertions

To say that a class *implements* a type means that any client designed to work with a specific type in a particular variable or parameter should be guaranteed to work properly with an instance of the class.

In Java, types are represented by interfaces and abstract classes. Even though the complete specification of the type (pre- and postconditions and so on) is not understood by the compiler, the following clause documents the designer's intention to satisfy the expectations of anyone who has read the spec associated with the interface Food.

    class Potato implements Food ...

Java allows many classes to implement one interface, directly or through class extension. The following clause should mean that the class implements the type represented by its superclass as well as extending the definition of its code.

    class HotPotato extends Potato ...

In each case, the interface and abstract class referred to should be documented appropriately with a type specification.

In C++, public inheritance is used to document extension and implementation. private inheritance is used for extensions that are not implementations (apart from the simple restrictions mentioned earlier); but the usual recommendation is to use instead an internal variable of the proposed base type.

3.13.8.2   Constructors

A *constructor* has the property that it creates an instance of the class and thereby a member of any type the class implements:

```
class Circle implements Shape {

    ...

    public   Circle (Point centre, float radius);
            // post return:Circle—the result belongs to this Class
            // — from which you can infer that return:Shape
```

Constructors should ensure that the newly created objects are in a valid state— that is, that they satisfy the expected invariants.

3.13.8.3   Retrieval

A fully documented implementation claim is backed up by a justification; the minimal version is a set of *retrieve* functions (see Section 6.7, Spreadsheet: Operation Refinement). Writing these functions often exposes bugs.

For every attribute in the type specification, a function (read-only operation) is written that yields its value in any state of the implementation. This retrieval can be written in executable code for debugging or test purposes, but its execution performance is not important. The functions are private. They are useful for testing but not available to clients.

```
interface Shape {
    attribute[20]   bool      contains (Point); // type model attribute
    public          void      move (Vector v);
                    // post (Point p,
                    //   old(self).contains(p) = contains(p.movedBy(v)))
}

class Circle implements Shape {
    private    Length    radius;
    private    Point     center;
    private    bool      contains (Point p)      // retrieval
               { return (p.distanceFrom(center) < radius); }
    public     void      move  (Vector v) { ... }
}
```

---

20. This takes liberties with Java syntax. A suitable preprocessor could convert attributes to comments after typechecking them or leave it as code for testing purposes.

3.13.8.4   Operation Specs

An operation can be specified in the style detailed earlier in this chapter. You can refer to the old and new values of the internal variables (and to attributes of their types, and of the attributes' types, and so on).

Eiffel is among the few programming languages to provide directly for operation specs, but they can, of course, be documented with an operation in any language. In C++, suitable macros can be used; Java could use methods introduced on the superclass Object. For debugging, pre- and postconditions can be executed.

Chapter 4 Interaction Models Use Cases, Actions, and Collaborations

Chapters 2 and 3 have described how to model the behaviors of an object by specifying operations in terms of attributes. However, the most interesting aspect of any design lies in the interactions among the objects: the way that the net behavior resulting from their collaborations realizes some higher-level function when they are configured together in a particular way.

Use cases, actions, and collaborations abstract the interactions among a group of objects above the level of an individual OOP message send. These interaction models let you separate abstract multiparty behaviors, joint or localized responsibilities, and actual interfaces and interaction protocols.

Section 4.1 provides an overview of the design of object collaborations. Section 4.2 begins with examples of object interactions to show that many variations in interaction protocols achieve the same net effect and so motivate the need for abstract actions. Section 4.3 introduces use cases and relates them to actions and refinement. Section 4.4 explains how actions and effects are related to abstract actions. Section 4.5 describes concurrency between actions and explains how to specify these constraints.

Collaborations—sets of related actions—are introduced in Section 4.6. Section 4.7 describes how to use collaborations to describe either the encapsulated internal design of a type specification or an "open" design pattern. The separation of actions internal to a collaboration from those that are external to a collaboration forms the basis for effective collaboration models and is the topic of Section 4.8.

4.1 *Designing Object Collaborations*

The big difference between object-oriented design (OOD) and the procedural style is that with OOD your program must not only work as a sequence of statements but must also be well decoupled so that it can easily be pulled apart, reconfigured, and maintained. You must make an extra set of decisions about how to distribute the program's functionality among many small operational units with their own states. In return—if you do it well—you get the benefits of flexibility.

There are three big questions in object-oriented design.

- *What should the system do?* This is the focus of type specification in Chapter 3. You'll find guidance on putting it together in Chapter 15.
- *What objects should be chosen?* The first draft is the static model we used for the type specification, although it is modified by design patterns to improve decoupling.
- *Which object should do what, and how should the objects interact?* The most important criterion is to meet the specification. In addition, our goal is to separate different concerns into different objects while balancing the needs of decoupling with performance.

The art of designing the collaborations is so important that many experts advocate making collaborations the primary focus of object-oriented design—with, of course, a reasonable type specification first. In Catalysis, collaborations, like types, are therefore first-class units of design. A *collaboration* is a design for the way objects interact with one another to achieve a mutual goal. A type represents a specification of the behavior seen at an interface to an object. By contrast, a collaboration represents a design of the way a group of objects interact to meet a type specification.

There are several situations in which collaborations should be used.

- When you're designing what goes on inside a software component.
- When you're describing how users (or external machines or software) interact with a component you're interested in. It is useful to understand how a component is to be used before constructing it.
- When you're decribing how real world objects in a business organization (or a hardware design) interact with one another. This description is typically used to help explain the business in which a system is to be installed or updated.

4.2 *Actions (Use Cases) Abstract Complex Interactions*

We've already said that it's often useful to talk about what is to be achieved in some part of a complex design before you go into how it is to be achieved. Type specifications are about hiding the "how" inside individual objects and stating only the end result of invoking a particular operation.

Abstract actions do the same for interactions *between* groups of objects (as opposed to inside them). We know that we want to achieve the transfer of information and that it might involve the participants having a complex dialog, but we may wish to leave the details aside for a separate piece of work. The interacting participants might be objects inside a program, or people, or people and computers.

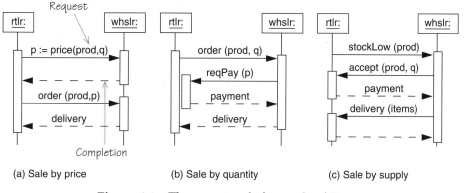

Figure 4.1   Three protocols for a sale of items.

For example, how does the sale of a product from a wholesaler to a retailer work? Here are three different possibilities, as illustrated in Figure 4.1.

a. The retailer first queries the price for a product and then requests a sale while providing payment; the wholesaler then delivers the items.

b. The retailer requests the sale, and the wholesaler calls back requesting payment of the appropriate amount. When the payment is provided, the wholesaler delivers the items.

c. The wholesaler triggers the retailer to buy the product, perhaps by monitoring the retailer's inventory systems. The retailer returns a payment, and the wholesaler then delivers the items.

But at some level of analysis or design, I don't want to bother with which of these protocols is used or whether all or any of them is available. What they have in common is the same net effect of transferring a quantity of items and money based on the wholesaler's price. They differ in who initiates which operation and the protocol of interactions.

In Catalysis, we can describe the whole dialog as a single interaction (Figure 4.2). On any sequence chart, a series of horizontal bars can be collapsed to a single bar, representing their combined effect. The horizontal bars connect objects that influence or are influenced by the outcome: there may be any number of them. If all the possible refinements have the same initiator, it can be marked with a shaded oval (Figure 4.2b).

4.2.1   Action Types and Refinements

Each horizontal arrow or bar represents an occurrence of an action. Just as object instances belong to types that group them according to behavior, so action occurrences belong to action types, to which descriptions of the action can be attached. An action type is shown as an ellipse associated with the types of object that can participate in it (see Figure 4.3). Participants are those objects whose states can be

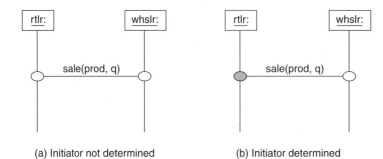

(a) Initiator not determined   (b) Initiator determined

Figure 4.2   A sale as one action, without the details of the protocols.

Figure 4.3   An action type with participants.

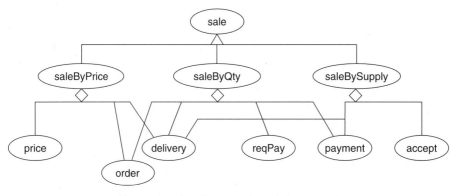

Figure 4.4   Different kinds of sale and and their constituent actions.

changed by, or whose states can affect the outcome of, an action; there may be any number of them.

The value of an action such as sale is that it represents all protocols that achieve the same postcondition. We can show its relationship to different possible protocols, as in Figure 4.4. The subtyping symbol is used to show that there are different variants of sale, all of them sharing and extending its description. The diamond aggregation symbol decomposes an action into more-detailed constituents. An aggregation doesn't show exactly how the smaller actions make up the larger one. They might be a sequence or might occur repetitively or concurrently;

that must be documented separately for each aggregation—for example, by using sequence diagrams such as that shown in Figure 4.1.

The most-abstract actions represent only the effect of an interaction. The more-detailed ones are directional, stating who intiates the request and who processes it. The most-concrete actions are object-oriented messages.

4.2.2   Preview: Documenting a Refinement

Chapter 6, Abstraction, Refinement, and Testing, discusses refinement in detail, but we include a short discussion here to show how to relate abstraction and realization to each other in the context of actions.

One of the finer-grained actions in a sale is the delivery of the product to the retailer. Consider a simple retailer warehouse object, WHA. One of its operations is re_stock, by which one of the products in the warehouse is restocked by some quantity. One abstract description of this action uses a simple type model:

> <u>action</u> WH$_A$::re_stock (p: Product, q: Quantity)
> <u>post</u>:   p.stock += q

One realization of this warehouse, WHB, provides a sliding door that can be moved to a particular product and then opened; then items are added to that product shelf one at a time before the door is closed. The actions at this level of realization need a slightly richer type model with a selected_product attribute:

> <u>action</u> WH$_B$::open (p: Product)
> <u>post</u>:   selected_product = p
>
> <u>action</u> WH$_B$::insert ( )
> <u>post</u>:   selected_product.count += 1
>
> <u>action</u> WH$_B$::close ( )
> <u>post</u>:   selected_product = null

It is clear that a certain sequence of these detailed actions constitutes a valid re_stock action. Thus the following sequence constitutes an abstract action: re_stock (p, n).

> open (p); insert$_1$(); insert$_2$(); ... insert$_n$(); close()

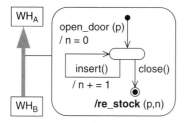

The refinement relation between the two levels of description documents this mapping. The state chart shows how the parameters and state changes in the detailed action sequence translate to the abstract action and its parameters. In this example we use a counter attribute to define this mapping; it is an attribute of a specification type representing a restocking in progress at the more detailed level (Pattern 14.13, Action Reification).

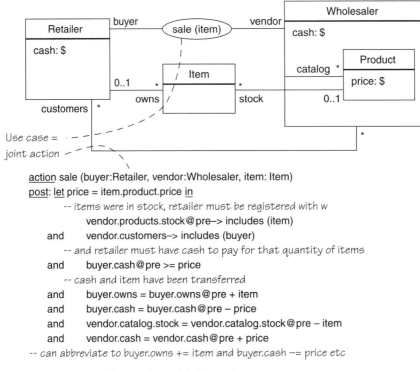

action sale (buyer:Retailer, vendor:Wholesaler, item: Item)
post: let price = item.product.price in
              -- items were in stock, retailer must be registered with w
                     vendor.products.stock@pre–> includes (item)
        and   vendor.customers–> includes (buyer)
              -- and retailer must have cash to pay for that quantity of items
        and   buyer.cash@pre >= price
              -- cash and item have been transferred
        and   buyer.owns = buyer.owns@pre + item
        and   buyer.cash = buyer.cash@pre – price
        and   vendor.catalog.stock = vendor.catalog.stock@pre – item
        and   vendor.cash = vendor.cash@pre + price
     -- can abbreviate to buyer.owns += item and buyer.cash –= price etc

Figure 4.5   A joint action, or use case.

4.2.3   Joint Actions (Use Cases)

In Catalysis we believe in the value of separating the various decisions that must be made during a design. We therefore require two things: a way to describe the overall effect of an interaction without any attribution of who does what and a way to document who does what after we have made that decision.

A *joint action* represents a change in the state of some number of participant objects without stating how it happens and without yet attributing the responsibility for it to any one of the participants. We can write its postcondition more or less formally in terms of the models of the participants as shown in Figure 4.5.

4.2.4   Localized Actions

To assign responsibility for the execution of an action, use a localized action. Draw the action attached to the type or (more conventionally) list it in the bottom section of the type box.

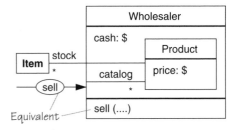

In accompanying text, a localized action is prefixed with its type using the context operator:

<u>action</u> Wholesaler :: sell (retailer : Retailer, item : Item, out price : $)
<u>pre</u>   catalog.stock->includes(item)   -- this item was part of our stock
<u>post</u>   price = item.product.price   -- price returned to caller
      and   cash = cash@pre + price
      and   stock = stock@pre − item

In the specification of a localized action, self is defined and refers to the *receiving* object. We do not know who the invoker is. Return values (e.g., price) can be defined.

4.2.5   Joint versus Localized Actions

Let's look at some differences between joint actions and localized actions. First, localized actions are invoked. A localized action represents an interaction in which the receiver (the object taking responsibility) is requested to achieve the postcondition. It should do so if the precondition is met.

The message (or operation) in an object-oriented programming language is one realization of a localized action. Localized actions are a bit more general, encompassing any way in which an object can be stimulated to do something.[1] For example, in specifying an application program such as a drawing editor, we can think of the editor as a single object; the user operations, such as cut, paste, and move shape, are actions localized on the editor. They are abstract in that each one is invoked using a sequence of smaller actions (keystrokes, mouse moves, and clicks); there may be no single message to a particular object within the editor corresponding to, say, move shape.

Joint actions represent possibilities A joint action represents a specification of something that may occur. It can be referred to in other specifications (e.g., "To achieve restocking, one or more sales must occur") but can't be invoked directly from the program code. To do that, you must have an implementation (such as one of the sequences in Figure 4.1), which will tell you one of the ways to start.

Localized actions provide preconditions. When a localized action is invoked, if the precondition is true we are assured that the postcondition will be achieved. Joint actions represent descriptions of history: Looking at the history of the world, wherever this and that has happened, we call that a sale. Wherever something else happened that started the same way but ended up differently, we call it something else, such as a theft.

(We sometimes find it convenient to write "preconditions" on joint actions, but they are really only clauses that should be wrapped up in a big (...)@pre and conjoined with the rest of the postcondition.)

---

1. A directed joint action encompasses any way one object may stimulate another to do something.

4.2.6   Action Parameters

The parameters of an action represent things that might be different from one occurrence to another. In any sale, the selling and buying parties may be different, and the item being sold is different; they are all parameters. The price also changes, so we could make it a parameter; however, we might assert that the price exchanged in our sales is always the price in the vendor's catalog. Therefore, although we could include it as a parameter, it would be redundant. Notice how different action parameters are from programming-language parameters: we are specifying the information content of the interaction and not its implementation.[2]

In a joint action, some of the parameters may be distinguished as participants and drawn linked to the use case pictorially, whereas other parameters are written in text style. For example, in Figure 4.5, buyer and vendor are participants, whereas item is a parameter. In business analysis, the difference is a matter of convenience and is analogous to the equivalence of the associations and attributes of object types. In a software design, the participants can be used to represent objects that we know will definitely exist in the final code and that will, between them, take responsibility for executing the action. The list of parameters, on the other hand, represents information transferred between them whose implementation is yet to be determined.

In text, the list of participants can be written in front of the action name as partially localized context:

```
action (buyer:Retailer, vendor:Wholesaler) :: sale (item: Item)
post:  let price = item.product.price in
             vendor.customers → includes (buyer)
```

4.2.7   From Joint to Localized Actions

A joint action is interesting because its effect says something important about all participants. Although some joint actions, such as the one in Figure 4.2, do not designate any participant as an initiator, in general you can designate initiator and receiver. Here is the syntax for each variation of a three-way use case, sale, between a retailer, a wholesaler, and an agent. (We use the convention that the names of untyped parameters imply their types.)

- (retailer, wholesaler, agent) :: sale (x: Item)

  This represents a joint action with three participants, with no distinguished initiator or receiver. The effect refers to all participants, parameters, and their attributes.

- retailer -> (wholesaler, agent) :: sale (x: Item)

  A joint action, this time initiated by the retailer. It is now meaningful to mark some parameters as *inputs*—determined by the initiator by means unspecified

---

2. Perhaps we should have used a markedly different syntax.

in the effects clause—and others as *outputs*—determined by other participants, used by the initiator in ways not fully specified in the effects clause.

- retailer -> agent:: sale (x: Item, w: Wholesaler)

  A directed joint action that designates the retailer as initiator and the agent as the receiver; the sale is initiated by the retailer and carried out principally by the agent. Again, the effect refers to all participants and parameters. In this example, the wholesaler is identified to the agent by the retailer as a parameter. An alternative arrangement might leave the choice of wholesaler to the agent, appearing only in the effects clause based on some attributes of the agent.

- initiator: Object -> agent :: sale (....)

  A directed joint action initiated by an object and received by the agent. Nothing is known about the type of the initiator or its role in this action; hence, initiator is declared to be of unknown type Object.

  Our use case template permits these additional distinctions to be made:

use case	sale	
participants	retailer, wholesaler	
initiator	retailer	-- also listed as participant
receiver	wholesaler	
parameters	set of items	-- can separate inputs/outputs for directed actions

A localized operation is a degenerate case of a joint action with a distinct receiver, in which nothing is known or stated about the initiator's identity or attributes. All relevant aspects of the initiator are abstracted into the input and output parameters of the operation. The following is a fully localized operation that cannot refer to the initiator at all.

Agent:: sale (....)

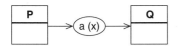

In the diagram notation, we show an arrow from the initiator to the action and from the action to the receiver if either one is known. Each action can have any number of participants and parameters.

4.2.8 Inputs and Outputs

Within the effects clause, there is no strong difference between participants and parameters: both can be affected by the action. The distinction is intended to document a partial design decision. The participants exist or will be built as separate entities, with some direct or indirect interaction between them to realize the action. Together, the parameters represent information that is passed between the participants, encoded in a form not documented here, and possibly communicated differently.

The concept of inputs and outputs is meaningful only for directed requests: either fully localized operations or joint actions with initiators and receivers, in which the invoker of an operation somehow provides the inputs and uses the outputs. In the case of joint actions that have no distinguished initiators or receivers, the effect is expressed in terms of, and on, all participants, and there is no need to explicitly list inputs or outputs.

The input parameters in a directed action are simply attributes of the initiator in a corresponding undirected joint action; they represent state information known to the initiator when it provides the inputs to a directed request. Similarly, the outputs of a directed action are state changes in attributes of the sender in the joint action. When parameters are used in a joint action, the parameter list represents information exchanged that is not fully determined by attributes in the participants; that is, they provide a degree of nondeterminism.

4.2.9   Abstracting a Single Operation in Code

We have seen how an entire sequence of interactions between objects can be abstracted and described as a single joint action. We will next see how even in program code, an operation invocation itself has two sides: the sender and the receiver. By using input and output parameters, a localized operation specification decouples the effect on the receiver from any information about the initiator.

Consider the following interaction sequence between retailer and wholesaler. The retailer first requests the price of some quantity of the product. It then requests a sale, paying the required amount, and gets as a return a set of items. Let us examine the sell operation. Its spec, based on the type model shown in Figure 4.6, could be

action Wholesaler::sell (prod: Product, q: integer, payment: Money) : Set(Item)
    pre: -- provided the request product is in our catalog, and payment is enough
        catalog->includes (prod) and payment >= prod.price * q
    post: -- the correct number of items has been returned from stock
        result ->size = q and catalog.stock -= result and cash+= payment

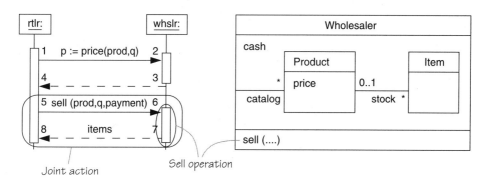

Joint action   Sell operation

Figure 4.6   Scope of operation versus joint action. The numbers represent
                 increasing points in time.

This spec says nothing about how the values of p, q, and payment are related to any attributes of the retailer. Nor does it say what effect the returned set of items has on the retailer. Although this lack of detail is useful when you're designing the wholesaler in isolation, in the bigger picture of the overall interaction between retailer and wholesaler, those details are important.

The numbers in Figure 4.6 will help you understand what is going on here. The numbers mark increasing points in time (although the separations may be a bit artificial for a procedure-calling model of interactions).

1. Retailer has just issued the first price request.
2. Wholesaler has received that request.
3. Wholesaler has just replied with the requested price.
4. Retailer has accepted the returned price.
5. Retailer has just issued the sell request.
6. Wholesaler has just received that request.
7. Wholesaler has completed processing the request and has just returned the items.
8. Retailer has accepted the items.

When we wrote our specification for Wholesaler::sell, the span we were considering was from 6 to 7, no more and no less. Thus, we ignored all aspects of the retailer in the specification.

If we wanted to describe the effect including points 5 and 8, we would include the fact that the product, quantity, and payment from the retailer are precisely those previously exchanged with the wholesaler (at time 5), and we would increase the inventory of the retailer (step 8). We can introduce attributes on the retailer to describe the product, quantity, and payment known to it at point 5 and the set of items that will be increased at step 8; we can then define a directed joint action.

```
action (r: Retailer -> w: Wholesaler) :: sale ( out items: Set(Item))
let ( prod = r.prod,      -- the product the retailer wants
      q = r.qty,          -- the quantity the retailer wants
      pay = r.pay ) in (                -- the amount to be paid
    pre:
          -- provided retailer has enough cash
          r.cash >= pay
          -- and product is available and in stock
          and w.catalog->includes (prod) and prod.stock->count >= q
    post:
          -- payment and inventory of that product have been appropriately transferred
          r.cash -= pay and w.cash+= pay and
          items.product@pre = prod and items->count = q
          r.items += items and w.catalog.stock -= items
  )
```

Note that the effect is defined almost completely in terms of attributes of the retailer rather than by parameters that would otherwise be unrelated to retailer attributes. Some of these attributes may even correspond to local variables within the retailer's implementation, in which the product, quantity, and payment due are stored after step 4. The particular set of items transferred has been modeled as an output because the specific items can be determined by the wholesaler in ways not specified here, provided they are of the right product and quantity.

4.3 *Use Cases Are Joint Actions*

Joint actions are useful for describing business interactions, interactions within a software design, and interactions between users and software. We like to separate the specification of an action from its refinement into smaller actions.

The analysis idea of a use case is a joint action specification at the business or user level. When describing a use case, you may prefer a diagram view without the type models and may want to use a form that looks a bit more like a narrative template for review by customers. Making it precise is still your job.

<u>use case</u>	sale
<u>participants</u>	retailer, wholesaler
<u>parameters</u>	set of items
<u>pre</u>	the items must be in stock, retailer must be registered,
	retailer must have cash to pay
<u>post</u>	retailer has received items and paid cash
	wholesaler has received cash and given items
	-- formal versions hidden

It is also useful to document informally the performance requirements of a use case. Such requirements include whether it is considered a primary or secondary use case (alternatively, priority levels), the frequency with which it is expected to take place, and its concurrency with other use cases.

<u>use case</u> sale

.....

<u>priority</u>	primary
<u>concurrent</u>	many concurrent sales with different wholesaler reps
	no sale and return by the same retailer at the same time
<u>refinement criteria</u>	*-- what to consider when refining this use case into a sequence*
<u>frequency</u>	300-500 per day
<u>performance</u>	less than 3 minutes per sale

In the rest of this book we will sometimes explicitly show the informal use case template equivalent of a specification. However, the joint action form can always be represented in the narrative use case template.

▶ *use case*   A joint action with multiple participant objects that represent a meaningful business task, usually written in a structured narrative style. Like any joint action, a use case can be refined into a finer-grained sequence of actions. Traditionally, the refined sequence is described as a part of the use case itself; we recommend that it be treated as a refinement even if the presentation is as a single template.

Many use case practitioners recommend listing the steps of the use case as part of its definition; we do not do this because it mixes the description of a single abstract action with one specific (of many possible) refining action sequence. Instead, first describe the use case as a single abstract action without any sequence of smaller steps; document its postcondition. This approach forces you to think precisely about the intended outcome, a step back from the details of accomplishing it.

When you separately refine the action (Chapter 6, Abstraction, Refinement, and Testing), it is useful to document the refinement textually in a use case template.

<u>use case</u>	telephone sale by distributor
<u>refines</u>	use case **sale**
	(the pre/post of sale could be shown here)
<u>refinement</u>	1. retailer calls wholesaler and is connected to rep
	2. rep gets distributor membership information from retailer
	3. rep collects order information from retailer, totaling the cost
	4. rep confirms items, total, and shipping date with wholesaler
	5. both parties hang up
	6. shipment arrives at retailer
	7. wholesaler invoices retailer
	8. retailer pays invoice
<u>abstract result</u>	**sale** was effectively conducted
	with amount of the order total and items as ordered

Some leading use case practitioners recommend adding an explicit "goal" statement to a use case. In Catalysis this is taken care of by refinement. Goals can usually be described as some combination of the following.

- *Static invariant:* Whatever happens, this must be true afterward.
- *Action specification:* This action should get me to this postcondition.
- *Effect invariant:* Any action that makes this happen must also ensure that.

Refinement allows us to trace use cases back to the level of such goals.

4.3.1   A Clear Basis for Use Cases

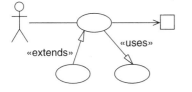

Use case has become a popular term in object-oriented development, where it is defined as "the specification of a sequence of actions, including variants, that a system (or other entity) can perform, interacting with actors of the system." This concept is given a solid foundation in Catalysis based on actions and refinements.

In the common literature, a use case is typically a joint action involving at least one object (called an *actor*) outside the system of interest; the granularity of the action is such that it accomplishes an objective for the actor. The use case is refined into a more detailed sequence of actions and is explored with sequence diagrams illustrating that collaboration. Use case diagrams can be used to capture the action refinement. Most current accounts of use cases fail to separate the specific action refinement (one of many that may be possible) from the single abstract action because the use case definition itself includes the specific sequence of steps followed to accomplish the use case; this lack of separation can make it difficult to handle alternative decompositions.

The use case approach also defines two relationships between use cases— *extends* and *uses*—to help structure and manage the set of use cases. These relationships are defined in UML as follows.

▶ *extends*   A relationship from one use case to another that specifies how the behavior defined for the first use case can be inserted into the behavior defined for the second use case.

▶ *uses*   A relationship from a use case to another use case in which the behavior defined for the former use case employs the behavior defined for the latter.

The extends relation serves two purposes. First, it is used to define certain user-visible behaviors as increments relative to an existing definition—for example, to define different interaction paths based on configurations or incremental releases of functionality. Second, it does so without directly editing the existing definition—a fancy editing construct. Catalysis meets these objectives within the framework of actions and packages, in which a second package may specify additional behaviors or paths for the same basic service from another package (Chapter 7, Using Packages).

The uses relationship between use cases is meant to let use cases share existing use cases for some parts that are common. There is, however, a conflict between the often-stated goal of having a use case correspond to a user task and the need to factor common parts across use cases. This leads to some confusion and variations in interpretation even among use case consultants. Catalysis provides *actions* and *effects* as the basis for this sharing; "using" another use case means that you use its effect or quote the action itself.

Based on refinement, Catalysis provides a more flexible mapping between abstract actions and their realizations. For example, here are two partially overlapping views of a sale. A customer views sale as some sequence of <order, deliver, pay>. A salesperson may view sale as a sequence of <make call; take order; wait for collection; file commission report; collect commission>. Both views are valid and constitute two different definitions of a sale.

Consider the following example from an Internet newsgroup discussion, which highlighted some of the confusion surrounding a precise definition of use case.

> *A system administers dental patients across several clinics. A clinic can refer a patient to another clinic. The other clinic can reply, accepting or otherwise updating the status of the referral. Eventually, the reply is seen back at the referring clinic, and the case file is updated. Later, the final treatment status of the patient is sent back to the referring clinic. Then there is a financial transaction between the two clinics for the referral.*

Several questions arise.

- Is this one large-grained use case, Refer Patient?
- Are there separate use cases for Send Referral, Accept Referral, Get Acceptance, Final Referral Status, and Transfer Money?
- Suppose that Accept Referral is done by a receptionist printing it from the system and then leaving it in a pile for the dentist to review. The dentist reviews the referral and annotates acceptance. The receptionist then gets back on the system and communicates that decision. How many use cases is that?

In Catalysis, all these actions are valid at different levels of refinement. There is a top-level action called Refer Patient. In our approach, the name you choose for a use case is helpful, but its meaning is defined by the pre- and postconditions you specify for that use case. As with any other action (see Section 3.1.5, Two Kinds of Actions), a use case can be refined into a sequence of finer-grained actions; alternative refinements may also be possible. The steps of a use case are also actions, just as the use case itself is an action.

Use cases give reasonable guidelines on how fine-grained a use case should become, if only at the bottom end of the spectrum: If the next level of refinement provides no meaningful unit of business value or information, do not bother with finer-grained use cases; just document them as steps of the previous level of use case.

4.4 *Actions and Effects*

An effect is simply a name for a transition between two states. We can define joint effects just as we define localized effects in Section 3.8.3.

    effect (a: A, b: B, c: C) :: stateChangeName (params)
        pre: ...
        post: ...

Actions and operations describe interactions between objects; an effect describes state transitions. You use effects to factor a specification or to describe important transitions before the actual units of interaction are known. Just as attributes are introduced when convenient to simplify the specification of an operation, independent of data storage, so can effects be introduced to simplify or defer the specification of operations.

Effects can also be used when responsibilities of objects (or groups of objects, in the case of joint effects) are decided but their interfaces and interaction protocols are not yet known. You can then express actions in a factored form without choosing interfaces or protocols.

    effect Wholesaler::sell (x: Item)
        pre: -- item must be in stock
        post: -- gained price of item, lost item

<u>effect</u> Retailer::buy (x: Item)
    <u>pre</u>:   *-- must have enough to pay*
    <u>post</u>:   *-- has paid price of item, gained item*

The joint action (or another effect) can then be written conveniently using a single postcondition:

<u>action</u> (r: Retailer, w: Wholesaler) :: sale (x: Item)
    <u>post</u>:   r.buy (x) and w.sell (x) and r: w.registrants @ pre

Every action introduces an effect, which can be referred to by *quoting* it. This is a way to use the specification of that action, committing to achieving its effect without committing to specifically invoking it in an implementation.

    .... [[(r,w).sale (x)]]

The joint action can also be *invoked*. This means that one of the protocol sequences that realizes the joint action will be executed; specific participants and parameters are bound, but how they are communicated is left unspecified.

    .... ->(r,w).sale (x)

It is not meaningful to "invoke" an effect.

4.5 *Concurrent Actions*

All actions take up some period of time. Some actions are more interesting because of what they do while they are in operation than what they have achieved after they have finished.

For example, a wholesaler and a retailer have an ongoing supply relationship in which the retailer's stock is maintained by regular sales by the wholesaler. We can show that supply consists of a number of sales (see Figure 4.7). A guarantee clause is used to state what the supply relationship means:

<u>action</u>   (retailer, wholesaler) :: supply
<u>guarantee</u>   retailer.stock->size >10   *-- the retailer's stock will never go below 10*
<u>rely</u>   wholesaler.in_business   *-- provided the wholesaler is always in business*

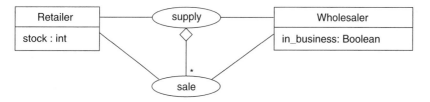

Figure 4.7   A supply activity consists of many sales.

The rely condition qualifies the description, saying that it is valid only if the stated condition remains true through the life of the occurrence. If a concurrent action causes it to be false for any of period of time, then we cannot point to any overlapping period and say, "There is an occurrence of supply." (Not according to this description at least; there may be other descriptions that define what supply means over such a period.)

If you want to define supply to mean that the retailer's stock is maintained whenever the wholesaler is in business even though this might vary during the period of a supply occurrence, you should put it all in the guarantee:

<u>guarantee</u> wholesaler.in_business => retailer.stock–> size > 0

In some cases, we are interested both in what an action achieves from beginning to end and also what it does while in operation. For example:

<u>action</u>   (retailer, wholsaler):: supplyForYear (amount:Money, from:Date, to:Date)
<u>guarantee</u>   retailer.stock–> size < 10 and (from:today<to)$\Rightarrow$
            retailer.orders[source=wholesaler]–>size > 0
<u>post</u>   wholesaler.income +=amount
     and   retailer.outgoings +=amount   *-- net effect is transfer of money*
<u>rely</u>   wholesaler.inBusiness   *--makes no sense if not in business*
<u>pre</u>   from < to   *--makes no sense if dates aren't in order*

Both the guarantee and the postcondition are qualified by both the precondition and the rely condition.

4.5.1   Rely and Guarantee

The rely and guarantee clauses contribute to an action speicification as follows:

- An action description has a signature and four clauses: precondition, rely, guarantee, and postcondition.
- A guarantee clause states a condition maintained while an action occurrence is in progress.
- A postcondition states a condition achieved between the beginning and the end of an action's occurrence.
- A precondition states what must be true at the start of an action occurrence for all of this description to be applicable.
- A rely condition states what must be true throughout the action occurrence for all of this description to be applicable.
- There may be more than one description of an action having different rely conditions and preconditions.

4.5.2   Granularity

The guarantee applies only between the beginnings and ends of actions in the next, more detailed level of aggregation. A sale might be implemented as making an order followed by a later delivery; in that case, the retailer's stock might temporarily go below 10, but only while a sale is in progress that will bring it up again.

The rely condition works on the same level of granularity.

4.5.3 Exploring Interference

Sequence diagrams are useful for exploring how concurrent actions may potentially interfere with one another. Suppose that we know that sales consist of making an order, delivering, and paying and that the order is not accepted unless the wholesaler has the items in stock (see Figure 4.8). The * against the sale action signifies that several sales may be in progress at once, although each sale is between one wholesaler and one retailer.

Suppose that a retailer orders 10 widgets; then another retailer orders 15 more; the wholesaler delivers the 10, and then has insufficient widgets to fulfill the order for 15. We can see this kind of situation more easily by drawing sequence diagrams (see Figure 4.9). (Remember that each vertical bar on a sequence dia-

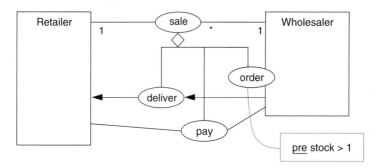

Figure 4.8 Constituent actions for a sale.

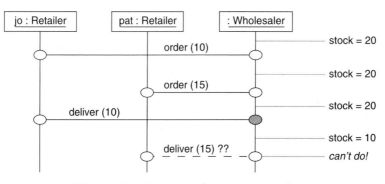

Figure 4.9 Attempted concurrent sales.

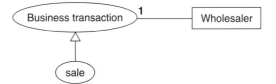

Figure 4.10   Action multiplicity = 1 bans concurrent actions.

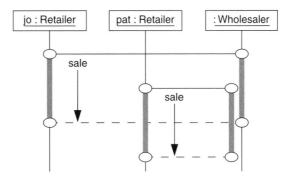

Figure 4.11   The extension of an action over time.

gram is an object, and not a type.) Also it's often useful to draw snapshots of the states, although here it is necessary only to write the single stock attribute.

Perhaps Wholesaler needs an "earmarked for delivery" attribute as well as a stock count. Alternatively, we may prefer to ban concurrent sales or even concurrent transactions of various kinds (see Figure 4.10). Explorations of potential interference scenarios are useful, although they are not a fully formal technique. If you are designing an operating system or a nuclear power station, please refer to a text on verifying concurrent designs.

We sometimes want to draw on a sequence diagram the extension of an action over time, indicating that its constituent actions (even if we don't know what they are) are interleaved with those of another action (see Figure 4.11).

4.5.4   Meaning of Postconditions

Given that actions may overlap, we must take a broader view of the meaning of a postcondition. For example, sale means that, somewhere between the start and the end of the action, the wholesaler's till gets fatter by the price of the items. But does it? If you compare the actual contents of the till before and after the sale, the difference is probably not the same as is documented. It depends on what else has happened during that interval: other sales may have been completed; the manager may have taken the cash to the bank; there may have been a refund or a robbery.

A postcondition therefore means not that the difference between before and after will always be literally what is stated. Instead, it means that if you take into account concurrent actions, the cumulative effect will be what you'd calculate from all the postconditions of the actions. So if you compare the till contents at the beginning and the end of the trading day, you should get a balance equaling the sum of all the sales, bankings, robberies, and so on.

4.6 *Collaborations*

A collaboration is a set of related actions between typed objects playing certain roles with respect to others in the collaboration, within a common model of attributes. The actions are grouped into a collaboration so as to indicate that they serve a common purpose. Typically, the actions are used in different combinations to achieve different goals or to maintain an invariant between the participants. Each role is a place for an object and is named relative to the other roles in the overall collaboration.

For example, the subject-observer pattern uses a set of actions that enables the following: the subject to notify its observers of changes; the observer to query the subject about its state; and the observer to register and deregister interest in a particular subject. These actions, taken as a set, form a collaboration. When several actions have the same participants, it is convenient to draw them on top of one another. The collaboration in Figure 4.12 describes a set of three actions between retailers and wholesalers. This collaboration is a refinement of the joint sale use case we specified earlier because particular sequences of these refined actions will realize the abstract action.

A collaboration represents how responsibilities are distributed across objects and actions, showing which actions take place between which objects and optionally directing or localizing the actions. The actions are related by being defined against the same model and achieve a common goal or refine a single, more abstract action.

Associated with a collaboration is a set of types: those that take part in the actions. Typically, they are partial views, dealing only with the roles of those objects involved in this collaboration. For example, the retailer in this collaboration may well have another role in which it sells the items to end customers.

Note that a type specification is a degenerate special case of a collaboration spec, one in which all actions are directed and nothing is said about the initiator.

▶ *collaboration*   A set of related actions between typed objects playing defined roles in the collaboration; these actions are defined in terms of a common type model of the objects involved. A collaboration is frequently a refinement of a single abstract action or is a design to maintain an invariant between some objects.

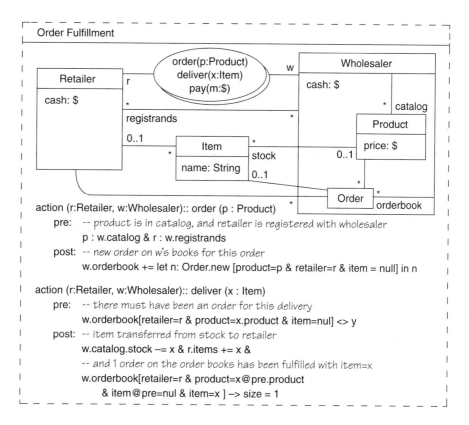

Figure 4.12   A collaboration that realizes the abstract sale.

4.7 *Uses of Collaborations*

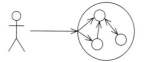

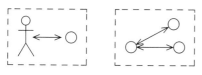

Collaborations are used to describe designs in two primary forms. In an *enscapsulated* collaboration the behavior of an object can be specified as a type; it can then be implemented, with the object comprising others that collaborate to meet its behavior specifications. Individual classes fall into this category.

In an *Open* collaboration, a requirement expressed as an invariant or joint action can span a group of objects; a collaboration is a design for this requirement. Services (infrastructure services—transactions and directory services—and application-specific ones—spell-checking or inventory maintenance), use cases, and business processes usually fall into this category.

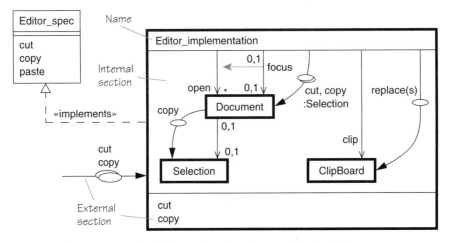

Figure 4.13   A collaboration implementing the Editor type.

4.7.1   Encapsulated Collaboration: Implementing a Type

A collaboration that has a distinguished "head" object can serve as the implementation of a type. Like a type, such a collaboration can appear within a three-part box. The difference is that the middle section now includes actions (directed or not) along with the collaborating types and links (directed or not) between them.

So in fact the "type" is now a class or some other implementation unit (such as an executable program whose instance variables are represented as global variables within the process). The collaboration describes how its internals work. The Editor_implementation type and those within its box are all *design* types (rather than hypothetical *specification* types, as discussed in Section 3.8.6). Any implementation of this collaboration must implement them in order to realize this collaboration.

The collaboration diagram in Figure 4.13 shows five actions indicated by the action ellipses on the lines between types: the external cut and copy operations that the editor must support according to the specification, and the internal cut, copy, and replace actions—between the editor, the focus document, its internal selection, and the clipboard—that will realize it. The lines without ellipses represent type model attributes—now containing directions and eventually denoting specific implementation constructs such as instance variables. As usual, we can choose to show only some of the actions in one appearance of this collaboration and show the remaining actions on other pages; all model elements can be split across multiple diagram appearances.[3] You would normally show all internal actions required for the external actions on that diagram.

---

3. Within the scope of a package, as discussed in Chapter 7, Using Packages.

4.7.2   Interaction Diagrams

A Catalysis collaboration diagram shows object and action types; it does not indicate what sequence of these internal actions realizes the specified effect of a cut. An *interaction diagram* (Figure 4.14) describes the sequence of actions between related objects that is triggered by a cut operation. It can be drawn in two forms.

• *A graph form:* Actions are numbered in a Dewey decimal manner: 1, 2, 2.1, 2.2, 2.2.1, and so on. For consistency, we prefer to show actions with an ellipse ─○─►; however, directed actions can be shown with simple UML arrows, optionally with a "message flow" arrow next to the action name. This diagram highlights interobject dependencies; sequencing is by numbering. The encapsulated objects could be shown contained within the editor, as in Figure 4.13.

• *A time-line/sequence form:* This diagram highlights the sequences of interactions, at the cost of interobject dependencies; otherwise, it captures the same information as the graph version. Again, multiparty joint actions, such as entire use case occurrences, require an alternative notation to the arrow.

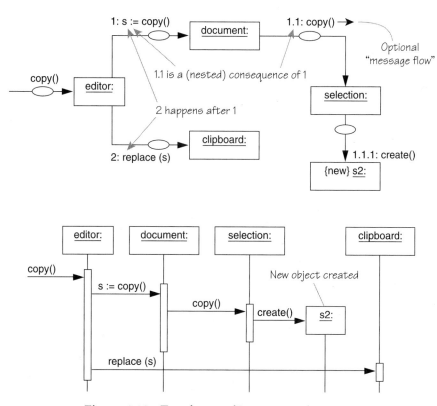

Figure 4.14   Two forms of interaction diagrams.

Typically, an interaction diagram shows only two or three levels of expanded interactions, with a specification of the actions whose implementation has not been expanded; presenting too many levels on one drawing can get confusing. Interaction diagrams can also be used at the business level (Section 2.7) and at the level of code (Section 3.3.1).

4.7.3 Sequence Diagrams with Actions

An action occurrence is an interaction between two particular points in time involving specific participant objects bringing about a change of state in some or all of them. An action occurrence is shown pictorially on a scenario or interaction diagram in one of two ways:

- As a horizontal bar (with arrows or ellipses) in a sequence diagram
- As a line with an ellipse ──○─► in an interaction graph; sometimes abbreviated to an arrow from initiator to receiver

In the action sequence diagram in Figure 4.15, each main vertical bar is an object. (It is not a type: If there are several objects of the same type in a scenario, that means several bars.) Each horizontal bar is an action. Actions may possibly be refined to a more-detailed series of actions—perhaps differently for different subtypes or in different implementations. The elliptical bubbles mark the participants in each action; there may be several. If there is a definite initiator, it is marked with a shaded bubble.

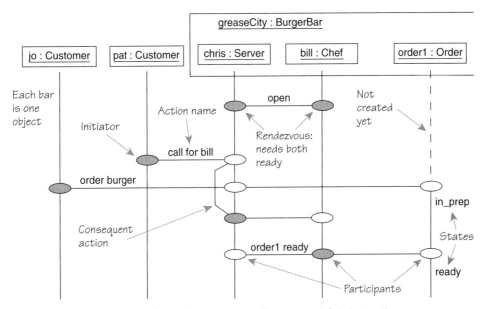

Figure 4.15 Scenario sequence diagram with joint actions.

We use horizontals with bubbles instead of the more common arrows because we want to depict occurrences of abstract actions, even of complete use cases. They often do not have a distinguished "sender" and "receiver" and may often involve more than two participants. Arrows are acceptable for other cases, including to illustrate the calling sequence in program code.

Starting from the initial state, each action occurrence in a scenario causes a state change. For joint and localized actions, we can draw snapshots of the state before and after each action occurrence. The snapshots can show the collaborators and their links to each other and to associated objects of specification types.

Other vertical connections show that participation in one action may be consequent on an earlier one. This situation might be implemented as directly, for example, as one statement following another in a program. Or it might be that a request has been lodged in a queue, or it may mean only that the first action puts the object in a suitable state to perform the second.

4.7.4   Scenarios

A scenario is a particular trace of action occurrences starting from a known initial state. It is written in a stylized narrative form, with explicit naming of the objects involved and the initial state, and it is accompanied by one of the forms of an interaction or sequence diagram.

scenario	order fulfillment out of stock
initial state	retailer has no more items of product p1;
	wholesaler has no inventory of p1 either
steps	
1	retailer places an order for quantity q of p1
2	wholesaler orders p1 from manufacturer m
3	wholesaler receives shipment of p1 from m
4	wholesaler ships q1 of p1 to retailer with invoice
5	retailer pays wholesaler's invoice

4.7.5   Open Collaboration: Designing a Joint Service

Unlike the previous editor example, some collaborations do not have a head object of which they are a part. There are no specific external actions on the objects that are being realized by the collaboration. These collaborations are shown in a dashed box to indicate the grouping. An open collaboration can have all the syntax of an encapsulated collaboration except that there is no "self." Like a type box, an open collaboration has a name, an internal section with participant types and internal actions, and an external section that applies to all other actions.

Figure 4.16 depicts a collaboration for lodging services, showing how responsibilities are distributed across three actions—check-in, occupy, and check-out—and across the two participant types. Lodges provide check-in, initiated by the guest; guests occupy rooms, initiated by the lodge; and check-out can be initiated by either.

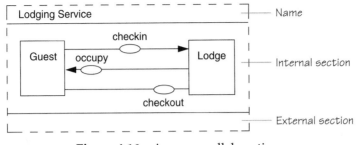

Figure 4.16   An open collaboration.

This style of collaboration is common when each participant is one role of many played by some other object and the collaboration is part of a framework. These generic pieces of design are rarely about one object. Instead, they are about the relationships and interactions between members of groups of objects. Most of the design patterns discussed in books and bulletin boards are based on such collaborations: for example, the observer pattern, which keeps many views up-to-date with one subject; or proxy, which provides a local representative of a remote object; or any of the more specialized design ideas that are fitted together to make any system.

As we discussed in Section 2.6, interface-centric design leads us toward treating these open collaborations as design units. Each interface of a component represents one of its roles, which is relevant only in the context of related roles and interactions with others. An open collaboration is a grouping of these roles into a unit that defines one design of a certain service (see Figure 4.17).

Collaborations, including encapsulated designs, are often built by composing open collaborations. The services in an open system are extended by adding new roles to existing objects and introducing new objects with roles that conform to a new service collaboration, subject to the constraints of existing collaborations.

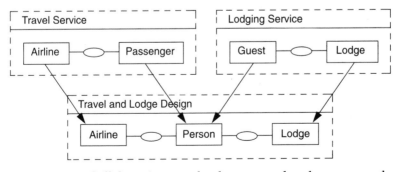

Figure 4.17   Collaborations can be decomposed and recomposed.

4.8 *Collaboration Specification*

Every interacting object is part of a collaboration and usually more than one. Every collaboration has some participants that interact with objects—hard, soft, or live—outside the collaboration. So every collaboration has external actions and internal actions, the latter being the ones that really form the collaboration. In the encapsulated collaboration in Figure 4.13, the external actions include the three specified operations on the editor implementation; in the open collaboration in Figure 4.16, all actions involving the guest or lodge—except the check-in, occupy, and pay actions—are external.

4.8.1   External Actions

If external actions are listed explicitly, they can be depicted as action ellipses outside the collaboration box or listed in the bottom section of the box. Encapsulated collaborations always have explicit external actions. Open collaborations typically have unknown external actions; you do not know what other roles, and hence actions, will affect the objects you are describing. External actions still have specifications in the form of postconditions.

For an encapsulated collaboration, if you wish to repeat an external action's spec (usually already given in the type specification for whatever this implements), it can be written inside the box in terms of self, representing any member of the implemented class. Equivalently, you can write it anywhere, context-prefixed with the class name Editor_implementation :: .

For an open collaboration, you can write an external action's spec outside the box; in that case, you must list the participants and explicitly give them names. External actions often take the form of placeholders in frameworks—actually replaced by other actions when the frameworks are applied, as described in Chapter 9, Model Frameworks and Template Packages. Or they are constrained by effect invariants as described in Section 4.8.3.

4.8.2   Internal Actions

Internal actions are depicted as actions, directed or not directed, between the collaborators inside the middle section of the box. These actions also have specifications either in the body of the box, with explicit participants, or within the receiver types if they are directed actions. Alternatively, the specs can be written elsewhere, fully prefixed with the appropriate participant information.

4.8.3   Invariants

Because collaborations explicitly separate external from internal actions, you can now define invariants—static as well as effect invariants—that range over different sets of actions. There are two useful cases: ranging only over external actions (internal ones are excluded and need not maintain these invariants) and ranging over all actions, both internal and external.

You can write in the bottom section of the box an invariant that applies to all the external actions. A static invariant would be anded with all their pre- and post-conditions; an effect invariant would be anded with all postconditions. This approach is useful for expressing some rule that is always observed when nothing is going on inside the collaboration but that is not observed by the collaborators between themselves. An open collaboration typically cannot list external actions explicitly, because they are usually unknown. Instead, you can use an effect invariant to constrain every external action to conform to specific rules. For example, the external effect invariant in Figure 4.18 states.

> *If any action on a guest causes that guest's intended location (**where**) on the following day to be different from the guest's current lodge location, that action must also cause a check-out to take place.*

This invariant applies to all external actions on a guest; hence, it excludes the checkin and occupy actions themselves. A guest who checks into a lodge when his intended location for the next day is not at that same location will *not* trigger a checkout. However, actions from other collaborations could trigger it: The home_burned_down action from the insurance collaboration, or the cops_are_onto_me action from the shadowy_pursuits collaboration definitely could trigger it.

Invariants can be written inside the middle section of the box and apply to both internal and external actions of this collaboration.

4.8.4   Sequence Constraints

You can draw a state chart showing in what order it makes sense for the actions to occur. This isn't as concrete as a program, because there may be factors abstracted away that permit different paths, and intermediate steps, to be chosen; a program usually spells out every step in a sequence. The state chart is a visual representation of sensible orderings that could equally, if less visibly, be described by the pre- and postconditions of the actions.

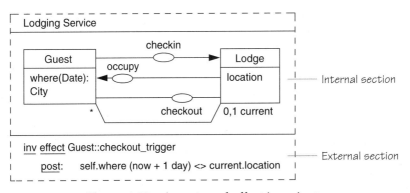

Figure 4.18   An external effect invariant.

This is not the same thing as a state chart showing how different orderings actually result in achieving different abstract actions. The actions of a collaboration may have many possible sequences in which they can sensibly be used, but each abstract action consists of only certain combinations of them. For example, there are many combinations in which it makes sense to press the keys of a UNIX terminal. The keystrokes and the responses you get on the screen are a collaboration. But there is a more abstract collaboration in which the actions are the UNIX commands. To form any one of these commands, you press the keys in a certain sequence given by the syntax of the shell language. The overall sensible-sequences state chart is more permissive than the state chart that realizes any one abstract command.

▶ *collaboration spec*   A collaboration is specified by the list of actions between the collaborators, an optional list of actions considered "outside" the collaboration, action specs, static and effect invariants that may apply to either set of actions, and an optional sequence constraint on the set of actions.

4.8.5   Abstracting with Collaborations and Actions

The most interesting aspects of design and architecture involve partial descriptions of groups of objects and their interactions relative to one another. Actions and collaborations provide us with important abstraction tools.

A collaboration abstracts a detailed dialog or protocol. In real life, every action we talk about—for example, "I got some money from the cash machine"—actually represents some sequence of finer-grained actions, such as "I put my card in the machine; I selected 'cash'; I took my money and my card." Any action can be made finer. But at any level, there is a definite postcondition. A collaboration spec expresses the postcondition at the appropriate level of detail—"There's more cash in my pocket, but my account shows less." Thus, we defer details of interaction protocols.

A collaboration abstracts multiple participants. Pinning an operation on a single object is convenient in programming terms, particularly for distributed systems. But in real life—and at higher levels of design—it is important to consider all the participants in an operation, because its outcome may affect and depend on all of them. So we abstract operations to "actions." An action may have several participants, one of which may possibly be distinguished as the initiator 1. For example, a card sale is an action involving a buyer, a seller, and a card issuer. Similarly, we generalize action occurrences, as depicted in scenario diagrams, to permit multiparty actions, as opposed to the strictly sender-receiver style depicted by using arrows in sequence or message-trace diagrams. A standard OOP operation (that is, a message) is a particular kind of action. The pre and/or post spec of an action may reflect the change of state of all its participants. We can thus defer the partitioning of responsibility when needed.

A collaboration abstracts object compositions. An object that is treated as a single entity at one level of abstraction may actually be composed of many entities. In doing the refinement, all participants need to know which constituent of their interlocutor they must deal with. For example, in the abstract you might say, "I got some cash from the bank," but actually you got it from one of the bank's cash machines. Or in more detail, you inserted your card into the card reader of the cash machine.

Hence, actions and collaborations are useful in describing abstractly the details of joint behavior of objects, an important aspect of any design.

4.9 *Collaborations: Summary*

Collaborations (see Figure 4.19) are units of design work that can be isolated, generalized, and composed with others to make up a design.

To help design a collaboration, we can use different scenario diagrams: object interaction graphs and message sequence diagrams for software; and action sequence diagrams for abstract actions (see Figure 4.20).

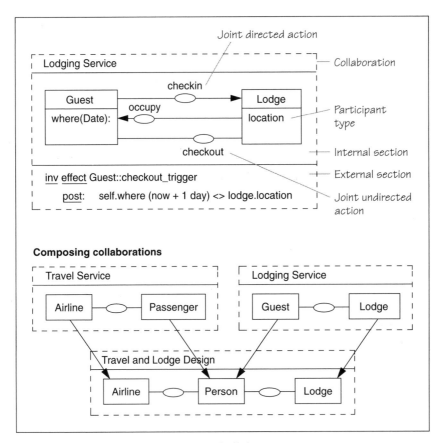

Figure 4.19 Collaborations.

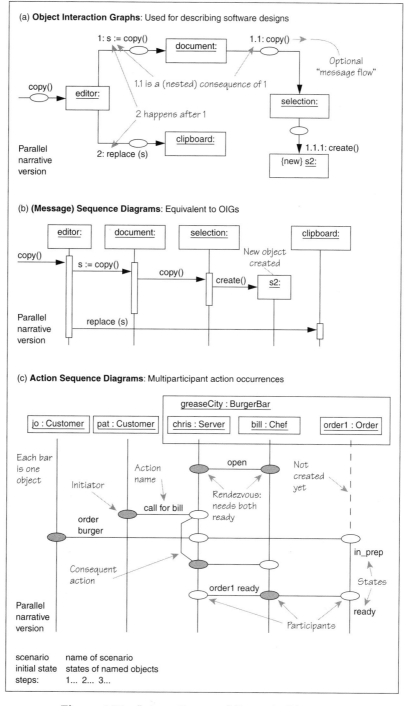

Figure 4.20   Interactions and Scenario Diagrams.

Chapter 5   Effective Documentation

The point of using an abstract, pictorial language for analysis and design is that you can say the most important things clearly. Each issue is dealt with only in as much depth as you require, unobscured by too much detail. Separate issues are presented separately.

The art of good documentation is the art of leaving things out; but in a consistent and useful way so that your documents are well structured, concise, and readable. In a sense, our ideal documentation would look like a cross between Knuth's "Web" of literate programming and a clear structure that separates specifications and external views of things from their internals.

The goal is not to create a nice, or large, or impressive-looking diagram; instead, the goal is to write an explanation of requirements, design rationale, and architecture. The diagrams help support the explanation, so you should structure the document with interleaved narrative, examples, and fragments of formal models and diagrams.

This chapter deals with how to use the notation to help convey your ideas both at the whiteboard and in documentation.

5.1   *What's It All For?*

Why are we drawing pictures and writing invariants and postconditions rather than writing program code? After all, it's the code that runs.

Well, first let's assume that you believe that there is something more to software design than just hacking the code; otherwise, you wouldn't be reading this book. We believe in early coding sometimes—for example, when we're building a small prototype from existing components. But for team work or for large projects and products that will last long enough to be updated, a proper design process is essential, and part of that is the use of a good design notation.

As we've already seen, program code is precise but tends to force you into too much detail. In design, you want to describe only the main scheme before proceeding to the detail. There are experimental "wide-spectrum" languages that cover both specification and coding; but unfortunately, most of us must work with the the most widely available tools rather than the technically best. (It's the same with operating systems, programming languages, videotape standards, and mousetraps.)

On the other hand, natural languages and ad hoc drawings are expressive and can deal with any degree of abstraction you like, but they are prone to ambiguity to the point of having no predictable interpretation, making it easy to gloss over inconsistencies. Part of the risk is that readers of design documents and participants in discussions can come away with divergent ideas about the design.

But a more significant problem is that in the early stages of a design you can leave things unspecified that need to be decided up front. We've all been in a meeting, not long before the delivery deadline, to decide an issue that should have been sorted out earlier. Sometimes, different designers have addressed the issue on-the-fly and have done it different ways, and now there is a panic about how we're going to reconcile them.

Experience with formal notations shows that the precision of the notation tends to flush out these issues at the appropriate stage. Anyone who has spent a day or two in a specification workshop, creating a model for a business or a new system, is aware of how quickly important questions are raised. Many of these issues would never have been thought of had the requirements document been in plain natural language (English or your local favorite).

A good design notation makes it easy to highlight the issues you care about at the moment, leaving other issues until later. Just as important, it gives you a well-defined way of combining different issues when it's time to implement the design.

Notation is used for two principal purposes:

- Discussions at the whiteboard, presentations, and so on
- Documentation—a clear statement expressing the project's current state of understanding of the design

It is during discussions that many people gain their first real appreciation of the value of design notations, but much of the way you use it at a whiteboard or in presentations follows from how you use it in documentation. The rest of this chapter will concentrate on the latter.

5.2 *Documentation Is Easy and Fun, and It Speeds Design*

Documentation is arguably the most sleep-inducing word in the English language. In part, this is because it is often seen as an extra chore, something you must do in addition to the real job to satisfy fretful management or neurotic QA people. In Catalysis, we think of documentation more as a tool to help do the job well. Far from being a deviation from the fast path, it is a moving walkway toward a solid, lasting product. And, like all tools, it can be misused.

(In those cases when you don't want a lasting product, omit the documentation. This suggestion is not meant to be flippant. In a later chapter, we'll discuss short-life products that are rapidly thrown together from robust existing components. By contrast, the components themselves are carefully produced and maintained, and they merit accurate and in-depth write-ups.)

5.2.1   Bad Signs

Here are some bad signs that indicate the wrong approach to documents.

5.2.1.1   Bad Sign: No Documentation

When new people come on board, they must ask everyone how it all works or guess from the code and the work of people before them. Code and source code debuggers have never been particularly good tools for understanding requirements, problem domain concepts, or design intent. New developers easily get the wrong impression and soon start doing things to the code that are inconsistent with the rest of the design. From then on, it's downhill all the way.

The usual excuse is, "We'll do it soon—when we get some time." Developers are too busy sorting out problems and late updates to do the write-ups. It's funny how these projects are always the ones that require a lot of heroic overtime. See Ed Yourdon's excellent book *The Decline of the American Programmer*. In such a case, a possible damage limiter is to hire a suitably skilled person to spend a few weeks writing the models. This person may be able to clarify some inconsistencies and at the same time transfer some skills to the existing team. But a lack of documentation is a cultural problem and is not easily fixed.

5.2.1.2   Bad Sign: All Documents, No Code

These folks are taking the sober approach: "We'll do the design when we've signed off the specification." Now, we have been aficionados of specification for many years; one of us has done and enjoyed mathematical program proofs in his time. But we have never tried to write the whole spec before doing some code. For one thing, you can't execute a spec,[1] and executing something is vital to finding out whether what you are specifying is really what is required. For another, it is bound to be wrong before it is finished.

---

1. You may have heard the phrase "executable specification." Mostly snake oil. The point about a spec is that it states the requirements of a particular user, which are usually partial. You must add decisions to make it work. An executable thing is usually a program even if it's written in a high-level language, or in pictures.

Producing code early is good for everyone's morale. One of the benefits of the high modularity of OO programming is that it is easy to do a sensible "vertical slice" of a program, try it out in isolation, and add the rest incrementally. Horizontal slices are also possible: What will ultimately be a database-resident distributed system can initially be written to run in the main memory of your laptop so that you can show it to prospective users.

The point about writing specifications and abstract designs is not to get them entirely set in concrete before implementing but instead to record what you've decided to provide. In the "How to" chapters in Part V, we look at the short-cycle incremental methods of delivery that have been found to be most effective in recent years. The main requirement of a specification is not that it be complete before the code is written but rather that by the delivery date it should be usefully complete and consistent with the code (and not too far off, in between).

The cure is to use RAD-style timeboxing: Put developers under a lot of stress to produce something demonstrably fast, with milestones for the specs and other documentation to get in sync.

5.2.1.3 Bad Sign: All Pictures

Pictorial models are a helpful part of documenting a design. Unfortunately, it is a common error to treat the pictures as the sole focus of documentation or design activities. Teams spend a real lot of money on modeling tools, draw lots of pictures using these tools, and then expect to press a button to generate well-structured, clear, explanatory documentation. Sadly, it does not usually turn out exactly that way.

Do not think of documentation as producing pictures; instead, you are trying to write a clear and concise explanation of the key decisions, whether requirements, design, or code. Precise definitions of terminology, coupled with well-written prose, goes a long way. The pictorial notations help summarize certain aspects of this; so do examples, tables, fragments of formalized specs, and informal sketches. You can sometimes write a clear explanation with an OCL fragment in a few minutes, whereas it would take an hour to create a diagram with the same information. We have seen extremely clear documentation in which the type model and action specs were described entirely in text, in the form of tables; a decent tool should keep such a view in sync with the underlying models just as easily as the pictures.

5.2.1.4 Bad Sign: Wall-Sized Documents

Sometimes you see a wall covered with a big class diagram that contains hundreds of little boxes. These diagrams are not very useful except for your boss to show off to her boss. It is difficult to find your way around such a diagram and difficult for people new to the project to know where to start. Diagrams should be used as part of a narrative explanation and not just on their own. Documentation should be structured so that the important, overall issues come first, with the detail filled in later.

The cure is to write a narrative document in normal requirements style. Every few paragraphs, use a diagram showing only those elements directly relevant to the text. The purpose of the text is to provide an immediately readable account; the purpose of the diagram is to disambiguate the text. Structure your document by separable issues.

The appearance of a type in more than one diagram means only that it has the attributes and operations gathered together from all its appearances. All OO analysis and design support tools allow you to separate big models into smaller diagrams. Some of them make it easy for the individual diagrams to be embedded within narrative text; with others, you must cut and paste.

5.2.1.5   Bad Sign: Big, Thick, Formal Documents

Sometimes we've come across a team busily engaged in writing a thick document that contains miles and miles of formally structured action specs. This is a write-only document, and it is likely to be a work of fiction by the time it is finished. Formal notation (pictures and formal text) is good at being unambiguous; pictures, in particular, are good at explaining complex relationships that would be difficult to get hold of in ordinary narrative.

Like software, documentation should be decoupled: the dependency relationships between different parts should be clear, and there should be not very many of them. Documentation should make it easy to find out about one particular aspect of the design; it should be clear what other things you must read.

The cure, again, is to embed the formal parts in narrative text. If the formal parts are getting too complex, look for ways to abstract, factoring out various aspects so as to better decouple your documents.

5.2.2   Good Signs

Not all documentation is bad! Let's look at some signs of good documentation in the sections that follow.

5.2.2.1   Good Sign: A Clear Document Structure

Document structure should be systematic, always separating external from internal views of things and further separating different aspects or areas of concern. Document structure corresponds to our "packages" and has a clear and uncircular structure of reference between them, as discussed in Chapter 7, Using Packages.

5.2.2.2   Good Sign: A Mix of Formal and Informal

Each section contains a natural-language description as well as a more formal one, interspersed as far as possible. The formal fragments are specifically used to clarify parts that might otherwise be unclear.

Informal text can also be substituted for or used as well as any part of a formal expression. For example, it is useful to write postconditions at least in natural language and then in precise terms if required.

Similarly, sketches of situations or phenomena in the problem domain are encouraged. Use informal or formal notations, including drawings and rich pictures, tables, and snapshots.

5.2.2.3   Good Sign: A Clear Glossary

In addition to a narrative, it is useful to have an index of the vocabulary. The glossary's purpose is to link the formal terms back to the real world. Rather than a single monolithic table at the end of the document, the definitions could be introduced as needed in the context of the document structure, together with additional explanation.[2]

5.2.3   The Art of Abstraction: Keeping It Short and Sweet

Part of the art of good documentation is to achieve a consistent level of abstraction. What should be left in, and what deferred? What tools can we use to leave things out? Here are some tips.

- Treat several objects as one. In a sequence diagram, consolidate several vertical bars into one. An example is to treat a company as one entity rather than to see only the individual employees. Another example is to treat a system you're about to design as one object: During design, you split it into its internal components.

- Treat several actions as one. In a sequence diagram, consolidate several horizontal bars. For example, talk about a complex transaction as one action rather than see the detail.

- Ignore how actions are initiated. Treat the information exchanged in an action as being a parameter. Later elaboration will discover how that exchange occurs.

- Model every useful concept, even abstract ones, as an object. Remember that specification types need not appear directly in an implementation.

- Characterize actions by their goals or effects rather than by the detail of how they work.

---

2. The table version could always be generated as an alternative view but not vice versa.

- Partition different views or aspects of whatever you are describing. Remember that you can write multiple specifications for the same action and have the same type appear in many drawings.

5.2.4   Separating and Joining Definitions

A good document takes one issue at a time, and each type will be involved in more than one issue. For this reason, OO analysis and design tools usually support the idea that each type or action may make an appearance in more than one drawing. This means that anyone wanting a full understanding of a type must search out all its appearances or, better still, get the tool to show the type's definition in full.

The operation of bringing together the different appearances is called *joining*. For a type, you list all the attributes that crop up in any of its appearances and do the same for its associations. Operations or actions in which the type takes part are also listed.

Actions (whether localized to a type or symmetric) can also appear in several places, and action specifications can be separated. You can give one postcondition spec in one place and give different ones elsewhere. This approach helps you to discuss separately the different constraints on the outcome of an action. For example, in one place you might say that the check_out action records that the given video is hired to the given customer; elsewhere, in a section about stockkeeping or marketing records, you say that check_out increments a count of the number of hires of the video. The join of the part specifications of one action is simply the AND of them all.

Invariants can also be separated: the joined actual invariant of the type is again the AND of the invariants given in its various appearances.

We will use the idea of join again when we discuss model frameworks in Chapter 9, Model Frameworks and Template Packages. Partial models kept in libraries can be composed to make complete models; their documentation need be kept only in one place.

Table 5.1 shows a few basic techniques for factoring models into parts that can be more easily recomposed. Well factored models have clearer documentation.

Table 5.1   Techniques for Factoring Models and Documentation

Construct	Usage
Effect	If actions have a common state change in their post-conditions; makes specifications more succinct and natural.
Invariant	To impose a static constraint on every action's post-condition; makes specs more succinct and natural.
Effect invariant	To impose a common state change on every action or on a specified subset using change1 ==> change2; makes specs more succinct and natural.
Convenient attributes	To simplify all specifications; to make algorithmic query operations trivial; to make specifications more natural.
Parameterized attributes	To avoid data-modeling explosion of artificial types and attributes; defer variation in how an attribute is computed.
Collaboration	To define a partial view of the roles of a set of objects separately from other roles they might play.
State type	To treat as a type those members of another type that satisfy some predicate; to make specifications more natural.
Subjective model	To describe constraints on objects of some types that are specific to their being in some relation with others.
Derived specifications	To highlight aspects of a specification that are of particular interest even though they are already implied by what is stated.

5.3   *Reaching the Documentation Audience*

The documents are intended to ensure that everyone has a consistent understanding of what's being built. So the audience is everyone interested in the system.

5.3.1   The Development Team

The first audience is you and your colleagues on the development team. The documents express your understanding of the business, the requirements, and the design you are engaged in. By creating an explanation of these things, you clarify your understanding of them, raise questions that otherwise would not have come up until coding, and iron out inconsistencies that otherwise would have been glossed over. This is a repeatedly observed effect, and the more precise you try to be, the stronger the effect. It is therefore a good investment to take the time to write Catalysis models as early as possible.

5.3.2   The Maintenance Team

These people will be doing the most work on the product. (Under maintenance, we include everything done after first delivery.) Few of them will have the time to understand the entire project completely before making the updates they've been asked to do.

Traditionally, this means that a programmer reads the code, makes a good guess at how the design works in the region of interest, and makes an update, which may be inconsistent with the overall design principles. After some years of these patches, many spurious couplings are introduced, and it becomes increasingly difficult to tweak one end of the system without the other end falling over.

The most valuable purpose of documentation, over the life of the system, is therefore to give maintainers a clear understanding of the architecture and design of the system so that they can quickly make changes that are just as good as if the system had first been designed that way. Pretty pictures of architectures, with no precise interpretation, do as much harm as good. By documenting it well, you are significantly extending the prospective life of your design.

5.3.3   The Clients

The people who will use your product need to see the requirements, although not the design. How this works depends on what sort of clients they are. If they are another design team using your software component, you can expect them to understand the documents directly. Still, it is essential that you clearly separate the external view from the internal workings. The requirements documents form part of the client's contract with you.

If they are not software people, your role as analyst is to interpret between them and the formal models. The models represent your team's clear understanding of what you are to provide. By writing them, you are taking the fuzzy and inconsistent desires of the client, crystallizing them into a more precise form, exposing the questions you need to ask, and going back to the client with questions, scenarios, storyboards, proactive proposals of precise definitions of terms and requirements, and prototypes (see Figure 5.1). The cycle continues until all

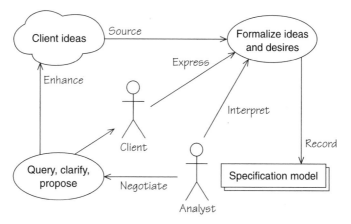

Figure 5.1   Typical interactions in building models.

the parties are satisfied that they know what is being discussed; your model should at that stage represent what is in the client's head (see Pattern 15.13, Interpreting Models for Clients).

The contract between you and the client can take the form of a requirements document of the traditional kind written in natural language. But having been through the process of formalization, both sides can be confident that it is achievable and consistent and masks no big unknowns.

5.3.4   Documentation Timing

As we've said, writing models improves your understanding of the system and raises useful questions. It therefore makes sense to start writing models as soon as possible. Once you are used to the technique, it becomes easy to sketch your ideas in this form. Sessions around the whiteboard with colleagues are valuable at an early stage, and Catalysis provides the language for it.

Although it is good to start writing as early as possible, it is not necessary or desirable to complete the models early. For one thing, this approach can lead to your getting hung up on writing specifications; for another, many of the details will change as time goes on. Don't expect to get the documents much more than 80% consistent or complete except at big milestones such as requirements sign-off and product delivery.

Don't insist on drawing a line under the spec before going on to the first prototype development. The RAD idea of timeboxing applies to each phase of development, including determination of requirements. Set a date by which requirements will be signed off, but start designing before then so that early storyboards or prototypes can be achieved. Section 10.11 presents an excellent example, using a system built from heterogenous existing components, of how and why models, designs, and implementation should not be done using the waterfall approach. The example, nevertheless, shows the value of models prior to code.

Formal documents take longer to write than traditional informal notes. And the more precise you make them, the longer it takes. The big fear from a managerial point of view is that people could get hung up on writing this sort of thing instead of getting on with the real job of writing the code.

To begin with, we believe in early delivery of prototypes and vertical slices, as you'll see from the "How to" chapters in Part V. And understanding what it is you are building is a major part of the real job of writing the code, and it is a lot more effective than just getting in there and hacking.[3]

---

3. Medieval architects would be shocked to see the amount of paper that gets produced before a stone is laid these days compared with their own methods; but we are aware that modern architects generally achieve a more reliable result—the landmarks we see today are the ones that didn't fall down—and can build bigger and more versatile buildings even if they are no more pleasing to the eye.

Think of the code as embodying all the requirements and design decisions that have been made during the development: They're all mixed up in there somewhere. Imagine pulling out the biggest decisions—the most important ones on which most others depend. Now rinse off any smaller ones that may be sticking to them. What you have left in your colander are the main requirements and the biggest design decisions.

By writing models up front, we identify these major ingredients. The more formality and precision we achieve now, the more we clarify the picture and ensure we haven't missed or mistaken any important ingredients and hence that we don't make a cake of it further down the line, when changes will be more expensive. Anyone writing formal models soon discovers that more questions are raised and clarified in the first afternoon of a modeling workshop than are often raised in a traditional development until the code has been written.

The main visible effect is that 100% completion of the requirements comes later than in the traditional process, but there is less work to do after that stage. Writing the code is relatively easy, because the big decisions have been made. However, because we overlap the phases, code certainly gets written before the requirements are complete.

The main worry is that requirements sign-off with the client could be delayed. In practice, this tends not to happen. Determination of the requirements is a cyclic process, and if it is reasonably well managed the main features can be brought out and agreed on first. If the client initially approaches you with an informal requirements document, the essential goal is to get most of its points modeled and clarified. In consultation with the client, you cycle through your model, regenerating the client's requirements from the model. An estimate, and hopefully a contract, can be formed on the basis of the first iteration, with the understanding that further questions will be discussed later.

5.4 *The Main Documents: Specification and Implementation*

There are two main kinds of documents.

• *Specifications:* A specification describes actions using postconditions (perhaps drawn with state charts); the postconditions are written in terms of a vocabulary of objects and their static relationships, which is described in a type model. These documents must be inspected at *external design reviews*. Types, rather than classes, are the main focus.

• *Implementations:* An implementation shows how a component works, describing the objects that are inside, how they interact, and in what order things happen. These documents are the internal counterpart to the specifications and are shared by the *design team*. Together with types, internal components and classes become an important element.

Specifications are defined by types. In an implementation, the interactions are expressed with collaborations, and the complete prescription of the design of any one component is called a class.

A component is anything you can design as a unit, whether it is a single C++ class, a complete software application, a part of an application, a piece of hardware, or even a business department.

Implementations always include some element of specification (but not vice versa), so the two kinds of document are never entirely separate. First, an implementation need not be complete down to the finest detail; it might interconnect a few smaller component specifications, leaving their implementations to be chosen separately. Second, the concepts the participants talk about when they interact can also be specified rather than implemented; using types, we can define what information must be sent without deciding its representation.

5.4.1 Spec and Implementation in a Typical Project

You typically start a design project by looking at how the existing business organization works—that is, how it is implemented. At this stage, you may reorganize the business (on paper at first) , including as interacting components a new or modified department, piece of hardware, or piece of software. You specify this new component so that it supports the interactions you require it to take part in and then go on to implement it. Figure 5.2 outlines this stage with new components B1 and B2 included in the envisaged business model.

So the following three main documents generally crop up in a standard software development project.

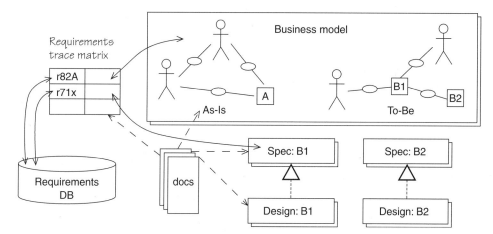

Figure 5.2 Typical separations of the documentation structure.

- *Business model:* The "outside." An implementation describing the users' picture of the world they work in: what concepts there are, how they are related, and how they interact. "Business" here means any part of the world in which you're interested, including software systems.

- *Component specification:* The "boundary." Specification of the behavior of a component, saying nothing about its internal design. The document may also show collaborations between the component and the objects around it (whether soft, hard, or live). It is frequently structured into different subject areas, which focus on different aspects of the system.

- *Component design:* The "insides." Implementation showing how the component works, detailing how responsibilities are distributed among the internal components.

These three levels, with various names, are found in most books about OO design. In practice, you might use only some of them, or you could introduce in-between layers such as an abstract spec, a detailed spec, a high-level design, or a detailed design.

Once you have decided on the levels, you should keep them separate. The business model will act as the basis for your component design, so you can edit a copy of the former until it becomes the latter; but use a copy rather than lose the original. When the business changes, update the business model and then update the derived models correspondingly. Good tools (which by no means includes all of them) let you keep track of the derivation trace from one model to the other, flagging the parts of the derived diagrams that need attention after changes have been made.

One business model may be common to many component designs. For example, an insurance company with many products and procedures may construct a business model to gain a clear understanding of what goes on in the company. The model can be used both to help improve the business organization and to serve as the basis for the specification of various support software. The business model will therefore be unbiased toward any particular software design.

In other cases, there is no strong need to construct a business model before you get on with a component spec, particularly if the software focuses on only one aspect of a very general business. Sometimes it is useful to create the static part of the business model, without any collaborations. For example, before designing a word processor, you first define what a document is. This is the business world in this case—the subject matter with which the software will deal but modeled separately from any concerns of what the software will do with it. This approach is particularly useful when there are standards of interchange between components: Web pages, RTF files, floppy disks, and TV pictures all have standard models of the objects without designing the equipment that handles them.

5.4.2   Continuity of Notation

One of the great things about OO analysis and design is that you use the same notation for every level of model and retain the problem domain concepts through to your code. That makes it easy to adhere to the Golden Rule of OO design: that the software have the same shape (more or less) as the business. It is possible to analyze or design the business organization, hardware, software, or any combination of them in essentially the same notation. The business, the tools that support it, and the interfaces between them are all seen as different parts of a single design.

We'll now look at the purposes of these three major models in more detail.

5.5 *Documenting Business Models*

A business model records your understanding of a business. As an analyst, you record your clients' views of the world in which they work. Suppose a client tells you, "Every customer has a name and an address; several customers may live at the same address; sometimes they move." You busily sketch a type diagram (Figure 5.3).

Type diagrams represent the static relationships between objects and the actions intrinsically applicable to them. Collaborations represent dynamic behavior, as when your client says, "A check-out means that a customer chooses a video from the shelves, shows it to the assistant, and takes it away." You can draw the diagram shown in Figure 5.4.

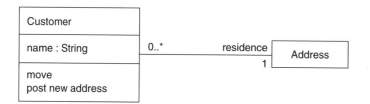

Figure 5.3   Simple business type model.

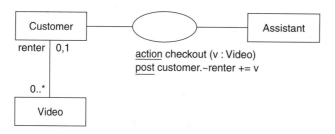

Figure 5.4   Actions, or use cases, in the business.

Part of your job as an analyst is to reconcile different views when they conflict and to clarify concepts when they are fuzzy. Suppose your client says, "Several customers may be renting the same video. Customers can reserve videos, and when a reserved video is returned, we hold it off the shelves for the reserver to come and collect it." Somewhere in there are two uses of *video*: one meaning an individual copy, and a second one meaning a title. Your job is to identify the two types.

You should also faithfully record redundant relationships and views. Your client sometimes speaks of the renter of a Video, which is a Customer, as shown in Figure 5.4. But you may also be told, "We record the date a video went out, whether a deposit was paid, when it is due back, and who rented it: That is called a rental." So the renter of a Video is the Customer named on the Rental; this is a derived relation (see Figure 5.5).

5.5.1   The Glossary in a Business Model

Annotate each type and collaboration with a summary of what its instances represent. Be careful to make it clear which real-world objects and events are included. For example, does a Customer include all the people we have ever sent brochures to, or is it only people we've actually done business with? Is a separate check-out deemed to have occurred for each separate video, or is a bundle of four (with one free) a single check-out?

The same principle applies to attributes and associations. Is the renter linked to the person who last rented the video, or does it exist only while the video is out on hire? Is the Customer associated with a check-out the person who takes the video away, or is it the person whose membership is used to rent it? (Or does a business rule prevent these from being different people?)

5.5.2   Document Different Degrees of Abstraction

For a clear understanding, it is important and useful to zoom out and in from the detail of the processes. For example, several actions can be considered to be part

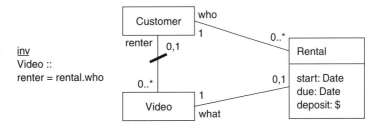

Figure 5.5   Business terms as redundant attributes.

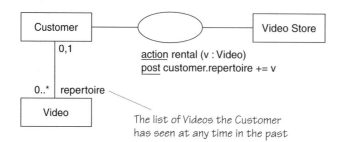

Figure 5.6   Abstract business actions.

of the use case of rental, the business of allowing a customer to have access to a video for a period of time (see Figure 5.6).

We should show how this zoomed-out view of things relates to the more fine-grained operations such as check-out and return. One way to do this is to associate a set of event charts with the rental action. They show examples of the ways in which the more abstract action can occur (see Figure 5.7). Each detailed action, such as checkout, should be specified somewhere.

An abstract action, together with a refinement, is called a use case. The story accompanying the event chart is called a scenario. Some tools can show the breakdown of the video store into its internal parts directly in the event chart; others make you show it in a separate diagram.

You'll find more on collaboration abstraction and refinement in Chapter 6, Abstraction, Refinement, and Testing.

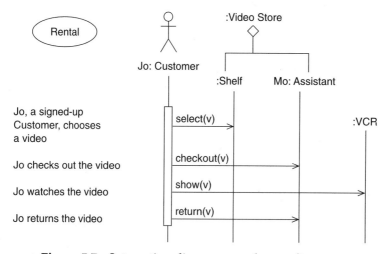

Figure 5.7   Interaction diagram can show refinement.

5.5.3   The Reengineered Business and Component's Context

After you analyze the business context, the typical next steps are to redesign the business interactions and to "install" a new component. This may involve redrawing the diagrams if the business process is to be much changed, or you may need only to refine the picture to sufficient detail to see how the abstractly specified business processes are supported by the system you intend to build. (More on the procedure will follow in the next chapters.)

The result should show how the business works, with the component of interest being one element. A component can (and usually does) play several distinct roles, providing a different interface to each of several other objects, or *actors*, as they are often called in this context; as usual, they may be other pieces of software, people, or equipment. A collaboration diagram can be used to illustrate the different interactions (see Figure 5.8). This is often called a system context diagram; it is traditional to draw the external roles as stick figures, although type boxes are also OK.

The collaborations rental support and stock keeping represent the overall business transactions our system is directly involved in. As we've seen, we can refine them separately to individual actions, using event charts and so on to show the relationship between abstract and detailed collaborations. The more-detailed collaborations can be summarized as shown in Figure 5.9.

5.5.4   Constructing the Business Model

You write business models and requirements documents by talking with people who know the business and will use the product that you are designing. They

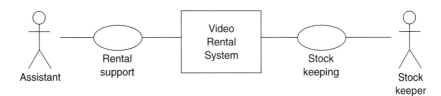

Figure 5.8   System context with abstract actions.

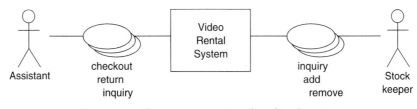

Figure 5.9   System context with refined actions.

may be end users, or they may be the designers of a larger system of which your component is a piece.

We recommend that you look at some of the excellent books on requirements elicitation (for example, [Graham]). The main message is to keep the users involved. Work on a short cycle: Interview, draft models, and send them back to users. Recast the story in your own words, and feed it back to them for comment.

Focus on scenarios: what people actually do in their work. Keep the scope broad to begin with. As they describe the business, construct static type models to represent their vocabulary of concepts; construct collaborations (use cases) to represent processes and tasks and the people and things involved in them. Follow use cases across departments; identify roles rather than follow departmental structure. Sketch snapshots whenever there is any questionable situation.

You will find that different users in a large business have different views of the business. Some of the differences reflect different areas of concern, others reflect differences in vocabulary, and still others are misunderstandings. Begin by making different models. Many of the differences can be resolved by writing invariants: The simple rental relationship to one user is a detailed object to another. You may find that your activities result in a clearer understanding by the clients of different parts of their own business and create a more consistent language between them.

On a practical note, it is worth making it clear, when you interview the client's staff, that your project is engaged in improving support for them in their work and that they are to be the prime consultants about what is required. After this is clear, enthusiastic cooperation is usually forthcoming. Nearly everyone loves the opportunity to explain what he or she does to a receptive ear. For that reason, do not be afraid to go back and ask again. Make it clear, when you leave the first meeting, that the usual procedure is to digest the information in your own terms and return later to ask for clarifications.

Another practical tip: to find out how a business really works, interview the people who do it and not their managers, who don't know the half of it. And don't believe what people say they do: Watch them doing it. It usually takes several visits to do the job properly.

5.6 *Documenting Component Specifications*

The purpose of a component specification is to say what the component does rather than how it works inside. (Once again, a component may be hardware, a software system or object, or a person or organization, on any scale.)

The component is treated as a single object, and its specification is a type spec. The actions that the component can perform are listed in the bottom section of the type box; they can be separated into protocols grouped by the more abstract use cases they form part of.

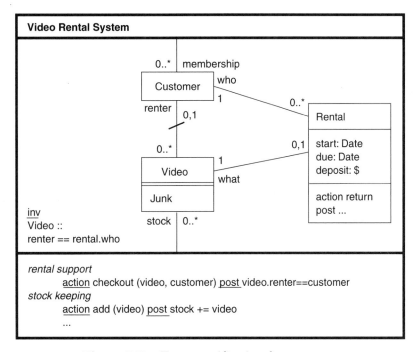

Figure 5.10   Type specification for a system.

The component's attributes are used to help describe the actions. The type spec can be shown pictorially (see Figure 5.10). Typically, we show the types nested inside the model part of the component spec because they represent what it knows about those types, which may be different from what another component knows about them. This nested model is only a model of the component's state and says nothing about how the component might be implemented (except, of course, that it must conform to the spec).

The full name of the Video type as used in the Video Rental System's model is Video Rental System:: Video. The full signature of operations of the component follow the form Video Rental System :: checkout(video, customer). This follows C++ convention.

5.6.1   Factoring Operation Specs

Operations attached to types inside the component model have a special "factored" interpretation. Everything the model says is part of the behavioral spec of the component: There are no internal parts. So if we attach a return operation to the Rental type, we mean that it is part of the abilities of the Video Rental System to deal with a return relating to a particular rental. Because this is only a model, the implementor is under no obligation to assign the return operation to the Rental class or even to have such a class. (A sensible OO design from scratch would do so in the interests of mirroring the spec; but the designer might reuse existing designs that do things a different way.)

The full signature of the return operation is Video Rental System :: Rental :: return ( ).

5.6.2   State Charts in Component Specifications

A state chart in a component spec refers to the component's behavior (see Figure 5.11). It can focus on one of the component's model types, but again, there is no guarantee that such a class will exist in an implementation, only that the information it represents will be implemented.

All the operations are those that the component as a whole makes available to the outside world. Some of them may be factored into a model type, and, in those cases, the diagram shows which objects the operations should relate to for the transition to occur.

One occurrence of a component operation may affect several model objects simultaneously. For example, a return puts the relevant rental into the "done" state and simultaneously (as we can see from Figure 5.11) sets the related Video into available. The diagram states that this occurs only for the Video whose rental is the one being returned.

In some complex cases, we want to specify that when a particular transition in one model object occurs, then some other transition should also occur in another. We do this by raising a *private event* in the component, writing ^ eventname against the causing transition (or in a postcondition). Its meaning is that all the effects of eventname elsewhere in the component should take place. For the specifier, the cause and the targets of the event are decoupled; for the implementor, it is necessary to find all the targets and ensure that the appropriate effect takes place.

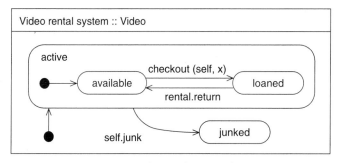

Figure 5.11   State chart of a specification type.

5.6.3   The Glossary in a Component Specification

The types, attributes, and associations should be annotated with what they mean to the component, rather than globally. This is only a shift of emphasis and might not be very different from the business model. However, because one business model may be associated with many component models, there will typically be a difference in what is included.

The glossary entries for the actions are the pre- and postconditions (formal or informal) with a general natural-language description.

5.6.4   Writing a Component Specification

As with business models, the main message is to keep the users well involved. The worst method is to take an informal requirements document, go off into a back room for three years, and then proudly present users with something that isn't what they wanted in the first place and is inappropriate now. You need to make it clear to users that their ideas are invited, take steps to stimulate ideas, and keep them in touch with the process.

Make a model by adapting the initial statement of requirements, by interviewing prospective users, and by using domain knowledge and existing systems and standards. Much of the static type model will be taken over from the business model. The big difference is in the system context: what the system is required to do and, more important, how people will do their jobs after it is installed.

Workshops are a good mechanism for stimulating and gathering ideas. Bring together key representatives of the user departments involved. The workshop also tends to encourage people to identify with the project and to help different groups of users to understand the issues of other groups.

A workshop should aim to produce scenarios, the most accessible notation to general users. Different small groups can work on different use cases. The main job of the facilitator is to show the groups how to abstract both actions and objects and not to get hung up on details. Once people understand it is acceptable to omit detail, they are reasonably good at it, especially if sessions are timeboxed.

In a system that has a GUI, storyboards—sketches of successive screens—are a well-tried method. Play-acting workflows and business interactions is also both effective and fun, as are snapshots.

Once the party is over, it is your job as analyst to abstract and refine, find generalizations, clean things up, and write a proper specification. This process will probably require much more detail on some of the collaborations. The workshop having established the main ground, you can go to individuals to ask for the details.

As you formalize the action specifications, you will find that the static types adopted from the business model contain superfluous information in some parts and inadequate information in others. Notions such as "currently logged-in user" are relevant only to a computer system. Adapt the model as required; but the changes should be extensions and deletions rather than alterations. If you find yourself altering something, it is probably a mistake in the business model that you should fix; or it may be that you are dealing with a slightly different concept, in which case you should give it a different name and model it separately.

Once a clear model of at least one aspect of the system is obtained, use it to construct slide shows and prototypes and to reconstruct the scenarios from the workshop in more detail. The process will have generated plenty of questions. Discuss them with the appropriate users.

Cycle until time runs out; meanwhile, implementation should be starting, beginning with key parts that can be delivered for trials ahead of the rest.

5.7 *Documenting Component Implementations*

An implementation uses collaborations to define interactions; types to define interfaces and roles between objects; and classes to define the implementation of individual objects.

5.7.1   Internal and External Views of the Implementation

Always be clear about who the document is for and why it has been created. A document, even of an implementation, that is meant for a client of the implementation should not bother with showing internal implementation decisions. Instead, it should show only the types that the client needs to know about along with their type specifications.

Documentation of a framework—a set of abstract and concrete classes and types that must be extended by the client before using it—should also explicitly include the superclass/subclass interface and describe what is expected of anyone extending and overriding methods in the framework.

5.7.2   Classes and Roles in Design

A class diagram is just a type diagram with a different emphasis. The purpose of a class diagram is to represent the classes that appear in the code and the roles that they take in the working software.

The emphasis in design shifts to the responsibilities of the instances of each class (or larger component). Each class has a defined purpose for its existence that determines which operations and information should reside in its instances. This purpose should be documented succinctly in the annotation of a class. A standard rule of thumb is that better designs have classes that can be more briefly described.

Because a class diagram is closer to code, navigability arrowheads appear on the links. Annotations relating to privacy can also be added.

One class of object often plans several distinct roles. Good documentation is structured to describe these roles separately as collaborations, and then shows how they are synthesized in one class. For this purpose in Catalysis, we use the join relationship between the roles. Different tools support different ways of doing this. For example, in Rational Rose, roles are shown as actor symbols that take part in collaborations (use cases); a class can be shown as implementing several roles (see Figure 5.12). (The «join» stereotype shows that this is not pure subtyping.)

5.7.2.1   Documenting Designs versus Specs

A design document should also explain how the design realizes the specification—that is, how the individual type models of the designed components together realize the specified type model—and how sequences of interactions in the design realize the required external behavior. The details are covered in Chapter 6, Abstraction, Refinement, and Testing.

5.7.2.2   Class Diagrams and Code

At the lowest level, class diagrams can correspond directly to program code: attributes and associations turn into pointers or (in languages such as C++) contained objects. Many OO design tools provide the means to turn a class diagram into skeleton code and vice versa. However, we should be careful not to use this facility too readily; it is useful only at the very bottom layer of design.

For example, your code could include mention of various classes and interactions that deal with making objects persistent; the extracted diagrams will also

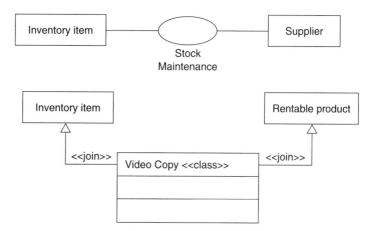

Figure 5.12   Classes can "join" roles in different collaborations.

include this persistence information. However, at a reasonable level of abstraction, I'd like to design my collaborations ignoring the practical need to move some things to and from disk. There are some very good packages, OO databases, and tools that help make this kind of thing reasonably transparent; unfortunately, they are not yet very well integrated with the OO analysis and design tools. Before you can generate code, you must take the design down to the level at which some persistence mechanism is explicit.

Code generation is nevertheless a useful facility, at least for creating prototypes. It is easy to take the packages from your business analysis and turn them into the skeleton of a rapid prototype.

5.8 *Summary*

The purpose of documentation is to explain the essential parts of a requirement, design, or implementation in a way that would not be obvious from the code itself. Think of all the documentation parts of development as writing this explanation. It includes model diagrams, examples, informal sketches, formal specifications, storyboards, tables, and so on only because they make the explanation clearer, uncover hidden issues and problems, and help you focus on some things while deferring details of others.

No less than the code, the documentation must have a clear structure. Documentation that is separated and decoupled typically follows a prototypical form.

• *Business model:* A (section of a) document that describes the business or problem domain, precisely capturing object types, attributes, invariants, and actions. This document may itself be structured based on

  – *Subject areas:* Different views of areas of concern in the business. For example, a video rental business may have subject areas for rentals, accounting, and marketing.

• *System or component specification:* One or more documents, each of which describes a black-box view of a software system or component, specified as a type. In turn, it may be structured as

  – *System or component contexts:* A section that describes the use of the system by external agents to accomplish business tasks. It includes system contexts as collaborations, scenarios, user-interface sketches, and prototypes.

  – *System or component type specifications:* A section that uses static type models and action specifications to specify the type of each system.

  – *Subject areas:* Different views of each component, including those of different users or interfaces it offers.

- *Internal design:* One document for each system or component, showing how it is built internally.
  - *Technical architecture:* The domain-independent pieces of middleware, databases, libraries, and so on that will be used in the implementation. This is documented with package diagrams and with collaborations.
  - *Application architecture:* The major components, how they partition the business logic, and how they interact, defined primarily with collaborations and types.
  - The main types offered between components, separated from the corresponding classes that implement those types.
  - Documentation of the refinement between the design and the specification.

Part III Factoring Models and Designs

Part II was about the basic Catalysis tools for modeling the statics, dynamics, and interactions of objects. When faced with complex systems, we need to decompose the problem into smaller parts. We use the basic tools to separately model and understand the parts; then we need a means of putting them back together, to model and understand how the parts interact.

Part III is about tools for separating the various aspects of a problem or a design and then rejoining them.

One of the most natural ways to deal with a complex system is to step back from the details, specifying only its essential aspects—an abstraction. However, when faced with the detailed version—a refinement—you must understand how it relates to the abstract version, and you must test that an implementation correctly meets the abstract specification. Chapter 6, Abstraction, Refinement, and Testing, shows how these fit together, using four specific kinds of refinement.

It also helps to separate aspects of the system that are mostly independent; they can be worked on, managed, and version-controlled separately. Chapter 7, Using Packages, shows how all descriptions are grouped into units called packages. The *import* relationship between packages determines which definitions depend on which others and how implementations and specifications are related. Every modeling statement is made within a package. Catalysis offers specific mechanisms for extending definitions across packages.

Chapter 8, Composing Models and Specifications, discusses what it means to compose models that have partial definitions from different views or packages, paying special attention to specifying exceptions.

Chapter 9, Model Frameworks and Template Packages, shows how recurring patterns of types, collaborations, and refinement can be captured using the idea of a framework: a template package. The resulting model can then be used as a skeletal model that is applied with various specializations to different problems. Frameworks enable you to define new modeling constructs.

Chapter 6   Abstraction, Refinement, and Testing

Abstract diagrams are good for many purposes. At the whiteboard, you want to exhibit the main ideas of something without all the details of program code. Perhaps you want to say what it does and not how, or what it requires of other components that plug in to it. And whether it's a single procedure or an entire planetwide distributed system, you want to fit it all on one board and convey useful things about it.

When it comes to documentation, a component description that makes clear the essential vision of your design will help future maintainers understand it quickly. Their short-order updates will more likely cohere with the rest of the design, thereby giving your brilliant ideas a longer life. For users of the component (whether end users or other programmers), you don't want to show how the thing works inside but only what they can do with it.

We have seen how to draw and write these abstract descriptions, but how can you be sure they accurately represent the code? The concepts of abstraction and refinement capture the essential relationship between these descriptions. This chapter is about different forms of abstraction and refinement, and it explains the rules for showing that a more detailed model refines (or conforms to) a more abstract one.

Refinement and conformance are a focal point in a Catalysis design review, in which you check that the design or implementation meets its specification(s).

Testing fits naturally into this approach to abstraction and refinement. This chapter also discusses how to test different kinds of refinement relations, including the one between the implementation of an operation and its specification.

You can read Sections 6.1 and 6.2 on a first pass, which touches all the main points.

6.1 *Zooming In and Out: Why Abstract and Refine?*

A major theme of Catalysis is precise abstraction: the ability to look at a design or a model in only as much detail as necessary and without loss of precision. You can precisely describe your code to your colleagues in documents or in presentations, or just sketching over coffee, without getting into superfluous detail. The abstract views can isolate different concerns; you can present the behavior of a component from the point of view of a particular user (or of another component) omitting details seen by another user (or through another interface). You can restrict yourself to the externally visible behavior, or you can describe the internal design scheme. You can describe only one component, a partial collaboration pattern, or the way the components fit together; or you can describe architectural rules followed by all the components.

The zoomed-out, abstract views and the zoomed-in, detailed views must be clearly related. If you write, "and we use the kwik-kache approach to cache information on the client," the link between this abstract intent and the code must be quite clear for it to survive the first few rounds of maintenance by new programmers.

Enter the refinement relation. Using it, you can tell whether the code for a component conforms to the interface expected by its clients and whether a system, if designed to behave as specified, would contribute to the business needs; you can also link individual requirements to specific features of a design. All this gives you a much better start on what is the real long-term problem: change management.

The degree of rigor of this traceability is variable. In a critical context, you can do these checks in mathematical detail. In more ordinary circumstances, you document the main points of correspondence to guide reviewers and maintainers and use these points as the basis for verification, design reviews, and testing.

Testing of object and component designs can be more difficult than in traditional systems because of the added complication of polymorphism, inheritance, and arbitrary overriding of behaviors. The essential idea of testing is to verify that an implementation meets its specification—the same goal as that of refinement except that testing tackles the problem by monitoring runtime behaviors under a systematically derived set of test cases. This chapter outlines a systematic test approach based on refinement.

▶ *abstraction*   (1) A description of something that omits some details that are not relevant to the purpose of the abstraction; the converse of *refinement*. Types, collaborations, and action specs are different kinds of abstractions.

(2) To *abstract* (verb) is to create an abstraction; also called *generalize, specify,* and sometimes *analyze.*

▶ *refinement*   (1) A detailed description that conforms to another (its abstraction). Everything said about the abstraction holds, perhaps in a somewhat different form, in the refinement. Also called realization.

   (2) The relationship between the abstract and detailed descriptions.

   (3) To *refine* (verb) is to create a refinement; also called *design, implement,* or *specialize.*

▶ *conformance*   One behavioral description conforms to another if (and only if) any object that behaves as described by one also behaves as described by the other (given a mapping between the two descriptions). A *conformance* is a relationship between the two descriptions, accompanied by a *justification* that includes the mapping between them and the rationale for the choices made. Refinement and conformance form the basis of traceability and document the answer to the "why" question: Why is this design done this way?

▶ *retrieval*   A function that determines the value of an abstract attribute from the stored implementation data (or otherwise detailed attributes); used with a conformance to show how the attributes map to the abstraction as a prerequisite to showing how the behavior specifications are also met.

▶ *implementation*   Program code that conforms to an abstraction; requires no further refinement (strictly speaking, it still goes through compilation and the like).

▶ *testing*   The activity of uncovering defects in an implementation by comparing its behavior against that of its specification under a given set of runtime stimuli (the *test cases* or *test data*).

Suppose you ask a hotel for "a room with a nice view, for five people; it should not be noisy in the morning"—an abstract requirement, A. The clerk responds by assigning you "the deluxe penthouse suite overlooking Niagara Falls; its three bedrooms each have two double beds; and it has a built-in Jacuzzi and gym"—a realization, B. B is a *refinement* of A—that is, it *conforms* to A—provided the hotel can *justify* to you that (1) overlooking Niagara Falls constitutes "a nice view"; (2) the humble penthouse suite can suffice as "a room"; (3) the six double beds will serve to accommodate your party of five; (4) the roar of millions of gallons of water will, in fact, be a soothing background whisper; (5) the built-in Jacuzzi and gym do not conflict with anything you've asked for.

6.1.1   Four Basic Kinds of Abstraction and Refinement

Our models center on either the behavior expected of individual objects (large and small) or the designs for how groups of objects collaborate. Each of the primary abstractions—type and collaboration—has two main forms of refinement. Collaboration refinements affect multiple participants in the collaboration; type refinement should not affect a client in any way. Most design steps are a combination of these basic four varieties.

6.1.1.1   Behavior of an Object

We describe an object's behavior using a type, with two parts to its specification: the operation specifications (usually pre- and postconditions) defining what it does; and the static model, providing the vocabulary of terms for the operation specs.

If the type spec and the implementation look different, we need ways of determining whether the code conforms to the type. We treat the two main parts of the type separately, giving us *operation abstraction* and *model abstraction.*

An operation spec (and a static model) is a bit like the usage instructions for a machine (with a simplified drawing of the machine): It tells us what to expect as users. But if we remove the top from the machine, we may see a more complicated mechanism at work. The same thing happens when we look at the implementation code that meets a type spec: Its stored data, variable names, and specific sequences of statements are not seen from the outside.

6.1.1.2   Collaborations among Objects

We describe designs for objects using collaborations—collections of actions. A joint action defines a goal achieved collaboratively between the participant objects, using postconditions whose vocabulary is the model of each of the participants. Collaborations range from business interactions ("banks trade stocks") to hardware ("fax sender sends document to receiver") to software ("scrollbar displays file position").

An abstract action spec states only the goal achieved and the participants it affects. But we can put more detail into the design by working out a protocol of interactions between the participants. Such refinements might include banks make deals, confirm deals, settle the accounts; fax connects, sends page, confirms, repeats; file notifies scrollbar of change of position.

Similarly, we may discover that each of the participants is itself an abstraction made up of distinct parts that play roles in the collaboration. The banks' traders make the deal, but their back offices do the settlement. Again, the two aspects of the collaboration can be treated separately, giving *action abstraction* and *object abstraction.*

The four basic kinds of abstraction and refinement are shown in Figure 6.1. Most abstractions can be understood as combinations of the four basic varieties shown in Table 6.1.

6.1.2   Refinement Trees

Big refinements are made up of smaller ones. A requirements spec and a completely programmed implementation of it may look quite different, but their relationship can be seen as a combination of several smaller refinement steps.

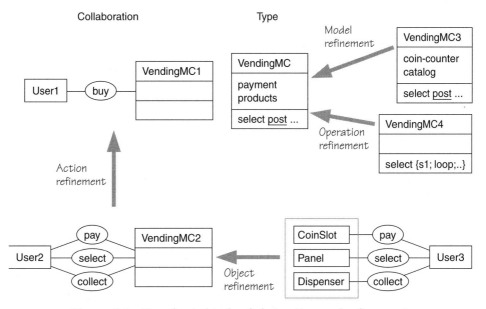

Figure 6.1   Four basic kinds of abstraction and refinement.

Table 6.1   Basic Varieties of Abstractions

Abstraction	What It Does	Conformance and Justification
Operation	Specifies what an operation achieves in terms of its effect on the object executing it rather than how it works	Does the sequence of statements in code have the specified net effect?
Model	Defines the state of an object (or component) as a smaller and simpler set of attributes than the actual variables or fields used in the design; or simpler than some other model that presents a more detailed view.	How would you compute each abstract attribute from the data stored in the implementation, or from the more detailed attributes?
Action	Describes a complex protocol of interaction between objects as a single action, again characterized by the effect it has on the participants.	What sequences of detailed actions will realize the effect of the abstract action? Use state charts, sequence or activity diagrams.
Object	Treats an entire group of objects (such as a component or subsystem or corporation) as if it were a single one, characterizing its behavior with a type.	How do the constituent objects (and their actions) correspond to the abstract object (and its actions)?

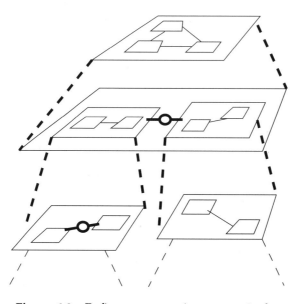

Figure 6.2   Refinements continue recursively.

So we can, in theory at least, relate a most abstract specification to the most detailed program code (or business model) through a succession of primitive refinements, each documented by a complete model (see Figure 6.2). If you have a great deal of time to spare, you might try it for a small design! This is what computers are for, of course, and appropriate tools can do a great deal to help. In practice, we use the ideas more informally and use design patterns as ready-made refinement schemes.

We'll now take a brief look at each of the four basic kinds of abstractions. Later sections treat them in more detail, describe how the conformance should be documented, and provide a full example.

6.1.3   Operation Abstraction

One of the most basic forms of abstraction is the operation specification: the idea that I can tell you some of the things that are achieved by an operation, omitting the detail of how it works and omitting things it achieves that I don't know or don't care about, such as sequences of algorithmic steps, intermediate states, variables used, and so on. The operation specs we usually encounter are pre- and postconditions, although they may also include rely and guarantee conditions. In a rely condition, the designer assumes the condition will remain undisturbed by anyone else while the operation is executing; a guarantee condition is one that the designer undertakes to maintain true during execution.

Operation specs can be used as the basis of a *test harness*: they can be incorporated into the code in such a way that an exception is raised if any of them ever evaluates to false. (Eiffel supports pre- and postconditions directly; the standard C++ library includes an assert macro.)

```
float square_root (float y);                        // specification
// pre:        y > 0
// post:       abs(return*return − y) < y/1e6                  -- almost equal

float square_root (float y)                         // implementation
{
    assert (y > 0);                                 // precondition
    float x= y;
    while (abs(x*x–y)>=y/1e6) { x= (x+y/x)/2; }                  // miracle
    assert (abs (x*x − y) < y/1e6);                 // post: x*x == y (almost)
    return x;
}
```

Quality assurance departments like operation specs because, apart from helping to document the code, they act as a definite test harness (see Figure 6.3). In a component-based environment, you frequently plug components together that were not originally designed together; as a result, integration testing becomes a much more frequent activity. Every component (which might mean individual objects or huge subsystems) therefore must come with its own test kit to monitor its behavior when employed in a new configuration.

In Catalysis, we characterize behavior using type definitions, attaching postconditions to the operations. In Java, the corresponding construct is the interface: Classes that implement an interface must provide the listed operations. Wise interface writers append comments specifying what clients expect each operation to do, and classes that claim to implement the interface should conform to those specifications even though each will do so in its own way. In C++, the pure abstract class plays the role of the Java interface in design.

Operation refinement, then, means to write code that conforms to an effects spec, which can be tested by writing the spec in executable form. Operational is the form of abstraction having the longest history, dating back to Turing. Those who crave mathematical certainty that their code conforms to the spec are referred to [Morgan] or [Hoare].

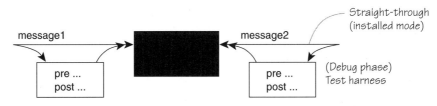

Figure 6.3   Operation specs: in testing versus in production.

6.1.4   Model Abstraction

The postconditions of the operations on an object usually must refer to attributes that help describe the object's state. It's difficult to describe any but the most primitive types without using attributes. We have also seen how we use associations as pictorially presented attributes.

Any implementation will also use internal stored variables operated on by the code of the operations, but they need not be the same as the model attributes used by the postconditions. Model attributes are only a hypothetical means of describing the object's state to help explain its behavior. For example, you might use the concept of its length to help describe operations on a queue (of tasks, orders, and so on), as shown in Figure 6.4.

We can think of several implementations of a Queue, but not all of them will have a length instance variable or method. Nevertheless, it is undeniable that every Queue has a length. That is what an attribute is about: it is a piece of information about the object and not necessarily a feature of any implementation.

An attribute can always be *retrieved* from an implementation. Suppose I publish the type in Figure 6.4 on the Web and invite tenders for implementation. A hopeful programmer sends me an array implementation:

```
class ArrayQueue implements Queue
{     private Object array [ ] ;              // the list of items
      private int insertionIndex;            // where items are put
      private int extractionIndex;           // where items are gotten from
      public void put (Object x)
      {     array[insertionIndex]= x;
            insertionIndex= (insertionIndex+1) % array.length;
      } ...
```

As a quality assurance exercise, I want to check whether the code of put (say) conforms to my spec. But my spec and this code talk in different vocabularies: It has no length. I need to translate from one model to the other—to map to the

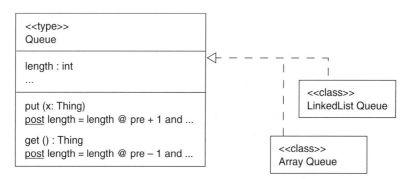

Figure 6.4   Different implementations of the same type model.

abstraction—before I can begin. So I write back to the programmer and say, "Where's your length?" The answer comes back:

```
private int length ( )
{ return (insertionIndex – extractionIndex) % array.length; }
```

In other words, I have been provided with a function that retrieves or abstracts from the implementation's terms to the spec's. (And, of course, it is read-only: It would be confusing if it changed anything.) Now I can see that the put code indeed increases the length, as I required. If working that out by only inspecting the code is not my style, I can ask that the designer include my pre- and postconditions as assertions in the code so that we can test it properly.

Again, quality assurance chiefs love this stuff. They demand that every implementation be supplied with a set of retrieval functions: that is, read-only abstraction functions for computing the value of every attribute in the abstract spec. This also applies to associations, which we have previously observed are merely pictorial presentations of attributes.

Another implementation of a queue is based on a linked list. There is not necessarily any variable that corresponds directly to the model's length, but you can retrieve it by counting the nodes.

It doesn't matter whether retrieval functions are slow and inefficient: They are required only for verification either by testing or by reasoning. The exercise of writing them often exposes mistakes in an implementation when the designer realizes that a vital piece of information is missing.

Notice that in Catalysis, we do not expect that attributes and associations will always be publicly supplied for use by clients. There are, of course, many attributes to which it is useful for clients to have "get" and sometimes "set" access; but modelers often use attributes to express intermediate information they don't expect to be available directly to clients.

On a larger scale, more-complex models can be used to represent the types of whole systems or components and are usually shown pictorially. In an abstract model, the attributes and their types are chosen to help specify the operations on the component as a whole and, according to good object-oriented analysis practice, are based on a model of the domain. However, anyone who has been involved in practical OOD is aware that the design phase introduces all sorts of extra classes as patterns are applied to help generalize the design, make it more efficient, distribute the design, provide persistence or a GUI, and so on. But we can still retrieve the abstract model from any true implementation in the same way as for the simpler models.

Model refinement, then, means to establish the relationship between the more abstract model used to define postconditions and the more complex practical implementation. Retrieve functions translate from the refined model attributes to the abstract ones.

Model refinement has the second longest history, dating back to VDM and Z in the 1970s.

6.1.5   Action Abstraction: Messages and Actions

At the programming level, *messages* are the interactions between objects (in most OO programming languages). Some messages have variants on the basic theme, such as synchronous versus asynchronous (waiting or not waiting for the invoked operation to complete). Envisaging complex sequences of messages can be difficult, so we draw sequence diagrams such as the one shown in Figure 6.5.

Sequence diagrams have the disadvantage of being bad for encapsulation, particularly when multiple levels of calls are shown on one diagram. Unfortunately, they allow you to see in one diagram the response to various messages of several objects at once and so encourage you to base the design of one object on the internal mechanisms of the others. They also show only one sequence of events and so make it easy to forget other cases and to forget that each object may receive the same messages in other configurations. However, sequence diagrams make it easy to get an initial grip on a design, so we use them with caution. It is often good practice to limit the diagram to only one level of nesting and to use postconditions to understand what those events achieve.

The same diagrams can be used to show the interactions between objects in the business world and interactions between large components.

But in any but the most detailed level of design, we usually deal in actions: dialog with an outcome definable with a postcondition but made up of messages we do not care about. For example, I might tell you, "I bought some coffee" rather than expect you to listen to a long tale about how I approached a vending machine, inserted several coins, pressed one of the selector buttons, and so on. The former statement abstracts the latter detailed sequence and includes any other means of achieving the same effects. In Catalysis, actions are characterized principally by their effects; to show how an action is achieved by some combination of smaller ones, you document a refinement.

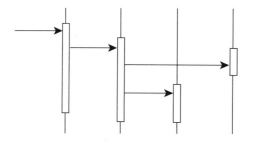

Figure 6.5   Sequences of messages realize abstract actions.

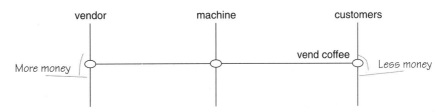

Figure 6.6   Occurrence of a joint action.

A single action may involve several participants, becuase it may abstract several smaller actions that may have different participants. On a Catalysis sequence diagram, the small ellipses mark the participating objects (vertical lines) in each occurrence of an action (horizontal lines). We also mark the states or changes of states of participants (see Figure 6.6).

OO messages in programming languages are only one subtype of actions: those that always have a distinct sender and receiver (see Section 4.2.7, From Joint to Localized Actions).[1] We can use action abstractions to represent interactions external to the software, those between users and software, and those between objects within the software. Within the software, action abstractions are very useful for abstracting the standard interactions that happen within certain frameworks and patterns, such as observer.

Sequence diagrams illustrate sample occurrences of actions, but an action type can be drawn with the types of its participants and a postcondition written in terms of the participants' attributes (again, whether the types represent software or domain objects), as shown in Figure 6.7. The ability to define the effects even at an abstract level is what makes it worth doing. Abstraction without precision is often just waffle; until some precision is used, it is typically not reliable.

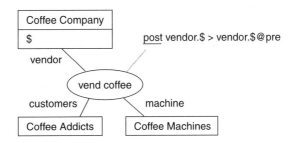

Figure 6.7   Action type shown on a collaboration.

---

1. CLOS is an exception: Its operations are not attached to any particular receiver. As with Java and C++, there may be several operations with the same name and different parameter lists; but the operation to be executed is chosen at runtime on the basis of the classes of all the parameters (not just the receiver, like the other languages). Catalysis works as well for CLOS as it does for Java and so on because multireceiver messages are a type of action.

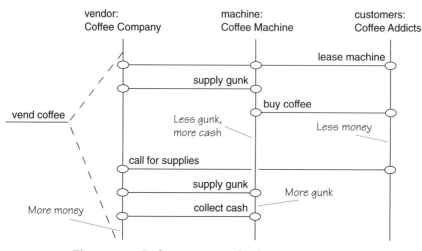

Figure 6.8   Refinement into further joint actions.

6.1.5.1   Refining Actions

We can zoom into, or refine, the action to see more detail. What was one action is now seen to be composed of several actions (see Figure 6.8). Each of these actions can be split again into smaller ones, into as much detail as you like. Some of the actions might be performed by software; others might be performed by some mixture of software, hardware, and people; still others might be the interactions between those things. At any level—deep inside the software or at the overall business level—we can treat them the same way. Catalysis is a "fractal" method: It works in the same way at any scale.

Notice that the abstract action has not gone away; we have only filled in more detail. It is still the name we give to the accomplishment of a particular effect by a combination of smaller actions, and that effect is still there.

These illustrations might suggest that an action is always made up of a sequence, but often the composition is of several concurrent processes that interact in some way. Recall that *action* is the Catalysis blanket word for process, activity, task, function, subroutine, message, operation, and so on.

We can summarize any kind of action abstraction on a type diagram, showing which collaboration (set of actions) can be abstracted into a single abstract action (see Figure 6.9). The diamond aggregation ("part of") symbol is used to indicate that the abstract action is an encompassing term for compositions of the smaller actions. It shows constituent parts of the abstraction, although we must state separately how they are combined—whether in parallel or sequence—and whether some are optional or repeated. Also, another diagram may show a different set of detailed actions abstracted to the same abstract action.

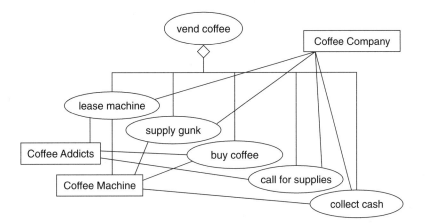

Figure 6.9   Abstract actions shown using aggregation.

6.1.5.2   Summary: Action Abstraction

Action abstraction is the technique of treating a dialog between several participants as a single interaction with a result definable by an effect.

Action abstraction and operation abstraction are both about treating several smaller actions as one. The differences can be summarized as follows.

- In operation abstraction, the initial invocation results in a sequence of smaller actions determined by the design; the abstraction still has the same initial invocation and captures the net desired effect.

- In action abstraction, no invoker need be identified: Any participant can initiate it. The exact sequence is determined by the designs of all participants (some of whom could be human); we can say only what the smaller actions are and the constraints on how they might be combined. Also, the abstract action may never be directly "invoked" at the detailed level.

Action abstraction comes from the idea of transaction, developed in the database world in the 1970s, although it is a natural usage in everyday conversation.

6.1.6   Object Abstraction

We can refine, or zoom into, objects, splitting any of the vertical bars on the diagram into several. Thinking about it in more detail, we realize that the vendor company has different departments that deal with different parts of the business. Also, the customer organization will have users as well as a site manager who establishes a liaison with the vendor (see Figure 6.10).

Again, the more-abstract objects have not gone away. The company is still there; it is what we call a particular configuration of interrelated smaller objects. Again, each object can be split further into smaller parts: servicing may turn out to be a department full of people having various smaller roles.

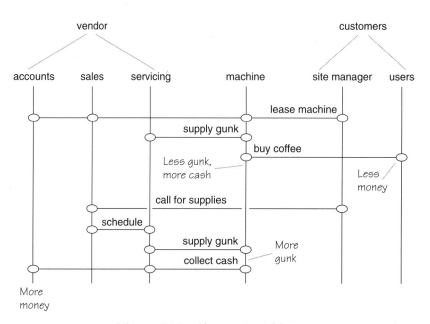

Figure 6.10   Abstracting objects.

Just as what characterizes an action is its effect, so what characterizes an object is the set of actions it takes part in—its type. There may be many refinements that will satisfy one abstract object type. (Indeed, there may be refinements that successfully satisfy several roles: Some small companies have only a single object that plays the roles of accounts, sales, and servicing.)

Some of the objects may be software components. For example, zooming in on the Accounts department would probably reveal some combination of people and computers, and more detail on the computers would reveal a configuration of software packages, and going into them would reveal lines of Cobol or, if we're lucky, objects in an OO language. The same thing would happen if we peered into the coffee vending machine. And we can continue using the same interaction sequence diagrams (and other tools) right down into the software.

The relationship between an abstract object and its constituents can be shown on a type diagram (see Figure 6.11). The diamond again indicates the refinement relationship. Again, it doesn't by itself give us every detail about any existing constraints between the constituents of one abstraction.

6.1.6.1   Summary: Object Abstraction

Object abstraction means to treat a group of objects—whether in software, in a human organization, or in a mechanical assembly—as one thing.

The idea is as old as language and was discussed by Plato, Michael Jackson, and others—often beginning with "How many parts of a car must you change

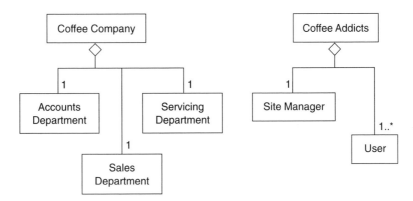

Figure 6.11   Abstract object shown using aggregation.

before it's a different car?" or "Are you the same person you were when you were born?" The examples serve to highlight the idea that the identity of anything is, in the end, a model constructed for our convenience rather than something inherent.

6.1.6.2   Abstracting Objects and Actions Together

It is usual to zoom in or out in both dimensions at the same time. As soon as you resolve each object into several, you must introduce interactions specifically with or between them. Conversely, when you put more detail into an action, you need more objects to represent the intermediate states between the actions.

When we looked inside the vendor company, we assigned **sales** to receive supply requests from the customers, who then schedule a visit by **servicing**.

By contrast, we left the collection of cash as one action involving both **servicing** and **accounts**. This means that we've deferred until later a decision about how that action splits into smaller steps.

Zooming in to an action often involves more objects. As an example, let's go the other way and abstract the original **vend coffee** action. If the overall requirement is only to get money out of people by giving them coffee, there are more ways of doing it than by installing a machine near them: You could run a café or street stall. So we could have started with this:

and then refined that to this:

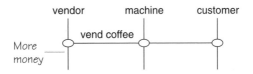

Note that the machine is required only when we go to the more detailed scenario of exactly how we're going to sell the coffee.

6.1.7   Zooming In to the Software

In Catalysis, the standard pattern for developing a software system or component is to begin with the business context and represent the business goals in terms of actions and invariants. Then we decide how to meet these goals in a more refined view, with the various roles and interactions within the business.

Some of these interacting objects may be computer systems. We can treat them as single objects and describe their interactions with the world around them. Subsequently, we refine the system into a community of interacting software objects (see Figure 6.12). (A standard OO design is based on a model of the external world so that we now have two of everything: a real coffee cup, a user, and a coin, plus their representations inside the software.) When we look inside the software, we can continue to use the more general multiple-participant actions along with objects that actually represent whole subsystems; but ultimately we get down to the level of individual message sends between pairs of objects.[2]

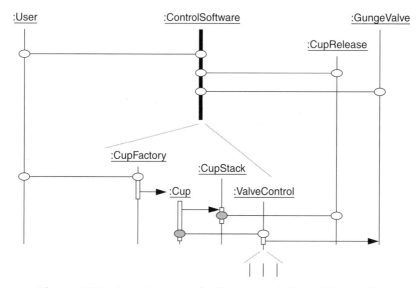

Figure 6.12   A continuum of refinement: real world to code.

---

2. A significant difference between Catalysis notation and UML version 1.1 (current at the time of writing) is that UML does not have generalized actions in sequence diagrams; nor are the messages in a sequence diagram understood as instances of use cases. However, at the message-passing level, our sequence diagrams are the same as UML.

Figure 6.13   Context diagram (collaboration) for one software component.

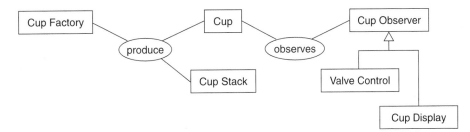

Figure 6.14   Collaboration between software components.

Again, the sequence diagrams help us illustrate particular cases, but we prefer to document the refinement using type diagrams. This gives us software component context diagrams (see Figure 6.13). It also gives us high-level design diagrams (Figure 6.14).

6.1.8   Reified and Virtual Abstractions

When designing objects inside the software, you have a choice about whether to *reify* abstract objects and actions—that is, represent them directly as software objects—or just to leave them as ideas in the design that help you understand the various configurations of objects and protocols of messages.

The usual approach is to represent each entire system and each component as an object because it gives something to anchor the parts to. A more difficult decision is whether to make it the *façade* for the group of pieces it represents—that is, the means by which all communication with the outside world should go. Sometimes this works well; it helps ensure that everything inside the component is consistent. In other cases it is not efficient, any more than insisting that every communication with customers go directly through the president of a company.

6.1.9   Composition and Refinement

Other forms of abstraction and refinement, more related to the separation and subsequent joining of multiple, mostly independent views, are covered in Chapter 8, Composing Models and Specifications.

6.1.10   Summary: Kinds of Abstraction

An abstraction presents material of interest to particular users, omitting some detail without being inaccurate. Abstractions make it possible for us to understand complex systems and to deal with the major issues before getting involved in the detail. In Catalysis, we can treat a multiparty interaction as one thing or treat a group of objects as one, and, at different layers of detail, we can choose to change the way we model the business and systems. But through all these transformations, we can still trace the relationships between business goals and program code and therefore understand how changes in one will affect the other.

We've identified four particularly interesting varieties of abstraction.

- *Operational*: Pre/post (or rely/guarantee) specs.
- *Model*: Model attributes may be different from actual implementations.
- *Action*: A complex dialog presented with a single overall pre/post or rely/ guarantee spec.
- *Object*: A group of objects presented as one object.

6.2 *Documenting Refinement and Conformance*

When you write a requirements specification (in any style and language you like), you want it to be a true statement about the product that ends up being delivered. If QA shows that the product falls short of the spec, you fix the code; or if it turns out to be impractical to deliver what was first specified, you can change the specification. But one way or another, you can't (or shouldn't!) call the job complete until the delivered design matches the specified requirements.

For valuable components (as opposed to throwaway assemblages of them), we believe in keeping the specification after you've written the code and in keeping it up-to-date. In the long run, the spec (and high-level design documents) helps to keep the design coherent, because people who do updates have a clearer idea of what the component is about and how it is supposed to work. Designs without good documents degenerate into fractal warts and patches and soon end up unmodifiable. Remember that more than 70% of the effort on a typical piece of software is done after it is first delivered and consider whether you want your vision of the design to be long-lived.

This is not to argue that you should complete the high-level documentation before embarking on coding. There are plenty of times when it's a tactical necessity to do things the other way around. Prototypes and rapidly approaching deadlines are the usual reasons. The most useful cycle alternates between coding (to obtain feedback from testing and users and to get things done) and specifying (to get overall insights). Never go beyond getting either cycle 80% complete without working on the other. All we need is that, by the appropriate milestone, the specs should correctly describe the code.

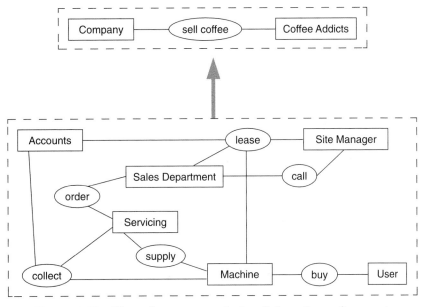

Figure 6.15   The refinement symbol: collaboration refinement.

6.2.1   Documenting the Refinement Relationship

The relationship between an abstraction and a refinement is the *refinement relationship*. It is an assertion that one description of a configuration of objects and actions is a more abstract view of another (see Figure 6.15).

6.2.1.1   Refinement and Subtype

The refinement symbol is a version of the subtype symbol.[3] It states that the more detailed model achieves everything expected from the more abstract one. But whereas a subtype symbol says to the reader, "The subtype is defined a priori as an extension of the supertype, having all its properties and more," the refinement symbol says, "The refinement, a self-contained model even without the abstraction, is believed to specify everything defined for the abstraction and more."

6.2.1.2   Refinement and Aggregation

There is also a slight difference between the refinement symbol and the diamond aggregation symbol. The diamond makes the abstract and constituent types (or actions) part of the same model. In these models, it is explicit that a wheel is a part of some particular car and that there is some way of knowing which buy action a

---

3. UML 1.1 makes mention of refinement, with a default notation that uses a stereotype on the generic 'dependency' arrow. Refinement is central to Catalysis; in our presentation here, we have chosen to highlight refinement with a distinguished arrow.

Figure 6.16 Refinement using aggregation.

particular pay is part of; some portion of the retrieval is implied by the aggregation itself, but the full justification is with the refinement.

The aggregation symbol is commonly used when, in a design, you have a reified and distinguished head object representing the abstraction itself (see Figure
6.16). But the refinement symbol is somewhat more general. It says that, even if
we didn't think of it that way when creating one model, the other model is nevertheless a more abstract or refined view of it; and we can deal with either model
separately.

In some idealized sense, every design project can be thought of as generating a
series of refinements even if some of them arise as a result of refactoring or
bottom-up abstraction. You begin with a general idea of what is required, refine it
to a solid requirements spec, refine it further to a high-level design, and so on to
detailed design and code. For example, you might start with very abstract actions
between users and system and refine down to the actual sequences of GUI actions
required for each action. If the project is critical enough to be fully documented,
each of these refinement layers is written up separately; just as important, the
refinement relationships themselves are documented and checked.

Documenting a refinement means writing down the following.

- The reasons for choosing this realization from the alternatives (so that those
  who follow won't fall down the same pits you fell into along the way).
- A justification for believing you've done the refinement correctly—that is, that
  the abstraction really describes the realization accurately. (Doing this is an
  invaluable sanity check and helps reviewers and maintainers.)

Because refinement is a many-many relation, the refinement documentation
shouldn't properly attach to either the abstraction or the refinement but rather to
the refinement relationship between them. (A component you found in a library
may be a good realization of your requirements, but presumably it will fit the
requirements of others as well.)

If you're designing a nuclear power station or a jumbo jet, we hope you would
take all the preceding writing and verification very seriously, with each layer individually written up and each refinement carefully established. But for most of us,
it's both acceptable and desirable to opt for the somewhat more practical solution
of clarifying some essential issues at the requirements level, then working on the
design and code while resolving other issues, and only then updating a few class
diagrams.

Well, maybe. In the new world of component-based development, the successful components will be those that interoperate with many others. Each interface

will be designed to couple with a range of other components and must be specified in a way that admits any component with the right behavior and excludes others. A designer aiming to meet a spec should be confident that the component works and should be able to justify that belief.

We should therefore have some idea of what it means to conform to a specification: what must be checked and how you would go about it—in other words, documenting the refinement relationship.

6.2.2   Traceability and Verification

It is important to be able to understand how each business goal relates to each system requirement and how each requirement relates to each facet of the design and ultimately each line of the code. Documenting the refinement relationships between these layers makes it easy to trace the impact of changes in the goals.

Traceability is a much-advertised claim of object-oriented design: Because the classes in your program are the same as in your business analysis, so the story goes, you should easily be able to see the effects on your design of any changes in the business. But anyone who has done serious OO design knows that in practice, the designs can get pretty far from this simple ideal. Applying a variety of design patterns to generalize, improve decoupling, and optimize performance, you separate the simple analysis concepts into a plethora of delegations, policies, factories, and plug-in pieces.

▶ *traceability*   The ability to relate elements in a detailed description to the elements in an abstraction that motivate their presence and vice versa; the ability to relate implementation elements to requirements.

Documenting the refinement relationship puts back the traceability, showing how each piece of the analysis relates to the design.

In safety-critical systems, it is possible to document refinements precisely enough to perform automatic consistency checks on them. However, achieving this level of precision is rarely cost-effective, and we do not deal with that topic in this book.

For the majority of projects, it is sufficient to use pre- and postconditions as the basis of test harnesses and to document just enough of a refinement that other developers and maintainers clearly see the design intent. We'll see how to do that later in this chapter.

6.3   *Spreadsheet: A Refinement Example*

The sections that follow look in more detail at the four main kinds of refinement we mentioned earlier. This section introduces an example that runs through those sections.

6.3.1   A Specification for a Spreadsheet

Let's look first at what can be done with a good abstract model. It's a model of a self-contained program, but it could equally well be a component in a larger system.

Figure 6.17 shows a model of a spreadsheet together with a dictionary interpreting the meaning of the pieces in the model. A spreadsheet is a matrix of named cells, into each of which the user can type either a number or a formula. In this simplified example, a formula can be only the sum of two other chosen cells (themselves either sum or number cells).

The model shows exactly what is expected of a spreadsheet: that it maintain the arithmetic relationships between the cells no matter how they are altered. In particular, the invariant Sum::... says that the value of every Sum cell is always the addition of its two operands.

Notice that this is very much a diagram not of the code but rather of what the user may expect. The boxes and lines illustrate the vocabulary of terms used to define the requirement.

The box marked Cell, for example, represents the idea that a spreadsheet has a number of addressable units that can be displayed. It doesn't say how they get displayed, and it doesn't say that if you look inside the program code you'll *necessarily* find a class called Cell. If the designer is interested in performance, some other internal structure might be thought more efficient. On the other hand, if the designer is interested in maintainability, using a structure that follows this model would be helpful to whoever will do the updates.

The model doesn't even say everything that you could think of to say about the requirements. For example, are the Cells arranged in any given order on the screen? How does the user refer to a Cell when making a Sum? If not all the Cells will fit on the screen at a time, is there a scrolling mechanism?

It's part of the utility of abstract modeling that you can say or not say as many of these things as you like. And you can be as precise or ambiguous as you like; we could have put the {Sum::... invariant as a sentence in English. This facility for abstraction allows us to use modeling notation to focus on the matters of most interest.

6.3.1.1   Using Snapshots to Animate the Spec

Although (or perhaps because) the model omits a lot of the details you'd see in the code, you can do useful things with it. For example, we can draw snapshots: instance diagrams that illustrate clearly the effect each operation has.

Snapshots illustrate specific example situations. Figure 6.18 shows snapshots depicting the state of our spreadsheet before and after an operation. (The thicker lines and bold type represent the state after the operation.) Notice that because we are dealing with a requirements model here, we show no messages (function

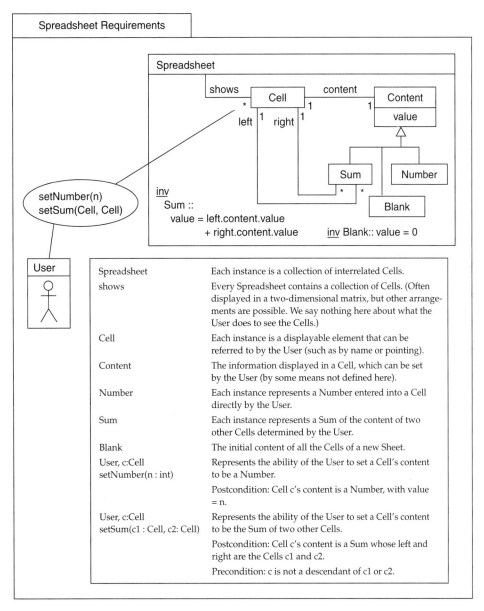

Figure 6.17   Model for a spreadsheet.

calls) between the objects; they will be decided in the design process. Here we're concerned only with the effects of the operation invoked by the user. This is part of how the layering of decisions works in Catalysis: We start with the effects of operations and then work out how they are implemented in terms of collaborations between objects.

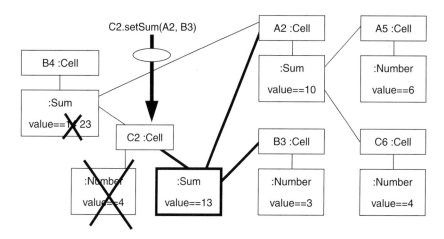

Figure 6.18 Spreadsheet snapshots.

6.3.2 An Implementation

Now let's consider an implementation. The first thing to be said is that the program code is much larger than the model, so we'll see only glimpses of it. Here is some implementation code for a spreadsheet:

```
package SpreadSheetImpl_1;

class SpreadSheet_I                  // This class implements SpreadSheet
{
    private Cell_I [ ] cells;               // array of cells of my spreadsheet
    ...        // various code here
}

class Cell_I
{
    private int m_value;                  // The current value of the Cell
      private Sum_I sumpart;              // Null if it's a plain number
      public int value ( ) { return m_value; }
      // will need some mechanism to keep m_value in sync with sumpart!
      ... // More code for manipulating Cells goes here
}

class Sum _I                              // Represents Sums
{
    private Cell_I [ ] operands;           // An array of several operands
    int get_value ( )
    {      int sum=0;
          for (int i= 0; i<operands.length; i++)
              sum += operands[i].value( );
      }
... // More code ...
}
```

The (|_|) suffixes distinguish the implementation. The first thing a reviewer might notice is that the classes I have written don't seem to correspond directly to the classes mentioned in the specification. Their attributes are different, and so on. "We are doing object-oriented design," says the reviewer. "Your code should mirror the spec. It says so in 50 different textbooks."

I am quick to my defense. Point (a): encapsulation. The spreadsheet as a whole, seen through the eyes of users (including other programs driving it through an API), does exactly what the spec leads them to expect. They won't know the difference. This is encapsulation, something that is "also mentioned in about 150 different books," I point out.

Point (b): engineering. Whereas the spec was written to be easily understood and general to all implementations, my particular implementation is better. It works faster, uses fewer resources, and is better decoupled than some amateur attempt that slavishly follows the model in the spec. And for many programs, there would be practical issues such as persistence not dealt with in the spec.

"And finally," I add, "my program is a whole lot more than just a spreadsheet. To use it as such is to play 'Chopsticks' upon the mighty organ of a grand cathedral; to ask Sean Connery to advertise socks." In other words, the spec from my point of view is partial, expressing the requirements of only one class of user; so the implementation classes you see here are chosen to suit a much broader scheme. Nevertheless, it is able to function merely as a spreadsheet when required, and I wish it to be validated as such against the spec.[4]

6.3.3   The Refinement Relationship

Whether you believe all that about my spreadsheet is not important here. Certainly, there are many times when performance, decoupling, or a partial spec leads to differences between model and code. So the reviewer is faced with trying to determine whether there is some correspondence between them: whether the code conforms to the spec (or refines it).

Naturally, proper testing will be the final judge. But understanding the conformance relationship allows an earlier check, which can clarify the design and the rationale for the differences. What's more, it provides traceability: the ability to see how any changes in either the spec or the code affect the other.

As we've seen, we can distinguish a few main primitive kinds of refinement. Combinations of them cover most of the valid cases: you can explain most design decisions in terms of them. In a large development, the usual layers of requirements, high-level design, detailed design, and code can be seen as successive refinements.

---

4. Presumably, the spec has not said anything about my program's 94MB size and the download time to Web users other than Sean Connery.

Understanding refinement has several advantages.

- It makes clear the difference between a model of requirements and a diagram that more directly represents the code (one box per class).
- It makes it possible to justify design decisions more clearly.
- It provides a clear trace from design to implementation.

Many of the well-known design patterns are refinements applied in particular ways. The refinements we're about to discuss are, in some sense, the most primitive design patterns; they are themselves combined in various ways to define the more popular design patterns.

We'll now see examples of the four refinements we looked at in Figure 6.1.

6.4 *Spreadsheet: Model Refinement*

The reviewer begins by getting me to produce a drawing of my code. Figure 6.19 shows a view focusing on the external user operations and their postconditions. You can see the direct correspondence between the static model and the variables. Indeed, there are tools that will take the code and produce the basis of the diagram.

```
class Cell_I
{ private int value;
   Sum_I sumpart;   // null for a Number
   ...
class Sum_I
{ Cell_I operands [ ];    // array
   ...
```

The reviewer begins with how the information in the model is represented.

"How is the spec's Sum represented?" she asks.

"By my Sum_I," I reply.

"So where are the left and right attributes of a Sum?"

"No problem," I answer. "All the information mentioned by the requirements is there—it's just that some of the names have changed. If you want to get the left and right operands of any Sum, look at the first and second items of my operands array. But because the requirements don't call for any operations that directly ask for the left or right, I haven't bothered to write them." Nevertheless, anyone using my code would see it behaving as expected from the spec.

6.4.1   What a Type Model Means and Doesn't Mean

The types in a model provide a vocabulary for describing a component's state. The terms can be used to define the effects of actions. However, the model does not provide any information about the internal structure of the component.

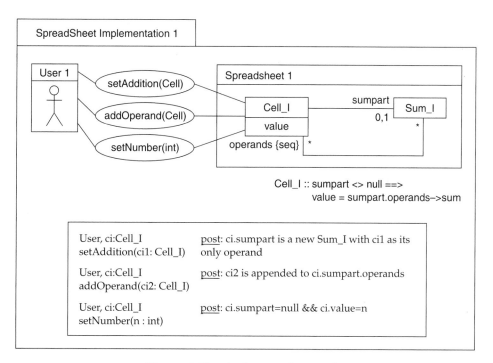

Figure 6.19   A picture of my code.

A static model (types, attributes, and associations) provides, by itself, no useful information about what behavior to expect. Only the action specifications based on it provide that. The complete specification is a true one if the statements it makes or implies about the component's behavior (response to actions) are always correct. Features of a static type model not used by action specifications are redundant, having no effect on the specification's meaning.

6.4.2   Documenting Model Conformance with a Retrieval

The general rule is that, for each attribute or association in the abstract models, it should be possible to write a *read-only* function in the implementation code that abstracts (or retrieves) its value. Here are the retrievals for Sum_I I've just mentioned to my reviewer:

```
class Sum_I
{    private Cell_I [ ] operands;    // array
     Cell_I left ( ) {return operands [0]; }
     Cell_I right ( ) {return operands [1];}
     ...
```

These abstractions happen to be particularly easy; the correspondence to the spec model is not very far removed. Others are more complex. But it doesn't matter if an abstraction function is hopelessly inefficient: It need only demonstrate that the information is in there somewhere. Nor does it matter if there is more information in the code than in the model. I can store more than two operands, although readers of the official spec won't use more than two.

6.4.3   Drawing a Model Conformance

Retrievals can be made more clear with a diagram. It can be helpful to draw both models (or at least parts of them) on a single diagram. You can then visually relate the elements across the refinement using associations and write invariants that define the abstraction functions for all attributes in the spec.[5] These associations, introduced specifically for this purpose, are distinguished with a <<retrieval>> tag or stereotype. (We often abbreviate that to a // marker, although in Figure 6.20 we've shown both.) Figure 6.20 shows that each Cell_I in the implementation corresponds one-to-one with a Cell in the spec; the same is true for Sum_I and Sum. All we need is to document how the attributes of Cell or Sum can be computed from the attributes of Cell_I or Sum_I. For example:

Sum ::	left =	impl1.operands[1].abs
and	right =	impl1.operands[2].abs
and	value =	impl1.container.value

Notice what's happening: we start with a part of the spec and go through its attributes, showing how they are realized in this implementation, which is called impl1 (not just impl—it might have many implementations we've not seen yet). The left is given by our implementation's first operand—well, not quite, because that's a Cell_I. Actually, it's the abstract Cell represented by its first operand—hence, the abs at the end.

We can say the same kind of thing about Cells:

Cell::   content.value = impl1.value
                 -- my content's value is represented by my implementation's value
  and   if (impl1.isBlank) abs.content : Blank
                     -- impl1's isBlank flag means I am a Cell with a Blank content
                 else if (impl1.sumpart = null) abs.content : Number
                     -- if my implementation has no sumpart, my content is a Number
                 else (content : Sum) and content = impl1.sumpart.abs
                     -- otherwise my content is a Sum, as represented by my
                         implementation's
                     -- sumpart --- see its retrieval for details

And finally we can say the same thing about the whole spreadsheet:

SpreadSheet_1 :: abs.cells = cells.abs
    -- I represent the Spreadsheet whose Cells are all the abstractions that my
        Cell_Is represent

---

5. The specification model will generally be in one package and the implementation in another. (Packages are dealt with in Chapter 7.) There may be more than one implementation, so we don't want to put them all in one package. The conformance retrieval information may be with the implementation or in its own package.

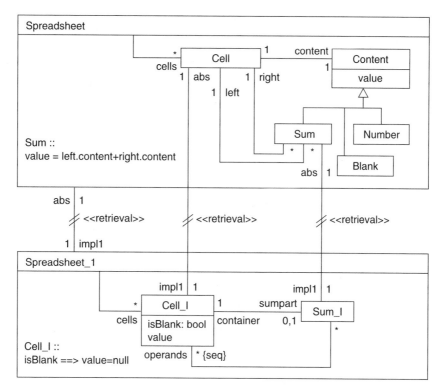

Figure 6.20   Retrieval diagram.

Writing the retrieval functions doesn't directly depend on drawing the retrieval relations, but it helps where the correspondence is more or less one-to-one. Notice that we don't, for example, have a direct correspondence to Number.

6.4.4   Testing Using Abstraction Functions

QA departments may insist that such retrieval (abstraction) functions should be written down or even written into the code. Even though these functions are not always used in the delivered code, they are useful.

- Writing them is a good cross-check, helping to expose inconsistencies that might otherwise have been glossed over.
- They make an unambiguous statement about exactly how the abstract model has been represented in your code.
- For testing purposes, testbeds can be written that execute the postconditions and invariants defined in the requirements models. These talk in terms of the abstract model's attributes, so the abstraction functions will be needed to get their values.

For example, recall that we wrote one of the invariants as

Sum:: value = left.content.value + right.content.value

Becuase we have defined what value, left, and right mean in terms of this implementation, we can rewrite it, substituting the definitions of each of them:

Sum :: impl1.container.value = impl1.operands[1].abs.content.value
                                                            + impl1.operands[2].abs.content.value

The impl1 at the start of each of these expressions says that we are talking about the implementations. So maybe it would be simpler to write the invariant so that it applies to all Sum_ls instead:

Sum_l :: container.value   = operands[1].abs.content.value
                                                            + operands[2].abs.content.value

This is an invariant we could execute in the implementation in debug mode. We could make one further simplification to make more clear what is happening. Evaluating the expressions operands[n].abs will give a Cell; and the retrievals say that Cell::content.value = impl1.value. So we could rewrite the invariant:

Sum_l :: container.value   = operands[1].abs.impl1.value
                                                            + operands[2].abs.impl1.value

But that's still a bit long-winded. Something such as abs.impl1 is running one way up a one-to-one association only to come back down it again—the two cancel out. So we get

Sum_l :: container.value   = operands[1].value + operands[2].value

6.4.5 Model Conformance: Summary

We've seen how a model can be very different from the code and still represent the same information. Now, as we've said before, the Golden Rule of object-oriented design is to choose your classes to mirror your specification model. When that is possible, the abstractions are trivial, a one-to-one correspondence. But there are several circumstances when it isn't possible, and model refinement gives us a way of understanding the relationships. Typical cases include the following.

- The model that gives best execution performance is very different from one that explains clearly to clients what the object does.
- The implementation adds a lot to the specified functionality. It is possible for one object to satisfy several specifications, especially when it plays roles in separate collaborations (as we will see in later chapters). Each role specification will have its own model, which must be related to the implementation.
- You specified a requirement and then bought a component that comes with its own spec. The first thing you must work out is how its model corresponds to yours.

We've also said before that it is a matter of local policy how formal your documentation must be. When you're plugging components together to get an early product delivery, you don't care about all this. But when you're designing a component you hope will be reused many times, it is worth the extra effort. And even if you don't go to the trouble of writing the abstraction functions, it is useful to do a mental check that you believe they could be written if you were challenged to.

6.4.6   Testing by Representing the Specification in Code

What the Quality Assurance department really wants is to be able to represent a spec in code so that it can be run as a test harness. They want to be able to write one set of invariants, postconditions, and so on that every candidate implementation can be tested against. As far as they are concerned, the spec writer writes a spec and associated test assertions. Each hopeful designer must supply two things: the design plus a set of abstractions that enable the test assertions to execute.

This rigorous view of specification and testing leads to a view in which all models can be cast into program code (something that is not so tedious as it was before code-generating tools). The types in a specification turn into abstract classes, of which the designer is expected to supply implementations. Figure 6.21 on the next page shows this done for the invariants; postconditions are omitted.

(In Java, you'd think spec types would be written as interfaces. Unfortunately, if we want to put the invariants and postconditions into the types themselves in real executable form, they must be classes. This has the uncomfortable effect of disallowing one implementation class from playing more than one role. An alternative is to put all the test apparatus in a separate set of classes that interrogates the states of the types. Again, we find ourselves applauding Eiffel, in which all this is natural and easy.)

If we can write the whole thing, spec and all, in code, we can also show both the abstract model and the more detailed design in one picture—see Figure 6.22 on page 245. The Cell and Sum refinements are only model refinements, because the abstraction did not promise any behavior requirements on those types.

But our reviewer has been thinking. "I notice your left and right return Cell_I, so that must be your representation of Cell, right?" she says. "So what's a Cell_I's content?"

"In my terms, that's its sumpart," I reply.

"But that only works if the Cell's content is a Sum," she says. "What if it's a Number or a Blank?"

Well, that's a good question. The spec always models every Cell as having a Content even if it's just a plain Number, whereas I keep the value in the Cell_I itself and use an extra object only to deal with Sums. The information is all in there but is distributed in a different way. But it presents an obstacle to the executable invariants idea: A term such as left().content().value() wouldn't work where left() is a plain number cell, because it doesn't have a content.

Specification as Code

```
package SpreadSheetSpec;

abstract class SpreadSheet
{
    public abstract Cell [ ] shows ();
        // Cell [ ]      --array of Cells
        // abstract      --header only, no body

// invariant true if all constituents OK
    public boolean invariant ( )
        { boolean inv= true;
            for (int i= 0;
                i<shows () .length; i++)
            inv &&= shows () [i] .invariant ();
            return inv;
}        }

abstract class Cell
{   abstract Content content ();
//invariant true if content is OK
    boolean invariant ( )
        { return content( ) .invariant(); }
}
abstract class Content
{   abstract      int value ( );
// default invariant - depends on subclass:
    boolean invariant ( ) { return true; }
}

abstract class Sum extends Content
{
    abstract   Cell left();
    abstract   Cell right();
// crucial spreadsheet invariant
    boolean invariant ( )
    { return super.invariant() &&
        value() ==
            left() .content() .value( )
        +   right() .content() .value( );
} }

abstract class Number extends Content
{
    abstract      void set_value (int v);
        // post:    v == value()
}

class Blank extends Content
{
    boolean invariant ( )
    { return super.invariant()
                && value() ==0 ;
    }
    // This is so obvious . . . let's just do it
    public int value ( ) { return 0; }
}
```

Implementation (part)

```
package SpreadSheetImpl;
import SpreadSheetSpec;

class SpreadSheet1 extends SpreadSheet
    // This class implements SpreadSheet
{ private Cell_I [ ] cells;
//retrieval:
    public Cell [ ] shows ( )
    {   Cell [ ] r= new Cell [cells.length];
        for (int i= 0; i<r.length; i++)
        r[i]= cells[i];
        return r;
}    }
class Cell_I extends Cell
{   private boolean isBlank= true;
    private int m_value;        // current value
    private Sum_I sumpart;   // null for Number
//   retrieval as a Cell:
    public Content content ()
    {   if (isBlank) return new Blank( );
        else if (sumpart==null)
            return new NumberCellAdapter(this);
        else
            return sumpart;
    }
    public int value () {if (sumreturn m_value)}
//   services retrieval of Number:
    void set_value (int v) { m_value= v; }
}

class Sum_I extends Sum
{   private Cell_I [ ] operands;
    public int value ( ) { . . .add operands. . . }
//   retrievals as a Sum:
    public Cell left ( )
    {   if (operands.length == 0)
        return new Cell_I ( ); //blank
        else return operands[0];
    }
    public Cell right ( )
    {   if (operands.length <= 1)
            return new Cell_I ( ); //blank
        else return operands[1];
} . . . }

// This class is used for retrieval
// when debugging -- not required in delivery
    class NumberAdapter extends Number
{   private Cell_I myCell;
    NumberAdapter (Cell_I c) // constructor
        {  myCell= c; }
    public int value ( )
        {  return myCell.value(); }
    public void setValue (int v)
        {  myCell.setValue(v); }
}
```

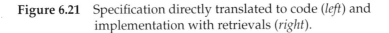

Figure 6.21　Specification directly translated to code (*left*) and implementation with retrievals (*right*).

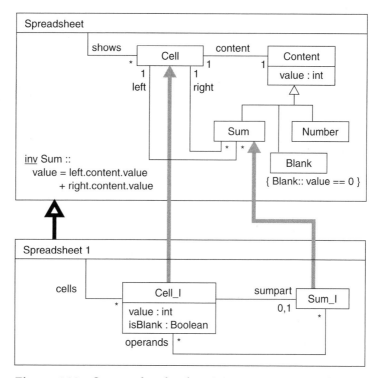

Figure 6.22 Spec and code, showing main correspondences.

What I want to say is that expressions in the spec such as content.value should be translated into the terms of the implementation as a whole: The content.value of a Cell_I is its sumpart.value if it's a sum and is its own variable m_value otherwise. This is perfectly reasonable if all I want to do is document the abstraction function and persuade my reviewer that my code is OK.

But for executable test assertions, content() must return something that will then return the appropriate value(). This leads to the invention of the class Number-Adapter (so now we have abstraction classes as well as functions). It can be kept fairly minimal. All it must do is know our implementation well enough to extract any information required by the test assertions in the spec type Number.

So the general pattern for executable abstractions is that for every type in the spec, the designer provides a direct subclass. Sometimes these can be the classes of the implementation; in practice they often must be written separately, mostly because your classes have more interesting things to be subclasses of. Each adapter retrieves from the implementation that part of the component's state that its specification supertype represents. Notice that our adapters are created only when needed (see Figure 6.23).

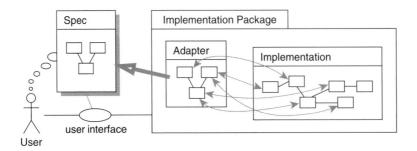

Figure 6.23   Test by adapting the implementation.

What has happened to our ideal of encapsulation? We started with the idea that internal workings unseen by the user could be designed in any way you like; now we've had to put back all the structure of the model.

Well, not quite. The adapter classes need only translate and are there only for verification. The real implementation still does the hard work. And you'll need them only if your QA department is pretty stringent.

As it turns out in practice, adapters of this kind are frequently needed for each external interface of a component, whether it is a user interface or an interface to another component (see Figure 6.24). This is because the component's internal state must be translated into the view understood by each external agent. (For human users, the GUI usually encompasses the adapter.)

6.4.7   Specifications in Code: Summary

Specifications can be written not only as pictorial models but also in the form of executable test frameworks. The benefit is a much stronger assurance of conformance, especially where there may be a variety of candidate implementations.

Implementors must provide executable abstraction functions to translate from the component's internal vocabulary to that of the specification. Often, this leads to providing an *adapter*, a set of classes directly mirroring the types in the spec. However, adapters can be useful at the interface of a component in addition to their role in verification.

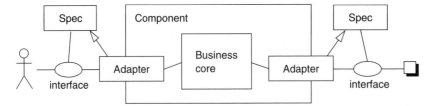

Figure 6.24   Adapters for other interfaces.

6.5 *Spreadsheet: Action Refinement*

The next thing my code reviewer notices is that nowhere is there a function set-Sum(Cell, Cell). I explain that I have decided to refine this action to a finer-grained series of interactions between the user and the spreadsheet (see Figure 6.19 earlier). To set a cell to be the sum of two others as per requirement, the user performs this scenario:

- Select the cell in question by clicking the mouse.
- setAddition: type = and click one of the operand cells.
- addOperand: type + and click on the other.

The requirement is provided for by a combination of features in my implementation. My "=" operation turns the Cell into a single-operand sum, and each "+" operation adds another operand. So although there is no single operation with the signature setSum(Cell, Cell)—either at the user interface or anywhere inside the code—the user can nevertheless achieve the specified effect.

It is an important feature of a Catalysis action that, without stating how, it represents a goal attained by a collaboration between the participants. The goal can be unambiguously documented with a postcondition or with a guarantee condition. A *conformant* implementation is one that provides the means of achieving the goal.

Different implementations require different behavior on the part of every participant, because they will involve different protocols of interaction. A user who knows how to use my spreadsheet implementation will not necessarily know how to use another design. It is the collaboration that has been refined here and not the participants individually.

6.5.1 Action Conformance: Realization of Business Goals

In general, the specification actions are about the business goals of the system—for example "The user of our drawing editor must be able to duplicate picture elements and must be able to copy them from one drawing to another." The actions that we provide break these larger goals into decoupled pieces. We invent a clipboard and provide cut and paste operations with which the user is able to achieve the stated goals.

Here's another example: "The customer of our bank must be able to get money at any time of the day or night." So we invent cash machines and cash cards and provide the actions of inserting the card into the machine, selecting a service, and so on. The user, with the help of a good user interface, uses these actions to achieve the stated goals.

6.5.2   Checking Action Conformance

We need to check that, for every action defined in the specification, there is a combination of implementation actions that the user could follow to achieve the defined goal. Let's take setSum as an example.

The action specs shown here were given in Figure 6.17 and Figure 6.19:

From the spec			
User, Cell c ::		Represents the ability of the User to set a Cell's content to be the Sum of two other Cells.	
setSum (ci1 : Cell, ci2 : Cell)	<u>Post</u>:	Cell c's content is a Sum whose left and right are the Cells c1 and c2.	
From the implementation			
User, Cell_l ci :: setAddition (ci1 : Cell_l)	<u>Post</u>:	ci.sumpart is a new Sum_l with ci1 as its only operand.	
User, Cell_l ci :: addOperand (ci2 : Cell_l)	<u>Post</u>: <u>Pre</u>:	c2 is appended to ci.sumpart.operands. ci.sumpart <> null. This is already a Sum.	

A little thought suggests that a setAddition followed by an addOperand should achieve the effect of a setSum. A comparison of snapshots in the two views will help; the arrows show which links are created by each action (see Figure 6.25).

Now we can see that performing the sequence

<ci.setAddition(ci1), ci.addOperand(ci2)>

should achieve an effect corresponding to the spec's c.setSum(c1, c2). To be absolutely sure, we can use the abstraction functions we worked out earlier.

setSum's postcondition talks about the left and right of Cell c. In our implementation, we claim that Cell_ls represent Cells, so in our example snapshot, cin represents cn. We also decided that content.left in the spec is represented by sumpart.operands[0]. So does this sequence of steps achieve that "Cell c's content is a Sum whose left is Cell c1"? Yes, because the first step makes ci.sumpart.operands[0] =ci1. And does it achieve that c.content.right = c2? Yes, because the second step achieves ci.sumpart.operands[1] = ci2.

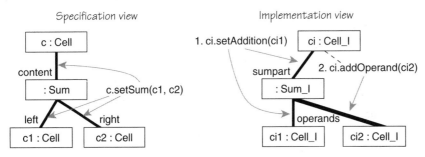

Figure 6.25   Snapshots in specification and implementation.

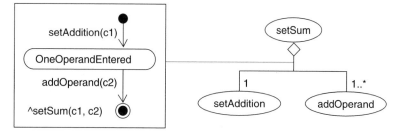

Figure 6.26   Action conformance.

6.5.3   Documenting Action Conformance

We can document the refinement as in Figure 6.26. The diamond "assembly" symbol says that there is some way in which the specification effect can be achieved by some combination of the implementation actions. But exactly what sort of combination—concurrent, sequential, some sort of loop—must be said separately.

In the case of a sequence, this can be done with a state chart.[6] Each implementation action is a transition on the diagram; each state represents how much of the overall job has been achieved so far. You may need to use additional attributes, with new postconditions on the detailed actions, to make the mapping clear.[7]

This one is simple. The initial setAddition takes us into an intermediate state, OneOperandEntered, from which an addOperand will complete the overall setSum action. This achievement is denoted by the caret mark ^. We do not specify here what happens if addOperand occurs when we're not in OneOpnd or what happens if setAddition is performed again when we're in OneOpnd. Those exceptions can be shown separately.

Names are chosen in the state chart (here, c1 and c2) to indicate how the arguments of the actions are related. You can use the names in guards and postconditions written in the chart to show other constraints and results in more detail.

As usual, diagrams are not intended to be a substitute for good explanation in your natural language. Instead, they are supposed to complement it and remove the ambiguities.

6.5.4   Testing Action Conformance

Testing action conformance at runtime isn't as easy as just inserting a few lines of code to monitor the postconditions. The problem is that nowhere does my user

---

6. We have found that temporal logic handles more general cases in a very concise form. The UML activity diagram is another alternative.

7. For example, Section 4.2.2, Preview: Documenting a Refinement, introduces a counter to count the number of individual item insertions and map to the single abstract action of some quantity of those items.

explicitly say to my implementation, "Now I want to do a setSum." It's the same with our other examples: A user doesn't say to the drawing program, "Now I'm going to move a shape from one drawing to another." Rather, the user just uses the select, cut, and paste operations.

Therefore, we have two options. We can write a test harness that performs the requisite sequences and checks the postconditions by comparing states before and after, or we can perform the equivalent checks manually by following a written test procedure. This is a matter of policy in your project. Each approach will be appropriate in different circumstances. Either way, you are systematically defining test *sequences* based on refinement of abstract actions. And, either way, the documented action conformance should be used to guide the creation of the tests, and the retrievals (whether only documented or actually coded as we saw earlier) provide the mapping between the different levels of the model.

6.5.5   Action Conformance and Layered Design: Action Refinement Brings Model Refinement

Action refinement is nearly always associated with model refinement. To represent the intermediate states, the more detailed model needs more information.

Action refinement is about taking a large interaction with many parameters and breaking it into several steps with fewer and simpler parameters. For example, get_cash(ATM, person, account, $) breaks down to several steps, such as insert_card(ATM, card) and enter_amount($), each of which identifies only a few parameters at a time. After the first step, the ATM system must remember whose card has been inserted so that when the later $ step happens, it knows which account to debit (see Figure 6.27). The association of "Account x currently using ATM y" is not needed at the more abstract level. Ultimately, the process can be taken down to individual keystrokes and mouse clicks.

In our spreadsheet, we glossed over something of this nature. We originally said that the user first selects a cell and then performs a setAddition operation to identify the first operand. In other words, select(Cell_I) sets some current_focus attribute of the spreadsheet as a whole; and setAddition's postcondition should properly have been written in terms of current_focus.

> <u>action</u> setAddition (ci1: Cell_I)

<u>post</u>: current_focus.sumpart is a new Sum_I with ci1 as its only operand.

We can take the action refinement even further. How is a setAddition performed? By typing = and clicking in a cell. For that we need an addition to the model to record that after the =, we're now in the "identify Cell for adding" state and to map mouse coordinates to Cells. Yes, finally, we've gotten down to something that uses the graphical layout of the spreadsheet.

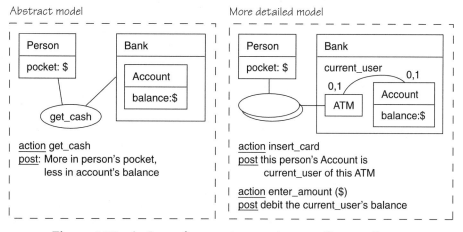

Figure 6.27   Action refinement means intermediate attributes.

6.5.5.1 Reifying Actions

Reification means to make real. We use it to mean making an object from some concept. In a model, we can feel free to represent any concept as an object; in a design, reification is the decision to write a class to represent that concept.

It is often useful to represent an action as an object, particularly an abstract action with refinements. Its purpose is to guide the refined actions through the steps that lead to the achievement of the abstract action's postcondition and to hold the extra information that is always required to represent how far the interaction has progressed.

In the bank example, we might create an ATM_transaction object as soon as a user inserts a card. This object would keep all the information about the account that has been selected, the current screen display, the menu options, and so on.

Reified action objects also form a record of the action after it has completed (for audit trail purposes) and keep the information necessary for an undo operation. This transaction object is also the place to put all the functionality about exceptional outcomes, rollbacks, and so on.

We can see reified actions in real-world business transactions. An order is the business concept representing the progression of a buy action through various subactions such as asking for the goods, payment, and delivery. An account is the reification of the ongoing action of entrusting your money to your bank.

Reified actions are often called *control objects* or *transaction objects*. Whenever we draw an action ellipse on a type diagram, we are really drawing a type of object, which might or might not be reified in an implementation. (See Pattern 14.13, Action Reification.)

It's easy to see the direct correspondence: The participants of the action are drawn as, and are, associations of the reified action; the action's parameters—

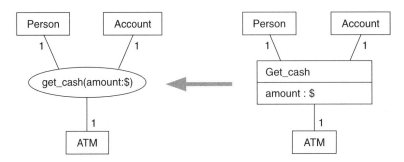

Figure 6.28   Reification of get_cash action.

variable values we don't bother to depict as links on the diagram—are the object's attributes (see Figure 6.28). As we add detail about the constituent actions, the extra information is added to this object. The state diagram we drew—depicting the correspondence between the abstract and detailed actions—becomes the state chart of this object.

6.5.5.2   Action Refinement and Design Layers

The relationships between abstract actions and their more-detailed constituents cover a scale from individual keystrokes or electrical signals to large-scale operations. The objects that reify these actions range from GUI controllers to entire application programs. For example, the operations of editing words and pictures in a drawing program can be seen as refinements of the overall action of creating or updating a document; the in-memory version of the document, and mechanisms such as the cursor and scrollbars, are part of the extra information attached to the object at the more detailed level. At an even bigger scale, workflow and teamwork systems help control the progress of a project through many individual tasks, with documents as intermediate artifacts.

Within a software design, the different levels of refinement are generally associated with different, decoupled layers in the software. We can see this, for example, in the conventional separation into business and GUI layers. We can also see it in communications protocols, from the individual bits up through to the secure movement of files and Web pages.

6.5.6   Action Conformance and Collaborations

We have seen how a more detailed static model is required to describe a more detailed action. The purpose of a model is to carry the effects of one action across to the next; there wouldn't be much use in using a different model for every action. A collaboration is a group of actions and the model that describes them (see Section 4.6).

Because we refine the model with the actions, we usually refine a complete collaboration together: first the model, according to the rules of model conformance,

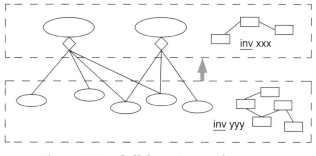

Figure 6.29   Collaboration conformance.

and then each action (see Figure 6.29). Each of the more-detailed actions can be used in several of the more-abstract actions.

Invariants are attached to collaborations or types and govern the actions that are part of the collaboration or the operations that are defined for the type. An invariant says, "If this is true when we start, it should still be true at the end." It can be conjoined with every pre- and postcondition of every action in its collaboration.

The actions in a collaboration do not observe the same invariants as the actions they refine. For example, when we look at a transaction between a shop and a customer at abstraction sufficient to see purchases, we believe in the invariant that the amount in the vendor's till plus the value of the stock should always add up to the same amount: Every sale simply swaps some stock for some money. But when we look in more detail, we can see that the money is transferred separately from the goods, so there are periods between payment and delivery when the invariant is not observed. Nevertheless, this layer still has its own invariants—for example, that the total of the vendor's and the customer's cash is always the same.

Therefore, invariants should always be quoted as part of a given type or collaboration. Before doing anything to correlate one level of abstraction with another, absorb the invariants into the pre- and postconditions.

6.5.7   Action Conformance within Software

Action refinement is not solely about user interactions. You can use the same principle when describing dialogs between objects in the software. This lets you describe collaborations in terms of the effects they achieve before you go into the precise nature of the dialog.

For example, one of the invariants of the spreadsheet implementation is that the value of a Cell_I with a sumpart is always the sum of sumpart.operands. To achieve this, my design makes each Sum register as an observer of its operand Cells. When any Cell's value changes, it will notify all its observers; Sums in turn notify their parent Cells. The effect is to propagate any change in a value.

-- for any action on Cell
inv effect Cell:: update_when_change
post   -- if its value changes, every sum using this cell as an operand is updated
    value <> value @ pre ==> ~operands->forAll (s | (self,s).update ())

action (c: Cell, s: Sum) :: update
    -- the change in value of cell is propagated to the sum
    -- we have not said what the protocol is for accomplishing this update
    post
    c.value – c. value@pre = s.~sumpart.value – (s.~sumpart.value)@pre

Figure 6.30   Deferring the update protocol.

We can document that requirement while deferring the details of how the change is propagated. Does a Cell send the new value in the notify message? Or does it send the difference between old and new values? Or does it send the notification without a value and let the observer come back and ask for it? In the midst of creating the grand scheme of our design, we don't care: Such details can be worked out later, and we want to get on to other important issues first. The art of abstraction is about not getting bogged down in detail! All we need do at this stage is to record the relationship and the effect it achieves. For this, we use an invariant effect that constrains all (see Figure 6.30).

6.5.8 Action Conformance: Summary

Actions are used to describe the way in which objects—people, hardware, or software—collaborate. Actions are primarily described by their effects on the participants and secondarily as a series of steps or another refinement to smaller actions.

Action abstraction allows us to describe a complex business or software interaction as a single entity. Action refinement can be traced all the way from business goals down to the fine detail of keystrokes and bits in wires.

A useful technique in documenting action conformance is to draw a state chart of the progress of the abstract action through smaller steps.

6.6 *Spreadsheet: Object Refinement*

Object conformance means recognizing that a particular single object is an abstraction representing several constituent parts and that the state and responsibilities attributed to the abstract object are in fact distributed between the constituents.

Object conformance often accompanies action conformance when it turns out that the detailed dialog is not conducted between the participants as wholes but

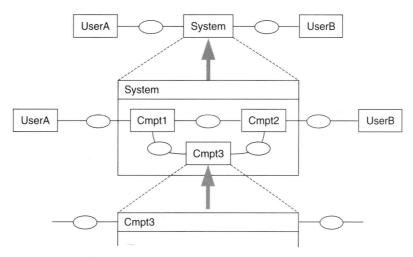

Figure 6.31   Fractal process of refinement.

rather between their parts. You can get cash from a bank, but more specifically from one of its cashiers or ATMs. In fact, looking at the actions in detail, when you receive cash from an ATM it actually comes from its money dispenser.

In Catalysis, we separate the act of writing the requirements of a system from the act of designing the internal messages that deal with each action. In requirements specs, we treat the system or component we're designing as a single object. The closer inspection of a system to treat it as a set of interacting objects is only one example of object refinement.

The process can be fractal: Like all our techniques, it applies as well to a complete system as to a small object inside the software (see Figure 6.31). A system design can start by refining into major components and then can define the high-level actions between them. Subsequently, those actions can be refined to provide more interactive detail. Each component can itself be refined into constituent objects and so on, until the actions are individual messages, and the objects are things you can write directly in your favorite programming language.

Looking in the other direction, the system we're interested in designing is part of a larger machine or organization or software system. By zooming out, we can understand better how our design will help fulfill the overall goals of the larger object.

This section uses the term *component* to refer to the object we are interested in refining, but the same principles apply on every scale.

6.6.1   What an Object Means and Doesn't Mean

We can use an object to describe any concept, including the active components of a system, whether people, hardware, or software or groups or parts thereof. Similarly, we can use a type to describe the behavior of such objects and use actions to describe its participation in interactions with other objects.

A type always describes the behavior of a linked-together collection of smaller constituents. A closer look reveals the parts and reveals that different parts deal with different behavior.

To specify the abstract object's behavior, we use a type model that tells us nothing about the abstract object's internal structure. The internal structure can be described as a set of linked objects participating in actions; the actions occur between the objects and with the outside world. A more detailed picture that reveals the internal structure must account for how the external actions visible in the abstract view are dealt with by the internal structure.

6.6.2   The Process of Object Refinement

The kinds of refinement we've already looked at can be used in a variety of ways, but they fit together particularly well as part of an object refinement. So let's review those techniques as steps forming part of object refinement.

We've looked at this process in other parts of this book. The point here is to see the steps in terms of the formal refinements defined in this chapter.

6.6.2.1   Start with the Specification

The model we begin with specifies the behavior of our component. Most objects are involved in more than one action: Our spreadsheet has addOperand, setNumber, and so on. Some objects are involved in actions with several other objects: Whereas the spreadsheet has one user, the bank's ATM has customers, operators, and the bank's host machine to deal with. Each of the actions can be specified at a fairly high level, with details to be worked out later (see Figure 6.32).

For each action, we have a specification, in terms of more-or-less rigorously defined pre- and postconditions (and possibly rely/guarantee conditions). Given this context, we work out which objects there are inside our abstract object and

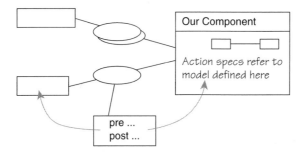

Figure 6.32   Joint action specified in terms of multiple participants.

how they collaborate to achieve the effects specified for each of the abstract object's actions.

Notice that we might be refining only one of these objects; perhaps the others are users whose behavior is the province of the GUI designer and the manual writer. Or it might be that we will be refining several of them if they are components in a larger system.

6.6.2.2   Design the Object Model

The actions are specified in terms of their effects on the participants, of which our component is one. For that purpose, each participant has a model. For simple objects, it may be only a few attributes; for complex ones, it will be a picture based on the business model. Our spreadsheet has cells and their various contents.

Focusing on the system we're interested in refining (the spreadsheet rather than the user), we may decide, as we did in this example, to use a different set of objects in the actual design. We have already seen how to use abstraction functions to relate the design model to the specification.

6.6.2.3   Refine the Actions and Mask the Specs

We refined the actions (so that setSum became <setAddition, addOperand>) and specified the more-detailed versions in terms of the design model (Cell_I rather than Cell and so on).

At this stage, we *mask*: remove anything from the action specs that talks about the other participants in the actions. For example, we don't care about the state of the ATM user's pocket as long as the ATM dishes out the cash. In the spreadsheet example, we didn't say much about the user's state anyway. In an action involving two or more software components, the team working on each component would make its own version of the action spec that would define only its effect on the team's component.

In some cases, masking is easy: The postcondition says, oneParticipant.someEffect AND theOtherParticipant.someOtherEffect. We simply throw away the clauses that don't apply to us. The other components' teams will worry about them.

Sometimes the postcondition is written so that the effect on our component depends on something elsewhere. In the ATM, for example: "IF the account in the user's bank is in credit, THEN the user gets the money." This means that, in refining the action, we must include an action with the user's bank that transfers that information here. (This also applies to preconditions, which are equivalent to an *if* clause like this.)

Masking should also make the actions directional, with a definite initiator and receiver, so that they are more like messages. However, they may still encapsulate a dialog refined later. This approach enables us to summarize the component spec in the form of a type diagram with model and action specifications (see Figure 6.33).

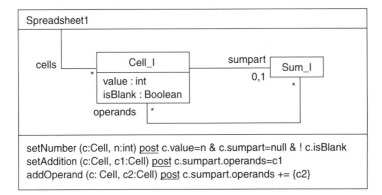

Figure 6.33   Localize and specify actions.

We refine the actions down from the highest-level business abstractions but not down to individual keystrokes or electrical pulses. We refine actions to the point where they make sense as individual actions on the objects we have chosen for our design—if you like, to the same conceptual layer as our design. "Make a spreadsheet" is too abstract for our design; "click mouse at (x,y)" is too detailed; but setNumber(n) makes sense as a message to one of our cells.

All such judgments are relative. Working in the GUI layer, mouse clicks and keystrokes are what we deal with, and the job is to parse them into actions that can be dealt with by the spreadsheet core. Working in a workflow system, the creation of a spreadsheet might be only one action, so that, from its point of view, the spreadsheet program is all a detail of the user interface that builds a series of cell-setting operations into one spreadsheet creation. A good guideline is this: "What would constitute a useful unit of work for the client?"—something the client would cheerfully pay for.

6.6.2.4   Localize Each Action to a Constituent Object

We now make each action the prime responsibility of one of the design objects internal to our component. Usually, a good choice is the proxy object that represents the external participant of the action, which might be a user, a piece of hardware, or a software object in a different component. If there is no such proxy—as in our spreadsheet, which has no representation of its user—then one of the action's parameters is the next choice. We'll choose the target Cell c. (In any case, a proxy often just sends the message to one of the parameters. But there is good pattern in which all messages to and from an external object should go through their local proxy, which thereby keeps abreast of what its external counterpart is up to.)

With the assignment of a component action to one of its constituents must, of course, go the specification of what it is supposed to achieve.

6.6.2.5   Operation Refinement for Each Component-Level Action

Now we work out how each component-level action is dealt with by the object it is assigned to—in other words, we design the sequence or write the operation code so as to meet the spec. Typically, this means sending messages to other objects.

We could put it more generally and say that each object can initiate actions with one or more other objects. You may know what you need to achieve and who should be involved, but you may not care (yet) how it is to be achieved or who should be primarily responsible for each part.

The receiving objects must themselves be designed, so they then pass messages to other objects. The result is that many of the component's internal objects now have their own specified actions.

We repeat the procedure for each of the component-level actions. The component's responsibilities are now distributed among its constituents. This is the essence of object refinement.

6.6.2.6   Visibilities

One last step is to decide who can see whom—in other words, object attributes—and we append arrowheads to the links in our model. The simple criterion here is that any object needs a state corresponding to a link to every other objects that it must "remember" across its operations. Again, these links need not correspond to stored pointers in program code; they can themselves be abstractions subject to further refinement.

In some cases, each object of a linked pair must know about the other. This in itself can add some final operations relating to the management of the link. An important pattern is a *two-way link*. When two objects refer to each other, it is important that they not get out of sync and point at different objects or point at a deleted object. Therefore, the only messages that immediately set up or take down the link should come from the object at the other end. When an object wishes to construct a two-way link with another object, it should set its own pointer and then register with the other. (See Pattern 16.14, Two-way link.)

6.6.3   Documenting Object Conformance

Interaction diagrams (also called object interaction graphs or OIGs) are snapshots with messages added. They are useful for illustrating particular cases. One or more collaborations can be drawn for each component-level action.

For example, our spreadsheet Cell will respond to an addOperand by sending the message to its Sum, which will set up an observer action with the target Cell (see Figure 6.34). The diagram shows the new links and objects in bold. A new observation relationship is created; It is an ongoing action characterized by its guarantee rather than its postcondition. It is treated as an object in these diagrams. We have decided that, at this stage, we don't care how it works, although we will specify what it achieves.

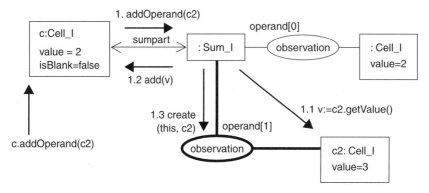

Figure 6.34   Internal interactions in the spreadsheet.

As is often the case when working out an interaction, we find we have brought new elements into the design. These elements should now be incorporated into the class diagram and specified. At the same time, we can begin to add localized actions to the classes (see Figure 6.35). (Recall that the [[action]] notation is used within a postcondition to specify that another action has been performed as part of this one.) We have specified the observation action; it may become an object in its own right or (more likely) will turn out to be only a contractual relationship between its participants.

Notice that although the interaction diagram is useful for illustrating specific cases, the class diagram (with associated dictionary, specifications, and code) is

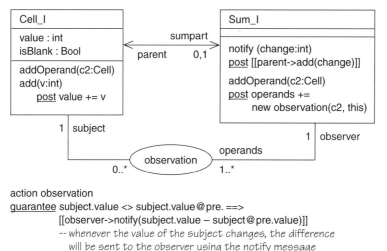

Figure 6.35   Update class diagram with localized actions and specs.

the canonical description of the design. As more collaborations are drawn, more detail can be added to the class diagram. Ultimately, we must also resolve observation to specific messages and attributes.

A sequence diagram is an alternative presentation of the same information as shown in a collaboration diagram and is better at showing the sequence of events; but the collaboration diagram also shows the links and objects. As an example, Figure 6.36 shows the sequence of the propagation of changes.

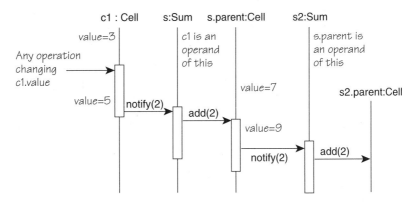

Figure 6.36 Sequence diagram alternative.

6.6.4 Object Access: Conformance, Façades, and Adapters

How do the external objects get access to the appropriate constituent objects within our component? The following sections discuss how access is implemented.

6.6.4.1 Direct Access

If the external objects and our component are all in the same body of software, there is a straightforward answer: All of them have references to those of our constituents they want to communicate with. When we do an object refinement, the main task is to work out how the externals will initially connect to the appropriate internal. Our abstract component object is a grouping of smaller objects, and we allow the boundary to be crossed arbitrarily (see Figure 6.37).

There can be a variety of drawbacks to the direct access scheme: making it more difficult to guarantee abstract object invariants and exposing more of the internal design decisions than necessary. Each of them applies only in certain circumstances.

6.6.4.2 Façade

A façade is a single object through which all communication to a component flows. It simplifies several aspects of object refinement.

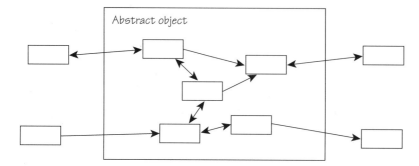

Figure 6.37   Direct external access to internal objects.

• You need not design the external objects to know which constituent to connect to. In the direct access scheme, refining our object also means designing the externals to work with our organization.

A business analogy is a company that provides a single point of contact for each customer or supplier. It saves the outside entity from having to understand the company's internal organization.

A corollary is that, if the design of the external objects is already finalized, a façade is necessary.

• Invariants applying to the component as a whole can be supervised by the façade, because it is aware of every action that could affect it. Conversely, the external objects have no direct access to any objects inside.

The supervision of invariants is a common motivation. Consider, for example, a SortedList object, in which the members of the list are NumberContainers; the value of a NumberContainer can be changed by sending it an appropriate message. The documented invariant of SortedList is that its members are always arranged in ascending order. But if external objects have direct access to the list's members, they can sneakily disorder the list by altering the values without the knowledge of the anchor SortedList instance.

Making the façade the only way of accessing the list elements is one way to keep control. The other approach is to implement a more complex Observation scheme whereby the elements notify the façade when they are changed.

A single façade can, however, be somewhat limiting. Every change to the internal objects to add or change the services they offer to the outside requires a corresponding change to the single façade even if particular clients never see that service.

6.6.4.3 Multiple Façades

The big drawback of a single façade object is poor decoupling: as soon as you change or add to any of the types in the component, you must extend the façade to cope with the new messages.

However, we can make the façade itself an abstract object consisting of a collection of *peers*: smaller façade objects, each of which handles communication with a given class of internal object. Most GUIs are constructed this way. Corresponding to each spreadsheet Cell, for example, is a CellDisplay object that deals with position on the screen and appearance and also translates mouse operations back to Cell operations.

In a more general scheme, different categories of external objects may have different *ports* through which to gain access, each of them a different façade.

6.6.4.4 Adapters

It's easy to draw links and messages crossing the boundary of a component; but what if the objects are in different host machines or written in different languages? Or what if the external objects are machines or people? How do the messages cross the boundary, and what constitutes an association across the boundary?

These objections are met by building an appropriate *adapter*: a layer of design that translates object references and messages to and from bits on wires (such as CORBA); or to pixels and from keystrokes and mouse clicks (the GUI). An adapter is a façade with strong translation capabilities.

Typically, you deal with references across boundaries by mapping strings to object identities. Your bank card's number is the association between the physical card and the software account object in your bank's computer; the spreadsheet cells can be identified by their row-column tags. The other common method is by mapping screen position to object identity, as when you point at its appearance on the screen.

It is because of the adapter(s) that we can always begin the object refinement by assuming that the appropriate internal object will be involved in the external actions. We leave it up to the adapter design.

In the case of the spreadsheet, a considerable GUI will be required to display the spreadsheet, to translate mouse operations into the specified incoming messages, and to direct them to the appropriate cells.

6.6.4.5 Boundary Decisions in Object Refinements

Object refinements, whether on a small or large scale, always involve a decision about how the boundary is managed: whether direct access is OK or whether a façade or the more general adapter layer is required.

Our original picture of an object refinement as a simple group of objects has now become a group of objects plus a layer of adapters (see Figure 6.38).

6.6.5 Object Conformance: Summary

Object abstraction gives us the ability to treat a whole collection of objects—people, hardware, software, or a mixture—as a single thing with a definable behavior.

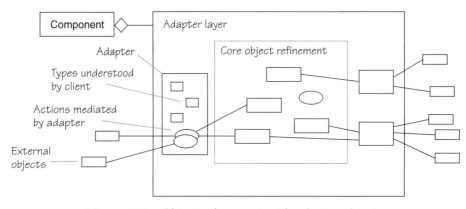

Figure 6.38   Object refinement with adapter objects.

This can be applied on the large scale of complete computer systems and businesses or on the small scale such as software sets and lists.

The key to documenting conformance is to show how the responsibilities of the abstract object are distributed to its constituents.

6.7 *Spreadsheet: Operation Refinement*

Operation refinement means writing a program that fulfills a given pre/post (and/ or rely/guarantee) specification. It is here that we finally get down to program code. In one sense, this is the part we need to say least about, because the point of this book is not to teach programming; you know how to put together loops and branches and sequences and can easily learn any (far more verbose) graphical representations of the same. However, there are some special considerations, most of them about decoupling, which is what OO programming is all about.

6.7.1   What Operation Abstraction Means and Doesn't Mean

An operation is a subtype of an action: operations are actions consisting of an invocation from a sender to a receiver, followed by an activity on the part of the receiver and possibly ending with a return signal to the sender. Operations are a one-sided view of the sender-receiver interaction.

If an operation is invoked in a situation when the precondition is false or if, during the execution of the operation, its rely condition becomes false, then the specification does not state what the outcome should be.

If an operation is invoked in a situation when the precondition is true and the rely condition is true throughout, then, by the end of the operation, the postcondition will have been achieved; and during the execution of the operation, the guarantee condition will have been maintained.

Preconditions and rely conditions, by default, are "true" and there is no obligation on the sender. Similarly, an empty postcondition or guarantee condition imposes no obligation on the implementor.

The operation should not alter variables that could be left untouched while achieving the postcondition and guarantee conditions.

Any invariant in the model should be considered to be ANDed to the pre- and the postconditions (but not the rely and the guarantee conditions).

6.7.2   Strong Decoupling

In conventional programs, you split a big program into subroutines so that common routines can be invoked individually and so that the program is easier to understand. In OO programming, the process goes even further. For every statement, you think, "Which object should this be attached to? Which object has the information and the other operations most strongly relevant to this?" Then you send a message to the appropriate object. Actually, that's not for every statement; rather, it's for every subexpression.

The purpose is to ensure that the program is well decoupled. If the preceding stages of design have gone well, many of these questions should be sorted out. However, you definitely have more decisions to make in an OO development than in procedural development.

The choice of types for a local variable—temporaries, inputs, and even return values—for an operation is crucial to good decoupling. As soon as you declare a variable or parameter that belongs to a particular class, you have made your part of the program dependent on that class. This means that any changes there may have an impact here. Instead, it is usually better to declare all variables as *types*; the only place in a program where you absolutely must refer to a concrete class is to instantiate a new object.

There is a variety of powerful patterns to help reduce dependencies.

• *Role decoupling:* A variable or parameter contains an object or a reference to one. Frequently, the component in which the declaration occurs uses only some of the facilities provided by that object.

Therefore, define a type (that is, an interface or pure abstract class plus a specification) that characterizes only the features that you will use. Declare the variable to be of this type. Declare the object's class to be an implementor of this type. This approach will minimize the dependency of your component on the other object. Related patterns are adapter and bridge [Gamma94].

(Role decoupling is particularly important for two-way links.)

• *Factory:* An object must be created as a member of a definite class. This gives rise to a dependency between your class and that one.

Therefore, devolve to a separate class the decision about which class the new object should belong to. By doing this, you encapsulate the class dependency behind a type-based creation method [Gamma95].

6.7.3 Documenting Operation Spec Conformance

Whether we have written it informally or in more precise form, we should have a specification of what is expected of each operation. We should attempt to check that the program code of each operation conforms to what is expected of it.

The most reliable method is to turn the specs into test harnesses, as we discussed earlier. But there is also the Deep Thought approach: as a general principle, it is possible to inspect both specification and code and to check that one meets the other by a judicious mixture of careful reasoning and guesswork. Although Deep Thought is not an economical method of verification outside safety-critical circles, being aware of the basic principles can help anyone root out obvious mistakes before getting to the testing stage.

There are two ways of fulfilling a spec. The hard way is to write the entire implementation yourself. The easy way is to find something that comes close to already doing the job and possibly bend the requirements to suit what you've found. The latter is usually more economical if you're fairly confident of its provenance and integrity (see, for example, Section 10.11, Heterogenous Components).

6.7.3.1 Comparing Two Operation Specs

Suppose we find some code in a library and we suspect that it does the job we require. Miraculously, it comes with a spec and model of some sort, which we want to compare to our requirements spec.

The rules for comparing two pre/post specs are as follows.

- Any invariants in each model should be ANDed with both pre- and postconditions written in that model.
- If the requirement has several pre- and postcondition pairs—which may come from different supertypes—they should be ANDed in pairs ((pre1=>post1) AND (pre2=>post2)) to give an overall requirement postcondition. If the pre- and postconditions are not from supertypes and are subject to joining (see Section 8.3.4, Joining Action Specifications), compose them accordingly.
- The implementation's vocabulary should be translated to the specification's by using retrieve functions as in Section 6.4, Spreadsheet: Model Refinement.
- The precondition of the requirement should imply the precondition of the implementation. For example, if the requirement says, "This operation should work whenever Cell c contains a Number," then an implementation that works "whenever c is non-Blank" is fine because it is always true that "a Cell contains a Number => it is not Blank."
- The postcondition of the implementation should imply the postcondition of the specification. (Notice that this is the other way around from preconditions, a feature called *contravariance*.) So if the implementation claims that "this oper-

ation adds 3 to the Cell's value" whereas the requirement is more vague ("this operation should increase the Cell's value"), then we are OK, because it is always true that "3 added to value => value increased."

6.7.3.2 Comparing Operation Specs with Code

More likely, you will have to compare your specification with code (whether you've written it yourself or someone else has). Again, the most effective strategy is to write test harnesses, as we discussed before.[8]

In debug mode, preconditions should be written as tests performed on entry to an operation; postconditions are tested on the way out. The only complication is that, because postconditions can contain @pre, you must save copies of those items while checking the precondition. (Or you may be lucky enough to be using a language with this facility built-in.) The main caveat is to ensure that the pre- and postconditions don't themselves change anything.

If you prefer the Deep Thought approach, many (unfortunately, rather academic-sounding) books have been written on how to document this kind of refinement (for example, [Jones] and [Morgan]). The following summarizes the key points in a pragmatic way.

- For sequences of statements separated by a semicolon (;), it is useful to write assertions (conditional expressions that should always be true) within the sequence. This helps you see how the requirements are built up with each statement and can be a useful debug tool if the expressions are actually executed. The assert macro provided with C++ has parallels in other languages.

- Where an operation is called within a sequence, its precondition should be satisfied by the assertion immediately before it; the assertion after it should be implied by its postcondition.

- If statements ensure preconditions for their branches. The postcondition of the whole thing is an OR of the branches:

  ```
  if (x>0) z= square_root(x)        // pre of square_root is 'x>=0'
      else z=square_root(–x);
  assert z*z == x  or  z*z == –x
  ```

- In a loop, it is useful to find the loop invariant: an assertion that is true every time through the loop. It works as both pre- and postcondition of the body of the loop. Together with the condition that ends the loop, it ensures the required result of the loop. For example, consider this routine:

  ```
  post sort queue into order of size
  {   int top= queue.length;
      while (top > 0)
      invariant everything from top to end of queue is sorted,
  ```

---

8. For more on the Deep Thought approach, see [Morgan88] or [Jones86]. For more on executing pre- and postconditions, see [Meyer88].

```
//    and everything before top is smaller than everything beyond top
{     post move biggest of items from 0 to top along to top
      { ... to be written ... }
      top = top −1;
}
// top == 0 and everything from top to end of queue is sorted
}
```

Here, the invariant separates the queue into two parts: unsorted and sorted. The top pointer moves gradually downward, until the whole queue is in the sorted part.

If you were called to review such a refinement, you should check that (1) the claimed invariant is bound to be satisfied on first entry to the loop (it is satisfied here, because there's nothing beyond top); (2) if the invariant is true before any iteration of the body, it is bound to be true after; (3) the invariant and the exit condition together guarantee the effect claimed for the whole thing (true in this case because when top gets to 0, the whole queue must be sorted).

Notice that a postcondition has been written to stand in for a chunk of code not yet finished; we are simply using known techniques to defer details, except that now we're using them in code. (How would you design it? What would be the loop invariant?)

6.7.3.3   Operation Conformance and Action Conformance: Differences

Both operation and action conformance show how a single action with an overall goal is released by a composition of smaller actions, and some of the techniques for establishing the relationship are the same. The differences are summarized in Table 6.2.

6.7.4   Operation Conformance: Summary

Operation abstraction makes it possible to state what is required of an object without going into the detail of how the requirements are met. The implementation will use whatever constructs are provided by the programming language, such as sequences, branches, and loops; it will choose its own set of variables and stored data. There are well-defined rules for verifying that the implementation meets the specification or, more pragmatically, systematic techniques for instrumenting and testing the implementation.

Table 6.2   Operation Conformance versus Action Conformance

Operation Conformance	Action Conformance
An operation begins with an invocation: a function call or message send. This prescribes the limits on the sequence of events that should happen. We know from the beginning of the sequence which operation we're dealing with	An action is identified only in retrospect. If someone selects some goods in a shop, it will often be the first step to a sale; but the shopper might decide not to buy or might walk off without paying; so it turns out not to have been a sale but a theft. An action is a name for an effect. We can provide a protocol of smaller actions whereby it can be achieved, but the same actions may be composed in some other way to achieve something different.
When we design a procedure that refines an operation spec, we can focus on the receiving object and devolve subtasks to other objects we send messages to. If we change the design, we are changing this one object.	When we design a protocol of actions that satisfies an action spec, we focus not on any one participant but on the interactions between them. If we change the refinement, we affect the specs of all the participants.
Refining an operation is like designing a computer monitor: You have the specs of the signals that come along the wires and their required manifestations on the screen. Your work is to define the insides of the box; you may involve others by specifying parts you will use inside. Your design talks about the specifications of the constituent parts and how they are wired together.	Refining an action is like devising an interface standard for the signals on a video connection. You must involve all the designers who might make a box to go on either end of this connection—or at least all those you know at the moment. You must agree to a specification for what is achieved and then refine it to a set of signals that, in some parallel or sequential combination, achieves the overall required effect. You cannot talk in terms of any thing inside the boxes, because they will all be different; you can only make models that abstract the various boxes and talk in terms of the signals' effects on them.
To test an operation refinement, you push a variety of signals in, from different initial states, and see whether the right responses come out. There are various ways to use a precise specification to generate test cases that reasonably cover the state space of input parameters and initial state.	To test an action refinement, you must see whether it permits a variety of different combinations of participants to collaborate and achieve the desired effect. Interoperability is the general goal. The goal here is to explore each sequence of refined actions that should realize the abstract one—a much larger, sequential state space. Scenarios defined during modeling form a useful starting point; the specs can be used to systematically get broader coverage than just the scenarios.

6.8   *Refinement of State Charts*

In the Catalysis interpretation, the states in a state chart are Boolean conditions and the transitions are actions. As such, actions may take time; there is a gap between one state going false and the next state lighting up (rather like the floor indicator in many elevators).[9] Most state charts focus on a given type, and the states are defined in terms of its attributes.

---

9. We prefer our state charts like this, because they are easier to reconcile with the actuality of the software compared with *instantaneous event* models; and they tie in better with the actions. In some notations, they would have an event representing the start of an action and another for the end of it, and a state in between representing the transitional period. But at a given level of abstraction, we do not know enough to characterize the intermediate state, because that is defined only in the more-detailed layers of the model.

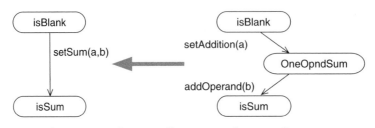

Figure 6.39 Intermediate states due to refinement.

A Cell can contain a Blank, a Number, or a Sum. Let's consider the abstract setSum action, which should set the target cell to be a sum of two others, shown on a simple state chart in Figure 6.39. We would have to wait for the user to enter two operands before the transition to a Sum was completed. During the interval, the implementation is in no state that the abstract spec understands. The addition of the intermediate state is a valid change specifically in a refinement.

Each state in a state chart should be documented with a condition stating when it is true. In this case, isBlank corresponds directly to the attribute of that name; isSum == (content : Sum) ("the content attribute is of type Sum").

Because states are Boolean attributes, retrieving a state is no different from retrieving any model. The abstract states can still be seen in the refinement, although you must use the abstraction functions to translate from sumpart to content (Figure 6.20). Also, the extra state must be given its own definition.

6.8.1 Distinguishing States of Spec Types from Design Types

Considering the GUI for a moment, it may be useful to make a small state chart about whether or not a Cell is selected (see Figure 6.40). The Cell type forms part of the spreadsheet's model; the actions are those of the spreadsheet as a whole (see Section 3.9.4, State Charts of Specification Types). The states diagram applies simultaneously to every Cell in the model. Any Cell that is the subject of a select operation gets into the selected state; all others go into unselected, as defined by the guard.

To accommodate the new bit of information, we could add an optional link to the model. It is then easy to write a definition for the selected state (see Figure 6.41). Now, when we come to the implementation, the pointer to the currently selected Cell comes from somewhere in the GUI, and, because the pointer is one-way, the Cell itself does not know that it is selected. (In fact, it would be common in an MVC design for the implemented cell to remain unaware of many such changes in UI state.) Is the original state diagram still valid if the Cell has no information about its state of selection (see Figure 6.42)?

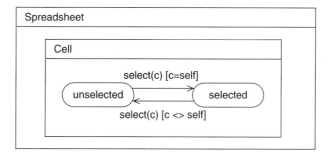

Figure 6.40 Cell selection state chart.

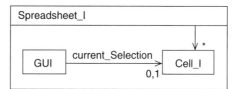

Cell:: selected = (~currentSelection <>null)

Figure 6.41 Link for indicating cell selection.

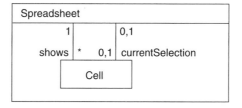

Figure 6.42 Implementation: Does a cell still have
a "selected" state?

Yes, the state diagram is valid. For one thing, the state diagram is of a Cell and not a Cell_I; and the abstraction function to Spreadsheet from Spreadsheet_I should yield all the information about each Cell. In any case, it would still be valid to draw that diagram for a Cell_I. We need only define the state with a little more imagination—something like this:

Cell :: selected = (there is a Spreadsheet_I si, for which
si.gui.current_selection = self)

The there is means in practice that you must search around the object space until you come to a Spreadsheet and try it for that property; but we said that specification functions need not execute efficiently to be meaningful.

6.8.2   Other State Chart Refinement Rules

If your project uses state charts extensively, you may wish to look at {Cook94], where a complete set of rules for refining state charts is provided.

6.9 *Summary*

The various kinds of abstraction make it possible to discuss the essentials of a specification or design without regard to the details and to define systematic approaches to verifying that an implementation does what it is supposed to do.

Catalysis provides a coherent set of abstraction techniques and also provides the rationale to relate more-detailed accounts to the abstractions and to document the conformance with specific descriptions.

The justification associated with a refinement can be formal or informal; it could even simply say, "Joe said this will work." The verification techniques can be applied in varying degrees of rigor, from casual inspection to mathematical proof. In between, there is the more cost-effective option of making refinements the focus of design reviews and basing systematically defined test code on the specifications (see Figure 6.43).

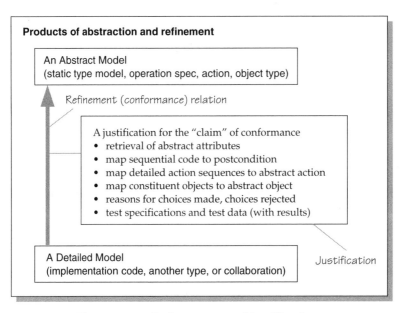

Figure 6.43   Refinements and justifications.

6.10 *Process Patterns for Refinement*

Following is a set of high-level process guidelines for applying refinement techniques.

- *Pattern 6.1, The OO Golden Rule (Seamlessness or Continuity)*: This shows how to achieve one of the most important benefits of objects: a seamless path from problem domain to code.
- *Pattern 6.2, The Golden Rule versus Other Optimizations*: This is the pattern to use when stringent requirements about reuse, performance, or flexibility keep you from maintaining the most straightforward continuity to code.
- *Pattern 6.3, Orthogonal Abstractions and Refinement*: Sometimes the most dramatic simplifications and flexibility come by adopting a whole new view of domain terms (e.g., spreadsheets, cells, and formulas can support accounting, inventory tracking, and baseball scores).
- *Pattern 6.4, Refinement Is a Relation, Not a Sequence*: Do not make the common mistake of thinking that refinement means top-down development; it is a fundamental relation between different descriptions regardless of which one was built first.
- *Pattern 6.5, Recursive Refinement*: The ideas of refinement apply at all levels, from describing organizations and business processes to program code. This means that it can form the single consistent basis for traceability.

Pattern 6.1   The OO Golden Rule (Seamlessness or Continuity)

In ths pattern, you build a system that clearly maps to a model of the problem or real world and keep it that way (also called *continuity* or *seamlessness*).

Intent

An object-oriented design is one in which the structure of the designed system mirrors, to the extent possible, a well-chosen model of the world in which it works. Many of the advertised benefits of object technology come from this principle. It is made somewhat easier because object-oriented languages provide mechanisms that roughly simulate the real world's dynamic interaction between state-storing entities; object technology has strong roots in simulation techniques and languages (such as Simula). Objects have a strong relationship to the artificial intelligence (AI) subculture's *frames*, which are units of an agent's understanding of the world around it.

Considerations

Truth and Reality. You must begin by making a model of the real world. But what does *real* mean?

- One person's view of reality will be different from another's. There are numerous views of reality. Many of them may be self-consistent but may be cast in terms different from those of others. It is important that the model of each class of user be clearly reflected in the system as the user sees and uses it.
- There are numerous ways to use the notation to model the same set of ideas.
- While constructing a model, you will ask and resolve many questions that have never previously been resolved. This is a good thing, but you must be aware that by forcing precise and consistent descriptions of reality you are actually constructing reality and not passively discovering it. And again, the various interested parties will have varying views on what the answers should be.

Compromise with Practicality. The design that mirrors the users' concepts most closely is not always the most efficient, and it sometimes takes significant factoring in design to achieve flexibility. Compromises must be made, and there is an architectural decision about how far to do so. Fortunately, this can be taken to different degrees in different parts of the design; see Pattern 6.2, The Golden Rule versus Other Optimizations.

Strategy

Build and Integrate Users' Business Models. See Pattern 14.2, Make a Business Model. This is always a good starting point. On a typical software project, an astonishing number of downstream problems can be prevented by clarifying and building a clear vocabulary of the problem domain.

Cast System Requirements in Terms of the Business Model. See Pattern 15.7, Construct a System Behavior Spec. Particularly if the domain model has been clearly defined, system requirements can be discussed, understood, and decided far more precisely.

Choose Classes Based on the Business Model. To maintain traceability, deviations forced by performance, current or planned reuse, and other constraints should be local and clearly documented as refinements.

Maintain Development Layers (Business Model to Code) in Step. This strategy clearly conflicts with the usual short-term imperative of getting changes done immediately and directly in the code; but a clear separation of domain, system, and technology infrastructure descriptions (and code) helps localize changes, and experience shows clear, long-term benefits. Furthermore, because the documents are more abstract as you go up the tree, you come to a point where there is no change. Performance improvements, for example, usually change the code but perhaps not the requirements or the model in which they are expressed; or some design refactoring for reuse and flexibility may have no effect on the external spec, affecting only the refinement and its associated mapping.

Build Many Projects on the Same Model. A problem domain model is useful across more than a single project. But don't take this as a reason for perfecting a model before building your first system; see Pattern 14.2, Make a Business Model.

Benefits

Many of the advertised benefits of object technology come from this pattern.

- The resulting system relates better to the end users because it deals in the terms they are familiar with (assuming a reasonable problem domain model) and traces back to the business tasks they perform.
- Making changes is easier because users express their requirements in terms that are easy to trace through to the model and implementation. In a good problem domain model, things are factored so that common requirements changes do not cause massive model updates; the design should reflect this structure.
- The same business model can be used for many projects within the same business. As a result, more of the code can also be generalized and reused.

Pattern 6.2   The Golden Rule versus Other Optimizations

Consciously tradeoff performance, reuse, and flexibility optimization against entirely seamless design; document a refinement clearly whenever you must stray significantly from a pristine domain model.

Intent

In an ideal sense, the structure of the design could be based directly on a model of the world in which it works (to an appropriate extent). Performance, flexibility, and reuse constraints sometimes dictate against naive continuity, and elements from architectural design down may need to differ from a real-world model. The question is how to balance the goals of seamlessness, maintainability, reuse, and tuned performance.

Considerations

Will the program code be object-oriented? If it is, should we choose the classes directly from the domain model or based on design patterns or following the gut instincts of the project guru?

Mirroring a good model of the world in your code is good for simulations: Every time you change your picture of the world, you can more easily find which parts of the simulation code to change. This is how OOP originated with the Simula language.

The flexibility provided by polymorphism and dynamic binding in an OOP language, combined with a well-factored design, makes it better suited for writing any kind of program whose requirements change regularly—that is, almost all of them. (It's been estimated that 70% to 80% of total spending in a program's life cycle is in the maintenance phase after first delivery.) However, we gain this flexibility at the cost of making many extra decisions about which object should take responsibility for each small part of the job—something that is often not obvious from the problem domain model itself—and at the cost to runtime performance of all those objects passing control to one another. The former can make a difference in initial project development time; the latter can make a big difference in performance-critical real-time control software such as communications or avionics.

Moreover, there is little flexibility and reuse at the level of individual problem domain objects. Each object plays roles in different collaborations; a far more likely unit of reuse is the collaboration or its manifestation as a framework in code (see Chapter 11, Reuse and Pluggable Design: Frameworks in Code).

Code that makes miraculous-seeming leaps from the domain vocabulary into design decisions, even if based on the best gut instincts, will not retain its intended form for long.

Flexibility comes from decoupling: making components independent of one another. Optimization for performance generally means that pieces of code that were ideally decoupled become dependent on one another's details. So the more you optimize, the more you mix concerns that were independent before. In the extreme, you end up with a traditional monolithic program.

Strategy

Make an early architectural decision about how much you will tradeoff performance, seamlessness, reuse, code flexibility, and so on. If your clients shout for little functional enhancements every day (something that is typical for in-house financial trading software), optimize the underlying communications and infrastructure but leave the business model pristine. But if your software will be embedded in a million car engines for 10 years, optimize for performance.

Eighty percent of the execution is done by 20% of the code. Design your system in a straightforward object-mirroring way and then abstract and re-refine the pieces that are most critical to performance. (Or analyze a prototype and worry about the execution hotspots.) See Pattern 15.12, Avoid Miracles, Refine the Spec.

Buy faster hardware and more memory. They're much cheaper than programmers.

Benefits

An OO program is one that is refined from an OO design. A clearly defined refinement carries a retrieval that relates it to the abstraction even when the design has been optimized from a real-world abstraction.

Pattern 6.3   Orthogonal Abstractions and Refinement

Sometimes the greatest improvements in reuse and flexibility come by adopting a significantly more abstract (or even orthogonal) view of problem domain terms. Use refinement and frameworks so that you don't lose traceability to domain terms.

Intent

Gain flexibility by using orthogonal abstract views of different parts of the problem, but retain traceability to the straightforward domain terms.

Considerations

You get only so much reuse and flexibility by adopting the most straightforward model of the problem domain. The terms have evolved to be specific to that domain and may be inconsistent with terms used elsewhere.

Consider a couple of examples. First, in an application for supporting a seminar business, we need to schedule instructors and rooms for seminar sessions; track customer preferences and trends to better target our marketing efforts; and maintain a stock of course materials, producing new ones as needed. Although we could analyze this problem in its simplest domain terms, there would be much more opportunity for reuse if we characterized the problem in an abstract, orthogonal way as follows: Assign resources (instructors, rooms) to jobs (seminar sessions); track customer trends for different products (seminar topics); and maintain a just-in-time inventory of items (course notes) of our products (seminar topics). Note that our requirements are now much more generic, merely specialized to our domain specifics. (This example is worked out in more detail in Section 11.4.1.1, Combining Model Frameworks.)

Second, in an application for processing credit cards at a gas station, there are many variations in choices (paying outside versus paying inside), in product offerings (optional car wash or discount items), and in sequences of interactions with the user and the remote financial hosts. We could tackle some of this variability by appropriate design of types and class hierarchies; however, we gain the biggest increase in flexibility when we recognize that we should reify the steps in the card processing (product offerings, payment authorization, amount entry) from the sequences in which these steps are executed. If we build an explicit representation of sequencing and other dependencies, we could even use a generic Petri Net interpreter as an abstract machine for handling arbitrary sequences and dependencies.

However, code that makes miraculous-seeming leaps from the domain vocabulary into design decisions, even if based on the best gut instincts, becomes irreversibly deformed by the first few modifications made by a new programmer.

Strategy

Do not lose sight of the domain terms even in your code. Use refinement to maintain traceability even as your code becomes more decoupled and reusable. Wherever possible, recast the problem domain descriptions themselves using these orthogonal and more abstract views; remember, you are actively constructing a model of reality and not passively discovering it. Use frameworks (see Chapter 9, Model Frameworks and Template Packages) to explicitly document the mapping from domain terms to terms and roles in the abstract problem descriptions.

Pattern 6.4   Refinement Is a Relation, Not a Sequence

Use refinement for any combination of top-down, bottom-up, inside-out, or assembly-based development; it does not imply sequential top-down development.

Intent

Refinement results in realistic deliverables for each development cycle depending on what development process is most suited to the project.

Considerations

We have a clear picture of the ideal refinement relations from business model to code. How is this related to the actual series of cycles of the development process on a particular project?

Clearly, there are some dependencies between prior and consequent phases. Even the most unregenerate hacker does not begin to code without at least a vague idea of an objective (well, not many of them, anyway!) .

But it is obstructive to be overly concerned about completing all the final touches on any phase before going forward to the next. It is a well-known demotivator, paralyzing the creative processes, and is often an excuse for people who don't know how to proceed.

But if too much is undertaken without clear documentation of the aims of each phase (as determined by the outcome of the preceding ones), all the usual misunderstandings and divergences will arise between team members and between the original target and the final landing.

In any case, it's an illusion that every design is determined entirely by the requirements. It's often the other way around. When technologists developed the laser, it was not so that they could make CDs. Few of us knew that we needed musical birthday cards before they were provided for us. We build and use what we have the technology for, and this will become increasingly relevant in a world of component-based development.

Strategy

The typical deliverables of a development cycle (see Pattern 15.13, Interpreting Models for Clients) are *not* individual completed documents from the linear life cycle. More usually, they might be first draft requirements; GUI mockup; client feedback; second draft requirements; critical core code version 1; requirements modified to what we find we can achieve; . . .

Get It 80% Right. To avoid "analysis paralysis"—the tendency to want to get a perfect business model, requirements, or high-level design before moving on— deliberately start the next phase when you know its precursor is still imperfect. Move to the next phase as early as you like but no later than when you estimate there's still about 20% to finish. (Personal wisdom about the exact percentage varies, of course.) The results from the next phase will in any case feed back to the first.

Bottom-up and Top-down Approaches. Our approach to refinement between spec and design (and other layers of documentation) in no way constrains you to begin with the requirements and end with the code. Called upon to write an article, you need not begin at the beginning. Instead, you edit the whole in any order you like as long as it makes sense when you've finished. Similarly, the context of a project may call for a different route through the method (see Section 13.2.1, Multiple Routes through the Method).

In the same way, consider the various documents of a development to be elements in a structure that you are editing (see Figure 6.44). The goal of the project is to fill in all the slots in the structure and make them all consistent when finished. Feel free to begin at the bottom, if appropriate, and don't worry if things get inconsistent en route provided that they come back in line at some planned milestone.

Coding Can Even Help with Analysis. People know what they *don't* want better than they know what they *do* want. (Ask any parent!) When you put a finished system in front of customers, they'll soon tell you what changes they need. And the system will alter their mode of work, so their requirements will change anyway. To circumvent some of this, deliver early a slide show or a prototype or a vertical slice—whatever will stimulate the imagination. OO can be great for this incremental design, but it must be a clear part of the plan.

- What information will be extracted and fed back to analysis from an early delivery? (And how will the information be obtained? Is the planned delivery adequate to expose that information?)

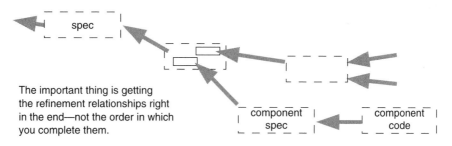

Figure 6.44   Refinement is a relation and not a sequence.

- What will happen to the code? Is it a throwaway? If not, all proper documentation and reviews must be applied. Often, prototypes are not exposed to proper QA—and then are incorporated into the real thing!
- What will happen to the other design documents? The design material usually represents more valuable work than the code itself, so you can build a prototype as a throwaway even in some other language. This assumes that, as a reader of this book, you're documenting the design in some form other than the code.

Pattern 6.5   Recursive Refinement

Establish a traceable relationship, based on refinement, between the most abstract spec and the detailed implementation (program code).

Intent

The abstract spec should bear a systematic relationship to the code, and this relationship should be expressed as a series of refinements. Many of these are decompositions, which break the problem into smaller pieces.

We wish to document the outcome of design.

Strategy

• Model separate views. Rather than build a single monolithic model, recognize when there are useful different external views of your component. Model each such view separately so that the model relates seamlessly to that part of the problem domain.

• Compose views into one spec. When designing, it helps to have a single combined spec on which you base your design; then you refine, and map to, only that single specification. Hence, compose your views into a single spec that you relate to your design and implementation.

• Refine the spec using one of the standard refinements. Some refinements are one-to-one; others are decompositions. The latter split the spec into several separate ones, each of which can be dealt with as a separate goal.

• Document each decomposition with a refinement that states how the constituents work together to fulfill the abstract spec.

• Each decomposition divides the job into a set of constituents, each with a specification that can be fulfilled separately. The same principles can be applied recursively to its design. Thus, you can specify an entire application as a type and then decompose it into internal collaborating components. If the components are of a nontrivial size, recursively model and specify each of them as a type.

• "Basic design" shortcuts some of the recursive refinement process by going straight for a set of decisions that accept the specification types as protoclasses. A judicious combination of basic design, subsequent optimization, and recursive refinement is practical for many projects.

• Use frameworks to build specifications and designs as well as refinements between the two. Frameworks (see Chapter 9, Model Frameworks and Template Packages) capture recurring patterns of types, collaborations, and refinements. Used properly and with the right tool support, frameworks let you document the main refinement decisions in a single place rather than duplicate them each place they are used. A single framework named Cache could have the design and refinement rationale independently of the many different contexts in which it is used.

Result

The result is a design that is traceable through the refinements.

Chapter 7   Using Packages

A *package* is a container for any piece of development work you want to treat as a unit. Packaging is concerned with the dependencies between pieces of design work, which package diagrams help expose. Good packaging reduces dependencies and is fundamental to good reusable design.

The principal relationship between packages is *import*. When you start a new piece of work, you almost never work from scratch; there are at least all the primitive definitions (the numbers and so on). More usefully, you write an implementation against a corresponding specification package, and you write that specification by importing a corresponding domain model package.

This chapter discusses packages, the relationships between them, and how to use them effectively. Section 7.1 introduces packages and explains how a package contains names and formal definitions within an informal narrative structure.

Packages are built by importing other packages and by extending the imported definitions (Section 7.2). This import facility can be used to effectively partition development work in several useful ways (Section 7.3) as well as to decouple units of work from changes in others (Section 7.4).

Packages themselves are subject to packaging as nested packages (Section 7.5), and a special form of encapsulation and decoupling applies to them (Section 7.6). When packages have multiple imports, you must be careful about what it means to import like-named elements from two sources and sometimes must explicitly rename some elements (Section 7.7).

Packages also serve as encapsulated units of builds and can help with versioning and configuration management (Section 7.8). Section 7.9 compares packages to the package-like constructs found in some programming languages.

7.1 *What Is a Package?*

The package is the basic unit of development product—something you can separately create, maintain, deliver, sell, update, assign to a team, and generally manage as a unit. A package might contain any logical unit of development artifact: types, classes, compiled code, frameworks, patterns, documentation, tests, and so on.

In the Catalysis model, all development work creates or modifies a package even if you don't give it a name. The package is the collection of all the names you define and all the statements you make about them, whether in diagrams or in text form. All the modeling work you do—drawing types, creating associations, specifying an operation—is done within a package.

Every package (except for some extremely basic ones) imports other packages. Import is analogous to Java's import or C's include. It means that all the definitions and statements in the imported package are usable within the importing package.

A package is its own "world": when working in a package, you can know or believe only what is within it—either introduced directly in the package or known in a package that it imports. You cannot refer to other things. In that sense, a package represents a unit of knowledge or belief. When you model a type with an integer attribute, you are using the imported package that defines what you know, and can say, about integers. When you write a C struct with an integer field within a package, you also import the package that defines what a C struct and its fields mean.

For example, it's common in large enterprises to make a model of the business domain—let's say, a telecommunications company with Calls, Circuits, and so on. When you are writing the requirements for a billing system for the company, you naturally use some of these terms, and you want to ensure that you use the same names for the same concepts and with the same relationships between them—as well as add extra material specifically about accounts. So your Billing Requirements package will import the Telecoms Business package; so will the Network Management package and others, thus ensuring that terms used throughout the company have the same meaning. (We have seen such companies in which wildly inconsistent vocabularies were used in various departments—until they got sensible and wrote a business model.)

Then when you design components of the system, you can import the relevant requirements model and use the types it defines.

But even a package that doesn't import anything locally defined uses names such as +, 42, true, integer, and and—all the primitives as well as the relationships they have with one another. These, too, are defined in packages.

User-defined models, such as design patterns, frameworks, and other architectural elements, are also defined in their own packages. The set of definitions composing each model is grouped into a package and can be used by many others. Even attribute definitions, associations, and refinement relations are defined within a package.

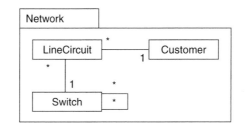

Figure 7.1   Basic telecomm package and contents.

7.1.1   Notation

A package is drawn as a box with a tab containing the package name. Figure 7.1 shows one that defines the basics of a telecommunications business. Inside the box, you can draw some or all the definitions the package contains. However, packages can be quite large, so this approach is often impractical. Tools allow you to click on the package symbol and browse the collection of type diagrams and so on that the package contains. In a document, you can make each major section, and the whole document, correspond to a package; you can structure subsections around actions, subject areas, nested or imported packages, or something else.

Within textual descriptions, it is sometimes useful to be explicit about which package originated the definitions you are talking about. Using the context symbol as follows means "What follows is part of the Network package" :

package Network :: ...

The package diagram symbol is often used without contents. In this case, many people (and tools) prefer to move the package name from the tab to the main box. This convention is inconsistent but looks nicer.

▶ *package*   A named container for a unit of development work. All development artifacts—including types, classes, compiled code, refinements, diagrams, documentation, change requests, code patches, architectural rules and patterns, tests, and other packages—are in some package. A package is treated as a unit for versioning, configuration management, reuse, dependency tracking, and other purposes. It also provides a scope for unique names of its elements.

7.1.2   What Does a Package Contain?

In the early days of object-oriented programming, attention was focused on the class as the fundamental unit of modularity. But there are other equally valid units of design work. Think of all the different pieces of work you could usefully transmit to a colleague or store in a database; here's a list of things a package might contain.

- Types and classes—specifications and implementations of objects.
- Source or compiled program code.

- Collaborations—partial schemes for object interactions.
- Top-level names of constants, variables, and functions.
- Refinements—documented abstraction relationships between types, collaborations, requirements, classes, and so on. A refinement is often placed in a separate package from the elements it relates by importing those packages into its own, and adding documentation justifying the refinement.
- A group of types or classes that form a coherent set and don't make sense without one another.
- Partial definitions of types or classes described from one user's point of view, with potentially different aspects of each type captured in different packages.
- Useful information about an existing type or class—for example, an observation stating, "Class Bicycle conforms to type WheeledVehicle"—that has not been explicitly stated by the designer of class Bicycle in the package.
- Patterns and frameworks—recurring schemes of types and collaborations that are abstracted into a pattern, optionally including generic implementation code, and then used in many places.
- Requirements—initially informal and then formalized descriptions of what is expected of a system or component.
- Change requests—a common form of requirement.
- Bug reports—with symptoms; hypotheses on the causes; justifications; scenario or test data to reproduce the bug, and so on.
- Modifications to code, including bug fixes, that can override or patch existing code in another package (with certain restrictions ensuring backward compatibility).
- Narrative documentation (or preferably, hypertext) accompanying the model.
- Diagrams—presentations of model elements in various visual forms.
- Other (nested) packages—as a grouping and macro-visibility construct.
- Tests or verification documents—specifications of correct behavior, concrete initialization and test data, expected results, and actual results.

In addition, there are many project-management-related attributes associated with the elements in a package and with packages themselves. These attributes include effort, priority, status, authors, schedules, and so on.

It is a central tenet of our approach that every picture should be translatable into text-based statements, not because you'd ever want to but because that gives it a clear and unambiguous meaning. For the same reason, the text-based notation we use can be translated into a small core syntax. Notice that this is more than a claim to have a clear syntax: It is an unambiguous semantics. So the names, definitions, and statements of a package[1] really carry all the information we will discuss in the rest of this section.

---

1. A package is a many-sorted theory, as in [Larch91] or [Mural91].

A package can contain definitions of constants. It can also contain descriptions of prototypical instances as used in snapshots, scenarios, or interaction diagrams or can even contain a global declaration of a name that refers to a particular object.

In short, the answer to "What can be in a package?" is the same as "What can be in a file?" or "What can be in a document?" A Catalysis package is similar to a package in Java or a namespace in C++; a Catalysis package contains not only code but also specifications and designs and, unlike programming languages, allows for some forms of factoring and then reconnecting partial descriptions.

In short, a package can contain any formal or informal description, program code or model, and textual or pictorial statements (see Figure 7.2).

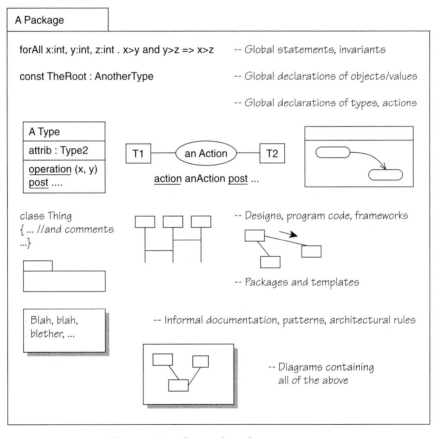

Figure 7.2   General package contents.

7.1.3   Model of a Package

A package consists of at least the following elements.

• *Name*: Its own name should be unique (within a given containing package) and may include a version identifier. A package has a planetwide unique effective name and in that respect is rather like a URL (the Internet addresses typically of the form http://someMachine/aDirectory/aFile). The name should not change once it is published. Conversely, no two published versions should have exactly the same name even if the package contains only a bug fix.

• *Administration*: Publication status, author, version, and derivation history.

• *Declarations*: Names that are declared in this package for types, actions, classes, invariants, constants, and nested packages.[2]

• *Facts and rules*: Statements involving the names—definitions of them (such as constant or type or class definitions) and constraints (such as invariants, pre- and postconditions, and cardinalities of associations). Facts can be stated pictorially—in the forms of all the static type models, action diagrams, and state charts that we have been discussing—or in text.

• *Dictionary*: With every declaration there should be a dictionary entry. Its purpose is to convey informally what the name represents and its relationship to its real world. Whether or not it is presented as a single table, the dictionary is notionally the holder of all the names and their definitions in a package even if the definitions are actually spread around narrative text or within other pieces of syntax.

• *Diagrams and appearances*: The total model defined by a package is split across a number of diagrams. Each model element can have multiple appearances in different diagrams or in fragments of formal text.

• *Notes*: Every diagram can have embedded informal notes. Any syntactical construct—for example, a type, an attribute, a postcondition, a subexpression, or a variable—can also have an informal note. A note can appear in addition to or instead of the more formal statement.

• *Narrative*: The formal contents of the package should be divided into digestible chunks and embedded with text and diagrams in a narrative document. This narrative need not be linear; it can be a web of information, including links that refer to imported packages. All documentation is also part of a package.

7.1.4   The Narrative and the Dictionary

It is an important principle of Catalysis that precise, formal notation be used to complement, structure, and render unambiguous the requirements, design, or

---

2. The very constructs "types," "class," "association," and so on are themselves defined in packages (see Section 9.9, Down to Basics with Templates).

Figure 7.3   Every package has a dictionary and a narrative.

other modeling documents that you write. The more informal, immediately readable material (such as what you are reading) is called the *narrative*. Every package has a dictionary and a narrative, as shown in Figure 7.3.

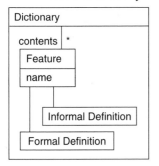

The dictionary is the interface between the informal and the formal. It has an entry for the name of each named *feature* together with both its formal and its informal definitions. Whether or not the dictionary is presented as an actual table (either in printed matter or on screen—a good tool should be able to extract it and present it if you so require), the dictionary is the notional holder of all the features defined within the package.

Features include types, collaborations, actions, patterns, classes, or extensions to classes—anything that has a name and a definition (see Figure 7.4).

The narrative of a package is the important structure of text, pictures, illustrations, anecdotes, footnotes, and all the other apparatus of good explanation directed at helping human readers to understand what you are describing. Embedded in that material are the the formal descriptions of the features you wish to display, just as we have used formal diagrams to illustrate what we are also trying to explain in words. Neither the formal nor the informal would be very good without the other. Informal is too vague; formal is too inscrutable.

Features may have several *appearances* in a narrative, each as part of a different diagram at a location in the text. For example, the type Feature has just appeared in three different places. Rather than display a single wall-sized diagram, it is better to split it into smaller topics and discuss each one in turn, using the formal

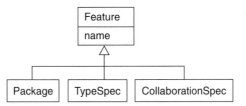

Figure 7.4   Features include anything that has a name and a definition.

notation to back up the flowing, exciting, erudite prose. Each appearance contributes to the overall definition of that feature within the package.

7.2   Package Imports

One package can import another package, and everything stated in the imported package is seen in the importer. It is as though the imported package contents were copied into the importer except that when you update the imported package, the importer also changes; and the importer cannot delete anything that was defined in the imported package; it can only add to it. The example in Figure 7.5 on the next page shows a structure of importing packages. Notice that the arrow goes from the importer to the package being imported. Thus, the Billing and Fault Management packages can both see the definitions of Line Circuit, Switch, and Customer that were defined in the Network package.

Furthermore, every definition is introduced within a package (even if we've forgotten to say which one!). The package identifies the context in which any diagram is drawn. If you draw a diagram on the tablecloth while having a project dinner, the drawing is in a package, and the imports are all the assumptions made by the people at the table about the terms you're using. You all know what a Thingamajig is, because it's in the project's business model (embodied, we hope, in a more conventional medium than the tablecloth).

If you take part in a different project that happens to use the term *Thingamajig* for something in the business, you recognize that you could be using different imports there. And if I write "2+3," you know what I mean because we both import the same package of arithmetic definitions we learned about in school.

Imports are shown as a dashed arrow from importer to exporter—strictly with the stereotype marker «import». An equivalent is to write an import statement inside the importing package (along with any other contents), as in this diagram. A formal text alternative to the import diagram is

Billing
import Network;

package Billing <u>imports</u> Network;
package Fault Management <u>imports</u> Network;
package Network <u>imports</u> Telecoms Stds;

7.2.1   Importing to Extend or Specialize

One package can import another package and extend it. The extending package adds more definitions; its reader knows everything there is to be learned from the original package plus more that the extender has defined (see Figure 7.6). Extension is drawn with a generalization or specialization arrow in UML; but our default meaning, whenever an import is drawn without other qualification, is extension.

In Catalysis you are allowed to make additional statements about an imported model element in the importing package; examples are new attributes, new

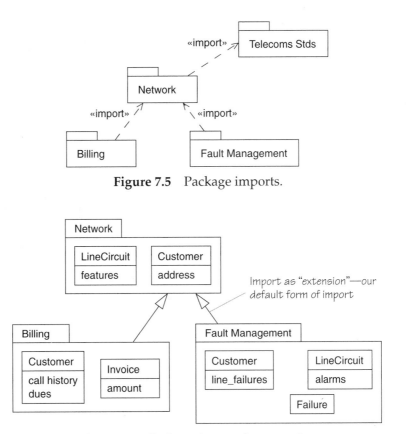

Figure 7.5   Package imports.

Figure 7.6   Package import for extension.

actions, or even new pre- and postcondition pairs for an imported action. In the Billing package you can define call-history and cost information with a Customer; in that case, the Fault Management package may find the history of failures reported by that Customer to be more interesting. This gives us a flexible mechanism[3] for defining multiple views or subject areas: Define a base package that introduces shared terms, such as Circuit and Customer; then define each view as an importing package, extending the definitions of Circuit and Customer for that view. Each view describes somewhat different aspects of an overlapping set of types and actions. Extension corresponds roughly to C++ include, Envy prerequisite, and the mathematical idea of theory extension.

You can draw an approximate analogy between package import and class inheritance. In both cases definitions from one package or class become available to another package or class. With packages, imported types become available;

---

3. The commonly used solution of subtyping does not address this problem.

with classes, inherited methods become available. In addition, with packages, the importing package can define additional properties about the same type; with classes, the inheriting class can extend the definition of a method by adding its own specific processing. One difference is that you can override a method in languages such as C++ and Java and thereby entirely replace the superclass method.

▶ *import, extension*   A relation between packages whereby all names and definitions exported by the imported package are accessible in the importer together with any new elements and added statements about the imported elements that the importer may introduce. A package exports all introduced elements as well as all elements accessible via extension imports. Import by extension is the default rule for import.

Extension has a number of typical uses. It is used for defining a component spec from a business model and for defining variations. In the first case, the component model builds on the definitions of the business model. So once you've read the Networking requirements, you know not only what a LineCircuit is but also how to point at one in your software system.

In the second case, the imported model contains partial definitions; the extenders add the missing pieces in different ways. For example, you might have two slightly different networking requirements: one for small offices and a second one for large offices. They could perhaps contain different collaboration or type definitions at a detailed level but be based on a common underlying abstract model.

It is sometimes useful to prevent a model element—a type, an operation, and so on—from being extended in another package. That element can be marked as «final»: Any importing packages can use it as is but cannot extend it. Specifically, an importer cannot add *new* information pertaining to that element, but new specifications that are *derived* are still permitted (see Section 3.5.2, Redundant Specifications Can Be Useful).

7.2.2   Import for Private Usage

An import for private usage is a private relationship between packages. If a package is used by another package, the user of the first package can see its definitions; but the user's users can't. This arrangement lets the importing package make use of definitions while keeping them hidden from other importers; it is used most commonly to document internal design relationships that should not be visible to others (see Figure 7.7). Malik's Accounts Receivable System can use definitions made in Pat's Billing Design as well as those in Billing Spec but cannot automatically use the contents of Jean's Generic Invoicing Component Spec. To do the latter, another import would have to be declared.

For packages that contain designs, this makes sense: Jean's . . . is used to help implement Pat's . . ., which Malik doesn't need to know about. It's the usual argument for encapsulation at the level of a complete package. For large systems, encapsulation at this level is more useful than it is at the level of individual objects or classes.

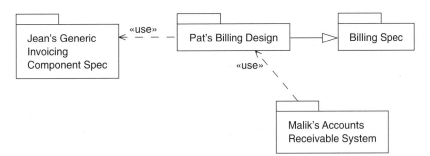

Figure 7.7   Import for private usage.

By contrast, we generally use extension on the level of models and specifications because each package in the chain defines concepts that are used all the way down the line. The basic concept of a Line Circuit will be used in nearly all the packages in a telecommunication business, and it will have been defined up at the level of the Network package; or perhaps ClockBuster extends an industry-standard package that defines a Line Circuit.

Some OO analysis and design tools automatically infer dependencies when you use a class from one package within another package. We prefer to state imports explicitly: You should use the contents of a package only if you explicitly have decided to use it. This policy ensures that we keep conscious control of the coupling between packages.

▶ *import, usage*   A relation between packages whereby all names and definitions exported by the imported package are accessible in the importer together with any new elements and added statements about the imported elements that the importer may introduce. However, elements accessible only via usage imports are not exported by a package.

7.2.3   Rules on Imports

The first rule is that import defines visibility. Every name or assertion you can use either is defined within the package you're working in or comes from the packages it imports. If you want to use something defined in another package, import it. If you do not want to import that entire package, you must refactor it into smaller parts that can be imported separately.

You can think of a package as a complete "world" of information: names, terms, definitions, and rules. The package within which you are working defines all the things you know about and all that is known about them.

Visibility is transitive for extension imports; your children's descendents can see your definitions. It is not transitive for usage imports; only a direct usage importer can see your definitions.

The primary reason for requiring transitivity is that individual types and classes almost never stand on their own. If you depend on a particular class, then you also depend on at least the type definitions of all its method input and output parameters, which could often be in its imported packages; if these definitions change or if a new version is released, your work will need examination.

The second rule is that circular extensions are forbidden. Extensions cannot form a cycle. Because visibility is transitive for extensions, a cycle in imports means that all elements are mutually visible. The entire cycle might as well be in a single package.

Note that there are always some elements that are intrinsically mutually dependent even for their definitions. It is futile to try to break these cycles; just put them into one package.

Usage imports, in contrast, can be circular. It is permitted, but not good practice, for usage imports of designs and implementations to be circular; if they are, it means that no one can use one in the circle without bringing all the others. Often the key to breaking circles is that an implementor should refer to someone else's specifications and abstract type definitions rather than implementations or classes. For example, A's reference to B's implementation is suspect: It would be better to depend only on the requirements spec that B has implemented. (See Section 7.4.1.)

Fourth, there can be no contradictions. An extender can add type or action definitions. It can also add new information about imported types and actions but should not contradict what is already known.

For example, in the early school years we learn a package of arithmetic in which the numbers have well-known operations. In college, we may learn another package that talks about statistical operators. The package does not define any new types. We are still talking about the numbers we have always known; it's just that we now have new information about the same types.

An example of a contradiction would be for one package to give a postcondition $x > y$ and an extender to give the postcondition $x < y$ for the same action.

The rules also allow multiple import. You can import multiple packages; it just brings in all the definitions and statements expressed in all the imported packages. (For more about this, see Section 7.7, Multiple Imports and Name Conflicts.) However, a package should not import very many others. The more packages it depends on, the more likely it is to be affected by any changes.

In general, there is no point in giving someone a package unless he or she also has access to the packages it imports: The meaning of the package is in part contained in the exporters.

7.2.4   Catalysis Import and Dependencies

UML has a relationship between packages called *dependency*, which can be annotated as an import; another relationship is called *generalization*. In Catalysis you must permit and track dependencies, by explicitly deciding to import a package, before you can use any of its contents. This approach is very much like the import and include schemes in programming languages. A general dependency is inferred after the fact, whereas an import is decided beforehand.

Two Catalysis packages may have different definitions (of types, classes, and so on) that happen to have the same name. This is because they may come from different sources. Moreover, using *extension*, an importing package can "say more" about the terms that were imported from another package. UML has another modeling element called *model*; it seems superfluous once you have packages.

⚠ 7.2.5   Virtual and Concrete Packages and Virtual Imports

A *concrete* package is one documented in the UML syntax; *concrete import* is the relationship whereby statements of one concrete package are adopted as part of another. However, we sometimes work from a common set of terms that was never documented as a concrete UML package—for example, some telecommunications standards.

A *virtual* package is a coherent set of ideas, whether written or not, that has not been explicitly documented as a UML package but that we still wish to reference in our work. It might be a consensus in your business or in a standards organization about the meaning of different terms and the properties of the things they refer to. Or it might be a document written in informal language.

For example, one of our clients in the telecommunications industry recently built a business model. In that world, all the manufacturers and operators adhere to several standards. So some of the client's model was determined by what the standards say and will have to be updated whenever the standards change; in other words, it imports the industry-standard virtual packages. So our client's business model contains definitions of the standardized concepts (or at least its interpretations of them) along with all its own definitions. Because there were not yet any UML versions of these standards, we simply consider the standards documents to be part of an implicit virtual package and proceed to "virtually" import it.

So a virtual package is a set of ideas that is represented in some part of your concrete package (see Figure 7.8). And to virtually import means to write the definitions into your own model because they were never formally defined in the package you import. But at least you have documented the set of things you assume. We can also talk about an informal import, in which some other document is referred to in an ad hoc way.

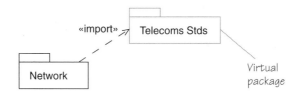

Figure 7.8   Import of virtual package.

It might have been better to have put the standards into concrete packages and thereby clarify which definitions were the client's own and which were imported. Also, should the telecomm standards organizations ever get around to writing UML packages with precise models, it would become easier all around to adopt them.

Virtual imports always raise the question, "Should we make a concrete package of this?" The answer is usually that it would be a good idea. But in some cases you may really use the external ideas only as a prompt but interpret and redefine them as you go along. This is fine as long as you've consciously decided to do so. The disadvantage is that you may be compromising future interoperability with others in the same area; how will you connect to someone else's system that uses those standards? And if you use the same terms for different concepts, you risk confusing people. BluePhone's LineCircuits were subtly different from those of everyone else in the industry, a common stumbling block for "cross the street" recruits.

One of the benefits of using an import (virtual or otherwise) is that you are forced to use a different name for a different concept: Redefinitions aren't allowed, although extensions are fine. (Maybe they should have called them BlueLineCircuits or something.) And one of the benefits of talking about virtual packages is that it makes you consider what the sources of your ideas are or should be and whether you are or should be using the same or different terms for some wider body of ideas.[4]

▶ *package, virtual*   A name that informally denotes (as opposed to actually containing) some set of terms and definitions that you want to refer to from other packages. A virtual package can be "virtually" imported by a "real" package.

7.3 *How to Use Packages and Imports*

Catalysis rules for packages and imports give you much flexibility in factoring your models into separate parts. There are some common idioms for using these facilities.

7.3.1 Separation of Concerns

Packages separate work into areas that can be dealt with individually, with explicit dependencies between them. This arrangement helps control the propagation of changes and the concomitant expense. Therefore, you should divide your work into manageable chunks and put them into different packages. The same principle applies at all levels of development, from business modeling to

---

4. Critics may wish to consider how well we have adhered to this advice with respect to the metamodels of Catalysis and UML.

program code. The typical methods for partitioning contents of packages are as follows.

- *Vertical slices*: This approach reflects the fact that different users have different views of a business or system—for example, accounting, call processing, and network monitoring. They may use different software applications, performing different actions on possibly overlapping sets of objects.

- *Horizontal slices*: This technique separates business models, specifications, and designs down to the level of technical infrastructure and communication protocols. These are different levels of description of the same phenomenon and are related primarily by some form of refinement relation.

- *Different domains*: This partitioning is based on domains such as user interface, persistence, or the primary problem domain.

- *Templates and patterns*: After different concerns have been separated, you often find that the same general schemes can apply in a variety of situations. With careful structuring, they can be made to apply simply by changing names. This is the basis of *model frameworks* based on *template packages,* which allow you to write generic models. The main aspects of most analysis and design patterns can be expressed in this way. These generic schemes can be used to express, among other things, connection protocols between components. We will look at template packages in Chapter 9, Model Frameworks and Template Packages.

- *Translation schemes*: One particularly systematic approach to development encodes a selection of patterns as translation schemes. To move from requirements spec to detailed code, you choose a succession of translations. Template packages can be used to represent translation schemes. Another variety of translation scheme expresses the semantics of a language, such as UML, by defining how it translates to more basic terms. This technique is especially useful for stereotypes, the variable part of the UML notation.

- *Assertions and proofs*: Particularly when you're specifying safety-critical systems, it is important to document all critical information about the beast being built. Sometimes, redundant or derived facts are useful: If "the coolant valve is open whenever temp > 700" and "whenever the coolant valve opens, an alarm rings," it may be worthwhile to explicitly state that "whenever the temperature *rises* above 700, the alarm rings." There are many less obvious properties of a software component, and sometimes the original author is not the one who documents them in the package. A separate package can then be written, not to define anything but only to contain this extra information.

The following sections look at vertical and horizontal partitioning in more detail using models and software applications for a telecommunications business.

7.3.2   Vertical Slices

One way to separate concerns at the business and requirements levels is according to the point of view of different categories of users—a particular kind of subject area. This approach gives you different models of the same types and actions (they must be combined at some stage before you can build a system). You base your views on the high-level actions of those users. Each action needs a model to specify what it achieves and needs additional static and dynamic models to refine it into finer-grained actions.

For example, BluePhone's analysts begin by looking at the business activities of their company. They produce the high-level collaboration diagram in Figure 7.9, which they would like to partition. This is a typical high-level business model obtained by asking people, "What do you do? Whom do you talk to?" Each of the actions shown here refines to a series of many smaller concurrent actions: making a call, chasing a fault, changing service level, making a charge and sending a bill, and so on. The actors refine from departments and groups of people to individual customers, roles within departments, and so on.

These major actions partition the model into vertical slices so that different teams can interview the actors separately. They will get different perspectives on the same types. Finance and Billing will be interested in the customer's bank details; Service Provisioning will want the customer's line characteristics; Fault Management needs alarm information about lines and circuits. All of them may be interested in name and address.

It is useful to establish a central package of shared basic definitions that are known throughout the business—the vocabulary the staff use in their work. The *viewpoint* packages can import this package. Like our earlier Network package, it tends to be a mostly static model (types and attributes).

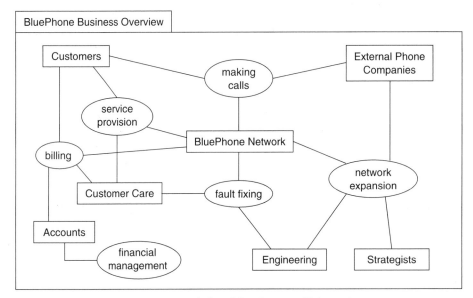

Figure 7.9   High-level business collaboration.

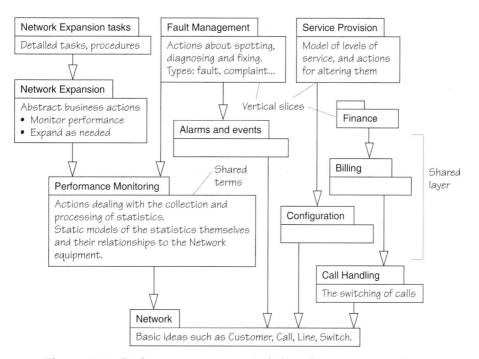

Figure 7.10   Packages segment vertical slices from a common base.

Sometimes another partitioning becomes apparent in a layer in between (see Figure 7.10). For example, BluePhone decided that many Fault Management and Network Expansion tasks are shared between the major activities and that they would have an intermediate layer of shared business model packages for different areas. Performance monitoring, for example, contains a number of actions concerned with gathering and processing connection statistics together with models of the performance figures produced. Strategists use the figures for planning network enhancements, whereas engineers look for unusual changes suggesting malfunctions.

All these packages are concerned with modeling business activities. Some of the actions at the detailed levels may be supported by a software application.

7.3.3   Horizontal Slices

In addition to separating different business areas, it is also useful to separate high-level business models, detailed business tasks, specifications of software supporting those tasks, and technology infrastructure in the software implementation. BluePhone decides to build a new software interface for the Customer Care role in Figure 7.9, integrating service and billing inquiries. Based on the package partition in Figure 7.10, we define a new software requirements package that imports

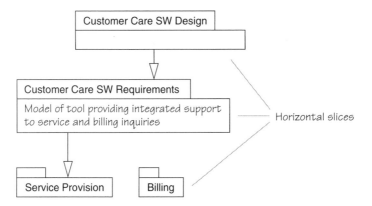

Figure 7.11   Horizontal packages slices: business, software spec,
software implementation.

the packages relating to abstract service and billing business activities; we separately design the application to meet the spec (see Figure 7.11).

BluePhone decides not to build specialized tools for Fault Management or Network Expansion. Instead, more basic tools for Performance Monitoring and Alarms will be used where necessary by the actors involved in the larger tasks of Fault Management and Network Expansion; they will, of course, need to do a larger portion of the abstract business tasks themselves because the tools are not specific to their needs.

The detailed tasks for Fault Management and Network Expansion are now rewritten to use these tools (see Figure 7.12). The old network expansion tasks are replaced by new procedures, but both the old and the new achieve the same high-level aims; the new tools provide a new refinement in which portions of the high-level tasks are performed by software tools. This is a good case for separating the detailed and abstract views of the business. We can then easily deal with the different realizations of the business processes, including those that involve software.

For example, the split_subnet abstract business action might be "Estimate network traffic and then purchase the cheapest equipment combination that can handle that load." In the new business, the worker may perform the estimation with the help of the new PM tools, and select the cheapest equipment combination using a Web browser and desktop calculator.

The two versions of Network Expansion Detailed Tasks import Network Expansion, because it specifies the overall abstract goals that each of them meets. Each includes refinement schemes showing how its detailed actions are composed to achieve these goals, so they must import the package containing the goals. Perhaps the old way of estimating traffic involved watching the lights flicker on equipment and monitoring user complaints, whereas the new way uses the PM tools proactively for the same purpose.

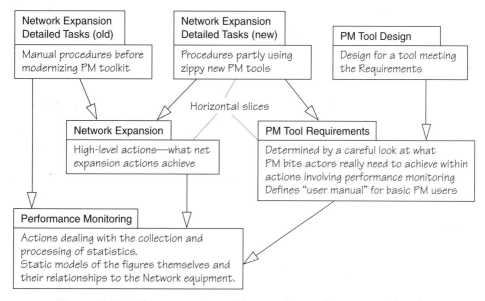

Figure 7.12 Abstract action with reengineered process and tools.

The new Detailed Tasks package also imports the Tool Requirements so as to define how actions involving the tool are used; interactions and scenarios of using the tool to accomplish network expansion tasks are included in this package.

Finally, a Design for the new toolset also imports the Tool Requirements, again because it includes refinement schemes showing how the spec is met.

7.4 *Decoupling with Packages*

You could contain all the work of a project in a single package and import only whatever was determined before you started. But making smaller packages helps manage the work and, in particular, dependencies.[5]

For example, BluePhone's type Call has an understandable meaning without the idea of a Customer Invoice. On the other hand, it would be difficult to understand what an Invoice was about if you didn't know what a Call was. So we can put into one package some core ideas that must be understood by everyone in the company, and then we can build separate packages for different areas of activity. Fundamentals such as Call, Line, and Customer would go in the Phone_Basics package, and then package Billing and package Network_Maintenance would import that. Such separations make it easier to manage the development work and its prod-

---

5. Good package design also helps with reuse and parallel development.

ucts and to reduce the impact of changes in one area on another. In fact, this is the basis of the decoupling that gives OO methods their flexibility.

But the appropriate separations often become clear only when the development work has progressed to some extent. Typically, a modeling or programming project evolves a mass of classes and there comes a point when you realize that order should be imposed on it.

A useful task for a chief designer at this stage is to draw a map of dependencies and then partition them into packages with a good import structure. As we noted earlier, this means that the designer should allow no circularities and that each package should import not too many others. These principles usually imply reviewing the model and applying decoupling patterns to pry apart the pieces.

An effective tactic is to stare at the diagram and think, "Does the idea of a Hat-stand make sense on its own without the idea of a Hat? Or vice versa?" and act on the results (substituting your own types for Hats). Beyond that, the tactics are a bit different for classes and types.

7.4.1 Role-based Decoupling of Classes

In a program (or an implementation model of it), the working elements are classes. Programmers have no difficulty writing a piece of software that is all classes and no types. Indeed, any program that is fairly directly based on a model of the business tends to end up with a class for every business type and not much else. This situation usually needs some remedy.

Remember that types are behavioral specifications of objects, pieces of documentation telling you only what can be seen of an object from the outside; any internal attributes are there only to help express the specification. Classes, on the other hand, are designs for objects, defining internal variables in which information is actually stored as well as program code for the operations. In a program, pure abstract classes (interfaces, in Java) represent types even though most programming languages do not provide for attributes, operation specs, and other apparatus for specification. Programs may also contain partial abstract classes, each of which may stand both to represent a type and to contain a partial implementation of it.

In a program, each object generally communicates with several others. Drawing a dependency diagram between the classes, you end up with many loops. For example, callbacks such as in an observer pattern result in loops. Simplistically, you may decide that each must know about the other, because it sends it a message (see Figure 7.13). In fact, this program is far more coupled than it need be. Each of these classes does not need to know about the "more operations" of the other class; they are used by other correspondents we've not shown here.

The general rule is that, for every class, you can work out a set of types it uses by looking at the messages it sends. LineCircuit needs, not specifically a UsageMonitor, but simply something that understands the notifyEvent(Stuff) message; let's call

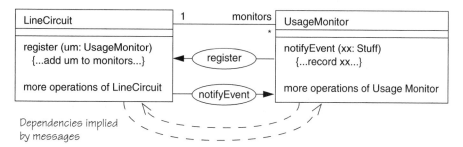

Figure 7.13   Overcoupled class dependencies.

it a CircuitListener. And UsageMonitor—well, maybe it is designed specifically to monitor LineCircuits, but maybe it could also handle a few other things. All it needs is something to which it can send the register(UsageMonitor) message that will send the right messages back.

We can do the same thing for all the other collaborations the two classes take part in. We end up with each class dependent on a set of types that represent only that behavior each class expects of its neighbors. As shown in Figure 7.14, each class implements the types required by its correspondents (here we've drawn classes in bold, types in light). The dependencies are now from each class to the types it implements and the types it uses but not to other classes. At the object level at runtime, nothing looks different: There are still LineCircuit and UsageMonitor objects that send messages to each other. All we've done is to pull apart the design to decouple the code.

This approach enables each class to be in its own package, importing only other types and not other classes. The interface types can be further partitioned into packages with unidirectional dependencies; MonitorableElement is dependent

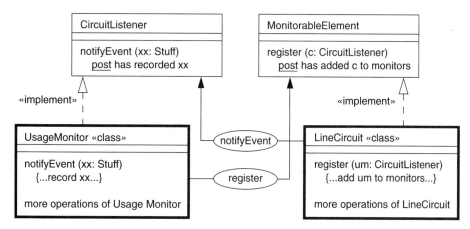

Figure 7.14   Decoupling via types.

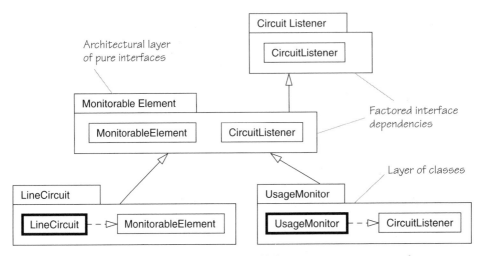

Figure 7.15   Horizontal separation: collaborating types versus classes.

on CircuitListener but not vice versa. The prototypical structure is shown in Figure 7.15. (This is analogous to the usual policy with C++ header files, but stronger: A header should contain only interfaces—that is, pure abstract C++ classes.) However, it may not always be useful to go as far as one class per package. Many classes work closely with each other and will always be interdependent and modified together. Such classes should be in the same package.

To summarize this pattern, extract from each class a definition of the minimal specifications of each type of object it needs to work with. This separates the roles played by each class, and they can be packaged more easily.

It's been suggested that this pattern can form a general design policy, one that is enforced by some research programming languages: that all variables and parameters be declared as types and never as classes. The monitors variable in LineCircuit could not be declared to be a list of UsageMonitors; you would be forced to invent the supertype.

7.4.2   Decoupling in Business and Requirements Models

Let's move back to BluePhone's business model. Let's suppose that after some brainstorming, we arrive at an unstructured draft that includes the fragment shown in Figure 7.16. Although we will discuss everything in this section in terms of type definitions, the same rules apply to all definitions, including actions and nested packages. There are extra complications to deal with for programming classes.

On reflection, we decide that it's possible to understand LineCircuits, Calls, and Switches without LineFaults and Engineers, but not the other way around. We want to separate the material into different packages (see Figure 7.17). As an additional benefit, these packages represent views of different departments in the company.

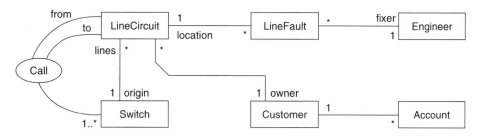

Figure 7.16 Desired overall model.

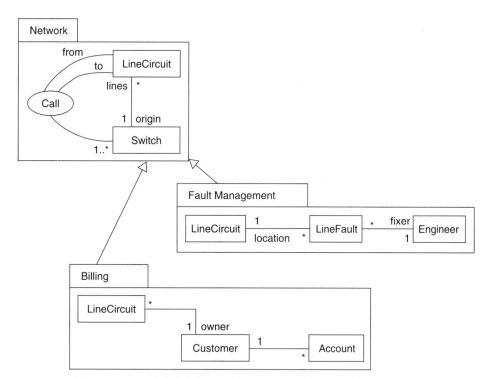

Figure 7.17 Model factored across packages with imports.

To see exactly what each package tells us, we can "unfold" the imports—that is, redraw everything as if it were in one package. For example, Billing unfolds as shown in Figure 7.18. In other words, within the Billing package, we can write postconditions and invariants that refer to LineCircuits, Calls, and Switches, as well as Customers and Accounts. But LineFaults and Engineers are not in scope here.

Within the Network package, we can write statements about LineCircuits and Calls and Switches but not about Customers, Accounts, LineFaults, or Engineers.

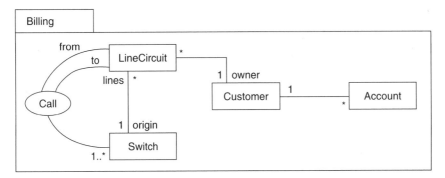

Figure 7.18   Unfolded model in Billing package.

7.5 *Nested Packages*

Any time you name an element (a type, an attribute, and so on) you must also know the scope within which that name uniquely refers to that element. A Cobol variable name must be unique but only within one program. The Internet address systems have managed planetwide uniqueness. A Catalysis type name must also be unique but only within its package. Importing a package gives access to all names and definitions (of types, collaborations, and so on) visible within it.

What about package names themselves? A package can be nested inside one other package. A package name must be unique only within its containing package; each package has an expanded name, prefixed by the expanded name of its container package. This arrangement gives us a flexible scoping mechanism for package names; the nesting lets us deal with a group of packages as a single thing to import, move, version, and so on.

When you import a package, the short names of its nested packages become visible to you; but the names and definitions within those nested packages remain hidden until you explicitly import those packages. You can always refer explicitly to a nested package by qualifying its name with the name(s) of its parent package(s). Nested within a package, the rules about usage and extension between subpackages are the same as usual. A nested package automatically imports its parent package and hence can see its sibling package names and element names and definitions in the parent package (see Figure 7.19).

Importing the containing package gives you access to the names of nested packages; you can then directly refer to those you are interested in by their shorter local names, for example to import them. A package automatically imports its containing package; for example, Billing automatically imports Finance (and, by transitivity, Network Business as well).

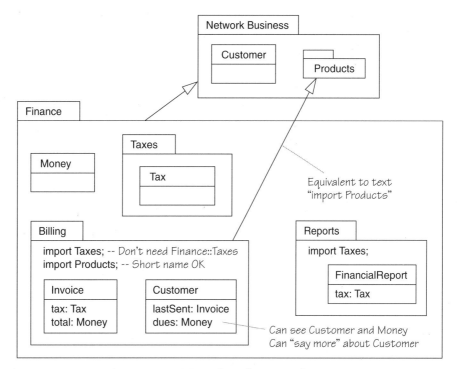

Figure 7.19   Nested packages and imports.

Provided that noncircularity is observed, a package can explicitly import the following.

- Sibling packages (nested within the same container as itself; their names are directly visible, because it implicitly imports its container). For example, Billing can import Taxes.
- Packages nested within those it has imported. For example, Billing can import Products.

Notice that there is always some package containing everything, whether or not it is explicitly delineated. This illustration forms a package, a world of its own. Outside this book, there may well be definitions of things called "Finance," but we know there is no guarantee that what we and they mean by Finance are the same.

▶ *package, nested*   A package whose name is itself scoped within a containing package. The contained package implicitly imports its container.

A nested package scheme could be understood as a convenient abbreviation for an unnested import structure, with additional scoping of nested package names. To translate to flattened form, qualify each package's name with that of its container and then import container packages (see Figure 7.20).

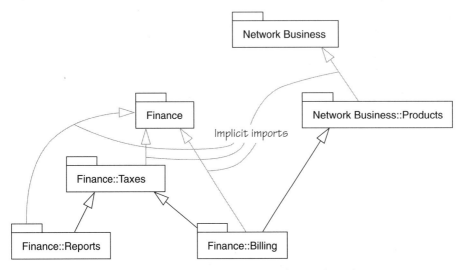

Figure 7.20   Equivalent flattening of nested packages.

7.6 *Encapsulation with Packages*

Let's look at two issues that arise with the use of encapsulation in packages: model decoupling with auxiliary definitions and the use of encapsulation in specifications.

7.6.1 Model Decoupling with Encapsulated Auxiliary Definitions

A type (or action or other definition) from a preexisting package may not directly provide all the definitions that you would like to associate with them.

Suppose in Corporate Management we issue annual reports and need an operation that compares two quarterly FinancialReports using a formula that includes the difference between taxes paid. It would have been nice if the comparison had been defined in the Finance::Reports package, but perhaps the package was written by someone else and we're stuck with it as it is. Hence, the issue of encapsulation for abstract models is similar to that for code except that we can make packages that add new material to any given type and thereby remedy an existing deficit. For example, a FinanceCompare package could import Finance::Reports and add a definition of the comparison (see Figure 7.21). Moreover, FinanceCompare could be a nested package, limiting its visibility and confining the dependency to a limited area.

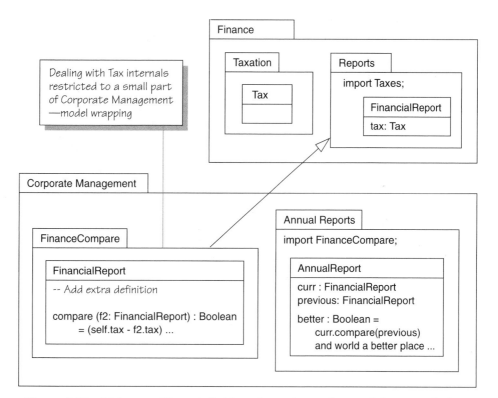

Figure 7.21   Using auxiliary definitions in packages for model encapsulation.

7.6.2   Is Encapsulation Relevant for Specifications?

Encapsulation is not quite as important for abstract models as for implementations. Suppose we implement a position on a surface as a class with (x, y) coordinates and provide operations for moving it, finding the distance from another position, and so on. Later, we decide it would be better, instead of (x,y), to store the position as (distance from origin, angle from x-axis). We must rewrite my operation code; if I did not encapsulate my code carefully, clients that used the (x,y) variables directly would no longer work.

Contrast all this with a model of a position. First we use x, y. How important is it that other parts of the abstract model avoid using the x and y attributes? Suppose we next decide that we'd rather model positions using (r,w). First, this is less likely to happen than with an implementation: there are no issues of efficiency but only considerations of appropriateness for conveying the ideas. Second, we can just as easily leave the old model as it is while defining the new one. All it needs is an invariant to state how the two are related.[6] Now anyone can use whichever model is preferred.

---

6. r*r = x*x + y*y and r*sin(w)=y and r*cos(w)=x, if we have our school math right.

If I get the model wrong, then I will have to really change it rather than only extend it; but in that case, my users would have to change anyway, and encapsulation is no protection. Encapsulation helps protect code changes when the spec remains the same; it is less effective at stopping the propagation of specification changes.

The same thing applies to larger pictorial models with associations. Some methodologists have argued that the tendency to draw models with several types and associations is antipathetic to encapsulation. This would be true if the boxes represented classes and if the lines represented their variables: Each class should be separately designed, independently of the others. But when the boxes are types and the lines merely abstract attributes, the issue of encapsulation is much weaker.

So we support the protest of these folks against those whose diagrams are merely pictures of their code, who simultaneously design parts that rightfully should be independent. We also support the argument against the blind use of tools that convert between pictures and code—and doubly so for people who do so in both directions and claim they have produced abstract analysis and design models.

Properly used, a type diagram is a model—and not an implementation—of a program component. In other words, it is a valid, retrievable abstraction of any correct implementation.

7.7 *Multiple Imports and Name Conflicts*

What happens when you import several packages? The unfolded importer has all the definitions of all the exporters. When the definitions in the different exporters are unrelated, this is simple.

Now suppose the BluePhone analysts extend their interest to CustomerCare and decide that the contents of that package need to refer to both faults and accounts (see Figure 7.22). If CustomerCare is unfolded, are there two copies of the definitions imported from Network? Not really.

Think of each package as a set of logical statements about the various types. If it makes it any easier, remember that every diagram can be translated into a set of statements in text form. The fact that every LineCircuit has an origin that is a Switch is one of the facts stated in Network. By import, the same fact is known within both Billing and Fault Management. By import from them, it is also stated within CustomerCare. If you like, you can think of that fact being stated twice within CustomerCare; but that doesn't make it any truer, nor does it mean that there are two kinds of LineCircuit.

So packages are just lists of facts about named ideas and their relationships. A package can add new facts about a type, about which relatively little is known in

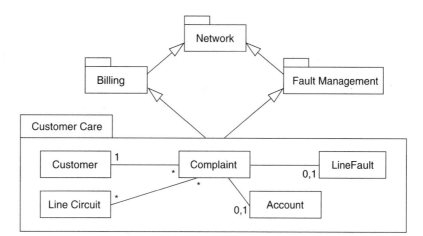

Figure 7.22   Dealing with multiple imports.

an exporter. A student of CustomerCare knows that attached to a LineCircuit there is a Customer, a number of LineFaults, and any number of Complaints: all properties unknown to anyone who has read only the Network package.

Does that make the type CustomerCare::LineCircuit different from Network:: LineCircuit? In a sense, yes; a type is just a list of facts you know about an object, so the CustomerCare version is a more fully defined one. There are many implementations of the Network version that would not satisfy the more stringent requirements of the more developed one. So should we perhaps give them different names? In Catalysis the answer is that "PackageName::TypeName" is the full name of a type. But we use the same type name from one package to another so that we can easily add properties in each importing package, as we've done here.

(An alternative convention would be to disallow additional statements to be made about a type by importers, allowing only that subtypes could be defined. This convention would be needlessly restrictive and would make it complex to define multiple views that could be recombined. Also, it is difficult to avoid seemingly innocent invariants on a new type actually constraining an existing one. So the policy of using subtyping would be difficult to enforce in practice, because such constraints would break subtyping rules.)

What happens if you import two packages that impose contradictory constraints? For example, one package asserts that attribute x must be > 0, and another says x< 0. The result is that you've modeled something that can't exist—something you can talk about but won't find any implementations of, such as orange dollar notes, dry rain, or honest politicians. If it's a model of a requirement, you'll find out when you try to implement it. Moreover, you can construct self-contradictory models within a single package: Whether importing is involved is irrelevant.

7.7.1   Name Mapping on Import

Nested packages alleviate name conflicts. But whenever imports are used a complication arises when two packages are imported from different authors who happen to have used the same name for different things. BluePhone might find it useful to import a ready-made accountancy model; but what accountancy calls an Account (of our company with the bank) might be different from what the Billing department calls an Account (of one of our customers with us). In that case, we don't want the two types to be confused.

Conversely, sometimes we want types with the same name to be identified: Maybe the accountancy package's idea of a Customer is consistent with ours. Or sometimes we want two differently named types to be identified: Perhaps what we call a Customer, an imported package calls a Client.

The first defense against unwanted results is that your support tools should raise a flag when you import a package that contains name conflicts (although this is not needed if the first definition of the name comes from a common ancestor package).

What do we do if we want the two definitions to be separate? In the importing package, one of them should be given a different name. We can show this on a diagram such as the one in Figure 7.23. The annotation [X \ Y] means "Rename X to Y in the importing package (the tail end of the arrow)." It doesn't mean that there is any change in the original package from which the definition comes. In the unfolded Finance package, there is an Account type that means what it does in Billing (perhaps with more information added in Finance) and a CorporateAccount type that means what Accountancy::Account did (again, perhaps Finance adds to it).

A tool should attach to each import a record of these mappings, at least for each name conflict (that does not arise from a common ancestor). When the designer opts to confirm that two types with the same name should be identified, that decision can be recorded with a mapping such as [Customer\Customer]. An interactive tool will also distinguish between a name and the name's string representation.

To deal with the case when different types should be considered the same, we can either write within the importing package an extra invariant such as Client=Customer or we can use renaming. The former approach ends up with two

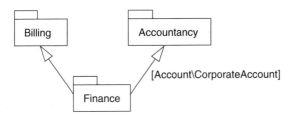

Figure 7.23   Import with renaming.

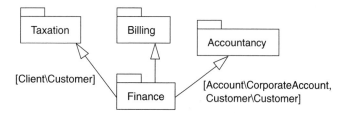

Figure 7.24 Using renaming to combine types.

names for the same thing, and that could potentially lead to confusion; so the latter is preferred. A typical package diagram with renaming is shown in Figure 7.24. Import schemes can also be written in text form:

package Finance   imports   Billing
                  and   Taxation [Client \ Customer]
                  and   Accountancy   [Account \ CorporateAccount,
                                            Customer \ Customer];

It is possible to write package expressions, directly composing large-grain units:

- Taxation [Client\Customer] represents a package that is exactly the same as Taxation but with the names changed.
- P1 and P2 represents a package that has all the statements of packages P1 and P2 and nothing further.
- P1 imports P2 is a Boolean expression stating that every statement of P1 can also be found in P2. You can also write P1 => P2.

Types and packages are only two of the many kinds of elements that can be renamed; other named elements of a package, including nested packages, are also subject to renaming. This facility is used to help create template packages in Chapter 9, Model Frameworks and Template Packages.

7.7.2 Selective Hiding

It is sometimes useful to explicitly render a name syntactically invisible to its importer. Rename to an empty substitute:

import SomePackage [someName \ , anotherName\ ];

Hiding a package hides all the names defined within it.

7.8 *Publication, Version Control, and Builds*

Packages are units that can be passed around and kept in repositories: They are the units of management of development work. It is therefore essential that different versions of a package not get confused.

The contents of a package are always evolving as long as it is being worked on. We will not discuss snapshots of that evolving package or the conveniences of a *sandbox* model that a repository-based tool may provide to insulate multiple users from the interim changes of others.

The Catalysis rule is that a package has an attribute publication state whose type at least includes Editable and Published. Once Published, a package cannot be altered and does not revert to Editable; all the packages it imports must also be Published. All you can do is release a new version or variant.

We also distinguish between versions and variants, two common relationships between packages that are revised after publication.

- A new *variant* may have any change compared with previous variants of packages of the same name. The contents might be completely different. Users know that a new variant may not be compatible with the old one.

- A new *version* is backward-compatible from a user's point of view. The new material is only an extension of the old. If the contents are program code, then the code may be different, but it should at least meet the previous version's spec.

These rules are fairly commonplace and are supported by good version and configuration management tools. Package-level versioning and configuration management can be used to structure the requirements or design for a beta version and a release version (see Figure 7.25). Nested packages (see Section 7.5, Nested Packages) make this approach even more useful, because an entire containing package can be treated as a single unit.

Packages contain everything including business models, change requests, component specifications, source code, bug reports and their test data, changes and bug fixes to code, test specs, concrete initialization and test data, expected results, and even actual results. It becomes simple to write queries to extract what you need in a package.

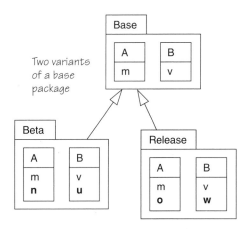

Figure 7.25 Package-level beta and release versions.

"Release 4.5 of the SunshineOS configuration of NetManic, with all changes made to fix bugs Gripe72 and Crib34 that have been approved by QA"

Or it might look like this:

"All interfaces that are believed to be affected by change request RedoItAll81"

A package is also a unit of *build*. Traditionally you perform a build by running various external programs (compilers, linkers, test scripts, documentation tools, and so on) over the contents of the package—to create various derived elements such as executable code and test results—and, recursively, over the contents of imported packages. In Catalysis, each package is associated with a special function called its build function, which, given a BuildEnvironment, creates a resulting BuildObject.

> Package::build (BuildEnvironment): BuildObject

The BuildEnvironment enscapsulates external development environment specifics about doing the builds. This technique keeps system construction modularized and separates the logical function that creates various derived artifacts (such as compiled code) from any specifics of the environment in which the build is taking place. The underlying machinery for evaluating a build function may cache information, perhaps using traditional versioning, time-stamping, or facilities such as make.

Packages can be used to deal effectively with variations and versioning across members of a product family. You build base packages containing either models or framework implementations. Each member of that product family then imports that package. Because a Catalysis package can "say more" about any imported element—including types, actions, and refinements—each product can define a variant suited to its own needs. Configurations and versions are defined by the import structure (see Figure 7.26).

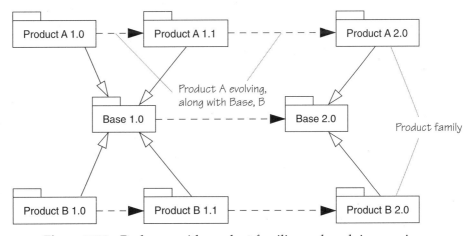

Figure 7.26 Packages with product families and evolving versions.

7.9 *Programming Language Packages*

Programming languages have a variety of forms of packaging.

Java packages can contain any combination of interfaces (types) and implementations (classes). Augmentation and redefinition of classes or interfaces across packages are not allowed. A Java package or group of packages can be used to implement the requirements expressed by a model package. A sensible use of Java packages to clearly layer the architectural design would be that from Section 7.4.1, Role-based Decoupling of Classes.

A C++ include file is a primitive form of package. Header files or groups of them can implement requirements expressed by a Catalysis model package. ANSI C++ has the namespace construct, which provides somewhat better packaging facilities.

In Smalltalk/Envy, an executing system is made up of a series of packages (or "applications") loaded in a specific order, starting with the kernel, which defines all the primitives. Each package can extend existing classes and redefine specific methods.

Smalltalk (in its marketed version) has no types, so types are at best a matter of documentation. A programmer can associate model packages with the code packages or can use conventions to group sets of messages to define named types.

The classes in a code package can be documented as implementing the requirements specified in a model package. If certain principles are followed, this can be preserved even though other code packages may be overlaid. The main points are as follows.

- Each redefinition of a method should satisfy all the specifications, from different model packages, that refer to that method.

- The packages loaded onto a particular target system may be different from those where any one package was designed. Nevertheless, packages that were designed independently should not be allowed to interfere with one another: A package may not redefine any method code that was not redefined as part of its own design.

7.10 *Summary*

Packages are the containers for all development work, from models to documentation to code and test (see Figure 7.27). Packages define units of versioning, configuration management, and reuse.

A package declares names and asserts facts about those names. The declarations and facts may be in pictorial form. A package has an associated dictionary or

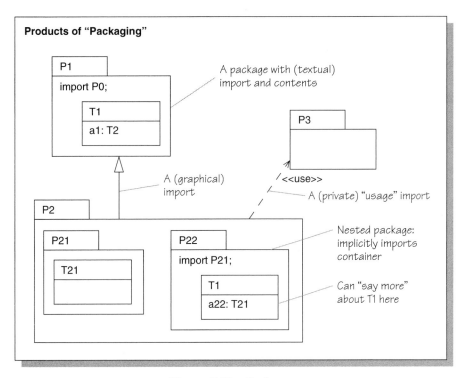

Figure 7.27   Packages.

narrative (or both), which explains the formal assertions in more readable language. The more formal presentations are used to disambiguate the text.

Packages import other packages either to extend them or to make private use of their contents. The import structure is a fundamental part of planning a project.

The purpose of packages is to make explicit the dependencies between different areas of the development work. A variety of patterns can be applied to help separate concerns, including vertical separation of different views, horizontal separation of different architectural and business levels, and code separations of interfaces from implementations.

Chapter 8 Composing Models and Specifications

⚠ When you're building models and specifications, it is important to be able to compose them with a clearly defined and intuitive meaning. This clarity makes reuse and learning easier, because you can understand the whole by understanding the parts and then recombine them in a predictable way. All descriptions in Catalysis can be composed—from attributes and actions on a type to entire packages.

A package is always built upon others that it imports. They provide the definitions of more basic concepts that it uses, all the way down to utter primitives such as numbers and Booleans.

A package augments and extends the material it imports. It can import several packages so that their different definitions are combined. In many cases, the different sources of material will deal with some of the same things. There must therefore be clear rules whereby the definitions that are found within a package are *joined* with others.

This chapter deals primarily with how to use packages in the building of other packages and how to interpret the resulting compositions. It also discusses some nuances of specifying and composing specifications of operations in the presence of exceptions.

8.1 *Sticking Pieces Together*

Every method of development must be good at building its artifacts—models, designs, plans, and so on—from smaller pieces. We can get our heads around only a small chunk at a time and can build big things only by sticking small ones together. Moreover, parts are more likely to be reusable if they can be put together in various ways with predictable results.

Note: Yes! Entire chapter is an advanced topic.

Much of this book is about building from parts. We'll discuss building models from frameworks and building software from components. The software has its own intricate plugging mechanisms; this chapter is about the much simpler matter of combining models, as used in type specifications and collaborations. Here, we are putting together specifications and high-level designs, so this is a design activity rather than one of integrating code.

There are three specific situations that call for composing models.

- The documentation chapter (Chapter 5) says that we can present a large model as a series of smaller diagrams. That's great for a guided tour through the model, but an implementor must see everything relevant to each action or type. So we need exact rules by which the diagrams recombine to make the big picture.

- The packages chapter (Chapter 7) talks about one package importing others. We need rules governing how to combine the definitions from the different sources. (The frameworks chapter, Chapter 9 takes this idea even further and combines generic models.)

- Our components (Chapter 10) can have multiple interfaces; that is, they must satisfy the expectations of several different clients, who might or might not know about one another. Each interface is defined by a type, so we need a way of working out what it means to satisfy two or more types at the same time.

This chapter deals with the basic combining mechanisms that are used in different ways in all these situations.

8.2 *Joining and Subtyping*

In Catalysis, we use two different ways of composing types: a type join and a type intersection.

▶ *Type join*   A way of composing types that combines two views of the same type; each view can impose its own restrictions on what the designer of the type must achieve (conjoining postconditions) or what a client must ensure (conjoining preconditions). Joining happens when two views of the same type are presented in different places; they might be in the same package or imported from different ones. Joining is about building the text and drawings of a specification from various partial descriptions.

▶ *Type intersection*   A way of composing types that combines two specifications, each of which must be fully observed (without restricting the other) by an object that belongs to the resulting type. The designer must guarantee each postcondition whenever its precondition is met regardless of the other's pre/post. Type intersection, or subtyping, happens when a component or object must satisfy different clients. Each specification must be satisfied independently of the other. A type specification defines a set of instances: the objects that satisfy that spec. Subtyping is about forming the intersection of two sets: those objects that happen to satisfy both specifications.

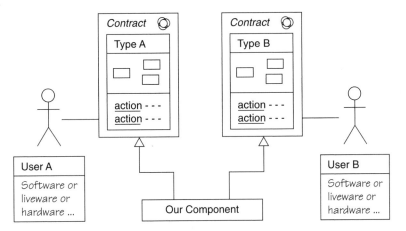

Figure 8.1   Component must satisfy multiple views.

The behavior of anything from a simple object to a large, complex system can be specified with a type specification, which has actions specified in terms of a model. The rules for joining and subtyping can be described as operations that you perform on the specifications. After a quick recap of type intersection, the rest of this chapter will focus on the joining operation.

8.2.1   Type Intersection: Combining Views

Type intersection means conforming to the expectations of more than one client, each of whom has a self-contained type specification you must conform to (see Figure 8.1). In any system that has more than one class of user, each of them has his or her (or its) own view. In software, the pluggable components that we want to build need the same capability. From user A's point of view, no matter what else Our Component does, it must always conform to the expectations set by Type specification A; the same thing is true of user B. In the most basic form of OO design, we use our type specifications as the basis for the design. But here there are two sets of models and actions. How do we go about designing it? Following are the basic steps for combining two types.

1. *Combine the two lists of attributes.* If any attributes from the two types have the same name, determine whether it's accidental or because the name is inherited from a common supertype. If it's the former, rename one of them; it won't make any difference to the meaning of the type. But if the duplicate names are inherited, they really do mean the same thing.
2. *Merge the two lists of operations.* If each action has a unique name, that's easy. For any operation that has specifications from both types, follow these steps.
   - and the precondition from each type with the invariant from that type.
   - and the postcondition from each type with the invariant from that type.

– Write the new operation specification using the anded expressions as

<u>pre</u>   pre1 or pre2
<u>post</u>   (pre1==>post1) and (pre2==>post2)

Why must the invariants be absorbed into the action specs? They must be absorbed because it's the pre- and postconditions that are the real behavioral spec: An invariant is only a way of factoring out common assumptions made by all those within its own context. Outside that context, the same common assumptions might not apply (see Section 3.5.5), so we must make them specific in any pre- and postcondition we want to move out of the context. After all the actions have been combined, you can probably factor out a common invariant that occurs in all the combined operation specs.

If we are talking about two 300-page type specifications, this process may take a little longer. This task is covered properly in the components chapter (Chapter 10), but the essence is the same on a larger scale.

- Build a new model sufficient to include the state information from both types; verify this (and assist the testing team) by writing two sets of abstraction functions (see Section 6.4) that will retrieve any piece of information from your component back into the language of each type.

- Then build your component using façades, each of which is dedicated to dealing with only one of these clients (see Section 6.7) and supplies the actions it expects, translated from your component's internal model.

8.3   *Combining Packages and Their Definitions*

So far, we've rather glibly talked about the way definitions are augmented and combined when packages are imported. This section looks in more detail at how the materials from imported packages are combined with each other and with the additional material already in the importer.

8.3.1   Definitions and Joins

What exactly does a type box in a diagram mean? What does it mean if boxes claiming to represent the same type appear in different diagrams in a package? Or are imported from different packages into one? Within one package, boxes headed with the same type name may appear in different parts of the same diagram, in different diagrams in the package, and in textual statements in the dictionary or the documentary narrative. Some of the diagrams in the (unfolded) package may have been imported from other packages, but that makes no difference. Whatever the source of the multiple appearances, it is always possible to join all of them into a single type definition.

The rules are the same for all kinds of multiple appearances, whether they are multiple diagrams in one package or definitions from multiple packages. The operation of combining them is called *joining*. Frequently, the individual splinters, taken on their own, don't denote any type; it's only when you put them together that they define a set of objects characterized by a particular behavior.

Each kind of definition that you can find in a package has its own joining rules. This section describes the rules for each kind.

8.3.2   Joining Packages

You form the join of two packages by forming a bag of all the statements and definitions from both packages and then joining those definitions with the same names (after any renaming, as discussed in Section 7.7.1, Name Mapping on Import). This join is applied to any nested packages along with everything else.

You obtain a package's full unfolded meaning by joining its imports to its own contents. There are specific rules for joining different kinds of definitions.

Type specifications are joined by joining their static models and their action specs.

8.3.3   Joining Static Models

To join multiple appearances of a type into a single type definition, follow these rules.

- and all invariants. The type has an effective invariant that is the conjunction of all the separate ones.
- Put into a set all the attribute names from the appearances; the completed definition should have the same set of attribute names. Include association names and parameterized attributes in the same way.
- For each attribute (or association) name in an appearance, consider any type constraint to be an invariant. So count:Integer means, "For any object x of this type, x.count always belongs to the type Integer." The completed type should contain an invariant that ands these together. So

$$\text{count : Integer} \quad \underline{\text{and}} \quad \text{count : Number} \quad ==> \quad \text{count : Integer}$$
$$\text{-- all Integers are Numbers anyway}$$
$$\text{thing : Boolean} \quad \underline{\text{and}} \quad \text{thing : Elephant}$$
$$\text{-- contradiction} - \text{can't join these definitions,}$$
$$\text{unsatisfiable spec}$$
$$\text{connection : Trasmitter} \quad \underline{\text{and}} \quad \text{connection : Receiver}$$
$$==> \text{connection:Transceiver} \quad \text{-- which is a subtype of both of these types}$$

- If the attribute has parameters (similarly, if the association has qualifiers), you can write the attributes as overloaded functions, provided that the parameter types don't overlap. So price(CandyBar):¢ and price(FreeFlight):FlyerMiles can remain as two attributes, because there is no CandyBar that is also a FreeFlight (yet). The general rule is that you first convert the attribute types into invariants of the form

> (param1 : Type1 <u>and</u> param2 : Type2) ==> attribute : ResultType

anding such expressions together gives a result that says, "If you start with parameters such as these, you get this kind of result; if you start with parameters such as those, you get that kind." If an argument ever belongs to both parameter types, then the result should belong to both result types.[1]

8.3.4   Joining Action Specifications

Action specifications are joined according to a covariant rule that permits any appearance of a type to reinforce preconditions and invariants. The rules apply to operations or actions localized to particular types and apply to joint actions.

Treat actions having different signatures (names and parameter lists) separately. For each action signature, take the individual pre- and postconditions and do the following:

- and the preconditions
- and the postconditions
- and the rely conditions
- and the guarantee conditions

anding preconditions means that in different packages or diagrams (or in different parts of your narrative) you can use preconditions to deal with different restrictions, confident that these restrictions will apply regardless of what is analyzed in other packages. Under Fault Management, we can say that a call can be made only if the Line is not under maintenance; under Billing, we can say that a call can be made only if the Account associated with the Line is not in default. Each package has no comprehension of the other's constraints; yet the net result is that a call cannot be made unless the line is free from maintenance and not in default.

anding postconditions means that, in different packages, you can use postconditions to deal with different consequences of an action: Under Billing, you can say that a charge is added to the associated Account; under Fault Management, we can say that the count of successful calls is incremented.

anding rely conditions means that in different packages, you can define different invariants the designer should be able to rely on while the action is in progress; anding guarantee conditions allows you do separate invariants your action will preserve.

---

1. All this conforms to the usual contravariant rules.

Thus, the two separate specs could be

<u>action</u> Agent::sell_life_insurance (c: Customer)
    <u>pre</u>:   c.isAcceptableRisk   *-- provided the risk factor is OK*
    <u>post</u>:   c.isInsured   *-- issue insurance when I "sell life insurance"*

<u>action</u> Agent::sell_life_insurance (c: Customer)
    <u>pre</u>: c.home : self.territory   *-- if the customer is a part of my territory*
    <u>post</u>: territory statistics updated   *-- update statistics when I "sell life insurance"*

The combined spec as the result of joining the two would be

<u>action</u> Agent::sell_life_insurance (c: Customer)
<u>pre</u>:   c.isAcceptableRisk <u>and</u> c.home : self.territory *-- combine restrictions*
<u>post</u>:   c.isInsured <u>and</u> territory statistics updated *-- combine outcomes*

The reason for using these join rules for actions is that each action specification could have been written without knowledge of the other specification or of its attributes. When I write my preconditions I do not know what other preconditions you may want to impose on that action; we both should be confident that, when our separate specifications are joined together, each can rely on its restrictions still being in force. The same principle applied to postconditions.

Sometimes, however, you want to write a specification that makes guarantees for certain cases when these cases may overlap with others. In this case you can use an alternative style for writing the spec: do not use an explicit precondition but instead describe the case within the postcondition itself. Here we use the same composition rules:

<u>action</u> Stack::push (<u>in</u> x, <u>out</u> error: Boolean)
<u>post</u>: self.notFull@pre ==> self.top = x and error = false
               -- provided I was not full beforehand, x will now be my top element

This spec tells us what happens in the successful case and might be, on its own, all we need. But perhaps in another part of your spec you want to write down what would happen in the other case:

<u>action</u> Stack::push (<u>in</u> x, <u>out</u> error: Boolean)
<u>post</u>: self.full@pre ==> error = true
              -- provided I was full beforehand, you will get an error flag.
              -- I'm not telling you what might happen to my contents!

The joined spec would make one guarantee for one case and another guarantee for the second case (the two cases happen to be disjoint in this example).

<u>action</u> Stack::push (in x, out error: Boolean)
<u>post</u>:   (self.notFull@pre ==> self.top = x and error = false)
    and   (self.full@pre ==> error = true)

It is possible to compute a resultant precondition from this specification:

<u>action</u> Stack::push (in x, out error: Boolean)
<u>pre</u>:   self.notFull **or** self.full
<u>post</u>:   self.notFull@pre ==> self.top = x and error = false
    and   self.full@pre ==> error = true

Hence, these two different styles of writing specs can be used to accomplish these two different goals of composing separate specifications. More details on dealing with exception conditions in specifications appear in Section 8.4, Action Exceptions and Composing Specs.

8.3.5   Joining Type Specifications Is Not Subtyping

A type specification denotes a set of objects: All objects that meet that specification are members of that type. Some ways of combining type specifications correspond directly to operating on the corresponding sets of objects; join does not.

When you join type specifications, you are combining the descriptions themselves and not directly the types (sets of objects) they specify. In the usual case, two type specifications are joined when a package, P1, imports two other packages—P2 and P3—each of which provides separate specifications (T_{s1} and T_{s2}) for the *same* type, T. Within package P1, the resulting specification of type T is the specification that results from a join:

    T_{s1} <u>join</u> T_{s2}

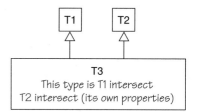

In contrast, when you define a subtype, you are defining a subset of objects; when you combine multiple supertypes, you are intersecting the corresponding sets. The rule for intersecting action specs is quite different from the rules for join. You can write a different expression—T1 * T2—which represents the type of objects that conform both to T1 and also to T2—that is, the intersection of the two sets. Type intersection or subtyping is a "no surprises" combination. Anything you're guaranteed by one spec can't possibly be taken away by the other. It is what happens when you have multiple supertypes, each of which provides specs for the same action; or when you combine a supertype action spec with a corresponding spec in the subtype.

Suppose we had the following explicitly declared specs:

    T1::m <u>pre</u>: A <u>post</u>: X
    T2::m <u>pre</u>: B <u>post</u>: Y
    T3::m <u>pre</u>: C <u>post</u>: Z

The resulting equivalent spec, after combining with the supertype specs, on the type T3 is obtained by anding all three pre/post *pairs*:[2]

    T3::m (<u>pre</u>: A <u>post</u>: X) and (<u>pre</u>: B <u>post</u>: Y) and (<u>pre</u>: C <u>post</u>: Z)

That is equivalent to

    T3::m <u>pre</u>: (A or B or C) <u>post</u>: (A @pre ==> X and B @pre ==> Y and C @pre ==> Z)

---

2. In a join, you separately and the precondition and then the postcondition.

An implementation of the resulting operation spec is guaranteed to meet the expectation of anyone who expected either T1 or T2. An invocation of m is valid whenever A is true (because that would make (A or B or C) true) and is guaranteed to result in X (and perhaps *also* Y, Z depending on whether B or C was also true).

When you join two type definitions, you are not usually intersecting the types, depending on how the action specs were written. For example, if I ask you for an object that conforms to Billing's idea of a Line, I would expect to be able to make calls whenever the Account is in order. If you give me something that conforms to Billing::Line join Fault_Management::Line, then I will find to my dismay that sometimes my Account is OK but I still can't make calls.

In fact, many partial specifications that you find in models don't constitute a complete type specification at all—they have attributes but no actions. Strictly speaking, any object would satisfy such a type spec, because it states no behavioral requirements. Types that are only attributes (and associations) are meaningful only as part of the models of larger types.

8.3.6   Joining Action Implementations

You can implement an action's specification by designing a refinement into a smaller set of actions—ultimately, in software, messages. Program code is the most detailed kind of action implementation. Implementations cannot be joined in the same way that specifications can be joined (see Figure 8.2). First, it isn't clear what anding two programs together would mean. The machine must follow one list of instructions or the other; which one should it execute? Both? In what order? Therefore, your support tool should complain if you try to provide code for two operations with the same name in the same class or for two refinements of the same action into different sets of smaller steps.

A second complication is that any implementation of the Call action provided by, say, the Billing package isn't likely to satisfy the requirements specified by Fault Management, because neither world understands the concepts of the other. So we cannot always accept an imported implementation even if there is no competing implementation from the other packages.

The only circumstance under which an implementation can be imported is when there is no difference between the pre/post specification in the imported package and the corresponding specification in the unfolded importer—that is, when there is no extra material about this action from the other imports, and no extra material is specified here. In that case, we know that the designer was working to the same spec.

Does this mean that we cannot bring together code written in different packages? Of course we can, but the code must be routines that can be referred to separately; and as designer of the importing package, we must design the implementation that invokes each of them in the right way. Some languages allow you to invoke super.method(); others permit Super1::method() and Super2::method().

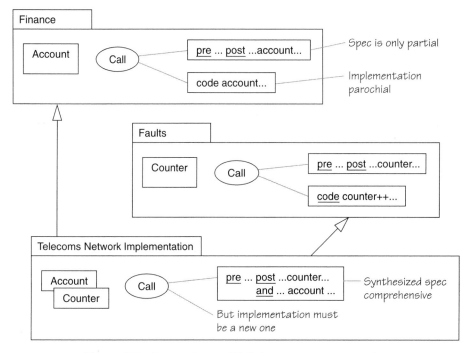

Figure 8.2   Importing and joining specs versus code.

Each of the packages for the telecoms network is a *view* of the whole system; it is constructed from the point of view of one department or business function. Knowing this, the package designers should not presume to provide their own implementations of overall actions. Instead, they should provide auxiliary routines that help implement their concerns. So Faults could provide successfulCallLog and Finance could provide callCharge. The designers of Telecoms Network Implementation can then choose to invoke these routines where appropriate in their own implementation of Call.

8.3.7   Joining Classes

A class defines an implementation or partial implementation of an object, with program code for localized actions and variables for storage of its state. A class can also be documented with invariants over its variables and pre/post specifications for each operation signature. Some programming languages support these features—notably Eiffel, which provides a testing facility that uses them.

The idea of joining class definitions isn't something you find in a programming language. By the time you get to compilation, it's assumed you've chosen your program code and there is no need to automatically compose it with any other code.

But some programming environments, such as Envy, allow a class to be synthesized from partial definitions imported from different packages ("applications" in Envy). There are restrictions that help prevent ad hoc modification of the behavior of the instances. Among other things, this arrangement permits a useful form of structuring development work. Because an object typically plays multiple roles and each role is meaningful in the context of interactions with objects playing other roles, the class is not the best unit of development work to assign to a person or team; instead, the collaboration between roles should be an implementation unit.

Other interesting work has been done in the area of *subject-oriented programming*, which strives to compose implementation classes that define different views, or roles, of some objects.

The rules in Catalysis are as follows.

- The joined class has all the variables in the partial definitions. Types must be the same. (If they were widened, the preconditions of some methods might fail, finding values in the variables they couldn't cope with; if they were narrowed, some methods might find they could not store the values they needed to.)
- The joined class has all the methods from the partial definitions. Methods are joined according to the rules for actions: Only one method for each signature is allowed (within this class) and not even that if there is a pre/post spec attached to that signature in one of the other joinees. Pre/post specs can be inherited from superclasses.
- Invariants over class variables, and pre- and postconditions attached to message signatures, are treated as for joining types: They are anded.

8.3.8 Joining Narrative

How shall we combine the narrative documentation of a package with those of the packages being imported? Perhaps the best that can be done automatically is to stick them end to end.

But decent support tools provide for a hypertext structure. Importing means that the points of reference in the original text can be referred to from the importer's text; and, in the context of renaming (see Section 7.7.1), the resultant imported text can actually be customized based on the importer's text and names.

8.4 *Action Exceptions and Composing Specs*

Exception handling adds complexity to any application. Even if the normal behavior of a component would be easily understood, the presence of exceptions often complicates things dramatically. We want to be able to separate exception specification to simplify the normal behavior specs, but we also want to address the specific characteristics of exceptions, and compose specs containing exceptions.

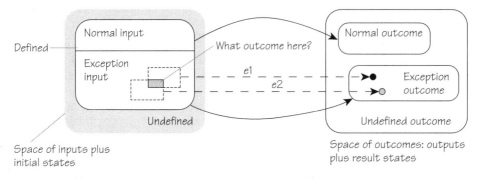

Figure 8.3   The spaces of normal and exception behavior.

8.4.1   Required Exceptions versus Undefined Behavior

The outcome of invoking an operation with some inputs and initial state will be either *defined*—the operation is required to complete and the outcome must satisfy some specification—or *undefined*—the specification does not constrain the outcome for those cases. Any defined behavior could, in turn, be considered as (1) *normal*—the operation performed the required task—or (2) an *exception*—the operation did not perform the required task because of an anomaly and signaled the failure as required. Figure 8.3 illustrates this behavior.

It is important to distinguish the exception case, in which the operation has met its specification with an exceptional outcome, from the undefined case, in which the operation has no specified behavior. Figure 8.3 shows that normal and exception outcomes are disjoint, because there should be unambiguous checks to distinguish required success from required failures; the caller should not be guessing: *"Hmm... I wonder whether that last call succeeded."*

Figure 8.3 also shows that the same input can give rise to different exception outputs (e1, e2); some inputs may cause more than one exception condition to be true.

8.4.2   Design by Contract versus Defensive Programming

Over the years, there has evolved an approach to programming called *defensive* programming. In essence, when you implement any operation you do the following.

- Consider the normal invocation of your code; implement it.
- Consider the countless abnormal invocations of your code; implement checks for those conditions and take defensive actions such as returning a null or raising an exception.

This approach can be quite damaging. Each implementor provides identified defensive checks *in the code*, but none of the interfaces documents what is guaranteed to be checked and by whom or what outcome is guaranteed in the event of those errors. Responsibilities become blurred, and the code becomes littered with disorganized, redundant, and inadequate checking and handling of exception cases.

Instead, you should be clear about the separation of responsibilities in the design itself. The specification of each operation should clearly state what assumptions the implementor makes about the invocations—the caller must ensure that those are met—and what corresponding guarantees the implementor will provide. This includes a specification of which failure conditions or paths the implementor guarantees to check and the corresponding outcomes. Then implement to that contract; allow for the defensive programming mode when you're debugging the code and when running tests (see Section 6.1.3, Operation Abstraction).

By all means, employ "defensive specification" at appropriate interfaces in your system; but make sure that the checking and exception handling are specified and documented as part of the interfaces and not just in the code.

8.4.3   Specifying Exceptions

We want to separate normal and exception conditions, both within one spec and across multiple specs. However, we still want our descriptions to compose with predictable and intuitive results.

In Catalysis, the approach of specifying using pre- and postconditions simplifies matters, because you can have multiple specifications for an action that compose following clear rules. However, exceptions pose unique requirements.

We introduce two special names: normal and exception. These names can be used in two ways.

1. As Boolean variable names that can be bound before the pre/post specification section; define normal and exception in terms of the success and failure indicators that the operation will use. They are treated as special names, as opposed to names introduced locally within a let..., because their binding must be shared across all specifications of that action.

> action Shop::order (c: Card, p: Product, a: Address, out success: Integer)
>   normal = (success=0) ... -- *success indication to the caller*
>   exception = (success < 0) ... -- *failure indication to the caller*
> <u>post</u>: ...

2. As Boolean variables that can be used within a postcondition. For example:

> action Shop::order (c: Card, p: Product, a: Address, out success: Integer)
> <u>post</u>:   c.OK ==> normal -- *success indication if card is OK*
>   if (....) then (exception and ....) -- *failure indication must be raised if ....*
>   if (exception) then (.....) -- *any failure must guarantee ....*

We can now require the operation never to have an undefined outcome:

> <u>post</u>:   (normal or exception) = true
>   -- *must indicate success or failure; returning +2 would be an implementation bug*

Or we require it never to raise any exception outside a particular set:

> <u>post</u>: exception ==> (success = -1 or success = -2)

We can now write the successful outcome, assuming that the success indicator will be defined somewhere. Effects are guaranteed with the success indicator:

> <u>action</u> Shop::order (c: Card, p: Product, a: Address, out success: Integer)
> <u>post</u>:   normal ==> (-- if success is returned, then caller is assured the following
>   Order*new->notEmpty and -- new order
>   c.charged (...) and   -- customer card charged
>   (p.noInventory ==> RestockOrder*new [...] notEmpty)
>   -- restocking order if out of stock

Or we can write conditions under which success must be indicated:

> <u>action</u> Shop::order (c: Card, p: Product, a: Address, out success: Integer)
> <u>post</u>:   c.OK ==> normal -- if the card is OK, definite success indicator

We could write the exception outcomes in the same manner (but see the later discussion of why this would be inflexible with multiple possible exceptions).

> <u>action</u> Shop::order (c: Card, p: Product, a: Address, out success: Integer)
> <u>post</u>:   not c.OK ==> (success = -1) -- specific indicator for bad card

> <u>action</u> Shop::order (c: Card, p: Product, a: Address, out success: Integer)
> <u>post</u>:   not a.OK ==> (success = -2) -- specific indicator for bad address

> <u>action</u> Shop::order (c: Card, p: Product, a: Address, out success: Integer)
> <u>post</u>:   exception ==> (Order*new–>isEmpty)
>   -- if failure is signaled, guaranteed that no new order was created

Typically, however, you want to deal with multiple possible exception outcomes in a more flexible manner. If you place an on-line order, given the preceding spec, what should happen if the credit card number and address are both invalid? Which exception should be raised? It is best to leave to the implementor the choice of *which* exception to signal as long as failure indication is guaranteed. This technique helps with composition of specifications, each with its own exception conditions, as is the case of failures in distributed systems. Hence:

> <u>action</u> Shop::order (c: Card, p: Product, a: Address, out success: Integer)
> <u>post</u>:   -- bad card means some failure indication
>   not c.OK ==> exception
>   -- a failure indication, with code -1, will happen only if the card was bad
>   (exception and success = -1) ==> not c.OK

This is a common form of specification for exceptions, so we introduce a convenient query isException on the predefined type Boolean and rewrite it as

> <u>post</u>:   (not c.OK) . isException (exception, success = -1)

This is exactly equivalent to the longer form. Our definition of isException is as follows:

```
-- a given trigger condition is Exception means...
Boolean::isException ( generalFailure: Boolean, specificIndication: Boolean ) =
            -- if the trigger condition was true, then some failure has been signaled, and
    (    (self = true) ==> generalFailure ) and
            -- the specific Indication will not be raised unless the trigger was true
            ( generalFailure & specificIndication ==> (self = true ) ) )
```

One final point: Suppose you write a specification that says simply

Success indicator = a; Failure indicator = b;

If a, then x is guaranteed to have happened;

If b, then y is guaranteed to have happened.

You would, strictly speaking, have to admit an implementation that simply failed every time, as long as it met the failure indication. Either you should be more strict about the kinds of exceptions that can be raised and when, or you should assume a reasonable convention in which the implementor is obliged to try to meet the success goals and should raise an exception only if that turns out to be impossible.

8.4.3.1   Other Exception Indication Mechanisms

Different languages have different mechanisms to indicate exceptions: return values, exception objects thrown, signals raised, and so on. For specification purposes, you can work with any of these, including some language-neutral mechanisms (such as return values; remember that the signature of an abstract action specification is itself always subject to refinements (see Chapter 6, Abstraction, Refinement, and Testing).

```
action T::m (....., out success: Boolean)
post:     not success ==>  (...guarantees about every indicated failure...)


action T::n (....) throws (Object) -- Java-like exception spec
    exception = thrown (Object) -- no using throw except to indicate failure


action T::n (.....) -- WrongState exception spec
post:     (self.wrongState) . isException ( thrown (Object), thrown (WrongState) )
```

Or to make a guarantee on any exception thrown

```
action T::n (....)
post:     thrown ( Object ) ==> (...e.g., all state cleaned up ...)
```

The meaning of the language-specific mechanisms, such as throw, is provided by working in a context where the appropriate packages have been imported (see Chapter 9, Model Frameworks and Template Packages).

8.4.3.2   Exceptions with General Actions

This approach extends to general actions. An exception in an abstract action can be traced across action refinements. You can specify traces or sequences of detailed actions as raising an exception on the abstract action (rather than having

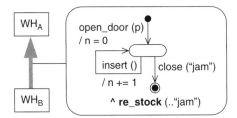

Figure 8.4   Mapping to an abstract exception action.

to invent a new abstract action for it or having to ignore it at the abstract level). The exception can be traced through action refinements down to the level of exceptions in program code.

Of course, when specifying an abstract action you should describe only those exceptions that have meaning at that level of abstraction, not every disk or networking failure!

Let us revisit the example in Section 4.2.2, Preview: Documenting a Refinement, on restocking of a vending machine (see Figure 8.4). Suppose that the warehouse inlet door for a product can jam when closed. If this outcome is an interesting exception at the abstract level, it could have been specified as such on the joint action. In the refinement, the appropriate sequence can be mapped to this abstract exception action.

This provides a precise basis for exceptions in traditional use case approaches.

8.4.3.3   Exceptions and Use Case Templates

Just as we introduced a narrative-style template for defining use cases, it is also useful to incorporate exceptions into use case narratives.

use case	sale
participants	retailer, wholesaler
parameters	set of items
pre	the items must be in stock, retailer must be registered, retailer must have cash to pay
post (normal)	retailer has received items and paid cash wholesaler has received cash and given items
normal indicator	confirmation to retailer
exception indicator	no sale confirmation to retailer from wholesaler
on exception	neither cash nor items transferred

Similarly, as part of the use case documentation it is useful to document those sequences that might give rise to an exception. The mapping from the formal refinement description (such as a state chart) to this narrative is straightforward:

use case	telephone sale by distributor
refines	use case **sale**
refinement	1. retailer calls wholesaler and is connected to rep
	2. rep gets distributor membership information from retailer

> 3. rep collects order information from retailer, totaling the cost
> 4. rep confirms items, total, and shipping date with wholesaler
> 5. both parties hang up
> 6. shipment arrives at retailer
> 7. wholesaler invoices retailer
> 8. retailer pays invoice

<u>abstract result</u>   **sale** was effectively conducted
                    with amount of the order total, and items as ordered

<u>exception</u>   retailer canceled order before it was shipped (step 6, use case **sale**)
     <u>exception outcome</u>   confirmed cancellation
                         -- implicit: non sales confirmation; no cash or items transfer

8.5 *Summary*

All modeling elements should be composable so that specifications and designs can be factored into smaller parts and recombined in predictable and intuitive ways.

Packages usually import other packages, those on which the importers' definitions are based. We have looked at the rules whereby imported definitions are combined with new material and with material from other imports.

Each package has a notional unfolded form, in which all the definitions from the imports and their imports are visible. New facts and definitions in a package can constrain its own declared names and those that are imported.

You need to take special care when you specify exceptions so that they can be composed and so that abstract actions with exceptions can still be refined. We outlined how to specify exceptions to meet both these needs, and we linked them to exception paths in use cases.

Chapter 9   Model Frameworks and Template Packages

It isn't only chunks of code that can be made into reusable assets. Designs and specifications, too, can be separated into parts, which can be kept in a library and subsequently combined in many different configurations. We call them model frameworks.

The basic tool for representing and combining frameworks is a generic form of package, called a framework or template package.

Pieces of design combine to produce only designs, and they still need to be implemented. But if you've read the book this far, you'll agree that a design represents much of the major decision-making that goes into finished code; being able to put a design together rapidly from prefabricated parts is a valuable facility. Moreover, later we will outline (Pattern 11.1, *Role Delegation*) a uniform design and implementation style that also lets you plug code components together.

This chapter deals with model frameworks and explains how to build and compose them using template packages. It also discusses how the fundamentals of the entire Catalysis approach are themselves defined as such frameworks and shows how they can form the basis for a modeling language that is truly extensible.

9.1 *Model Framework Overview*

After you've been modeling and designing object systems for a while, you start noticing certain patterns recurring. We can see the same set of relationships, constraints, or design transformation in different designs. We call this set of relationships a *model framework*. Many popular design patterns boil down to a model framework combined with surrounding how-to, when-to, and whether-to advice.

A suitable tool should be able to support the building of models and designs by application of model frameworks. Suppose, for example, that our business model has a type Stock with a numeric attribute level; choosing a package of user-interface pieces, we find a type Meter for displaying numeric readings.

Now we want to specify that Meters can be used to display Stock levels, using the well-known Observation[1] pattern. As usual, we can focus on different aspects of a model in different diagrams, so we don't have to repeat all the stuff that has already been said about the two types. We need only define the extra attributes and operations needed to connect them.

This is where model frameworks are useful. Let's assume that because Observation is a common pattern, we have defined a model framework for it; using it gives us an abbreviated way of defining what we need (see Figure 9.1).

The vehicle for a framework is a generic, or *template*, form of package. Inside the template, some types and their features can be defined using placeholder names. Looking at its definition in the library, we find that the Observation template has two type placeholders Subject and Observer; we have imported that package, substituting Stock and Meter. The sustituted definition becomes part of the model. In other words, whatever attributes and operations are defined for Subject within the template's definition are now defined for Stock. Other names can be substituted, too. The template uses an attribute called value for the aspect of the Subject that we want observed; so we substitute it for the Stock's level.

▶ *framework*   A template package; a package that is designed to be imported
with substitutions. It "unfolds" to provide a version of its contents that is specialized based on the substitutions made. (Note that our usage of *framework* is somewhat broader than its traditional usage as a collection of collaborating abstract classes.)
A framework can abstract the description of a generic type, a family of mutually dependent types, a collaboration, a refinement pattern, the modeling constructs themselves, and even a bundle of fundamental generic properties (associative, commutative, and so on). Frameworks are themselves built on other frameworks. At the most basic level, the structure of frameworks represents the basis for the organization of all models.

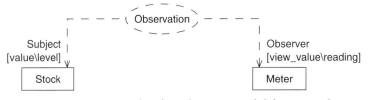

Figure 9.1   Example of applying a model framework.

---

1. State in one object tracks state changes in another; see Figure 9.11.

Notice that what the Observation framework does is to represent a cluster of design decisions about how two types of objects should collaborate to provide the required effect. It does not discuss any other roles and collaborations of those objects, and it decouples this design work from any specific domain. This is one of the most effective uses of model frameworks.

A *pattern* is a set of ideas that can be applied to many situations. A framework is at the heart of many patterns, but a pattern usually also includes less-formal material about alternative strategies, advice on when to use it, and so on. When you keep a framework in a library, it should be packaged with this documentation.

Some programming languages have *class templates* or *generic classes*; UML has them, too. The notation is slightly different, but a class template is a model framework that contains only one class. We'll discuss class templates in more detail later.

A variety of techniques can be used to build executable frameworks, from which programs can be quickly generated by subclassing, by plugging in new components, and by interpreting purpose-built languages. We will look at these kinds of frameworks in Chapter 11, Reuse and Pluggable Design: Frameworks in Code. This chapter is about frameworks of abstract models.

Tools that support model frameworks and templates should allow you to unfold each application of a model framework so as to see the full resulting model with all the substitutions made. Ideally, the tool should keep the definitions of the framework, the original definitions of the types to which it is applied, and each diagram in which the framework is applied. If the user changes any of these, the resulting unfolded model should change in step. Furthermore, the tool should allow you to define your own frameworks in the same notation as the models themselves.

Among current popular tools, there is some support for templates in a restricted way. Typically, the template works more like a *script*: a series of operations that is applied once to a model, adding the necessary attributes and operations. This technique has the disadvantage that the simpler original definitions are lost and changes are less easy to make. It is also less easy to see what the template is about, because it is written in a scripting language.

In summary, templates provide a powerful way to capture reusable model frameworks, whether at an abstract specification level or down in the detailed design. In particular, templates are good for capturing collaborations. Even without tools, the template notation is a useful form of abbreviation even when the template is not very rigorously defined. It's an easy way to say on a diagram, "This, this, and this type have such-and-such a relationship."

The rest of this chapter begins by looking at how frameworks work to help build static models using only attributes and associations; then we will go on to deal with actions. Subsequent sections add further ideas, and a summary of concepts appears at the end of the chapter.

9.2   *Model Frameworks of Types and Attributes*

Suppose a plumbing company asks us to do an analysis of its business prepara-
tory to getting some computerized support. After a day or two with them, we
arrive at the central model shown in Figure 9.2. Each Plumber is at any one time
scheduled to do a list of Jobs, each of which takes place on some date and is for a
particular Customer. There are only a certain number of kinds of Job, and each is
described by a JobDescription. Among other things, this model says which Skills are
required for the job (electrical wiring, excavation, denial of responsibility, and so
on). Each Plumber is qualified with a list of Skills. A key invariant is that no Plumber
should be assigned to a Job for which he or she lacks the appropriate skills—or, as
we've written it in the invariant, every Job's description's requirements must be a
subset of the qualifications of the assigned Plumber.

There's more to the model than this, of course, and work continues. Meanwhile, our consultancy gets involved in another modeling contract, this one with
a commercial teaching organization. We soon realize that we can make some savings here: Course Offerings, which happen on particular dates, are occurrences of
Courses—just as Jobs and JobDescriptions; and Courses call for certain Instructor
Skills (arm-waving, blustering, hypnosis, and the like).

So we generalize our model into a framework by creating a template package,
as shown in Figure 9.3. (We will later drop the «framework» stereotype. We've
taken the opportunity to add more details, particularly about Resources not being
double-booked. (TimeInterval will have to be defined somewhere; we've assumed
it has a Boolean function noOverlap that compares two TimeIntervals.)

Now our plumbing model can easily be generated from a *framework application*
(see Figure 9.4). Notice that several of the names inside the framework definition
are written within angle brackets (< >); they are *placeholders* that should be identified with actual type names when the framework is applied. This is the effect of
the labeled arrows when the framework is applied.

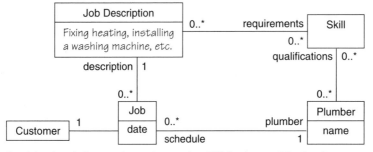

inv Job:: description.requirements –> subsetOf(plumber.qualifications)

Figure 9.2   Model of allocating plumbers to jobs.

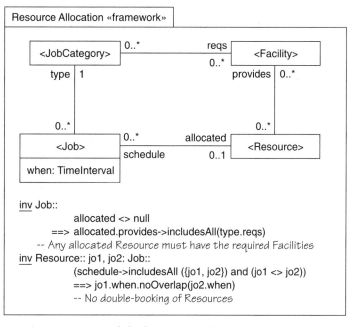

Figure 9.3   Model of resource allocation framework.

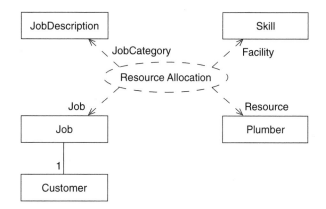

Figure 9.4   Application of resource allocation to plumbing.

In the resulting model, each type has all the features given to it explicitly (such as, the Job's Customer) and also all the features defined by the framework, as name-substituted by the application. Working out the complete model is called *unfolding*. A good tool can show an unfolded version on demand.

Turning again to seminar scheduling, we produce the model shown in Figure 9.5. This happens to apply the same framework twice. Both Rooms and Instructors are constrained to provide the right stuff: Instructors have skills, Rooms have vari-

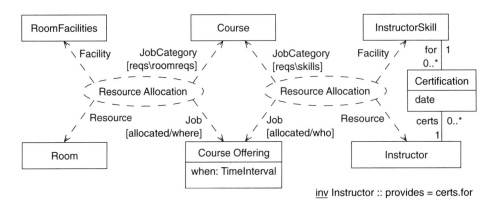

Figure 9.5   Double application of resource allocation to seminar scheduling.

ous facilities (projectors, whiteboards), and neither must be overbooked. We have also added an extra idea: that instructors' skills, determined by dated certifications, define the provides association from the framework. We have modeled this explicitly and tied it into the provides association with an invariant.[2]

This example also shows name substitution in the form [framework-name \ applied-name]. We have used it to rename some of the associations to avoid Courses having different attributes with the same name. This text form and the arrows are equivalent. It is sometimes convenient to write instead of drawing pictures:

ResourceAllocation [JobCategory \ Course
                                    [reqs \ roomreqs],
                             Resource \ Instructor ...]

When unfolded, statements from each framework application, after the necessary substitutions are made, are composed with each other and with any local definitions that are applicable. The unfolding is shown in Figure 9.6. Clearly, using frameworks reduces complexity and duplication. It also provides a higher-level view of the model, making it clear that each loop of four associations forms part of a single relationship, the one we've called Resource Allocation. So frameworks are a useful kind of abstraction.

▶ *unfolding*   Depicting the results of an import, possibly including substitutions, in the context of the importing package with the appropriate elements substituted.

▶ *framework applicaton*   An import of a framework with substitutions; usually depicted graphically using a UML "pattern" symbol, with labeled lines for the type substitutions and text annotations for finer-grained substitutions (attributes, actions, and so on).

---

2. The UML symbol for a pattern is a dashed use case, although pattern semantics have nothing to do with UML use cases. UML 1.1 does not have any semantics for patterns, only a notation; perhaps our semantics will be adopted.

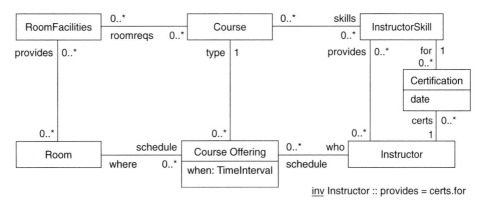

inv Instructor :: provides = certs.for

CourseOffering:: who <> null ==> who.provides->includesAll(type.skills)
    -- Any allocated Instructor must have the required Skills
CourseOffering:: where <> null ==> where.provides->includesAll(type.roomreqs)
    -- Any allocated Room must have the required RoomFacilities
Instructor:: jo1, jo2: Job:: (schedule->includesAll ({jo1,jo2}) & jo1 <> jo2) ==> jo1.when.noOverlap(jo2.when)
                                        -- No double-booking of Instructors
Room:: jo1, jo2: Job:: (schedule->includesAll ({jo1,jo2}) & jo1 <> jo2) ==> jo1.when.noOverlap(jo2.when)
                                        -- No double-booking of Rooms

Figure 9.6   Unfolded view after applying frameworks.

9.2.1   Framework Applications Are Not Subtypes

Could we have used subtyping to express the similarity between Courses and plumbers' JobDescriptions (Figure 9.7)? Not really. This would imply that plumbing Jobs might require (or could be used with) overhead projectors, and other mix-ups. It isn't the individual types that are specialized but rather the entire group of them along with their relationships and interactions.

Another example is the faulty old syllogism "Animals eat Food; Cows are Animals; Beefburgers are Food; hence Cows eat Beefburgers." The mistake is that the first statement should not be taken to mean that every object conforming to the

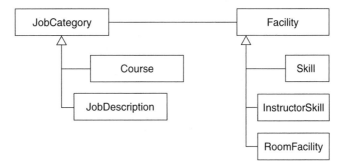

Figure 9.7   Why subtyping does not correctly reflect frameworks.

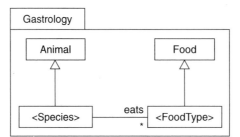

Figure 9.8   A gastrology framework.

type Animal can eat every instance of the type Food. A more explicit statement would be "For every subtype A of Animal, there is a subtype F of Food such that all members of A can eat any member of F." Using frameworks, this can be written as shown in Figure 9.8.

Now we can explicitly apply the framework to those pairs that are acceptable (see Figure 9.9). The association eats might represent the assignment of food items to specific animals in an automatic feeding system. We thus ensure that instances of Grass will be the only members of Food proffered as fodder to any Cow instance.[3]

A framework can use nonplaceholder types, such as Animal and Food. So by applying the framework to Cat and to Cow, we are asserting that both of them are subtypes of Animal.

9.3 *Collaboration Frameworks*

A collaboration describes the interactions between a group of objects that are designed to work together. They send one another messages intended to attain a goal that they are designed to achieve jointly. Much of the skill of object-oriented design is about designing collaborations. The CRC technique (classes, responsibilities, collaborations) is basic to OO design and is all about dividing the responsi-

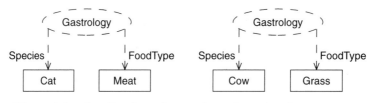

Figure 9.9   Application of gastrology framework.

---

3. Would that it were so.

bilities for a task among collaborating objects. These design decisions distinguish OO programming from merely structured design, in which all the work is lumped into one program. In return for the extra decision making (if you do it well), you get a decoupled design that is flexible and extensible. Doing it badly leads to an unmanageable mess.

The careful design of collaborations is of such value that, when you have done it well, it is worth recording the ideas and using them again. This is the motivation of many patterns. Some tools explicitly provide a way to define collaborations and then compose them into bigger designs.

In Catalysis, frameworks are our reusable pieces of design; so now let's use them for reusable pieces of collaboration. The interesting thing about a collaboration is that it defines the interactive relationship between two or more objects; but when you define it by itself, you avoid saying anything about the other relationships each role player might have.

As a real-world example, if you describe what it means to be a parent, you're talking largely about your interactions with your children and the effects you have on one another. When you describe what it means to be an employee, that's a different role with a different set of interactions with an object described in different terms. But although the collaborations can be described separately, the fact is that every object usually plays a role in several collaborations: perhaps you are both a parent and an employee. Each object conforms to the spec of its roles in the various collaborations it takes part in.

Separate collaborations can have effects on the same object attributes. Parenthood affects the bank balance; fortunately, that's the same attribute that is improved by employment. So when we combine roles in one object, we usually must take into consideration this interference between the different roles. Indeed, if two roles didn't interfere in this way, it wouldn't make any difference whether they were assigned to the same object.

The Subject-Observer collaboration is a more technical example. In Figure 9.10, we try to show each object's external interface as split into different roles in different collaborations, whereas the internal attributes may be shared. The collaboration governs two roles: Subject and Observer. The Subject has some sort of value, and the Observer has another; let's call it its value_view. An update action is initiated by the Subject to keep the Observer up-to-date.

Of course, any pair of classes that conforms to this relationship in some chunk of program code will probably not be called Subject and Observer. They'll have bigger, more interesting roles in their program, perhaps as pieces of a GUI or proxies in a distributed system. But this is exactly what frameworks are about: We can define only the aspects about which we have something to say and then allow users to use other names and extend the definitions when they apply our framework.

So, as we've shown in Figure 9.10, we really know only about part of each object we're describing: The rest depends on whoever chooses to use the framework. In this example, we don't know how or why the Subject's value gets

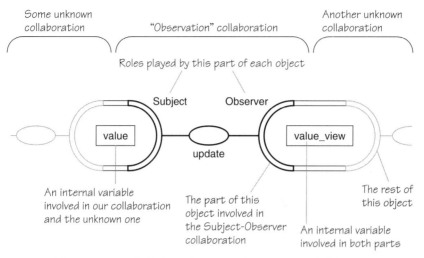

Some unknown
collaboration   "Observation" collaboration   Another unknown
                                                               collaboration

Roles played by this part of each object

Subject   Observer

value   value_view

update

An internal variable   The part of this   The rest of
involved in our collaboration   object involved in   this object
and the unknown one   the Subject-Observer
                                collaboration   An internal variable
                                                            involved in both parts

Figure 9.10   Collaborations are about parts of objects.

changed. We know only that it can happen and that when it does, the Observer
must be updated.

9.3.1   Using Invariant Effects in Collaboration Frameworks

The big difference between this framework and the ones we have discussed so far
is that this one has actions. In fact, there are several:

- The update action between the Subject and Observer
- All the other actions we don't know about, which might change the Subject's
  value

  Specifying the first one is easy:

  <u>action</u> Observer :: update ( )
      <u>post</u>   value_view = subject.value
                - - I now correctly reflect my subject's value

(As always, an action might abstract a sequence of smaller messages, but we'll
leave it to someone else to refine it.)

The crucial thing we have to say in this framework is that the update action
occurs as part of *any* other action that changes the Subject's value. To say this formally, we use an effect invariant (see Section 3.5.4, Effect Invariants) on the *external*
section of the collaboration (see Section 4.8.1, External Actions). It is a postcondition without an action name or signature:

<u>inv effect</u> Subject ::
    <u>post</u>   value@pre <> value $\Longrightarrow$ [[observers.update()]]
              -- Any action that changes my value also ensures
                that the observers correctly reflect the new value.

(Recall that [[anAction]] means that the postcondition of anAction is achieved as part of this action. If there are several observers, the same applies to all of them.)

The idea is that this postcondition applies to every other action performed by a Subject no matter where the rest of the spec of that action comes from. So when we use this framework, we must and the effect to all the postconditions of each of the other operations. When we finally come to program the Subject class (or rather the class playing the Subject role when we've applied the Observation framework), we'll find that wherever the spec tells us to change its value, we must also update the corresponding Observer (or whatever the user has changed the names to).

9.3.1.1   Completing This Example

Our framework can be applied to any pair of types and will add to them the necessary specification to say that one of these types can be an observer of the other. But there must be some way of telling which Subject instances are observed by which Observer instances. We can define that as an association and add another action for making links that belong to it.

Figure 9.11 on the next page shows the collaboration framework as we would normally draw it. The subject-observers association links particular instances of the two types, and the update action applies only to Observers that have a current Subject. The register action links a particular Subject to a particular Observer. It is a joint action: We have not specified here how it happens or even to whom you send the message to make it happen; we have specified only that there should be such an action, with responsibility for executing it distributed somehow between Subject and Observer. When designers apply the framework to a particular pair of types, it tells them to provide this facility.

9.3.1.2   More Abstract Models

To illustrate how Catalysis lets you choose how detailed or abstract to be, we could have written the overall requirement without mentioning the update action at all, with an even less detailed external effect invariant:

> <u>inv effect</u> Subject::
>
> <u>post</u>   value@pre <> value ==>
>   observer.value_view = value
>   -- Any action that causes a change in value
>   must ensure that the observer's latest 'value_view'
>   is the same as our latest 'value'

Further, we could have written an invariant external to the collaboration, defining the overall goal and saying nothing about how it is achieved:

> <u>inv</u> Observer :: subject.value = value_view

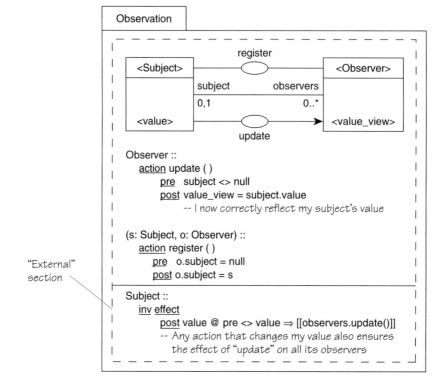

Figure 9.11   Collaboration template.

9.3.2   Applying a Collaboration Framework

One of the authors' clients designed a call management system for telephone sales teams. One of the types in the model was a CallQueue: the list of calls waiting for a particular group of operators. Let's suppose we have that type defined in one package; in another package, we have a kit of GUI widgets, one of which is a Thermometer—a useful display for numeric values. Figure 9.12 shows parts of their models.

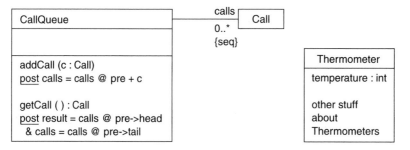

Figure 9.12   Target type model for using observation.

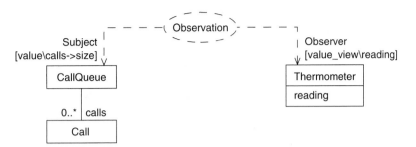

Figure 9.13   Framework application and substitutions.

Now we are designing the bridge between business logic and GUI, and we make a package into which we import (among other things) the CallQueue and Thermometer. We'd like to make it possible for the "temperature" of a Thermometer (the number it displays) to be used to show the number of Calls on a particular CallQueue. So we apply our Observation framework as shown in Figure 9.13. This has the effect of adding the necessary specifications. Now let's suppose we have a tool that can display the unfolded model if we wish; it shows the result of applying the framework and gives the spec (see Figure 9.14).

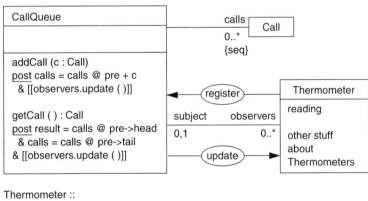

Thermometer ::
   <u>action</u> update ( )
      <u>pre</u>   subject <> null
      <u>post</u> reading = subject.calls->size
               -- I now correctly reflect my subject's value

(s: CallQueue, o: Thermometer) ::
      <u>action</u> register ( )
         <u>pre</u>   o.subject = null
         <u>post</u> o.subject = s

Figure 9.14   Unfolded result of framework application.

Notice that the Observer and Subject names have been replaced. (We've actually made a slight abbreviation here: The addCall and getCall operations will always change the calls size every time, so we can drop the value <> value@pre ==> from their postconditions.)

So far, we have used frameworks for building models; what we end up with is a specification, which still must be implemented. In this particular example, some work is left to the framework's user, because we have not been told how to realize the register and update actions as specific operations on the objects. (Some other framework might choose to provide more.)

The update action could be realized as a single notify(newValue) message or, in the Smalltalk MVC style, could consist of an update( ) message to the Thermometer, which then must come back to the CallQueue asking for details of the changes.

The register action would typically be initiated by a supervising object telling a particular Thermometer to observe a particular CallQueue; then the Thermometer must introduce itself to the CallQueue so that each knows about the other.

9.3.3   Using One Framework to Build Another

The idea of registering and unregistering is common to any situation in which each of two objects needs to know about the other. So we could separate this scheme into its own framework (see Figure 9.15). Any instance of A and B can be linked; aa and bb are the links in each direction. (The arrows indicate that we've definitely decided to make the link navigable in each direction.) The operations intended for use from outside this collaboration are register, sent to an A to link it to a particular B; unregister; and release, sent to a B to unlink it from everything. The other operations on Bs—link and unlink—are intended only as an internal part of the design of this collaboration. We've written the specifications so that they are quite explicit about how the two-way links are maintained.

Now we see that we could have used this framework to help define the Observation framework (see Figure 9.16). (In fact, it can say more than before, because it now tells how the register action works rather than just calls for one.) Again, comparing Figure 9.16 with Figure 9.11, we can see that the use of a framework imposes a higher-level order on the appearance of the model, substituting a meaningful single pattern on the diagram for a variety of links and operations.

9.4 *Refining Frameworks*

Frameworks are an expressive abstraction tool and are used throughout Catalysis, even in the definition of basic modeling constructs. Still, as a template-like mechanism, they can be used only when the problem at hand is suited to the parameterization and the level of granularity of the framework.

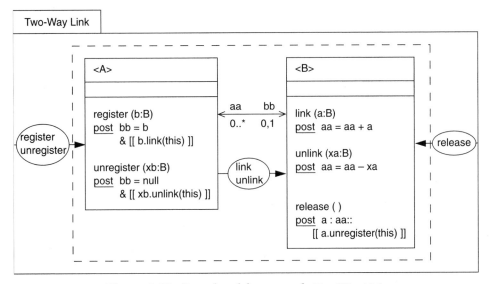

Figure 9.15   Low-level framework: Two-Way Link.

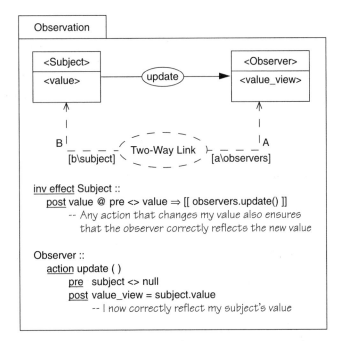

Figure 9.16   Observation framework using Two-Way Link framework.

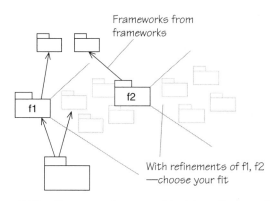

Figure 9.17   Frameworks are subject to refinement.

Fortunately, our frameworks have an additional dimension of flexibility: *refinement* (see Figure 9.17). There is no restriction that a framework be defined at a fixed level of detail; frameworks themselves are subject to refinement, abstraction, and composition in exactly the same ways as other models are. Furthermore, some of these refinements are themselves defined as frameworks.

9.4.1   A Requirement

The framework in Figure 9.18 illustrates a relationship between a Trader who makes Orders from a Distributor. In the framework, we don't care how the Trader gets rid of stock, nor how the Distributor acquires it. We have shown this as a degenerate collaboration, as it will next be refined as a unit. (Notice that we've made all the types substitutable except Date. So we would likely have Date defined as an actual type somewhere in the package in which this framework definition appears or in the packages it imports.)

This tells us that a Trader must always have an Order pending for low stock; in that way, we hope to avoid outages. Designers might find it convenient to use this framework by itself and then go on to define within their own models how Orders are made. Or we could go on to define another framework that includes that information.

9.4.2   A Collaboration Refining the Requirement

According to the Trade Supply framework (see Figure 9.19), when the stock of any Product gets low, the Trader makes an Order with the Distributor using the make_order action. Once an Order is established, the Distributor can deliver the goods, and the Trader can pay.

There are different kinds of Traders in the world, and they get rid of their stocks in different ways. Some only sell them; others cook them up and serve them; still others build things from them. But no matter how stock depletion happens, the

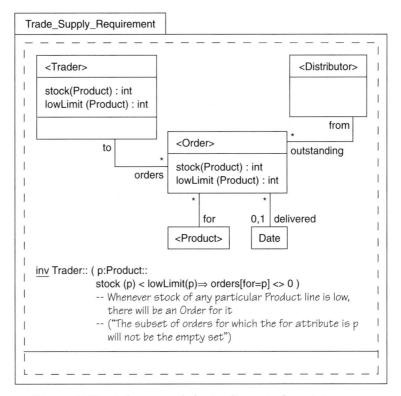

Figure 9.18   A framework for trading: stock maintenance.

Trade Supply framework still manages to tell us that make_order should happen when stocks get low.

In an earlier example, we used only one effect clause. Here, we have split the cause from the effect. First, we've invented an effect name depletion (p) as a place-holder name for any action (no matter where defined) that causes stocks of p to be reduced: An invariant effect clause tells which (unknown) actions are considered to have the depletion effect. Second, we have defined a postcondition for depletion in the usual way for an effect: This says that we require to perform the make_order action.

Separating cause and effect in this way is useful when they have a many-many relationship and are the essential reason for the effect construct.

9.4.3   Documenting the Refinement

We want to claim that anyone who uses the Trade_Supply framework, using the same placeholder substitutions, will achieve the goals set by Trade_Supply_Requirement. More precisely, we must document a reason for believing that if we combined the two models, we'd end up saying no more than we've already said in Trade Supply:

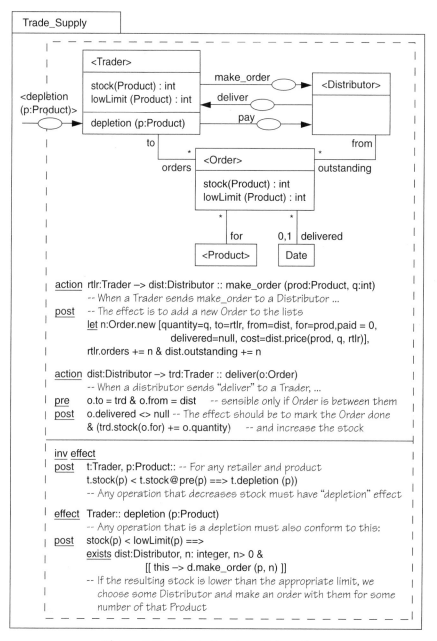

Figure 9.19 Trade Supply collaboration.

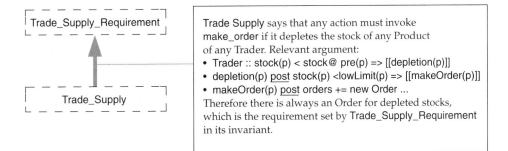

Trade Supply says that any action must invoke
make_order if it depletes the stock of any Product
of any Trader. Relevant argument:
- Trader :: stock(p) < stock@ pre(p) => [[depletion(p)]]
- depletion(p) post stock(p) <lowLimit(p) => [[makeOrder(p)]]
- makeOrder(p) post orders += new Order ...

Therefore there is always an Order for depleted stocks,
which is the requirement set by Trade_Supply_Requirement
in its invariant.

Figure 9.20   Documenting a framework refinement.

that all its statements (pictorial or otherwise) already imply those in Trade Supply
Requirements.

The general rules are the same as those discussed in Chapter 6, Abstraction,
Refinement, and Testing. In this case, the static models are the same; the only
thing we have to worry about is that invariant in the Requirement.

We can write it as shown in Figure 9.20. (Actually, a more rigorous treatment of
this argument reveals a hole regarding when Orders get removed. You might like
to tighten the reasoning and the spec of Trade Supply.)

9.5 *Composing Frameworks*

A commercial retailer plays many roles, participating in many collaborations. One
such collaboration is its interactions with customers (see Figure 9.21). The

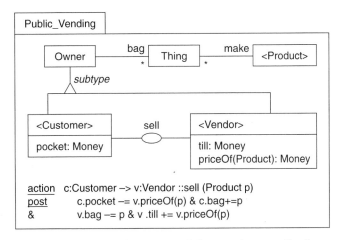

Figure 9.21   Another view of the vendor: retail sales.

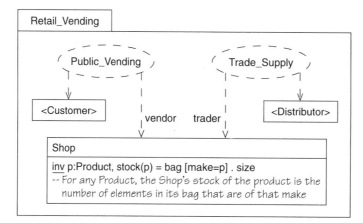

Figure 9.22 Joining roles by applying two frameworks.

collaboration shows the relationship of Customers to Vendors. In the sell operation, cash and Products are transferred in opposite directions.

A Shop is a type of object that plays the roles of both Trader and Vendor. So now we compose the two frameworks into a single picture, with Customer, Shop, and Distributor as the key players (see Figure 9.22). In Public_Vending, the Vendor's stock was represented as a set of Things, each of which is an example of a Product; so this model must be tied, using an invariant, to the Trader's stock that had been modeled as an integer for any Product.

The final step is to implement the types with classes. Supposing that Shop:sell is not refined further but is implemented as a single message, the designer must observe Trade_Supply::depletion whenever stocks get depleted; so a call to make_Order must sometimes be part of executing sell. Because the design has been so fully thought through, the class implementation will be simple.

9.5.1   Building Systems from Collaborations

Shop is a synthesis that plays two roles. Each role is about the interaction with another type of object—or rather, a role of another object. The Shop functions by having enough roles to make a coherent unit—in this case, ensuring the throughput of stock.

Given a variety of different collaborations, it is possible to construct many different role-playing objects. Collaborations are plugged together by making objects that play roles in each (and sometimes more than one role in one collaboration, just as a person may wear more than one hat in an organization). For each object, it is necessary to state how participation in one role affects the other by tying together their vocabulary of state changes, as is done with the Shop's bag and stock.

But the main work of the design resides in the collaborations themselves, and plugging them together is relatively straightforward. Collaborations are the best focus for design, and objects are secondary. Following this principle results in designs that are more flexible.

⚠ 9.6 *Templates as Packages of Properties*

Suppose you frequently find yourself modeling bananas, with a keen interest in their curvier-than relation; elsewhere, you trade commodities that have a pricier-than relation; in a class library you model strings with a dictionary-precedes. Some objects have several such relations; physical objects can be compared separately for weight, size, and price.

All these objects have a comparison operation that works largely the way "<" works on numbers in that they observe certain rules: a banana can't be curvier than itself; it is either less curvy or not less curvy than any other banana; and if mine is less curvy than yours and yours is less so than your friend's, then mine must be less curvy than hers. These properties are quite important in some contexts, for example if they are to be sorted into a unique linear order.

How do we avoid repeating these rules every time we state them? It is not a solution to say that those types (or their attributes) are all subtypes of, say, Magnitude, which packages operator < (Magnitude) with all the rules. That would mean that any Magnitude could be compared with any other, and a String's dictionary position could be compared with a Banana's curvature. (For the same reason, we didn't use subtypes for the Jobs and Skills in Section 9.2.1.)

Treating operators as functions (as in C++), we instead make a template package (see Figure 9.23). TotalOrdering is being used as a convenient package for a set of assertions or properties that we can apply to different types. Because we're

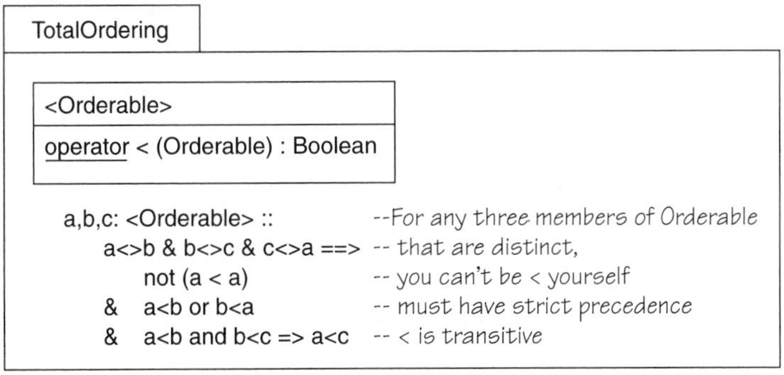

```
┌────────────────────────────────────────────────────────────────┐
│ TotalOrdering                                                    │
│  ┌──────────────────────────────────────────────┐               │
│  │ <Orderable>                                   │               │
│  ├──────────────────────────────────────────────┤               │
│  │ operator < (Orderable) : Boolean             │               │
│  └──────────────────────────────────────────────┘               │
│                                                                  │
│    a,b,c: <Orderable> ::        --For any three members of Orderable │
│        a<>b & b<>c & c<>a ==>   -- that are distinct,            │
│            not (a < a)          -- you can't be < yourself       │
│        &   a<b or b<a           -- must have strict precedence   │
│        &   a<b and b<c => a<c   -- < is transitive               │
└────────────────────────────────────────────────────────────────┘
```

Figure 9.23   Framework for TotalOrdering.

going to use the template many times, we take the trouble to set out the rules precisely. Groups of useful properties such as TotalOrdering are sometimes called *traits*. With a rich enough library of traits,[4] you can make a wide variety of type definitions by combining several traits in "mix and match" style.

Not all operators have the TotalOrdering properties. For example, when you make a project plan, the tasks have only a partial ordering with respect to the must-precede operator. Task A must be finished before B and C, and both B and C must be finished before D is started; but the order of finishing B and C might not matter. Figure 9.24 shows some types whose properties can be defined in part with the help of this template.

9.6.1 A Template Can Have Provisions

A sorted list keeps its items in a uniquely determined linear order. You can make sorted lists of almost any type of object provided that it has a comparison opera-

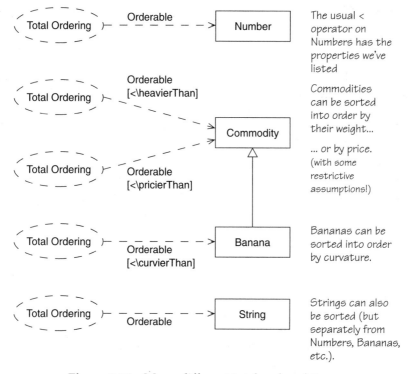

Figure 9.24 Many different total-ordered items.

---

4. Including the obvious ones—associative, commutative, and idempotent—and many not-so-obvious ones that help factor fundamental commonality in structure and behavior.

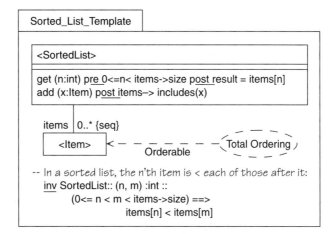

Figure 9.25   Sorted List framework: What kinds of items are OK?

tor with the TotalOrdering properties. The template in Figure 9.25 defines what a SortedList means and includes the TotalOrdering properties on its items.

A Sorted List Template can be applied to any type; when applied, the imported TotalOrdering template will impose its properties on the type substituted for <Item>. The fragments in Figure 9.26 define different types that represent sorted lists with different content types.

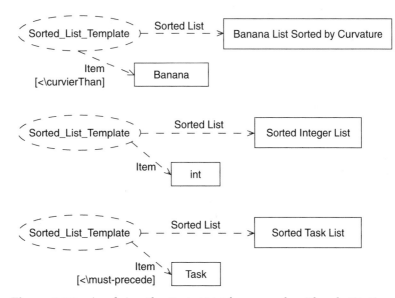

Figure 9.26   Applying the Sorted List framework with substitutions.

We have explicitly identified a separate new type for sorted lists of each item type (you can't put a Banana in a Sorted Integer List). The template *imposes* on the item types the properties of the relevant operators. Notice that we also substitute "<," which the Sorted List Template has imported from TotalOrdering. If you put a bunch of Bananas into a BananaListSortedByCurvature, they may end up in different relative positions than in a BananaListSortedByPrice.

What happens if you try to model a sorted list for something like project Tasks, which should not really be totally ordered based on must-precede? The TotalOrdering properties would be imposed on Task, something that (1) is probably not what you intended, because it imposes a linear order on all tasks, and (2) could be inconsistent with the definitions of the must-precede operator itself.

What we really want is to state that, as a prerequisite, the type substituted for <Item> should independently have the properties described by the TotalOrdering template; if it does not, it is not suited to the Sorted List template.

In a separate section of the package we provide a way for the designer of a template to say, "This template should be applied only to things that you already intend to have certain properties." The idea, called a *provision*, is a bit like a precondition, except that it typically works at design time.[5] Figure 9.27 shows an improvement of Sorted List Template. It says that if you have a type to which the TotalOrdering properties already apply, then it is OK to make Sorted Lists of it.

In the provisions section, you can put any model to which the substituted types must *already* conform.[6] Thus, you can require that one substituted type be a subtype of another; or that they have some relationship (see Section 9.2.1, Framework Applications Are Not Subtypes) or satisfy some predicate. The designer who applies the template must check, perhaps with help from a tool, that all the other parts of his or her model imply the properties laid down as provisions, and this should be documented much as a refinement is documented.

To see exactly what this means, we must recall that all models are defined within a package and that models are usually structured into packages. The people who use our template will probably apply it in a separate package, into which they will have to import both the package defining our template and the packages in which their item types are defined (see Figure 9.28). The imported packages must provide definitions that imply everything given in the provisions clause; and a conformance justification should be attached to the application of the template (Figure 9.20).

In general, when you build a framework you must make certain assumptions about the things that are substituted for your placeholders in order for that appli-

---

5. Using *reflection*, you can write generic code that does similar checks at runtime.

6. This lets us correctly describe C++ template design and usage, including the Standard Template Library.

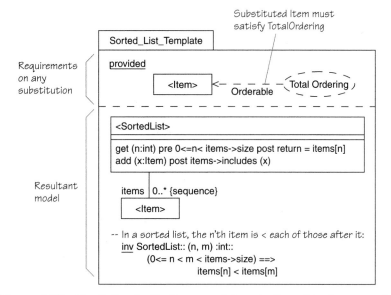

Figure 9.27   Explicit substitution provisions in SortedList framework.

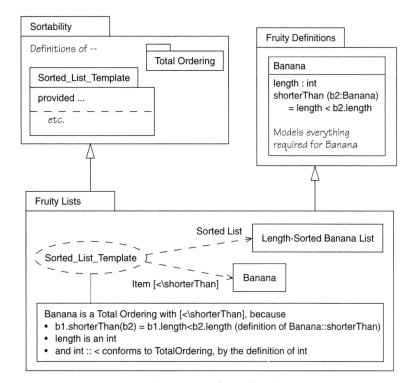

Figure 9.28   Applying templates that have provisions.

cation of the framework to work as intended. Use the provisions section to document these requirements.

▶ *provisions*   A set of prerequisites associated with a framework; any elements substituted when applying this framework must meet those prerequisites in order for the framework to be applicable. Provisions are analogous to "design-time" preconditions.

9.6.2   Template as Generic Types and Classes

Many templates exist to define a single family of types, such as the Sorted Lists. It is inconvenient to explicitly invent a new type name every time we want to make a new sorted list of something and then to explicitly substitute that for the placeholder in the template. An abbreviated notation covers these cases.

Within the definition of the template package, you can use its name as one of the placeholder names—for example, the name of a type. Using UML conventions, add an inset dashed box at the corner of the type and list the placeholders of the template (see Figure 9.29).

To use the template, draw a type using the name of the template package (this is also the name of the primary template type, which the type drawn implicitly substitutes). Place the template parameters in the UML inset dashed box or show them as explicit textual substitutions[7] in the form shown in Figure 9.30. Either one is equivalent to drawing the syntax shown in Figure 9.31. (In C++, the equivalent would be roughly SortedList < Banana, shorterThan>.)

Nested packages are useful when they are generic; a standard package can contain definitions of several generics (see Figure 9.32). A user can import the container, making the names of the nested generic packages visible, and then apply the generics. Package provisions also work well with package nesting.

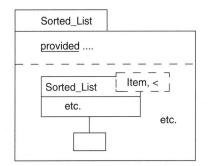

Figure 9.29   Defining a template with convenient syntax.

---

7. The text version also works for nongraphical things such as attributes and inline declarations such as x: Sorted_List. UML would treat this as an uninterpreted string.

Figure 9.30   Alternative convenient syntax for applying a template.

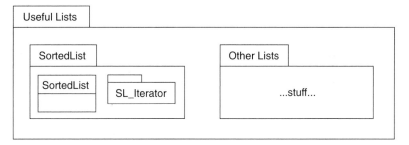

Figure 9.31   Equivalent "full" syntax.

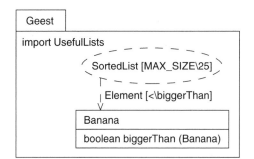

Figure 9.32   Templates and nested packages.

9.6.3   Using Substitution as Parameterization

You can substitute any name when you do an import—not only types and attributes but also variables, constants, and more. A substitution can be used to parameterize a spec. For example, if an integer constant MAX_SIZE is used within SortedList but is not set to any value, it can be substituted when SortedList is applied (see Figure 9.33). Figure 9.34 shows the graphical version.

Figure 9.33   Substituting "values": textual version.

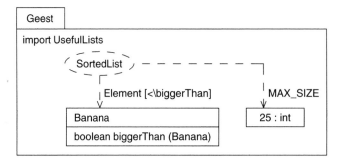

Figure 9.34   Substituting "values": graphical version.

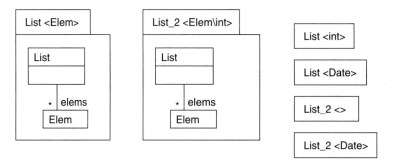

Figure 9.35   Explicit template parameters and parameter substitution.

9.6.4   Explicit Template Parameters

In general, we do not constrain the types that can be substituted, because we sometimes substitute just to avoid name clashes between multiple imports (see Figure 9.35). The "<..>" markers simply suggest places for substitution; but unmarked types can be substituted, and marked types can be left unsubstituted. Any substitutable type that isn't substituted when imported remains as a substitutable type in the importer.

Packages can be given explicit parameters. These are substitutable elements that must be explicitly substituted by the importer (even if only by one of its own parameters). They also can be given default arguments.

9.7 *Templates for Equality and Copying*

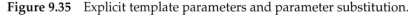

What does it mean for two objects to be equal? For one to be a copy of the other? These questions arise often in different forms and have an answer that is domain-independent. This section defines what they mean and provides standard template packages to use. These standard template packages can be used to define standard copy and equality as well as for features such as replication and caching.

9.7.1 Type-defined Equality

Are these two shapes equal? Some people might say yes, because all their lengths and angles are the same; others might say no; they are in different positions and hence different. It all depends on what exactly you mean by *equal*; sometimes there are different degrees and kinds of equality (such as "congruent" and "similar").

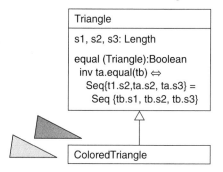

So whereas object identity is treated as an intrinsic property, equality must be defined separately for each type: There's no automatic meaning for it. There may be several useful equality-like relations, or none, and it's up to the inventor of a type to define them.

Equality is relative to type. Suppose that you define that two Triangles are equal if the lengths of their sides are equal. Then someone produces two members of the Triangle type that happen to be colored. One is blue and the other red, but their sides are the same. Are these objects equal?

People who are aware of the type Triangle but not ColoredTriangle would say yes. For their purposes, the two Triangles are equal; they never ask about a Triangle's color. The fewer differences you're interested in, the more things look the same; The more you know, the more differences you can discern.

Moreover, it would be wrong to contradict our definition of equality in a subtype. Triangle is the set of all triangles, colored or not, and it should be the place where you put statements that are true about all of them. Equality on colored triangles could further discriminate on color. But the supertype has stated that as long as the sides are the same, two triangles are equal.

So the equality definition typically cannot simply be inherited, and we must do one or both of the following.

- Have a differently named equality-like relation for every type. This isn't as bad as it might first sound. It forces you to think through the differences.
- Have a single notion of equal but be more careful about what we promise about it. For example, we could say that for two triangles to be equal they must have equal sides, but not necessarily the reverse:

$$ta . equal (tb) \Rightarrow ta.s1 = tb.s1 \ \& \ ta.s2 = tb.s2 \ \& \ ta.s3 = tb.s3$$

The same considerations apply to almost all comparison relations between members of the same type (for example, $\leq$ and $\geq$). An "equality-like" relation is one that conforms to the template shown in Figure 9.36. This principle can be applied to Triangles in a variety of ways (see Figure 9.37).

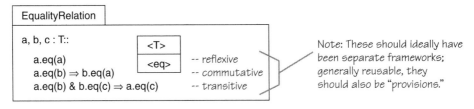

Figure 9.36   Template for equality relations.

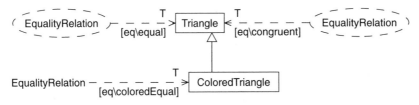

Figure 9.37   Defining different equality relations.

▶ *equality*   A generic relation on a type. The relation must satisfy certain mathematical properties. Defined as a standard framework.

Sometimes you can make an equality-like relation that seems reasonable for all subtypes. For example, we could define equality for shapes of any form by assuming they all have some Boolean contains(p:Point), as follows:

Shape::equivalent (s: Shape) = --'self' and 's' are equivalent
    -- if there is some vector, offset (conceptually, the difference in their positions) for which
    Vector->exists (offset |
        -- any point is in "self" exactly when (point - offset) is in s
        Point->exists (p | self.contains(p) = s.contains (p-offset)))

Although this is more general, it may still fail to adequately address colored points.

A user of a graphical editor can make a Group of other Shapes, which then behaves as one Shape, for the purposes of moving it around and so on. It's also possible to ungroup a Group, restoring the individual parts. This means that the two examples shown here before ungrouping, although equivalent by the preceding definition (looking the same), are *significantly unequal*—that is, unequal in a sense that is likely to be important to their users. Similarly, a rectangle may happen to be temporarily shaped like a square; however, if you stretch it horizontally and stretch a true square horizontally, very different things happen.

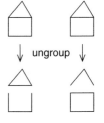

Here, equality-like relations need to be considered on a per-type basis; they should take into account dynamic and mutative behavior.

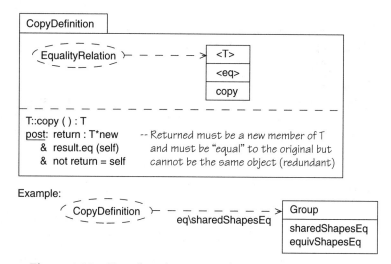

Figure 9.38   Template for copy with prerequisite of equality.

9.7.2   Copying an Object

It's often necessary in an action spec to require that a new copy of an object be made—that is, one that is equal (by some definition) but not identical. Just as equality must be defined separately by type, so must copying. To copy a Triangle means to copy its three sides; to copy a Grouped collection of Shapes means to copy the constituents of the Group.

You can use the template in Figure 9.38 to conveniently define a copy operation provided that your chosen comparison operator is a valid equality relation.

This copy definition could be used on Groups with either of two different equality operators: sharedShapesEq (two group objects are considered equal provided that they share the same shapes) and equivShapesEq (the shapes themselves need not be shared but must be equivalent by some definition of equivalent).

In contrast to equality, the name of the operation doesn't need to be changed across subtypes for copy. If you know only that you've been given a Shape, you know that getting a copy will give you the same visible result; you have no expectations about anything more, because you have no information on type-specific operations. However, a subtype of shape would have to copy in accordance with its specialized definition of the equality operator; so colored shapes would have to copy the color as well.

⚠ 9.8 *Package Semantics*

Template packages define the meaning of recurring patterns of models and designs, but the idea extends to the basic modeling constructs themselves. If two designers draw a pair of type boxes, with a 1-1 line between them, both designers have the same intent except for the specific domain they work in; the same thing is true for using subtype arrows, a state transition, or superstates. And if they put the same stereotype on two elements, they mean the same thing (presumably).

Templates can be used to define fundamental modeling constructs, as well as any extensions, in Catalyisis. This includes associations, associative classes, qualifiers, and even types and subtypes. Of course, most of them will have convenient syntactical forms, such as those UML provides. This section describes how new notations and semantic extensions can be defined precisely in Catalysis.

9.8.1   Interpreting Package Contents

We've already observed that the diagrams we draw in UML could as easily be written in the form of textual statements. The advantage of the diagrams is that they are easier to find your way around in and to grasp as a whole. Presumably they put your visual processing capabilities to work on the problem, leaving your linguistic processor free to mouth punchy-sounding businessspeak.

But diagrams can't express everything you want to say, so for details such as invariants and postconditions, we usually resort to text.[8] The pictures themselves can be converted to textual statements in a similar style. So the entirety of a model can be thought of as a collection of assertions. A package is a chosen set of such statements, and importing means only that you are including the statements from one package within another.

It's possible to write a precise set of rules (that is, a program) for converting each diagram element into text. And given any complex piece of text—such as an action specification, with its pre- and postconditions and odd constructs such as @pre and so on—it is possible to write a set of rules for converting it into a longer set of statements in terms of a much more basic set of ideas. These sets of rules are called the *semantics* of the language.

Books such as this one, which explain a notation and how to use it, are informal versions of the semantics: informal in the sense that they aren't written as an executable program and include ambiguities and inconsistencies. No one has yet written a full formal semantics for UML, Catalysis, or Objectory, although several projects are under way. Still, there is a wide range in how precisely their various visual notations are understood and how much reinterpretation will be required by practitioners. The closest things most people see in practice are the consistency-checking facilities of various support tools. Unfortunately, the different tools have slightly different ideas about the semantics, and that is why it would be nice to get an agreement on one of them.

---

8. Although Stuart Kent has shown how to move some of these assertions into the pictorial domain.

What has been written is a description of the abstract syntax: the constructs that exist and some of the constraints on them. These are sometimes called *meta-models*. However, they are far from being a full semantics.

9.8.2   Stereotypes and Dialects

Another disadvantage of a pictorial notation is that there aren't enough symbols to cover all the subtly different things we want to say. You can invent only so many variants of boxes and lines and round things; if there are too many of them, newcomers soon despair of remembering what they mean.

We use UML stereotypes for this reason. A *stereotype* is a tag that you can attach to any box, arrow, or other pictorial construct to tell you exactly which meaning is intended. In other words, it tells you which translation rule to use from the semantics (assuming there is one).

Stereotypes can be used on an individual model element as an alternative syntax to apply a framework (similar to Section 9.6.2, Template as Generic Types and Classes). The shorthand rules are as follows.

- If a type has the same name as its package, then using that name as a stereotype on a target type means to import the package, substituting the target type.
- If an attribute has the same name as its package, then using that name as a stereotype on a target attribute means to import the package, substituting the target attribute and its source type. It works similarly for other elements.
- Just as with other template shortcuts, stereotype application can use additional explicit substitutions: «name[x\a, y\b]». Or you can provide parameters defined on the template: «name⟨a,b⟩» (see Figure 9.39).

However, freely adding individual stereotypes leads to inconsistent models. Rather than attach stereotypes to every construct in the picture, we establish a set of defaults: a particular default meaning for each pictorial element without stereotypes, or a consistent family of stereotypes. This default set is a called a *dialect*. To specify which dialect a package should use, quote the dialect in the package tab. Naturally, the use of consistent dialects will simplify things; but if the dialects

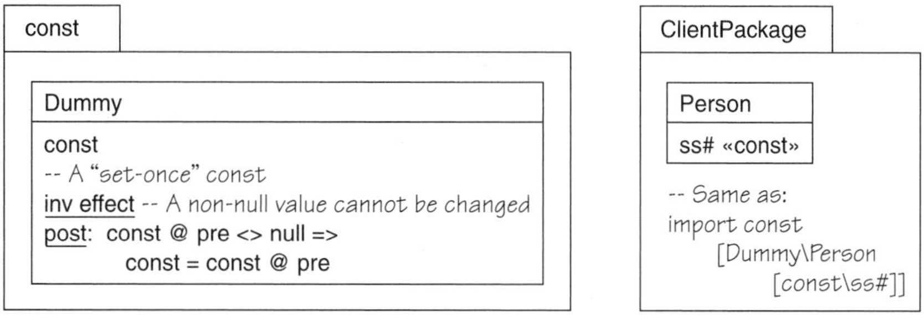

Figure 9.39   Defining the meaning of stereotypes using templates.

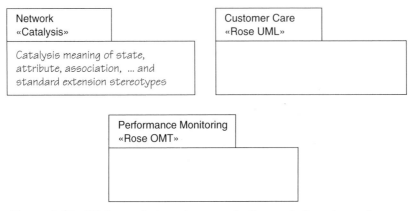

Figure 9.40   Dialects of stereotypes and other notations in packages.

have a common underlying translation (see Section 9.8.3), you can even use custom dialects best suited to each portion of the problem (see Figure 9.40).

Stereotypes make the language extensible. This can be a disadvantage or an advantage depending on whether you make your money by using the notation or by pontificating about it. Every self-styled expert has a pet variant on the basic ideas; all of them are, of course, improvements. It is widely agreed, though, that UML is by no means the last word on modeling languages and that it would be neither possible nor appropriate to make it entirely fixed at the present time.

▶ *stereotype*   A shorthand syntax for applying a framework; a stereotype is used by referring to its name as «name» attached to any model element. Frameworks provide an extensibility mechanism for the modeling language; stereotypes provide a syntax for using this mechanism.

▶ *dialect*   A package that contains a useful and agreed set of mutually consistent stereotypes, together defining a particular dialect of the modeling language. All modeling work is done in the context of selected dialect(s).

9.8.3   Examples of Semantic Rules for a Dialect

To close full circle, as perhaps you may have guessed by now, dialects and semantic rules themselves are defined within packages, although, as we've said, consider them virtual until further notice. But here is a short example to show the idea.

Semantic rules are expressed as templates; a dialect contains nested packages for its semantic rules. Each rule translates a slightly higher-level notation into its equivalent lower-level one. Here, any line between two type boxes that contains an explicit stereotype means the same as *inverse attributes* (see Figure 9.41). So what should an association line mean if it has no stereotype tag? To define a default, you identify the untagged feature with the appropriate tag[9] (see Figure 9.42).

---

9. A template could also introduce customized textual and graphical syntax for the application of that template; we do not generalize to such visual grammars in this book.

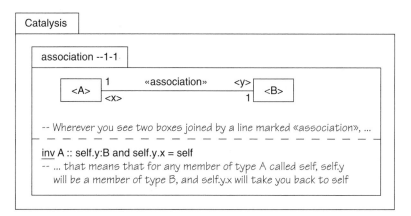

Figure 9.41   Template for what an association is.

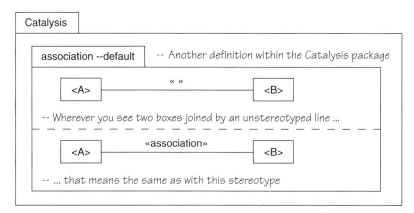

Figure 9.42   Template defining the meaning of default notation.

Figure 9.43 on the next page shows some equivalent ways to define an association. The top part (a) uses the highest-level notation: a line. In (b), you see the pattern notation for applying a template; in (c), a straight textual form, and in (d), the expanded result of any of the previous forms.

9.9   *Down to Basics with Templates*

We have seen that templates can be used to define domain-specific patterns, providing a higher-level notation for describing problems. The same templates can be used to define the modeling language itself, down to its formal basics.

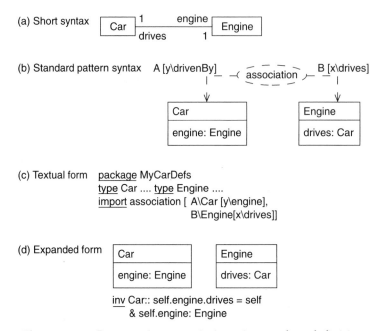

(a) Short syntax

(b) Standard pattern syntax

(c) Textual form

package MyCarDefs
type Car .... type Engine ....
import association [A\Car [y\engine],
                    B\Engine[x\drives]]

(d) Expanded form

Figure 9.43   Interpreting association via template definitions.

9.9.1   Template Packages to Represent Inference Rules

Templates can be used to represent general facts that are useful in understanding or reasoning about types. They can be presented as diagrams or as Boolean expressions. For example, at the very basic level, we can write things such as or-definition. It means that, if you happen to find an expression involving or and two Boolean expressions on either side of it, you can match them to <A> and <B> and rewrite the whole thing using not and and. Figure 9.44 shows a few others.

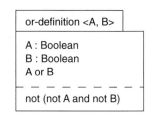

It is sometimes useful, with these kinds of rules, to use placeholders that themselves take arguments (see Figure 9.45). This may sound mind-bending at first, but this is as bad as it gets. We're now outside the realm of practical daily application for most software developers. But briefly, in case you're interested, the induction rule can be used to verify statements involving a progression. For example, here's how to prove that all cricket scores are boring.

- A score of zero is clearly boring, because nothing has happened.

    A score of 0 is boring.

- Given any score, whether it is 42 or 103 or anything—call it x—then a score of x+1 is bound to be more boring than x. This is because x+1 can be achieved only after more cricket has occurred, and clearly that is incrementally boring. So if x was boring, then x+1 definitely also will be boring. We can write this as

A score of x is boring.
A score of x+1 is boring.

an inference of which we have satisfied ourselves; we don't need to give it a name, because we won't be needing it for long. Clearly, cricket is boring.

- Let's choose a particular score, say 200. You will agree that

   200 : Integer and 200 >= 0

- At this stage, all the requirements of the Induction template have been met, with these substitutions:

   P [<x>]   -->   A score of <x> is boring.
   i   -->   200

- The Induction rule tells us that we can now safely conclude

   A score of 200 is boring.

Note that negative cricket scores might yet prove interesting.

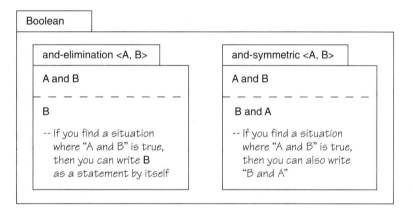

Figure 9.44   Templates for typical inference rules.

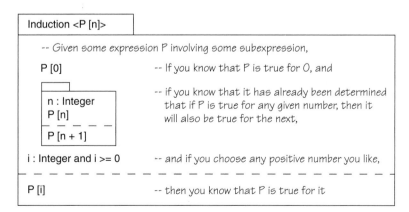

Figure 9.45   Induction template.

9.9.2   Template Packages for Primitive Types

The primitive types that we use in every model and design—Boolean, arithmetic, sets, lists, and dictionaries—can be defined in basic packages that are imported by all others. These types are most easily defined in an axiomatic style—that is, by simply stating a number of fundamental facts (*axioms*, mathematicians call them) that are true about the types, from which other facts follow. For example, the package defining Boolean operators contains the propositions shown in Figure 9.46.

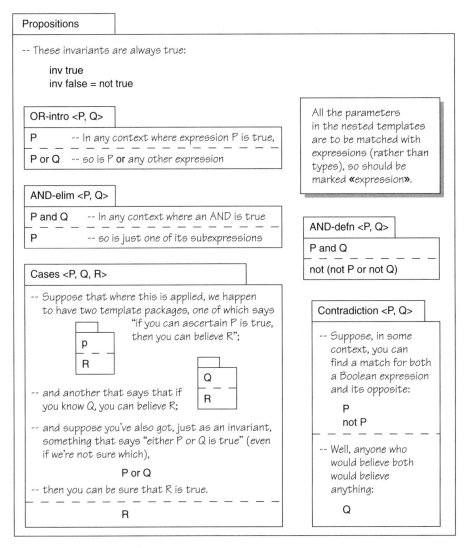

Figure 9.46   Propositions: a packaging of Boolean operators.

We can create another package that imports this one, defining Predicate Logic, which gives the meaning of the quantifiers "for all x, [some expression about x]" and "there is an x such that. . . ." A package about Sets comes next, and together with Predicates is imported to help define the rules of arithmetic. Other kinds of collections (lists and dictionaries or maps) can also be defined with the help of sets and predicates.

9.9.3 Layered Semantics

The ideas of objects and types can also be defined in this style. Membership of a type is implied by observance of all the constraints (invariants, postconditions, and so on) imposed by the type definition.

In this fashion, we can build up a hierarchy of basic types and operators—not only the syntactic definitions but also their meanings! And because the basics can be different for different modeling and programming languages—for example, not all have exactly the same idea of the passage of time—different packages can be supplied for users of different dialects and can be referenced as stereotypes.

In fact, the entire semantics of the modeling and programming languages that you use can be defined in this way. Choose your basic modeling package on which to build your specification, and choose the Java package to be able to check that your code matches your spec. A typical hierarchy for modeling is shown in Figure 9.47. But for most users, it is not necessary to know about the details of these basics, any more than you bother with the formal semantics of your programming language. Still, it is nice to know that this foundation can be made explicit and that the details can be made a matter of choice.

And, of course, most of these packages—especially the complex semantics ones—are virtual at present. But some research projects have indeed built up the packages of primitives. (The example given here comes from [Mural91].)

One interesting feature of these packages is that they define many "if you already know that this fact is true, then you can also assume that" rules. These packages talk about the fundamental properties of the expressions we can write: In the arithmetic package, for example, there is something that tells us that x+y is the same as y+x, a likely fact to use in programming. In the extreme case of safety-critical systems, designers can use these rules (and similar ones dealing with programming language statements) to check that their programs fulfill robustness criteria and indeed meet their specs. Designers can also build higher-level rules around them. The rules are checked once and then institutionalized as templates.

For the writers of support tools, these basic packages are a way of discussing and defining the exact details of the languages they support. This should have the benefit of making the languages more interoperable and should allow these writers to define more-sensible consistency checks. But for most of us, the importance of this level of detail is secondary, arising from its relevance for tool designers.

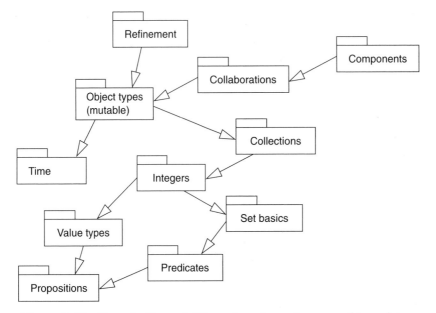

Figure 9.47   No primitives: full layering via packages and templates.

9.9.4   Standard Packages

We have seen that nested packages can be used to define a related set of stereo-types, such as those needed for a particular method or language (see Figure 9.48). There is a Standard Catalysis package that is imported automatically into all others. It defines numbers, logic, and other basics. It is called catalysis.spec.lang. If you explicitly import any other *.spec.lang packages, catalysis.spec.lang is no longer automatically imported.

There are standard packages for various programming languages, enabling you to embed code in Catalysis designs. They are called catalysis.java.lang, catalysis.cpp.lang, catalysis.eiffel.lang, and catalysis.smalltalk.lang. These packages define the valid syntax and semantics of programming constructs in these languages.

9.10   *Summary of Model Framework Concepts*

A model framework is a generic package containing both normal and placeholder definitions. A placeholder is a name that can be substituted when the framework is used. Each use or application of the framework provides its own substitutions of the placeholders. Placeholder names are distinguished with angle brackets (<>). The names of attributes and associations of placeholder types are themselves placeholders. (This is not automatically true of actions.)

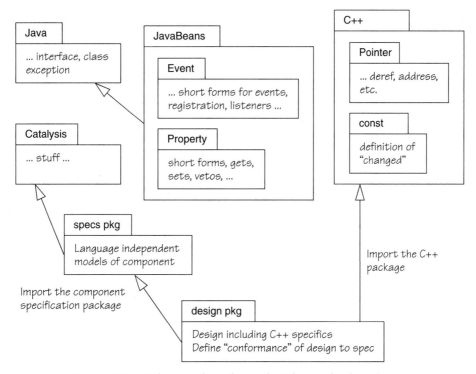

Figure 9.48 What can be achieved with standard packages.

If the framework has a provisions section, an application is considered meaningful only if the requirements are already conformed to, prior to the applicaton, with the same substitutions. A justification should be attached to each application to document how the requirement is met.

9.10.1 Composition of Definitions

Recall that every model can be regarded as a list of individual statements: All the pictures can be translated into formal text. A template package is a collection of statements; when it is applied, the statements (subject to substitutions) are added to the model.

Each type and action in the model is defined by all the statements made about it in its various appearances. Some, all, or none of these may come from template applications. All these statements compose following the standard composition rules.

Figure 9.49 summarizes the model framework concepts.

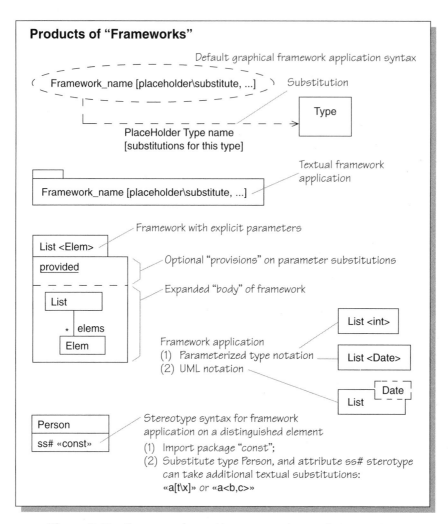

Figure 9.49 Frameworks: patterns, generics, and stereotypes.

9.10.2 Usefulness of Model Frameworks

Model frameworks can be used to express relationships that straddle type boundaries and to encapsulate relationships made up of a collection of types, associations, and actions. They are a powerful tool for abstraction and a useful unit of reuse.

Part IV Implementation by Assembly

Part III, Factoring Models and Designs, describes how you can factor specifications and models into parts and then compose them to readily build larger models. Although the basic idea of factoring and composing carry over to design and implementation, a different set of constraints is imposed by the implementation technology.

This part is about the reuse of implementation code and discusses approaches to designing and building components so that they can be readily extended or adapted for use in different contexts.

Chapter 10, Components and Connectors, describes the richness of component-based developmemt and explains how it raises the level at which implementation units can be connected to build larger systems. Because there is no single answer to what constitutes useful component and connection mechanisms, we use frameworks (see Chapter 9, Model Frameworks and Template Packages) to define the generic building blocks of different component architectures.

Chapter 11, Reuse and Pluggable Design: Frameworks in Code, discusses the design and development of pluggable components, including how it affects the development process.

Chapter 12, Architecture, shows how the architecture of a system—views of its components structure and their relationships to one another—is defined by the set of available design and implementation building blocks and the set of rules and patterns for applying those blocks coherently and consistently.

Chapter 10 Components and Connectors

Many software managers, harried by budgets and delays, envy hardware designers. To design a steam engine, the engineers did not start by designing screws from scratch. Electronic systems are built by plugging together chips, boards, or boxes that are widely interoperable. A well-chosen set of components can have many possible configurations: many end products that can be made quickly and reliably.

Over the past few years, the same thing has begun to happen in software. Word processors can talk to spreadsheets, and graphs to databases. Standards such as COM and CORBA allow you to plug together components in different languages and platforms. JavaBeans, or any similar protocol, allows separately designed objects to find out more about each other's capabilities before negotiating a collaboration. Visual building tools help you plug components together pictorially.

Large-grained components are becoming a practical part of an enterprise component strategy. These components interact with one another as much as their smaller cousins do, and they must be analyzed and designed so that they interoperate as expected.

This chapter explains how to meet requirements using component-based designs and how to design components that work well together. After introducing component concepts, discussing pluggable parts, and describing how components have evolved over the years, we look briefly at three component standards: JavaBeans, COM+, and CORBA.

Rather than limit ourselves to a specific component technology, we then introduce the port-connector model of component architectures. We discuss a typical example of such an architecture and show how to specify and design with components in this architecture. Then we show how even ad hoc and heterogenous component systems are amenable to systematic development in Catalysis.

10.1 *Overview of Component-Based Development*

By itself, the use of object-oriented programming is not enough to get stupendous improvements in software delivery times, development costs, and quality. Some people wonder why, having bought a C++ compiler, they're not seeing all the glorious benefits they've heard of.[1] But it doesn't work that way. The greatest benefits depend on good management of the software development process. The bag of techniques, languages, methods, and tools lumped under the "object-oriented" heading is an *enabling* technology: It makes it easier to achieve fast, cheap, robust development, but only if you use it properly.

If you want to achieve significant improvements in software productivity, one of the most important shifts is to stop writing applications from scratch every time you embark on a new project. Instead, you should build by using software components that already exist. The building blocks that you use for software development should not be limited to those offered by the programming language but should also include larger-grained, encapsulated units.

Over the past five years or so, we have seen this change happening. Many applications are now built on purchased third-party frameworks or by gluing together existing applications. Many programmers have come across Microsoft's OLE/COM (and before it, DLLs), which provides a way of bolting together entire applications. The OMG's CORBA provides similar facilities.

For example, an application that reads stock figures from a newsfeed can be "wired up" to a spreadsheet; this component does some calculations and passes the results to a database, from which a Web server extracts information on demand. Each of these components may be a stand-alone application, perhaps even with its own user interface, but is provided with a way to interact with other software.

Many development teams think only of gluing together large third-party components that can also work as stand-alones. But the spreadsheet in our example doesn't need a user interface: It is used only as a calculating engine within a larger chain. The example could be built more efficiently by using a calculating mechanism designed to be used as a component in a larger design and so lacking all the GUI overhead (perhaps with a suitable GUI as an optional add-on). And the persistence mechanism need not be a part of the spreadsheet itself. It could use a separate data-access component for that; again, it could include a default one.

Most development teams could benefit from thinking more in terms of building their own components for their application area. This is the key to fast, reliable development: to do it the way hardware designers have been doing it for two centuries and build components that can be assembled together in many combi-

---

1. And some of them then go around saying, "It doesn't work"!

nations. Most end products—and indeed most components—should be assemblies of smaller components, built either elsewhere or in-house.

The aim must be to invest in the development of a component library as a capital asset (see Figure 10.1). Like any investment, this one requires money to be spent for a while before any payback is seen. A conventional software development organization requires a considerable shift of attitudes and strategy to adopt a component-based approach. Like all big shifts, it must be introduced in easy stages, and you must plan carefully the risks, fallbacks, and evaluation of each phase.

A lot of marketing hype surrounds the terms *component* and *component-based development*. It includes radical pronouncements suggesting that object technology is dead and components are the next salvation. Separation of concerns, encapsulation, and pluggable parts continue to distinguish good, flexible designs from bad.

10.1.1   General Components

What is new about components? If they are reusable software pieces, how are they different from modules? If they are like objects, in what ways are they different? At the most basic level, components are parts that can be composed with others to build something bigger. Let's start with some basic definitions.

▶ *component-based development (CBD)*   An approach to software development in which all artifacts—from executable code to interface specifications, architectures, and business models; and scaling from complete applications and systems down to small parts—can be built by assembling, adapting, and "wiring" together existing components into a variety of configurations.

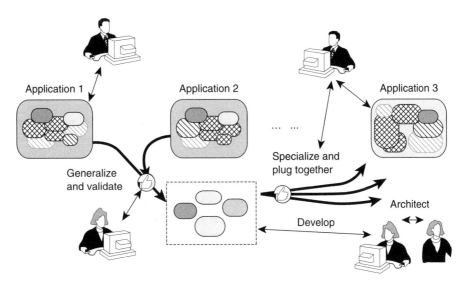

Figure 10.1   Component development and distribution.

▶ *component (general)*   A coherent package of software artifacts that can be independently developed and delivered as a unit and that can be composed, unchanged, with other components to build something larger.

Based on this broad definition, all the following items conform to the general spirit of component-based development:

- Dropping a user-interface widget, such as a master-slave pair of list boxes, onto a canvas and connecting the lists to the appropriate data sources from the problem domain.

- Using the same C++ List template to implement any number of domain classes by specializing the template parameter:

```
class Order {
    private:  List<LineItem> items;
};
```

- Using an off-the-shelf calendar package, word processor, and spreadsheet in an assemblage of several heterogenous components and writing scripts so that these components together fulfill a particular business need.

- Using a class framework, such as Java's Swing components, to build the user interfaces for many applications and to connect those UIs to their domain objects.

- Using a model framework, such as resource allocation, to model problems ranging from seminar room allocation to scheduling machine time for production lots in a factory.

- Using predefined language constructs in an infinite variety of contexts:

```
for ( ...; ...; ... ) { ... }
```

A component can include anything that a package can include: executable code, source code, designs, specifications, tests, documentation, and so on. In Chapter 9, Model Frameworks and Template Packages, we show how the idea of composing software based on interfaces also applies to designs and models, leading to a more general idea of component-based modeling: All work is done by adapting and composing existing pieces. To make effective use of implementation components, we should start with componentization of business models and requirements. In this more general sense, a Catalysis package constitutes a component.

10.1.2   Implementation Components

In this chapter we focus on implementation components: executable code, source code, interface specs, code templates, and the like. In this context, a component is similar to the well-known software engineering idea of a *module*, although we have standards in place and technology infrastructure that makes building distributed component systems a reality.

For one component to replace another, the replacement component need not work the same internally. However, the replacement component must provide at least the services that the environment expects of the original and must expect no more than the services the environment provides the original. The replacement must exhibit the same external behavior, including quality requirements such as performance and resource consumption.

▶ *component (in code)*   A coherent package of software implementation that (a) can be independently developed and delivered, (b) has explicit and well-specified interfaces for the services it provides, (c) has explicit and well-specified interfaces for services it expects from others, and (d) can be composed with other components, perhaps customizing some of their properties, without modifying the components themselves.

10.1.2.1   A Unit of Packaging

A component is a "package" of software that includes implementation, with a specification of interfaces provided and required. The mechanics for this packaging differ. In some component technologies, such as JavaBeans and COM+, the compiled code for a component includes an explicit runtime representation of interfaces; you can programatically inquire about these interfaces and use the information to establish suitable connections between components. In other component technologies, the compiled implementation may be stripped of this extra information and reduced to a minimal executable or DLL; in this case, the packaging unit must include separate and explicit descriptions of interfaces provided and required. COM (prior to COM+) required a separate and explicit type library containing component interface information to be registered in the shared system registry.

A component package typically includes the following.

- *A list of provided interfaces:* These are often imported from other packages, containing only the specs of these interfaces.
- *A list of required interfaces:* These are often imported from separate packages, just like the provided interfaces.
- *The external specification:* This is a specification of external behavior provided and required, relating all the interfaces in a shared model.
- *The executable code:* If built according to a suitable and consistent architecture, this can be coupled to the code of other components via their interfaces.
- *The validation code:* This is code, for example, that is used to help decide whether a proposed connection between components is OK.
- *The design:* This includes all the documents and source code associated with the work of satisfying the specification; it may be withheld from customers.

Components can also contain modifications to, and extensions of, existing classes. This is used often in Smalltalk—in which existing classes and methods can be dynamically modified and extended—and also is generally useful for any system that cannot be halted to install software upgrades. The interesting thing in terms of modeling is to provide mechanisms and rules for ensuring that the components do not interfere improperly with one another after they're installed in a system.

In some situations it can be useful to further distinguish the specification of a component, an executable that implements that spec, a particular installation of that executable, and a "running" incarnation of that executable that is available as a server. We will use the term *component* loosely to include all these. A tool or metamodel that dealt more fully with component deployment and management would separate them.

10.1.2.2 A Unit of Independent Delivery

Being independently deliverable means that a component is not delivered partially. Also, it must be specified and delivered in a form that is well separated from any other components it may interact with when deployed.

10.1.2.3 Explicit Provided and Required Interfaces

The only way one component can interact with another is via a provided interface. The specification of a component must explicitly describe all interfaces that a client can expect as well as the interfaces that must be provided by the environment into which the component is assembled.

For components to be *plug-replaceable*, it is essential that the component specs be self-contained and symmetrical; it is the only way to be able to design reliably using parts without knowledge of their implementations. In contrast, a traditional *server*, in a client-server setting, is one-sided: It provides a set of services, but the services it expects from others are not documented explicitly. Object-oriented languages have also focused almost exclusively on services implemented by a class without any explicit description of the services it expects from other objects.

10.1.2.4 Complete Separation of Interfaces from Implementation

Component software demands a complete separation of interface specifications from implementations. The interface specs, rather than the source code, define what a component will provide and expect when used. In fact, if you are ever forced to use an existing component that does not have an explicitly documented interface, it is usually worth writing a specification of it "as perceived and used"; this document greatly simplifies testing and reduces the time to evaluate the suitability of new and alternative versions of the component.

10.1.2.5 Component Composition

The basic idea is that, to assemble a larger component or application, the composer of components (a) selects which components to compose; (b) connects required interfaces of one component to provided interfaces of others to plug them together; and (c) perhaps writes some *glue* using scripting or adapters between components. Composites often provide standard services to structure their child structure at runtime and to expose some of their children's services.

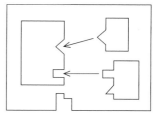

As with packaging, the exact form of component composition varies across different component technologies and tools. The key point is that the composition can be done by a different party, and at a different time, from the building of the components themselves. Section 10.7, Component Architecture, discusses a component-port-connector model for describing compositions in a simple way. Ports are the access points in a component where its services can be accessed or where it can access another's services; connectors couple ports. The kinds of compositions supported by a particular technology or style can be described by its connector kinds.

10.1.3   Components and Binding Times

Components are designed and built in one activity; they are composed with others in a separate step. When designing and building a component, you can relate it to the others it will (eventually) be composed with only by their contractual interfaces. Actual implementations are selected at composition time or, sometimes, even at runtime. We usually want to delay the bindings made when components are composed so that the composition can be done as late as possible. One view of the range of binding times is shown in Table 10.1.

Exhibit 10.1   Binding Times for Composition

Binding Time	How It Works
Coding time	Straight-line code, without even procedural separation.
Compile time	The standard separation of procedures; all calls are bound to an implementation at compile time.
Link time	Separate compilation units, with interfaces declared separately from their implementations; calls are compiled against interfaces and are bound when the compiled units are linked into an executable.
Dynamic linking	Separate compilation units that do not need to be linked into a single executable up front; instead, a compiled unit (a DLL) can be dynamically linked into the running system. Calls are compiled against interfaces and are bound the first time the implementation is loaded.
Runtime	Calls are compiled using a level of indirection; this indirection is used to dynamically bind a call against an interface to a specific implementation at runtime based on the "receiving" object; this can be combined with dynamic linking (Java) or static linking (C++).
Reflective	Calls are not compiled against interfaces at compile time. Instead, the runtime keeps an explicit representation of interfaces offered; calls are issued dynamically against these at runtime based on "reflection" about the services and (of course) are resolved dynamically. Scripting services, in which components are coordinated by interpreted scripts, are best built on such a facility.

10.1.4   Objects Versus Components

There is confusion in popular writings about the similarity and differences between an object and a component. Some of this confusion stems from the fact that component technology is often best implemented using an object-oriented language; more fundamentally, it stems from loose usage of the terms *object, class,* and *component.*

10.1.4.1   Is an Object a Component?

Components are software artifacts and represent the work of software developers and their tools; objects are identifiable instances created in running systems by executing code that is a part of some component. So, in that strict sense, an object is not a component. It is the component code that is reused—the calendar package, perhaps with some customizable properties—rather than a specific calendar instance and its state.

That said, a running component is often manifested as a collection of objects and can be usefully treated as though it were one large-grained object, based on our approach to refinement. So we sometimes use the term *component* a bit more loosely in this chapter to refer to the object or set of objects that manifest a particular usage of a component in an application.

▶ *component instance*   The object, set of objects, or predetermined configuration for such a set of objects that is the runtime manifestation of a component when composed within a particular application.

10.1.4.2   Is a Class a Component?

Only if packaged to include explicit descriptions of the interfaces that it implements and the interfaces it expects from others. Consider the following Java class:

```
class C1
    implements I1, I2      -- interfaces this class implements
{
    public T0 foo (T1 x);
    private T2 y;
}
```

The minimal component that could contain C1 would also have to include the specifications of I1, I2, T0, T1, and T2. A package with a single class; the interfaces it implements (perhaps those interface specs are imported from another package); and the interfaces it requires of any other objects it deals with (input parameters, returned objects, factory objects it uses to instantiate other objects, and so on) would constitute a minimal OO component.

If class C1 inherited part of its implementation from another class, there would be a direct implementation dependency between the classes. Many people believe that implementation inheritance, although often useful, should not cross component boundaries. When the boundary must be crossed, it may be better to adopt a composition or delegation style approach (see Section 11.5.3, Polymorphism and Forwarding).

In general, a component could implement its interfaces by directly exposing them to clients or by implementing classes that provided the interfaces; to use the interfacer, clients would need to obtain a handle to an instance of such a class.

10.1.4.3   Component-Based Design versus OO Design

When you build a design from components, you don't need to know how they are represented as objects or as instances of a classes or know how the connectors between components work.[2] In federated systems, just as in OO programs, each component is a collection of software; it is chosen for the support it provides of the corresponding business function and uses local data representations best suited to the software. Just as in OO programs, objects must access the information held by other objects, so in a component architecture, components intercommunicate through well-defined interfaces so as to preserve mutual encapsulation.

The smaller-grained components in Section 10.6.1 and Section 10.6.2 are also very similar to objects. In fact, they would be easiest to implement as objects in an object-oriented programming language. This shows that the differences between component-based design and object-oriented design are mainly of degree and scale and are not intrinsic to either type of design.

- Components often use persistent storage; although objects in an OO programming language always have local state, they typically work only within main memory, and persistence is dealt with separately.
- Components have a richer range of intercommunication mechanisms, such as events and workflows, rather than only the basic OO message. These mechanisms support easier composition of the parts.
- Components are often larger-grained than traditional objects and can be implemented as multiple objects of different classes. They often have complex actions at their interfaces, rather than single messages.
- A component package, by definition, includes definitions of the interfaces it provides as well as the interfaces it requires; a traditional single class definition focuses on the operations provided and not on the operations required.
- Objects tend to be dynamic; the number of customers, products, and orders you have, and their interconnections, changes dynamically. In contrast, larger-

---

2. Components can also be built without explicitly using object-oriented design techniques at all; but OO makes it a lot easier. If you tried to build a component architecture without mentioning objects, much of the technology you'd use would amount to object orientation anyway. We've recently read a few reports proclaiming "Objects have failed to deliver! Components are the answer!" The authors either have a poor understanding of how componentware is built, or, being journalists and paid pundits, they enjoy a disconcerting headline. The reality is that OOP, like structured programming before it, has become part of the body of ideas that constitute good software engineering. Having learned how to do it, we can now move on to putting it to work.

grained components may be more static; there will probably always be only one payment control and one finance component, and their configuration will be static.

Components, like objects, interact through polymorphic interfaces. All our modeling techniques apply equally well in both cases, including the more general connectors for components. Plus, we can usefully talk about a component instance, component type, and component class.

10.1.5   Components and Persistence

A component instance has state represented by its object(s) and is part of a larger component. Hence, its persistence needs to be in the context of its containing component. Java and COM provide differing versions of such protocols.

In simple cases, persistence can be achieved by a protocol by which a component instance serializes itself into a stream that is managed by its container. For larger, server-side components, each component can manage its own persistent storage and transactions; effective composition now requires that the container be able to coordinate nested transactions that cross its subcomponent boundaries. Enterprise JavaBeans, CORBA, Microsoft Transaction Server, and COM+ provide their own versions of this.

10.2 *The Evolution of Components*

We should not assume that objects are intrinsic to component-based development; in fact, one of the advantages of components is that they can encapsulate legacy systems regardless of how the systems are implemented inside. The idea of components goes back almost as far as the idea of software, but a number of things have changed significantly over the years.

* The granularity of the components and the corresponding unit of pluggability: from monolithic systems, to client-server partitions, to the operating system and its services, to today's object-based component approaches.
* The effort and ease of dynamically connecting components to compose larger systems, from writing screen-scrapers for host-based systems (discussed in a moment) to creating complex applications by visually configuring and connecting server-side components to one another and to user interfaces.
* The overall effort and cost of creating applications: from monolithic custom-made systems to gigantic "package" solutions[3] to the assembly of smaller components built on standard infrastructure and interfaces.

---

3. These are sometimes so inflexible that they either work wonderfully for your business or your business must adapt to fit what the package solution offers.

The earliest mainframe-based systems were written as monolithic applications manipulating data shared across all the application procedures. Internal procedures could rarely be considered encapsulated; they typically operated on shared data, making composition at that level difficult and error-prone. The only visible interface was to an external dumb terminal, and the nature of the interface was primitive: paint to the terminal screen and read character commands from the keyboard.

Calling these host-based applications "components" is a stretch; composing them was painful. Because the only interface offered to the outside was to a dumb terminal, the only way to connect two such "components" was to write pieces of code called *screen-scrapers* and *terminal emulators*. These programs acted as dumb terminals to the host but interpreted the screen painting commands and generated character commands. The granularity of components was very large, connections could not be established dynamically, and the technology for connecting parts was primitive.[4]

At the time, it was possible to deliver complete applications only in the form of an executable. Moreover, the executable had to be prebuilt in a static manner and could be replaced or upgraded only as a single unit. Software libraries contained source code, which you used by including the text and compiling it with your own.

But software vendors aren't keen on letting people see their source code; they'd rather give you the executable and (if you insist) the spec. This meant providing ways in which applications could communicate. In the early days, this meant that they passed files to one another, a slow process that required that every output and input from a program be converted to the form of external records. It lent itself to pipeline processing rather than dialog between programs.

This led to the development of the application program interface—which could be seen as a way in which a program could pretend to be an application's user using facilities standardized at the level of the operating system—and dynamic linking, which enabled code to be linked at runtime without further processing. Two distinct forms of large-grained components evolved from this.

The first form led to client-server-styled systems, with the client combining user-interface and application logic and communicating via SQL requests with a database server that dealt with persistence, transactions, security, and so on. All communication involved database processing requests in SQL, and clients did not communicate with one another (except indirectly through shared data on the server).

Finer-grained application components also started to interact, using operating system support. In the world of Windows, generic applications were built with

---

4. This is changing substantially, with mainframe applications reborn as *server-side components* using technologies such as Enterprise JavaBeans.

APIs that enabled them to be interconnected and interact via the operating system, exchanging information through standardized data representation schemes. Thus, a spreadsheet application could communicate with a word processor and a stock feeder to produce a formatted financial report. In UNIX, we saw the emergence of the elegant, but limited, pipe-and-filter architecture.

The first APIs were sets of functions that an external component could invoke. If there was any notion of an object receiving the function calls, it was the entire running executable itself. But the most recent developments in this field have put the executable program into the background (see Figure 10.2). The objects are the spreadsheet cells, the paragraphs in the document, the points on the graph; the application software is only the context in which those objects execute. The component architecture determines what kinds of object interactions are allowed.

Clearly, the granularity of components became much finer with object technology. No longer was it only the spreadsheet interacting with the database; now it was the sheets and cells that were connected to the columns and rows in the database, generating paragraphs and tables in the word processor. These relatively dynamic objects connect to other objects, regardless of the applications within which they exist.

The virtual enterprise of the future is built with components and objects locating each other, connecting, and interacting on a standardized infrastructure. This happens for components of all granularity, from large server applications to fine-grained objects, across boundaries of language, processor, and even enterprise, and with binding times from completely static to highly dynamic.

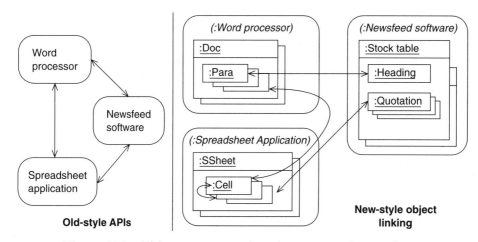

Figure 10.2   Old versus new styles of component interactions.

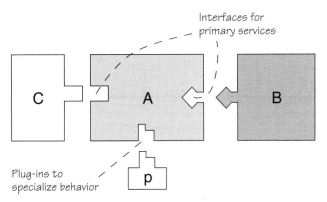

Figure 10.3   Primary and customization interfaces.

10.2.1   Components and Pluggable Reuse

Reuse comes in a wide variety of flavors ranging from cut-and-paste through complete application frameworks that can be customized. The component approach to reuse mandates that a component not be modified when it is connected to others; components should simply plug together, via defined interfaces for their services, to build larger components or systems. This makes it easier to replace or upgrade parts; if they support the same (or compatible) interface, one part can be replaced by another (see Figure 10.3).

The fact that a component should not be modified does not mean that it cannot be customized externally. A component can be designed to provide, in addition to the interfaces for its primary services, additional interfaces for plug-ins that customize the behaviors of its primary services; settable properties are a special case of this. This style of pluggable design is discussed in Chapter 11.

The precise meaning of a connection between components varies depending on the needs of the application and the underlying component technology. It could range from explicit invocation of functions via the connection to higher-level modes such as transfer of workflow objects, events being propagated implicitly, and so on. Section 10.7, Component Architecture, examines this in detail.

10.2.2   Components and Standardization

If we are to build systems by assembling components, we need a set of standards that are agreed to by component developers so that these components can interoperate and reduce the development burden of common tasks. Many of these issues would need to be addressed even without components, but the need for standardization would be less. There are three broad categories of standards: horizontal, vertical, and connectors (see Figure 10.4).

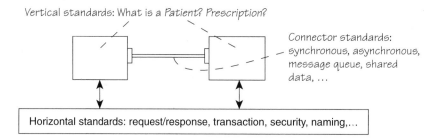

Figure 10.4 Horizontal, vertical, and connector standards across components.

10.2.2.1 Horizontal (Infrastructure) Standards

Components need a common mechanism for certain basic services, including the following.

• *Request broker:* This mechanism maintains information about the location of components and delivers requests and responses in a standard way.

• *Security:* This category includes mechanisms for authentication of users and authorization for performing various tasks.

• *Transactions:* Because each component potentially maintains its own persistent state information, business transactions must cross multiple components. A common mechanism is needed for coordinating such distributed transactions correctly. These transactions will be nested rather than flat.

• *Directory:* Many components need access to directory services—for example, to locate resources on a network or subcomponents within a component. They must be based on a common interface, with a uniform way to reference entities inside different components and across different naming schemes.

• *Interface repository:* Component interfaces and their specifications must be defined in a common way so that they can be understood both by people and by other components.

10.2.2.2 Vertical Standards

In addition to the underlying mechanisms being shared, components must agree on the definition of problem domain terms—usually manifested as problem domain objects—on which they will jointly operate. Components in a medical information system, for example, must share a common definition of what exactly a Patient is and what constitutes an Outpatient Treatment. They must share this definition at least in terms of the interfaces of those objects.

As of 1998, the OMG was actively working toward such *vertical* standards in domains that include telecommunications, insurance, finance, and medical care. Microsoft has a less coordinated effort under its DNA project. Every project must invariably also define its own domain-specific standards.

10.2.2.3   Connector Standards

We must also use standard kinds of *connectors* between components, defining a variety of interaction mechanisms for various kinds of components and compositions. The basic object-oriented message send is not the only, nor even the most suitable, way to describe all interactions.

- *Connectors that support explicit call and return:* The call could be synchronous or asynchronous. Asynchronous messages could be queued until processed, and return values could be treated as *futures*[5] or callbacks.

- *Connectors with impicit event propagation:* Certain state changes in one component are implicitly propagated to all components that registered an interest in that event.

- *Connectors that directly support streams:* Producers insert values or objects into the stream, where they remain until consumed by other components.

- *Connectors that support workflow:* Objects are transferred between one component and the next, where this transfer is itself a significant event.

- *Connectors that support mobile code:* Rather than just receive and send data and references to objects, you can actually transmit an object, complete with the code that defines its behaviors.

10.2.3   Why the Move to Components?

Components and *component-based development* are rapidly becoming buzzwords; like those before them, they bring a mixture of hype and real technical promise. The main advantages of adopting a component-based approach to overall development are as follows.

- It permits reuse of implementation and related interfaces at medium granularity. A single domain object may not be a useful unit of reuse; a component—packaging together an implementation of services as it affects many domain objects—can be.

- Effective components also form the basic unit for maintenance and upgrading. There should no longer be a need to upgrade entire "systems"; instead, components get replaced or added as needed.

- Component partitioning enables parallel development. Identifying medium-grained chunks and focusing on early design of interfaces make it easier to develop and evolve parts in parallel.

- Interface-centric design gives scalable and extensible architectures. By letting each component have multiple interfaces, we reduce the dependency of any one component on irrelevant features of another component that it connects with. Also, adding new services incrementally can be accommodated more eas-

---

5. An encapsulation of a "promise" of a value; it may block if the value is accessed before being available.

ily; you can introduce new components and add the relevant interfaces to existing ones. Scalability is somewhat more easily addressed, because replication, faster hardware, and so on can be targeted at a finer grain. Moreover, modern component technologies such as Enterprise JavaBeans move many of the burdens of resource pooling and scaling away from the business components to the containers within which they run.

- It lets you leverage standards. Because component technology implies a base set of standards for infrastructure services, a large application can leverage these standards and save considerable effort as a result.
- It can support capabilities that are impractical for "small" objects, such as (1) language-independent access of interfaces—so that you can use components written in other languages—and (2) transparent interaction between distributed components.

10.3 *Building Components with Java*

JavaBeans is the component technology for building components using Java. A JavaBean can be a single Java class whose external interfaces are described using the following.

- *Properties:* Object attributes that can be read and written by access methods
- *Methods:* Services with specified effects that a client can invoke
- *Events:* State changes that an object will notify its environment about, with no expectation of any resultant effect

Properties and methods represent services provided by the component. Events represent notifications from the component. There is no explicit way to represent services required by the Bean.

JavaBeans was designed to distinguish properties, methods, and events without any change to the basic Java language. It does this by using a facility called reflection.

10.3.1   Reflection

Java retains an explicit runtime representation of class, interface, and method definitions in its compiled class form; the *reflection* API is a facility for accessing this information. For every class that is loaded into a running system, Java instantiates a single instance of the predefined class Class. There is a static method for dynamically loading any class based on its name and several methods for examining the structure of a class definition.

```
class Class {
    static Class forName(String);        // load class by name, instantiate Class
    Class getSuperclass();               // return the superclass
    Class[] getInterfaces();             // return list of interfaces implemented
```

```
        Method[] getMethods();          // return list of methods
        Field[] getFields();            // return list of stored fields
        Method[] getConstructors();     // return list of constructors
        Object newInstance();           // create a new instance
    }
```

There are several other related classes, of which the most interesting one is Method.

```
    class Method {
        Class getDeclaringClass();      // return home class
        String getName();               // return method name
        Class getReturnType();          // return type
        Class[] getParameterTypes();    // list of parameter types
        Class[] getExceptionTypes();    // list of exception types
        void invoke(Object target);     // (very late bound) method invocation
    }
```

The following example illustrates a runtime use of these facilities:

```
    // locate and load the class dynamically
    Class c = Class.forName ("UserDefinedClass");

    // instantiate the class
    Object o = c.newInstance ();

    // get one of the methods on that class
    Method m = c.getDeclaredMethod ("userMethod", { } );

    // invoke that method on the new instance
    m.invoke (o);
```

In addition to supporting the mechanisms needed by JavaBeans, as explained later, reflection enables very late binding of calls by dynamically looking up interfaces and methods and invoking them against objects of statically unknown types.

10.3.2   Basic JavaBeans

The simplest way to write a JavaBean is to program a single class, following certain naming patterns for the methods on your class. Using the reflection API on an instantiated Bean (a process called *introspection*), a visual tool or other application can categorize the methods into properties, methods, and events.

- *Property:* Write a pair of methods named Y get<X>() and set<X>(Y) to define a property named X of type Y.
- *Event:* Write a pair of methods named add<X>Listener (XListener) and remove<X>Listener (XListener) and add the event signature to the operations that the XListener interface must support; this defines a single event your bean can publish to registered parties.

- *Method:* Write a method that follows neither a property nor an event pattern.

You can implement Beans without following the naming rules. You implement additional methods on the bean that (indirectly) explicitly identify the methods corresponding to properties, events, and methods on that Bean. We omit the details here.

10.3.3   Improved Components with JavaBeans

Attempting to program a Bean as a single class is not practical for nontrivial components; a component instance would typically consist of several connected objects of different classes, each implementing some of the external component interfaces. The more recent specifications for JavaBeans make it simpler to build complex Beans from several classes.

- Do not use language primitive "casts" to access other interfaces of a component, because they would understand only language-level objects. Instead, there is a prescribed explicit query protocol for getting to other interfaces.
- Bean instances will be nested. The containing "context" may (1) provide standard containment services and (2) interpose its own behavior before its parts execute their methods. Standard interfaces are defined for this purpose.

10.3.4   Persistence

Java provides a light-weight serialization mechanism; the implementor need do no additional work for objects to serialize and restore themselves correctly. The mechanism uses the underlying reflection services to implement generic save and restore functionality only once.

10.3.5   Packaging Using JAR Files

Compiled Java components are packaged into JAR files and include the class files that implement the component services, additional class files (if any) for explicitly defined properties, methods, and events, and some additional information.

10.3.6   Enterprise JavaBeans

Server components typically implement significant business functions and run on a server. In a multitier architecture, most business logic in an application runs on dedicated servers rather than on the client machine. In general, a multitier design increases the application's scalability, performance, and reliability—because components can be replicated and distributed across many machines—but at the cost of some "middleware" complexity. Java's Enterprise JavaBeans (EJB) standard is a server component model that simplifies the process of moving business logic to the server by implementing a set of automatic services to manage the component.

The Enterprise JavaBeans model lets you implement business functions as JavaBeans and then plug them in to a standard *container* that provides automatic management of resources and contention from multiple threads, transaction programming based on two-phase commit across multiple independent components, and distributed programming. An EJB component, packaged into a JAR file, has four main parts.

- *Home interface:* The client interface to a factory object that instantiates the main server Bean. A client locates this factory using a standard directory-based name lookup.
- *Remote interface:* The interface to the primary server Bean itself, providing the business operations to the client.
- *EJB class:* The class that implements the business operations.
- *Deployment descriptor:* A description of the preceding parts and additional attributes such as transactional and security behaviors that can be decided at deployment time rather than in the code for the main server component itself.

When the component, packed into its JAR file, is deployed, you must designate a

- *Container:* A component implemented by a middleware vendor; it acts as a container for your server component. It provides exposure of your services to clients (who actually do not directly access your implementation), remote access, distributed transaction management, security (including authentication and authorization), resource pooling, concurrent service for multiple clients, clustering, and high availability. In short, a container gives you all the things that, if they were absent, would make implementing a multitier system a nightmare.

Java presents a compelling technical base for component-based development, including enterprise-scale server components. Its main drawback is the single-language model, which is addressed by the integration of Java and CORBA.

10.4 *Components with COM+*

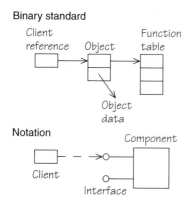

Binary standard

Client reference   Object   Function table

Object data

Notation

Client   Component

Interface

As it does almost everyplace else, Microsoft proceeds to define its own set of standards in the area of components. The foundation of its component software starts with COM: a binary standard for interfaces. A client reference to any object via an interface is represented by a pointer to a node that refers to a table of interface functions. If the reference is to an object with state, the intermediate node will also contain or refer to that object's state representation. A component offers some number of interfaces, each referred to by the client in this way. The implementation could involve many objects and classes or could involve none.

Every interface supports QueryInterface, a common function that queries for other interfaces based on unique identifiers assigned to interfaces. Each interface is immutable once published; a new version is a new interface. Because references to an object via different interfaces are physically different pointers, determining whether two references refer to the same object is not direct. Instead, COM prescribes that each component possess a single distinguished interface called IUnknown, which reliably serves as the identity.

COM is an interface standard and not a programming language; hence, it does not prescribe specific mechanisms for implementation reuse, such as class inheritance. However, it offers two mechanisms for composition.

- *Containment:* In this simple and straightforward approach, a container object receives every client request and explicitly forwards all requests as needed to its child objects.
- *Aggregation:* A container can directly expose references to (interfaces of) its inner objects; a client can then directly invoke operations on it. To behave like a single object, each inner object delegates all its QueryInterface requests to its container.

New objects are instantiated by a library call to CoCreateInstance, with a unique identifier for a particular implementation to be instantiated and the identifier of the interface of the new object that should be returned. The appropriate *server* is identified (from those registered in the system registry), started, and requested (via a factory) to create a new object; it returns an interface reference to the client.

COM interfaces are defined in an interface description language called IDL.[6] These interfaces can be compiled to produce *type libraries*—the runtime representation of the structure of interfaces and methods—and to produce appropriate proxy, stub, and marshaling code for the case of remote object references.

COM does not have the equivalent of Java's reflection, relying instead on the type library. Consequently, scripting and other applications that require very late binding—in which even the method called is not compiled against an interface but is looked up at runtime—require explicit support in the component itself. Each component can support what are called *dispatch interfaces*, in which a client requests an operation by a number; the component resolves the mapping from numbers to methods to invoke. COM uses *outgoing interfaces* to define events, just as JavaBeans uses its events.

COM includes a model for compound documents called OLE (a collection of standard COM interfaces) and includes ActiveX controls, another set of COM interface standards that include outgoing interfaces to permit events to be signaled by a control to its container. ActiveX controls also have properties that are similar to JavaBeans properties.

---

6. It is different from the OMG's IDL.

COM+, a relatively recent entry in the furiously renamed space of Microsoft's component technologies, has serious technology merit. It essentially defines a virtual machine model for components, similar in many respects to the Java virtual machine. COM+ provides garbage collection (eliminating the pesky reference counting approach of COM), extensive metadata (permitting reflection and eliminating dispatch interfaces), and infrastructure services (security and transactions) for server-side components. One of its more interesting features is called *interception*: the ability for the virtual machine to intercept requests sent to a component and interject special processing. This feature could be used to provide late-bound cross-component services, much as Enterprise JavaBeans uses the container as an intermediary to access component services.

10.5 *Components with CORBA*

CORBA (Common Object Request Broker Architecture) was designed by the Object Management Group (OMG) to support open distributed communication between objects across a wide variety of platforms and languages. Interestingly, despite the "Object" in its name, CORBA does not directly expose the notion of object identity; it could more properly be considered a distributed component framework.

To meet its goals of heterogenous computing, CORBA opted to become a source code standard rather than a binary one. Component interfaces are defined within modules using the CORBA IDL; different programming languages have standardized bindings to the IDL. Programmers either (a) manually write IDL and then compile it into the source code versions needed to write their implementations or (b) use a vendor's programming language compiler that offers direct generation of IDL.

The OMG's Object Management Architecture looks somewhat like the drawing in Figure 10.5. The architecture comprises four parts:

- *CORBA bus:* The base level of IDL-based interface definitions, the interface and server repositories, and the request broker

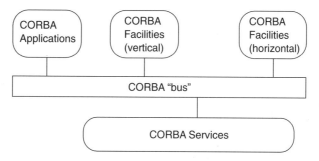

Figure 10.5 The CORBA architecture.

- *CORBA Services:* A variety of largely infrastructure services ranging from events to transactions, relationship, naming, life cycle, licensing, and externalization
- *CORBA Facilities (horizontal):* Printing, e-mail, compound documents, structured storage, workflow, and so on
- *CORBA Facilities (vertical):* Standards for business objects in "vertical" domains, including health care, telecomm, financials, and so on

CORBA recently defined mappings for the Java language and aligned closely with JavaBeans and Enterprise JavaBeans for its component model. In fact, the Java Transaction Service is defined based on the CORBA model.

10.6 *Component Kit: Pluggable Components Library*

This section is about component *kits*: collections of components that are designed to work with one another. The contents of a kit need not be completely fixed; you can add to it and have various accessory kits and subkits of pieces that work particularly closely together. But a kit has a unifying set of principles—the kit's component architecture type—that makes it easier to plug together the members of a kit successfully compared with components built separately or chosen from different kits. Plugging arbitrary components together usually requires that you build some sort of glue. We deal with that in Section 10.11, Heterogenous Components.

We'll begin our discussion of component kits with an example to illustrate the basic principles and later show how they apply to larger-scale (and more business-oriented) components. These examples use various kinds of connectors between component instantiations, coupling service requirement points (ports) in one to service provision points (ports) in another. We use arrows and beads to represent connectors: $\longrightarrow\!\!o\!\longrightarrow$. Section 10.8.2, Defining the Architecture Type, shows how varying kinds of connectors can be defined.

10.6.1   Graphical User Interface Kit of Components

GUIs form the most widely used kits of components. Windows, scrollbars, buttons, text fields, and so on can be put together in many combinations and coupled to your database, your Web server, or some other application. You rarely need to program the software that sets up and builds the forms: Instead, you use a GUI wizard to design them directly.

Using the connector notation discussed earlier, a typical design might look like the configuration of component instances shown in Figure 10.6. The connectors represent couplings between properties of two components ($\longrightarrow$; a pair of values is kept continually in sync) or events of two components ($\longrightarrow$; a published occurrence from one component triggers a method of another component).

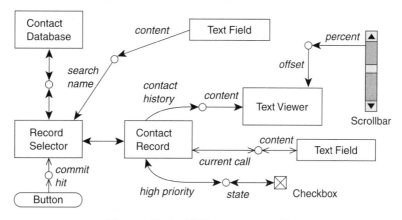

Figure 10.6   GUI component kit.

There is some need for adapters between, for example, the content of the Text Viewer and the contact history of the Contact Record. The design calls for continuously updated properties, such as the scrollbar's connector to the Text Viewer, as well as events such as the Button's hits. Some of the connectors are bidirectional: The checkbox both sets the priority and immediately shows a change in the property.

10.6.2   Kit of Small Components

Suppose you are given a collection of pieces of hardware: a motor of some sort, a couple of push-button switches, and a meter. Suppose the motor has a few wires attached: one labeled "start," another "stop," and a third tagged "speed «output»." The buttons and meter also have labeled connections. Now imagine connecting the components as shown in Figure 10.7.

Of course, a push-button can be used for many other purposes; if you had a lamp, you might use the push-button to switch it on and off, and your Meter might be used to display a temperature. There might be other ways of controlling the motor and other ways of using its speed to control other things. Let's root around in the box of parts and do some creative wiring (see Figure 10.8).

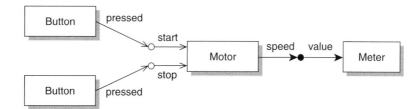

Figure 10.7   Electronic hobbyist component kit.

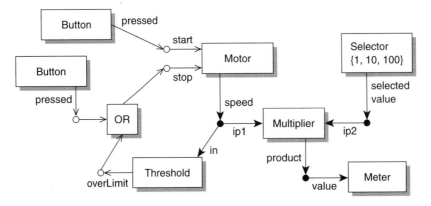

Figure 10.8   Electronics kit: a nontrivial configuration.

When the motor is running slowly, the meter doesn't show the low speed very clearly, so we've decided to multiply the speed by 10 or 100 before it gets to the meter. From the box of components we've pulled a Multiplier and a Selector. A Selector is a user-interface widget that provides a fixed choice of values, which in this case we've set to the factors we want to allow.

We're also worried that the Motor might run too fast sometimes (perhaps if its load is removed), so we've pulled out a Threshold.[7] It converts a continuously varying value, such as the speed, into a Boolean off/on, switching on when its input rises above a certain limit. Then we've connected it and the stop button (through an OR gate) to the Motor's stop input. So the Motor will be stopped either by the button being pushed or the Motor running too fast.

Any model railroad enthusiast will recognize this as a neat kit of parts with which you could build a lot of different projects—many more potential products than the number of components in the box. Note the ease of modifying the first version to realize the second. It's not difficult to imagine such a kit in hardware nor to visualize it in software. The Motor could be a software component controlling a hardware motor; the Buttons, Meter, and Selector could be user-interface widgets; and the other components could be objects not directly visible to the user.

10.6.3   Large Components

Components need not be little things; they can be entire applications or legacy systems. The nature of the connectors between these components differs. The components shown in Figure 10.9 are the support systems for some of the departments in a large manufacturing company.

---

7. Hardware people call it a Schmitt trigger.

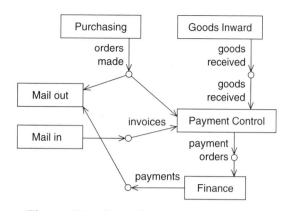

Figure 10.9   Large business components.

The components and their lines of communication mirror those of the business. The diagram could represent a business structure of departments and flows of work, or a software structure of components and connectors. Just as departments are composed of teams and people, so a closer look at any one of these components would reveal that it is built from smaller ones.

The company places orders, which are mailed and forwarded to payment control for subsequent payment. When the shipping department receives goods, it forwards a notification to payment control. Invoices received are also forwarded. When an invoice is received for goods that were delivered, a payment is generated.

Whereas the smaller example sent primitive values across the connectors, these components send larger objects, such as orders, invoices, and customer information, to each other. The connectors between these components serve to transfer objects, in one case with a duplication or split to two or more destination components.

The configuration is a modern one. Rather than a single central database with clients all over the enterprise, there are separate components, each holding appropriate data and performing appropriate operations tailored to support the business operations. There are several benefits of this *federated* scheme.

• *Flexibility:* It is more extensible and flexible than centralized systems clustered around one database. Business reorganization is rapidly reflected in the support systems.

• *Scalability:* It is more scalable to serve more people and buy more machinery. You are not constrained by having a single server that will scale only so far.

• *Graceful degradation:* Each business function is supported by its own machinery, so one malfunction doesn't stop the whole enterprise.

• *Upgradability:* You do not have to set up and subsequently update the system as a single entity. As the business grows and is reorganized, new software can be added. You can plug in commercial off-the-shelf components rather than build every enhancement into a single program.

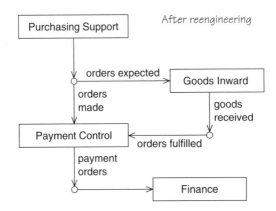

Figure 10.10   Reconfigured business components.

- *Appropriateness:* Because it requires less central control, it is less prone to local political and bureaucratic difficulties. There is no one authority that must agree to every change or must be persuaded to address the evolving requirements of every department. Instead, the business users hold much more responsibility for providing support appropriate for themselves.

An inefficiency was diagnosed in the process; goods were being delivered and paid for that had never been ordered, and reconciling purchase orders with goods received was becoming expensive. The company reorganized its departmental roles and the software to match (see Figure 10.10). Goods Inward now has records of all orders that have been made and will turn away spoof deliveries.[8] Because the component structure reflected the business structure at the level of granularity of the change required, the change was accommodated fairly well. Finer-grained business changes, such as the introduction of a new pricing plan for existing products, require a corresponding finer-grained component (or object) structure to accommodate the change.

10.6.4   Component Building Tools

Component technology is often associated with visual building tools. Once a systematic method of connecting components has been established, tools can be devised that let you to plug the components together graphically. Digitalk's Parts and IBM's Visual Age were early examples; Symantec's Visual Café works in Java, as does Sun's Java Workshop. Similar-sounding *visual programming* tools are restricted to building user interfaces rather than composing general components. There are tools (for example, Forté) that specialize in distributed architectures, in which the components may be executing on different machines. Others are good

---

8. Thanks to Clive Mabey, Michael Mills, and Richard Veryard for this example.

at defining workflow systems in which components of one kind—work objects—are passed for multiple stages of processing between components of another kind, the work performers.

10.7 *Component Architecture*

An *architecture* is an abstraction of a system that describes the design structures and relationships, governing rules, or principles that are (or could be) used across many designs. Here are examples:

> *"Four-tier with Web servelets."*
>
> *"We shall all write in Java."*
>
> *"Here's how we make one property observe another."*
>
> *"Use these interfaces and protocols to implement a spell-checking feature."*
>
> *"Use Fred's class whenever you want to wongle foobits."*
>
> *"Never use return codes to signal exceptions."*

The architecture is what lends the coherence and consistency to the design.

An architecture broadly comprises two parts (we defer a more detailed discussion to Chapter 12, Architecture).

- The generic design elements or patterns that are used in the architecture, such as subject-observer, Fred's class, the event-property connectors, or the generic design for spell checking.
- The rules or guidelines that determine where and how these architectural elements are applied, such as "For any composite user-interface panel that may be reused, make all internal events available via the composite." In the extreme case, these rules can be formalized to fully define a translation scheme.

Design is about relating several independent pieces together and claiming, "This particular way of combining these pieces will make something that does so-and-so."

The pieces might be the result of applying architectural rules, or they might be a sequence of statements making up a subroutine. They might be a group of linked objects, an assembly of hardware components, or large software subsystems that intercommunicate in some way. Or they might be a composition of several collaboration patterns on problem domain objects. The essence of design is that the composition of various pieces, each one designed separately, somehow meets a requirement.

That said, we sometimes refer to a high-level partitioning structure as architecture, either technical architecture (having to do with underlying component technology, independent of business logic) or application architecture (having to do with partitioning of application logic).

10.7.1   The Component-Port-Connector Model

The rest of this chapter deals with how to model and specify components: executable units that can be plugged together with different interaction schemes connecting them. Our modeling approach is based on the ideas put forth in three definitions.

▶ *ports*   The exposed interfaces that define the *plugs* and *sockets* of the components; those places at which the component offers access to its services and from which it accesses services of others. A plug can be coupled with any socket of a compatible type using a suitable connector.

▶ *connectors*   The connections between ports that build a collection of components into a software product (or larger component). A connector imposes role-specific constraints on the ports that it connects and can be refined to particular interaction protocols that implement the joint action.

To us, a component architecture defines the schemes of how components can be plugged together and interact. This definition may vary from one project or component library to another and includes schemes such as CORBA, DCOM, JavaBeans, database interface protocols such as ODBC, and lower-level protocols such as TCP/IP as well as simpler sets of conventions and rules created for specific projects.

Component models are specifications of what a component does—based on a particular component architecture, including the characteristics of its connectors—and descriptions of connections between components to realize a larger design.

▶ *component-based design*   The mind-set, science, and art of building with and for components and ensuring that the result of plugging components together has the expected effect.

It's impossible to allow a designer to stick components together just any old way: An output that yields a stream of invoice objects can't be coupled to an input that accepts hotel reservation cancellation events. But we would like to be able, at least within one kit of components, to couple any input with any type-compatible output if their behaviors are compatible. To be able to do this confidently across independently developed components means that certain things must be decided across the whole kit.

• *Specification:* What must you do to specify a particular component, with its input and output ports?

• *Instantiation:* What must you do to create an instance of a component and to couple components together?

• *Connectors:* How do connectors (connections between components) work—as function calls, messages on wires, data shared between threads, or some other way? If there are different kinds of connectors, what are they, and how do their implementations differ?

- *Common model:* What types are understood by all the components (only integers or Customers too?)? How are objects represented as they are passed from one component to another?

- *Common services:* How does a component refer to an object stored within another? How are distributed transactions coordinated?

The answers to these questions are common across any set of components that can work together (see Section 10.2.2, Components and Standardization). Together, they form a set of definitions and rules called a "component architecture." Microsoft's DCOM, the Object Management Group's CORBA, and Sun's JavaBeans are examples. Project teams often devise their own component architecture either independently or (more sensibly) as specializations of these types. Highly generalized architectures cannot provide, for example, a common model of a Bank Customer, but this would be a sensible extension within a bank.

In this chapter, we concern ourselves with architecture at the generic level of the kinds of ports and connectors supported, although, more broadly, an architecture definition could include much more.

10.7.1.1   Component Connector

We use arrows and beads to represent connectors, ——⟶○——⟶ based on the UML notation for defining an interface and a dependency on it. However, our use of connectors between ports is more refined.

A type of connector is defined as a generic collaboration framework (see Chapter 9). The interactions between components can be complex, and part of the complexity comes from the techniques that permit them to be coupled in many configurations. The same patterns are repeated over and over—each time, for example, we want work to flow from one component to another or we want a component to be kept up-to-date about the attributes of another.

Connectors hide complex collaborations. The stream of payment orders from Payment Control probably requires a buffer along with a signaling mechanism to tell the receiving component to pick up the orders. The stream of invoices from Purchasing follows the same pattern. The continous update of the Meter's value from the Motor's speed requires a change-notification message; other values transmitted in that example need the same message.

Rather than describe these complex collaborations from scratch for each interface, we invent a small catalog of connectors, which are patterns of collaboration that can be invoked wherever components are to be plugged together. Then we can concentrate on only the aspects that are specific for each connector, mainly the type of information transmitted.

A design described using connectors doesn't depend on a particular way of implementing each category of connector. What's important is that the designer know what each one achieves. We can distinguish the component architecture model (which connectors can be used) from the component architecture implementation (how they work).

10.7.1.2 Example Connectors

Each project or component library can define its own connectors to suit itself. In the Motor example in Section 10.6.2, Kit of Small Components, we can identify two principal kinds of component connector:

- *Events:* Exchanges of information that happen when initiated by the sender to signal a state change (shown with an open arrow: $\longrightarrow$)
- *Properties:* Connectors in which an observer is continually updated about any change in a named part of the state of the sender (shown with a solid arrow: $\longrightarrow$)

The approach we discuss here also applies to other kinds of connectors such as the following:

- *Workflow transfers:* In which information moves away from a sender and into a receiver
- *Transactions:* In which an object is read and translated into an editable or processable form, is processed, and then updates the original

These are examples; you can define your own kinds of connectors to meet the needs of your enterprise. Being able to separately and explicitly define connector types lets us further decouple intercomponent dependencies from the component implementations and better abstract the structure of components when they are composed later.

10.7.2 Taxonomy of Component Architecture Types

There can be many different implementations of a given architecture model, and the same architecture model can be applied to many different applications. A given component architecture describes its type, or style, and its implementation.

▶ *component architecture type, or style*   Which categories of connectors are permitted between components, what each of them does, and the rules and constraints on their usage. Some (unary) connector types can even be used to define standard infrastructure services that are always provided by the environment.

▶ *architecture implementation(s)*   How each category of connector works internally, including the protocol of interactions between ports.

Each component architecture does this, whether it uses widespread standards or is defined by the architect of a particular project. Although the use of the big standards is important for intercoupling of large, widely marketed components, we believe that purpose-designed architectures will continue to be important within particular corporations and projects and also within application areas (such as computer aided drafting, geographical systems, and telecommunications) that have particular needs (such as image manipulation, timing, and so on). Therefore, it is necessary to understand what an architecture defines, how to define your own architecture (see Section 10.8, Defining Cat One—A Component Architecture), and how various architectures are related.

Like everything else, architectures have types (requirements specifications) and implementations. A type defines what is expected of the implementation, and there may be many architecture implementations of a single architecture type. One architecture implementation may be clever enough to implement more than one architecture type if they do not make conflicting demands. For example, most television broadcasts now carry both pictures and pages of text, thereby accommodating separate architectural requirements within a single design of signal. Similarly, some architectural implementations allow two architectures, such as CORBA and COM, to interoperate.

Like object types, architecture types can be extended: Extra requirements can be added (just as the transmission of color pictures was added to the original monochrome). A simple version of the architecture discussed earlier defines event and property connectors; an extension might add transfers and transactions.

It's important to remember that an architecture does not necessarily define any code. The type lays down rules for what the connectors achieve, and the architecture implementation defines the collaborations to achieve that. The collaborations tell the designers of the components which messages they must send and in what sequence.

An architecture gives a component writer a set of ground rules and facilities. It does not necessarily limit the kinds of interactions a component can have with another component; rather, it provides patterns for the most common kinds of interaction.

Suppose you are writing a component that accepts print jobs, queues them, and distributes them among printers. An empty architecture is one in which nothing is predefined and every component and interface must be defined from scratch. Without a laid-down architecture, the documentation of your component must define

- Which operating system clients must use
- Which programming language (or set of calling conventions) must be used
- Which calls the client must make to inquire whether you can accept a job, to pass a job to you, and confirm that you've received it

If you have a simple component architecture, it could minimally define operating system and language or clarify how to couple components working in different contexts. If it defines no notion such as our transfer connector, you must define all the messages you expect to send and receive.

But if it is a more sophisticated architecture that defines transfers, your job is much simpler: You only need to say exactly what type of object you're transferring. The architecture defines what "transfer" means and what messages achieve that effect; wherever you need to, you simply use the transfer connector (as in using a framework application, discussed in Chapter 15) and omit all the details.

So an architecture doesn't limit the kinds of work that components can do together, but it makes it easier to document certain categories of interaction and thereby encourages the use of components.

10.8 *Defining Cat One—A Component Architecture*

There are an infinite number of interesting architectures, and the principles of component-based design we discuss apply regardless of specifics. Components can be connected in a great variety of ways—using CORBA, COM, or even a daily manual FTP transfer—but all of them can be seen as examples of the basic notion of self-contained components coupled together using a set of connectors. The kinds of components and connectors and the way they are implemented vary from one architecture to another; for example, JavaBeans (see Section 10.3) offers a specific set.

In Catalysis, we view all component architectures as follows.

• *Component:* Any active element that performs a useful task we call a component. Components can be individual objects or large subsystems; they can even be the departments in an organization. In general, components differ from plain objects in being packaged more robustly.

• *Connector:* Any means of communication between components we call a connector. A connector can be something as simple as a function call or a group of calls that provide for a collaboration, or it can be something more complex such as a dialog across an API. Or it might be a message sent via CORBA or COM or a file transfer, a pipe, or even the delivery of a deck of punched cards by courier. And of course, a GUI is a connector, just as a user is a component.

• *Port:* In general, each component has several identifiable means of being connected to others. We call these *ports*; connectors connect ports together. Each port can be given a name (and, if there are a variable number of them, an index). For example, the operations on a plain object have their message names; the ports to an Internet host have numbers; the pins on a logic chip and the sockets on the back of your PC are tagged with specific functions; and many large systems have interfaces directed at different user roles.

Some architectures allow for restrictions on *fan-out:* the number of inputs supplied by each output. In general, connections can be made and unmade dynamically, although this can be restricted in a particular architecture.

• *Port category:* In any architecture, there are different *categories* of ports characterized by the style of information transfer: whether isolated events or streams of values, whether buffered, whether interactive, and so on. They are also differentiated by implementation: C++ function call, database transaction, FTP transfer, dictation over the phone, and so on.

- *Component architecture:* A component architecture is a choice of categories of connectors. They are specified first by what they achieve (signaling an event, updating values, transferring objects, and so on) and secondarily by how they are implemented (COM operation, e-mail, carrier pigeon, and so on).

Most categories of port have a *gender* (such as «input» and «output») and a type of value that is transmitted, from simple numbers to complex objects such as reservations or stock dealings. These elements also are defined by the specific component architecture, which also must define the rules whereby the ports can be connected (for example, an input always to an output).

10.8.1   Cat One: An Example Component Architecture

For the sake of concreteness, we will introduce a specific hypothetical architecture called Cat One. It provides a fairly typical basis, and its connectors are similar to those in COM and JavaBeans. However, the component model is itself extensible.

Cat One has several port categories: «Event», «Property», «Transfer», and «Transaction Server». All the port implementations are described in terms of function calls, but you could easily extend Cat One to support more-complex implementations crossing application and host boundaries.

The information carried by each port has a type. Each port can be coupled only to another port that has a compatible type. Compatibility is defined separately for each port category; for Event and Property couples, the sender's output type must be a subtype of the receiver's input.

A connector is implemented as the registration of the receiver's input with the sender's output. When a connection is to be made, the sender must be informed that the required output is to be sent to the required input of the required receiver. This explains what an output port is: It represents an object's ability to accept registration requests and to maintain a list (a separate one for each of its output ports) of the interested parties. An input port represents an object's ability to accept the messages sent by the corresponding output ports.

There are various ways of implementing the messages that occur in a connector. One way is to use only one universal "event" message, with parameters that identify the sender, the name of the output port (as a string), the name of the input port, and the information to be conveyed. This approach is convenient in languages such as C++. In Smalltalk it is easier to use a different message name for each input port; the name corresponds to the port's label. (Only in reflexive languages can the sender be told at registration what message to send.)

A connection can be implemented by an adapter object, whose job is to receive an output message and translate it into the appropriate input, translating the parameters if necessary at the same time.

Events are the most general category of port: An event is a message conveying information about an occurrence. The only difference between an event and an ordinary object-oriented message is that in an event the receiver is registered to receive it. More generally, an event can be implemented as a dialog of messages initiated by the sender; in Catalysis we know how to characterize that with a single action.

Properties convey the value of some attribute of the source component. A property output sends a message (or initiates a dialog) each time the attribute changes. (The attribute may be the identity of a simple object such as a number or of a complex object such as an airplane.) A variation on this theme calls for updates at regular intervals rather than immediate notification of every change. A further variant provides for the source to ask the permission of the receivers each time a change is about to happen. Obviously, this approach calls for more messages at the implementation level; but in a component design, we consider all that to be part of one port.

A Transfer port passes objects from the source to the sink. Once accepted by the sink, a sent object is no longer in the sender. Strings of components with Transfer ports can be used to make pipelines and workflows. In an implementation, the source asks the sink to accept an object; if and when the object is accepted, the source removes it from its own space.

Each Transaction Server port provides access to a map from keys to values. Key-value pairs can be created and deleted; the value associated with any key can be read and updated. Many Transaction Client ports can be coupled to one Server; each one can seize a particular key so that others cannot update it. On release, the client can choose to confirm or abort all the updates since seizing.

10.8.2   Defining the Architecture Type

An architecture is a set of definitions that you can take for granted once you know you're working within that context. Defining an architecture is therefore about writing down the things that are common to every component and its connectors. In other words, it's about defining a design package that can then be imported wherever that architecture is used and gives a meaning to the shorthand port and connector symbols.

An architecture package generally specifies a number of connectors. In addition, it may define collaborations that implement the connectors. Third, it may define generic program code that a designer can use to encode one end of each connector.

10.8.3   Connector Specification

Each component can have several named ports; each port can take part in a connection with several others (see Figure 10.11). The connect action between two ports links them together with a connector. One of the ports must be unlinked; if the other one is already linked, the existing connector is used. Other connectability criteria, not yet defined, must be satisfied as a precondition.

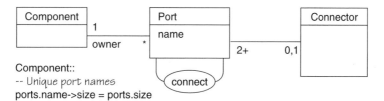

Component::
-- Unique port names
ports.name->size = ports.size

Figure 10.11   Basic port and connector model.

<u>action</u>   connect (a : Port, b : Port)
<u>pre:</u>   (a.connector = null or b.connector=null)
          and connectable(a,b)   -- *to be defined for each category*
<u>post:</u>   a.connector = b.connector and
          a.connector.ports =
                a.connector@pre.ports + b.connector@pre.ports + a + b

<u>action</u>   disconnect (a : Port)
<u>pre:</u>   a.connector <> null
<u>post:</u>   a.connector = null

A port may have a gender. No more than one source port may be coupled to the same connector.

10.8.4   Connector Design

Figure 10.12 shows a design (one among many possible) of gendered ports, in which a connection is established by registration. To distinguish the types of this implementation from the types they represent in the model in Figure 10.11, we alter the names slightly.

The connect action is realized as a collaboration between the owners of the ports.[9] The owner of the sink port is sent a registration message:

<u>action</u> Component1::couple(sink: SinkPort, source:SourcePort)
<u>pre:</u>   sink.source = null and connectable(sink, source)
<u>post:</u>   sink.source = source and
          source.owner–>register(source, sink)

Registration does two things: It records the source and port to which this sink is connected and results in a message to the source owner:

<u>action</u> Component1::register (source: SourcePort, sink: SinkPort)
<u>pre:</u>   sink.owner = self
<u>post:</u>   source.sinks += sink

This code adds the sender to the registry of sinks for this source.

---

9. If the connect takes place in a component assembly tool, the registration may be hidden within initialization code generated by the tool.

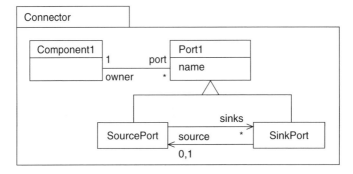

Figure 10.12   A design for establishing connections.

The abstract model's Connector is realized as the pair of links sinks and source. A Connector exists for each non-empty set of sinks; its ports are the linked SourcePort and SinkPort.

10.8.5   Interpretation of Connector Diagrams

Now we must define how the notation we've been using for components should be interpreted in terms of our component model. We define each box on a component diagram as a Component1 instance; each emerging arrow is a SourcePort, and each ingoing arrow is a SinkPort. A connection between components is a Connector in the sense of our abstract model, which we've realized as a complementary pair of links between the ports.

We can translate a typical fragment of componentry[10] (see Figure 10.13). This illustration shows that an architecture gives a meaning to a component diagram by making it an abbreviation for an object diagram.

10.8.6   Property Connector

Having given a meaning to the basic idea of a connector, we can go on to define the various categories we are interested in for Cat One.

A property connector has a value in the source port that is maintained by its owner. Whenever the value changes, all currently connected sink ports are updated (see Figure 10.14). The PropertyConnector framework is applied for each connector marked «property» (for which an abbreviation is the filled arrow). The

---

10. We could use explicit stereotypes to indicate the component frameworks being applied; instead, we assume that a distinguished connector and arrow notation has the same semantics within a particular component architecture. Also, the semantics work equally for types and instances.

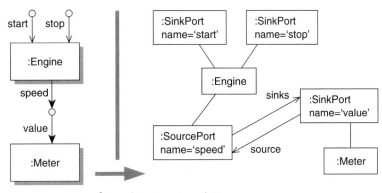

Our architecture translation

Figure 10.13   Unfolding of a component diagram based on framework.

ports are labeled with the appropriate substitutions for SourceType and SinkType; the type names should also be used to generate separate types for the ports.

Suppose that we want to see how our architecture interprets the example shown in Figure 10.15. The intent of this figure is that the aircraft shown in the aircraft display always tracks the current plane from the runway control; the ready status of the approach control tracks the clear status of the runway control.

We can translate first to a framework application: In the context of our composed component type, the framework relationships shown in Figure 10.16 on the next page

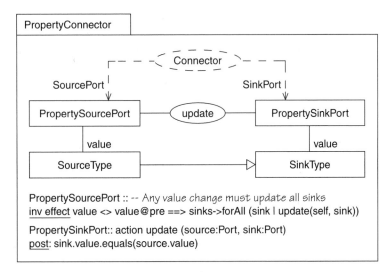

Figure 10.14   Template for a property connector.

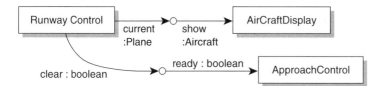

Figure 10.15   Component diagram to interpret.

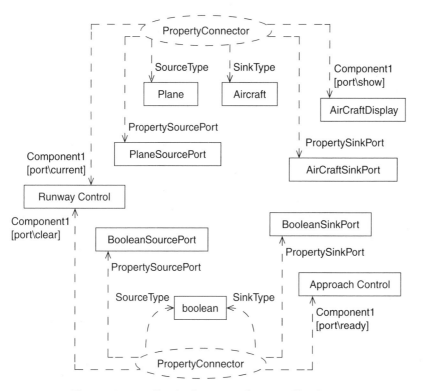

Figure 10.16   Equivalent template applications.

hold between the parts. The unfolded framework definitions are shown in Figure 10.17.

The complexity of this result is persuasive of the utility of the component notation. The same technique can be used to give meaning to any additional layer of notation and not only to components. All this could be defined in a syntax section of the architecture package itself along with a suitable mechanism for defining a visual grammar (see Chapter 9, Model Frameworks and Template Packages).

A straightforward generalization uses a recursive definition of port and connector, allowing us to make connections either at the level of individual events and properties or at higher-level bundles of them.

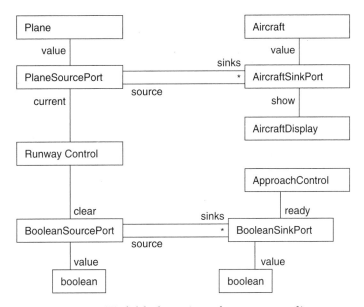

Figure 10.17   Unfolded version of component diagram.

10.9 *Specifying Cat One Components*

When we specify a component, we take for granted the underlying architecture—mechanisms for registration to receive an output and the like—and focus on a higher-level specification. Including outputs in a specification (marked «output property», «output event», and so on or the equivalent solid arrow notation) implies that all this is assumed. A component specification takes the form of a single type description; but as always in Catalysis, it can be refined and implemented as a collection of objects.

Let's now look at the main categories of ports in our Cat One architecture one by one and see how to use specification techniques to define them.

10.9.1   Specifying Input and Output Events

We already know how to specify input events: this category corresponds to the actions or operations that in previous chapters have been used to specify objects. The only difference comes in the implementation and runtime effect. An object designed as a component accepts events according to the protocol defined in a chosen component architecture so that it can be coupled to other components' outputs, including any registration required for those output events. Mechanics for mapping from the output event to the corresponding input events—including string-based mapping, reflective techniques, or an adapter object—are defined by the implementation of the architecture.

An output event occurs when a given change of state occurs. We can specify the change that stimulates the output, using the "old and new state" notation of postconditions within an effect invariant (see Section 3.5.4, Effect Invariants). Notice the caret mark denoting that this message is scheduled to be sent. Here, we've declared the output event superfluously both in text and pictorially. («output event» pressed could have been omitted.) Output events can have arguments, which deliver information to the receiving input events. The usual type matching rules apply.

Button
down : boolean

«output event» pressed
  down and not down@pre
  ==> ^pressed

pressed ↓

Certain details of an output event are not specified in this style. For example, how soon after a qualifying transition takes place must the output be made?[11] Nor have we said who will receive the output, because this will differ for each design in which the component is used; the architecture guarantees that all connected ports are notified.

Output events aren't always coupled purely to a state change: an output may happen only when the change is caused by a given input action. For example, our Button is a graphical user interface widget that responds to various mouse messages from the windowing system: let's assume mouseUp, mouseDown, mouseEnter, and mouseLeave. The latter two happen if the user drags the mouse in or out of the Button's screen area; the Up and Down messages are sent only when the mouse is within that area.

Let's suppose that we want the operation stimulated by the button to take place when the user has pressed and released the mouse. As the user presses, the Button changes color, and it changes back to normal as the release occurs. But after pressing, the user can make a last-moment decision not to do the action, signaling the change of mind by dragging the mouse away from the Button before releasing the mouse key. In this case, the Button returns to the normal state but does not send the output event.

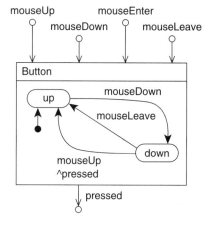

The required behavior can be readily illustrated with a state chart. Alternatively, we can show the ^pressed requirement as part of the postcondition of each action that causes it:

> <u>action</u> mouseUp
> <u>post</u>: up and (down@pre ==> ^pressed)

Here are some useful abbreviations for events:

> «input event» action (params)   action(params)
> «output event» operation(params)   ^ operation(params)

---

11. We can easily add performance specifications either informally or formally.

At a business level, a Warehouse component might publish an event outOf-Stock(Product) specified as

«output event» outOfStock (p: Product)
<u>inv effect</u> p.stock@pre >= p.minumum & p.stock < minimum ==> ^outOfStock(p)

10.9.2   Specifying Properties

Input and output properties provide a simple way to connect state variables across components.

10.9.2.1   Specifying Output Properties

Counter
count : int
«input property» stepSize : int
«input event» step( ) post:count = count@pre + stepSize
«input property» scale : int
«output property» current: int <u>inv</u> current = count * scale

An output property is an attribute that the component architecture specifically allows to be visible to other components. A chosen component architecture provides a pattern for implementing attributes tagged with the «output property» stereotype.[12]

Like any other attribute, a property can be used in and affected by postconditions of events.

In the component's type definition, properties are shown textually below the line that separates model from behavior; the implementor is obliged to make the property externally visible. But, as usual, the attribute need not be implemented directly as a stored variable but can instead be computed when required.

10.9.2.2   Specifying Input Properties

An input property is an attribute exposed according to a component architecture so that it can be controlled by the output of another component. It can be linked with invariants to other attributes. There is an implied invariant: that an input property will be equal to whatever output (of some other component) it may be coupled to. Therefore, although an input property can be used in a postcondition, it doesn't make sense to imply that it is changed by the action:

wrongOp (x : int) <u>post</u>:stepSize = stepSize@pre + x

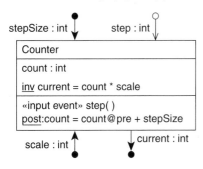

An input property must always be coupled to exactly one output property, although it can be coupled to different outputs at different times. (The next section deals with creating and connecting components.)

Pictorially, input and output properties can be shown with solid arrows, as distinguished from the open arrows of events. (The shadow emphasizes that this is a component—that is, something intended to

---

12. An example is the get/set method pattern used in JavaBeans for component properties.

be implemented according to a component architecture. But it's only for dramatic effect and can be omitted.)

A property value may be an object (and may itself be a component). Updates should be notified whenever a change in a property would significantly change the sending component. A "significant" change is one that would alter the result of an equals comparison between this component and another component.

If the property changes to point to another object, that would normally be a significant change. If there is a change of state of the object pointed at, then the significance of the change depends on whether the property object's state is considered part of the state of the component. This is the same issue as the definition of equals in Section 9.7, Templates for Equality and Copying.

10.9.2.3   Require Condition

A require condition is an invariant that it is the responsibility of the component's user to maintain. By contrast, a regular invariant is one that, given that the require condition is true, is maintained by the component. A require condition governs the relationship between properties. A typical one might be

    require scale * stepSize < 1000

As with a precondition, it is a matter of design policy whether the implementor assumes that the require condition will always be observed by a careful client or whether the implementation performs checks to see that it is true.

10.9.2.4   Constrained Connectors

A constraint can be imposed on an input and written either against the port in a diagram or in the type description:

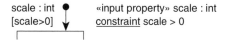

Different component architectures treat constraints differently. The simplest approach is to treat the constraint as a form of require condition: the user must ensure that it is not violated.

Alternatively, the architecture can support constraints with a protocol whereby an output requests permission before each change. One such architecture gives the implementation of every port a method with a signature such as change_request_port_x (new_value). By default, this returns true. Before altering an output, a component should send a change request to all the inputs currently registered with that output. If any of them returns false, this change at this output must not happen, and the component must think of something else to do.

Another alternative is for the architecture to support an exception/transaction abort scheme. This approach could be described using the techniques for describing exceptions in Chapter 8.

Using such a mechanism, constraints can also be applied to outputs and more generally to combinations of inputs and so on.

10.9.2.5   Bidirectional Properties

An «in out property» can be altered from either end: changes propagate both ways.

10.9.2.6   Port Attributes

In our approach, every port has several attributes; as before, attributes and specification types need not be directly implemented.

- port.component: The component to which this port belongs.
- inputPort.source: The output port to which an input port is currently coupled.
- outputPort.sinks: The input ports to which an output port is currently coupled.
- propertyPort.value: The object or primitive that is output or input by this property port. Generally, when there's no ambiguity it's convenient to use the name of the property port by itself, omitting the .value.
- propertyPort.constraint(value): A Boolean function returning, for an input property port, whether the associated constraint is true for the given value—that is, whether it is permissible to send this value to this port. For an output port, it is true if true for all the currently coupled inputs.

Port attributes can be used in specifications. For example, suppose we want to insist that the Counter always be wired so that the component that sets its scale is the same one that sets its stepSize:

```
requires
stepSize.source.component = scale.source.component
```

10.9.3   Specifying Transfers

A transfer connector sends an object from the source component to the sink. In contrast with events and properties, each «output transfer» port can be connected to only one «input transfer»; but the basic library of components includes a Duplicator component that accepts one input and provides several outputs.

Like properties, transfers are characterized by the type of object transferred.

10.9.4   Specifying Transactions

A transaction connector provides for a property of the component to be locked against alteration or reading by others; altered; and then either released in its new state or rolled back to its original state.

10.10 *Connecting Cat One Components*

Big components are made by connecting smaller ones. In this section we explain how the connector types in our example architecture support composition.

10.10.1 Connector Properties

An input property can be driven by an output property, and each output can generally drive any number of inputs. A connection must match types: The output type must be the same as, or a subtype of, the input type. The input and output can have different labels.

It is sometimes useful to make simple transformations between output and input—for example, multiplying a value by a fixed constant or translating an object from one type to another. In the implementation, such things can be done either by an appropriate small component or by some flexibility in the architecture that permit inputs to accommodate straightforward translations on-the-fly. For example, in C++, it is easy to define a translation from one type to another (with a constructor or user-defined cast), which is automatically applied by the compiler where necessary.

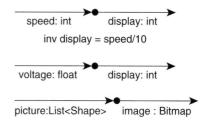

In our notation, a transformation can either be shown as an explicit annotation to the connector or, where the output and input types differ, can be left implicit, as the default translation between those types.

10.10.2 Connecting Events

Unless a particular restriction is specified, an output event can be connected to any number of inputs, and an input can be connected to any number of outputs.

An output event has a name and a set of arguments; an input event has a name and a set of parameters. In the simplest connector, only the names differ; then the occurrence of the output event causes the input to be invoked on all currently registered targets. The arguments must match the parameters in the usual way.

If the parameter lists of the output event differ from those of the input to which it is coupled, a mapping must be defined at the connector. If the transformation is too complex, an intermediate component should be defined for the purpose.

An output event can transfer information in two directions: via parameters and via the return value normally associated with function calls. For that reason, an output event can have a postcondition at the sending end.[13]

---

13. In contrast, in JavaBeans an output event cannot expect any postconditions; this means that it cannot be used to describe actual services expected from another component.

10.10.3   A Basic Kit of Components for Cat One

A basic kit of components can be defined to which you can add components that are more domain-oriented. The following is a selection of basic pieces that can be used in many ways. It's intended to provide a general flavor of what can be achieved.

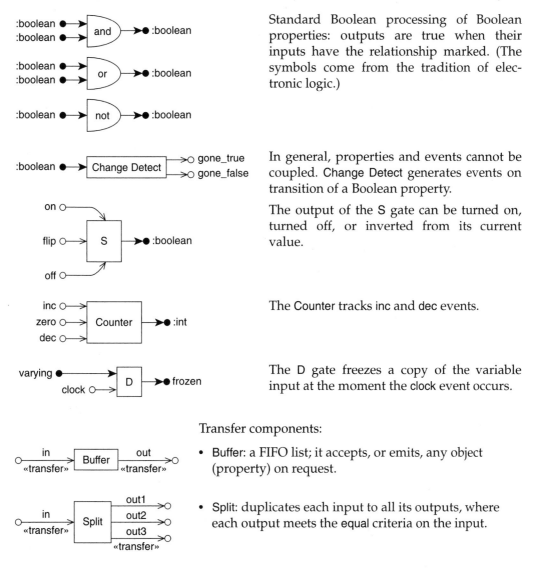

Standard Boolean processing of Boolean properties: outputs are true when their inputs have the relationship marked. (The symbols come from the tradition of electronic logic.)

In general, properties and events cannot be coupled. Change Detect generates events on transition of a Boolean property.

The output of the S gate can be turned on, turned off, or inverted from its current value.

The Counter tracks inc and dec events.

The D gate freezes a copy of the variable input at the moment the clock event occurs.

Transfer components:

• Buffer: a FIFO list; it accepts, or emits, any object (property) on request.

• Split: duplicates each input to all its outputs, where each output meets the equal criteria on the input.

10.10.4   Dynamically Creating and Connecting Components

Components can be instantiated and connected dynamically.

10.10.4.1   Connecting Components

The port attributes allow us to specify a connection in a postcondition, as in the following example:

```
Desk :: login(userName:String)
post:directory.userWithName(userName).gui.source = self
```

10.10.4.2   Instantiating Components

Components are instantiated in the same way as types are instantiated in a post-condition: by using ComponentType.new. Consider an operation that causes a component to permanently invert the value of a Boolean output property.

```
action Comp::invert (out: Port)
post:      -- a new Not is created
          let (n : Not.new) in (
                -- whose output connects to the original sink ports
                n.sinks = out.sinks@pre
                -- and it is attached to the port
                out.sinks = n.input
          )
```

A particular component architecture (such as COM+) might intercept the instantiation and connection operations. (Remember, many of them need to be a part of the standard infrastructure services; see Section 10.2.2, Components and Standardization.) That component infrastructure can monitor the known components and their connections to provide richer extensions of behavior.

10.10.4.3   Visual Notations

All the standard notations for dynamic creation of objects, links between objects, and cardinality constraints on the connections extend also to components. In addition, visual builder tools may provide alternative visualizations for instantiating components and connecting their ports.

10.11 *Heterogenous Components*

A kit of components is designed to a common architecture and can readily be plugged together in many ways. But more often, we must use components that were not designed to work together and may not have been designed specifically to work with any other software.

An assembly of disparate components is prone to inconsistencies and gaps in its facilities. And as components are rewritten or substituted, it is easy for its specification to drift.

When you're building with a heterogenous collection of components, you think less about making a beautiful architecture into which all the pieces fit. You don't have the opportunity of designing them. Instead, you worry about how you can nail together the pieces you are given to achieve your goals.

You can considerably alleviate these problems by building a requirements model and then using retrievals to relate the assembly of components back to the requirements. Used systematically (see Section 13.2.1, Multiple Routes through the Method), this approach helps keep a consistent vision of the system's objectives. The work required to construct a requirements spec and models of the components is repaid by the savings from greater coherence of the result and the rapidity of assembly that is inherent in component-based design.

10.11.1   A Requirements Spec

Let's suppose we are starting a company that sells office equipment. There will be no showroom—only a catalog mailed to customers—and we'll have a warehouse and a telephone sales organization. We want to put together a system to assist its operations.

10.11.1.1   Requirements Model

Figure 10.18 shows a quick and rough model of what we'll deal with.

Most of the types and attributes shown here have an obvious meaning. The primary use cases in this business include makeOrder, makeCustomer, recordContact,

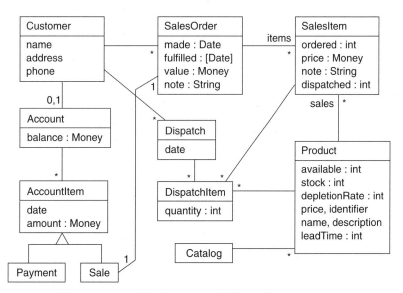

Figure 10.18   Business model for sales company.

and dispatchShipment; others, such as findOrderDispatches, are more like queries and look up information. Let's elaborate a bit on one sample:

<u>use case</u>	dispatchShipment
<u>participants</u>	dispatch clerk, shipping vendor
<u>parameters</u>	list of <sales items, quantities>
<u>pre</u>	sales items not yet fulfilled, all items for same customer
<u>post</u>	a new Dispatch created, with dispatch items for each
	sales orders that have no more pending items marked fulfilled

10.11.1.2   Business Rules

When a sale is made, the sales staff creates an appropriate Customer object (unless one already exists) and a SalesOrder. The SalesOrder may have several SalesItems, each of which defines how many of a cataloged Product are required. Products are chosen from a Catalog. To avoid confusion, there can't be two SalesItems in a Sales-Order for the same Product:

<u>inv</u> SalesOrder::
item1 : SalesItem, item2 : SalesItem :: item1 <> item2
    implies   item1.product <> item2.product

An availability level is recorded for each Product: this is the number of items available in stock that have not been earmarked for a SalesOrder. Any operation that adds a new SalesItem also reduces the availability of the relevant Product:

<u>inv effect</u> Product:: newItem: SalesItem ::
        sales = sales@pre + newItem
        implies availability = availability@pre − newItem.ordered

By contrast, the stock level is the number of items actually in the warehouse; they may have been ordered but not yet dispatched. Availability can fall below zero (if we've taken orders for products we haven't got yet), but stock can't be negative. It is reduced by any operation that adds a new dispatch:

<u>inv</u> Product :: stock >= 0
<u>inv effect</u> Product :: newDispatch : DispatchItem ::
        dispatches = dispatches@pre + newDispatch
        implies stock = stock@pre − newDispatch.quantity

(When availability gets low, we start purchasing more stock; but let's not go into all that in this example.)

When items are sent to a Customer, a Dispatch object is created. One Dispatch may satisfy several SalesOrders (to the same Customer); and one SalesOrder may be dealt with over several Dispatches as stocks become available. The total number of items dispatched must be no more than the number ordered:

<u>inv</u> SalesItem ::   dispatched = dispatchItems.quantity->sum
       and   dispatched <= ordered

We must also send the right things to the right Customer:

<u>inv</u> DispatchItem ::
        dispatch.customer = salesItem.salesOrder.customer
    and product = salesItem.product

A fulfilled SalesOrder is one all of whose SalesItems have the same dispatched and ordered counts. The fulfilled attribute is an optional Date:

<u>inv</u>   SalesOrder :: (fulfilled <> null) =
        (item : salesItems ::item.dispatched = item.ordered)

Any operation that changes the order or dispatches must observe this invariant and set fulfilled to something other than null after the order is fully satisfied. But we should also say that the "something" should be the date on which this happened:

<u>inv effect</u> SalesOrder :: (fulfilled@pre = null and fulfilled <> null) ==>
        fulfilled = Date.today

Every SalesOrder is recorded as an item in the Customer's account:

<u>inv</u>   SalesOrder:: sale.amount = value
    and value = items.price->sum

A further feature is that the sales staff keeps a note of contacts with potential Customers to remember when and why to pester them next and how much chance there is of getting some business (see Figure 10.19). Some people do this with sticky notes; others use electronic organizers. A Contact here is an occasion on which a Customer was spoken to or sent mail; Customer includes prospects who have not yet made an order.

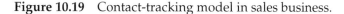

Figure 10.19   Contact-tracking model in sales business.

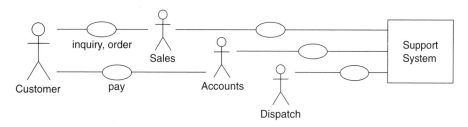

Figure 10.20   Target context diagram.

10.11.1.3   Target Operations and System Context

The new system should support sales, dispatching, and accounts staff (see Figure 10.20 on the previous page). Here's a rough list of the actions we'd like the system to perform for the Sales staff:

(Sales, Support System)::

nextProspect	Display a Customer due to be contacted today.
addContact	Add details of call and date for next try.
makeCustomer	Create details of a new Customer.
findCustomer	Find a Customer from a name or order reference.
makeOrder	Make a SalesOrder for the currently displayed Customer.
findProduct	Display a product from the catalog.
addOrderItem	Add the currently displayed product to the currently displayed SalesOrder.
confirmOrder	Enter payment details such as card payment or payment on account; complete order creation.

The Accounts staff should be able to check on the state of a Customer's account and enter payments. The Dispatch staff should be able to see the orders and create Dispatches.

10.11.2   A Component-Based Solution

In ancient history (earlier than, say, five or six years ago), we might have set to and launched a two-year project to write from scratch a mainframe-based system that integrates all these facilities. But that seems very unlikely these days.

Our chief designer immediately recognizes that the contact-tracking requirement corresponds closely to a single-user PC-based application she has seen in use elsewhere. This will suffice; customers are assigned to sales staff by region, so each salesperson can keep his or her own contact database. There are several mainframe-based general accounts systems; and the designer knows of an ordering system that can be brought in and adapted quickly.

In the interest of meeting rapidly approaching deadlines, therefore, separate systems are set up to accommodate the preceding requirements (see Figure 10.21). Each salesperson works at a PC running four applications: his or her own contacts database that tracks customers in the assigned region; a products catalog browser (hastily constructed as a local Web site); and two virtual terminals, each to the Orders and the Accounts systems. The staff in the warehouse and the Accounts department have their own user interfaces on these terminals.

Does this design fit the bill? That depends on what each of the chosen components actually does.

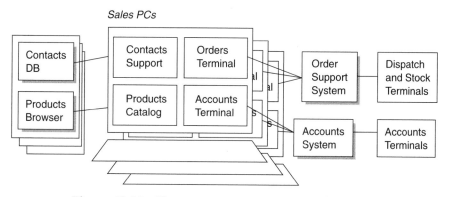

Figure 10.21   Heterogenous component architecture.

10.11.2.1   Model of the Whole

Let us first build a model of the components in the complete solution as envisioned (see Figure 10.22). We have annotated it with the types from the requirements model, with a first guess of where these types will "primarily" be maintained. Life will not be so simple, of course.

10.11.2.2   Models of Constituent Components

Before we can plan any meaningful interaction between the existing components or start to develop glue code, we need a model of what they do. Of course, none of them comes with such a model handy!

By a mixture of experiment and reading the manuals, we build a behavioral model for each component (their designers have omitted to provide one for us). This procedure is highly recommended when you're adopting a component made elsewhere; the same applies when you're reviewing an aging component built

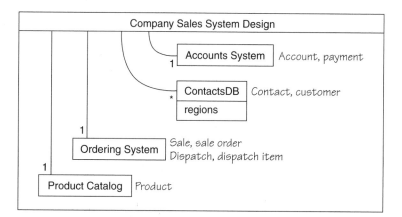

Figure 10.22   Large-grained components modeled.

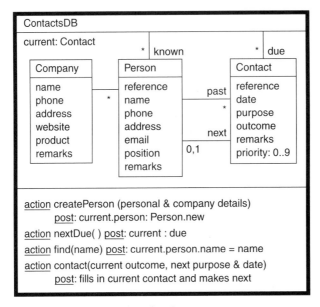

Figure 10.23   The Contacts system.

locally. The exercise clarifies your understanding of the component, reveals useful questions about its behavior that you can research further, and also tends to make it clear where its shortcomings lie.

The Contacts system has the type model shown in Figure 10.23. Each known person has a history of past contacts and a scheduled next contact. There is a set of due contacts: those that should be worked on. In the reference fields you can put a unique reference number that can be used externally to identify objects.

Like many simple data storage applications, its operations don't seem very interesting: they are different ways of entering, searching, and updating the attributes. There is a current Contact and, by implication, a current Person and Company: these are displayed on the screen. createPerson makes a new one; nextDue selects a Person who is due for pestering again; and there are various find operations that can select a person by name, reference, company, postal code, and so on.

When a contact is made (a call, e-mail exchange, and so on) the outcome of the current contact is filled in, and a new Contact attached to the same Person, with suggested date and purpose of call. There is no way of deciding never to call this Person again or of leaving it to the Person to call when interested. Sales staffers insist that such a course of action is unthinkable.

The Ordering system attaches Orders to Customers and provides information about the demand for Products, although not the actual stock (see Figure 10.24). There are operations for creating new Customers, Orders, and Items. On a longer-term basis, new Products can be created. When an Order is fulfilled, it is removed from the outstanding list and linked to a new OrderFulfillment on the completed list.

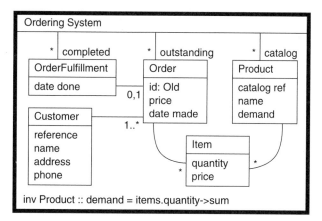

Figure 10.24   The Ordering system.

The Accounts system keeps a record of payments against accounts (see Figure 10.25). The reference attribute of an account enables it to be cross-referenced to external records.

10.11.2.3   Cross-Component Links

The system is now made up of a disparate set of components; each one keeps a part of the information needed by the whole system. The Accounts in the Accounts system refer to the People in the Contacts database. How do we represent these cross-references?

Links between types represent any association of the members of one type with the members of the other type no matter how the association is implemented. Within a single component, associations typically may be implemented with memory address pointers; within a single database, associations may be implemented as pairs of keys in a table. Between components, an association represents a form of identification that each one recognizes as referring to a single object within itself. For example, we could draw an association between Person (real ones) and the Personal_Records in a national Social Security database: the Social Security number identifies members of one type with those of the other.

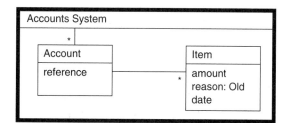

Figure 10.25   The Accounts system.

In the company Sales system (see Figure 10.26), the link from Customer to Account is not held in one component. The Accounts system doesn't have a notion of Customer. But we can decide to use reference fields to cross-link them as *foreign keys*. Within each component, the CID (customer identifier) attributes uniquely identify one Person, Customer, and Account. The CID type itself is understood by all the components (and may be just a number or a string). So the Person::Account link, which tells us where to find accounting information for a Person, is implemented as the Account in the Accounting System that has the same reference as the Person's ref. We have chosen to show both the link and the CID attributes; the link is a derived one, so we should write an invariant that relates them.

Notice that this is an invariant of the company Sales system design. There is nothing that constrains a Contacts database in general to have cross-references to Accounts databases; after all, it's a third-party component. Therefore:

> Company Sales System Design :: -- *within any instance of this design,*
> inv
>> Person :: ref = account.reference
>> -- *each Person's ref is the same as his or her account reference*
>> -- *(We already know from the type diagram that the account is within the*
>> -- *Accounting System that belongs to the same Company Sales System Design)*

We can do similar things with the other cross-component links. The oscustomer link is optional, and that makes it more convenient to state more directly how it is represented:

> Company Sales System Design :: -- *within any instance of this design,*
> inv
>> Person ::   -- *for any Person,*
>> oscustomer = orderSys.customerDB [c | c.ref = ref]
>> -- *my oscustomer is the only member of the (Company Sales System's)*
>> -- *order system's customer database whose ref attribute is the same as*
>> -- *my ref attribute. (So if there is no such customer, oscustomer = null.)*

In effect, reference numbers, identifiers, and keys of all kinds are implementations of links that cross system and subsystem boundaries (see Figure 10.27).

10.11.2.4 Retrievals

Now we must show how all the information mentioned in the business model is actually represented somewhere in the system design. (See Section 6.4, Spreadsheet: Model Refinement.) This is essential for review and testing, and generating these relationships tends to expose mistakes.

For example, our business model mentions a customerBase, a set of Customers. Where and how are they represented in the system? There is something called Customer in the design, but that is a Company Sales System Design::Ordering System::Customer, which is not the same as a Company Sales Business Model :: Customer. Where do we look to find the complete set of Customers?

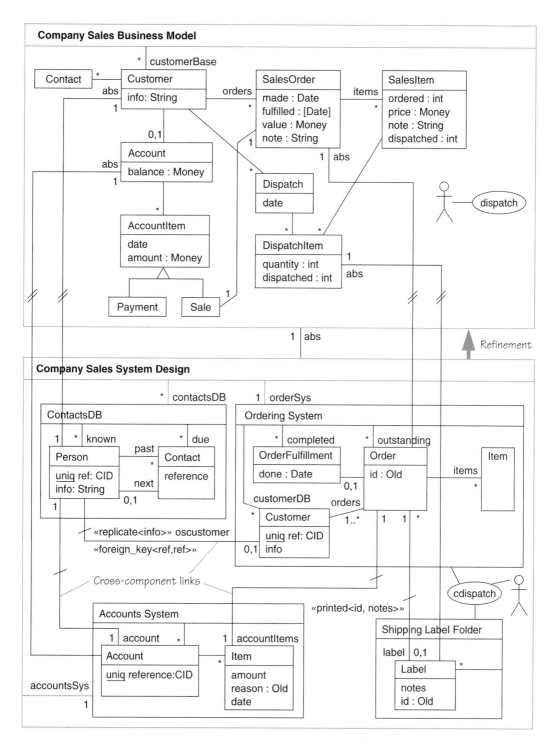

Figure 10.26 Mapping component models and new business process to requirements.

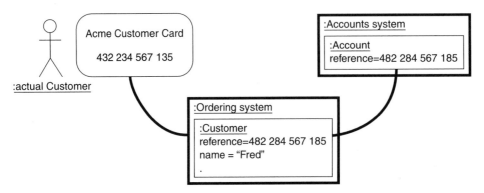

Figure 10.27   Cross-component links.

For every Customer we know about businesswise, there is a Person in the System Design. We've shown the relationship as the association abs. There are similar direct correspondences for several other types. In fact, the whole business model is implemented by the whole system design, so we've shown that association, too. (The outer type boxes are shown in gray to reduce clutter in Figure 10.26. In real documentation, you'd show them separately.) So we can say that

> Company Sales System Design ::   -- *for any member of this particular design,*
> abs.customerBase   -- *the customer base of the business model*
> = contactsDB.known.abs   -- *is represented by all the Persons in all*
>   -- *the contacts databases*

(In another implementation, there might not be any one place where all the customers are stored. For example, there might be Customers in the Ordering system that are not in the Contacts database. In this case, we'd say

> abs.customerBase = contactsDB.known.abs + orderSys.customerDB.abs.)

The abs at the end says that it's not the Person that is the Customer but rather the abstraction represented by that part of the implementation. So we should now define what abs means for a Person:

> Company Sales System Design ::
> Person ::   -- *and for each Person, the corresponding Customer's*
>   abs.info = info   -- *attributes are got by following various links and then*
>   and abs.account = account.abs   -- *finding what they represent*
>   and abs.orders = oscustomer.orders.abs
>   and abs.dispatch = oscustomer.orders.label.abs

Notice the style here: starting with a type in the implementation, we say that it represents something in the more abstract model—a Customer in this case—which we call abs. Then we go around all the attributes of that abstraction, saying how each attribute is represented within the implementation: abs.info = ..., abs.orders = ..., and so on.

Each of these pieces of information can be retrieved from the implementation by following some links. Sometimes, that is enough: the info is a String, which is what we modeled. But often, we navigate to an implementation type, such as Order; so we end up by saying that it's not actually the implementation's Orders, but rather the abstractions they represent. So we say oscustomers.orders.*abs*. Then in a separate retrieval, we can define how Orders are represented, in the same way.

```
Company Sales System Design ::
Order ::
            abs.fulfilled = orderFulfillment.date
and         abs.value = accountItem.amount
and         abs.items = items.abs ... etc
```

In this way, we can gather together, or *retrieve*, the attributes of the business model's types that are scattered about in the implementation.[14, 15]

10.11.2.5   Implementing Actions and Business Rules

Now that we know how the requirement's model is represented in the components stuck together for the design, we can work out whether and how the required actions are properly catered to. We need to coordinate the business transactions across our ad hoc components. Let's look at makeOrder, addOrderItem, and confirmOrder.

The requirement for makeOrder is to "create a new Order for the currently displayed Customer." In our hastily contrived system, there can be two Customers displayed on a sales PC screen: one in the Contacts database and another one in the Ordering system. Because the components are entirely separate, the system provides no guarantee that they are consistent.

But makeOrder is an action: a specification of something that must be achievable *with* the system, although not necessarily something it must take the entire responsibility for. Remember that we have modeled it as a joint action (see Section 4.2.3, Joint Actions), and the responsibility partition has not been decided. Our implementation of makeOrder is shown on the next page.

---

14. You might like to try completing the retrieval. In doing so, you may find that some business attributes are missing from the implementation.

15. The technique illustrated here is very general. For example, in the highly regulated business of financial services (banking, insurance), there are many rules about the permitted and prohibited flow of information in different business areas. At the technology level, the CORBA security service provides some machinery to implement this. Explicit as-is and essential business models were constructed, as was a separate technology model. The formal retrievals highlighted many holes that needed addressing and established confidence that the solution met the complex requirements.

- The salesperson gets the same Customer displayed in the Ordering system window as in the Contacts database. This may involve creating a new Customer in the Ordering system, using the PC's cut-and-paste facilities to transfer name, reference number, and address from one window to the other.

- The salesperson uses the Ordering system's Order creation operation.

The Ordering system provides this action directly, although you must first look up the Product in its list, which carries less information than the separate Web-browsable product catalog.

The spec says, "Enters payment details, such as a credit card or payment on account." According to one of the business rules (see Section 10.11.1.2), the order must be entered as a sale in an Account associated with this Customer.

The Accounts system is entirely separate from the Ordering system, so it is up to the sales staff to copy the right numbers into the right accounts.

Again, we're using the idea of action as specifying the outcome of a dialog between actors (people and components in this case). When people are involved, this generally means relying on them to do the right thing.

How would we describe the use case findOrderDispatches in our new business process? Let's first look at the original requirements model; this use case is a query, and it is best to make the specifications of queries trivial by adding convenience attributes to the model. So we add an attribute on SalesOrder:

SalesOrder::dispatches
     -- it is all dispatches for any of my SalesItems
     items.dispatchItems.dispatch

<u>action</u> Agent::findOrderDispatches (order, out dispatches)
<u>post</u>:   result = order.dispatches

This requirements specification applies whether the underlying process is manual or automated. The new version refines the required one:

<u>action</u> Agent::findOrderDispatcher (order#)
        -- the dispatches with labels whose orders include the target order#
<u>post</u>:   result = shippingLabelFolder.labels[order.id->includes(order#)].dispatch

Similarly, the abstract dispatch use case is refined to cdispatch, which now involves the agent, the ordering system, and the shipping labels folder.

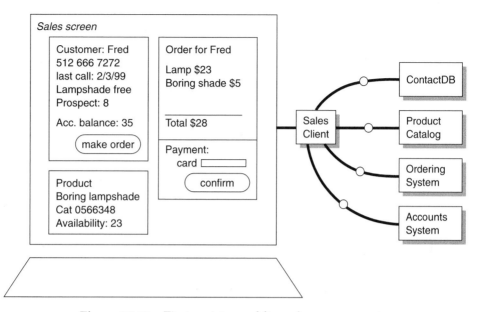

Figure 10.28   First revision: adding glue components.

10.11.3   Glue Components

Once the dust of setting up shop has settled a bit, we can make some improvements to the first support environment. We will move some work from the staff into the machine.

Sales staffers will now work through a Sales Client component (see Figure 10.28). This is an evolutionary change: the other components will stay exactly as they are. The Sales Client provides a single user interface to all the components used by the sales staff. It implements some of the cross-component business rules such as the Account-Order tie-up, eliminating that area of human error.

In this design, the Sales Client (which runs in each sales PC) integrates the third-party components; but notice that they still do not talk directly to each other. Often, there is no facility for this in older components. In a similar way, a Dispatch Client (used by the warehouse staff) can integrate the Ordering system with a dispatch-tracking system and stock control.

Now that the Sales Client has become the sales operator's sole interface with the system, it should take complete responsibility for implementing the actions and business rules associated with sales. Its spec is the sales part of the requirements. It should therefore provide complete operations for making an order, adding the currently displayed product to the order, and creating and adding the proper amounts to the Customer's account.

It is characteristic of third-party components that there is little that is coherent about their interfaces: they all talk in integers, floats, and characters, and that's as far as it goes. There are few standard protocols between components, and locally built glue such as Sales Client tends to be written to couple to specific components. Nevertheless, if the glue can be kept minimal, adaptations are not difficult.

Glue components are not always user-interface or client components. Components can be "wrapped" in locally built code to work to a standard set of connectors, making them look more like members of a coherent kit.

10.11.4   Federated Architecture

A federated system is one in which the division between components more nearly matches the division between business roles.

Improving our system still further, we write our own components. We divide the functions of the Ordering system (see Figure 10.29). One part runs on the salespeople's PCs, and the other part runs on the dispatching department's machine.

Each sales support component has a list of Products and Customers and can generate Orders. Orders are sent (either immediately or in batches) to Dispatch Support, and corresponding debits are posted to the appropriate accounts. The lists of products and customers are shared between all sales staff by intermittent replication to a Sales Master component.

(The pattern of replication is the same for all objects, involving comparison of modification dates followed by transmission one way or the other. This suggests

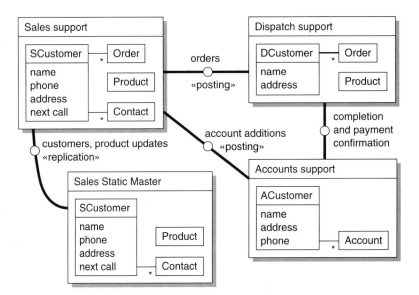

Figure 10.29   Eventual version: federated architecture.

«replication» as a connector category. The same principle applies to «posting», which is about appending an item to a list that cannot otherwise be altered.)

Each component has a version of the types that support its function. Taken together, these types retrieve to the requirements types.

Federation brings a number of benefits, including decoupling of outage: Each staff member can keep working even if other machines are down. It also supports scalability—the number of sales and dispatching staff is not limited by the power of one machine—and geographical decoupling: a high-bandwidth connection is not necessary between a salesperson and other parts of the system, so salespeople could work from home.

On the downside, some replication is necessary of the product catalog and the customer database. (*Replication* means ensuring consistency between datasets using intermittent updates, such as when a user logs in occasionally.) However, disk space isn't very expensive, and the technology of replication has been much developed in recent years, particularly since its popularization by Lotus.

10.11.5   Summary: Heterogenous Components

A designer using a set of components that were *not* designed as a kit is faced with two problems:

- Matching their different and redundant views of similar concepts (such as Customer)
- Making their different connectors work together

Glue components can be built to translate the concepts and adapt the connectors; in the simplest case, the users can perform those functions.

We have seen how a clear, high-level requirements specification, and the retrieval relationship, helps clarify the relationship between the disparate designs of the components. We have also seen what needs to be done to unify them.

Pattern 10.1   Extracting Generic Code Components

Reuse code by generalizing from existing work to make pluggable components.

Intent

Make an existing component reusable in a broader context. Resources have been assigned for work outside the immediate project need (see Pattern 10.2, Componentware Management).

Considerations

It is often better to make a generic framework model, which requires less investment in the plug technology needed to make code components plug together. A framework model provides only the specs for each class that fits into a framework and is typically specialized at design time. This arrangement is better for performance and requires less runtime pluggability.

It takes hard work to find the most useful generalization that fits many cases—and to get it right. This effort is worthwhile only for components that will be reused at least four or five times; the investment doesn't pay off for some time.

Strategy

Components Cross Projects. It is unusual for someone without much experience to design a good generic component in advance; such components become apparent only after you find yourself repeating similar design decisions. It is also not very helpful to find components in isolation: They work best as part of a coherent kit. Within a small project, there is not much payoff in developing components: It's easy to spend too much time honing beautifully engineered components that aren't used anywhere else. It's therefore a far-sighted architectural job to decide which components are worth working on and integrating into the local kit.

Identify Common Frameworks. Separate objects and collaborations that have common features into framework packages and reimport them to apply.

Don't Overgeneralize. If you simply dream up generalizations, they will not work.

Identify Variable Functionality and Delegate to Separate Plug Objects. Any time you can encapsulate such variability into a separate object, do so.

Specify Plug Interfaces. Define what you need from anything that plugs into your component as well as what you provide to it. Provide the simplest model that makes sense. "Lower" interfaces generally need to know less than "upper" ones.

Package Your Component. It should be delivered with the following.

- Its plug specifications.
- Its test harness for clients' plugs—based on the plug spec. This takes one of two forms:
  - A stand-alone harness that drives the plug-in and pronounces judgement
  - A switchable monitor that checks pre- and postconditions during operation
- A selection of demo or default plug-ins.

The component may be part of a suite of components that can plug together in different ways.

Pattern 10.2   Componentware Management

In this pattern, you devote resources to build, maintain, and promote use of a component library. There is no free lunch.

Intent

Reuse Motivates the Adoption of OT. Surveys show that of the main three motivations managers quote for taking up object technology, reuse is the leader. But objects do not automatically promote reuse; rather, they are an enabling technology that will reduce costs if well applied. If OT is badly applied, it

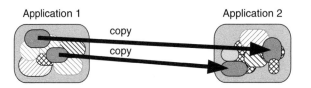

Relative Number of Managers

increases costs. These costs always increase in the short term: Investment is required to move to a reuse culture. The good news is that there are a growing number of success stories when objects are done right.

Considerations

Maturity. You need a well-defined process already followed by your developers.

What Is Reuse? Cut and paste, also known as "Adopt, adapt, and improve," is cheap and easy but provides limited benefits; enhancements to the original do not benefit the reusers at all.

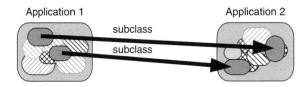

Programming by adaptation means that if something looks similar, you inherit and override methods as required. It takes more effort and gives limited benefits. Unless you adhere to strict rules, superclass enhancements need review of overrides in subclasses.

The third approach is to build generic components and import them to reuse. You must devote substantial resources to a library, but this approach yields the best benefits. It requires the most investment.

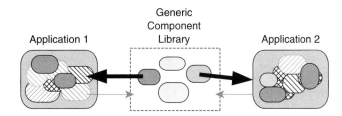

Caveats. Expect limited success initially. For example, payback should not be expected until after a year or two; pilots will show some success in the short term. It also takes time for management and technical staff to consistently support the idea long-term, and the skills required—for generic component design and interface specification—are more demanding.

Strategy

- Apply the spiral model, with deliberate activities for abstraction and re-refinement.
- Develop a reuse team whose members know and develop the library. Use people with a perfectionist turn of mind and the right skill set.
- To encourage reuse, offer the services of some reuse team people to development projects.
- Do not underresource; it is your design capital.
- Apply models, patterns, frameworks, and designs to all stages of the process.

Pattern 10.3   Build Models from Frameworks

Do not build models from scratch but instead build them by composing frameworks.

Intent

The idea is to generalize modeling work so that you focus on reuse and componentware as early as possible (see Pattern 10.2, Componentware Management).

Considerations

Large models can be repetitive within similar business environments just as program designs are. And models also have variability that can be captured by different forms of factoring and parameterization.

A framework can be only a specification or can also include code implementation (see Chapter 11, Reuse and Pluggable Designs: Frameworks in Code). The latter requires more investment in its design and may run slower. Pure specification frameworks help you build a spec, and then you must implement the result; it does not have the same runtime overhead of pluggability.

Strategy

Model-only Strategy. In this strategy, you build and use model frameworks.

- Look out for similar patterns within business models, type specifications, and high-level designs. Also, make frameworks for common design and analysis patterns.
- Extract common models and use placeholders, effects, invariant effects, and abstract actions to allow you to separate the parts of the models.
- Compose your framework with others. When one type has definitions from more than one framework, use join composition (see Section 8.3.4, Joining Action Specifications).
- Implement the composed framework. Each type in the composition will have a spec, which can be implemented as for the basic design.
- Use a tool that will help you compose model frameworks.

Pattern 10.4   Plug Conformance

Two components fit together if their plug-points conform. Document them with refinements.

Intent

Ensure that two components you've acquired (or built) will work with each other.

There are two specifications at a plug-point: the "services offered" advertisement of one component and the "required" of the other. We must ensure that one matches the other.

How hard this is depends on whether the two components use similar terms. If one happens to be designed specifically for the other, it's easy. If that's not the case but they are based on the same business model, it's not very difficult. If the models are entirely different, there's more work to do (for example, see Section 10.11, Heterogenous Components).

Every model is based on imported others; with luck, components concerned with the same business will import the same packages. Indeed, for this reason it is important to base your specifications on imported models as much as possible.

Strategy

Document a refinement that shows how one component meets the other. See Chapter 6, Abstraction, Refinement, and Testing.

Pattern 10.5   Using Legacy or Third-Party Components

Make a model of an existing component before using it. Create proxies to act as local representatives of the objects accessed through the component.

Intent

This pattern produces a uniform strategy across component boundaries, including legacy components.

Some of your software may be in the form of a third-party or legacy component. It may be an infrastructure that you use to serve your middleware or may be part of the core of the system that implements part of the main business model.

For example, a library management system deals with loans, reservations, and stock control. A third-party component is bought to deal with membership. This is a conventionally written component (probably built atop a standard database) with an API that allows members to be added, looked up, updated, and deleted.

Considerations

Model Translation. The component may (if you're lucky!) come with a clearly defined model. If it doesn't, it may be useful to build your own type model. The model will show the component's view of the information it deals with, together with the operations at the API. The model will not correspond precisely to your system model.

- It will not contain all the information. For example, the library manager knows each member's address, which books the member is currently holding, and what fines are owed. Only part of this data will be stored in the membership manager.
- The component may be capable of storing other things we aren't interested in for this application, such as credit history.
- If the component's model was written by someone else, its attributes and associations may be radically different from those of your system model. For example, it may be designed to associate "reference numbers" with several "short strings," which you intend to use for the member name and address.

Associations across Component Boundaries. Any kind of association crossing a component boundary—for example, between members and loaned books—must be represented in some way, typically by a handle that both components map internally to their own ends of the links. So there may be a reference number used to identify members at the API of the membership manager; this reference number would be stored wherever we need to associate our other objects with members.

Strategy

Use proxies outside the component to represent objects stored more completely within it. Create proxies only when they're needed. For example, the library looks up a member by name and gets back a reference handle from the membership manager, which you wrap in a Member object created for the purpose. Further operations on the Member are dealt with by that object, which sends changes of address through the API; it can be garbage-collected when we process another member.

To check that the component as described does what you require, make a partial retrieval between its model and the system's. Check for conformance of the API specs to your requirements.

10.12 *Summary*

The Catalysis approach to design is about standing back from the detail so that you can discuss the most important parts without the clutter of fine detail. You prolong the life of a design by making your overall vision clear to maintainers, enhancers, and extenders. Earlier in this book we saw how to use models to abstract away implementation details. Pre/post specifications abstracted what was required of an object rather than how it achieved it. Joint actions represent, as one thing, an interaction that may be implemented by a series of messages.

This chapter takes the abstraction one level higher (see Figure 10.30). We have defined a notation in which components—separately deliverable chunks of software—can be specified and designed and then plugged together to make bigger components and complete systems. We have also defined a variety of ways in which components can be interconnected, abstracting away details of the connectors, and outlined a framework for the definition of more categories of connectors.

We have applied the Catalysis ideas of modeling and behavioral abstraction to enable us to specify components aside from their implementations. We have also shown how to check that plugging a set of heterogenous components together meets a given set of requirements.

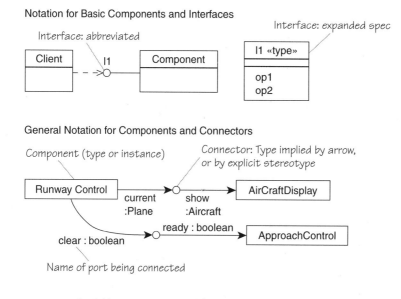

Figure 10.30   Notation for the products of component modeling.

Chapter 11 Reuse and Pluggable Design Frameworks in Code

Code reuse is a sought-after goal, but it does not happen automatically. It costs money, and it requires explicit attention at the level of design and in the structure of the development process within and across projects.

Reuse requires that components be built in a manner that is both generic—not overly tied to a specific application—and customizable so it can be adapted to specific needs.

Reuse comes in many flavors, from cut-and-paste to building libraries of low-level utility routines and classes to creating skeletons of entire applications with plug-points that can be customized. The latter requires a particular mind-set to extract commonality while deferring only those aspects that are variable.

There are two keys to systematic use of frameworks in code: The first is to make problem descriptions more generic. Second, you must have code techniques for implementing generic or incomplete problem specifications and then specializing and composing them.

11.1 *Reuse and the Development Process*

One of the most compelling reasons for adopting component-based approaches to development, with or without objects, is the promise of reuse. The idea is to build software from existing components primarily by assembling and replacing interoperable parts. These components range from user-interface controls such as listboxes and HTML browsers to components for networking or communication to full-blown business components. The implications for reduced development time and improved product quality make this approach very attractive.

11.1.1   What Is Reuse?

Reuse is a variety of techniques aimed at getting the most from the design and implementation work you do. We prefer not to reinvent the same ideas every time we do a new project but rather to capitalize on that work and deploy it immediately in new contexts. In that way, we can deliver more products in shorter times. Our maintenance costs are also reduced because an improvement to one piece of design work will enhance all the projects in which it is used. And quality should improve, because reused components have been well tested.

11.1.1.1   Import Beats Cut-and-Paste

Something like 70% of work on the average software design is done after its first installation. This means that an approach, such as reuse, aimed at reducing costs must be effective in that maintenance phase and not just in the initial design (see Figure 11.1).

People sometimes think of reuse as meaning cutting chunks from an existing implementation or design and pasting them into a new one. Although this accelerates the initial design process, there is no benefit later. Any improvements or fixes made to the original component will not propagate to the adapted versions. And if you're going to adapt a component by cut-and-paste, you must first look inside it and understand its entire implementation thoroughly—a fine source of bugs.

Good reuse therefore implies using the same unaltered component in many contexts, a technique much like the idea of importing packages described in Chapter 7, Using Packages. Texts on measuring reuse don't count cutting and pasting as proper reuse.

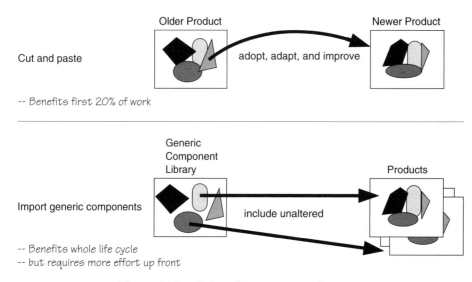

Figure 11.1   Cut-and-paste versus Import.

11.1.1.2   The Open-Closed Principle and Reuse Economics

But there is a difficulty. If alterations are not allowed, a component can be useful in many contexts only if it is designed with a good set of parameters and plug-points. It must follow the well-known Open-Closed Principle:

> *Every component should be open to extension but closed to modification.*

It takes effort to work out how to make a component more generic, and the result might run slower when deployed. The investment will be repaid in savings every time the component is used in a design and every time maintenance must be done on only one component rather than many slightly different copies. But it is not always certain exactly when or how a component will be reused in the future. So, as with all investments, generalizing a component is a calculated risk.

11.1.2   What Are the Reusable Artifacts?

A reusable artifact is any coherent chunk of work that can be used in more than one design. Following are examples.

- Compiled code; executable objects
- Source code; classes, methods
- Test fixtures and harnesses
- Designs and models: collaborations, frameworks, patterns
- User-interface "look and feel"
- Plans, strategies, and architectural rules

This list includes all kinds of development work. We have already discussed model frameworks and template packages, which can be valuable to an enterprise. They are *white-box* assets: What you see is what is they offer. By contrast, an executable piece of software, delivered without source code, can perform a useful and well-defined function and yet not be open to internal inspection. Software vendors prefer such *black-box* components.

11.1.3   Reuse Truths

What should you reuse? The executable? Source code? Interface specifications? Problem domain models?

▶ *Reuse Law 1*   Don't reuse implementation code unless you intend to reuse the specification as well. Otherwise, a revised version of the implementation will break your code.

▶ *Reuse Lemmas*   (1) If you reuse a specification, try a component-based approach: Implement against the interface and defer binding to the implementation.

    (2) Reuse of specifications leads to reuse of implementations. In particular, whenever you can implement standardized interfaces, whether domain-specific or for infrastructure services, you enable the reuse of all other implementations that follow those standards.

(3) Successful reuse needs decent specifications.

(4) If you can componentize your problem domain descriptions themselves and reuse domain models, you greatly enhance your position to reuse interface specifications and implementations downstream.

11.1.4   A Reuse Culture

In a reuse culture, an organization focuses on building and enhancing its capital of reusable assets, which would include a mixture of all these kinds of artifacts. Like any investment, this capital must be managed and cultivated. It requires investment in building those assets, a suitable development process and roles, and training and incentives that are appropriate for reuse.

But designs must be generalized to be reusable. Generalizing a component can't be justified in terms of its original intended purpose. If you write a collision avoidance routine for airplanes, there's no reason you should do the extra work to make it usable by your maritime colleagues: You have your own deadlines to meet. And if your product deals only with air traffic, you have no reason to separate out those pieces of the airplane class that could apply to vehicles in general. All these generalizations require broadening of requirements beyond your immediate needs.

On the other hand, if you notice three lines of code that crop up in six different places in your own product, then you will easily see the point of generalizing them and calling a single routine from each place. That's because you're controlling the resources for all the places it could be used; and the problem is small enough that you can easily get a handle on what's required.

On the larger scale, reuse of components between individuals, between design teams, and across and outside organizations takes more coordination. It's usually someone who holds responsibility for all the usage sites who can assign the resources to get the generalization done. To make it happen, reuse needs an organization and a budget.

A significant part of identifying large-grained reuse comes from careful modeling of the problem domain and of the supporting domains—UI, communications, and so on—that would be a part of many applications. This activity also crosses specific project boundaries and so needs organization support.

Should a component be made sufficiently general for reuse? How generic and reusable should it be? These are decisions that must be made consciously and carefully. We have all made such generalizations when deciding that a few lines of code could be moved to a subroutine of their own. Parameterizing a whole class or group of classes follows the same principle but employs a wider variety of patterns and should be more carefully thought through.

Some components can be reused more widely than others. Some objects, routines, or patterns might be useful only in several parts of the same software product; but if it is a big product or a product family, several teams may need coordinating.

"Galloping generalization" is the syndrome wherein a group spends months producing something that runs like a snail on dope and has hundreds of interesting features, most of which will never be used. The best strategy seems to be to generalize a component only after it is earmarked for use in more than one context; and then generalize it only as much as is necessary for the envisaged applications.

Naturally, the organization that measures developer productivity in terms of lines of code written has some rethinking to do before reuse can succeed. Suitable incentives schemes should be based more on the ratio of code reused to new code written.

11.1.5   Distinct Development Cycles

In a reuse culture, development tends to split into two distinct activities.

• *Product development:* The design and creation of applications to solve a problem. This phase is centered on understanding the problem and rapidly locating and assembling reuse capital assets to provide an implementation.

• *Asset development:* The design and creation of the reusable components that will be used in different contexts. This is carried out with more rigorous documentation and thought. Because software capital assets will be used in many designs, the impact of a change can be, for better or worse, quite large.

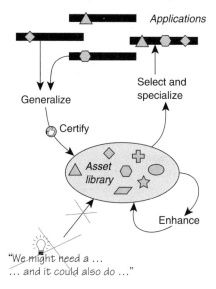

It is therefore worth putting much serious effort and skill into assets. Of course, the products must work properly; but whereas much may be gained by, for example, tuning a reusable asset's performance as far as possible, a product that is used only in one context often must be good enough only for that purpose. Strong documentation also pays off more with assets than with products.

For developing reusable assets, you would generally want to apply many of the techniques in this book. Reuse means investing in the quality of software; the old argument that "we don't have time to document" can have only a negative effect in a reuse culture. The development of products or applications will also use many of the same techniques, but the process can be quite different (for example, see Section 10.11, Heterogenous Components).

11.2   *Generic Components and Plug-Points*

For a component to be reused in different contexts, it must be sufficiently generic to capture the commonality across those contexts; yet it must also offer mechanisms so it can be specialized as needed.

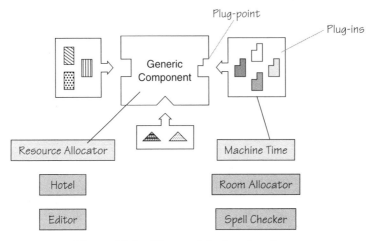

Figure 11.2   Plug-points for plug-ins.

This means that you must understand what parts of the component are common across those contexts. Design it so that those parts that vary across contexts are separated from the component itself at carefully selected *plug-points* where that variation can be encapsulated and localized—places where specialized components can be plugged in to adapt the overall behavior. As Figure 11.2 illustrates, a resource allocator component might be specialized to allocate machine time on a factory floor; a hotel component might accommodate various room allocation policies; and an editor might accommodate any spell checker.

11.2.1   Plugs: The Interfaces

Let's look at a couple of ways in which components can be made to plug together. In particular, it helps to distinguish between (1) composing components to build something bigger and (2) plugging parts into a generic component in order to specialize its behavior to current needs. Although both approaches place similar demands on modeling and design, the intent of each one is different. These distinctions may get blurred in the presence of callback-styled programming and reentrant code; when an architecture is layered, with calls restricted to a single direction from higher layers to lower, the distinction remains sharp.

11.2.2   Upper Interfaces: For "Normal" Use

The components we use are made from other components. Figure 11.3 illustrates how a larger component (a video rental system) might be assembled by assembling components for membership, reservations, and stock management. We think of this as the "upper" interface; it is the direct and visible connecting of parts that provide well-defined services. Examples of such upper interfaces are the public operations of a class, APIs of databases, windows systems, and, of

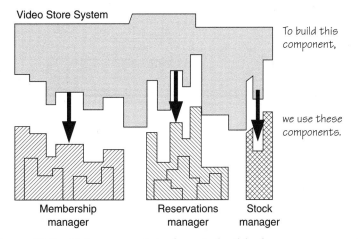

Figure 11.3   Using upper interfaces to build a larger component.

course, the primary services offered by the membership, reservations, and stock management components.

11.2.3   Lower Interfaces: For Customization

Each of the components whose "normal" interface we used is itself an incomplete implementation; to provide its services, it needs additional parts to be plugged in to it. Figure 11.4 illustrates the use of "lower" interfaces via which a generic component is specialized with several plug-ins that customize its behavior to the problem at hand. In this case, a generic membership manager is being adapted by plugging in specifics for video store members and their accounts.

Generic components have plug-points—parameterized aspects that can be filled in appropriately in a given context—both for implementation components and for generic model components that are built to be adapted and reused. When designing a complex component, we might reach into a component repository and build our specific models from generic model components in this library. Of course, the generic versions must provide mechanisms for extension and customization to the specific domain at hand.

Modern desktop software bristles with plug-points. Web browsers, as well as word processors and spreadsheets, accept plug-ins for displaying specialized images; desktop publishing software accepts plug-ins for doing specialized image processing. In those cases, the plug-ins usually must be designed for a particular parent application. Using dynamic linking technologies, the plug-ins are coupled with the parent application when it begins to run.

Every OO language provides some form of plug-ins. The most common form is the use of framework classes: the superclasses implement the skeleton of an application—implementing methods that call operations that must be defined in the

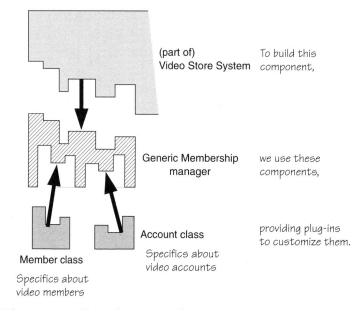

Figure 11.4   Using lower interfaces to customize a component.

subclasses—and a set of subclasses serves to specialize the application. The plug-points are the subclasses and their overriding methods. In C++, a template List class can be instantiated to provide lists of numbers, lists of elephants, or lists of whatever class the client needs; the plug-point is a simple template parameter.

The principle is not limited to single classes but rather can span multiple abstract classes that collaborate and must be jointly extended before use. Many class libraries provide user-interface frameworks (such as Smalltalk's Model-View-Controller). You make a user interface (either manually or with a visual builder tool) by inheriting from the framework classes and plugging specializing methods in to your subclasses.

11.2.3.1   Infrastructure Services: A Special Kind of Lower Interface

To operate properly, many components need an underlying set of infrastructure services (see Section 10.2.2, Components and Standardization). These services do not customize the behavior of the component in any interesting way; they simply provide an implementation of a common *virtual machine* for use by all components.

Obvious examples include the POSIX interface, which provides a common view of many different operating systems, and the Java virtual machine, which provides all the services needed to run Java components. However, this underlying virtual machine may be more specialized to the problem at hand—for example, a state-machine interpreter or a graph transformation engine.

11.3 *The Framework Approach to Code Reuse*

In object-oriented design and programming, the concept of a framework has proven to be a useful way to reuse large-grained units of design and code while permitting customization for different contexts. The style of reuse with frameworks, and the mind-set for factoring out commonality and differences, is quite distinctive.

11.3.1   OOP Frameworks

An object-oriented framework is often characterized as a set of abstract and concrete classes that collaborate to provide the skeleton of an implementation for an application. A common aspect of such frameworks is that they are adaptable; the framework provides mechanisms by which it can be extended, such as by composing selected subclasses together in custom ways or defining new subclasses and implementing methods that either plug in to or override methods on the superclasses.

There are fundamental differences between the framework style and traditional styles of reuse, as illustrated by the following example.

Design and implement a program for manipulating shapes. Different shapes are displayed differently. When a shape is displayed, it shows a rendering of its outline and a textual printout of its current location in the largest font that will fit within the shape.

In the next two sections we will contrast the traditional approach to reuse with the framework style of factoring for reuse.

11.3.1.1   Class Library with Traditional Reuse

A traditional approach to reuse might factor the design as follows. Because the display of different shapes varies with the kind of shapes, we design a shape hierarchy. The display method is abstracted on the superclass—because shapes display themselves differently—and each subclass provides its own implementation.

There are common pieces to the display method, such as computing the font size appropriate for a particular shape given its inner bounding box and printing the location in the computed font. Hence we implement a computeFont and printLocation method on the superclass (marked protected in Java so that it is subclass-visible).

```
class Shape {
    // called from subclass: given a Bounding Box and String, compute the font
    protected Font computeFont (BoundingBox b, String s) { .... }
    // called from subclass: print location on surface with Font
    protected void printLocation (GraphicsContext g, Font f, Point location) { ... }
    public abstract void display (GraphicsContext g);
}
```

A typical subclass would now look like this:

```
class Oval extends Shape {
    // shape-specific private data
    private LocationInfo ovalData;
    // how to compute my innerBox from shape-specific data
    private BoundingBox innerBox() { .... }
    // rendering an oval
    private void render (GraphicsContext g) { ... trace an oval ... }
    // display myself
    public void display (GraphicsContext surface) {
        render ();
        BoundingBox box = innerBox();
        // let the superclass compute the font
        Font font = super.computeFont (box, ovalData.location.asString());
        // let the superclass print the location
        super.printLocation (surface, font, ovalData.location);
    }
}
```

A class model is shown in Figure 11.5. The dynamics of the inheritance design can be shown on an enhanced interaction diagram, separating the inherited and locally defined parts of an object to show calls that go up or down the inheritance chain.

11.3.1.2 Framework-Style Reuse and the Template Method

With framework development, the skeleton of the common behavior is one of two things: either (1) an internal method specified on an interface that must be implemented by a specialized class, or (2) a *template method* in the superclass with the variant bits and pieces deferred to the subclasses. We will illustrate the latter design here.

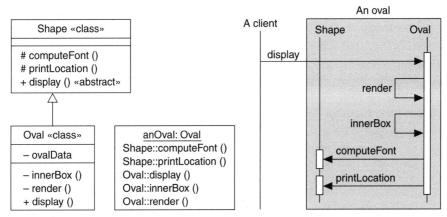

= "protected"; + = "public"; − = "private"

Figure 11.5   Inheritance design and enhanced interaction diagram.

With a framework approach to reuse, our factoring looks quite different from that of the traditional approach. We start with the assumption that all shapes fundamentally do the same thing when they are displayed: render, compute a font for their inner bounding box, and print their location in that font. Thus, we implement at the level of the superclass:

```
class Shape {
    public void display (GraphicsContext surface) {
        // delegate to subclass to fill in the pieces
        render (surface);              // plug-point: deferred to subclass
        BoundingBox box = innerBox(); // plug-point: deferred to subclass
        Point location = location();   // plug-point: deferred to subclass

        // then do the rest of "display" based on those bits
        Font font = computeFont (box, location);
        surface.printLocation (location, font);
    }
}
```

The actual rendering and computation of the inner box and location must be deferred to the subclasses: *plug-points*. However, if a subclass provides the appropriate bits as *plug-ins*, it can inherit and use the same implementation of display. Thus, we are imposing a consistent skeletal behavior on all subclasses but permitting each one to flesh out that skeleton in its own ways.

```
class Oval extends Shape {
    // implement 3 shape-specific "plug-ins" for the plug-points in Shape
    protected void render (GraphicsContext g) { ...trace an oval ...}
    protected BoundingBox innerBox () { ... }
    protected Point location () { return center; }

    // private shape-specific data
    private Point center;
    private int majorAxis, minorAxis, angle;
}
```

Figure 11.6 illustrates this approach. Although this example focuses on a single class hierarchy, it extends to the set of collaborating abstract classes that are characteristic of frameworks.

To display itself, the Shape hierarchy, for example, requires certain services from the GraphicsContext object. There could also be different implementations of GraphicsContext—for screens and printers—using a similar framework-styled design. It is this partitioning of responsibility—among different shape classes and among shapes and the GraphicsContext—that gives the design its flexibility. Thus, any packaging of a class as a reusable unit must also include a description of the behaviors expected of other objects—that is, their *types*.

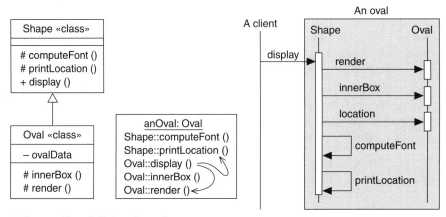

Figure 11.6 Framework-style inheritance design.

Table 11.1 Contrast between Traditional and Framework Styles

Traditional	Framework
Begin with the mind-set that the display methods would be *different* and then seek the *common pieces* that could be *shared* between them.	Assert that the display methods are really the *same* and then identify the *essential differences* between them to *defer* to the subclasses.
Focus on sharing the *lower-level* operations such as computeFont and printLocation. The higher-level application logic is duplicated, and each one calls the shared lower-level bits.	Share the *entire skeleton* of the application logic itself. Each application plugs in to the skeleton the pieces (such as render, innerBox, particular GraphicsContexts) required to complete the skeleton.
	Most (many) calls go from the framework skeleton to the individual applications; in fact, one of the hallmarks of a framework is, "Don't call me—I'll call you."
	Define an interface representing demands that the reusable skeleton framework makes on the applications—the plug-points for extension.
	Application contains newer code; however, the existing (base) code calls newer code to delegate specialized bits.
	The framework implements the architecture and imposes its rules and policies on the applications.

11.3.1.3 Contrast of Styles

Table 11.1 summarizes the contrast between the approaches in terms of factoring of code, degree of reuse, and consistency of resulting designs. These differences are summarized in Figure 11.7, which show the contrast between base and application levels in the two approaches.

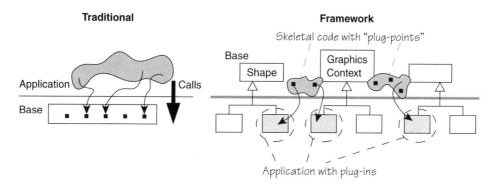

Figure 11.7   Traditional versus framework-style designs.

A significant part of framework design is factoring the plug-points that are provided for adaptation or customization. This example requires that a subclass provide the missing behaviors. A more frequently recommended design style for frameworks is based on delegation and composition; by composing an instance of a framework class with an instance of a custom class that implements a standard framework interface, we adapt the behavior of the framework.

11.3.2   Non-OOP Frameworks

Object-oriented programming provides novel ways to implement with plug-points and plug-ins by using class inheritance. However, you can use other techniques to achieve the underlying style of implementing a skeletal application and leave places in it that can be customized. The central such technique is delegation (see Section 11.5.3, Polymorphism and Forwarding). The framework approach to building systems extends to component-based development as well (see Section 1.9.2, Component Frameworks).

11.4 *Frameworks: Specs to Code*

In the preceding section we saw how framework techniques in object-oriented programming can help build a skeletal implementation, with plug-points for customization to specific needs. We saw in Chapter 9, Model Frameworks and Template Packages, that pieces of code are not the only useful reusable artifacts; recurrent patterns occur in models, specifications, and collaborations. Moreover, the basic OOP unit of encapsulation—a class—is not the most interesting unit for describing designs; it is the collaborations and relationships between elements that constitute the essence of any design.

11.4.1 Generalizing and Specializing: Models and Code

To systematically apply framework-based techniques to development, we start with template packages to construct domain models, requirements specifications, and designs from frameworks. We could construct the specifications for a particular problem by applying the generic framework and plugging in details for the problem at hand. On the implementation side, an implementation for the generic specification should be correspondingly customizable for the specialized problem specification (see Figure 11.8).

A framework implementation thus provides a customizable solution to an abstract problem. If it is done right, the points of variability in the problem specifications—plug-points on the specification side—will also have corresponding plug-points on the implementation side.[1]

11.4.1.1 Combining Model Frameworks

Consider the operations of a service company that markets and delivers seminars. Different aspects of this business, and hence its software requirements, can be described separately: allocation of instructors and facilities to a seminar, on-time production of seminar materials for delivery, trend analysis for targeted marketing of seminars, invoicing and accounts receivable, and so on.

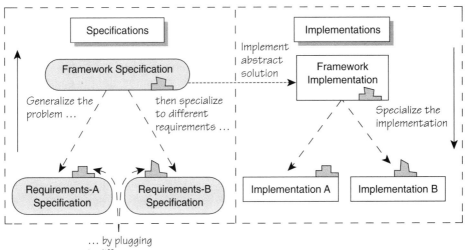

Figure 11.8 Frameworks for specification versus implementation.

---

1. The relation between these plug-points is analogous to refinement.

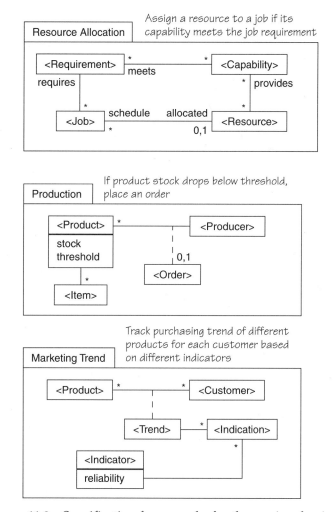

Figure 11.9   Specification frameworks for the seminar business.

Each such aspect can be generalized to be independent of seminar specifics, creating a library of reusable abstract specification frameworks, shown in Figure 11.9 with details of invariants and action specs omitted.

This model framework uses abstract types such as Job, Requirement, and Resource and abstract relationships such as meets, provides, and so on. These types will map in very different ways to a car rental application (Resource=Vehicle, Job=Rental, meets=model category matches) than to assigning instructors to seminars (Resource=Instructor, Job=Session, meets=instructor qualified for session topic).

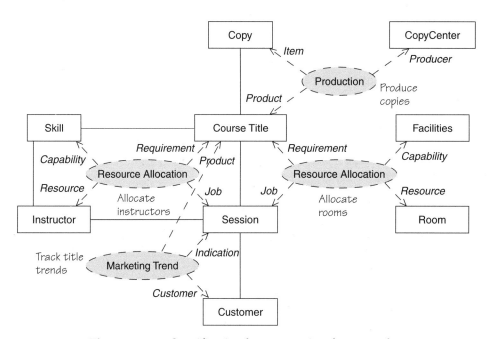

Figure 11.10   Specification by composing frameworks.

These frameworks must now be mapped to our problem domain and must be related to one another by shared objects, attributes, and so on. Figure 11.10 shows the overall problem model as an application of these frameworks. Of course, these frameworks must interact. A session must have both an instructor and a room assigned; failure of either means that the session cannot hold.

When a session holds, copies of course materials must be produced, and the customer trends are updated. Note that each problem domain object can play multiple roles in different frameworks. For example, a Course Title serves as a Requirement in the two applications of the Resource Allocation framework and serves as a Product in the applications of the Marketing and Production framework.

11.4.1.2   Combining Code Frameworks

Each of the model frameworks in Figure 11.10 could come with a default implementation framework. Our design, at the level of framework-sized components, would look like Figure 11.11. Each of the framework components has its plug-points suitably filled by implementation units from this problem domain. Thus, the instructor allocator has Instructor and Session as plug-ins for Resource and Job; and the trend monitor has Session and Topic plugged in for Indication and Product.

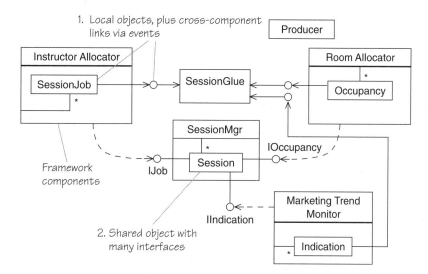

Figure 11.11   Two alternative ways to compose code frameworks.

Here are two (of many) schemes to implement the plug-ins while making these frameworks interact correctly with each other.

1. Separate objects (SessionJob, Occupancy, Indication) within each framework capturing the framework's view of a session so that we have a federated component system. We also need some form of cross-component links between them and a mechanism to keep them in sync. This is often best implemented with a central session object, SessionGlue, that acts as the glue between each of the role objects; it registers for events from the roles and uses the events to keep the other roles in sync. Each of these role objects can inherit a default implementation that is part of the generic framework itself:

```
// the role of a session within the instructor allocation framework
class SessionJob implements IJob extends DefaultJob {
    // link to the "glue" object, SessionGlue, via an event notification interface
    ISessionJobListener listener;

    // just became confirmed from the allocation framework
    void confirm () {
        super.confirm () // do normal inherited confirmation stuff
        // notify the listener object about confirmation
        listener.confirmed (self);
        // could also update the marketing indicators directly; simpler, more coupled
        // MarketingTrendMonitor::indicationConfirmed (trendIndication);
    }
}
```

```
class SessionGlue implements ISessionJobListener, ... {
    // maintain the cross-component links
    // code to receive events from one of the role objects
    // update any shared state, invoke methods on other role objects
}
```

2. Shared objects for the sessions, perhaps implemented in a SessionMgr component (which might be the shared database). Each session offers different interfaces for each role a session plays in each of the frameworks: IJob, IOccupancy, IIndication. Its class will implement methods on each interface to make explicit invocations into the other frameworks if necessary.

```
// one interface for each role this shared object plays
class Session implements IIndication, IJob, IOccupancy {
    // just became confirmed from the allocation framework
    void confirm () {
        ...do normal confirmation stuff
        // but confirmation must also update the marketing indicators
        MarketingTrendMonitor.indicationConfirmed (self);
    }
}
```

A third way is to uniformly compose roles (see Pattern 11.1, Role Delegation).

11.4.2   Issues of Composing Multiple Code Frameworks

Combining independently designed frameworks is not easy. As discussed in Section 11.3.1.3, Contrast of Styles, a framework attempts to codify and prescribe the policies and rules for interactions among its application's objects; in particular, the framework usually takes control, and the applications simply plug in the parts they need. We need explicit attention to interframework coordination at the level of the interframework architecture.

One way to open up the control is to adopt a more component-oriented approach across frameworks. Each framework instance might publish a variety of "internal" events to other interested framework instances; these events expose selected state changes from one framework and offer the others a chance to react to the change.

A somewhat more sophisticated approach would refine the event notification to a negotiative-style protocol: Rather than announce "I've done X," a framework announces, "I'm about to do X; any objections?" Other frameworks then have a chance to veto the proposed event if it would compromise some of their rules. This approach is particularly useful when each framework imposes its own restrictions on what can be done in the other rather than only extending the behaviors (as described in the discussion on joining of specifications in Section 8.3.5, Joining Type Specifications Is Not Subtyping). JavaBeans offers a facility of vetoable events that uses exceptions to signal the vetoing of a proposed event. At the level of federated business components, an alternative is to use cross-component transactions to the same effect: either all, or none, complete.

11.5 *Basic Plug Technology*

There are several implementation mechanisms for achieving the effect of plug-points and plug-ins. This section discusses the main ones, emphasizing the value of black-box composition over white-box inheritance for large-grained reuse.

11.5.1   Templates

C++ provides a compile-time template facility that can be used to build generic classes or families of generic classes. One way to implement a framework for resource allocation is to use a family of C++ template classes that are mutually parameterized:

```
template <class Job>
class Resource {          // a resource is parameterized by its job
    Set<Job*> schedule;
    makeUnavailable (Date d) {

        ...
        for ( each job in schedule overlapping d, if any )
            job.unconfirm ();
    }
}


template <class Resource>
class Job {               // a job is parameterized by its resource
    Resource* assignedTo;
    Range<Date> when;
    unconfirm () { .... }
}


template <class Resource, class Job>
class ResourceAllocator {// a resource allocator manages resources and jobs
    Set<Resource*> resources;
    Calendar<Resource*, Job*> bookings;
    ...
}
```

We can use inheritance to have a domain class, Instructor, act as a resource for a seminar session:

```
class Instructor :public Resource<Session*>, ...
```

We might use multiple inheritance[2] to have our Session play the role of Job for two resources:

```
class Session :public Job<Instructor*>, public Job<Room*> {
    ....
}
```

---

2. Some circularities in type dependencies will not work with C++ templates.

11.5.2   Inheritance and the Template Method

For an inheritance-based design, the template method (see Section 11.3.1.2, Framework-Style Reuse and the Template Method) forms the basis of plug-ins. This design style, common initially, has now fallen somewhat out of favor.

11.5.2.1   Inheritance Is One Narrow Form of Reuse

Inheritance was initially touted as the preferred object-oriented way to achieve reuse and flexibility. In the early days of Smalltalk (one of the earliest popular OO programming languages), several papers were written promoting "programming by adaptation." The principle was that you take someone else's code, make a subclass of it, and override whichever methods you require to work differently. Given, for example, a class that implements Invoices, you could define a subclass to implement BankAccounts: Both are lists of figures with a total at the end.

Although the code runs OK, this wouldn't be considered good design. The crunch comes when your users want to update their notion of what an Invoice is. Because a BankAccount is a different thing, it's unlikely that they'll want to change that at the same time or in the same way or that the overrides retain the behavior expected of an Invoice. It then takes more effort to separate the two pieces of code after the change, losing any savings you gained in the first place.

The programmer who uses inheritance in this way has forgotten the cut-and-paste keys: They provide the proper way to start a design that borrows ideas from another one. If the concepts are unrelated, then the code should also be unrelated.

> *Do not inherit code unless you also intend to inherit its specification, because the internal implementation itself is always subject to change without notice.*

11.5.2.2   Inheritance Does Not Scale for Multiple Variants

What else might inheritance be good for? Perhaps multiple variants of a basic class. Consider a hotel booking system. When a guest checks in, the system does various operations, including allocating a room. Different hotels allocate their rooms using different strategies: Some of them always choose the free room nearest the front desk; others allocate in a circular way to ensure that no room is used more than another; and so on.

So we have several subclasses of Hotel, one for each room-allocation strategy. Each subclass overrides allocateRoom( ) in its own way. The main checking-in function delegates to the subclass.

```
class Hotel
{     public void check_in (Guest g)
      { ... this.allocateRoom (g); ...}
      protected abstract Room allocateRoom (Guest g);
}
class LeastUsedAllocatingHotel extends Hotel
{
      public Room allocateRoom (Guest g) {....}
```

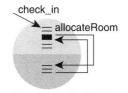

LeastUsedAllocatingHotel

But the problem is that it is difficult to apply this pattern more than once: If Hotels can have different staff-paying policies, does that mean we must have a different subclass for each combination of room allocation and staff payment? That would not scale very well even if you used multiple inheritance.

11.5.3   Polymorphism and Forwarding

The solution is to forward these tasks to separate specialist *strategy* objects that implement different policies behind a common interface [Gamma95]; this is the essence of good polymorphic design.

```
class Hotel {
     Allocator allocator;
     public void checkInGuest (Guest g)
     {... allocator.doAllocation(g); ...}
}

interface Allocator {
     Room doAllocation (...); // returns a free room
}

class LeastUsedAllocator implements Allocator {
     Room doAllocation (...) {...code ...}
}

class EvenSpaceAllocator implements Allocator {
     Room doAllocation (...) {...code ...}
}
```

Each Hotel object is coupled to a room allocator object, to which it delegates decisions about allocating rooms. Separately, it is coupled to a staff payer, and the same is true for whatever other variant policies there may be. Different policies are implemented by different classes, which may be completely different in their internal structure. The only requirement is that all room allocator classes must implement the doAllocation( ) message—that is, they must conform to a single interface specification.

This polymorphic coupling between objects is far more important as a design principle than inheritance is. It is what enables us to link one component to many others and thereby to build a great variety of systems from a well-chosen set of components. Both component-based and "pure" object-oriented approaches can take good advantage of this delegation-based approach via interfaces.

Let's return to the BankAccount and Invoice example: If there is any common aspect to the two things, the proper approach is to separate it into a class of its own. A list of figures that can be added might be the answer; so whereas BankAccount and Invoice are separate classes, both of them can use ListOfFigures.

11.5.4   Good Uses for Inheritance

Is there any good use for inheritance? Extremists would say we can do without it—and write good object-oriented software—provided that we have the means (a) to document and check interface implementation and (b) to delegate efficiently to another object without writing very much explicit forwarding code. All object-oriented programming languages support these techniques, although some do so better than others. Java, for example, has good support for interfaces, whereas C++ mixes implementation and interface. Smalltalk has support for inheritance but no type-checking. Few languages properly support delegation; it can be done in Smalltalk, and Java gets halfway there with its inner classes. Perhaps the next fashionable successor to Java will have explicit support for delegation.

More pragmatically, class inheritance has its place and value but should not be used when delegation via a polymorphic interface would work. It's reasonable to inherit from an abstract class, which provides an incomplete or skeletal implementation, and then extend it to plug in bits specific to your need. Inheritance with arbitrary overriding of methods is not advisable.

11.5.5   A Good Combination

One good way to combine these techniques is as follows.

- For every role, define an interface:

    ```
    interface IResource { .... }
    ```

- For every interface, define a default implementation with inheritance plug-points:

    ```
    abstract class CResource implements IResource {
        protected abstract plugIn ();
        public m () { ..... plugIn(); ...}
    }
    ```

- Each default implementation should itself delegate to other *interfaces*:

    ```
    abstract class CResource implements IResource {
        private IJob myJob;
    }
    ```

- Concrete classes typically inherit from the default implementation, but they could also independently implement the required interface.

- Use a factory to localize the creation of new objects of the appropriate subclasses:

    ```
    class ResourceFactory {
        IResource newResource () {
            return new CResource;
        }
    }
    ```

In that way you can make a local change to the factory and have entirely new kinds of resources be created and used polymorphically.

11.5.6   Replacing Inheritance with Type-Based Composition

Any inheritance structure can be replaced by a more flexible and late-bound composition structure provided that you don't use language primitives for checking object identity.[3] The key idea is to treat the different portions of an instance of a subclass as though they were separate objects that are composed; explicitly forward calls for inherited *up calls* as well as template-method *down calls*; and define explicit types to describe the call pattern between super- and subportions.

Figure 11.12 shows an example. For external clients, class A implements a type TA with its two public methods. The class A implements this type but expects to have the method Z() implemented by B; hence, the type of B as required by this implementation of A would be TBA. Similarly, the implementation of B provides the operation Q in addition to X and Y and expects the type TAB from its "super" portion. This results in four distinct types, which can be mapped directly to the two implementation classes.

When an instance of B is created, it must be passed an object that implements TAB. The code for B includes a reference to this object. Similarly, when an instance of A is created, it must be passed an instance that implements TBA. If the initialized references are thereafter frozen, the effect is very similar to inheritance except through a more robust and documented black-box type interface (see next page).

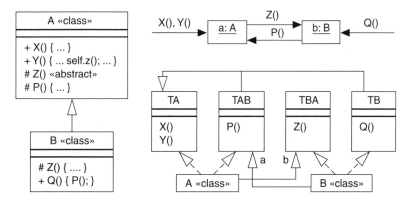

Figure 11.12   From inheritance to type-based composition.

---

3. We hope that the next generation of component-aware languages can make an assembly of objects appear as one, with intelligent query of object identity and interfaces.

```
class B implements    TB, TBA {
    private TAB a;      // the "super" part

    // interface for general clients: TB
    public X()    { a.X(); }
    public Y()    { a.Y(); }
    public Q()    { a.P(); }

    // interface for the "template-method" calls from A: TBA
    public Z()    { .... }

    // constructor: accepts an instance that implements TAB; or can create one itself
    B (TAB super)    { a = super; }
}

class A implements    TA, TAB {
    private TBA b;      // the "sub" part

    // interface for general clients: TA
    public X()    { .... }
    public Y()    { b.Z(); }

    // interface for the "up-calls" calls from B: TAB
    public P()    { .... }

    // constructor: accepts an instance that implements TBA;
    // circularity may need an additional "setter" method
    B (TBA sub)     { b = sub; }
    public setB (TBA sub) { b = sub; }
}
```

Although this structure may seem heavy for everyday use, keep it in mind as a possible transformation. You may use some variant of it to replace implementation inheritance with black-box reuse across component boundaries.

11.5.7 Specifying the Super/Sub Interface

One of the problems with inheritance frameworks is that they are white-box in nature: The extender of a framework must study and understand the source code in order to make extensions and to understand which methods to override, which other (template) methods that override will affect, and how the set of overridden methods must behave for the framework to function properly. The real reason for this legacy is that the "vertical" interfaces of class frameworks have rarely been documented explicitly, abstracting away from the code.

We have explained at length how type-based specification of interfaces lets us specify accurately, and yet precisely, the behavior expected of an object; and you have just seen how any inheritance structure can be analyzed, and even coded, using a type-based composition structure. Even if you do not change the implementation to composition, you can now document the super/sub interfaces using all the tools of type specification.

11.5.8   Component- and Connector-Based Pluggability

Let's not forget that components and connectors (see Chapter 10) provide yet another level of abstraction in building and plugging together components. Different, possibly customized, forms of connectors can make it much simpler to describe and implement the component configurations you need.

11.6   *Summary*

This chapter deals in some detail with the business of building reusable code components that are pluggable.

Reuse of software is not simply a matter of cut-and-paste; it should involve the reuse of interface specifications before implementation code is reused. Successful reuse poses many organizational challenges (culture, development processes, and so on) as well as technical ones (designing components that are adaptable to many different contexts and devising techniques for plugging in the adaptations).

The framework approach to code reuse provides a concrete, yet incomplete, implementation of the architecture: The rules and policies about how application objects interact are codified and enforced by the framework itself. Frameworks can be both white-box—a template method in the superclass must be overriden by a subclass after understanding the calls made in the superclass implementation—and black-box, in which interfaces for the plug-in calls are explicitly specified and implemented according to the spec.

The frameworks approach also works at the level of problem domain models. The ideal approach is to formulate requirements themselves in a modular fashion by using model frameworks and plugging in the specifics for your problem; implementing a code framework solution to the generic problem specification; and specializing that implementation framework to construct your system. A typical system consists of numerous such code frameworks and demands careful use of component-based techniques—such as event protocols across frameworks—so that the parts work together correctly.

The basic idea of plugging in to a code framework shows up in different ways in different languages, including C++ templates, component/connector technologies, and class hierarchies. The latter tend to be overused; it is often better to replace the inheritance with composition and explicit forwarding and to use types to document the subtle call patterns between superclasses and subclasses.

Pattern 11.1   Role Delegation

Adopt a uniform implementation architecture based on composition of separate role objects to allow plugging together of code components.

Intent

The idea is to compose separately implemented objects for different roles.

Objects play several roles, each of which may have several variants. We don't want a separate class to implement every combination of all the variants—for example, a Person can be a Full-time or a Part-time Employee; a Natural, Foster, or Step-Parent; and so on. The set of roles (and the choice of variant) may change at run time. We need to change the type without losing the object's identity.

Combining two specifications is easy: You just and them together (that is, you tell the designer to observe both sets of requirements). You can't do that with code, so we look for a standard mechanism for cooking up an object by systematically combining roles from several collaborations. This approach enables us to stick with the big idea that design units are often collaborations (and not objects) but retain the convenience of plugging implemented pieces together like dominoes.

Strategy

The technique is to delegate each of the role-specific pieces of behavior to a separate object (see Figure 11.13). One conceptual object is then implemented by several: one for each role, and (usually) a *principal* to hold them all together. The principal object keeps those parts of the state to which access is shared among the roles. Each role conducts all dialog with the other participants in the collaboration from which it arises. Generally, the roles are designed as observers of various pieces of the principal's state.

Make the group behave to the outside world as a single object, which was the original intent, by always keeping them in sync and being careful with identity checks. You must design an interface for all plug-ins to the same principal so that new plug-ins can be added for new roles. Never use a language-defined identity check (== in Java). Instead, have a sameAs(x) query; plug-ins pretend they're all the same object if they share the same principal. Calls to self within plug-ins usually go to the principal.

For example, the basic trading principal has a stock of products and cash assets. Into this can be plugged a role for retailing that knows about a Distributor and monitors the stock level, generating orders when necessary. Or we could make it a Distributor, plugging in the appropriate role; perhaps a Dealer would be something with both the Retailer and the Distributor roles.

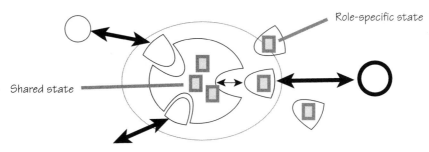

Figure 11.13   Building objects by connecting role objects.

Pattern 11.2   Pluggable Roles

Make role objects share state via observation of a shared object.

Intent

We need to supply complete implementations of frameworks, but frameworks are often about collaborations among roles rather than complete object behaviors.

Strategy

- Implement components as collaborations between role plug-ins. Each role implements the responsibilities of its framework spec, and each role is an observer of the shared state.
- Ensure a common interface for plug-ins. To build new collaborations, designers couple principals to collaborations.

Roles Observe the Shared State. So that a fully coded component can mimic the structure of the corresponding specification frameworks, each role should incorporate the code necessary for implementing placeholder actions. Most placeholder triggers boil down to monitoring changes of state. Each role can therefore be built as an observer of the parts of the common state that it is interested in.

The principal provides a standard pluggable interface allowing each role to register its interests and makes each shareable attribute a potential subject.

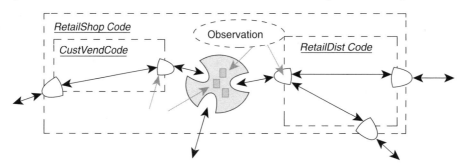

Collaborating Components Mirror Framework Specs. After building a specification by composing framework models, you can implement it by plugging together the corresponding fully implemented collaborations (if they are available).

This scheme could exact a performance penalty compared with purpose-built systems. There is overhead in the wiring of the observers wherever components are plugged together, although more-efficient versions of Observation, such as the JavaBeans event model, may adequately address this. In exchange for performance, you get rapid development; and you always have the option of designing an optimized version by working from the composed framework specifications.

Chapter 12   Architecture

Architecture is a word used loosely to mean many different things; yet it is one of the most important aspects of the design of a system and has far-reaching effects on its success.

An architecture is, first, an abstraction of a system's implementation. There are many different architectural models that help you understand the system: process, module, usage dependencies, and so on. These models help you analyze certain *qualities* of the system: runtime qualities, such as performance, security, or reliability; and development-time qualities, such as modifiability and portability. These qualities are important to different system stakeholders: not only the end user but also the system administrator, developer, customer, maintainer, and so on. Different kinds of usage scenarios, including system modifications and deployment scenarios, can help you to evaluate architectures against such qualities.

You should clearly define the vocabulary of element types that can be used to describe an architecture: processes, replicators, buffers, caches, and events. The same is true of the roles played by the different components: controllers, mediators, routers, and so on. A good architecture exhibits a coherence and simplicity by being based on a small number of such elements and patterns that are used consistently throughout the design.

In practice, it is useful to distinguish the application architecture—how the business logic is split across components and how they interact—from the technical architecture: all the infrastructure and other domain-independent pieces that support that collaboration. The four-tier Web-enabled architecture presents a typical case for making this distinction.

12.1   *What Is Architecture?*

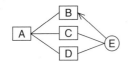

Because the term *architecture* is often used quite loosely, let us start with what it is not.

A neat-looking drawing of boxes, circles, and lines, laid out nicely in Powerpoint or Word, does *not* constitute an architecture.

Such a drawing leaves many critical questions unanswered. What is the nature of the blocks A–E: Are they objects, modules, libraries, or processes? Based on the shapes drawn, are A–D of a similar kind, and is E somehow different? Does the layout imply that A plays a special role relative to B–D (for example, it is created before them)? What do the lines between these blocks mean: interprocess communication, compile-time dependencies, data flow?

In short, if given a complete implemented system—source, design documents, development structure of the project, and running installation—how would you determine whether it conformed to this architectural drawing?

▶ *architecture*   The architecture of a system consists of the structure(s) of its parts (including design-time, test-time, and runtime hardware and software parts), the nature and relevant externally visible properties of those parts (modules with interfaces, hardware units, objects), and the relationships and constraints between them (there are a great many possibly interesting such relationships).

An architecture must define the parts, the essential external characteristics of each part, and the relationships between the parts.

12.1.1   Architecture Imposes Decisions and Constraints

In our view, architecture is not only about Gothic-scale structures but is also about all structures and relationships used down to the level of code.[1] The decision to use a four-tier structure, with a thin client, a Web server, a business application server, and a database, is architectural. But, in the extreme, we consider a consistent use of getX() and setX(x) methods also to be part of the (detailed) architecture. This view leads to a somewhat less formal definition of architecture.

▶ *architecture*   The set of design decisions about any system (or smaller component) that keeps its implementors and maintainers from exercising needless creativity.

Here is a sampling of such decisions across a range of granularity:

1. Use a three-tier client-server architecture. All business logic must be in the middle tier, presentation and dialog on the client, and data services on the server. In this way you can scale the application server processing independently of persistent storage.

2. Use CORBA for all distribution, using CORBA event channels for notification and the CORBA relationship service.

3. Use Collection Galore's collections for representing any collections; by default, use its List class or else document your reason for not using it.

4. Use Model-View-Controller with an explicit ApplicationModel object to connect any UI to the business logic and objects.

5. Start every access method with get_ and set_.

---

1. Provided that it influences the externally visible properties of the parts.

6. Every computation component must have update_data and re_compute operations, to be invoked by the scheduler.

This does not mean that there is no creativity in implementation. Rather, it means that any level of refinement involves a set of constraining design decisions that define a limited and consistent toolbox of techniques for downstream work. To continue our lower-level example, use your creativity to address the problems that matter rather than come up with your own convention for dealing with get and set methods.

We use the same philosophy in type modeling: When stating behavior requirements, you have a limited set of terms and their definitions, defined by the type model, that you can refer to. When implementing a system at any level, your design vocabulary is defined by a limited set of well-defined constructs.[2]

12.1.2 Architectural Models

The architecture of a system frequently remains undocumented. If documentation exists, it may be hopelessly out of date with the implementation; or it may be so fuzzy and ambiguous that there is no way to tell whether it is accurate. To be useful, architecture must be described in a clear, explicit way to serve as the basis for understanding, implementation, reuse, and evolution of the system.

Unfortunately, in some contexts, the word *architecture* is dropped into a discussion to lend instant credibility to someone's position: If it is about architecture, it must be abstract, and surely it cannot be bothered with the difficult questions about what it all means to an implementation. This leaves us with ill-defined terms and diagrams of boxes and lines. As with any model, their value is severely degraded if the underlying terms and notations do not have a clearly defined meaning or if the number and complexity of design elements render them incomprehensible.

12.1.3 Many Architectural Views

An architectural description is an abstraction; there are many such abstractions that contribute to understanding a system, each one focused on one aspect and omitting other details. As with any model, there is some definition of conformance—that is, does a given implementation conform to that architecture? Some views are more focused on the design and development-time activities; others are relevant when you're testing or running the system; still others focus on deployment and upgrade activities. Table 12.1 shows some useful architectural views and the system parts each one focuses on.

---

2. Down to the primitive constructs of your programming language; you could almost certainly be more creative in assembler.

Table 12.1   Various Architectural Views

View	Parts	Properties and Relations
Domain	Types, actions, subject areas	Attributes, associations, refinements, import relations between subject areas
Logical	Components, connectors	How business logic is logically partitioned in software; how parts collaborate
Process	Process, thread, component	Synchronization relations: precedes, excludes, controls; assignment of software components to processes and threads
Physical	Hardware units, networks	Processing and communication capabilities (speed, latency, resources), communication relations, topology, physical containment
Distribution	Software components, processes, hardware	Deployed on or runs on CPU, can dynamically move to, network protocols
Calls	Methods, classes, objects, programs, procedures	Call invocations, parameters, returns, synchronous versus asynchronous, data volumes, processing time
Uses	Packages	Imports, uses, needs the presence of (more general than "calls")
Data flow	Actions	Provides or sets up data for (independent of call-specific protocols)
Modules	Design-time units of development work	Design decisions hidden in work units (packages); refinements used for submodule decompositions; justifications, including rationale for choices made and choices rejected

A small project may need only one of these views. The domain view can map directly into classes, which also constitutes the units of work without any higher-level component structuring; and the domain view can run in a single process on a single machine. A large project can use all these views and can even introduce new ones. These views are not independent and it is critical to know how they relate to each other.

In Catalysis, we can use refinement to model abstract objects that do not necessarily correspond to an instance of an OOP class and abstract actions that may not correspond to a single OOP message send. Based on this, we can use all the modeling techniques—including attributes, types, collaborations, refinement, justifications, interactions, snapshots, and states—to describe architectural models and their rationale.

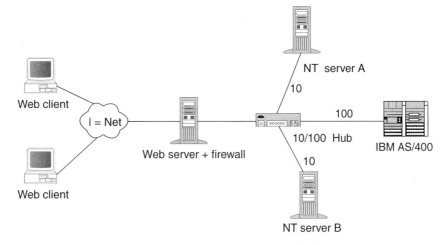

Figure 12.1 Networking symbols.

12.1.3.1 Physical Architecture

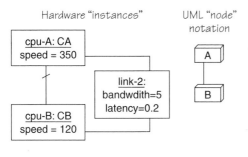

The processors in a physical model can be modeled as objects, their states modeled as attributes, their capabilities modeled as attributes, and communication links shown as explicit objects. It is useful to make visual distinctions between categories using stereotypes or a distinguished notation such as the one UML provides; or, you can use traditional network diagram symbols for the different hardware objects. Base operating systems can be shown as part of this hardware architecture (see Figure 12.1).

12.1.3.2 Software Distribution

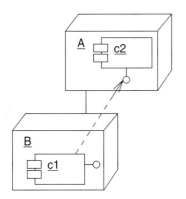

Deployment of software is shown here against this physical model, with different software components shown on different hardware nodes; for example, the software components in the four-tier system are shown in Figure 12.5. Note that software component requirements, such as memory and storage space, can be modeled as attributes and matched against the corresponding attributes of the hardware. If needed, you can also explicitly specify the effect of actions, such as node failures (failover requirements) or network load, against such a model.

12.1.3.3   Process Architecture

Processes and threads can be introduced into a design to deal with essential concurrency in the problem itself or to handle performance requirements. Both can be modeled as objects with suitable stereotypes «process» and «thread», and all the tools of object modeling applied. Processes are mapped to CPUs.

Abstract actions can proceed concurrently with others provided they satisfy concurrency constraints. When specifying essential concurrency, we use rely and guarantee clauses on actions to implicitly constrain what can happen concurrently, or we can explicitly define concurrent actions by multiplicities and other explicit constraints.

12.2   *Why Architect?*

Assuming that *to architect* means to go through the analyses and reasoning required to come up with an architecture, why bother?

12.2.1   Multiple Stakeholders and Their Requirements

The architecture largely determines how well the system will meet its requirements. Much of our earlier focus in this book has been on describing the functional behavior that an end user would perceive; however, the overall requirements and conflicting objectives are frequently much broader and vary among the different *stakeholders*—roles of people who will be involved in the construction of the system (see Table 12.2).

Table 12.2   Concerns and Requirements of Various Stakeholders

Stakeholder	Concerns and Requirements
End user	Intuitive and correct behavior, helps do tasks, performance, reliability
System administrator	Intuitive behavior, tools to aid monitoring and administration
Marketer	Competitive features, time to market, fits into larger market positioning with other products
Customer	On time, low cost, stable
Developer	Clear requirements, simple and consistent design approach
Architect	Familiar domain, infrastructure, architecture; buildable; meet others' requirements
Development manager	Predictability and tracking of project, schedule, productive use of resources including existing or familiar code, cost
Maintainer	Understandable, consistent and documented design approach, easy to make commonly required modifications

A clearly defined architecture defines constraints on the implementation: The components must have the required external characteristics, and their interactions and relationships must conform to the prescribed constraints. Architecture describes some of the most far-reaching design decisions about a system, having the greatest impact on how well the system meets its diverse requirements.

The architectural models are the primary vehicle for communication among all these stakeholders and for formal review of the models against the system requirements. They form the basis for an early prototype, against which many qualities can be evaluated even though there is minimal end-user functionality implemented.

The architecture directly influences the work-breakdown structure of the system and influences the package structure for the project, project planning and scheduling, team structure and communication needs, configuration management, testing, and deployment—in other words, all organizational aspects of the project. On a larger scale, a shared architecture for a family of products strongly influences the business that owns it.

12.2.2 Many Qualities Are Affected by Architecture

The quality of a system is a measure of how closely it meets all its requirements; it is an attribute of the design itself. Some qualities can be observed only during runtime because they relate to the dynamic behavior of the deployed system; others must be observed during development or maintenance activities because they relate to the design structure itself and how it can be manipulated.

Achieving system qualities is an engineering task: Frequently they conflict with one another. Some of the main qualities—often traditionally partitioned into functional and nonfunctional requirements—are briefly discussed next:

12.2.2.1 Development-Time Qualities

The following qualities most directly concern the development and maintenance teams; certain aspects of the architecture can make their life easier.

Modifiability: Is the system design structure amenable to effective modification? Are frequently requested changes achieved by changes that are fully localized within a single module or few modules without affecting public interfaces? Modifiability has become the single most important quality in most systems. Careful separation of concerns, grouping and hiding of design decisions that are likely to change together, separation of business functions from infrastructure technology, isolating computation from data and control transfer strategies, and interface-based specification are all important techniques to support modifiability.

Reusability: Are there implementation or design units in the system that are good candidates for reuse in another system? Does the system make good use of existing standard designs, interfaces, or implementations? Interestingly, systems that are designed to be easily modifiable for expected changes are also those that are the most reusable and the most maintainable.

Portability: Does the system design permit easy porting to other platforms? Are hardware and infrastructure dependencies localized in the implementation? Portability is governed almost completely by how well any idiosyncrasies of its computing environment have been encapsulated.

Buildability: Will the system as designed be easy to implement and build? What third-party components or libraries does it take advantage of? What tools will be used to assist in the construction process? Do these tools adequately support working with the components or libraries that will be used? Although this is rarely a stated requirement for the end user or customer, it is an important factor for the development team. Buildability is affected by the complexity of the design; whether it is counting on new, unproven technologies and tools; the appropriateness of the tools for the components being used; and the experience of the development team.

Testability*:* How easy is it to demonstrate defects in the system by stimulating it with test data? Is it clear how to systematically define the test data based on the documented system architecture? At a technical level, testability is determined by how easy it is to access the internal state and inputs of the component so that they can be stimulated and observed. What's more, testing is an effort to show conformance (or, more properly, lack of conformance) of an implementation to a specification; so testability is determined to a great extent by clear specifications and rules about how to map from an implementation to the specification (see Chapter 6). Tests are an important part of any refinement relation in Catalysis. At least as much attention should be paid to specification and testing as to actual implementing. For large systems, it is worth explicitly documenting a *test architecture*, which can include hardware and software configurations, test tools used, and packages containing the test cases and results.

System qualities that do not correspond to runtime behaviors—modifiability, portability, buildability, and testability—must also be captured as part of requirements-gathering activities, although evaluating them can be more difficult (see Section 12.3, Architecture Evaluation with Scenarios).

12.2.2.2   Runtime Qualities

Many requirements can be measured only against a running system. The following most obvious ones—the requirements of the end user—fall into this category.

Functionality: Does the system, when deployed and running, assist its users in their tasks? Our previous discussion of business models and system type specification addresses this quality.

Usability: Does the system at runtime provide an intuitive interface and easily support the users' tasks? Does this apply to all categories of users? Building good business models so that system operations are designed as refinements of business tasks, and getting early user input on user-interfaces, are both important aspects of usability. There are also other, deeper issues of designing human-computer interactions that are outside our scope.

Performance: Does the system perform adequately when running—response time, number of events processed per second, number of concurrent users, and so on? In most large systems, communication and synchronization costs between components, particularly across a network, dominate performance bottlenecks. Perceived response time can often be addressed by using multiple threads of control for asynchronous processing of a request. Performance can be modeled using the arrival rates of different stimuli to the system, the latency for different kinds of requests (processing time), and an approximation of delay caused by interference due to resource contention. The model can be checked as a back-of-the-envelope calculation, fed into a stochastic queueing model or simulation, or used to build a load driver for an architectural prototype. For many systems, raw performance is no longer the single most dominant quality.

Security: Does the system at runtime prevent unauthorized access or (mis)use? Security concerns typically include at least authentication—ensuring that the apparent source of a request is, in fact, who it claims to be—and authorization: ensuring that the authenticated user is permitted to access the needed set of resources. Security should be modeled as any other behavioral requirement is modeled. If an existing security mechanism or product is being used (for example, Kerberos), use a model of that mechanism as a part of your design models.

Reliability and availability: Does the running system reliably continue to perform correctly over extended periods of time? What proportion of time is the system up and running? In the presence of failure, does it degrade gracefully rather than shut down completely? Reliability is measured as the mean time to system failure; availability is the proportion of time the system is functioning. Both qualities are typically dealt with by making the architecture fault-tolerant: using duplicated hardware and software resources.

Scalability: Can the system as designed and deployed be scaled up to handle greater usage demands (volume of data, numbers of users, rate of requests)? Scalability is achieved primarily by replicating resources—processors, memory, storage media—and their software processing counterparts. Component-based designs in which the components can be deployed on separate processors, and where the overhead of cross-component coordination is proportionately small, enhances scalability.

Upgradability: Can the system at runtime be upgraded with new features or versions of software without bringing operations to a halt? Some systems must be operational continuously, and shutting them down for maintenance or upgrades is a serious matter. Systems that have a reflective core—the runtime keeps an explicit representation of the software structure, classes, interfaces, and so on and permits operations on that structure itself—can be the easiest to upgrade in this manner.

All the qualities that relate to runtime behavior should be captured as part of the behavioral specification of the system,[3] including requirements about security, availability, and performance, because they contribute to the definition of acceptable behavior. For example, the need to authenticate users before permitting them to access certain operations should be captured as part of the state transition model of the system. Similarly, the system may need to complete processing of certain requests in a timely manner for the components around it to function correctly.

12.2.2.3   A Single Key Quality

Other qualities also influence the design and development of a system. They include time to market, customizability to different products in a product family, development organization structure, distributed teams and their areas of expertise, and so on.

But despite this large number of different aspects of the "goodness" of an architecture, there is one single quality that dominates all others: the *conceptual integrity* of an architecture. This ephemeral quality summarizes an architecture's balance, simplicity, elegance, and practicality. A clean unifying architectural vision, and a consistency of design structures, can never be achieved by accident or by committee.

12.3   *Architecture Evaluation with Scenarios*

Although we can broadly state that an architecture that is simple is preferred to one that is not, we may want a more systematic way to evaluate architectural alternatives.

In Section 12.2.2, Many Qualities Are Affected by Architecture, we explained that there are many different qualities, both runtime and design-time qualities, that are affected by the architecture. Quantifying these qualities can be extremely difficult; for example, a design may easily permit one kind of modification but be resistant to another modification.

Hence, we must recognize that most "qualities" of a system are not absolutes but rather are meaningful only in specific contexts. A system is efficient only with respect to particular resources being consumed under particular usage profiles; it is modifiable under certain classes of requested changes.

Because each quality attribute corresponds to a stakeholder performing an action on the system either at design time or at runtime, we can use scenarios of such interactions to explore and evaluate an architecture. The main difference here from our original use of the word *scenario* (see Section 4.7.4, Scenarios) is that

---

3. They can often be in a separate section of the documents; our facility of joining combines all specifications of the same actions.

now we are not restricted to only runtime behaviors but include scenarios of system modifications, reuse, and so on.

The scenarios are used to rank the architecture qualitatively based on how well it handles the requirement, such as the number of components changed. Also, if scenarios that are largely independent affect common components, the responsibilities of those components may need reconsideration. Scenario-based evaluation is a relatively new technique, and we merely mention it here.

Here are some sample scenarios for the less obvious quality attributes.

- Make a batch program operate in an interactive mode and vice versa.
- Change an internal representation.
- Change an external interface that is known to be unstable.
- Add a new user function.
- Reuse a component in another system.
- Encrypt data being transmitted across a communication link.
- Integrate with a variety of e-mail systems.

12.4 *Architecture Builds on Defined Elements*

Simple digital systems are assembled from well-known libraries of parts: combinational logic gates (and, or, inverters, tri-state buffers); storage elements (flip-flops, registers, RAM); synchronization parts (clocks, dividers). From these parts are assembled a huge variety of systems, but all of them can be understood in terms of these basic parts.

Similarly, an architectural model is built from some number of elements: processors, modules, components, objects, class libraries, threads, and so on. A good architecture is based on a small set of design elements and uses them in a regular and consistent manner so that the system substructures are simple and similar.

The starting point for describing an architecture is to define the kinds of elements that constitute it. At the simplest level, interfaces and implementations are the elements of architecture. Beyond that, concrete implemented elements—specific kinds of buffers, synchronization primitives, coordinators, kits of parts to be assembled—can be specified as types or interfaces; more-abstract ones—design patterns, patterns of connectors and components—can be described using model frameworks. It is even possible for certain architectural qualities to be quantified, in a parameterized form, on the framework level. After these elements have been defined, the architecture itself can be described using these as "primitives."

12.4.1   Components and Connectors

As explained in Chapter 10, Components and Connectors, a component kit defines a set of components that are designed to work naturally together. The underlying idea is quite general, and frameworks let us define our own new kinds of components, ports, and connectors.

A sample architecture might be based on Cat One (see Section 10.8.1, Cat One: An Example Component Architecture. Its categories of ports include <<Event>>, an outgoing notification from a component to all other registered components; <<Property>>, a value that can be kept constantly in sync with another; and <<Transfer>>, wherein an object is moved from an output port to an input port. Using these ports, we can build a general-purpose set of components, such as those shown in Figure 12.2. An architecture can now be described as a configuration of such elements and their interconnections using the defined connectors.

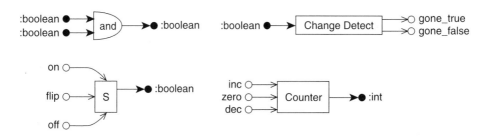

Figure 12.2   Sample low-level component kit.

12.4.2   Concurrency and Threads

A *thread* is a totally ordered set of events, or a sequential trace of execution, that can run concurrently with other threads. A thread is conceptually orthogonal to an object,[4] and its trace can involve the methods of many objects. Programming multithreaded systems is a tricky business, because you constantly must worry about the effects of concurrent activities; specifically

- Interference, in which one thread inadvertently interferes with state information that is being used by another
- Cooperation, in which two threads that are progressing concurrently at their own pace need to coordinate their activities at specific points in their execution

Just as programming language constructs relieve you of the tedium of assembler, multithreaded systems benefit from a library of concurrency and synchronization primitives.

- Bounded buffer, a thread-safe buffer with bounded capacity.

---

4. Except in the "active object model," which associates a thread with each active object.

- Future, a "promise" of a return value that can be returned eagerly and passed around. When its value is finally accessed, it may block the accessor if the value is not yet available.
- Semaphore, an integer variable with an associated queue of waiting processes.
- Condition variables, state variables that a thread can synchronize on. A waiting thread is notified precisely when those variables change.
- Timers, which wake up at programmable times, take an action, and then go back to sleep.

12.4.3   Pipes and Filters

The well-known *pipe-and-filter* architecture can be described as another set of components and connectors. The components are filters: stateless components that transform their inputs into outputs; they have input and output ports corresponding to each input and output. The connectors are the pipes the interconnect filter outputs to inputs.

12.4.4   Third-Party Libraries and Tools

Packages and their import structure define a development-time architectural model. In Catalysis, the imports define definitional and usage dependencies.

One architectural view includes all third-party libraries that will be used and import relations from packages that make use of these libraries. This view also explicitly describes the packages for tools (compilers, UI builders, and so on) that are used to populate other packages (containing object code, UI screens, and so on), documenting all project and module usage dependencies.

12.5 *Architecture Uses Consistent Patterns*

Having a set of design elements—components, connectors, object types—provides a higher-level language for describing an architecture. The use of these elements should also follow consistent patterns, and many of these patterns can themselves be formalized using frameworks. This section outlines a few such patterns; the details of formalizing them as frameworks is omitted. These examples are only illustrative not intended to serve as general prescriptions for architecture.

12.5.1   Event Notification Design Pattern

An event is an interesting change in state. There are many ways to design with events; this pattern defines one consistent style. To publish an event, E, from a component to interested subscribers, follow these steps.

1. Define the signature of E on an interface named E_Listener.

2. Add a pair of methods add_E_Listener and remove_E_Listener to manage the set of registered listeners on the component.

3. Document the event information in the parameters passed with E.

12.5.2 Subsystem Controller Pattern

Subsystems can interact with each other in many ways. This pattern defines a consistent scheme governing those interactions. For every subsystem, you may choose to uniformly have a distinguished *head object* that controls the connections between its children's ports and those in other subsystems based on a naming scheme. The head object also mediates all control and asynchronous communication between the subsystem and its parent system and coordinates the activities of its child components (see Figure 12.3). This arrangement gives a consistent structure for every subsystem: a head object, a defined role relative to its children, and a consistent protocol regardless of actual subsystem function.

12.5.3 Interface Packages Pattern

Packages can be structured in many different ways. The separation of an interface from classes in separate packages provides a pattern for setting up the project package structure. Combined with consistent naming conventions, it makes certain aspects of the architecture very visible in the project development structure (see Section 7.4.1, Role-based Decoupling of Classes).

12.5.4 Enterprise JavaBeans Pattern

The 1.0 specs of Enterprise JavaBeans are a good example of standard architectural patterns and how they can be used to define a simple and consistent architecture even for large-scale business systems.

12.5.5 Architectural Rules and Styles

In addition to the patterns themselves—event notification, subsystem controller— the architecture often dictates the rules that govern when these patterns must be

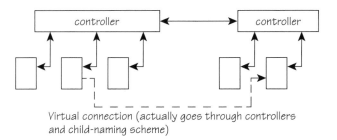

Figure 12.3 Consistent structure on subsystems.

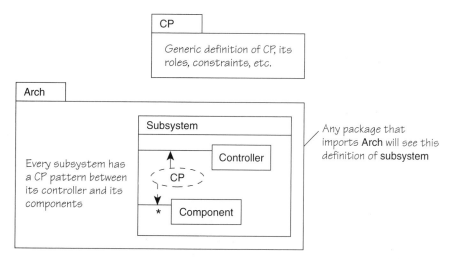

Figure 12.4   Defining the architectural rule for subsystem controllers.

applied and when they should not be used. Thus, we may decide that every single subsystem must follow the subsystem controller pattern (CP). We can document this in an architectural package (see Figure 12.4).

Architectural rules can be documented using frameworks and other modeling constructs, including the ability to "say more" about a modeling element in another package. You can introduce shortcut notations to *tag* design elements as belonging to certain architectural categories, using stereotypes or customized notations. If formalizing the rules seems too heavyweight for some rules, describe them in concise prose or use whatever mechanism is appropriate. Regardless of how they are documented, all such rules should be explicitly placed into an architecture package that is imported by all relevant detailed design packages.

▶ *architectural style*   An architectural style (or *type*) is defined by a package (with nested packages) that has a consistent set of architectural elements, patterns, rules for using them, and stereotype or other notational shorthands for expressing their usage.

For example, *layered* architectures frequently use a special notation. A catalog of such architectural styles can be built in a way that's much like the use of frameworks in Section 9.8.2, Stereotypes and Dialects.

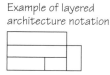

12.6 *Application versus Technical Architecture*

It is useful to separate the application architecture from the infrastructure parts (which we will call the *technical* architecture).

12.6.1   Application Architecture Partitions Business Logic

Application architecture is the partitioning of business logic across components and the design of their collaborations to meet the specified behavioral requirements. Application architecture is high-level logical design. In one sense it is entirely technology-independent, or at least the models are. However, how well a design fulfills other quality attributes, most notably performance, depends quite dramatically on the underlying technology: machines, networking, middleware, and so on.

Hence, even though logical application architecture can be started early, it should piggy-back on the physical and technical architecture to determine feasibility.

12.6.2   Technical Architecture Is Domain-Independent

The technical architecture includes all domain-independent design decisions, including the communication middleware that is used to enable communication between application architectural components; the patterns and rules that are followed in using the middleware; all domain-independent libraries that may be needed to build the system; and the rules for using them. The domain-independent facilities include the following:

- Communication middleware, the infrastructure that mediates between distributed components
- Command-line parser, a component to read commands and parse them against a command grammar
- State-machine interpreter, a means to interpret a reified representation of a state machine regardless of what the machine does
- Event logging, a facility to record all notable events, including communication, exceptions, and alarms
- Data access services, a layer that centralizes services to access the databases
- Exception signaling, the mechanism to signal, handle, and recover from various kinds of exceptions
- Start-up, monitor, shutdown, and failover, the mechanisms to start up the system, monitor its operations for things such as time-outs, shut the system down gracefully, and deal with failures
- Query processor, a means to deal with general ad hoc queries against any data model

12.6.3   Implement the Technical Architecture Early

Most project risk comes from two sources: business requirements and technology infrastructure. It is common for a project team to evaluate complexity based mostly on the business requirements—the problem domain itself—and vastly underestimate the effort it will take to implement all the plumbing and supporting pieces that are not domain-specific.

Unfortunately, until component-based development becomes the norm and until project managers understand the economics of buying the kinds of domain-independent components described earlier, we will still be building many of them. If most of the elements of the technical architecture are already *implemented*, then estimating the development time for business functions becomes much less like a black art.

Hence, you should implement the technical architecture as early as possible. Have all communication paths working—from user input and command-line parsing to the data access services—even with the minimum of end-user functionality; and test that architecture for performance.

12.7   *Typical Four-Tier Business Architecture*

A typical Web-enabled business system might adopt an architecture with four physical tiers, as shown informally in Figure 12.5. The four tiers are as follows.

- *Clients:* Browsers and traditional GUIs can connect using HTTP to a Web server.

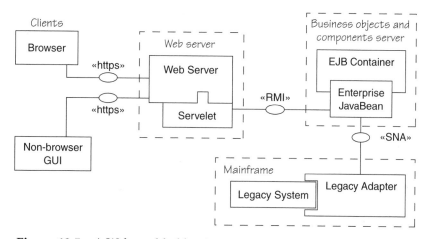

Figure 12.5   A Web-enabled business system with four physical tiers.

- *Web server:* This tier forwards appropriate requests to a *servelet*, a request handler that uses a standard API to plug in to the Web server. It translates CGI-encoded requests into proper method calls using distributed object invocations on an enterprise component. Then it formats and returns the results to the client.

- *Enterprise JavaBean:* This business component provides a meaningful business service using an uncluttered business type model via method invocation protocols such as Java RMI, or CORBA IIOP, or COM+ and communicating via a proprietary protocol to a legacy system and database. This component is also plugged in to an EJB container supplied by the legacy system vendor to provide security, transaction, threading, and other infrastructure services. This tier adds load balancing and failover behaviors, mostly provided by the container.

- *Legacy adapter:* This thin layer shields business objects from idiosyncrasies of the legacy system and its representations.

We can describe this architecture with a combination of a physical model, a component deployment model, and frameworks for the protocols used between these components. Moreover, the four-tier structure itself can be described as a framework.

12.8 *User Interfaces*

The Model-View-Controller (MVC) architecture (or some variant) is commonly used in the design of user interfaces. A user-interface element is associated with a single model—the object that acts as the source of the information presented, and the recipient of user requests. Each element is designed as a pair of a view, which deals with the presentation aspects of information from the model; and a controller, which is responsible for interpreting user inputs and gestures for the view and the model. The view and controller roles are combined into a single object in some variants.

When initially describing the system context, we avoid describing UI specifics, because these can vary. Detailed interactions via the user interface are better treated as a refinement of the abstract use cases that are being carried out. The basic MVC architecture applies to many forms of user interfaces, including graphical, character-based, touch screen, and voice-response.

At a higher level, it is useful to document the dialog flow of the UI, shown as a state transition diagram, where each state corresponds to a particular window that is active at that point in the interaction. At a more detailed level, we need uniform mechanisms to assemble the user interfaces and respond to their events.

There are various ways to build and connect user interfaces to business objects. The scheme you use depends largely on your user-interface frameworks. Following is a simple scheme broken into two main phases: configuration (creates and connects the appropriate objects) and run (user interacts with the widgets).

12.8.1   Configuration

For each window (or major panel within a window), follow these steps to configure the UI.

1. Create one application object. This object coordinates and mediates among the UI widgets and between the widgets and the business objects. The application object is created at the appropriate point in the dialog flow; in contrast, the business objects are created from persistent storage.
2. The application object creates its corresponding UI panel and populates it with its widgets.
3. The application object registers the widgets as its observer; later, a single changed method will inform all these widgets to update themselves.
4. The application object registers itself as the listener for events from each relevant widget; if necessary, it creates intermediate adapter objects to listen directly for these events and to translate them into callbacks to the application object (for example, if you have two buttons, both of which generate a pressed event).
5. The application object registers itself as an observer for the relevant business objects. When they change they update the application object, which updates the widgets if necessary (see Figure 12.6).

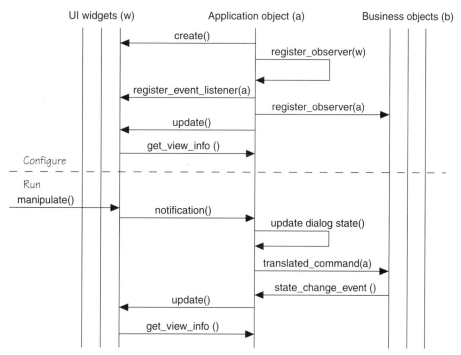

Figure 12.6   A typical UI interaction.

12.8.2 Run

During the run phase, the following actions occur.

1. The user manipulates a widget.
2. The widget generates the appropriate event to the application object (possibly through an intermediate adapter object).
3. The application object makes necessary changes to its state to reflect the progress of the interaction dialog; then it generates a command to the business object; then it propagates updates to the widgets.
4. The widgets update themselves by calling back to the application object for the state information they need (again, possibly translated by the intermediate adapter).

12.8.3 Reuse and the UI

You can sometimes make the user interface elements and the application object reusable so that you can create larger panels and application objects such as the following:

- video_title_selector: application object plus panel to help select a video title
- video_copy_scanner: application object plus panel to scan in a video copy
- member_selector: application object plus panel to select a member

Follow these steps.

1. Devise an event protocol to make these elements composable. For example, each application object checks with its container before it sends commands to its business objects.
2. If the application object represents an action in progress, name it as such.
   - check_out_video_application_object
   - return_video_application_object
3. Use typed event channels instead of generic subject-observer where necessary (see Section 12.5.1).
4. Use a scheme to batch the updates as needed.

12.8.4 Patterns in the UI

Define standard patterns to be followed in constructing the user interfaces. Many of these patterns can be formalized as frameworks. Examples are a master-slave listbox for navigating any 1-N association and a drill-down into data details using a tree panel.

12.9 *Objects and Databases*

In most applications the state of the business objects must persist even when the process or application that created them exits. There are three main approaches to providing this persistence.

12.9.1 Flat Files

Each object has the ability to serialize itself and also to initialize itself from a serialized representation. If the programming language has a reflective facility, you can write a single piece of code to determine the structure of the object and perform serialization and initialization. Java serialization works this way. Of course, flat files do not provide any of the multi-user, concurrency, meta-data, schema evolution, transaction, and recovery facilities that a database provides.

12.9.2 Relational Databases

In using a relational database, the interlinked object structure is translated into a representation based on tables and rows. Each object typically is a row in a table; one table is defined for each class (sans inheritance).

- The object identity is a primary key, usually generated by the database.
- Simple attributes are stored directly (if they correspond to built-in database types).
- Single-valued "object" attributes are stored as a foreign key referring to another table.
- Multivalued associations cannot be stored directly. Instead, they are stored as an inverse foreign key, and a join is performed to traverse the association.
- Inheritance cannot be mapped directly. There are several alternative schemes, well documented elsewhere, that are systematic and make different trade-offs.

The overall disadvantages of relational databases are as follows.

- Because of the different models of programming and persistence, impedence mismatch becomes a major development cost. It is alleviated by products that help automate the mapping.
- The cost of multiple joins can become prohibitive for a highly structured data model. However, some relational databases have recently shown tremendous improvements in this area.
- The data access is usually not integrated with the programming language.

  Conversely, relational databases have a number of advantages.

- Relational technology has been around for a while. It is mature and well understood at both a formal and a practical level.
- Query languages include declarative access and querying using SQL.

- Relational technology permits the use of multiple views: virtual "schema" that can be treated like the real schema, at least for query purposes.
- Relational databases are scalable and easily handle the terabyte range and hundreds of users.

12.9.3   Object-Oriented Databases

With object-oriented databases, the interlinked object model is transparently carried over to persistence, and the developer is concerned with logical things—transaction boundaries, concurrency, how far to propagate locks—rather than mapping between two dissimilar models.

The disadvantages of this approach include the following.

- Object-oriented databases scale to very large datasets but they do not have the maturity of relational products.
- OODBs traditionally have not supported declarative query access, choosing explicit navigation instead. This situation is starting to change, with standards such as the ODMG.
- Commercial OODBs do not provide a flexible mechanism for multiple views of a common underlying schema.
- The simplicity of the mapping can be deceptive. You still have to carefully design the volume of persistent data, granularity of objects that are made persistent, and transaction boundaries.

The advantages are as follows.

- OODBs present no major conceptual barrier for persistence.
- Within their scaling limits, OODBs traditionally have vastly outperformed relational databases.

12.9.4   Hybrid Object-Relational Databases

These purport to provide the best of both worlds. They are a relatively new technology and are worth watching as they mature. The growth of the World Wide Web has spurred on this segment significantly, because WWW demands better support for complex structured documents and other data.

12.10   *Summary*

The architecture of a system is the set of design decisions that constrain its implementors and maintainers. A good architecture is one that defines a small set of elements to be used in a consistent and regular way, and one in which conformance to the architecture can be clearly defined.

The architecture of a system has a direct impact on its qualities—performance, funtionality, understandability, maintainability, portability, testability, functionality, scalability, and so on. Scenarios are a promising way to evaluate an architecture against these qualities.

There are many different architectural views of a system, calling for different kinds of elements. These elements include hardware and networks, packages and their structures, object types and relationships, concurrent processes and threads, tables and columns, and the patterns that dictate how they are to be used. An architectural style, or type, defines a consistent set of elements and rules for their use.

Part V   How to Apply Catalysis

Parts II, III, and IV cover basic techniques for modeling with objects and advanced techniques for factoring and then recombining models and designs using packages, frameworks, and components. They do not describe a development process: the steps to validate and document these models.

Although good modeling tools can help you build useful descriptions of your design, an effective method must also define how to apply those tools and must provide a predictable and repeatable process for development and documentation that is understood by all team members. Developing software without an understandable process can be costly in terms of guesswork, communication problems, inconsistency, and quality shortcomings. A clearly defined process and concrete techniques for building models also shortens the learning curve for those adopting the approach and eliminates one element of uncertainty on the project.

For a bit of perspective, a recent study by the Standish Group found that the 83% of projects that either failed or seriously missed the target in time, cost, and function blamed a large portion of their problems on lack of user input and involvement, unclear requirements and specifications, changing requirements, and lack of executive support.

Part V shows how to use basic techniques to model and design using Catalysis in a clearly defined (although contrived) sequence of steps.

Chapter 13, Process Overview, is an overview of the development process, its objectives, and the typical structure of a project. This chapter introduces a set of process patterns that can be customized to different approaches and routes through the method.

Chapter 14, How to Build a Business Model, shows how to go about building a business model. Chapter 15, How to Specify a Component, describes the process for clearly specifying what is expected of a given component. Chapter 16, How to Implement a Component, describes how, given an external specification of a component, you can design and implement it.

Chapter 13   Process Overview

This chapter provides an overview of the Catalysis development process, describing how development artifacts can be structured, developed, and evolved on a typical project. The case study used in the next four chapters illustrates specific application of this process to a sample problem but does not illustrate all nuances of a complete development.

Section 13.1 provides a short recap of modeling, designing, and implementing with objects, from business to code and specification to deployment.

Section 13.2 is a general introduction to the process. It covers various routes through the method, its parallel and iterative nature, the continuous attention to QA and testing, and its early emphasis on architecture (both static dependencies and dynamic aspects).

Section 13.3 outlines how a typical project might evolve over time and explains how the development of various artifacts may overlap.

Section 13.4 describes a typical structure of packages for a project. This structure shows up in project planning, certain elements of system architecture, and the structure of documentation.

Section 13.5 introduces a set of process patterns that are elaborated on throughout the case study. These patterns describe some of the broad contexts for development and a reasonable strategy for each one. *Pattern 13.1, Object Development from Scratch*, outlines an approach for developing a system from scratch. *Pattern 13.2, Reengineering*, addresses the case when an existing design is being reworked. Pattern *13.3, Short-Cycle Development*, motivates development in short incremental cycles as a useful basis for many projects.

13.1   *Model, Design, Implement, and Test—Recursively*

The process of modeling and designing is recursive throughout business, component specification, and internal design. Similarly, specification and implementation activities are also recursive across the business or domain model, component spec, and internal design.

13.1.1   Models and Designs: Business to Code

A model of real-world objects and their inter-actions—or rather, some users' understanding of them—is called a *business model*. The outcome of each interaction depends on (1) the types to which its participant objects belong and (2) the states they are in at the time. For any participant types, you can describe the effects of an action by relating the values of the attributes before and after any occurrence of that action.

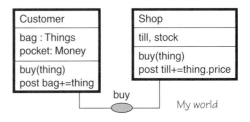

Components of a designed system can be described in the same way: as interacting objects. The same notation can be used for designing interacting software objects as is used for analyzing things and concepts in the users' world.

Each component is then designed as a collaboration of interacting objects in the same way, and so on recursively until we get to programming-language primitives or (preferably) an existing component. The same techniques are used to design the internal structure of a piece of software as are used to describe or design an organization or machine, which may or may not use software. Although it is not necessary or practical to produce the layers in top-down order, there is a notional hierarchy of designs. In the topmost layer, the complete system consists of a few interacting objects.

A useful principle of object-oriented specification (and design) is that the structure of a software system should be based on a well-chosen model of the world with which it deals; that approach makes the design easier to update with business changes. Each real-world object (whether physical or more abstract: orders, meetings, menus) has its counterpart inside the system. A first step in building an object-oriented program from scratch is therefore to make a business model and then declare it to be the first draft of a type model of the software. The objects and their relationships are used as the type model of the system.

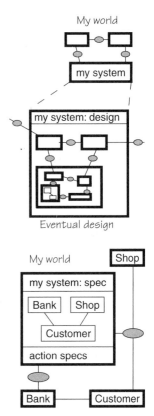

The attributes of a complex object are usually expressed in terms of types, which themselves are modeled with other attributes and so on. Drawing them pictorially shows the relationships more clearly. When an object is specified, the types of attributes are chosen for their expressiveness rather than for execution efficiency.

Some of these "specification" types invented to help model a set of actions may never be implemented directly; however, the type model must constitute a valid abstraction of the implementation, as documented in a refinement and its justification. The types that are implemented are those generated by decomposition: they must exist because the design calls for them to interact with one another.

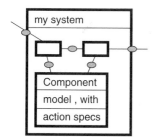

Intermediate step

The behavior that each object provides to the others is specified, and the specification is kept separate from its internal collaboration design and code. Thus, each internal designed component has its own type model, with some refinement that maps it to the type model of the containing component. This arrangement allows us to define a more general architecture, with a variety of different components able to plug in to the basic design. Some components may be bought, and others may be purpose-built. The idea of specifying the interfaces well is crucial for component-based development.

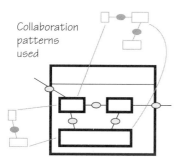

Collaboration patterns used

The design of any system embodies several partial designs of how the pieces collaborate. These designs constitute some of the key architectural elements used in the system design. The resulting design is a composition of these partial collaborations, unified via objects that participate in more than one collaboration. The architecture is often best described and understood in terms of recurring patterns of such collaborations.

An important principle of this recursive decomposition is that, at each level, the components can be designed independently if the specifications are accurate enough.

Accurate specification of the actions depends on careful models. When all the components are designed by the same team, we can afford to be relaxed about this: If the spec of a component you use is unclear, you can walk down the hall to whoever is designing it. But in a world that takes component-based design seriously, you won't know the designers of many of the parts you use, nor many of your own clients. More effort must be put into specification, with the understanding that the economies of CBD will pay it back.

The extent to which the code reflects the business model is related to the architecture. If the code must be changed every few days to keep competitive with others (for example, financial dealing systems), the requirements of users should translate directly to code changes, which must closely reflect a suitably flexible business model. If high performance is needed and changes are rare (as in an

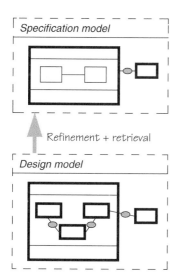

undersea multiplexor), optimizations must be done. The analysis and design models are kept separate. If the refinements are localized and well documented, the benefits of traceability are preserved. Refinements fall into a small number of categories and useful patterns that are documented in standard ways (see Chapter 6, Abstraction, Refinement, and Testing).

13.1.2   Specify, Document, Implement, and Test: Business to Code

For every specification activity there is a corresponding activity that deals with implementation and testing; every refinement claim has a corresponding justification and test (see Figure 13.1). At the level of a single interface, the implementation may be a single class that is tested against operation specs. For a collaboration, several classes or components are implemented and integrated, and then their interactions are tested against the collaboration specification. At the level of the system specification, all external operation and abstract action specifications are tested. At the level of the business or domain model, to implement means to deploy the "to-be" model, conducting training and other more conventional forms of upgrades, and acceptance testing.

Documentation is structured around specifications and implementation and their refinement and import relationships. A user manual—a description of how a user accomplishes tasks by using the system(s)—is a particular form of documentation associated with a refinement: how the abstract business model and actions are realized by more-detailed actions performed by the users and systems. Test specifications are also associated with refinement relationships. The rules for system architecture are documented in a package that specifies the patterns and frameworks that will be used in other packages that import it.

13.2 *General Notes on the Process*

Before we jump into specifics of the case study, let's review some general notes on how the method is applied.

13.2.1   Multiple Routes through the Method

There are many possible routes through the method, each with a different prototypical sequence of tasks and deliverables that is better suited to certain project characteristics; one route may omit activities and deliverables that another one includes. Different routes can be used or combined for any project or subproject. A lightweight route would be a good way to get started with Catalysis.

For example, for a project in which requirements should be specified early and accurately, we might follow the "Build" route in Figure 13.2; the case study in this section of the book roughly follows this route.

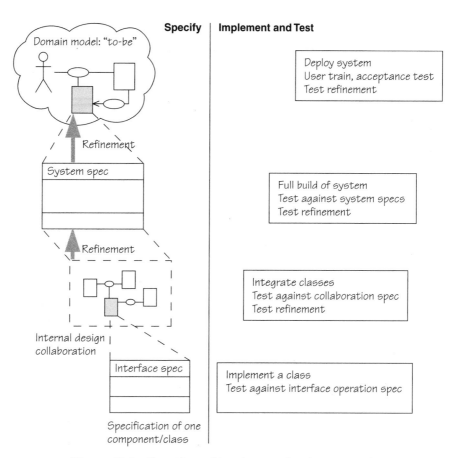

Figure 13.1   Specify and implement: business to code.

1. **Build1.** Build a domain model to capture terms, domain rules, business tasks.
2. **Build2–3.** Refine it to specify the system by building its local type model of the domain; the retrieval mapping is defined top-down.
3. **Build4–5.** Partition and refine it to build the internal design model; again, the retrieval mapping is defined by forward-engineering the system type model and distributing it across the design components.

In contrast, if the system must be built from many heterogenous components and if the requirements can be shaped significantly by the ease of assembling those components, we can follow an "Assemble" route like this:

1. **Assy1.** Start with a domain model—optionally, a rudimentary system spec.
2. **Assy2.** Build type models of each component, reverse-engineering if necessary.
3. **Assy3.** Define the retrieval mappings between type models of individual components and the domain model or system type models.

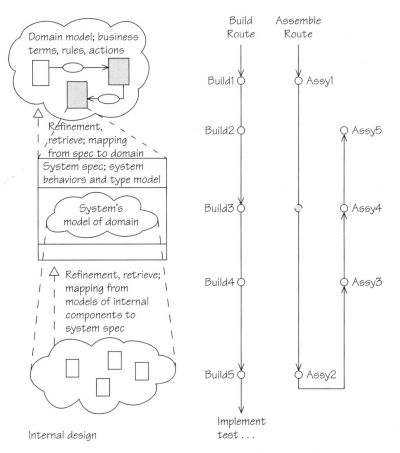

Figure 13.2   Many routes through a method.

4. Assy4. Define an achievable type model and behavior spec for the system.
5. Assy5. Refine the domain, defining how external components and users interact with this achievable system to accomplish the original tasks.

See Section 10.11, Heterogenous Components, for a complete example of how this
might be done in practice.

The relationships between all the models and documents are clearly defined in
Catalysis and can be clearly documented regardless of the sequence in which they
are built. When one model or document is changed, those that are related to it
may also have to change and must be reviewed.

13.2.2   The Process Is Nonlinear, Iterative, and Parallel

Although they are shown in these chapters in a linear sequence, these documents
are almost never produced in sequential steps. There will be a gradual shift in

focus from the "earlier" aspects to the "later" ones, but the creative process and prior constraints may in general develop the various parts in any order. Good management should impose discipline, not by forcing a linear sequence but rather by seeing the process as one of successive enhancement. Appropriate milestones, corresponding to multiple iterations, are the completion of *vertical slices* of functionality visible to the end user or *horizontal* services, components, and end-to-end implementations of the technical architecture that will be used for end-user functions.

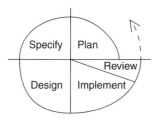

The *spiral* model works well in any context in which the current plan must depend on the outcome of earlier work expenditure increases along the spiral; each cycle includes a review of results and risks, and it drives a refinement of the goals and plans of the next cycle. An early spiral typically covers a much broader area in requirements and a much narrower piece of design; the situation reverses in later cycles. Lessons learned from any spiral feed back into the most abstract level of models that are affected. There are many colorful names for variants of this basic idea, including fountain, tidepool, and tornado.

The design of the spiral cycles is usually driven by an understanding of project risk, with high-risk items being tackled early. Some of the highest risks in a project come from unclear requirements,[1] so they should be tackled early. For large projects, the technical architecture—with all the infrastructure needed for communication, transactions, messaging, and systems management—also poses a serious risk. To help reduce this risk, practice explicit and early architectural modeling, evaluation, and implementation, and build on standard infrastructures. Other risk factors include team communication and dynamics, the age and maturity of technologies, management commitment, and project funding.

Cycles can be overlapped and carried on concurrently, because many activities can proceed in parallel with low risk of rework; these activities should not be needlessly serialized. Catalysis provides the appropriate consistency rules between artifacts even if they are developed in parallel. However, in some situations the best approach is for a small group of people to resolve critical issues, often at the requirements or architecture level. It is a mistake, simply to keep some developers from twiddling their thumbs, to force concurrent development if it is dependent on these issues being resolved.

Iterations and increments involve development cycles but play different roles. An *iteration* aims to improve the design of existing work; iteration is fundamentally about rework. In addition to dedicated iteration cycles, each development spiral might have a *consolidation* stage at the end, for refactoring the design and making it more robust for downstream work. In contrast, an *incremental* cycle

---

1. Many requirements "changes" are actually the result of initial lack of precision.

adds new functionality to what already exists: either a new end-user function or supporting functions that will be used toward that end.

Iterations and increments must have clear objectives or else they can become a euphemism for structured hacking. Increments should be planned at multiple levels, from end-user increments to those that are internal to the development team or visible and demonstrated up to the project manager. Packages and their import relations are used to plan iterations and increments.

13.2.3 Rigor, QA, and Testing Are Continuous

Quality assurance is not an after-the-fact activity in Catalysis. From the onset of requirements, the method is focused on ensuring quality in intermediate deliverables and documentation and ensuring a quality final delivered product.

Pre- and postconditions, invariants, and refinements offer "on-demand" rigor. Experience shows that writing in a more precise notation flushes out ambiguities and questions that would otherwise lie dormant until coding and testing. Even after there is code, an abstract model can help make a clear picture, whereas design pragmatics might obscure the big picture with complications. This kind of rigor saves time later, so the benefit is long-term rather than short-term. Using the formalisms is a skill akin to programming; some aspects may be a bit less familiar to some people, but no more difficult.

Adjust the degree of formalism to the life expectancy of your product. Components that will be reused a lot justify (and need) more investment in getting things right up front. "Quick and dirty" developments can be hacked to appear to work, but bear in mind that these solutions tend to end up being the bedrock! Cool-headed management is required. In general, you should adjust the degree of formalism within the development. Always use informal descriptions, but use greater formalism for crucial issues. Interleave narrative descriptions with formal diagrams and specifications.

For example, the GUI of a typical development might be documented only with storyboards and GUI mock-ups that are annotated with explanatory notes, with an optional mapping to the type model. Other design discussions, and specification of business behavior, use proper action specifications. Exceptions may be done more or less formally, depending on project needs.

All behavior specifications in Catalysis are precise enough to be used for testing, both at the unit level (type specifications and class refinements) and at the level of integration (collaborations and action refinements). In particular, specifications written in terms of abstract attributes become testable against the implementation by virtue of the *abstraction functions* that are part of the refinement; user tasks are specified as abstract actions and are documented and tested as sequences of refined actions (yes, the user manual starts early!). Static invariants can be tested at any time the system state is stable. More-general constructs, such as effects and effect invariants, also map cleanly to test specifications. In general, any claim of refinement between a concrete and an abstract model has a corresponding strategy for testing (see Chapter 6, Abstraction, Refinement, and Testing).

Catalysis models have clear semantic relationships to one another. At any level of abstraction, they form an important part of the inspection criteria for those models. Across levels of refinement, these rules, together with the rules for refinement, provide a concrete basis for design reviews.

The impact of change in Catalysis is clearly defined. A change at any level of description must be propagated up to the highest level at which the change has an impact. Specifically, the change at a concrete level need not be propagated to an abstract level if the refinement mapping can be updated so that the abstract specs are still valid.

Packages provide the unit of configuration management and release control. Catalysis packages are flexible, because one can model different aspects of the same type or action in two different packages. A versioned package is frozen; every package it imports is also versioned.

Safety-critical projects can further exploit the precision available with Catalysis, using advanced facilities (see Section 3.5.2, Redundant Specifications Can Be Useful) to formally check important properties that the design should exhibit.

13.2.4   Emphasis on Architecture

There are at least two interesting aspects to architecture: (1) static dependencies between units of work and (2) the runtime patterns of component and object structure and interactions.

The structure of packages defines one aspect of architecture: the static dependencies between units of development work, whether business models, interfaces, or implementations. The documentation and code structure reflects the package structure. Documentation, always combining informal with rigorous descriptions, is part of a package; within a document you can refer only to model elements visible to that package. Packages also provide the unit for change management and upgrades.

Using refinement, you can model objects and interactions at all levels of granularity. This arrangement provides a "fractal" view of architecture, from the business roles and processes to large-grained interacting architectural components including a "system" to individual interfaces and classes. Any refinement has associated architectural decisions.

In addition, good use of packages facilitates full separation of interfaces from implementations. As an extreme example, a single class might be implemented in a package that imports the packages with the type definitions of all types that class must implement; each such package contains the minimal model of any other types that it must interact with.

Therefore, you should structure the macroscopic view of the development around type models, frameworks, packages, and refinements.

Collaborations, as partial definitions of object roles and types and their interactions, provide support for a "pattern" view of the dynamic aspects of an architecture. A design is often best understood as a composition of such patterns onto the objects involved rather than in terms of individual objects or interactions.

The basic constructs of type, collaboration, and refinement support all levels of specification, architecture, and implementation. However, we also pay explicit attention to specific levels of architectural design: logical and physical database mapping, technical architecture (including client-server and multitier peer-to-peer architectures), and user-interface modeling. The case study touches only on some of these aspects.

13.2.5 Unambiguous Notation

The notation used is based on that of the Unified Modeling Language (UML 1.1). What we add is a systematic way to use this language, a way to establish and maintain the relationships between the documents, and a clear semantics for abstract models.

Much of the notation is useful throughout different stages of the process. For example, we use the same tools to describe the interactions between people and a machine we propose to build, to describe the interactions between objects collaborating inside the machine once designed, and to describe business tasks and processes. For this reason, many of the notational tools are introduced early in the case study and are then reapplied in each phase.

The notation here is not limited to complete documents delivered within a standard development process. Designers sketch these diagrams on whiteboards when they are discussing their designs with their colleagues. In short, this is a specialized language for communication models and designs.

Some informal and ad hoc notations are always useful as long as you recognize that they are informal; they should sometimes be cast into a more precise form as their purpose becomes clear. Useful new formal notations also will no doubt be invented; their semantics should be described clearly using frameworks, as illustrated in Section 9.8.3, Examples of Semantic Rules for a Dialect.

It is our experience that familiarity with the toolbag demonstrated here makes such discussions much less ambiguous and far more productive than they are when the only tools for debate are ad hoc pictures and natural language. And a single designer's own thoughts are clarified when cast into the forms shown here. This is often the greatest benefit of taking up a more rigorous notation.

So although this study demonstrates (parts of) an analysis-to-code document structure, there are other equally valuable ways to use the tools in the bag, including completely different routes (see Section 13.2.1, Multiple Routes through the Method).

13.2.6   Typical Process for Business Systems

A typical large business system has human users and a back-end database. The development process for these systems still goes through the levels outlined earlier, with some specialized activities required within the levels. Figure 13.3 outlines these activities and shows how they map to the three essential levels we discussed; the corresponding implementation and test activities are not shown.

There are still three conceptual levels: the domain models (the outside, describing the environment in which the software will reside), the component specifications (the boundary, describing its externally desired behaviors), and the component implementation (the inside, describing its internal design). These three levels continue recursively: Each subcomponent itself has a context (the collaboration with others that should realize the external spec), a specification, and its own implementation.

In traditional terms, requirements and analysis are mostly concerned with the outside and boundary, from identifying and understanding the problem to specifying each externally visible component of an envisioned solution; design focuses on

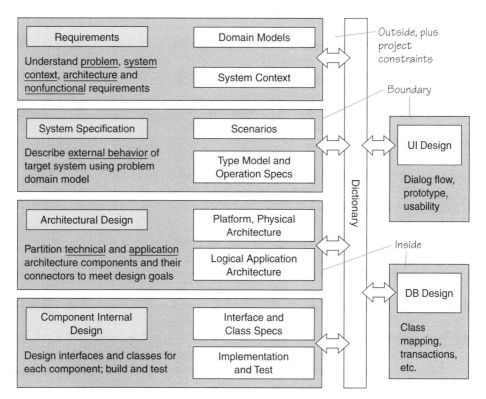

Figure 13.3   Main activities for a typical business system.

internal structure and architecture. However, externally visible decisions often have some design flavor; think of these as "external" design or "business" design.

13.2.6.1   Requirements: Spanning Outside, Boundary, and Inside

The requirements activity is aimed at understanding the problem and how the proposed solution will address it. The primary deliverables are as follows:

- *A business model:* Collaborations, types, and glossary (possibly an as-is model and a to-be version that includes the envisaged systems)
- *Functional requirements on the system:* Usually in the form of a system context diagram with use cases and scenarios
- *Nonfunctional requirements:* Performance, reliability, scalability, and reuse goals
- *Known platform or architectural constraints:* Machines, operating systems, distribution, middleware, legacy systems, and interoperability requirements, all captured by a package structure and collaborations
- *Project and planning constraints:* Budgets, schedules, staff, and user involvement

Specific techniques and constructs used to describe the business model and requirements include the following.

- *Storyboards:* Sketches of different situations and scenarios in the problem domain, possibly using a domain-specific notation.
- *Concept maps:* An informal but structured representation of related terms in the domain. The notation, which is similar to a mind map, is simply concepts or phrases with labeled directed lines between them indicating a relationship; it can include rich pictures or storyboards of the domain.

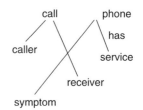

- *Business collaboration:* Identifies the actors in the domain and their interactions (the actions, or use cases, and information exchanged). The actors typically represent the roles of people (such as buyer) or software systems (such as inventory system). The as-is and to-be versions form the basis of deployment and transition plans for the systems.
- *System context:* A collaboration centered on the target software system, intended to clearly define the

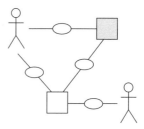

boundary of "the system." The use cases in which the system is an actor are those that must be developed as part of the system.

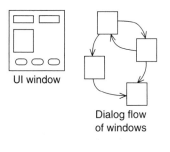

Scenario

A does ...

B inputs ...

System ...

- *Scenarios:* Aprototypical sequence of interactions in a business collaboration or the system context. These scenarios can be used to formalize specifications of the actions, even at the business level.

13.2.6.2   System Specification: The Boundary

UI window

Dialog flow
of windows

System specification proceeds much as before but has an added element of user-interface design. The normal artifacts of system specification—a type model and operation specs—are now accompanied by prototypes and UI specs describing the screens, dialog flows across windows, information presented and required, and reports. These user-interface elements are kept consistent with the type model and are reviewed through scenarios.

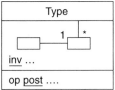

    The primary deliverable is a *type specification*: the system being developed specified as a *type*, with a *type model* (attributes and associations) and a set of *operations* specified against that type model. Defining the type involves identifying each action in which the system participates and specifying it as an operation on the type. The behavior can be described with state charts in addition to operation specifications and can be exercised with scenarios and snapshots.

The specification can be split across subject areas—broad areas of usage or function that help partition the system behavior—so that one area can be analyzed somewhat separately from the others. Packages can be used to structure all work on a large system across multple vertical views or horizontal layers.

13.2.6.3   Architectural Design: The Inside

The internal implementation of the system is split into two related parts: the application architecture and the technical architecture. The main deliverables are described on the next page.

- *The application architecture:* A package structure and collaborations. This implements the business logic itself as a collection of collaborating components, with the original specification types now split across different components. The components can range from custom-built to common off-the shelf components, such as spreadsheets, calendars, and contact managers, to purchased domain-specific components such as factory-floor schedulers. This application architecture lives "atop," and uses, the technical architecture.

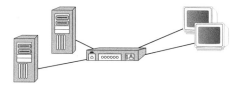

Packages   Collaborations

- *The technical architecture:* Apackage structure (for static dependencies) and collaborations (across technology components, such as UI, business object servers, and databases). These cover all domain-independent parts of the system: hardware and software platforms; infrastructure components such as middleware and databases; utilities for logging, exceptions, start-up, and shutdown; design standards and tools; and the choice of

Hardware architectures and distribution

component architecture, such as JavaBeans or COM. It also includes the design rules and patterns that will be used in the implementation. The technical architecture is designed and implemented early and is evaluated against nonfunctional requirements such as throughput and response time.

- *Database architecture:* The design of the database portion should start at this stage and includes mapping of the design object model to the database, definition of transaction boundaries, and so on. Depending on the choice of database and supporting tools, this activity may or may not take significant effort. Database performance modeling and tuning usually take some effort.

13.2.6.4   Component Implementation: The Inside

Individual application components are designed and built down to the level of programming language interfaces and classes or preexisting components, or to a point where the implementation can be mechanically generated from the detailed design.

The goal of component implementation is to define an internal structure and interactions that satisfy the behavioral, technological, nonfunctional, and software engineering requirements for a component. In Catalysis the component specification (type) mentioned earlier identifies the behavioral requirements.

In simple cases, you can start with the assumption that every type identified in the specification model will be implemented directly as a separate class; for large components you may go through a recursive step of subcomponent partition and specification. We determine intended responsibilities of each class and then build interaction diagrams to design their interactions to realize the specified behaviors.

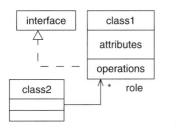

We can now define the design's class model: the classes that compose the system, the interfaces they implement and use, their attributes and operations, and the references between them. The initial class model is derived by reifying each model type to a class, adding the operations that the class must implement from the interaction diagram, and designing the attributes and directed associations that the class needs to implement those operations.

This design can then be refactored. In this activity, you separate interfaces on a class for different clients, migrate behaviors to abstract superclasses or collaborating classes, split data and behavior of one class into two, and refactor packages to separate architectural layers.

13.2.7   Modeling the Catalysis Process

Many aspects of the Catalysis process can be modeled using the concepts of type, collaboration, and refinement. When you're modeling the development process itself, the interesting development objects and actions include the following:

- Objects
  - *Packages:* Get populated, documented, import other packages
  - *Model types, actions, refinements, etc.:* Get specified, implemented, tested
  - *Other deliverable artifacts:* Documents, source code, tests, executables
  - *Developers:* Create and modify artifacts, get trained
  - *Development tools:* Evaluate, purchase, install, use to create artifacts
  - *Project and iteration plans:* Get reviewed, revised
  - *Deployment plan:* From as-is to to-be via a transition plan, including installation scripts, upgrade and migration tools, user documents, user training
  - *Paths and routes:* Different sequences of activities for various project types
  - *Project, subproject, activity, task, cycle:* Things to be done following some route
- Actions
  - *All development activities:* Actions by developers using tools on artifacts
  - *All planning activities:* Planning actions by developers
- Refinements
  - Detailing of development activities, artifacts, plans, and schedules

Although the rigor supported by the method may not be fully utilized in this context, its facilities for types, refinement, and frameworks become more interesting when the process and project management needs are supported by tools. We will not expand further on this point here but mention it for completeness.

13.3 *Typical Project Evolution*

A project produces a subset of models and diagrams that describe the design. For some projects, the order in which these are produced will be mostly top-down; for others, more bottom-up. In almost all cases there are multiple development tasks that can proceed in parallel depending on project resources and constraints. In all cases, the relationships among the artifacts are the same, and the most important initial methodology question for any project to answer is

> *"Which of these decisions will I explicitly document? And when and how?"*

Figure 13.4 illustrates a typical project evolution for a large business project; it shows the activities that take place across time (horizontal, not to scale) and different levels of development (vertical). Numbered items in the figure are discussed next. The circles indicate interesting points in time, perhaps with an associated artifact. The partitioning of work across packages, the degree of opportunistic development, and the specific path through the method vary across projects. The figure does not show iterations or increments explicitly; all deliverables are subject to revision or refinement based on downstream work within the rules established for configuration management.

1. *The business case:* This provides initial requirements, defining the business problem or opportunity that this project addresses. It typically includes a high-level list of numbered functional and nonfunctional requirements[2] (1b), the business reasons and risks for the project (1a), the scope of the project in terms of things definitely included or excluded, linked clearly to a business model in terms of business objectives, actions or use cases, and user roles that must be supported (1a), known requirements on the architecture, design, and implementation (1c), and constraints on project budget and schedules (1d).

2. *Domain or business models:* These describe the domain or business at hand, often independently of particular software solutions. It can include as-is and to-be models of the business. It is sometimes useful to analyze the as-is model, decide which aspects of it represent essential requirements, and abstract out an essential domain model that can then be refined to the envisaged to-be solution model. Domain models are reusable across multiple projects.

---

2. See Section 12.2.1, Multiple Stakeholders and Their Requirements.

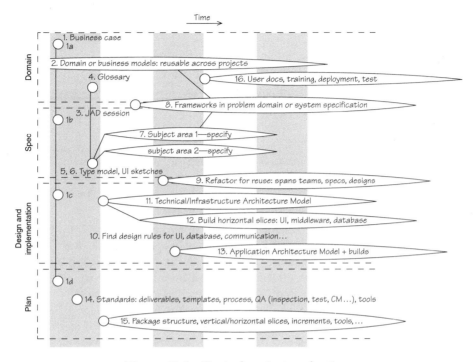

Figure 13.4   Typical project evaluation.

3. *Joint-Application Development (JAD) sessions:* Many projects can benefit from early structured sessions conducted by the development team and customers or users, whose purpose is to build a joint understanding of the requirements of the system to be built. They typically produce a running list of issues and the items listed under 4, 5, and 6.

4. *Glossary:* This is an initial set of definitions of terms used to define the problem or requirements. The glossary is developed in parallel with a type model, either for the system specification or of the domain itself. The glossary will be maintained through the iterations of the system specifications.

5. *Type model plus system specs:* The system context is defined, and the primary actions that the system participates in are first specified as abstract actions, and then refined to a level of an approximately *atomic* interaction with the system. Atomic interactions are those that, unless completed, would not constitute meaningful or useful operations on the system.

6. *UI sketches:* For systems that have user interfaces, initial sketches of the UIs are produced to define how user tasks might translate into system interactions, what information is exchanged in these interactions, and the dialog flow through these tasks. The user-interface elements are tied to the underlying type model. The names and labels for UI elements must map directly to attributes and types; their visual relationship to one another maps to relationships in the type model; the nature of the UI widgets used (lists, trees, fields, and so on) maps to static type model constraints such as multiplicity; and visual feedback, such as colors and highlights, maps to states. Do not get bogged down in UI design at early stages. The underlying type model, information exchange, and action specifications are more important.

7. *Subject areas:* These are broad areas of usage or function that help partition the description of the system behavior so that one area can be modeled and specified somewhat separately from the others. They need not correspond to separately implemented components; that would be an internal view.

8. *Frameworks:* Across the business models and system specification, there often are generic problem frameworks that appear in specific forms. For example, the business description (and hence system spec) for a seminar company might have frameworks for resource allocation (assign instructors and rooms), inventory and production (maintain course notes inventory for deliveries), and customer loyalty (monitor product preferences and usage levels of clients). Factoring the models to use generic frameworks (see Chapter 9, Model Frameworks and Template Packages) simplifies the descriptions and also gives you a basis for downstream design partitioning of application components and code frameworks (see Section 11.4, Frameworks: Specs to Code).

9. *Refactor for reuse:* This activity spans system specification and internal design. It involves rearranging parts of the models, sometimes extracting them into newly created packages and frameworks that are promptly reimported. This is an ongoing activity.

A common version is type-centric refactoring. A package containing a type model, either in specification or in design, shows a set of related types. However, to implement a particular type we need not know all the context-specific properties of all other types, only a subset. We could refactor the contents of this package into separate parts, each centered on a single primary type of interest and including only those aspects of other types that it must rely on to provide its services (see Section 7.4.1, Role-based Decoupling of Classes). This form also often shows up when you're designing class-based frameworks with plug-points (see Section 11.3, The Framework Approach to Code Reuse).

10. *Design rules for technical architecture:* This defines the elements used and patterns followed systemwide for dealing with the computing infrastructure aspects of the design. It includes hardware and software platforms and tools, middleware and databases, and the choice of API standards and component architecture, such as JavaBeans or COM. These rules emerge in parallel with the activities in items 11 and 12: architecture models and implementations.

Creating design guidelines against commercial or custom components and tools (some such design patterns can be formalized as frameworks), it defines standard mechanisms for mapping a type or class model to the chosen database, for presenting to and interacting with the user, for system boot-up and graceful failure, error handling, and so on.

11. *Technical architecture model:* This describes the package structure of and collaboration between infrastructure components at the technical architecture level, often treating each component as a single large object. All the techniques and diagrams for describing interactions apply, including collaboration, refinement, scenarios, and state models. The import structure of packages defines the static usage dependencies between component definitions and should be explicitly documented. The architecture should be explicitly evaluated against the runtime quality objectives (behavior, performance, scalability, and so on) and nonruntime quality objectives (modifiability and maintainability) for the system and should be documented and enforced in the implementation.

The component descriptions here typically belong to different domains than the primary business problem at hand. Database components are described by generic models of tables, columns, and keys (or types, classes, attributes, and IDs); transaction servers are described by transactional object, recoverable object, and resources; communication components could have sessions, channels, and messages; user-interface components have buttons, lists, panels, and scrollbars.

12. *Horizontal slices:* The technical architecture model should not be just a paper exercise. Instead, slices of the architecture model should be prototyped in a horizontal fashion: where each slice helps complete the end-to-end communication paths but does not introduce new end-user functionality. Nonfunctional requirements—throughput, scalability, data volumes, response time, and so on—should be tested carefully by using architectural simulation tools or by writing drivers to load the prototype appropriately.

13. *Application architecture:* This is the design of application logic itself as a collection of collaborating components. The nature of the component connectors—events, properties, workflows, replication, and transactions—is dictated by the technical component architecture selected. The specification types in the system spec are split across different components, possibly with multiple threads or processes.[3] These components can range from custom-built to common off-the shelf components, such as spreadsheets, calendars, and contact managers, to purchased domain-specific components such as factory-floor schedulers. The development activities here may include reverse-engineering, for those cases in which the application is being built from heterogenous off-the-shelf components (see Section 10.11, Heterogenous Components).

14. *Development standards for the project:* This project planning activity, which starts as early as possible, defines the deliverables, standard development tools,

---

3. Some of these choices will be influenced by the technical architecture. For example, Enterprise JavaBeans does not like its components to implement multiple threads, because it tries to manage that at the level of the vendor-provided containers.

documentation structure and templates when appropriate, process guidelines, team and stake-holder roles, quality assurance standards including inspections and metrics, testing, change and configuration management, and so on. All these standards should themselves be documented in some of the top-level packages for the project.

15. *Project plan:* This project planning activity also starts early but is subject to monitoring and refinement as the development progresses. It includes defining the high-level structure of packages. These packages define the basic units of work and configuration management and serve to separate different subject areas, separate interfaces from implementations, separate business logic from infrastructure components, and also enable parallel development. Appropriate iterations and increments are defined, following a typically spiral development model, and new tools may be introduced in the process.

A large part of project planning in Catalysis is centered on the structure and intended content of packages, including documents, models, tests, and code. All other development work is done within the context of a package; the project planning directly depends on the architecture, because it is concerned with partitioning, relating, and scheduling of these packages.

It is quite common for a Catalysis project leader to set up a structure of empty packages and use them to enter "stub" specifications, designs, and relations (such as refinements) between them that must be completed in downstream development. These packages also need an appropriate build mechanism that traverses and evaluates the contents of each package, generating results that will be checked, compiled, and linked.

16. *Deployment:* It is in this phase that the business or domain makes its transition to the to-be model, adopting new processes, hardware, and software. It involves things such as software and hardware installation, tools to upgrade or migrate to new releases, documentation, acceptance testing, and user and administrator training. Note that user documentation is not an after-the-fact activity. Because modeling starts with abstract user actions, refined eventually to system operations, the refinement definitions form the basis for many user documents: *If you want to accomplish task X, then do operations a, b, and c.*

13.4 *Typical Package Structure*

The separation of outside, boundary, and inside—covering business models, system or component specification, architectural design, interfaces, and implementation—holds for all projects (see Section 7.3, How to Use Packages and Imports). The package structure reflects static definitional and usage dependencies, including third-party interface and implementation units and even development and test tools. Packages reflect versioned units, documentation structure, and even tools for builds (see Section 7.8, Publication, Version Control, and Builds). A package can contain collaborations to define the dynamic aspects of architecture. Figure 13.5 shows a typical package structure.

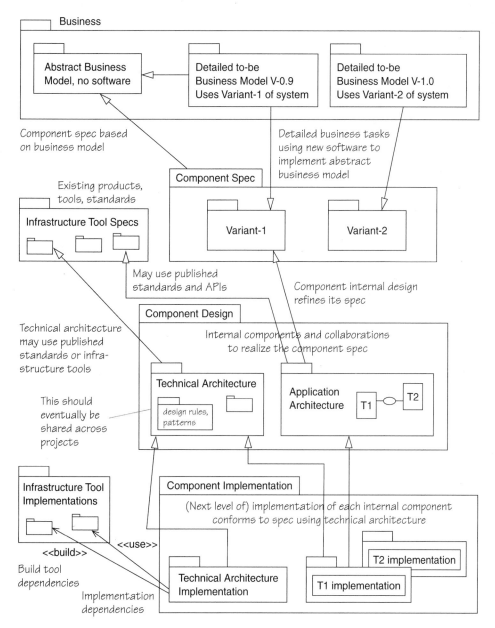

Figure 13.5   Typical package structure.

13.4.1   Levels of Description in the Case Study

In this case study we found it useful to distinguish six descriptions; a different project might make a somewhat different separation. The primary separation of domain or business (the outside), system specification (the boundary), and internal architectural and detailed design (the inside) will always hold. The following two features are common to each level.

• *Progressive formalization:* A progressive formalization turns natural-language statements into a less-ambiguous specialized notation. Casting statements into this more precise form clarifies them, exposing gaps and inconsistencies. (Programming language has comparable precision but is designed to deal with the solutions rather than the problems.) Although this formalization lengthens the analysis phase (compared with more traditional natural-language requirements), the design part of the process is clearer and shorter; and although the overall process is longer, the resulting system is more flexible and less costly to adapt and maintain.

• *Refinement:* Different levels of abstraction are supported by refinement. Giving an overall view helps everyone gain a better understanding of the problem. Sometimes the abstraction is written before the detail. In other cases, an abstraction is made after an initially detailed view—for example, to clarify issues after interviewing end users or to revise an external specification after a cycle of prototyping.

Following is a summary of the levels used in the case study; subsequent chapters treat each level in more detail.

13.4.1.1   Business (Domain) Model

This model describes the processes going on in that part of the world in which we are interested. These processes might be interactions between people or companies, physical processes, or the design of an existing computer system. The idea is to get a clear and agreed understanding of the concepts and rules important to all parties, especially the users and the designers of any existing systems.

The lightest-weight domain model is simply a problem statement, with a glossary of terms that are used in the statement. More-precise models use types, collaborations, and refinements to define static and dynamic business rules.

The description can be made without reference to a particular system we propose to design. It can be used either as the basis for a system analysis or just to get a clear view of the business processes, with a view to improvement or reengineering of business processes.

If the model is to be used as the basis for a system development, we would expect to see many of the object types identified at this stage carrying through the system analysis, design, and ultimately into the program code. The same business model should be relevant to many systems.

13.4.1.2   System Context

This involves understanding the role the system we wish to build will play in the context of the business: the interactions it will have with other objects in that world. Our system is part of a larger design, whether of software or hardware components or people, that may or may not have been explicitly described elsewhere. The objective of this part is to capture that information.

13.4.1.3   System Specification

This is a precise description of what is required of our system. It should be documented independently of how the requirements may be achieved. Clearly it will be necessary to think ahead, and consider some implementation questions, in part because there's no point in specifying something that cannot be made and in part because the creative minds of the analysts inevitably speculate about how it will work. We've already discussed the difference between doing these steps in parallel and documenting them separately.

13.4.1.4   Component Models

In this study, we assume that there are several large components from which we wish to build. They may already be purchased or may exist from a previous piece of design.

We make specifications of each component; again, they may already exist, or we may build them from our understanding of the components. In dire cases, this means reverse-engineering models for these components, experimenting with them in testbeds. The process of formalizing the spec exposes the questions that need to be answered.

13.4.1.5   System Architecture: High-Level Design

Here, the components are connected to form a design that meets the system spec. It is also important to document a justification for believing that it does so properly. As a high-level design, this describes only the overall scheme of interactions: large-grained components and their collaborations as well as corresponding static dependencies needed between different development packages. The detailed coding will be left until coding.

In this case study we have not adopted any particular component architecture such as Cat One (see Section 10.8.1, Cat One: An Example Component Architecture). So our connectors have been limited to standard requests or responses between large-grained components rather than higher-level facilities such as events, properties, and workflow transfers.

13.4.1.6   System Detailed Design

Further work is required for those components that are used in the design but not yet implemented—not purchased or adapted from previous projects. Just as we had a specification of the whole system and broke it into successive pieces, so each component can be broken into subcomponents, which in turn are specified and implemented until we get down to units directly implementable in program code.

13.5 *Main Process Patterns*

The patterns in this section form the basis of a customizable process of developing software; they show how the techniques are also applied to engineering business processes. Customization of these patterns would result in different routes through the method. Many, but not all, of these patterns have been applied and tested in practice.

13.5.1 Development Context: Defining Routes

The first few patterns offer a breakdown of how to proceed along a route through the method, given different assumptions about your goals.

- *Pattern 13.1, Object Development from Scratch*, shows how to proceed assuming that you have no existing design.
- *Pattern 13.2, Reengineering*, assumes an existing design and shows how you should go about improving it.
- *Pattern 14.1, Business Process Improvement*, is about applying object technology to organizations other than software.
- *Pattern 16.6, Separate Middleware from Business Components*, offers one strategy for handling legacy systems as well as for insulating the project from certain technology changes.

Regardless of which route, or combination, is appropriate, most projects would benefit from carefully managed iterations (see Pattern 13.3, Short-Cycle Development) and from concurrent development work (see Pattern 13.4, Parallel Work).

13.5.2 Phases

Each of the development context patterns applies some combination of the following patterns, which deal in different phases and activities of the development process. The idea is that they form a kit of tools rather than a fixed procedure. To begin with, you apply them by following one of the development context patterns; with experience, you apply them as needed.

- Business or domain models
  - *Pattern 14.2, Make a Business Model*: Understand the terms your clients are using before anything else; capture business rules, behaviors, and constraints that are independent of software solutions.

- System or component specification
  - *Pattern 15.5, Make a Context Model with Use Cases*: Understand the collaborations with and around an object.
  - *Pattern 15.7, Construct a System Behavior Spec*: Treating your system as a single object, define the type of any implementation that would meet the requirements.
  - *Pattern 15.8, Specifying a System Action*: Specify an action with the help of snapshots.
  - *Pattern 15.9, Using State Charts in System Type Models*: Building state charts of specification types is a useful cross check for completeness and uncovers missing cases of actions and effects.
  - *Pattern 15.12, Avoid Miracles, Refine the Spec*: Go into more detail about actions and the corresponding attributes; alternatively, abstract away from details to a higher-level, more task-oriented model.

- Internal design: technical architecture
  - *Pattern 16.6, Separate Middleware from Business Components*: Keep separate your legacy systems, business models (newly built or wrapped around legacy systems), and infrastructure middleware elements.
  - *Pattern 16.7, Implement Technical Architecture*: Define major technical components of your design as an architectural collaboration. These components might be GUI, business logic, persistence (database or file system), communications, and other middleware elements.

- Internal design: application architecture and detailed design
  - *Pattern 16.8, Basic Design*: Take each system action and distribute responsibilities between collaborating internal components. For small systems, begin by assuming that there is a direct implementation for every specification type of the system type model. For larger systems, use intermediate levels of collaborating large-grained components.
  - *Pattern 16.10, Collaborations and Responsibilities*: Document and minimize coupling by designing responsibilities and collaborators; compose patterns of collaborations to define the design.
  - *Pattern 16.11, Link and Attribute Ownership*: Decide and document the directionality of links and the visibility of attributes.
  - *Pattern 16.12, Object Locality and Link Implementation*: Locality of an object— where it resides and executes—can be decided independently of basic design, employing appropriate patterns to implement links and messages crossing locality boundaries. This applies across boundaries of hosts, processes, applications, and media.
  - *Pattern 16.13, Optimization*: Apply localized refinements to make the project run faster.

- Implement, test, deploy

    The line between design and implementation/test is a fine one; unfortunately, some people believe that textual descriptions, including code in C++ or Java, represent implementation and that diagrams represent design. Others use terms such as *diagrams* versus *specifications*. But that is simply a matter of notation; you can draw diagrams to assemble components and generate executable code. The Catalysis distinction between interface specification as a type—refined to an internal design as a collaboration—covers implementation in any form, whether expressed as diagrams or text.

    A Java class chooses its internal data members that collaborate to implement a Java interface; similarly, a traditional program with a set of global variables referring to its collaborating top-level objects implements a specification of the entire process as a type.

    Moreover, as discussed in Section 13.1.2, Specify, Document, Implement, and Test: Business to Code, activities to build, install, and deploy a system are consistently thought of as implementation steps at different levels: implementation of internal design, system spec, and the to-be business model.

Pattern 13.1   Object Development from Scratch

This pattern describes how to build a design starting from scratch. This route is suitable when you're designing a computer system or subsystem with no existing installation, no available major components to reuse, and no existing model of the business.

Considerations

Is there really no legacy? Consider people who have worked on an earlier system, or existing implementations that could perhaps be componentized and reused to reduce the development effort (see Pattern 10.5, Using Legacy or Third-Party Components). What are the business changes that accompany deployment? Use Pattern 13.2, Reengineering, to plan the transition and successive deployments.

Strategy

Apply Pattern 14.2, Make a Business Model, and Pattern 15.13, Interpreting Models for Clients, to the following series of phases.

• *Pattern 14.2, Make a Business Model*: Describe your understanding of the users' concepts and concerns and the vocabulary in which they express them. This activity is not limited to any single set of requirements and can serve as the basis for more than one development project.

• *Pattern 15.5, Make a Context Model with Use Cases*: Focus on the collaborations between your proposed system and other objects—people, machines, other software systems—with which it will interact. Also include relevant collaborations between them not involving your system, improving your understanding of what's going on around it.

• *Pattern 15.7, Construct a System Behavior Spec*: Treating your system as a single object, create a type specification for any system that would meet the requirements. Actions (and hence the type model) should be as abstract as possible at first cut—not individual keystrokes!

• *Pattern 15.12, Avoid Miracles, Refine the Spec*: Define more-detailed actions and attributes as a refinement.

• *Pattern 16.7, Implement Technical Architecture*: Define and implement major components of design as a collaboration. Typically, these might be GUI, client, business logic, persistence (database or file system), and communications.

• *Pattern 16.8, Basic Design*: Take each system action and distribute responsibilities among collaborating internal components. Begin by assuming that there is a class for every type of the system type spec. For larger systems, design an intermediate level of large-grained collaborating components.

- *Pattern 16.11, Link and Attribute Ownership*: Extract common components and recast the design in terms of the components.

- *Pattern 16.12, Object Locality and Link Implementation*: Decide how the basic design is split among machines, applications, and hosts.

- *Pattern 16.13, Optimization*: Perform localized refinements for performance.

An object-oriented design according to these principles can be fully traceable from business requirements through to code, whether or not the correspondence is direct.

Pattern 13.2 Reengineering

In this pattern you make an OO system using both the knowledge derivable from legacy code and the legacy code itself.

Intent

The idea is to gain the benefits of OO, but without throwing away old code. You want to be able to make systems that remain flexible as your organization and its structure and working methods change. You want to build many applications from a set of basic components. These are features of object-oriented designs.

You have a great deal of code written in an older tradition—for example, a relational database and its driving software. You cannot afford to hold everything while you rewrite it all.

For example, one of the authors worked a while ago with a GIS system that had been conceived 10 years earlier and written in Fortran. It was successful, so over the decade many features were added by popular demand. As the system gradually lost its original coherence, it came to the point that you couldn't tweak one end without the other falling over. Most of the patch-makers weren't around during the original development, so they understood only as much as they needed to. Many local changes were made that should ideally have been done at a more global level, and even from the outside it looked like a bit of a mess. It was decided to reimplement the system gradually as an OO design so as to give it another lease on life. However, there was no way for the organization to stop for a couple of years and rewrite it all: The company depended on income from maintenance contracts, and that meant providing customers with regular new features. How should it proceed?

In another case, a bank was writing an inquiry and loan application processing system. We wanted to get the benefit of object technology so that we could easily fashion variants of the system for different banks. But there was no point in building it entirely from scratch: The conventional databases were already in place, although each bank had a different one. How could we integrate the new technology with the old?

Considerations

Are you going to reuse the old code; or only the old design ideas; or only the old business model? In general, each of these elements can be reused using appropriate techniques. In each case, it is essential to capture the existing concepts first (using the modeling notation in earlier chapters) and, separately, to document where you'd like to be.

Are you going to wrap old code and gradually rework it, or leave it wrapped and rework only when essential, doing redesign in the wrapping layer?

Are you going to reengineer the business process of which the software system forms a part? (See Pattern 14.1, Business Process Improvement.)

Strategy

Make As-Is and To-Be Models. This can be done at several levels: business, system requirements, and system design.[4] The as-is model keeps fairly strictly to what exists at the present. (Because of ad-hoc changes over the years, it may be horrible. You're allowed some omissions when early reworking is an obvious necessity.) The to-be model is your vision of the ideal future. In practice, you should also make an intermediate near-term objective. It is often useful to abstract from the as-is model a truly "essential" model of what must be done; the as-is was the previous refinement of this model, and the to-be will be an alternative, improved refinement (see Figure 13.6).

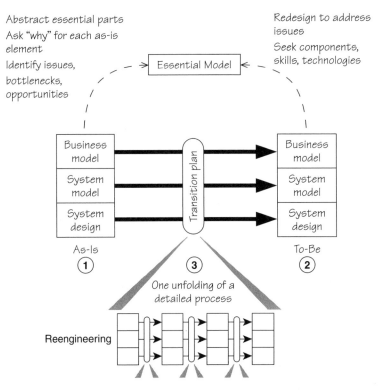

Figure 13.6   Reengineering and transition plan.

---

4. This strategy was formulated by the methods groups at TI-Software, London.

Plan the transition from as-is to to-be via intermediate steps, perhaps based on your chosen path or process. Be more specific in planning for the earlier transitions, because subsequent ones will inevitably be replanned as you approach them (see Pattern 13.3, Short-Cycle Development).

As-Is informs To-Be. The as-is model may be the best starting point for the to-be model. The original architects of the old system probably had a clear model, which has been obscured by numerous fixes and add-ons through the years, typically by younger folk who haven't entirely cottoned to the beauty of the original conception. (You can often find some of the old-timers still hanging around: They get excited about building these models, because they see it as a great opportunity to clear out all the indignities their brainchild has suffered over the years. Be sure not to leave them out of the activity, but don't be surprised if they come to blows with one another about the precise details of the original big idea.)

On the other hand, do not take legacy terminology as Gospel truth; always seek a more essential description if the terms used seem contrived or artificial. Be particularly suspicious of legacy terms that are purely artifacts of an ingrained way of doing things—for example, complex "codes" that are used to label business objects with compound meanings.

Abstract and Re-refine. This is an important technique for reengineering (see Chapter 6, Abstraction, Refinement, and Testing). Abstract the as-is model to form a more general statement of requirements. For example, the sequence of actions <customer inquiry; issue loan application; receive application; approve application> can be abstracted to the single action make loan. Then consider whether you can redesign the abstraction a better way (but don't do so just because you can!). For example, you might redesign the abstraction to <customer-inquiry(details); approve application>, eliminating the steps to transfer an application.

Apply Abstraction and Re-refine to Each Development Layer. Do this for the business model, the system context model, and the abstract and detailed layers of design, as listed in Section 13.5, Main Process Patterns. Each of the three principal layers can be approached differently.

Reengineering Business Model and System Requirements. These can often be reengineered directly toward the ideal. There isn't always so much complexity in the processes of human interaction that they can't be altered, although you should proceed with caution through people's sensitivities (see Pattern 14.1, Business Process Improvement).

Reengineering System Designs. You can apply small changes by the usual patching process. But radical changes require bigger solutions, and some systems should be explicitly designed to allow upgrades while they're running. Furthermore, the prospect of continuing change demands that business logic be decoupled from the underlying system. These considerations lead to the three-layer model, or middleware (see Pattern 16.6, Separate Middleware from Business Components).

An alternative is to consider gradually carving out and redeveloping the software. In many cases, realistically, such a process would not end within the life of the software and could ultimately represent much wasted effort. Instead, it is better to develop new components in OO terms, leaving the old stuff cleanly wrapped.

Pattern 13.3   Short-Cycle Development

In this pattern, you set specific short-term targets and more-general longer-term ones, and you use early feedback through scoped and managed short development cycles. This pattern is also known as "one step at a time," "don't chew off too much in one go," "walk before you run," the "spiral model," and "proceed with caution."

Intent

In any project in which the outcome of one phase will affect the plan for what follows, we need a systematic and realistic approach to planning by successive approximation, when the outcome and success of each piece of work is known only when complete. This does not apply (apart from exceptional circumstances) to building a house or baking bread, when the requirements, inputs, and outcomes of all steps are fully understood in advance. It does apply to all design projects, whether software or hardware, to all changes of organization, such as adopting new design methods, and to all research and development.

Considerations

It is unrealistic to write a linear plan for a research project; if you knew how each stage would go and what it would lead to, it wouldn't be research. The same holds for any intellectual work. But we need some way of planning.

Reaching a project goal is a bit like leaping from one spot to another. If you try to do it all in one leap, you must aim carefully to begin with, because it's difficult to change course in midflight. Object technology is good at handling changes and so enables us to do the job as a series of shorter jumps. There's less investment risked in each one, and because we can correct our direction at each step, we're surer of reaching the goal in a predictable and controlled fashion.

Customers like short cycles because they see results early and can take part in the development early. They don't like hearing nothing for a year and then getting a system that doesn't do what they want.

Developers like short cycles because it gives them a periodic feeling of achievement.

Project managers like short cycles because they feel they're in some sort of control as long as it does not degenerate into a euphemism for undirected hacking. They also like the Böhm's spiral model because it gives a respectable name and rationale to the fact that they don't know exactly what will be happening in week 42. That was always the case anyway, but it could feel a little uncomfortable in front of senior management.

Strategy

Plan in short cycles, each of which ends with the assessment of a deliverable that is measurable in terms of the ultimate goal, which then feeds into the planning of the next few cycles. Expect only an approximate idea of the cycles ahead of time.

Begin with cycles that use small investments to tackle issues that represent high project risk. Typically, these risks fall into two categories: requirements and technical architecture. More resources can be fed into successive cycles as confidence is gained. The idea is fractal: a big project's single cycle can be composed of several smaller cycles of subprojects.

Let cycles overlap and proceed in parallel (see Pattern 13.4, Parallel Work).

Each cycle consists of plan, execute, and evaluate phases. Set goals, level of investment, and acceptable risks; plan and decide what will be evaluated and how it will affect future cycles; determine fallbacks; execute the plan; evaluate the outcome. For software development cycles this often translates into plan, specify, design and implement, and evaluate.

Typical cycles in software development might include feasibility study, GUI mock-up, requirements analysis and prototype, single-user, single-machine vertical incremental slices, tightening of relations between documentation layers, distribution across hosts, and multiuser deployment. A typical 10-person software development might use cycles ranging from two to six weeks.

Make your package structure reflect the separations needed across iterations so that different work products can be managed and developed separately.

User-visible cycles should deliver meaningful functionality to users. Plan deliverables for these cycles in terms of abstract business actions (use cases) for the users based on their prioritization and on dependencies between these actions that are uncovered by system specification. For each use case delivered, track all refining system actions and corresponding internal component interactions, and schedule cycles accordingly. For any design element (action, effect, attribute, invariant), schedule its development based on the earliest scheduled use case that uses it.

Other cycles can be horizontal: one that does not deliver new user-visible functionality but instead carries a minimal use case through increasingly deep layers of the application and infrastructure components, exercising all communication channels. An example is a single user interaction carried from the user interface through the business object layer via an object request broker (ORB) to the applicable databases and back.

Early user cycles need not build on the technical architecture; instead, treat them as prototypes that will yield early feedback from users. These cycles—vertical slices of user-visible functionality—are focused on correct visible functional behavior at the user interfaces. They might be implemented purely as a single-machine, single-process prototype.

Adoption of new methods within a company might have cycles that begin with a small demonstration by a few people. Their experience feeds into something bigger, training for more people, selection of tools, and so on. With careful planning, the new methods may be taken on by a large project or complete division over a period of many months to years. (Trying to do it overnight doesn't work!)

Pattern 13.4   Parallel Work

Structure your packages to enable units of work to be done in parallel without excessive risk of rework. Do this early in the project, and sustain it throughout the project.

Intent

A project development team completes a multitude of tasks over the project lifetime. Some tasks are heavily dependent on others and should be serialized, perhaps using Pattern 13.3, Short-Cycle Development; others are largely independent and should proceed in parallel because downstream work is dependent on them.

Considerations

Some tasks are best done by small groups. For example, clarifying requirements and defining a precise, even if high-level, system specification is an activity best done with a few key people. Similarly, coming up with an initial definition of system architecture, and subsequently maintaining and evolving this architecture, is best done by a small team.

On the other hand, projects are often staffed early. Keeping the larger team constructively involved throughout the project, while minimizing rework, is good for the project schedule as well as team morale.

Strategy

As early as possible, define the system context and all known constraints on the system, its initial architecture, and internal components. Examine interfaces to external systems. There is often significant work in realizing the connections to those systems, whether it involves communications, hardware interfaces, database requests, and so on. This work can be started early.

Across the entire specify-implement-test cycle (Figure 13.3), there are several mostly independent tasks that can be run in parallel, ranging from setting up development tools and environment, to writing installation programs, to defining process and QA standards.

Partition system specification into subject areas. Define early the key type model attributes or effects that one subject area depends on; another subject area can specify the detailed constraints on those attributes or effects. Always have a mechanism (such as attributes or effects) that relates subject areas to one another.

Start work on the technical architecture early. This may involve acquiring and learning third-party packages. Build architectural prototypes based on a test slice of the system spec, and evaluate the architecture against nonfunctional requirements—throughput, scalability, data volumes, response time, and so on—by using architectural simulation tools or by writing drivers to load the prototype. Understand the capabilities of middleware packages; databases and transaction servers often offer services that can reduce the development work on the main application logic.

If there are external components—software or hardware—that define objects you need to use, spin off a task to evaluate whether to use these objects exactly as defined or whether to build a layer that offers a model closer and more natural to the one you would like to use internally in your development. If a core component defines widely shared and widely used objects, you may need to design a generic architectural scheme for extensible object data and behaviors.

Start user-interface prototyping when the high-level system actions and type model have been identified. Focus on a consistent UI metaphor, and cross check the user interfaces against the type model as the latter becomes better defined.

Structure packages to consistently separate interfaces from implementations, and aim for early initial definition of interfaces. Also, designate team roles that cut across parallel activities, watching for issues or overlaps that should be addressed separately.

Chapter 14   How to Build a Business Model

This chapter and the next two chapters illustrate the use of Catalysis on a sample problem and discuss the how-to of applying Catalysis. This chapter focuses on building a business model; this is usually the model of a problem domain or business and not of a software "business object" layer sitting behind a user interface. The software objects in the subsequent chapters are based on the business objects, and a naming scheme is used to associate them.

We start with a set of patterns that describe the process of building a business model and then illustrate their use in the case study.

14.1 *Business Modeling Process Patterns*

This section outlines the major steps in building a business process model.

Pattern 13.2, Reengineering, describes reengineering activities in general and discusses building as-is and to-be models to guide that effort.

Pattern 14.1, Business Process Improvement, discusses specifics that apply to business process modeling.

Pattern 14.2, Make a Business Model, covers how to go about constructing a useful business model.

Pattern 16.6, Separate Middleware from Business Components, discusses a specific and common concern in business modeling: designing and extending heterogenous and federated software components so that they directly track the business independently of changes in technology.

Pattern 14.13, Action Reification, introduces a common modeling pattern. When a use case is refined into a sequence of finer-grained actions, it is useful to model the abstract use case in progress as a model type in the detailed level, going through a life cycle as the detailed actions take place.

Whereas this section's patterns are about organizing the process of business modeling, Section 14.2, Modeling Patterns, covers some of the most essential patterns that are useful in the actual construction of a business model.

Section 14.3 shows how some of these patterns have been applied to the case study of a video rental business at an abstract level. Section 14.4 details this model using action refinement, showing the finer-grained actions involved in the business.

Pattern 14.1 Business Process Improvement

In this pattern, you abstract and re-refine to get an improvement in business organization.

Intent

The intent is to improve the organization of a business, a process not necessarily involving software or computing machinery. In the process, we can review roles and processes in the organization and can also require software systems development.

Considerations

A business improvement effort may be triggered by the installation or upgrade of a software system, a perceived quality problem in business performance, or the hiring of a new senior executive. Although the explicit request may be simply to work on a software project, the analyst's scope often expands to include business improvement. This is part of what the system context diagram (see Pattern 15.5, Make a Context Model with Use Cases) is about—the computer system as one element in the design of a business process.

Companies, departments, people—and hardware and software systems—can all be thought of as interacting objects; so can the materials and information in which they deal. Designing the way in which a company or department performs its functions—whether making loans, manufacturing light bulbs, or producing films—is principally a matter of dividing the responsibilities among differentiated role players. It also involves defining the flow of activities and the interfaces and protocols through which they collaborate to fulfill the responsibilities of the organization as a whole (which is one role player in a larger world).

This activity is similar to the problem of object-oriented design, and the same notation and techniques can be applied. (Indeed, an effective help in deciding the distribution of responsibilities among software objects is to pretend that they are people, departments, and so on, although the analogy can be carried too far!) This similarity should not surprise us, because the big idea of OO programming is that the software simulates the business.

Strategy

Approach this problem as a particular case of Pattern 13.2, Reengineering.

Make a business model (see Pattern 14.2, Make a Business Model), including associations and use cases, in which you reflect the existing process. This example is merely a sketch, less formal and less comprehensive than would be useful.

For any as-is element, ask, "Why is it so?" Abstract the collaborations to single use cases. Abstract groups to single objects (for example, individual person roles to departments). Specify abstract use cases with postconditions rather than sequences.

It may be useful to reiterate this to several levels of abstraction. Each abstraction generally represents a goal or goals of a part of the process or organization.

Refine the abstract model to a different design. Create the new design and document it as a refinement of the abstraction (see Chapter 6, Abstraction, Refinement, and Testing).

Evaluate the result in relation to quality aspects, including those not readily expressed as postconditions, such as error rate, cycle time, and costs. In the end, this technique can only suggest alternatives. Human, political, and many other constraints will influence the decision.

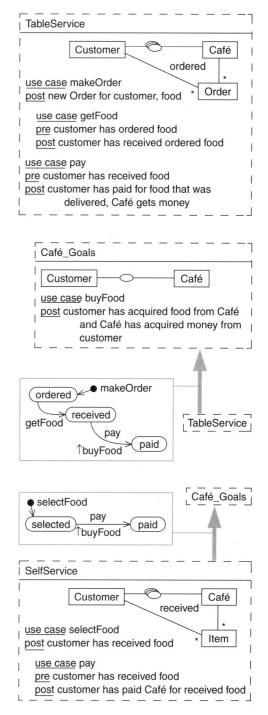

Consider how to plan the changes so as to cause minimal upheaval and at minimal risk (see Pattern 13.2, Reengineering).

Benefit

As always, there are many benefits to the act of formalizing your understanding of the situation in a well-defined notation, even at the business level.[1]

- It exposes gaps and inconsistencies and prompts questions you might never otherwise have thought to ask.
- It facilitates clear discussion and mutual understanding among those concerned.
- It provides an unambiguous method of encoding your current understanding even if your clients don't understand it directly (see Pattern 15.13, Interpreting Models for Clients).

The abstract and re-refine technique helps ensure that overall goals of the organization are still met insofar as they can be expressed in a functional notation.

---

1. Experience suggests the benefit might be even greater here, where we are conditioned to accept outrageously loose terminology.

Pattern 14.2   Make a Business Model

This pattern describes how to build a type and/or collaboration model that expresses your understanding of some part of the world, making it the final description of your understanding of your client's terminology.

Intent

The intent is to understand clearly the terms your clients are using before anything else and to ensure that they understand the terms in the same way that you do.

You can build a business model as a prelude to

- Pattern 14.1, Business Process Improvement
- System development, Pattern 13.1, Object Development from Scratch

Because a business model is not oriented to any single design, it can serve as the basis for many designs and structures within the business.

Considerations

The term *business* covers whatever concepts are of primary relevance to your clients and is not necessarily business in the sense of a commercial enterprise that makes money. If you're being asked to design a graphical editor, your business is about documents and the shapes thereon. Cursors, windows, handles, and current selections are possible parts of the mechanics of editing, but clients don't care about these mechanics except as an aid to produce their artwork. If you're designing a multiplexor in a telecommunications system, your users are the designers of the other switching components, and the business model will be about things such as packets and addresses. If you are redesigning the ordering procedures of a company, the business model is about orders, suppliers, people's roles, and so on.

There can be many views of a business. The concerns of the marketing director may overlap those of the personnel manager. Even when they share some concepts, one may have a more complex view of them than the other. See Chapter 6, Abstraction, Refinement, and Testing.

You may have frameworks available from which this model can be composed.

Strategy

You should end up with a model showing the types of main interest. They should have static associations and attributes, and they should have action links showing how they interact. The model consists of diagrams, invariants, and a dictionary (see Chapter 5, Effective Documentation). You should be able to describe any significant business event or activity entirely in terms of the model.

In making a business model, you will draw on a number of sources.

• *Existing procedures, standards documents, software, and user manuals*: When these exist, they should be consulted. But keep in mind that procedures as written often do not reflect the actual operations. User manuals for existing systems are a rich source of information. They act as a key input to reverse-engineering an abstract model of a system and therefore of a business.

• *Observation and interviews*: These include actual observation of procedures at work combined with interviews with the persons involved. Techniques such as CRC cards can be effective for eliciting information on as-is processes.

• *Existing relational or entity-relational (E-R) models*: These provide a quick start on the terminology and some of the candidate object types in the business. However, because of the mores or normalization and the exclusive focus on stored data, these models can often be considerably simplified to build a type model. Where used, triggers and stored procedures often encode many business rules.

• *Existing batch-mode systems*: Often, late-night COBOL batch jobs encode critical sets of business rules. Many of these rules can be captured as time-dependent static invariants on the type model (the batch job cuts in to make sure that no objects will be in violation of these invariants, come sunrise) or as effect invariants, of the form "Whenever this thing has changed, that other thing must be triggered."

• *Feedback from prototypes, scenarios, and models*: As always, any "live" media provides valuable feedback and validation of models being built. For example, storyboards, prototypes of UI screens, CRC-card-based scenarios, and model walkthroughs can all be used.

There are useful rules of thumb for finding objects, attributes, and actions. Looking through existing documents (business requirements, user manuals, and so on), map nouns to object types, verbs to actions, static relationships to associations, rules to static and dynamic invariants, and variations to subtypes or other refinements.

Focus on one type at a time and consider the interactions its members have with other objects. Draw use-case ellipses linked to participating objects. Some actions may have several participants of the same or different types. What roles are the participants playing within this collaboration? What information do they exchange?

What is the net result of an action? For example:

> *For an airplane: control*—Pilot; *check position*—GPS, GroundStation; *lift*—Atmosphere.

Focus on one type at a time and ask yourself, At any one moment, what information would we want to record about this type of object? Write this information as attributes and associations sourced at this type. For each one, ask what the type of that information is, giving the target type. Don't confuse static information

with actions; actions abstract interactions, whereas attributes represent information known before and/or after the actions. For example:

> For an airplane: pilot, copilot: both of type Pilot; airspeed, groundspeed: Speed; scheduled-to-
> land-at: Airport; previous 100 destinations: set of Airports; pilot's-spouse's-favorite-shoe-color:
> Color.

Use snapshots to verify that all the information of interest can be represented
by the static associations.

Determine a consistent level of abstraction in relation to actions: Are you going
to worry about individual keystrokes or talk only about broad transactions? The
highest-level action that could be useful should accomplish a business task or
objective or should abstract a group of such actions. The lowest-level action that
could be useful should constitute an indivisible interaction; if the interaction fails
to complete successfully or otherwise is aborted, there should be no effect that
would be useful at the business level.

Some business models focus on the types that a single client can manipulate,
such as the Drawing example here. In this case, all the actions are shown localized
in the Drawing and its constituents. Other models must be more concerned with
interactions between objects, such as the Library example. Figure 14.1 illustrates
both models.

The resulting business model acts as the central glossary of terms for all projects
associated with it: business engineering, software requirements, and so on.

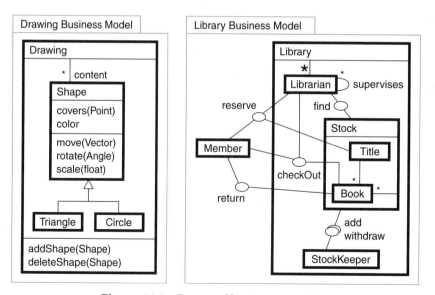

Figure 14.1   Range of business models.

Pattern 14.3   Represent Business Vocabulary and Rules

The purpose of the model is to represent both the terms used in the business and the rules and procedures it follows. Reduce business rules to invariants, generalized effect invariants, action specs, and timing constraints.

Intent

The intent is to reduce misunderstandings between colleagues about the terms and parameters of the business. Making some of these business rules explicit and precise aids identification of software requirements (which parts of the rules are dealt with by which component, which by users), type models (the models provide the vocabulary that helps specify the rules), traceability from software to business, and enterprise-level knowledge management (explicit representation of business knowledge and rules).

Strategy

Seek business rules in the current actual business process, the process as documented, and rules encoded in existing software systems (from user manuals, database triggers, and batch mainframe programs; see Chapter 17, How to Reverse-Engineer Types). Restate these business rules in terms of the following (in descending order of preference):

- Static invariants over the model
- Effect invariants that must apply to every action
- Timing constraints ("This must be done within . . .")
- Action specifications, including time-triggered actions

If an informal rule cannot be formalized in this way or starts to look complicated, you should suspect that the static model is inadequate and add new convenience attributes to make it simpler. Adding new named effects can also simplify things.

Wherever business rules are susceptible to change, exploit packages to separate them out. Remember that, in Catalysis, you can always say more about a type, action, and so on in another package; separating certain rules makes versioning and configuration management easier.

Pattern 14.4   Involve Business Experts

The idea here is to keep the end users involved in the business model.

Intent

The business model should be owned by the people who run the business. (The IS department is there only to coordinate writing it down.)

Strategy

Create the first draft of the model by interviewing experts and by observing what they do. Goals, achievements, tasks, jobs, and interactions of any kind should be sketched as actions; nouns are sketched as types.

For each action that appears on your sketch, ask, "Who's involved in this action? Whom does it affect? Looking at different specific occurrences of it, what could be different from one occasion to another?" These questions yield the participants and parameters. Don't forget to distinguish objects from types and parameters from parameter types.

For each type that appears on your sketch, ask, "What can be known about this? (Does it have a physical manifestation? What do you record about it? What creates it? What alters its state?" Or if it is an active object (a person or machine), "Whom does it interact with? What tasks does it accomplish?" These questions yield attributes and associations of the type as well as actions it participates in.

For each action, ask, "What steps are taken to accomplish this?" For each type, ask, "What constituent parts can it have?" These questions yield action and object refinements (see Chapter 6, Abstraction, Refinement, and Testing).

For each type, ask, "What states does it go through (or stages of development, phases, or modes)?" Draw state charts and check state transition matrixes (see Section 3.9.7, Ancillary Tables). The transitions yield more actions.

Remember to include abstract concepts (such as "Problem" or "Symptom") as well as concrete things (such as "Fault Report") and relate them together.

Ask, "What rules govern this action/state/relationship between types?" This will yield invariants.

With your analyst colleagues (who have perhaps been interviewing other experts concurrently) work out how to make the picture cohere. Formalize action specifications, define states in terms of attributes, make conjectures, and raise questions. Then go back to the experts with questions. (Don't be afraid to do so—people love explaining their jobs!)

After a reasonable (although still imperfect) model is drafted, hold workshops for the experts to review it. Take these in stages: static model first; then actions;

then invariants and use case specs. Use snapshots to communicate the intent of the model.

Post parts of the model around the walls in a large room. Begin with a general presentation about types, associations, and actions so that your colleagues can read the diagrams. Then have everyone walk around the room—don't permit sitting—congregating around the subject areas they are most interested in. Have one of the analysis team on hand to walk people through the details. Also have scribes on hand to note all the comments.

Cycle until everyone more or less (although not entirely) reaches agreement.

Pattern 14.5   Creating a Common Business Model

Rather than build a business model first, you create a common model from several components in the business and from the definitions of the interfaces.

Intent

The intent is to deliver a business model, given that you have a variety of components, each with its own model. The components have been developed separately. You need to connect them, whether through a live interface, by enabling files to be written by one and read by another, or with a manual procedure.

Considerations

This problem is found wherever different software deals in the same area: Most of us have encountered the problems of translating from Word to or from some other documentation tool. The writers of the import, export, and translation modules must begin by building a model of the document structure.

It is also a common problem in large organizations; each department has bought its own software, and the IS department has the task of making them talk together more coherently. (See Section 10.11, Heterogenous Components.) The problem is particularly acute when two enterprises merge and they have two different systems talking different languages.

The most high-profile cases involve communication across the boundaries of organizations: from banks to the trade exchanges; from one phone company to another; or between airlines and ticket vendors.

The important thing is that we are not dealing with a model of any of the programs that communicate. Instead, at issue is a model of what they are talking to each other about, whether documents, financial transactions, aircraft positions, or talking pictures.

Strategy

First, agree with whomever is in charge of the various components that you are going to create a common standard. Try to ensure that the most powerful player doesn't just go ahead and do things his or her own way.

Second, accept that there will never be a standard model that everyone works to: There will always be local variants and extras. Adapters will be used to translate from one to another. Therefore, timebox the generation of the common model.

Now we come to the technical part. Consider the models of each of the components and write a common model of which all of them can be seen as refinements. Write abstraction functions (see Section 6.1.4, Model Abstraction) to demonstrate this, mapping each component model to your new model.

There will be interesting features within some of the components' models that not all of them can deal with. Not all televisions can deal with color signals; not all fax machines understand Group III compression; not all word processors understand tables; not all of the software components running a library will understand the concept of the acquisition date of a book even though most of them will understand its title.

Add to your common model these additional features (perhaps in different packages). Work out whether and how each component will deal with the additional information when it gets it and can't deal with it or doesn't get it when it expects it.

Pattern 14.6   Choose a Level of Abstraction

This pattern discusses the need to reach agreement with your colleagues concerning how much detail you're dealing with at each stage.

Intent

We have seen that it is possible to document objects and actions at any level of detail or abstraction. This is a powerful tool, but two problems commonly arise.

- It is very difficult for programmers (especially good ones) to keep away from the detail and implementation.
- Misunderstanding about the level of detail you're working at is a common source of arguments.

Strategy

Use the abstraction and refinement techniques (see Chapter 6, Abstraction, Refinement, and Testing) to explore the levels that are more abstract and more detailed than you have. For example, after you have identified some actions, ask yourself, "What more-abstract action or object are these part of?" And "What more-detailed actions or objects would form part of this?"

Make sure that for each action at any level, you at least sketch out the effects. Do this with sufficient precision to be aware of which types in the model are necessary to describe the effects.

Each layer of abstraction will have a coherent set of actions that tell the full story at that level of detail and will have a static model that provides the vocabulary in which that story is told. Different layers will have different sets of actions and static models. Programmers can write test code before writing implementations.

This process of exploration tends to provide insights leading to a more coherent model.

Begin by sketching the various layers. Decide in advance how much time you will spend in this exploration—anything from half an hour to one day, depending on the size of the model. By the end of it, you should be able to make a more informed choice about what level to focus on and elaborate completely.

14.2 *Modeling Patterns*

The preceding patterns have been about planning the development process. The next few patterns are more in the style of conventional analysis and design relating to the construction of a business model.

There are many good sources for patterns appropriate to this modeling. Our main concern here is to point out the patterns that we see as most essential. The Catalysis frameworks repository will eventually hold such model frameworks, and a project team can always define new model frameworks.

Pattern 14.7 The Type Model Is a Glossary

In this pattern, we ensure that every term used within the field appears in the model.

Intent

The intent is to ensure that the type model fully represents the business domain.

Considerations

The purpose of the business model is to represent all the vocabulary that is used by the people in the business. It can augment or form a more structured variant of the company or project glossary. Its advantage over the plain glossary or dictionary of terms is that it can summarize complex relationships readily.

On the other hand, in an alphabetical dictionary it is easier to look up the terms. But this loses the context and motivation for those definitions.

Strategy

Model the business by drawing the glossary explanations in pictures. Ensure that every concept written in documents that describe the business, or uttered by experts in the business, is represented somewhere. Generally, nouns map to object types, and verbs map to actions.

Remember that you are modeling the business, and not writing a database schema or program or modeling purely physical relationships. The associations are attributes drawn in pictures and not lines of communication or physical connections. (The latter would normally be drawn as an action.)

Feel free to include redundant terms: if people talk about it, include it. Write it as an invariant and describe how it relates to the other terms. An example is shown in Figure 14.2.

A level of detail you would have to optimize in an implementation is OK in a business model. For example, some pages in a library book may be torn. In an implementation, a list of integers, representing damaged page numbers, could be

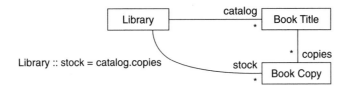

Figure 14.2 Business model with convenient terms and invariants.

optionally attached to each book copy; but to model the world more directly, let's model a book as a list of pages and give every page a Boolean torn attribute.

Although the static type model tells what snapshots could be drawn at any one moment, a snapshot may contain plans for the future (schedules and timetables) as well as historical data (audit trails). So a list of past loans would be a valid attribute of a book.

Complement the pictures with explanatory prose. Attach to every type and action a glossary-style description of what it is. Have your tool dump an alphabetical list of these descriptions.

Divide the model into smallish type diagrams and write a narrative description of the business in which these diagrams are embedded. Use a modeling tool that supports embedding within narrative. (See Chapter 5, Effective Documentation.)

Pattern 14.8   Separation of Concepts: Normalization

Starting with a draft model, you enhance it by considering a number of rules.

Intent

Analysts who have experience with entity-relational modeling sometimes ask whether constructing a static object-oriented model is any different. Much is the same, and some aspects are different.

- In business and requirements modeling, the objective is not to design a database. Therefore, we do not need to be so strict about normalization, and we need not distinguish attributes from associations.
- Redundant links and associations are OK, if defined with invariants.
- Object models have sub- and supertypes.
- Object models include actions, whether joint or local to an object type. Sometimes the only distinction between one type of object and another is how it behaves (that is, how the effects of actions depend on it). An entity-relational model would not make these distinctions.
- In an entity model, each type should have a key: a set of attributes that together define the object's identity and distinguish one object from another. In an object model, every instance has an implicit identity: two objects may have all the same attribute values and yet still be different objects.

    Nevertheless, we can use some of the techniques from E-R modeling to improve a model.

Strategy

Look for the following triggers to re-factor your model.

- For a type having many associations and attributes, consider whether it should be split into several associated types (see Figure 14.3).

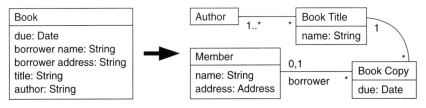

Figure 14.3   Splitting types.

- For any association, but particularly many-many associations, consider modeling it as a separate type (see Figure 14.4).

Book Copy :: borrower = loan.member

Figure 14.4   Reifying associations.

- For object identifiers, names, keys, tags, and similar attributes, use associations.

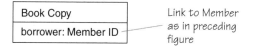

Pattern 14.9   Items and Descriptors

This pattern distinguishes things from descriptions of things.

Intent

When someone says, "I wrote a book" and someone else says, "I bought a book," do they mean the same thing by *book*? If the latter speaker is a publisher, then maybe; but when most people buy a book, they are buying one copy.

In a Library control system, we would have to distinguish individual Copies of books from the book Title. When Members borrow a book, they borrow a specific Copy; if they reserve a book, they're actually reserving a Title and don't usually care which copy they get. There are many Copies for one Title. Titles have attributes such as author and the actual title in the sense of a name (oops—another potential confusion here).

We often find the same potential confusion. A manufacturer's marketing people will discuss the launch of a new car; the customer will buy a car: But one means a model or product line, and the other means a specific instance of it. On the restaurant's menu, we see a variety of meals, with descriptions and prices; the meal a customer eats is not a description or a price but rather a physical item that conforms to the description. The flight you took the other day is one occurrence of the flight on the timetable.

The item/descriptor distinction is exactly the same as instance/class. (We use different words to avoid any additional confusion between the modeling domain and the software.) Indeed, in some programming languages (such as Smalltalk), classes are represented by objects, and each instance has an implicit link to its class. The class objects are themselves instances of a Class class, and new ones with new attributes can be created at runtime. This property of the language is known as *reflection*.

Strategy

In the most straightforward cases of items and descriptors, reflexive techniques are not necessary. The attributes of interest are the same for every book Copy in the library: who is borrowing it, what its Title is. Once we have spotted the distinction, there is no further complication.

A more difficult situation arises when we need to model a system in which the users may decide, while the system is running, that they need essentially new classes of items, with new attributes, business rules, and actions.

Few systems genuinely allow end users to make arbitrary extensions; those that allow it must provide a programming or scripting language of some sort.

Normally there is some restriction; all the additions fit within a framework. An example is a computer aided design (CAD) system, in which new kinds of mechanical parts can be added and the users can write operations that extend the code. Another example is a workflow system, in which users can define new kinds of work objects and their flows through the system.

In these cases, a framework can be defined (see Chapter 9, Model Frameworks and Template Packages) that imposes global constraints. The scripting language can be defined separately.

Pattern 14.10   Generalize and Specialize

Subtyping and model frameworks are used to simplify and generalize the model.

Intent

The intent is to make the model applicable to a wider range of cases and to provide insights to broaden the scope of the business or make it easier to understand.

Considerations

A supertype describes what is common to a family of types. A new variant can be created by defining what is different in the new type (see Chapter 3).

A model framework describes a family of groups of types. A collaborating group of types can be created by parameterizing the template. (See Chapter 9, Model Frameworks and Template Packages.)

The effort of generalization, either to a supertype or to a framework, usually leads to useful insights into the model. Also, it tends to simplify things: You find common aspects where you didn't notice them before, and you recast the model to expose them. Furthermore, the result is more easily extensible.

Strategy

Find common aspects between types in your model. Check that the similarities are real—that the users use a concept covering them both. Construct a supertype, and redefine the source types as its subtypes.

Find common aspects between groups of types in the model. Construct a template package containing everything that is common to the different occurrences, then rewrite them as framework applications.

Following are some specific triggers.

- Same types of attributes and associations in different types: form a supertype.
- Several associations with the same source and mutually exclusive 0,1 targets: form a supertype for the targets.
- Several *n*-ary associations with a common source, in which invariants and postconditions frequently need to talk about the union of the target sets: Form a supertype for the targets.
- Invariants and postconditions focused on type A use only some subset of the attributes of B, an attribute (or association) of A (see Figure 14.5): put the unused attributes in a subtype of B. (This reduces spurious dependency.)
- Similar "shapes" in different parts of the type and action diagrams: form a model framework that can be applied to recreate the collaborating groups.

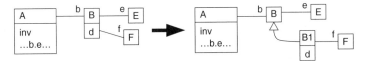

Figure 14.5   Introducing subtypes to decouple.

Pattern 14.11   Recursive Composite

Model an extensible object structure with a recursive type diagram.

Strategy

Let's look at a general framework for modeling extensible structures (see Figure 14.6). For a tree, set np to be 0,1; for a directed graph (with shared children), set np to *.

You must decide whether you will permit loops in the instance snapshots. If you will not, import instead the no-loops package (see Figure 14.7).

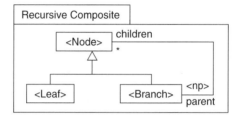

Figure 14.6   Template for recursive composite.

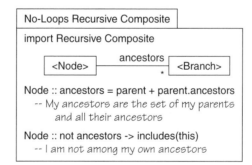

Figure 14.7   Recursive composite without instance loops.

Examples

The recursive composite pattern shows up in many problems. With np=1, no loops:

- *Programming languages*: Some statements (if, while, blocks) contain other statements; others do not (function calls, assignments).
- *Graphical user interfaces*: Some elements of a screen are primitive, such as buttons or scrollbars; others are composites of the smaller elements.

- Military or organizational hierarchies

With np=2, no loops:

- Family trees

With np=*, no loops:

- Macintosh file system
- Spreadsheets (each cell may be the target of formulas in several other cells)

With np=*, loops allowed:

- Road maps
- Program flowcharts

Pattern 14.12   Invariants from Association Loops

Loops in a type diagram suggest the possibility of an invariant.

Intent

The intent is to flush out useful constraints. You encounter this pattern when building a static type model (as part of a business model or component spec); it helps you to capture static invariants.

Motivation

A static invariant is a condition that should always be true, at least between the executions of any action that forms part of the same model. As a Boolean, it is composed of comparisons between pairs of objects. They might be < or = comparisons between numbers or other scalars; or more-complex comparisons defined over more-substantial types; or identity comparisons (whether one object is the same object as another).

Many invariants can be constructed when there is a loop[2] in the static type model: two different ways of coming at items of the same type. For example, a Library's books can be lent only to its own members. We could write

    LoanItem :: borrower <> nil ==> borrower.library = library

We can see the loop easily (see Figure 14.8). Here's another:

    Member :: age >= library.minimumAge

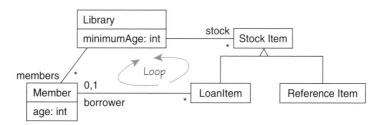

Figure 14.8   Association loops need invariants.

---

2. We are not referring to loops in instance snapshots here, as in Pattern 14.11, Recursive Composite.

Where's the loop? We said that attributes and associations are interchangeable in analysis. We could have drawn int as a type in its own box as shown here.

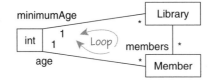

The only exception is to write a constant into the invariant itself.

Strategy

Whenever you notice a loop in the static type diagram, ask yourself whether there is any applicable invariant. The loop can have any number of links, from two upward; and a link can traverse up to a supertype.

14.3 *Video Case Study: Abstract Business Model*

In this section we begin our case study of a video rental business.[3]

14.3.1 Informal Description of Problem

The business sells and rents, or hires, videos to people through many stores. To rent a video from a store, a customer must be one of its members; becoming a member takes a few minutes. Anyone can buy a video without being a member.

Members can reserve a video for rent if all copies of it are currently hired. When a copy of the video is returned, the member will be called and the copy will be held for as long as three days, after which time the reservation will be canceled if not claimed.

Only a limited stock of videos is kept for sale, but a member can order a video for purchase. A store can order and acquire copies of a video from the head office.

The business head office sets the catalog of videos and their sale prices; this is common to all stores.

Each store keeps copies of a subset of the catalog for rent and for sale, and each store sets its own rental prices (to adjust for local competition). For strategic purposes, statistics are kept of how often and when last a video has been rented in each store. It is also important to know how many are available in stock for rent and for sale.

14.3.2 Concept Map

It is often helpful to start with an initial informal sketch of the main terms and concepts, drawn as a *concept map*. It serves as a concrete starting point for capturing the vocabulary used and the relationships between terms (see Figure 14.9). A concept map is simply a graph of labeled nodes and labeled (preferably directed) edges. We do not try to formalize the map or even worry much about distinguishing objects, types, actions, and associations. The concept map can serve as the starting point for the type model and collaborations.

14.3.3 Formalized Model

The aim is to get a more precise statement of the requirements. We segment the requirements into overlapping areas of concern, or subject areas, but focus in this

---

3. Thanks to Texas Instruments Software/Sterling Software for permission to use the video case study in the book; the authors originally developed this example for IT software.

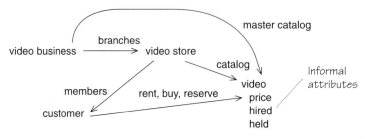

Figure 14.9   Concept map for video store.

description on the primary subject area of customer rentals and sales. There could be other subject areas for things such as marketing, purchasing, collections, and so on; they would define overlapping types and attributes and might add further specifications to common actions.

There are two distinct forms of abstraction at work on objects and actions. We must be clear about the boundary of objects and actions being modeled. We could model abstract actions, such as a complete rental cycle; or we could describe finer-grained interactions, such as reserve, pick up, return, and so on.

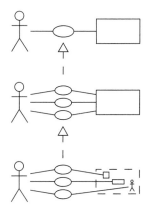

Similarly, we could model a video store as one large-grained object—an external view; or we could describe internal roles and interactions, such as the store clerk, the stockkeeper, the manager, and the video system—an internal view. We illustrate two levels of action abstraction in this chapter; the object granularity will be refined later, when we define the system context and user roles.

14.3.4   Subject Area: The Customer-Business Relationship

> *Rq 1   The business rents and sells videos through many stores.*

The type model in Figure 14.10 summarizes the interactions between Stores and Customers. The elements on the diagram are as follows.

• *Object types*: The boxes represent types of objects. There can be many Video Businesses, Video Stores, and Customers in the world.

• *Associations*: The arc corporation is a link type (or association). It shows that for any given Video Store, there is exactly one Video Business, which is its corporation (although different Stores may have different Businesses). The * shows that there may be any number of Video Stores that share a single Video Business as their corporation.

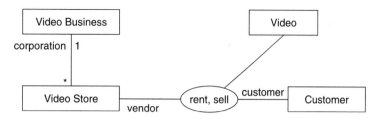

Figure 14.10   High-level business collaboration.

• *Use cases*: The ellipse (oval) represents a use case action called sell. (Actually, because exactly the same set of participants is involved in rent, we have written two labels in the same ellipse; but there are really two action types here.) Sell is an action each of whose occurrences involves one Video Store, one Customer, and one Video. (If there were several of any participant, we could use cardinality decorations.) We have not visually distinguished action participants from parameters here.

An occurrence of a use case action is a dialog of interactions, usually causing a change of state in some or all of its participants. The participants are all those objects whose states affect or may be affected by the outcome. An action is spread over time; when we look at it more closely, it is composed of smaller actions (such as scan shelves, choose, pay, and take away).

14.3.5   Dictionary

Accompanying the diagrams should be a dictionary carrying definitions of each object type, attribute, and action.

• Video Business   A company with branches that sell and rent Videos.
• Video Store   One of the branches of a Video Business.
• Customer   A legal entity to whom videos may be sold or hired.
• Video   An individual item that can be sold or hired.
• sell(VideoStore, Customer, Video)   The interaction between a Video Store and a Customer whereby the Customer acquires ownership of an instance of a particular Video previously owned by the Business in exchange for money.
• rent(VideoStore, Customer, Video)   The interaction between a Video Store and a Customer whereby the Customer is given possession, for some period of time, of an instance of a particular Video owned by the Video Business and normally kept at the store in return for a payment to the Store.

14.3.6   Use Case Actions: Precise Specs

It would be better to describe the use case actions more precisely. This cannot be done without the ideas that both VideoStores and Customers can own Videos and can possess money. Something like this:

> use case sell (vendor:VideoStore, cust:Customer, v:Video)
> post:
>> v is removed from stock of videos owned by vendor and is added to the videos owned by customer; the vendor's cash assets are increased by the price of v set by the vendor, and the customer's are depleted by the same amount.

What exactly do we mean by "the stock of videos owned by the vendor"? Let's augment the model to include this and then rewrite this statement more succinctly (see Figure 14.11). VideoStores and Customers are kinds of Owner; Owners have cash assets and own Videos. A VideoStore has a price for many Videos. We should augment the dictionary with these new types and attributes.

An attribute, like a link, is a read-only query. The main difference is that it is shown as text rather than pictorially. In theory, the two forms are interchangeable, but in practice the attribute form is used when the target type is defined in some other body of work. The inventor of Money does not know about Owners or Video-Stores.

Now we can rewrite the description of sell. It should be written both in natural language (more readable) and precise terms (less ambiguous):

> use case sell (vendor:VideoStore, cust:Customer, v:Video)
> post:
>> -- v is removed from the stock of videos owned by the vendor:
>> vendor.owns −= v
>> -- and added to the customer's stock:
>> and cust.owns += v
>> -- The vendor's cash is increased by the vendor's price for v:
>> and vendor.cash += vendor.priceOf(v)
>> -- and the customer's assets are depleted by the same amount:
>> and cust.cash −= vendor.priceOf(v)

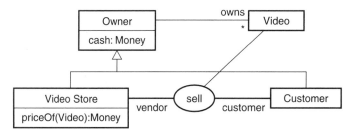

Figure 14.11   Revised and improved business collaboration for sell.

Every postcondition is a predicate (a Boolean, true/false condition) stating what must be true if the designer has done the implementation properly. So the clauses are connected by and, and there is no sequence of execution implied.

The purpose is to state properties of the result at the end of the use case, abstracting away from any details about sequences and how it is achieved. It is a relation between two states, before and after the use case has occurred. In later examples, you can sometimes see the "before" value of a subexpression referred to as expression@pre.

The construct x += y is an abbreviation for x = x@pre+y. x is what it used to be, plus y; it is predefined as an effect. This is not an assignment as in programming language. Instead, it is only a description of a part of the relationship of the two states.

There are many uses for operations on sets in abstract descriptions. Because the traditional mathematical symbols are not available on most keyboards, OCL defines ASCII equivalents. It is easier to use + for union, * for intersection, and – for set difference (see Section 2.4.5, Collections), and in Catalysis these features can be extended by the modeler.

14.3.7 Preconditions and More Modeling

Now let's try to describe the rent use case. To be comparable to sell, the intention is to let it encompass the whole business of renting a video, from start to finish. We will separately describe how this refines into a sequence of constituent actions such as renting and returning.

There's a slight conceptual difficulty here. Although there's an obvious transfer of money from one participant to another, what you've gotten for it once you've returned the video is less concrete than in the case of a sale. The most you're left with as a souvenir is whatever impression the video has made on your mind. Nevertheless, there's no reason that we shouldn't model this abstract notion as a Past Rental and model the rent use case as adding to your list of them (see Figure 14.12).

In another part of the document, we've said that VideoStores and Customers are kinds of Owner, which have cash and own Videos; so it is unnecessary to repeat it

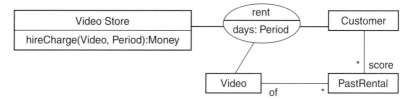

Figure 14.12 Model for rent.

Figure 14.13   Incorporating the term members.

here. Each diagram is in effect a set of assertions about the elements that appear in it; if an element appears in several diagrams, then all their assertions apply to it. Rather than show all the parameters pictorially by linking the use case to the types, we can show them as attributes within the use case ellipse.

One further complication is this requirement:

Rq 2   To rent a video from a store, a customer must be one of its members.

At present, there is nothing in our model representing membership, so we add it (see Figure 14.13).

Now we can state a precise description of the use case:

<u>use case</u> rent (hirer:VideoStore, cust:Customer, v:Video, days:Period)
<u>post</u>:
-- if customer is a member, then...
hirer.members→includes (cust) implies
    (-- a new PastRental of v is added to customer's 'score':
       cust.score += PastRental.new [of=v]
       -- The vendor's cash is increased by
       -- the hirer's hire rate for v at the time of commencement of the hire:
  and hirer.cash += hirer.hireCharge@pre(v, period)
       -- and the customer's assets are depleted by the same amount:
  and cust.cash −= hirer.hireCharge@pre(v, period)
)

Notice that nothing is said about the meaning of rent if the precondition is false. There might be another description of this use case elsewhere that covers that eventuality; but if there isn't, then we are saying nothing about what that might mean. Because we're describing rent and not "attempt to rent" or "inquire about renting," we leave it to a later, more detailed description to define precisely what happens when a nonmember demands to rent a video. It's part of the value of the postcondition approach that it allows you to paint the big picture, leaving the less important detail until later.

We could have modeled the hire charge as a per-day rate and multiplied it by the length of the hire. But doing it this way leaves the charging scheme open, allowing for reductions for longer rentals.

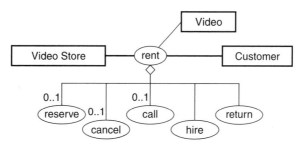

Figure 14.14   Refinement of rent.

14.4 *Video Business: Use Case Refinement*

Deciding we're interested in looking into one of the preceding use cases in further detail—let's choose rent as an example—we can show how it breaks into smaller constituents. The entire business of renting may involve reserving beforehand. So we could think of a rental as possibly reserving, followed by hiring and returning (see Figure 14.14).

The diamond indicates the relationship between an abstraction and its more-detailed constituents; it can include annotations such as multiplicity. Here it states that some combination of the constituent actions can be used to accomplish a complete rent; but we have yet to detail exactly how and in what order. This is only a summary diagram.

There may be other actions not mentioned here that can also be composed to make a rent; and these constituents may also be used in some other combination to make other abstract use cases. The constituent actions have their own participants, which we could have shown here or separately. They generally intersect with, or at least are mapped to, the participants of the abstract use case.

The relevant part of the informal business description is as follows.

> *Rq 3   Members can reserve a video for rent if all copies of it are currently hired. When a copy of the video is returned, the member will be called and the copy will be held for as long as three days, after which the reservation will be canceled if not claimed.*

To show the possible sequences of constituent actions and to specifically define which sequences correspond to an abstract rent use case, we model Rental as an object that goes through a sequence of states. In the transitions, s, v, c, and d refer to a store, video copy, customer, and rental period (see Figure 14.15). Frequently, such a reified action exists in the type model as an actual object, such as a progress record.

Round-cornered boxes are states, which can have substates; black dots are starting points. Arcs are state changes; they are labeled with the actions that cause them. The square brackets are guards: the transition happens only if the guard is true. A forward slash (/) marks a postcondition. This diagram formally docu-

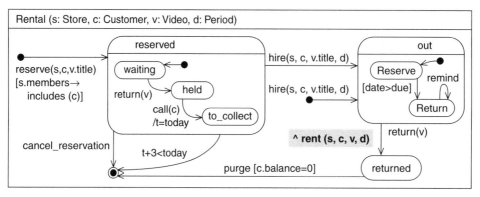

Figure 14.15   Refinement sequence for rent.

ments an action sequence refinement; any sequence of detailed actions starting
from a top-level ● and ending with ^rent constitutes an abstract rent use case.

14.4.1   Refined Model

We should write down descriptions of the more-detailed actions; in this case we
would likely still call each finer-grained action a use case. To begin with, let's keep
it relatively informal, extending the dictionary with action definitions.

- reserve (VideoStore, Customer, VideoTitle)   (At this point, we notice that there is a
  distinction between individual copies of a video—objects of type Video—and
  titles or catalog entries.) This use case represents the reservation of a given title
  by a member of a store. The title must be available at that store. The reservation
  will be recorded pending the return of a copy of that title to the store.

- return (Video)   The return of a copy to its owning store. If there is a reservation
  for that title at that store, it will be held for the reserver to collect; otherwise, it
  goes back on the shelves. The hire record is marked "returned."

- call(VideoStore, Customer, Video)   Applies when a returned Video has been held
  for this reservation. The reserver is notified by telephone that the Video can be
  collected. The reservation record is date-stamped, and, if the member has not
  picked up the copy within a fixed time, the reservation may be canceled.

- hire(VideoStore, Customer, VideoTitle, Period)   A member takes away a copy of a
  particular title for an agreed period. If this customer had a reservation for this
  video and there is a copy held, then that copy should be the one taken. It makes
  sense only if there is a copy on the shelves beforehand or a held copy. A record
  of the hire is kept.

- cancel_reservation(VideoStore, Customer, Video)   Occurs when the store becomes
  aware that the customer no longer wants the video. If a copy has been held, it is
  reallocated to another reservation or put back on the shelves. The reservation is
  deleted from the records.

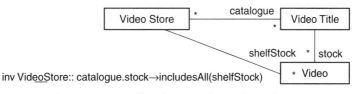

Figure 14.16   Clarifying video title and copy.

The distinction between Videos (individual copies) and VideoTitles has now become apparent. It gets documented together with an invariant (see Figure 14.16).

- VideoTitle   The set of individual Videos having a particular title.
- VideoStore::catalogue   The set of VideoTitles known to a VideoStore.
- VideoStore::shelfStock   The set of Videos currently available for hire. A subset of the total stock of all titles.

We could also draw pictures showing the participants in each use case, duplicating the dictionary entries for the use cases. In practice, this seamless switching between text and diagrams may or may not be supported by particular tools.

14.4.2   Formalized Refined Use Case Specs

Looking again at the preceding spec of reserve, it's clear that we must represent the idea of a reservation in the model (to be able to state that the use case creates a record of one). The same thing applies to rentals. In fact, there may be some advantage in regarding these two records as two states of the same thing; then it will be easy to include any initial reservation as being part of the history of a rental.

A useful pattern here is Action Reification (see Pattern 14.13). We'll reify the use case as Rental but preserve the distinct idea of a Reservation as a state type (see Figure 14.17).

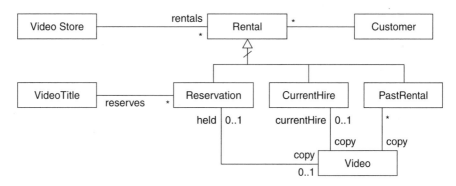

Figure 14.17   Using state types for a rental.

Now the finer use cases can be expressed more formally:

use case reserve (store:VideoStore, cust:Customer, title:VideoTitle)
pre: store.catalogue→includes (title) -- *The title must be available at that store,*
        and store.members→includes (cust) -- *the customer must be a member*
post: store.rentals→includes (
            Reservation.new[reserves=title and customer=cust and copy=null])
    --*There is a new Reservation in the store whose title and customer are as requested;*

Notice that we are still talking about the interactions between the real-world objects here. The Rental is not an object in the store's computer system but rather is an abstraction representing the agreement between the parties.

Notice also that the postcondition restates (perhaps in more detail) what is shown in the state chart, given an interpretation of the states in terms of the model. This reminds us that we should never write a state chart without defining the states in terms of the model attributes.

inv Rental::
        reserved self:Reservation -- *reserved state is a Reservation state type*
        and waiting = (reserved and copy=null) -- *waiting means reserved with no copy*
        and (held or to_collect) = (reserved and copy<>null) -- *other substates*
            -- *we'll need a boolean attribute to distinguish held from to_collect*
        and out = self:CurrentHire -- *'out' state is a CurrentHire state type*
        and hired = (out and date=<due) -- *substates of 'out'*
        and overdue = (out and date>due)
        and returned = self:PastRental -- *the returned state*

Continuing with the other use case specs, return can be specified separately for its two effects on the state chart (of two separate Rentals):

use case return (v:Video)
pre: v.currentHire<>null   -- *v is rented out*
post: v.currentHire@pre : v.pastRental -- *the rental is now part of v's past*

use case return (v:Video)
pre: v.title.reservation<>null and v.reservation.waiting
            -- *v is a copy of a title that is the subject of a Waiting Reservation*
post: v.title.reservation[waiting@pre and held and copy=v]→size = 1
            --*Of the resulting set of reservations for this title, there is exactly 1*
            -- *that was waiting and is now held for this video*

The spec of hire can conveniently be split into a general part and two effects: one for hiring based on a reservation and the other without a reservation.

use case hire (store:VideoStore, cust:Customer, title:VideoTitle, period:Period)
pre: -- *title from catalogue, and customer among members*
            store.catalogue→includes (title) and store.members→includes (cust)
post: -- *an available video copy of the title has been hired by the customer*
            (Video→exists (v | v.title=title and v.currentHire@pre = null
                and v.currentHire.videoStore=store
                and v.currentHire.customer=cust

-- *either based on a reservation, or without a reservation*
and (hireFromReservation (store, cust, title, video)
or hireFromCold (store, cust, title, video))

-- *we hire the video kept for this reservation*
<u>effect</u> hireFromReservation
(store:VideoStore, cust:Customer, title:VideoTitle, video:Video)
=   (title.reservation@pre <> null and title.reservation@pre.copy=video)

-- *we hire the video without a reservation*
<u>effect</u> hireFromCold
(store:VideoStore, cust:Customer, title:VideoTitle, video:Video)
=   (title.reservation@pre = null)

Canceling a reservation clears it from the ken of customer, store, and the video:

<u>use case</u> cancel_reservation (r:Reservation)
<u>post</u>: (r.copy@pre <> null implies r.copy@pre.held = null) -- *any held copy is released*
and r.videoTitle@pre.reservations −= r -- *remove r from reservations for its title*
and r.videoStore@pre.rentals −= r and r.customer@pre.rentals −= r

We omit further detailing of these use cases and coverage of other subject areas.

Pattern 14.13   Action Reification

This pattern supports systematic progression from succinct abstract actions (or use cases) to detailed dialog, supporting the strategic aim to expose the most important decisions up front and keeping reliable traceability to the details.

Intent

A sequence of action occurrences can often be seen as a group with a single outcome, which can be documented with its own postcondition. (This sequence is not necessarily contiguous—there may be other unrelated actions in between them.) Conversely, when you're specifying a system, you should omit detailed protocols of interactions so as to understand overall effects.

Example

Consider the transaction of obtaining cash between a customer and an ATM. It has a clear postcondition, is often mentioned in everyday life, and can usefully be discussed between ATM designers and banks. The detail of how it happens—log in, select a service, and so on—can be deferred to design and may vary across designs.

Terms

The *finer* actions *refine* the *abstract* one, and the relationship is documented as an *action refinement* consisting of a *model refinement* and an action refinement sequence. Many refinements of one action may be possible.

A *sequence constraint* may govern actions, stating the possible sequences; it may be expressed in the form of a state chart. Of all possible sequences of finer actions, only some may constitute an occurrence of the abstract action; for example, the card reader and ATM keys can always be used, but only some sequences constitute a withdraw action. An *action refinement sequence* relates finer sequences to specific abstract actions, and can be expressed in the form of a state chart.

Strategy

Model the abstract action as an object—reify it. Implementations are not constrained to follow models, but refication often corresponds to a useful object.

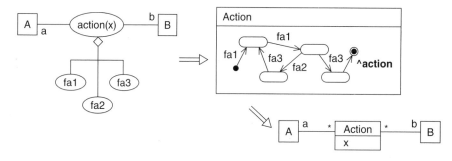

Chapter 15   How to Specify a Component

To specify a type means to describe the behavior required of any object that may claim to be of that type, regardless of its implementation. An object is a member of that type if its behavior complies with that specification.

Documenting a type specification involves describing the relevant actions an object participates in and expressing the effect of those actions in terms of a type model of that object. The specification should be satisfied by any correct implementation, and the type model is an abstraction of any correct implementation.

In this chapter we describe concrete steps toward building a system or component type specification to describe how an object behaves in response to any external stimulus such as a request to perform an action. The approach here is mostly top-down—Chapter 16, How to Implement a Component, describes how to design the insides of a component.

This chapter has two main parts. Section 15.1, Patterns for Specifying Components, describes patterns that often are useful when you're building a component specification. Section 15.2 and the remainder of the chapter illustrate the construction of a specification for the case study.

15.1 *Patterns for Specifying Components*

This section covers the major steps in building a component specification.

Pattern 15.1, Specify Components, motivates the extra effort involved in separating specification of expected behavior from its implementation.

Pattern 15.2, Bridge Requirements and Specifications, outlines a pragmatic view of requirements, as stated and understood by a user, and the more-precise specifications that a developer might use to understand what must be built.

Pattern 15.3, Use-Case-Led System Specification, explains why a use-case-driven approach to requirements capture is prudent but should always be interleaved with tools of more-precise specifications.

Pattern 15.4, Recursive Decomposition: Divide and Conquer, discusses the role of specifications within the design process.

Patterns 15.5, Make a Context Model with Use Cases, and *15.6, Storyboards,* deal with methods of determining a system's role within a business.

Pattern 15.7, Construct a System Behavior Spec, Pattern 15.8, Specifying a System Action, and *Pattern 15.9, Using State Charts in System Type Models,* describe concrete techniques to build the specification of the system of interest.

Pattern 15.10, Specify Component Views, and *Pattern 15.11, Compose Component Views,* explain how to show that separately specified components, when composed together in a particular way, realize the required behavior.

A development process should not leave large "leap of faith" gaps between models. *Pattern 15.12, Avoid Miracles, Refine the Spec,* describes how techniques of refinement and refactoring can help to reduce such gaps to a manageable level.

Pattern 15.13, Interpreting Models for Clients, provides concrete guidelines for reviewing formal specifications for clients or users.

Pattern 15.1 Specify Components

In this pattern, you specify what you are going to build separately from actually building it and specify most of it before you build it.

Intent

This pattern has three objectives.

- Identify conceptual problems and obstacles early.
- Reduce misunderstandings between stakeholders and reduce confusion in each developer's mind.
- Lengthen product life.

Considerations

Getting straight into the code can be useful for building a quick prototype. It can also be all you need to do in small projects (one person-month or so). And when you start with existing components, a detailed specification may not be achievable with the parts you have.

But for anything bigger, it is useful to separate out the more important design decisions from the less important ones. In this way, they can be thought about and discussed separately before much effort is committed to generating the dependent details. Even for existing components, a slightly more abstract spec is still invaluable.

After the code has been written, a spec is valuable for two purposes:

- Those who will maintain the code after you will understand your concepts and update it in accordance with your vision.
- Users (whether external or software) will have a clear understanding of what to expect from your component. This is especially important for a component that will be reused in contexts that you are not aware of. We are no longer in the days when the designer of the only component that talks to yours is sitting in the next cubicle.

Strategy

Write a specification for each component, whether it is a complete software product or a group of only a few objects in a larger program. Exceptions can be made for small components and rapid-assembly products that are not expected to have a long life.

It is not always necessary to write the specification before writing the code. Indeed, it isn't unusual to write some experimental code and then go back and try to make sense of what you've done.

Nor should you get the spec more than 80% finished without some implementation.

Consequences

It is a common experience with anyone who uses more-formal specifications that a single afternoon's work on a model at the beginning of a project can raise all kinds of subtle but important questions that would not have been noticed in writing conventional informal requirements. Often, such questions would not have been noticed until the coding stage—too late to solve the problem coherently.

The objection is sometimes raised that it is easy to get tied up in writing a specification in preference to getting on with the real work. First, you should never wait until the specification is 100% finished. Second, the decisions you are writing down in a spec are only the most important decisions that would have to be taken sometime in the design no matter how you approach it. We're only separating them out to avoid needing to backtrack later. Any extra time spent writing and maintaining a document is repaid within the 70%–80% of the product's life that comes after its first delivery.

Pattern 15.2   Bridge Requirements and Specifications

Requirements are for users; specifications are for analysts and developers.

Intent

The intent here is to bridge the gap between users and developers, without loss of accuracy, when you're specifying a software product with nonsoftware users.

Considerations

The notations we discuss in this book form a specialized language for developing and discussing software and other systems' behavior. This language provides the benefit that we, the analysts and designers of the system, can use it to form a clear picture of what we intend to provide for the users.

Like the language of an electrical hardware specification, a formal specification (with diagrams and formal descriptions) is not directed at end users.

Strategy

Write and maintain two views of the specification: one in terms that users understand and the other in more formal terms. They can be in separate documents or interleaved in a single document, as we saw in Chapter 5, Effective Documentation.

There is a cycle between the two documents (or two views): Use the formal statements to form questions you use to improve the informal statements (see Figure 15.1). In this way, you build a good understanding of the users' views, help them understand what's possible, and keep them well involved in the development. (Any book on rapid application development elaborates on this point.)

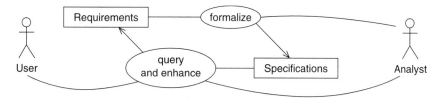

Figure 15.1   Typical user/analyst cycle with requirements
and specification.

Vocabulary

A *requirements* document is a document written in terms that can be discussed with users.

A *specification* is a document primarily intended for our own use as developers. It represents our current understanding of what we're providing for the users.

Consequences

Requirements Management. Use a suitable tool to link clauses in the informal narrative to the relevant elements of the specification (such as invariants and postconditions). These requirements management tools perform a kind of configuration management function: If any modifications are made to one end of each mapping, the other end is highlighted. Many-many mappings are allowed, and the linked elements can be in the same or different documents. The tool cannot know what links to make nor how the different elements should be brought into line after a change occurs, but it is very useful in tracing the propagation of updates.

Requirements and Specification Cycle. Narrative requirements statements often look quite solid when you first look at them; but as soon as you start a specification model, gaps and dislocations become painfully apparent.

Pattern 15.3   Use-Case-Led System Specification

Working from use cases, you can create a specification for the requirements of a system.

Intent

The aim is to create a specification for a substantial software component or for a product.

- *Deliverable*: Unambiguous specification of system requirements.
- *Inputs*: There may be a business model, either written as a precursor to this step or shared with other systems in the same business. See Pattern 14.2, Make a Business Model.

Considerations

The specification of a component goes hand-in-hand with the design for the process within which it is used. You cannot specify the component without having some idea of how it is going to be used; you cannot define how it will be used without knowing something about what it does.

Strategy

Explore and document the context within which your component will be used as well as defining its behavior. See Pattern 15.5, Make a Context Model with Use Cases, and Pattern 15.7, Construct a System Behavior Spec.

Often, the context model will yield several classes of users, each with a different view of the system. See Pattern 15.10, Specify Component Views, and Pattern 15.11, Compose Component Views.

Consequences

There is not usually a clear order in which to perform context analysis (use case analysis) and system behavioral specification. There is some element of negotiation between the two: How the users will work depends on what will be provided; and what is provided depends both on how they wish to work and on what is possible.

Therefore, don't attempt to finish one before proceeding to the next, and don't insist on doing them in one order or the other (although most people start with

use cases). Specifically, do not generate many detailed narrative use cases without
iterating through a precise modeling cycle (see Figure 15.2).

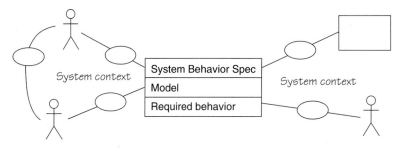

Figure 15.2   Use case model of system context.

Pattern 15.4   Recursive Decomposition: Divide and Conquer

Every specification is part of a larger implementation, and every implementation composes a solution from specified components.

Intent

The aim of this pattern is to promote practical design.

Considerations

We need to break large problems into smaller ones. We also must decouple the design efforts on the various smaller problems so that we don't have to keep them all in our heads at once—or indeed in any one head.

Strategy

Construct the implementation to a specification as some form of composition of smaller components (see Figure 15.3).

Specify each component. There may be many (or many potential) implementations of each component. When you're devising the present implementation, do not consider the internal details of the components. They will have their own decompositions.

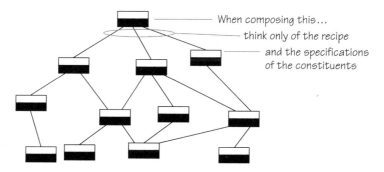

Figure 15.3   Each design should be constructed in terms
of specifications of its parts.

Do not confuse the use of a component with the definition of the component. One component may be shared between the implementations of several others. In each use, there may be particular restrictions or simplifications that apply; they are not part of the intrinsic definition of the shared part. Use packages to distinguish them.

It is not usually sufficient to say what the constituents are; the way in which they are combined is also required.

Vocabulary

- *Composite* is a relative term: the object of which a constituent forms part.
- *Constituent* is a relative term: an object that makes up a composite.
- A *recipe* is the extra information that defines how the constituents are composed together to make the composite.

Known Examples

A subroutine fulfills a requirement. It is implemented as a sequence of invocations of constituent subroutines.

An object's behavior is implemented with a composite of instances of smaller objects linked in a collaboration.

A hardware component is a composite of smaller components wired according to a defined scheme.

The specifications of a component you are asked to design may come from a larger design. This situation contrasts with that of an end-product design, in which your team's responsibility includes documenting the system context use cases (see Pattern 15.3, Use-Case-Led System Specification).

Pattern 15.5   Make a Context Model with Use Cases

Capture collaborations with and around an object, component, or system by building a context model that shows all abstract actions (use cases) involving the system.

Intent

This pattern's objectives are to define the scope and boundary of a system and its relation and interactions with its immediate environment; to build the requirements spec for a system or subsystem to be installed; or to review the context of a legacy system.

Context

If this is a subsystem within a larger design, much of this work may already be done. Otherwise, we begin by understanding how our system works within a larger system to meet larger objectives. For example, if we are asked to write an order payment application, we need first to understand the relevant procedures of the financial department, the role envisaged for our software, and the functions to be performed by the users themselves or by other pieces of software.

Considerations

In general, each of the different parties that interact with an object has a separate view of its concerns. A context model should cover all external roles and interactions, at least at an abstract level, even if they are split across multiple collaborations.

Many of the collaborations will follow stereotypical interaction patterns—for example, an interaction that consists of logging in, conducting transactions, and logging out; or making a selection and then operating on that selection. These patterns can be abstracted as frameworks (see Chapter 9, Model Frameworks and Template Packages), and then applied and composed to define the system context collaboration.

It can be difficult to understand all the operations on a system. It is easier to identify the main user roles, which can then help define the operations and flow of information across the system boundary.

However, there is a subjective choice here: What should you model as two separate roles? For an interaction sequence—log in, conduct transaction, and log out—should you have three separate user roles? For order fulfilment, should the order placer be modeled as a separate role from the receiver?

How far out should you show actions? Should you include only those actions that directly involve the system? How fine-grained should the actions be?

What about time-triggered actions that have no explicit external initiator?

Strategy

Scope the Context Model. A context model consists of one or more collaboration models (see Section 4.6, Collaborations) focused on the object we are principally concerned with (typically a software system or component) and its interactions with others (typically people, other software, or hardware).

Summarize the interactions with the system as collaborations between the system being specified and other objects, building scenarios to validate the collaboration and modeling actions at a consistent level of abstraction. Show all external roles as types—also called *actors*—that participate in these actions. Also, document those actions that can proceed concurrently on a single system, including constraints on concurrency. For example:

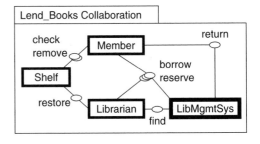

> CONCURRENT ACTIONS: *Any number of members can be borrowing or returning book copies or reserving book titles at the same time; a given book copy can have only one borrow or return involving it at any time.*

In addition to all actions that directly involve the system, also show actions between the external actors if they are relevant to the collaboration. If there are relevant actions even further removed from the system, either show actors and actions one level further out or model them as effects (see Section 4.4, Actions and Effects) on the external actors already included.

Treat the system of interest as a single object without internal roles or objects. Be precise about the boundary of the system you are describing in a collaboration; for example, is the database within or outside that boundary? If it is outside, you should describe interactions with the database; if it is inside, the database and all interactions with it are abstracted into a simpler type model and effects on that model (see Figure 3.10 for an explanation).

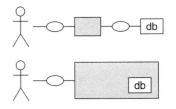

Define for each object a set of responsibilities and list them in the action section of that type. In particular, list and document the responsibilities of the system within the context of the larger organization (or larger system); treat the system as part of the design of the larger context.

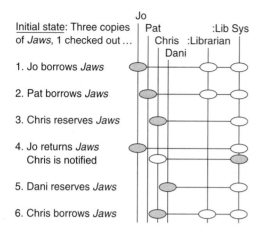

Jo

Initial state: Three copies
of *Jaws*, 1 checked out …

1. Jo borrows *Jaws*

2. Pat borrows *Jaws*

3. Chris reserves *Jaws*

4. Jo returns *Jaws*
   Chris is notified

5. Dani reserves *Jaws*

6. Chris borrows *Jaws*

Scenarios. Construct scenarios and storyboards of the projected use of the system, starting from a known initial state. Pay particular attention to cases when the system's dealings with one object affect those with another, and cover interleavings of these in a scenario. Create interaction diagrams for the scenarios, combining scenario narrative with the diagrams; the interaction diagrams can depict directed arrows or joint action occurrences (see Section 4.7); this example uses the joint action notation. A scenario should show named objects; it is usually sufficient to use generic names for them, such as c1, c2, c3: Customer, and t1, t2: Title.

As a rule, each step of the scenario that involves the system should start with an externally initiated action and include all subsequent system response, including resulting system-initiated actions such as step 4 in the example. This will serve as the starting point to identifying and specifying system operations.

Abstract and Re-refine. Abstract some of the actions to understand goals more clearly; good high-level actions often reflect goals of the user. For example, suppose we are told that we must deal with separate actions:

```
made_order(agreed_price, items);
received_invoice(amount);
received_goods(items)
```

We could abstract this to a higher-level action buy_goods(price, items). The postcondition is that we get and have paid for goods we have ordered. Re-refining this, we can question whether the receipt of an invoice is relevant: As long as the goods have been ordered, we can pay for whatever we receive, cutting out some administrative work. This option can then be discussed with our client.

You can model the system context and the corresponding scenarios, system type model, and action specs at any consistent level of granularity. The actions should be refined to the level at which completion of the action accomplishes an atomic transaction with the system and must be completed in its entirety by the actor to be meaningfully handled by the system.

Separate Roles. Make separate context models for the system as used by different groups of collaborators. In general, the separation works best by considering the abstract collaborations rather than individual collaborators.

For example, the member and the librarian both interact with the library system about the different stages of an abstract lend-books action (which encompasses borrowing, returning, and reserving). Theirs would be one view; the system plays one role in that collaboration. The stockkeeper's add-books would affect the other collaboration—you can't lend books you don't have—but it isn't part of the lend-books collaboration, and the system plays a distinct role. So in this example, one collaboration is separated from the rest.

Do not go overboard in separating actor roles. Specifically, if there are strong dependencies in state or attributes of the actor involved across two actions, do not needlessly split into two actor roles. For example, if the system requests authorization from an external system for a credit card and follows with an approval request for a payment amount on that same card, it would be better to use a single external role for the authorization system. Similarly, it would not be helpful to distinguish reserver, borrower, and returner as separate roles in a library. Map the user roles in the system context to roles in the business model and perhaps eventually to job descriptions.

Time-Triggered Actions. In addition to explicit stimulus from exernal actors, a system may need to respond on its own to the passage of time. Model this also as an external input to the system, driven by a clock of arbitrarily precise frequency. Pick a suitable name for this action, such as end_of_day or tick. For clarity, separately define named effects to specify what happens at that time, such as clear_outdated_reservations. As always, you can have multiple specifications for the action.

```
action System::end_of_day
    post:    clear_outdated_reservations
                -- all expired reservations have been cleared
effect System::clear_outdated_reservations
    post:     -- specification of the effect of clearing all outdated reservations
```

Many time-triggered actions are better specified as static invariants initially:

```
inv System:: -- there must never be any expired reservation in the system, or,
inv Reservation:: -- cannot ever be expired
```

Benefit

Many of us have experienced a development project in which the designers didn't get to meet the end users: That is the analysts' prerogative. (They know how to wear smart suits, I guess.) The effect is that although the designers may implement the stated requirements, they may do so in a way that isn't very user-friendly simply because they don't have a clear vision of the context in which the system works. The context model and its documentation gets around this and provides a clearly scoped connection to the business model.

Pattern 15.6   Storyboards

In this pattern, you make pictures of the user interface.

Intent

The intent is to animate the system use cases in a form that can be discussed with end users when you construct a specification of a system that will have a graphical user interface.

Considerations

A rigorous specification expresses the developers' common understanding of what they intend to provide for the users. The act of constructing the specification raises useful questions to put to the clients. But it is not readily accessible to end users who are not themselves computer people. We therefore seek techniques that animate the specification for the end users. They relate most directly to what they see on the screen.

Strategy

Make a slide show or prototype of what the users will see on the screen.

Summarize the screens in a chart that shows all the possible transitions from one to another: This is the *storyboard*. Annotate the transitions with the names of actions, which you should have documented with their effects on the system's state. Also annotate with the story: the reasons people would choose different routes through the user interface.

The chart forms a state chart of the refinement of the user actions. (See Section 6.5, Spreadsheet: Action Refinement, and Pattern 14.13, Action Reification). After the chart is complete, abstract the major actions from the GUI detail: The latter may change between now and the implementation, but the major actions are what you require at present.

When discussing the storyboard with users, let them get involved in the detail of the GUI at first; it will help fire their imaginations. But make the point that the detail can be changed later and that what we want now is the major actions.

See Section 15.2.3 (Storyboards) for an example.

Pattern 15.7 Construct a System Behavior Spec

Treating your system as a single object, define the type of any system implementation that would meet the requirements.

Intent

The purpose is to construct a type specification (a view, or role) of a system we are to build. The deliverables are a type specification of any implementation objects meeting the requirements of this system (in the chosen role), embedded in narrative documentation, and a dictionary with specific meanings of types in this model.

Snapshots are thinking tools rather than true specifications (because they deal only in particular scenarios) but can be used for illustration in the narrative.

Context

We already have a system context model (see Pattern 15.5, Make a Context Model with Use Cases).

Considerations

The result will nominally be a type box that defines our system as if it were a single object (see Section 6.6, Spreadsheet: Object Refinement). As with all types, the behavior presented to the external world—in the bottom section of the box—is specified in terms of the hypothetical static type model—in the middle section (see Figure 15.4).

The whole thing won't usually fit in one box on one page. So we split it into multiple drawings or use refinement (see Chapter 6, Abstraction, Refinement, and Testing) to separate it into subject areas.

Strategy

Separate Roles. As we noted in Pattern 15.5, Make a Context Model with Use Cases, most objects play several roles, and when you're specifying requirements it is useful to focus on one at a time.

So in the example shown, we have listed only the operations from the lend-books collaboration and will specify those operations. Ultimately, the system's roles may be recomposed in preparation for designing it.

Summarize the Set of Actions for this Role. This can essentially be read from the context model. Actions (and hence the model) should be as abstract as reasonable at first cut—not individual keystrokes.

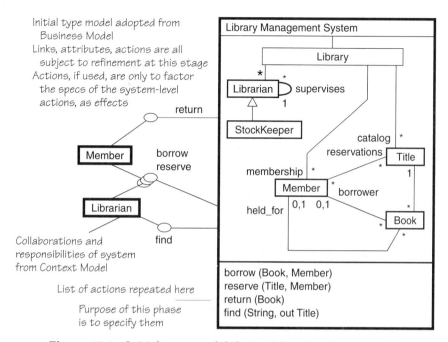

Figure 15.4   Initial type model derived from business model.

Each action must be given a parameter list. The parameters represent other information that will be available to the action when implemented. They could be the parameters of an API operation or information that a user can be asked to enter as part of a dialog to which this action is refined. They can usually be read from the participants and parameters in the corresponding action in the business model. For example, reserve(Title, Member, Librarian) indicates that there is a way in which those pieces of information can be entered; we don't yet care how. (See Chapter 6, Abstraction, Refinement, and Testing, for information about how parameters relate to action refinement.)

In some cases, we may immediately decide that some information is not required—for example, Librarian in the reserve operation. This doesn't stop you from putting that information back in a later refinement. The refinement rules allow you to add parameters but not to take them away; so by paring down the parameter list at the most abstract level, you are keeping your options open.

Adopt the Business Model as the Initial Type Model. That is, the model part of the type box defining the system. Note that this gives us two of everything: the external real object and its model inside the system. To distinguish where this might be ambiguous, use LibraryManagementSystem::Member and ::Member. Note, however, that actions from the business model do not translate into internal actions that must be implemented in the system. They are candidate effects and are there to conveniently factor out parts of the system behavior specification.

The ultimate purpose of a type model is to support the action specs; expect to add to it and eventually to drop parts as irrelevant. So for a drawing editor, we might add the idea of a current selection. For a library management system, we might drop the business model's Librarian-Librarian supervises link, because the actions expected of the system never use it.

An alternative approach is to start minimalist. The initial type model is not known—it is empty—and you draw elements from the business model into the system type model as you uncover a need for them in describing the system behaviors.

Note that the model represents the state of the whole system from its external users' point of view—not only the business logic and not only the software: Hardware may also be included. So if a display shows the result of a calculation and if that display is part of the boundary of the system, then that value can be an attribute in the model even if the software forgets it immediately after sending it to the display. It's the system context model that sets this boundary.

It's important to be aware that, at this stage, we are not intending to design the system internals. The type model is only a model: although the design may well be based on it, the designer is free to produce anything that exhibits the same list of system operations. In particular, the actions adopted from the business model illustrate only the model objects that may be involved in system-specified actions.

Exercise system queries. The most interesting actions are the ones that change the state of the system; but that state would be unnecessary if no information ever came from the system. It should be possible to represent in a snapshot any piece of information that a user may wish to extract from the system. For example, from the earlier library system type spec it would be possible to draw snapshots showing who is in possession of each book; but there is nowhere to record how long someone has been borrowing it.

Build State Charts of Key Types. This helps to clarify what is required of each action and to cross-check the model for overlooked states, operations, and combinations of them (see Figure 15.5). Each state chart shows the effect of actions in which the *system* collaborates on the *model* component of interest. See Pattern 15.9, Using State Charts in System Type Models.

For each state, define an invariant that relates it to other attributes in the type model. States are Boolean attributes and can be parameterized just as attributes are.

```
LibraryManagementSystem::Book::
        -- State definitions for the following diagram:
        lentTo(member) = self : (member.loaned)
                -- to be lent to a Member means to be in the 'loaned'
                -- set of books for that Member.
        holdingFor(member) = self : (member.held)
                -- wasn't in Business Model, had to add it!
        on_shelf = (~loaned = null) and (~held = null)
```

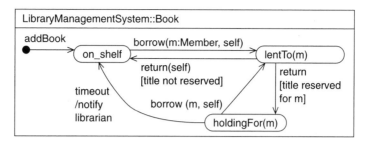

Figure 15.5   State chart of a spec type.

Specify Each Action. See Pattern 15.8, Specifying a System Action. The result is an effects clause and a review of the model.

    action borrow (book, member)
        pre: book.on_shelf
        post: book.lentTo(member)

Exercise the Spec with Scenarios. Perform a walk-through of a scenario and exercise the specification, starting from the initial state of the scenario. Check that the progression of states and system responses is as expected from the action specs.

Review Model. Delete attributes that are not used in any action spec; add attributes that are needed or that simplify the specification, and relate them to other attributes by invariants. Delete types not used for any query or action parameter. Update the dictionary with definitions that relate model elements to the business or domain model, its objects, and its events.

In the library example, drop Librarian and StockKeeper from this model. They may be required in models for other roles of this system.

Benefit

The exercise of writing a type spec in an unambiguous language always raises issues that are relatively inexpensive to debate at this stage. In our experience, the more precision you aim for, the more questions you raise and the more gaps you fix.

Pattern 15.8   Specifying a System Action

Specify an action using snapshots to help create the formal spec.

Intent

Each system action, no matter how abstract or concrete, can be characterized by the relation between its inputs, outputs, and states before and after the action. We want to write action specs with pre- and postconditions expressed informally and formally.

Context

We are specifying the type of a system playing a role in a collaboration—that is, the view that its collaborators have of it. We already have an initial type model. We can improve it in the light of what we need to say about this action and can iterate between specifying actions and updating the type model.

Strategy

Write the Spec Informally. State in natural language what is required of it. Think in terms of outputs, effects on external objects, and the initial and final internal state. Think also of preconditions—interpreted precisely as the conditions under which this particular postcondition make sense.

<u>action</u> return (book)
<u>pre</u>:   -- book is lent to someone
<u>post</u>:   -- book is either back ready to be loaned again,
               -- or, if someone has reserved its Title, it is held

Draw Snapshots. Draw a snapshot conforming to your type model that shows the system in a state conforming to the action's precondition. Then modify it (preferably in a different color) to show the state after the action. Intermediate states and the order in which things happen are of no concern. Draw a snapshot regardless of how complex the system is, introducing convenience or parameterized attributes to simplify matters (see Figure 15.6).

Delete links rather than whole objects. If necessary, draw an entire sequence of snapshots for a scenario, starting from the initial state.

Write Formal Pre- and Postconditions. Using the snapshots as a guide, write pre- and postconditions in the more-precise terms of the links or states. Expect to discover gaps and inconsistencies. (See Section 3.4.1, From Attributes to Operation Specification, for detailed steps.) Be aware of how your spec will be combined with other specs for the same action (see Section 8.1, Sticking Pieces Together).

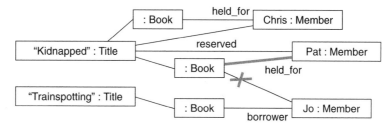

Figure 15.6   Snapshots of an action.

In this example, drawing snapshots helps us notice an inaccuracy in the initial attempt at the informal postcondition.

<u>action</u> LibraryManagementSystem:: return (book: Book)
<u>pre</u>:   *-- book is lent to someone*
                book.borrower <> null
<u>post</u>:   *-- book is either back ready to be loaned again,*
                -- or, if someone has reserved its Title but doesn't already have a copy held
                -- it is held for them
       -- the book is definitely not loaned out any more
       book.borrower=null <u>and</u>
       -- if this title had more reservations than held books
       if book.title.reserved@pre –> size> book.title.books[held_for<>null]→size
            -- it goes on hold; the new holder used to hold no books of this title
            <u>then</u>   book.held_for <> null
                    &   book.(not title.books@pre.held_for->includes(held_for))
       -- otherwise it goes back on the shelf
       <u>else</u> (book.held_for = null)

Look for Cases Not Covered by the Snapshots. The snapshots represent only a typical example, whereas the spec must cover every possibility within the scope declared by your precondition.

In the library example, it would be easy to overlook the case of returning a reserved book. But drawing snapshots for the documented scenarios (see Pattern 15.5, Make a Context Model with Use Cases) usually exposes these cases, as do state charts (see Pattern 15.9, Using State Charts in System Type Models).

Factor the Spec into Specification Types. If some parts of the pre- or postcondition seem to be particularly associated with types in the model, write them there as effects that you use in the system operation specs (see Section 3.8.3, Effects Factor Common Postconditions). This technique helps avoid replication in the spec and allows it to be polymorphic. Although the type model is not necessarily a blueprint for its design, this distribution (see p. 602) of concerns obviously looks forward to the distribution of responsibilities in design.

<u>effect</u> LibraryManagementSystem::Book:: return ()
    <u>pre</u>: borrower<>null <u>post</u>: etc...
<u>action</u> LibraryManagementSystem:: return(book)
    <u>post</u>: book.return()

Don't Try to State All the Effects at Once. In general, we don't specify every aspect of an action in one go or in one place. We will be specifying its effect from other collaborators' viewpoints when we come to them; and we will probably also keep exceptional circumstances separate, dealing only with the main cases at first. An advantage of specification with pre- and postconditions is that it is easy to combine different views later; a decent tool will readily present the combination of specifications when needed, yet the documentation can focus on different issues separately.

Benefit

The process of formalizing the action spec always raises questions about ambiguities and omissions in requirements. It is far better to deal with them at this stage than at coding time. Formalization also tends to expose shortcomings in the type model and leads to a clear and concise vocabulary shared by team members. This vocabulary will ultimately be the basis of the design.

Pattern 15.9   Using State Charts in System Type Models

In this pattern, you build state charts to find actions and effects and overlooked cases.

Intent

The objective is to cross-check the models and behavior specs. To that end, you tighten the type model to capture different modes in which different combinations of attributes make sense. Take a different perspective on the behavior specs; from the point of view of each specification type, what are all the actions that have an effect on it? Make state charts of principal types in a model.

This is a supplementary approach to finding the actions and their effects when creating a system specification. Except for special cases, state charts are not good at representing the whole story, because they form a single object's view of all the actions; designers ultimately work better from postconditions. But when there are clear changes in state, state charts work well and provide a valuable cross-check for completeness.

Considerations

Choosing States. The states are as you choose them. By a *state* in a state chart, we mean the truth or falsity of a predicate; it is just like any Boolean attribute, including parameterized attributes as well. A library book is or isn't out on loan; it is or isn't withdrawn from circulation; it is or isn't on the shelf. Some choices of states are obvious, because they make a significant difference to the postconditions and preconditions of the applicable operations. The point of a state chart is to illustrate these broad relationships between state and actions. But depending on your point of view, you can always choose a different set of states to illustrate: whether the book is or isn't in poor repair, whether it is more than 10 years old, whether it is currently passing through the checkout desk, whether it is overdue for return.

Other state differences can be too subtle to record effectively on a state chart. For example, there is a difference between a book that has been loaned five times and one that has been out on six occasions. But unless the library's loan policy changes qualitatively at that number, it would be pointless, although valid, to draw separate states for "loaned more (or less) than five times" and still more so to draw separate states for each separate number of times out.

State Charts and Types. State charts can (but need not) focus on a single type. In this pattern, we use state charts to represent the state of the members of a particular type within a system type model. A state chart can potentially be about universal truths; but we usually quantify over one type, such as any book, so that the states depicted are truths about any one of its members. We also use state charts to describe action sequence refinements in Chapter 6, Abstraction, Refinement, and Testing.

When devising a system type model (see Pattern 15.7, Construct a System Behavior Spec) we usually play an extra trick. As we've said, the types within such a model are at that stage there only for the purposes of specifying, and although the design would typically be based on them, there is no mandate to follow them provided that the externally visible behavior is as modeled. (Although we usually want the design to closely follow the specification model, it may sometimes differ because of performance optimizations or design reuse goals.) The trick is to draw a state chart for one of these specification types—for example, Book in the library system model—but in which the actions are those of the system being specified—for example, reserveTitle, returnBook, deleteMember. A state chart can be drawn for each of several types in the system model.

Keep in mind that when a system action occurs, it may affect several objects simultaneously; for example, deleteMember may have the effect of marking "lost" any book held by that member. It is as if the operations are broadcast simultaneously to all the objects inside the system, some of which take notice. The job of design can be seen as one of enhancing the performance of this mechanism and of deciding how the information modeled as these objects will really be represented.

Strategy

Identifying a Type. Identify a type with interesting states and transitions. Some types don't have any. Any Boolean attributes are candidates for states. Similarly, if you have "optional" attributes or associations, there are frequently states in which those attributes must be defined. Some continuous attributes may have values that signify a qualitative change in behavior; for example, speed > 75mph may qualify as a "speeding" state. Look also for radical differences in behavior—for example, can be lent or not—and for equivalent manual system stages or phases. Look for temporary tags or marks or locations of an item or piece of paperwork. Examples are books on shelves or held at desk or with member; hotel reservation in "future" folder or "today" pile.

Draw Transitions. At every state, decide the applicability of each operation and then link to its result. You may discover more states at this stage, but it is ok to leave some things underspecified for later refinement.

Label the transitions with the operations that cause them. Also, mark preconditions; the transition is guaranteed to occur only if the precondition is true. You can also write postconditions not indicated by the change of state, such as incrementing a counter.

Use only external operations; stages in the internal workings of the system are not states in this abstract picture. It is also sometimes useful to show state transitions for effects that you introduced as a way to factor the action specifications. You can consider time-outs or the arrival of particular times as external operations.

Use snapshots to illustrate what is happening to each object on each transition. This technique is especially useful for clarifying situations in which different things are happening simultaneously to different objects.

Formalize. States and transition labels are usually defined informally at first. An attempt at formalization raises more useful questions.

- Add each state to the dictionary. Define its meaning in the users' world view, taking care to exclude and include exactly what is intended. Does "on shelf" include times when a browser is inspecting the book within the library?
- Define each state as a Boolean function of the other attributes. It should be distinct from the other states in the diagram (except those explicitly parallel or nested). If it cannot be made distinct from another state, information is missing from the model.
- Such state definitions are often combinations of a few Boolean terms: an optional link present, an attribute > 0, and so on. Make a table of the combinations, showing how each state has a different combination and identifying combinations that do not correspond to any state. The complete set of allowed states is an invariant that should be documented for the model.
- Define pre- and postcondition labels of transitions in terms of links and attributes of this object in the system model. Each state chart applies to each object of the relevant type and can refer to self and to action parameters.
- As another cross-check, write a state-transition matrix. List all states on one axis and all actions on the other. Check that each combination has been considered, and mark it as either specified, unspecified, or impossible.
- Be aware that state charts have more than one interpretation. Does the absence of a transition between two states mean that there will never be any way in any member of this type (including all its subtypes) of getting directly from one state to the other? Or does it mean only that there are none we know about in this type, but subtypes might have some? If it is the former, mark the chart, or a state therein, as "closed" using a UML stereotype <<closed>>.

Intergrating Information. Integrate state chart information into specs for each system action. Each transition implies something about what an operation does to the relevant type of object. Some operations affect several types of objects; and the effects of these operations together.

Benefits

The model is usually improved by defining states. Some specifications become simplified by directly referring to states (including parameterized states) and letting the state invariants implicitly deal with the details.

Actions cover more cases than initially envisaged. The state chart visually highlights less-usual states in which actions can also take place. A state-event matrix (see Section 3.9.5) is a particularly powerful tool to highlight combinations of states and actions that might otherwise be missed. This fleshes out holes in the action specs.

The model is exercised in some detail by adopting an alternative view of the behavior of the component from the perspective of each of its specification types.

Pattern 15.10   Specify Component Views

Define partial views of a component, specifying behavior as seen from each interface.

Intent

The aim is to create a specification of a system that has multiple interfaces, or many different users, without being forced into a single description. The deliverable is a type model of a partial view of a component.

Context

The context is Pattern 15.3, Use-Case-Led System Specification, or Pattern 15.4, Recursive Decomposition: Divide and Conquer.

Considerations

When you're specifying a very large system (say, a telecomm network and its surrounding management software), it is usual to find that different users have different terms and different detailed models. What Engineering thinks of as a Phone has attributes such as line_impedance; what Accounts thinks of as a Phone has attributes such as call_charges. What the stockkeeper thinks of as a Book includes its purchase date and so on; but the desk staff members are interested in how long it has been on loan.

We must keep these models separate so that we can go back and talk sensibly to the different users in their own terms. But we also must merge them at some point so that we can implement an integrated system.

When you're specifying any component (with user or software interfaces), there are usually several interfaces. The different interfaces are aware of only part of the component's state and behavior. There may be several different classes of components that possess an interface conforming to a particular model.

We must keep the models separate so that we can pick which interfaces a new implementation conforms to.

In a hardware analogy, many different classes of devices generate a video signal; and many different implementations accept it. Each of those devices (such as a monitor or projector) also has other interfaces.

Strategy

Following Pattern 15.5, Make a Context Model with Use Cases, separate the different interfaces, one for each external role (or one for each group of roles that always occur together). Alternatively, you can identify the component and its interfaces during Pattern 15.4, Recursive Decomposition: Divide and Conquer.

Write a separate model for each interface. For each interface, consider only the concepts that the user of that interface requires to understand. Write the model in terms meaningful to that class of user.

Notice that one actor's view of the component often includes some understanding of the component's effect on third parties if the actor has some means of access to them outside the system. For example, suppose I press some buttons on my phone and then say, "Come to dinner at 8 P.M." to it. I do not expect the phone to appear at the table in the evening; nor do I imagine that my only access to my invitees is by shoveling the food down the wire. Instead, I understand that what I do to the phone has an effect on people with whom I have other means of interaction.

Pattern 15.11   Compose Component Views

Join several views of the requirements of a component.

Intent

The aim is to make a single combined model of a component before implementing it.

Context

We have several separately constructed views—see Pattern 15.10, Specify Component Views.

We are developing a component that must conform to an existing interface specification either from Pattern 15.4, Recursive Decomposition: Divide and Conquer, or from an externally defined standard.

Considerations

It is not unusual to have requirements provided from several sources, each of which is defined according to a separate set of terms and rules. The differing views can come from

- Different interfaces to different external actors
- Different industry, legal, and business constraints imposed by different organizations and expressed in different terms

For example, a financial system typically not only has the bare functional requirements (of settling trades or whatever) but also must conform to the company's business rules, the legal constraints, and the interface conventions of the external accountancy systems. Each of these sets of rules is defined with its own model, and each may impose its own rules on the system.

Strategy

Construct a common static model encompassing the concepts in each of the constituent models. This will be the static model for the component. The simplest way of doing this is to import the models into a single package and then define invariants defining how the attributes from one view are related to those from another, just as you would for redundant attributes. However, you may then need a separate refinement stage to get to the code.

The component model is a refinement of each of the views. Construct abstraction functions from the component model to the attributes of the views (see Section 6.4.2, Documenting Model Conformance with a Retrieval). If done fully, the abstraction functions provide a way in which the assertions of the views can be checked against the implementation.

If the implementation directly mirrors the spec, the abstraction functions are trivial.

Join the action specifications and invariants from different views, as decribed in Chapter 9, Model Frameworks and Template Packages. The covariant join semantics permits different views to impose their own restrictions on the whole.

This approach works equally well when you're designing components from scratch and assembling them from existing components. An example can be found in Section 10.11, Heterogenous Components.

Pattern 15.12   Avoid Miracles, Refine the Spec

Systematically go into more detail about actions and models, always mapping back to the abstract versions as a sanity check.

Intent

The objective is to bridge the gap between the abstract model and the implementation.

Considerations

Most people have seen the cartoon: a big, complex diagram of some outfit's Methodology; it has all sorts of purposeful-sounding tasks, numerous feedback loops and checkpoints, extensive forms and documentation templates to fill out, matrixes to put check marks against, and metrics to tell you how well you are doing. It has inputs to analysis at one end, code out at the other. But in the middle of all this busy activity, all arrows converge sooner or later on the box labeled "And Then a Miracle Happens"!

Catalysis reduces such magic. The miracle is your creativity as a designer. There's no algorithm for that, but it is spread evenly over the whole process, without a phase transition in the middle. In part, this has to do with the object approach: The software's structure mirrors reality. But we also can document refinements, which show the relation between a detailed description (often a design) and a more abstract one (often a specification), map between them, and justify choices made and key options rejected. We can also use frameworks (see Chapter 9, Model Frameworks and Template Packages) to memorialize common forms of refinement as recurring patterns, again helping eliminate the miracle.

Strategy

Follow the Golden Rule. Wherever possible, let your design reflect the model of the problem domain (see Pattern 6.1, The OO Golden Rule (Seamlessness or Continuity)). This strategy makes it much easier to bridge the gap from business models to implementations.

Focus on refinement during a design review. The designer should explain

- How the design is a valid refinement of the specification, including documenting conformance (see Section 6.4.2, Documenting Model Conformance with a Retrieval)
- Justifications for particular choices made based on performance, understandability, previous systems, and so on
- Architecture decisions, including patterns and rules applied

The resulting description provides the context of the problem (the specification), the context and considerations involved (the justification), and the solution (resulting design).

Rearrange the spec. When the gap between the specification and design gets larger, try to rearrange the specification so that its structure is somewhat closer to the implementation. It may be easier to rearrange the problem description itself and then map to the solution.

When you find a recurring pattern of transformation between spec and design, abstract that pattern into a framework.

Pattern 15.13   Interpreting Models for Clients

Use concrete examples with familiar notations, while still enforcing strict rules about terminology and definitions, to review and interpret formal models for customers who may not want to see models. Strictly separate external and internal views.

Intent

Building models helps to clarify requirements and designs, but the models themselves may not be appropriate to present to the customers. You need a way to validate the requirements, or designs, as captured in your models.

Strategy

Concrete Review. Specification models capture all possible behaviors (action specs and state charts) and all possible states (type model). It is always simpler to understand concrete examples rather than generalized specs. To do this, review the following.

- *Scenarios*: Narrative and interaction diagrams that trace through a collaboration with the system, with named objects in the initial state and consistently named objects for any information exchanged with the system. If you show the graph form of interaction diagrams, use a consistent layout and position for all objects involved; this helps comprehension across multiple interactions.
- *Snapshots*: Drawings of the state of the business or domain or of the state of the system. Illustrate how the snapshots change as they go through a scenario; this is the surest way to communicate their meaning to customers. The snapshots interpret the type model and static invariants; snapshot pairs interpret the action specs and dynamic invariants.

Positives and Negatives. Review positive and negative examples. When reviewing concrete examples of behaviors and states, include both an example that is valid according to the spec and one that is invalid. Include the constraints imposed by static and dynamic invariants. Generalize from the invalid ones and discuss how the informal specification prohibits them. Similarly, generalize the required valid cases and discuss how the formal specification enforces them.

Informal Specs. Review informal specs. The formal behavior specifications start with informal narrative and end with much clearer narrative description (see Section 3.4.1, From Attributes to Operation Specification). Always review this narrative specification and the definitions in the dictionary. Explain to the customer that the terms reflect the system's view of the domain and not necessarily every aspect of the domain itself.

Notations and Terminology. Use familiar notations. When you're showing objects, either in snapshots or scenarios, feel free to substitute graphical icons that are more suggestive of the objects involved. Use problem-specific drawings to show attributes and relationships between objects (such as a batch of silicon wafers positioned inside a particular crucible in a machine) to explain the meaning of corresponding snapshots.

Despite using largely informal and narrative descriptions to review the models, you should be particular about terminology. Treat the dictionary as the definitive glossary; terms outside it are suspect and should be avoided as much as possible. Reinterpret the customer's descriptions in terms of the dictionary and have the customer validate your description; update the dictionary with terms to make communication easier (see Section 3.8.2, Convenience Attributes Simplify Specs). If discussions with the customer regularly evolve into long and unfocused discussions of ill-defined terms or if the same issue is being repeatedly revisited, take on a more proactive role. Build models and use them to suggest defintions and proposed interpretations of requirements.

Conduct a Review. Conduct a user-interface review. Customers are happy to discuss what they should see on the user interface. Start user-interface sketches early, but use them appropriately. Do not get caught up in look-and-feel issues too early; instead, focus on information exchanged, expected behavior seen on the UI, and the flow of actions and corresponding UI elements for the user.

Any drawing of a user interface is a particular visual presentation of a snapshot. For example, attributes may translate into colors; an association between two objects may show up as a master-slave list or relative visual positions of the graphical presentations of each object. Every element on the user interface should map to an element on the underlying model, although the names may not be exactly the same. For example, presentation labels map to attributes or parameters, window names map to types, and buttons and menu items map to actions. Keep this mapping consistent and make it a part of your dictionary (at least in the package that includes both the models and the user-interface specification or prototypes). You are responsible to ensure that the user-interface bits are kept consistent with the underlying models.

An appropriate review would include scenarios, corresponding user-interface prototypes and flows, and the dictionary corresponding to the type model.

External versus Internal Review. Be very conscious of whom you are presenting a model to and why. It is a common mistake to review internal mechanisms and design decisions with a customer who should never even know whether you implement things that way. This is probably the most common error made when reviewing models among developers (as opposed to end users). Distinguish carefully between a review of a component from an external perspective (end users or clients who will call your code) and a review of the internal design (for the team that will implement that design of collaborating pieces).

The former is always centered on type models and operation specifications and should rarely discuss classes and inheritance. The latter is focused on collaborations between objects and includes the corresponding type models of each one; it can include many more details of code structure and reuse, such as class inheritance.

Prototyping and Vertical Slices. In short-cycle development (see Pattern 13.3, Short-Cycle Development), the most effective way to get the users' feedback is to produce something that works minimally. The only drawback is the users' tendency to imagine that you have already done the whole thing.

15.2 *Video Case Study: System Specification*

In this section, we are going to begin to build a system specification for the video business.

15.2.1   System Context

Here we introduce the idea of a software system we wish to build and explore the roles it plays from the viewpoints of various users and areas of activity. Effectively, this means zooming in on the interactions of the business model to understand exactly what goes on when, for example, a customer hires (rents) a video. It is often useful to build and compare descriptions of what happens now (with a manual or old system) and what will happen when our new system is installed; only the latter is illustrated here.

Some of the techniques described in this section are things you might do to try to think ahead to how people (or other pieces of software) will work with your system. It is rare to start with clearly defined system behavior requirements. Even in cases, such as telecommunications standards, in which voluminous "specifications" are available, a clear and understandable statement of requirements is usually not a part of these specs.

Building a prototype is an important option for many projects, and it can be used as a vehicle for finding and asking the same questions. It can be built in parallel with the scenarios of this section and the system specification illustrated in the next section and will be based on a set of classes that reflect the business model's types directly. See Section 13.3, Typical Project Evolution, and Pattern 13.3, Short-Cycle Development, for a discussion on prototyping.

15.2.2   Scenarios and User-Interface Sketches

A scenario is a story about how the system will be used. It has several benefits. First, it works as a medium for communicating with end users, who would not be expected to understand the more formal notation of the system specification. Most scenarios should be defined *by* the users, with the goal of capturing their ideal task flow and sequence.

A scenario also helps people understand the likely frequencies and sequences of the use of various operations, influencing the user-interface design and internal architecture.

In the scenario in Figure 15.7, we have highlighted the *commits* of major transactions on the video store system. These are points at which the interaction is not only with the user interface, and not only reading the business core, but also represents important changes to the state of business objects in the software. We focus on these actions first when we specify the system's behavior.

The scenario makes it clear how the responsibilities are divided among the various parties. For example, the system expects the member card before anything

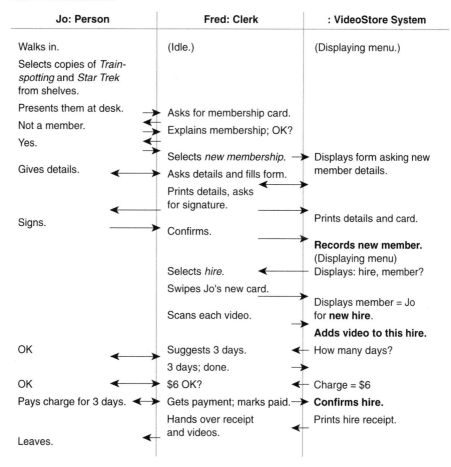

Figure 15.7   A scenario for a video rental.

Jo hires Trainspotting (2)

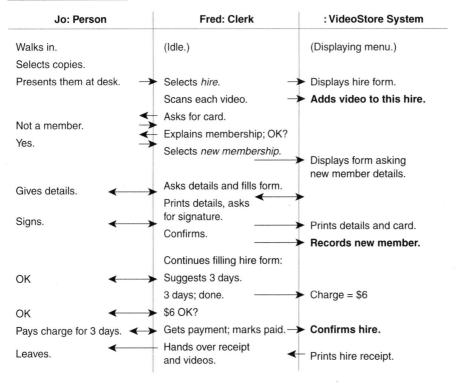

Figure 15.8   Scenario: rental with new member creation.

else, and the clerk therefore finds out at an early stage that Jo is not a member. Contrast that with the scenario in Figure 15.8, in which the clerk breaks off the hire operation to record the new member.

This scenario makes it clear that the user interface is essentially modeless; but there is no reason that the system should not be able to accommodate both scenarios. Each is only a single example of the system's use: This semiformal description does not capture all of the variations, so we must do quite a few to get a clear idea of the main patterns. In the end, the system specifications of the next section are the definitive specification.

We like this style of showing scenarios because they distinctly separate what each participating object does without using any technical notation. Popular modeling tools do not support writing narratives in this manner but instead support interaction diagrams (see Section 4.7.2, Interaction Diagrams). These diagrams can sometimes be annotated with narrative for each interaction arrow.

Making a Reservation

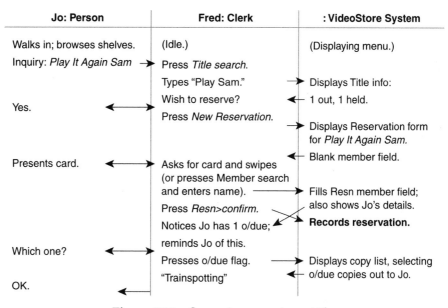

Jo: Person	Fred: Clerk	: VideoStore System
Walks in; browses shelves.	(Idle.)	(Displaying menu.)
Inquiry: *Play It Again Sam* →	Press *Title search*.	
	Types "Play Sam." →	Displays Title info:
Yes. ← →	Wish to reserve? ←	1 out, 1 held.
	Press *New Reservation*. →	Displays Reservation form for *Play It Again Sam*.
Presents card. ← →	Asks for card and swipes (or presses Member search and enters name). →	Blank member field. ← Fills Resn member field; also shows Jo's details.
	Press *Resn>confirm*.	**Records reservation.**
	Notices Jo has 1 o/due; reminds Jo of this.	
Which one? ← →	Presses o/due flag. →	Displays copy list, selecting o/due copies out to Jo. ←
OK. ←	"Trainspotting"	

Figure 15.9   Scenario: reserving a title.

The next scenario (see Figure 15.9) describes a member making a reservation for a title. Figure 15.10 shows a scenario for hiring and returning videos. Figure 15.11 shows a scenario for reminding customers to pick up reserved copies.

15.2.3   Storyboards

Individual user-interface windows and the flow between them can be captured as storyboards (see Figure 15.12). Each window is often associated with a particular task at some level of abstraction; a flow sequence refines a more abstract use case. Again, users should be actively involved in the actual design of the interface, even if that means teaching them a bit about what is achievable with the target system.

Of each type of window, no more than one is visible at a time. Those outlined in bold are always visible: the current title, copy, member, and hire. Italics show information displayed only in certain states. Underlined items are hypertext links; navigation proceeds as shown.

Only one subject area is dealt with here: the scenarios of the hires and reservations. Moreover, only those aspects immediately visible at the user interface are shown. If the system is expected to compile statistics about the monthly hirings of each title, that is not apparent here, and the user interface for it is not illustrated.

It is usually necessary to draw scenarios and storyboards dealing with several subject areas.

Returning and taking out copies

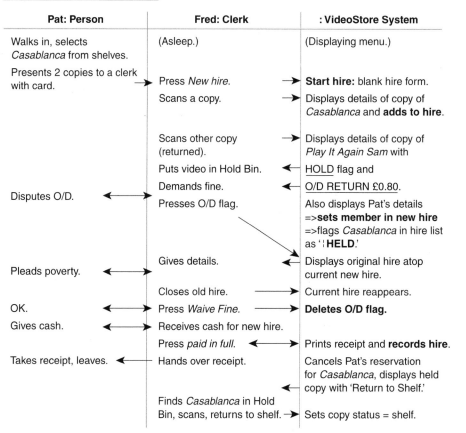

Pat: Person	Fred: Clerk	: VideoStore System
Walks in, selects *Casablanca* from shelves.	(Asleep.)	(Displaying menu.)
Presents 2 copies to a clerk with card.	Press *New hire*.	**Start hire:** blank hire form.
	Scans a copy.	Displays details of copy of *Casablanca* and **adds to hire**.
	Scans other copy (returned).	Displays details of copy of *Play It Again Sam* with
	Puts video in Hold Bin.	HOLD flag and
Disputes O/D.	Demands fine.	O/D RETURN £0.80.
	Presses O/D flag.	Also displays Pat's details =>**sets member in new hire** =>flags *Casablanca* in hire list as '¦**HELD**.'
Pleads poverty.	Gives details.	Displays original hire atop current new hire.
	Closes old hire.	Current hire reappears.
OK.	Press *Waive Fine*.	**Deletes O/D flag.**
Gives cash.	Receives cash for new hire.	
	Press *paid in full*.	Prints receipt and **records hire**.
Takes receipt, leaves.	Hands over receipt.	Cancels Pat's reservation for *Casablanca*, displays held copy with 'Return to Shelf.'
	Finds *Casablanca* in Hold Bin, scans, returns to shelf.	Sets copy status = shelf.

Figure 15.10   Scenario: returning, waiving fines, check-outs.

15.2.3.1   Animations and Prototypes

A slide show illustrating the scenarios is valuable for discussing requirements with end users. Better still is a prototype that can be taken through many situations. A prototype should be viewed as an analysis tool and is usually designed very simply from the principal types in the specification model (see the next section) together with a user-interface generator. In some cases, the core design of the prototype can be adapted to form the core of the system. However, it should be clear in the development plan exactly which parts of the prototype are to be carried forward and which are to be thrown away. Proper development practice should be applied to those parts to be carried into the design.

15.2.3.2   Predefined Context Design

Throughout this study, we conjecture that we're concerned with building a computer "System" that will work within a human context. Of course, many of the

Pestering Customers

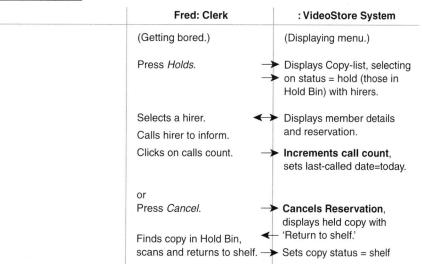

	Fred: Clerk	: VideoStore System
	(Getting bored.)	(Displaying menu.)
	Press *Holds*.	→ Displays Copy-list, selecting → on status = hold (those in Hold Bin) with hirers.
	Selects a hirer.	←→ Displays member details
	Calls hirer to inform.	and reservation.
	Clicks on calls count.	→ **Increments call count**, sets last-called date=today.
	or Press *Cancel*.	→ **Cancels Reservation**, displays held copy with
	Finds copy in Hold Bin,	← 'Return to shelf.'
	scans and returns to shelf.	→ Sets copy status = shelf

Figure 15.11 Scenario: reminding customers about reservations.

contracts that software designers have with their clients or employers are about building components within a larger piece of software or building a system embedded within a complex design of many pieces of hardware.

In such cases, most of the work illustrated in this section should already have been done and in considerably more formality than shown here. In fact, the relationship between our system and its context is then exactly that of a major component as illustrated next in Section 15.3, System Context Diagram.

15.3 *System Context Diagram*

From the scenarios, we arrive at a picture of the system's situation within its context. We can summarize the major use cases that we identified as being core state changes (see Figure 15.13). This makes it clear that we regard our system as spanning the entire business: There is one per VideoBusiness. It will probably be designed as a distributed system of independent subsystems in each store, but that aspect will be captured separately.

More generally, any single system can be seen as an object that interacts with its environment, which we can characterize with a type specification. The operations it performs can be specified in terms of a model of its state. This system model is based on the business mdoel—it represents what the system knows about its surroundings.

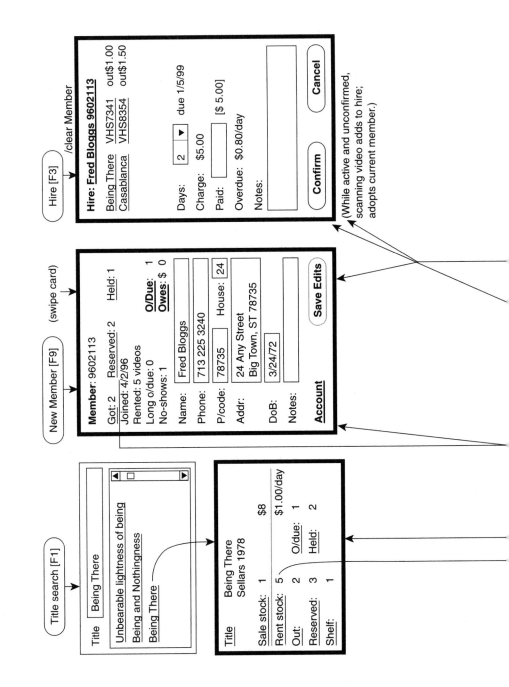

Title search [F1]

Title | Being There |

Unbearable lightness of being
Being and Nothingness
Being There

Title	Being There
	Sellars 1978	$8
Sale stock:	1	
Rent stock:	5	$1.00/day
Out:	2	O/due:	1
Reserved:	3	Held:	2
Shelf:	1	

New Member [F9]   (swipe card)

Member: 9602113

Got: 2	Reserved: 2	Held: 1
Joined: 4/2/96		
Rented: 5 videos		
Long o/due: 0		O/Due: 1
No-shows: 1		Owes: $ 0

Name:	Fred Bloggs
Phone:	713 225 3240
P/code:	78735	House:	24
Addr:	24 Any Street
	Big Town, ST 78735
DoB:	3/24/72
Notes:	

Account   Save Edits

Hire [F3]   /clear Member

Hire: **Fred Bloggs 9602113**

| Being There | VHS7341 | out$1.00 |
| Casablanca | VHS8354 | out$1.50 |

Days:	2 ▼	due 1/5/99
Charge:	$5.00	
Paid:		[$ 5.00]
Overdue:	$0.80/day	
Notes:		

Confirm   Cancel

(While active and unconfirmed, scanning video adds to hire; adopts current member.)

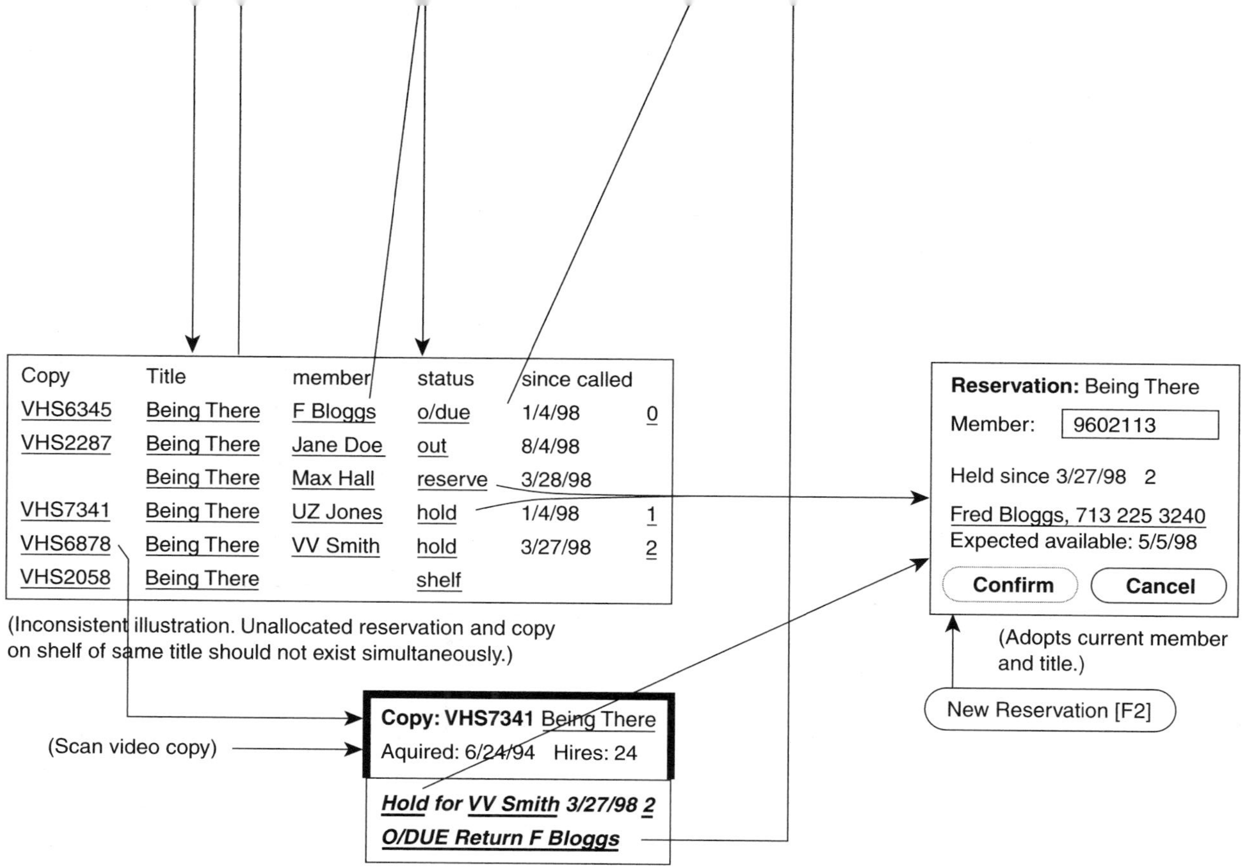
Copy Title member status since called
VHS6345 Being There F Bloggs o/due 1/4/98 0
VHS2287 Being There Jane Doe out 8/4/98
Being There Max Hall reserve 3/28/98
VHS7341 Being There UZ Jones hold 1/4/98 1
VHS6878 Being There VV Smith hold 3/27/98 2
VHS2058 Being There shelf
(Inconsistent illustration. Unallocated reservation and copy on shelf of same title should not exist simultaneously.)
(Scan video copy)
Copy: VHS7341 Being There
Aquired: 6/24/94 Hires: 24
Hold for VV Smith 3/27/98 2
O/DUE Return F Bloggs
Reservation: Being There
Member: 9602113
Held since 3/27/98 2
Fred Bloggs, 713 225 3240
Expected available: 5/5/98
Confirm
Cancel
(Adopts current member and title.)
New Reservation [F2]

Figure 15.12 Storyboard: user-interface sketches and flow of windows.

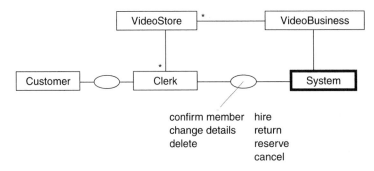

Figure 15.13   System context diagram.

15.3.1   Business versus System Context Models

Software systems are a part of the business and its operations and should be a part of business models, at least at some level of detail. What is the link between business models, the system context for a particular software component, and the subsequent software specifications and designs?

Suppose we want to improve some part of the business, as shown in Figure 15.14. Suppose the video business today conducts its operations by some combination of manual and automated processes. Memberships are recorded by issuing cards that have unique numbers; video rentals and returns are tracked in an Excel spreadsheet; and reservations are recorded by placing a slip with the member number into the cassette cover for the title.

An as-is model of the business (A) represents one refinement of the essential business requirements (B). A corresponding to-be model, incorporating the new target system (S) and revised business processes, will be an alternative refinement of the essential business model; this model is based on certain expected behaviors of the system (its specification) being used in particular ways by the business actors.

Section 10.11.2.4, Retrievals, illustrates with an example how a model comprising multiple software components and manual business processes can be shown to map to the essential business model. Similarly, an internal design of the system is one refinement of the system specification. It, in turn, is based on the individual specifications of each of the internal components in the design, which are configured so that they interact in specific ways.

15.3.2   UI Scenarios versus System Operations

In identifying the system context and use cases, we have actually considered some details of user interfaces and fine-grained interactions; yet the system con-

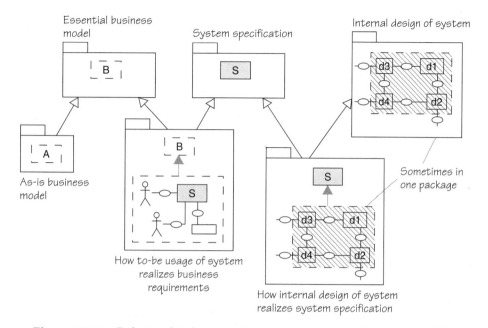

Figure 15.14   Relationship between business, system, and design models.

text seems to step back to a more abstract level of use case. This process can be rationalized as follows.

It can be helpful to make scenarios detailed enough to animate the imagination about how the system might be used in reality and to engage its users more actively in designing[1] this interface. However, you must realize that the GUI may change dramatically from a traditional window and dialog-box approach to direct manipulation to a voice-driven command interface. We would like to specify the main functions on the system independently of the interface mechanisms used for those functions.

So we look at the scenarios and think, "What are the core state changes, and what are the less stable GUI aspects?" These are what DB or IS people would call *transaction commits*; we have already begun the process by highlighting them in the scenarios. Each of these constitutes a "success unit" that delivers some value to the user.

Now we specify these more-abstract actions and separate the interface details to another package, such as when a refinement adds a particular user interface to the business core. We also separate out queries on the core: how to look up member details, titles, and so on. Typically, these queries are not specified in detail so

---

1. Yes, this is a design activity, albeit "external" or "business" design.

long as the type model offers the required information. The user-interface prototypes will capture the required query paths that the design must support.

15.4   *System Specification*

The system specification is the deliverable of the analysis phase, although it can
be somewhat more detailed than the traditional deliverables of analysis so as to
provide a less ambiguous and more consistent understanding of what is required
of the system. A feature of an OO analysis (in contrast with other rigorous methods) is that the description centers on a type model derived from the business
model. It is therefore easier to relate to the business, especially when changes
must be made.

A specification is best presented as a set of subject areas: an informal division
that relies on the idea that different things can be said about a type in different
places. In this way, we can focus separately on different aspects of a type's relationships and the behavior associated with it.

For each subject area, we will present the following:

- An informal description of the system's role and knowledge in this area
- A type model of the relevant aspects of the system's state, which is a vehicle for
  describing the operations the system can perform in this area
- Each operation spec, given as a postcondition and written both informally and
  formally, in terms of links in the system type model

15.4.1   Subject Areas

15.4.1.1   Membership

> *Rq 4   The System records membership of each store, including making new members, chang-
> ing their details, and deleting them. Members who have not been heard of for ages are periodi-
> cally deleted.*

At present we are able to give only informal descriptions of these operations:

<u>action</u> confirmMember (store: Store, person: Person)
   -- If person is not a member of store, makes new membership relation between them
<u>action</u> changedDetails (m:Member, p:Person)
   -- Replaces old personal details for m with the new ones in p.
<u>action</u> delete (m:Member) *-- Deletes m from records*
<u>action</u> purge (Store, today:Date)
   -- remove from members list all those who have not hired in > 2 years

We can achieve more-precise descriptions if we model the system's state using
types adapted from the business model. In other words, we will assume that the
system's internal state can in some way represent some aspects of the business.

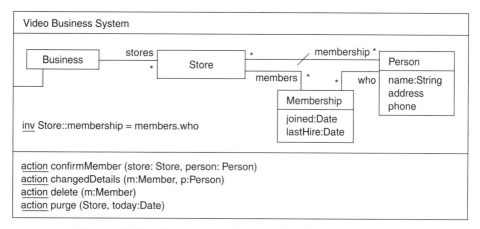

Figure 15.15   Type model for membership management.

Parts of the business model relevant to membership are shown in Figure 15.15.

> *Rq 5   A video business services its customers through its stores. A person can be a member of any number of stores.*

As we said earlier, the (Video Business) System knows about exactly one Business, with its many stores.

This is an abstract model of the state of the whole System and says *nothing* about its construction: whether it is distributed or centralized, whether the links are database keys or pointers, or whether the types can be found in the implementation as individual classes. All these matters are left to the design phase; a distributed object implementation, or a server-based one with remote screen-control clients, would both be equally valid choices.

We've represented the membership twice: as a direct association and also refined to a type. The first representation makes it directly obvious how the relation works; the second makes it easier to attach more detail. The invariant tells how the two are related.

This is of course only part of the system type model (more in a moment). The diagram can be interpreted as a set of assertions about video business systems; and it so happens that other assertions are presented later.

The actions can now be written in more detail, stating exactly what effects they have on the links in this abstract picture of the system's state. (All of them could be written inside the diagram, but we'll move them outside to save clutter.) Snapshots help visualize the intention of the more formal statements:

```
action Video_Business_System:: confirmMember (store: Store, person: Person)
post      -- insures person is a member of store
        store.members.who -> includes (person)
    and
```

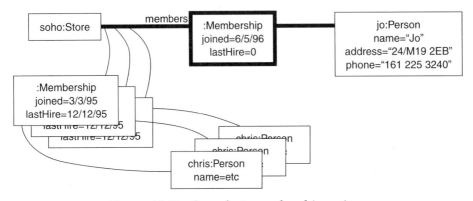

Figure 15.16   Snapshot: membership action.

```
-- define initial attributes for new members
(not (store.members.who -> includes (person))
==> store.members[who=person]::(joined=today & noShows=0)
```

To understand exactly what these statements are saying, it often helps to draw snapshots of relevant parts of the system's states before and after the operation occurs (see Figure 15.16). From the object type diagram, we see that each Store can have many links to Memberships and that the sheaf of links' name is members.

This snapshot, or object instance diagram, shows an example store with its members. Two states are shown, before and—outlined in bold—after the action has occurred. In this case, a preexisting Person object (perhaps set up by the user interface) has been linked to the store through a new Membership object.

Snapshots show only an example of a particular occurrence of an action in a particular situation. They are therefore used only for illustration and are not adequate documentation by themselves.

Now let's continue with the other action specs:

action Video_Business_System:: purge (store:Store, today:Date)
post   -- remove from members list all those not hired for > 2 years
                store.members −= store.members[today−lastHire > 2.years]

action Video_Business_System:: changedDetails (m:Member, p:Person)
post   m.who = p

action Video_Business_System:: delete (m:Member)
post   -- remove m from list of members of what used to be its store
                (m.~members@pre).members −= m

15.4.1.2   Rental

Rq 6   The system records Rentals *made by members. Each* Rental *is a contract whereby several* Copies *of a video may be taken away for an agreed period in exchange for a set charge. If any copy is kept beyond the date it is due for return, the system records a fine for it; the charges are made*

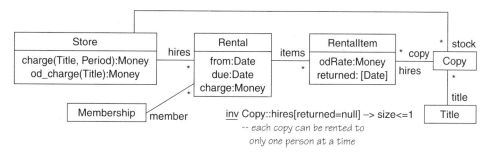

Figure 15.17   Type model: rentals.

separately. The store's rates may vary, are different for different video titles, and may include discounts for long periods; but rates charged for a rental are as they were at the time of hire.

Rq 7   Records of rentals are kept until they are no longer needed for statistical and accounting purposes.

Figure 15.17 shows the type model for Rental. A RentalItem represents the hire of an individual Copy. Each Copy may have many RentalItems, although at most one may not yet be returned.

A Copy is said to be out iff[2] it has an unreturned hire; it is o/due iff it is out and today is later than the rental due date. It is in iff not out.

> Copy:: (isOut = (hires[returned=null] <> 0)
> &   isOD = (isOut & hires[returned=null].~items.due < today)
> &   isIn ==> not isOut)

A Rental is said to be complete iff all of its RentalItems are returned.

> Rental:: isComplete = (items[returned=null] = 0)

The following system operations involve these types:

> <u>action</u> hire (store:Store, to:Date, copies:Set(Copy), m:Membership)
>   <u>post</u>   -- a Rental for these copies is added to this store's list of rentals
>   store.hires += Rental.new[member=m & from=today & due = to
>   &   charge = (store.charge(copies.title,to–today))..sum
>   &   items=(RentalItem.new[copy:copies
>   & odRate=store.od_charge(copy.title)
>   & returned=null])]

> <u>action</u> return (copy:Copy, store:Store)
>   <u>post</u>   -- if this copy is out, this copy's rental is marked returned
>   copy.~stock=store & copy.isOut@pre)
>   ==> hires[returned@pre=null].returned=today

> <u>action</u> purge(store:Store)
>   <u>post</u>   -- get rid of all complete Rentals made longer than 6 years ago
>   store.hires –= hires@pre[isComplete & (today–from)> 6.years]

---

2. iff = "if and only if."

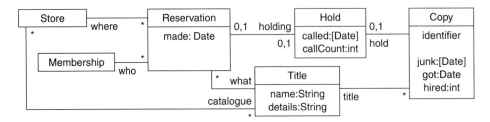

Figure 15.18   Type model: reservations.

15.4.1.3   Reservation

Figure 15.18 shows the type model for Reservation. A Hold represents the fact that a Copy is being kept aside for a Reservation, waiting for the Reserver to come and get it. A Hold not linked to a Reservation represents a Copy that is in the Hold Bin, having been held and for which the reservation has been canceled, so that it should be returned to the shelves.

If it is in, a Copy is said to be held if it is in the Hold Bin for some Reservation; Hold-Cancelled if it is in the Hold Bin but has no Reservation; shelf if available to be hired; sale if it can be sold; junk if it has been withdrawn from circulation.

```
Copy:: (  isHeld = (isIn & hold <> null)
    &    isHoldCancelled = (isHeld & hold.holding=null)
    &    isShelf = (isIn & not isHeld)
    &    isSale = (hired=0)
    &    isJunk = (junk <> null) )
```

The following actions are relevant to these types:

```
action reserve (member:Membership, here:Store, title:Title)
post      -- if title is in the store's catalog, add a Reservation for this title
    title : here.catalogue
            ==> Reservation.new .
                    [made=today & where=here & who=member &
                        what=title & holding = null ] -> notEmpty
```

```
action return (copy:Copy, here:Store)
post      -- if there are pending reservations for this title, hold copy for one of them
    copy.title.reservations@pre[holding=null & where = here].size>0)
==> copy.hold.reservation:: (holding@pre=null & what=copy.title & who)
```

```
action hire (here:Store, to:Date, copies:Set(Copy), m:Membership)
post      -- clear any reservations for these titles and member,
            -- and clear the Hold of any copies actually taken away
    delete copies.title.reservations[who=m & where=here]
    &    delete copies.hold
```

Figure 15.19   Type model: accounting.

15.4.1.4   Account

Figure 15.19 shows the type model for Account. The following operations are relevant to these types.

<u>action</u> credit (ac:Account, what:Money, why:String)
<u>post</u>   ac.items+= AccountItem.new[amount=what &
                                        reason=why and when=today]

<u>action</u> hire (store:Store, to:Date, copies:Set(Copy), m:Membership)
<u>post</u>   -- add hire charge to account
            (store.hires–store.hires@pre))::
            (member.account.items+= AccountItem.new [
                amount = charge & reason="hire" & when=today])

<u>action</u> return (copy:Copy, here:Store)
<u>post</u>   -- add overdue charge, if any, to account
            <u>let</u> thisHire= copy.hires [returned@pre=null],
            (thisHire::(rental.due<returned))
            ==> thisHire.rental.member.account += AccountItem.new [
                amount=thisHire::(odRate*(returned–rental.due))
            &   reason="overdue" & when=thisHire.returned]

15.4.2   Putting It All Together

Let's summarize the pieces of the model we've seen so far in a single diagram (see Figure 15.20). A good tool would make it easy to switch between the subject-area-specific views and this large view. We could also bring together the various pieces of specification we've seen for each action. For example, return has cropped up in several places. Its spec is the conjunction of them all:

<u>action</u> return (copy:Copy, here:Store)
<u>post</u>
(
            -- if this copy is out, this copy's rental is marked returned
            copy.~stock=store & copy.isOut@pre
    ==> hires[returned@pre=null].returned=today
) &
(-- add overdue charge, if any, to account
            <u>let</u> thisHire= copy.hires [returned@pre=null],
            (thisHire::(rental.due<returned))

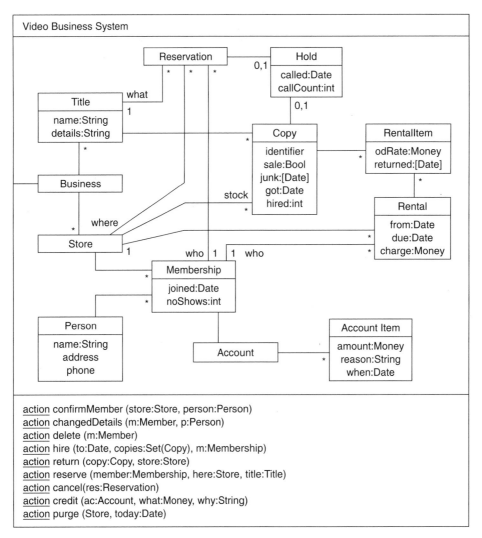

Figure 15.20   Combined type specification.

```
            ==> thisHire.rental.member.account += AccountItem.new [
                amount=thisHire::(odRate*(returned–rental.due))
            &    reason="overdue" & when=thisHire.returned ]
    ) &
    (            -- if there are pending reservations for this title, hold copy for one of them
                copy.title.reservations@pre[hold=null & where = here]->size>0)
        ==> copy.hold.reservation:: (hold@pre=null & what=copy.title)
    )
```

15.4.3   State Charts

It is often useful to express the behavior of a system by showing diagrammatically the effect of each of its operations of some part of its state. The part of its state we consider is usually (although not necessarily) one object in its model. By doing this for all the parts, we can build a picture of the behavior of the whole thing.

15.4.4   Copy

We've already defined various states for Copies (under Rental and Reservation earlier). Figure 15.21 shows a state chart for them. (Technically, it's a state chart for the entire system, wherein each state represents the truth of a predicate about any given Copy recorded within it.) Most of the guards needed in a state chart can be simplified by introducing convenience attributes, including parameterized ones, on the type model.

When a copy is created or returned, it is either held for an outstanding reservation or put on the shelf. It is held if it is wanted—that is, if there is a reservation for this title and in this store that does not have a Hold.

A copy ceases to be in when it is hired (that is, when a hire event occurs in which it is one of the copies hired). If a copy is held and the reservation is canceled, the copy is either reallocated to another reservation or becomes HoldCancelled until the clerk checks it back to the shelf. The same thing happens if another copy of the same title is hired to the member it's held for.

A state chart frequently brings up questions not noticed previously. For example, how is a new Copy introduced? What is the operation whereby the clerk puts a HoldCancelled copy back on the shelf? Are there system-enforced timeouts?

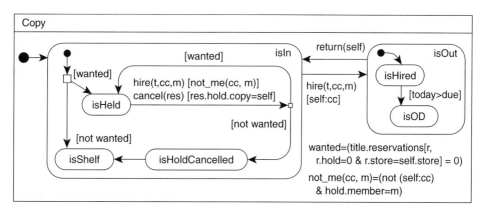

Figure 15.21   Copy state chart.

15.5 *Using Model Frameworks*

We've already seen (in Chapter 9, Model Frameworks and Template Packages) that a spec can be written in different parts, each one dealing separately with a different area of concern. By generalizing the components into frameworks, we can make a library from which many specifications can be composed. Key features of this approach are as follows.

- To get away from the notion of types as components. Every type has certain necessary relationships with other types. They are part of any coherent piece of work on the type and cannot sensibly be separated from it. So the components in a library are actually about relationships between types, often with one type as the central focus.

- To parameterize the components so that they can be applied in a wider range of situations and to build a repository of model and design frameworks that become a reusable asset across projects.

By separating and generalizing some components from the video store system, we can see what the typical contents of a specification library might be, and we can speculate about which other applications each component might be useful for.

15.5.1   Relation Detail

Something initially conceived of as an association may come to be modeled as an object. Although the association is then technically redundant—that is, an invariant fixes it precisely to other parts of the model—it need not be thrown out. It can still be useful to refer to it in postconditions and general discussion. We encapsulate this generic model in a framework called **Assoc-Type** (see Figure 15.22).

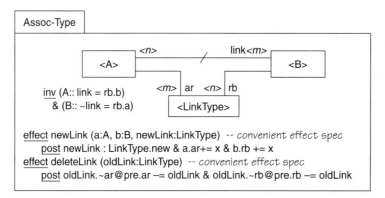

Figure 15.22   Framework for associative types.

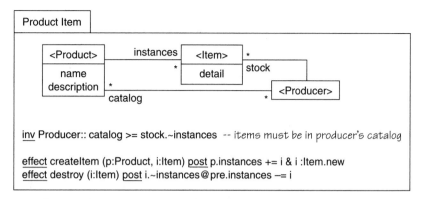

Figure 15.23   Framework for Product Items or Item Descriptors.

15.5.2   Products and Items

The distinction between Titles and Copies is a common one. Other examples are Menu items and actual dishes; training courses as in the catalog and specific occurrences on given dates; product lines and individual goods; or more generally, any description of a class of things as distinct from the individual instances of that class.

Indeed, Class and Object would be excellent names for these types, but instead let's call them Product and Item to avoid confusion (see Figure 15.23). An even more generic name might be Item Descriptor (see Pattern 14.9, *Items and Descriptors*).

This is a *framework*. It describes a relationship that is intended to be only part of the story within a full application. The types shown within the framework are *roles*. An object nearly always plays several roles in several frameworks. After introducing some more components, we'll see how the framework can be used.

15.5.3   Generalized Reservations

Reservations and bookings are a general concept that is applicable outside video businesses. A Reservation can be seen (in part) as a linkage between Users and Products. The relationship between products, items, and producers is unchanged from that in Instantiation. The framework diagram in Figure 15.24 repeats some of the links for convenience and adds extra assertions.[3] The main utility of the import of Instantiation is to simplify the action specs. The resulting framework is called Booking.

---

3. Each imported framework can actually be treated as a big assertion. It can be used directly as a term in a larger predicate.

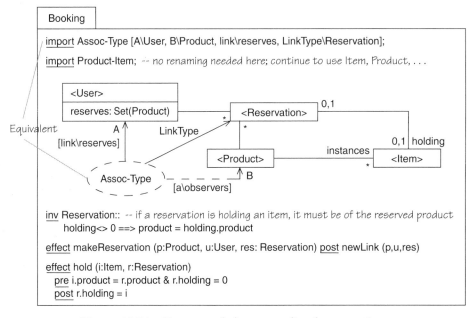

Figure 15.24   Framework for generalized reservations.

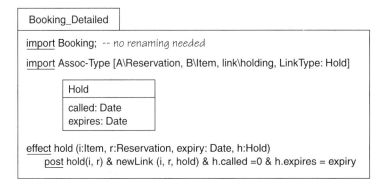

Figure 15.25   Reservations with detailed hold information.

15.5.4   More-Detailed Reservations

It may be useful for many booking applications to add more information to the holding link. So let's make it a Linkage and add some details to the LinkType. We do this in a separate package, extending our previous definitions (see Figure 15.25).

The new four-parameter version of hold uses the previous version and additionally sets the new attributes. Both versions are still available, but because the previous one leaves the date indeterminate, other specifiers would tend not to use it.

15.5.5   Other Framework Candidates

We could further factor out frameworks for generic accounts, accounting as specialized for rental organizations, and so on. We have not shown all these details here. The net result, upon unfolding the composition of these frameworks (in the manner outlined in Figure 9.6), would be a model that would be almost identical to Figure 15.20 except that almost none of it would have been built from scratch.

Chapter 16   How to Implement a Component

To implement a component means to devise a partition into smaller components and to define (a) the behavior of each one as a type and (b) the interaction between the smaller components that realizes the originally specified behavior.

There are many considerations to partitioning the components, with trade-offs on flexibility, reuse, and performance. This chapter discusses these trade-offs and provides a set of patterns for making these decisions.

To claim that we have implemented a specification, we must also document how the design meets the spec: Retrieve the specified model from the design and map design action sequences to abstract action specs. This chapter also outlines how to document this refinement.

16.1 *Designing to Meet a Specification*

The Catalysis refinement techniques make it possible to layer the design process so that the decisions that have the most far-reaching effects are clarified and are taken before the more trivial ones. A significant boundary in this layering lies between specifications of behavior (characterized by types) and descriptions of how that behavior is achieved (characterized by collaborations).

This chapter is about how you design a component to conform to a given type (behavioral spec). Again, it might be a complete suite of software, a component part of such a system, or a small object within the software. Or perhaps it is a mechanical system or human organization that you have decided to design using object-oriented methods (in which case, let us know how you get on!).

The spec might also be only a partial one: the view seen by an external actor through a particular interface.

The principal objectives to be met are as follows.

- Conform to the spec; we have this in common with all methods of software design.
- Build from well-decoupled components; this is a particular strength of object-oriented design.
- Retain precise traceability from spec to code; this is a speciality of the more serious development methods.
- Balance all the preceding within a design process that takes account of different development circumstances; this can be achieved with Catalysis.[1]

Decoupling tends to introduce much more separation between concepts than is typically found in an analysis. For example, any aspect of an object's behavior that could conceivably be varied tends to get delegated to a separate plug-in module. Thus, we end up with many more types of objects than were mentioned in the specification. Nevertheless, our refinement techniques (see Chapter 6, Abstraction, Refinement, and Testing) enable us to keep the traceability between the two models.

---

1. If you want us to write *your* advertising copy for you, we are very affordable.

Pattern 16.1   Decoupling

This pattern reduces the dependencies between parts of the design to make them able to function in many configurations.

Intent

This pattern is useful in creating a design of any kind, in which dependencies between parts must be reduced.

Considerations

Decoupling means minimizing the dependencies between the different pieces of a design. The more coupled a piece is to others, the less easy it is to reuse in a different context because it would have to be redesigned to work with its new neighbors. Creating any design from decoupled parts means that we can design new ones more rapidly, because we don't have to start from scratch. The designers of a new lamp, printer, phone, kitchen, or car does not begin by considering a lump of raw metal.

Work of Generalization. Reuse extends from simply calling the same routine from different parts of a program to publishing a design on the Internet. Whatever the scope, some work is necessary to generalize the design, as we discussed in Section 11.1.4, A Reuse Culture.

Importance of Interfaces. At one time, modularity in the software world was principally motivated by the need to divide a big job into manageable tasks. The interfaces of your module worked with the modules of the people in the neighboring cubicles; it was easy to discuss any issues about the interfaces. In a culture that reuses the pieces, you are unlikely to know all the components that yours will connect to: You must therefore be much more careful about your interface definitions (and about reading those of others).

Strategy

Coupling is introduced when one piece of a design mentions another by name: another class, another procedure or method, a variable in another class, or even (heaven forfend) a global variable. Explicit mentions of other classes may come in parameter or variable declarations; in type casts; when objects are created explictly of a particular class; and when one class inherits from another.

Therefore, you should avoid accessing variables outside your own class; always go through access methods instead and try to provide higher-level services instead of only get_ and set_ methods.

Separate concerns into different objects (and abstract objects; see Section 6.6, Spreadsheet: Object Refinement). Compose those objects together to provide the overall behavior. In general, prefer composition and black-box reuse over sub-classing.

Minimize the number of explicit mentions of other classes. Refer to other objects by their types or interfaces. When you need to instantiate another object, use a factory method rather than directly name the class to instantiate.

Minimize interfaces—that is, reduce the number of methods within each class that are used by another.

Draw dependency diagrams (see Section 7.4, Decoupling with Packages) between operations, classes, packages, and components. Study the package-level dependencies and seek ways to refactor across packages to reduce coupling.

Pattern 16.2 High-Level Component Design

In this pattern, you design large-grained components and connections.

Intent

Define component boundaries; you have a type specification of a system that you are to design.

Considerations

Object-oriented design is about decoupling; the major aspects of the way a component functions and connects to its neighbors can be separated into different subcomponents.

Strategy

Identify each major interface to the world outside the component: user interface, hardware monitor or drivers, and links to other components. This process provides a horizontal layering of the component.

Consider whether a façade is required for each of these interfaces (see Section 6.6.4, Object Access: Conformance, Façades, and Adapters, and Pattern 16.4, Separating Façades). Each façade is a subcomponent in its own right. If the interface is to another component within the same piece of software, the answer may be no: The interaction is direct. If the interface is to a person, the façade is a UI of some kind.

Reify the major continuous use cases (see Section 6.5.7.1, Reifying Actions, and Pattern 16.3, Reifying Major Concurrent Use Cases) that the system supports—often corresponding to business departments—such as loan books and manage stock. Each of these use cases can become a component that itself can be further reified. This approach provides a vertical partitioning of the component.

In deciding the functions of each major component, consider what can be most easily implemented with existing components or frameworks.

Consider whether the components should be in separate machines or separate languages. (See Pattern 16.5, Platform Independence.)

Choose the infrastructure components that will constitute your technical architecture (see Pattern 16.7, Implement Technical Architecture).

Use Pattern 16.8, Basic Design, to sketch interactions between subcomponents. While drafting a basic design, also apply appropriate design patterns (see Section 16.2, Detailed Design Patterns) to improve decoupling.

Specify each major component, particularly the core business components. Recurse this procedure on each subcomponent until the interacting subcomponents are simple classes.

Pattern 16.3   Reifying Major Concurrent Use Cases

This pattern describes recursive use-case-driven design.

Intent

The aim is to divide a large component into its major functional blocks, by use case.

Strategy

A business can be considered to comprise several large-scale use cases, each of which can be supported or run by a computer system. Frequently, the importance of the major use cases has already been identified, and they have been reified as business departments. Usually, these functions operate continuously and are interconnected in some way (see Figure 16.1).

The major use cases can now be reified to become objects that support those use cases. In this case, the use cases are complex, so the corresponding objects will be large enough to be refined separately. They might be set up in different computer systems. We can also show the actions whereby the objects interact with each other (see Figure 16.2).

Each of these objects should now be designed as a component in its own right, preferably starting with a specification. Each object will have its own model of

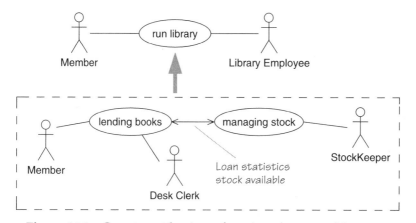

Figure 16.1   Concurrent business functions (use cases) interact.

what a book is (see Section 10.11, Heterogenous Components). Each of them has one façade to a human user and another façade to the other component.

These components could be distributed among various host machines.

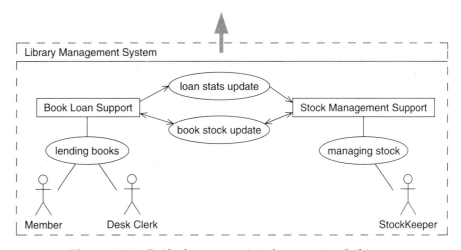

Figure 16.2   Reified use cases into large-grained objects.

Pattern 16.4 Separating Façades

Separate the GUI (and other layers that interface externally) from the core business logic.

Intent

The objective is to achieve horizontal layering, separating business from technology components.

Considerations

One principle of OO design is that you mirror the business types in the software. But in addition to the business functions, there are practical things to be dealt with, such as the presentation of pictures on the screen or the interpretation of mouse clicks or of signals from other machines. It's possible for a naïve designer (or a mediocre visual interface-building tool) to get the user interface well mixed with the business logic; but it is not recommended. We may wish to change the GUI without changing the business, so it is preferable to have everything separate.

The GUI involves more than one class—usually several classes for every kind of shape and display and every displayed business object. So we are talking here about another substantial component. Considerations that apply to the user interface also apply to interfaces to other external objects, so an interface to a separate component would also use a façade. Once these façades have been separated out, we are left with a core component in the middle that reflects the business types and represents the business logic in its code.

Strategy

Take each of the major components identified from major use cases—in a simple system, there may be only one—and separate out subcomponents, each of which is concerned with an interface to an external object (user, hardware, other software). Figure 16.3 shows an example.

Notice that each component could be broken down further if required. This is object refinement (as described in Section 6.6, Spreadsheet: Object Refinement).

Each component could be in a separate machine if required (as in client-server and the Web).

Each of the components has its own model of objects it is interested in. They include static types and reified actions (use cases). Examples are an object controlling the interaction with a user or, in the business logic, a long-term action such as loan.

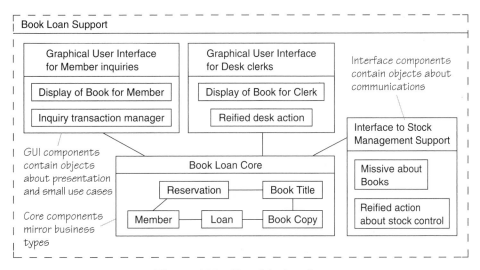

Figure 16.3   Possible façades.

Façades as Transparent Media. The need for a façade is largely to provide a way for messages to be sent across system boundaries. For example, we can define a message in the book loan core called reserve(title, member) in which each of the parameters is a pointer to an object of the appropriate type.

Now consider how that gets invoked. If the invoker is another piece of software in the same platform, the procedure call mechanism deals with the message send; memory addresses represent the object references. But if the invoker resides on another machine, some kind of remote method invocation must be employed; instead of memory addresses, some other kind of identifier must be used for the objects.

The situation is even worse when the invoker is a person. There is no one-shot way for a user to invoke a subroutine with multiple parameters: You must go through some interaction that gathers the information one piece at a time. This is half of what the GUI is for; the other part is the presentation of the states of core objects, something that is also a job of translation.

At the other end of the communications medium—be it a wire or screen + eyeballs + keyboard + fingers—there is another façade doing the translation in the opposite direction. In this way, the cores of the two components communicate[2] (see Figure 16.4).

---

2. This idea is similar to that of the OSI protocol stacks used in communications.

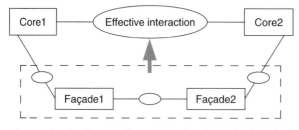

Figure 16.4   Layered communication via façades.

Façades between Components in the Same Platform. Sometimes there is no need for a façade: The two components send messages and keep pointers directly to each other. Because each component may be an abstract object (see Section 6.1.7, Object Abstraction), it may be that there is no single memory address representing each component: The two have numerous pointers directly between their consitutent objects.

Pattern 16.5   Platform Independence

Localize, in one component, ideas that are dependent on a particular platform.

Context

By "platform," we mean the technology that underlies the execution of your design. Here are examples:

- *Programming language, operating system, runtime environment*: Java, C++, Windows, UNIX, Smalltalk, Forté, Javascript on Netscape, workflow systems, and so on
- *Persistence*: How the state of the component is preserved for any length of time (file systems, databases)
- *Distribution mechanisms*: COM, CORBA, RMI, TCP/IP, and other technology (but consider which component is run on which machine)

All these infrastructure questions can be separated from the main issues of design. Outside their own layers, they should not make much difference to the design.

Strategy

Adopt techniques that keep as much of your design and code as possible independent of these layers.

This means that you should design using an insulating layer or virtual machine of objects in which the differences between one platform and another are concentrated. In this way, porting means changing only that layer. Also, keep the design well documented. Although porting would mean rewriting the code, it could be done quickly from the existing design.

Examples

The Java language provides a virtual machine that runs the same on all hardware.[3] The public GUI classes in the Java library are the same for all hardware, but they are façades for a layer of *peer* classes that adapt to the local operating system.

---

3. Never quite true, though, eh?

Pattern 16.6   Separate Middleware from Business Components

The point of this pattern is to separate business components from others. Wrap legacy systems behind a layer of objects representing the business concepts. Transition from custom infrastructure solutions to standardized middleware, enabling integration and extension of disparate systems in a way that is shielded from technology changes.

Encapsulate persistence mechanisms in a small number of platform-dependent objects with platform-independent interfaces. Separate out technology-dependent infrastructure components that serve primarily to connect other components, such as message queues, transaction servers, ORBs, and databases.

Intent

The objective is to build new business components that can integrate with legacy systems and across disparate systems while shielding the system from technology changes.

Considerations

The legacy system might be only a file server or a relational database. Or it might be a higher-level component, such as a spreadsheet with an API, or a complete application such as a reservations manager.

It may be "legacy" in the sense that there is a lot of code and data already built for a given application or only in the sense that compatibility constraints force the use of more-traditional technology such as RDBs.

Integration of disparate systems involves a lot of infrastructure support: communication, coordinating distributed transactions, load distribution, and shared resource management. The costs of developing infrastructure components of high quality would dominate a typical large business project compared with that of the actual business logic involved.

Strategy

Make a layer of business objects. In a client-server system, they typically reside on the server (although this strategy is independent of their location). The business objects correspond closely to the types found in the business model and deal with users' concepts, roles, departments, and so on (see Figure 16.5). As the business changes, it is this layer that is updated.

The GUI is a separate layer. In contrast to an older client-server (two-layer) architecture, the user interface should deal only with presenting business objects to users and translating user typing, mouse clicks, and so on to business object commands. Business rules should be embodied within the business objects.

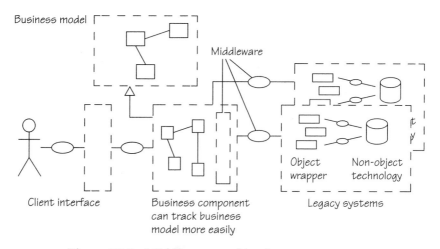

Figure 16.5   Middleware and business components.

The underpinning or old technology of database, communications, and so on is represented by a set of wrapping objects that drive them.

A variety of techniques exist for driving legacy components. You can use the API if you're fortunate enough to have one, or you can generate and send SQL or similar queries if it is a database component. For a host-based terminal application, you can use screen-scraping—pretend to be an old-style user terminal. These techniques should be encapsulated in middleware so that other components are not too dependent on the legacy communication. Whenever possible, buy the middleware components.

To use such a component accurately, it is helpful to build a model of it.

Benefits

The first benefit is platform independence. The business objects can be written independently of the legacy systems and can be ported. Using middleware, you can integrate new application components with existing application code and purchase components to build seamless business systems.

In addition, the software tracks business reorganizations. As usual in OT, the strength of reflecting the business organization in the software is that it can readily be rearranged when the business is reorganized.

Software location also tracks business location. Distribution of the objects among hosts comes after and is independent of object design (see Pattern 16.12, Object Locality and Link Implementation). This applies whether there is a central server or several servers or whether the business objects are hosted on server machines or clients or in their own machines. The strength of this independence is that the hosting can easily be rearranged—dynamically, if appropriate—as people and departments are relocated.

Pattern 16.7 Implement Technical Architecture

In this pattern, you document the selection of all infrastructure components and describe how they relate to the physical and logical architecture to be used. Implement the supporting pieces as early as possible and build an early end-to-end architectural prototype.

Intent

Reduce feasability and scalability risks of technical architecture.

Considerations

Much of the complexity and development cost of a large system can come from issues related less to the business logic than to technology factors: database access, general querying capabilities, message passing paradigms, exception signaling, interpreters for command languages, logging facilities, a framework for startup and shutdown, user-interface frameworks, and so on. These factors can be the most important ones in reasonable estimation of design and development times.

Coherence and maintainability of the system degrade rapidly if different developers choose their own schemes to solve these technology issues. Large-scale performance and scalability are determined primarily by how the components are partitioned and distributed across machines and by the nature of communication across machines.

Strategy

Make the design, implementation, and rules for using any infrastructure components a high priority. Separate distinct technology pieces.

- *Presentation*: Select a standard mechanism for all user-interface presentation— for example, MVC or document-view—and an implementation to go with it.
- *Business*: This category covers application components that partition application logic and business rules and collaborate to achieve the required business function.
- *Middleware*: This is the communication and coordination mechanism to enable components to collaborate across machine boundaries.
- *Component technology*: This includes the kinds of components and connectors that define more-expressive modeling and design constructs such as events, properties, workflow transfers, and replication.
- *Data storage and access*: This is the database access layer along with a logical layer above it to coordinate shared access to the data.

- *Utility classes*: Design and implement other domain-independent services, such as querying, exception signaling, message logging, command interpreters, and so on.

Use package diagrams to show the third-party and library components you will use. If you use a layered architecture, in which higher layers can call only layers below them, you can visually structure these diagrams to show the static dependencies corresponding to architecture layers. Explicitly capture tool dependencies (language versions, compilers, UI builders) across lower-level packages, introducing virtual packages for these tools if needed.

Use collaborations to show interactions between large-grained components and stereotypes or frameworks on the interactions (for example, «SQL», «RMI»).

Document in a package the overall guidelines or cookbook rules, including design and coding standards, that you want to follow for all these issues and particularly the rules to follow when adding new features to the system.

Pattern 16.8   Basic Design

Take each system action and distribute responsibilities between collaborating internal components. Begin by assuming that there is a class for every type of the system type spec.

Intent

The aim is to generate classes for coding based directly on specification types.

Context

A component specification has been written. It may come from requirements analysis (see Pattern 15.7, Construct a System Behavior Spec) or may be a part of the design of something larger (see Pattern 16.3, Reifying Major Concurrent Use Cases).

The component has been characterized with a type, specifying the actions it can take part in, in terms of the vocabulary of a static model. Figure 16.6 shows an example. These actions can later be refined to more-detailed interactions.

Considerations

Basic design is the first attack on a design before any consideration of optimization (see Pattern 16.13, Optimization) or generalization (see Pattern 16.11, Link and Attribute Ownership).

Classes, Specification Types, and Design Types. The types in a component's model are often called *specification* types because their reason for existence is to help specify the component's actions. A designer could invent a completely different internal structure that would still conform to the specified behavior as seen by external clients—a decision that would be justified by performance or other constraints.

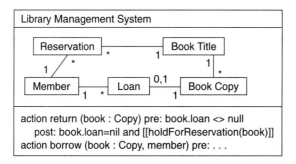

Figure 16.6   Type specification to be designed.

When you do a design, you define collaborations that divide responsibility among different types. These are often called *design* types, meaning that we know we must implement them at some stage; we indicate this by drawing them with slightly thicker boxes. In fact, the difference between specification types and design types is not intrinsic nor hugely important but reflects only the way you use them. You could just as easily use a design type—that is, one that you happen to possess an implementation of—as part of someone else's model.

The distinction between class and type also boils down to how you use it. After some quantity of refinement and design, you will end up with a type diagram in which all the actions are localized (that is, there are arrows showing which end is sending and which receiving), all the associations are directed (arrows showing who knows about whom), and all the actions have interaction schemes. At that stage, it is natural and easy to translate it all systematically into your favorite programming language. Nevertheless, you could stoutly maintain that it's all only a model. But generally, when we draw a box with directed links and localized actions that have interaction schemes, we'll refer to it as a class rather than a type.

Encapsulation. According to the principle of encapsulation, the internal structure of each unit should be invisible to others. In that way, each unit is designed to depend only on the behavior of those to which it is coupled. So what's a *unit*?

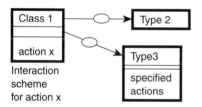

Ideally encapsulated design: one class uses several types and each class implements many types

The class (or the object) is conventionally taken to be the unit of encapsulation. But this isn't invariably the optimal solution: It may be useful to have a variable assortment of state-holding objects within a single design. If there is no intention ever to separate the design and if the pieces couldn't possibly make sense apart and will never be modified one without the others, then the unit of encapsulation is sensibly bigger than the object. It makes more sense to make the unit of design the unit of encapsulation (something that Java acknowledges by permitting visibility between classes in the same package).

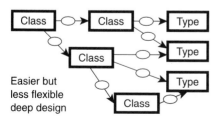

Easier but less flexible deep design

In any case, it can be difficult to begin a new design by working immediately with abstract types. It is easier to design the drawing editor beginning with example shapes and then generalize, carefully specifying in the Shape type what you require of any new shapes. Similarly, it's easier to design a library with books in mind and then generalize to videos and car rental. Brains work bottom-up.

We have found that it works well to begin with a large unit of encapsulation spanning several classes and then gradually draw the boundaries in. So we typically design sequences of operations that trace the flow of control several levels deep through the object graph. Generalizing is a subsequent step, which is done by defining a type for each class and then making it as general as possible. These then become cross-package interface specs.

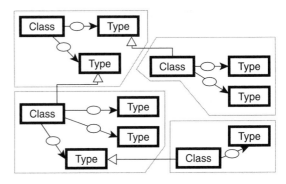

Strategy

Assign each system-level action to an internal object. In another part of the development (see Pattern 16.4, Separating Façades), the task of interfacing our component to its neighbors was delegated to a subcomponent. We can make some assumptions about how we will design the façade.

- Presentation of the state of the core to the external world will be handled appropriately by the façade. It will use observers (see Pattern 16.17, Observer) so that we need not consider the detail about how things appear on the screen. All we need do is keep the business objects' own state right.

- To the core the façade will send messages corresponding to the main actions we identified for the component as a whole.

- Each message will initially arrive at the most appropriate object in the core, which will then delegate some of the work to others. This object is called the *control* object for that component-level action.

The library is typical of many designs in that each type of external user talks to its internal proxy: each (real) ::Librarian through an instance of LibrarySystem::Librarian, each ::StockKeeper through an instance of LibrarySystem::StockKeeper, and so on (see Figure 16.7). Logging in establishes these connections via the screen, keyboard, and windows (each of these pieces of hardware has its software counterpart).

Program each system-level action. For each action specified for the component as a whole, design how its spec will be fulfilled by a collaboration of objects within the component. Make the starting assumption that the classes and pointers available are the types and associations from the component spec's static model.

To design each action, draw a before-and-after snapshot of a typical component state for this operation. Do them on the same drawing, with the after links distinguished, for example, by color. Work from the action spec: Ensure that your before situation satisfies the precondition.

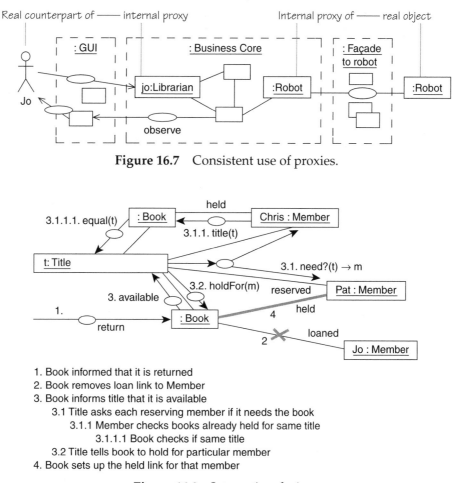

Figure 16.7   Consistent use of proxies.

1. Book informed that it is returned
2. Book removes loan link to Member
3. Book informs title that it is available
    3.1 Title asks each reserving member if it needs the book
        3.1.1 Member checks books already held for same title
            3.1.1.1 Book checks if same title
    3.2 Title tells book to hold for particular member
4. Book sets up the held link for that member

Figure 16.8   Interaction design.

Work out which operations each object must invoke on its neighbors, beginning with the head object, to achieve the after situation. To stick to basic design, your messages should only follow links. Draw them on top of the snapshot. It usually helps to number them in sequence of occurrence. Also number creations and deletions (see Figure 16.8).

The benefits of encapsulation become clear in this example. Do we really want to chase all the way down 5 and 6 to see how a book knows its title in this piece of design? See Pattern 16.9, Generalize after Basic Design.

Write stub operation specs wherever the interactions become too deep. For example, you can write a spec for Title::available (b: Book) and omit all details below 3 in this interaction diagram.

Title::available (b: Book)
<u>post</u>   book put on hold for one member with needy reservation for title
              (needy reservation for title = reservation for title, with no held copy)

If there are any different cases described in the postconditions not dealt with by the sample situation you have illustrated in the snapshot, repeat for the other cases. (With experience, of course, you can often skip all the tedious drawing. However, it's good to do some.)

It may be useful to redraw the design as an action sequence diagram (see Section 4.7.3, Sequence Diagrams with Actions). This technique shows the sequence more tidily and makes it easier to see how to move responsibilities "sideways" from one object to another. The role-activity variation also shows potential interference clearly (when one object is concurrently engaged in several threads).

When you're programming, follow the principles of coherence (see Pattern 16.10, Collaborations and Responsibilities): assign responsibility where it is appropriate.

Review Responsibilities and Collaborations for Each Class. After you program each system-level operation, each of the classes on which operations are invoked has a list of operations it is required to do. Document these operations as detailed in Pattern 16.10, Collaborations and Responsibilities, and review.

Consider Ownership of Each Link. That is, who knows about it? See Pattern 16.11, Link and Attribute Ownership.

Decide Distribution. That is, where does each object reside? On which machine? On what storage medium? In which major component? This can be done independently of the design. See Pattern 16.12, Object Locality and Link Implementation.

Decide How Objects, Links, and Actions Are Implemented. This is highly dependent on the answers to the preceding question. Each component may have its own internal representation of objects: as C structures, as Java or C++ objects, or as files or database records. Links may be memory addresses, URLs, CORBA identifiers, database keys, or customer reference numbers, or they may be refined to further objects. Actions may be further refined and ultimately be function calls, Ada rendezvous, signals, or Internet messages.

The implementation of links typically induces further message sends. For example, setting up or taking down a two-way link requires a housekeeping message (see Pattern 16.14, Two-Way Link).

The head class of the design is one possible implementation of the type represented by the system spec. The implementation class should have a separate name. If there is likely to be only one implementation, a reasonable convention (following [Cook94]) is to call the type ILibrary and the class CLibrary, for interface and class. The refinement relationship should be documented in the dictionary. (In Java, class CLibrary implements ILibrary.)

Collate Responsibilities of Each Class. The actions in which each class takes part can now be listed. Each one can be specified (if only informally).

Generalize. Push encapsulation toward each class being independent of all the others. Each action diagram should go only one level: the actions used by any method should depend only on the *specifications* of others.

It doesn't make much sense to encapsulate certain classes separately: you know that they will always go together. For example, how a current user selection is represented depends heavily on the design of the document. So, for example, the TextDocument and TextSelection classes will generally form part of one package and can be coded in a single Java package, C++ file, and so on.

On the other hand, an Editor may be able to handle many kinds of Document, so it makes sense to define a Document design type, with all the behavior the Editor expects, and provide several implementations. Defined fully, Document would have a complete model and operation list just as Editor does.

Reiterate for Each Design Type. The design has now been decomposed, and each design type can be implemented by designing it or finding a suitable library component.

Coding. Translate the classes and associations into program code.

Benefit

The benefit is that the system is designed to a spec. You can start easy, generalize, and optimize locally later.

Pattern 16.9   Generalize after Basic Design

Work with particular cases first and then generalize using decoupling patterns.

Intent

The aim is to achieve good decoupling by re-factoring an initial design.

Context

A draft design has been achieved using Pattern 16.8, Basic Design.

Considerations

There is a tendency for the design to be poorly decoupled after you do basic design. That pattern works with an overall view, using sequence charts and snapshots to show how messages propagate through the various layers of objects. But that very advantage works against encapsulation and decoupling: You are designing each object in a context in which the other classes are known, and the tendency is to make it work with those specific neighbors.

That does not mean we should throw out basic design or the notational tools that help it, although that has been suggested in some respectable quarters. We believe that human brains work best with concrete examples and that you cannot design a generalization without first creating something concrete.

Strategy

Apply generalizations after you complete the basic design. A wide variety of design patterns are directed at generalization and decoupling. Most notable are Pattern 16.15, Role Decoupling and Pattern 16.16, Factories.

In the library example, we can begin by lending books and then diversify into videos. Then we can privatize the library and start charging money.

Pattern 16.10   Collaborations and Responsibilities

In this pattern, you document and minimize responsibilities and collaborators.

Intent

The intent is to distribute responsibilities among objects in such a way as to produce a flexible, coherent design.

Context

The context is action refinement: making decisions that implement or put more detail into an abstract (set of) actions. This may be part of a computer system design (Pattern 16.8, Basic Design) or part of the reengineering of a business process (Pattern 14.1, Business Process Improvement) and may in particular be the engineering of the business process of which using a computer system is a part (Pattern 15.5, Make a Context Model with Use Cases).

A collaboration diagram defines interactions between objects. A collaboration is a set of actions that are related in some way, usually a common goal. Here are some examples.

- The maintenance of an invariant

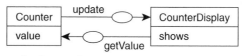

inv Counterdisplay :: shows=myCount.value

- Forming a refinement of a more abstract action (involving [some subset of] the same participants)

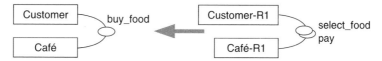

- Forming the implementation of an action (in which one object employs the services of others to fulfill its responsibilities to someone else)

The dictionary details the responsibilities of each type or class.

Considerations

Each participant in the collaboration should have a responsibility that can be succinctly stated: "displays integer values" or "sells food" or "represents recently deleted items in an editor." The actions should be a small set all of which relate directly to this responsibility.

The more specialized the collaborators of an object—the further down the type hierarchy—the less generally its design can be applied and used. The objective is to make the set of objects with which it will work as wide as possible.

Classes, Types, Design Types, Abstract Classes. The collections of methods for the actions now form classes. The boxes to which you sent messages without programming them further are design types: You know what you want them to do but haven't yet decided how. The process can be repeated for them later.

Strategy

Document Responsibilities and Collaborators. Record the following in the dictionary:

- The responsibility statement for each class or type
- The collated list of actions and collaborators for each class or type
- The specifications of each action
- The refinement of each action (for example, as skeleton method code)

Localize Actions. A general joint action ▭─○─▭ represents an interaction between the participant types without saying who does what. But at this stage, neither of the participants can be understood independently of the other. Localizing the action doesn't by itself reduce this coupling but is a useful preliminary to generalizing

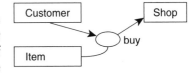

the sender end (see next point). Decide who is the sender and who the receiver. Mark them with arrowheads. Any other participants remain as parameters. (Writing the name and signature of the action within the behavior section of the receiver's type box is also a way of indicating localization.)

Minimize Coupling (Dependencies). The list of collaborations should be small. The well-known CRC technique of detailing responsibilities and collaborations on a single index card gives some idea of their preferred sizes. If the list is too large, suspect that a redistribution of responsibilities is required.

For each type, consider whether it is possible for its collaborators to have more-general types. For example, an Editor might work with Documents of any type (such as Texts) rather than only Drawings; conversely, a Document need not be driven by an Editor. Redraw using the more-general types.

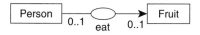

If you wish to focus on one participant type for the present, you can indicate that this is not the whole range of possibilities by using an "optional" mark.

In the most extreme case of decoupling, the receiver doesn't care at all what type the sender possesses, because the receiver never sends any messages back to the sender. This implies that the action we're looking at is never going to be refined further, and it is at this stage that we usually start calling it an operation or message or function call and expect it to be coded directly in the program. The sender's type is then Object, the type of which all others are subtypes.

Actually, this is not quite true. Even at the message level, there is some dialog, that depends on the sender's understanding what it gets back. An operation coded to be invoked as a function call needs a different sender than one invoked through an ORB or a dynamic linking system. Asynchronous and synchronous calls are different again. So strictly speaking, you must always know something about who is calling you, at least to the extent that you impose some requirements on its proper behavior.

For each type, consider whether the number of its collaborators can be reduced by a rearrangement of responsibilities. For example, we get the Editor to transfer deleted material to the Clipboard rather than get the Documents to talk to the Clipboard at the Editor's behest. That avoids the need for the Document (or its designer) to know about Clipboards, with the benefit that Documents can be reused in other designs where there is no Clipboard.

Consider the many other forms of decoupling listed in design pattern texts. The decoupling results in designs that are easier to pull apart, using the parts as components in different contexts. Decoupled designs also are more resilient to change; each interface impedes the propagation of change.

Pattern 16.11   Link and Attribute Ownership

The aim here is to decide and document the directionality of links.

Context

The context is late-stage design. You have worked out the collaborations (see Pattern 16.10, Collaborations and Responsibilities).

Considerations

A link (or attribute) in an abstract spec or design represents the fact that somewhere, somehow, there is a member of one type associated with every member of the other type. The link says nothing about how the types are associated.

There are various possibilities. The most straightforward are as follows.

* Each type knows about the other (see Pattern 6.4, Refinement Is a Relation and Not a Sequence), something that is frequently represented using a two-way link. Although simple, this link often results in excessive coupling. A simple measure would be to decouple using types (see Section 7.4.1, Role-based Decoupling of Classes).
* One type knows about the other, but not vice versa. This is usually the preferred solution: It layers the dependencies and makes testing simpler.
* Neither type knows about the other, but a third object keeps a mapping between them. When used systematically, this approach can be used to make objects appear more extensible: Its basic implementation is already defined, but an external mapping helps define extensions to its properties and behaviors.
* No one stores the information directly, but it can be computed.

A link is needed in a particular direction if an object must retain a reference to another across its public methods—for example, it must send a message down that link—or must keep the identity of an object for someone else—for example, as a list does.

Strategy

Notice that this issue is separate from link implementation, which has to do with Pattern 16.12, Object Locality and Link Implementation.

Pattern 16.12   Object Locality and Link Implementation

Locality of an object can be decided independently of basic design, employing appropriate patterns to implement links and messages crossing locality boundaries. Locality applies to hosts, applications, and media.

Intent

Decide where an object will reside and whether and how it will move around.

Context

This work is done after object design (see Pattern 16.8, Basic Design) and link ownership (see Pattern 16.11, Link and Attribute Ownership).

Considerations

Essentially, these issues are all the same, or very closely related.

- Which host an object resides on in a distributed system
- Which storage medium and platform an object is in (database, serialized in file, main memory, on a listing, in a bar code, on a magnetic stripe card, and so on)
- Which application or major component an object is in (in a spreadsheet or word processor; in a banking application; in a tax authority program)

In each case, we must worry about the following questions.

- How is the object represented in that locality? Can it execute there?
- Does the object move across locality boundaries (for processing or storage or to be processed locally for efficiency)? What makes this happen?
- If it crosses boundaries, are there then two copies (for economy or robustness)?
- If there are copies in different localities (temporarily or permanently), how are they kept in sync (paging or transaction tactics)?
- What are the performance implications of this distribution?
- How are cross-boundary links represented (URLs? keys? reference numbers?)?
- How do actions between objects in different localities work? How are parameters represented in transit?
- How should we handle different views and capabilities in different localities (for example, a picture in a CAD program imported into a word processor)?
- The basic object design should be independent of locality and boundaries and movements. How is this made to work?

Strategy

Use standard frameworks for distribution, including CORBA, Active-X, and COM+.

Because these decisions can be taken late, the basic design is changed very little by distribution across localities in a functional sense. This means that a distributed system can first be implemented on a single machine as a prototype. However, the performance implications can be significant, so, depending on the amount of interaction with the object and the bandwidth of the communication medium between them, architectural prototypes should be built early to validate both locality and responsibility decisions.

Pattern 16.13   Optimization

Apply localized refinements to make the application run faster.

Intent

The objective is satisfactory performance.

Context

Optimization should be undertaken after object design (see Pattern 16.8, Basic Design) and link ownership (see Pattern 16.11, Link and Attribute Ownership). Juggle with object locality (see Pattern 16.12, Object Locality and Link Implementation).

Object-oriented programs typically run 25% slower than their traditional counterparts, and they take up more space. And the more they are engineered for reuse, the slower they run. The cause? It's the dynamic name resolutions, and it's all those message sends between objects politely observing their demarcation rules, carefully deferring to the responsible person for each part of the job like a bureaucracy gone mad. (Is this an argument against applying the OO paradigm to business processes?)

Considerations

See Pattern 6.2, The Golden Rule versus Other Optimizations—optimization balances against flexibility.

Strategy

Eighty percent of the time is spent on 20% of the code. The majority of the code can mirror the business model: After running profiling tools to ascertain performance bottlenecks, concentrate on the worst 10% of the 20%.

Initial optimization should usually be focused on the levels of algorithmic improvements while trying to retain encapsulation. Beyond that, optimization is largely a matter of specialization and coupling—making one piece of code more dependent on its neighbors—and of technology-level optimization—improving locality and paging behavior, reducing network traffic, and tuning the database structures.

- Direct access to data; use friends (C++) or in-package access (Java)
- Less delegation; bring more of the job within one object
- Use static data structures
- Make standard optimizations as for conventional code

Object locality (see Pattern 16.12) is also an issue. Various patterns, such as caching and proxies, can be used to bring an object closer to the point of application while minimizing overhead and impact on the design.

Benefit

A basic design built directly from the business model can very quickly be constructed and run as a prototype, feeding back to the requirements analysis process. Optimizations can be kept as a separate task.

16.2 *Detailed Design Patterns*

There is a rapidly growing literature on design patterns. Patterns enable designers to discuss their designs clearly with their colleagues and to convey sophisticated ideas rapidly.

We believe that all programmers should have a basic vocabulary of design patterns, and we consider it inexcusable for a college now to release a computer graduate into the world without this knowledge.

This section highlights some essential patterns and shows how they serve the major objectives of decoupling. References to more-detailed discussion on these patterns can be found in the Bibliography.

Pattern 16.14   Two-Way Link

In this pattern, you make the participants in a two-way link responsible for linking and unlinking.

Intent

In the latter stages of design, it is decided to implement a single abstract association as a pair of pointers:

Various messages sent by other parties to A or B may cause instances of the association to be created or destroyed, adding or removing B instances from an A instance's list.

Objective

The aim is to ensure that the pointers are always reciprocal. Although the membership of the list may change, every item on an A instance's list must have a ~list pointer back to that A instance.

> (a:A:: a.list.~list=a) and (b : B:: b.~list.list->includes(b))

Strategy

When one end of the link wishes to alter the list, it must first inform the other. In general, the message must include self so that the recipient knows who it is being linked to. We therefore have two messages:

> void B::makeLink(a: A);   // pre (~list=null)
> void B::breakLink(a: A);   // pre (~list = a)

The same thing applies in the other direction if it is required that B should be able to initiate a change.

These messages should be used only between the participants in this link and should not be the same as any other messages (for example, the messages from outside that initially prompt the objects to set up the link). This approach gives better flexibility.

makeLink is often invoked as part of a constructor initializing a newly created object. *Either* the destructor of each object must send **breakLink** to all its list members, *or* it must be demonstrated in the design documents that the object will never be destroyed when there are list members.

Variants

The links may be one-to-one or many-many. If the cardinality is multiple at A's end, then B::breakLink(a) has a precondition (~list includes a).

One end may "own" the other—that is, making and breaking the link coincides with creating and destroying the object. In that case, the job of makeLink is performed by each of the constructor functions, and the job of breakLink is performed by the destructor. If ownership can be transferred, a separate transfer function should be used.

The links are not necessarily pointers in memory: They can be database keys, names, or any other kind of handle.

Pattern 16.15   Role Decoupling

Declare every variable and parameter with an abstract type written for that purpose.[4]

Intent

The intent is to decouple by minimizing the number of operations a client explicitly requires.

Context

We have a draft of a basic design; we seek to improve and generalize it.

Considerations

Few of the objects you design need to use all the messages understood by those it collaborates with. To put it another way, most objects provide a variety of messages that can be divided into separate interfaces; each interface is used by a different class of client. This situation enables substantial generalization.

Strategy

Declare every parameter and variable to be an abstract class or interface that specifies only the operations used by that variable, and no more. (A less extreme version is to permit some sharing of interfaces between variables.)

To show this technique pictorially, for every directed association between classes, draw the link instead to a type specification (in C++, a pure abstract class; in Java, an interface). The original target of the link is a subclass (Java: implementor) of this specification. In Figure 16.9 we have decided that a Book is loaned not to a Member but to a BookHolder, of which Member is only one possible implementation.

(Concrete classes are outlined in bold, abstract types with light rules.) Each type represents a role that the instances play in relation to the source of the link. Now it is easy to imagine BookHolders other than Members and to imagine LibraryUsers other than Members.

---

4. This principle is enforced in some programming languages, such as CLU.

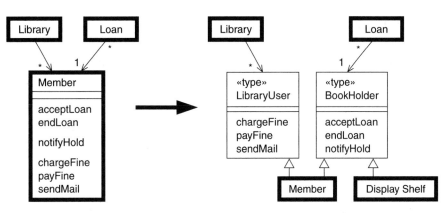

Figure 16.9   Using types as roles to decouple.

Benefits

The design has been generalized.

The designers of the surrounding classes are less likely to spread into using messages not intended for their use, so there is a tighter control on decoupling.

Variations

Fanatics may apply this pattern to every variable and parameter and hence every link on the diagram—two, for two-way links. Each class is surrounded by a cloud of the interfaces it requires and the interfaces it implements.

Notice that a collaboration framework (see Section 9.3, Collaboration Frameworks) is a set of roles coupled by actions—a logical extension of this pattern.

Pattern 16.16   Factories

The idea here is to use classes and methods whose speciality is knowing what class to instantiate.

Intent

The goal is to reduce coupling caused by explicit mentions of other classes in instance creation.

Context

After we have rid every declaration of any explicit mention of a class, we find that there are still one or two class names lurking in the code.

Considerations

Role decoupling allows a Loan to work with any BookHolder and any LoanableItem so that new variations could be invented every week; we could end up loaning geysers to Martians and never have to change a line of code outside those classes. But somewhere the objects must be created, and at that point you must stipulate a particular class and not just a type.

Strategy

Avoid distributing object creations all over the program. Instead, centralize the job of creating objects within *factories* [Gamma94]. The object-creation service provided by a factory has access to information with which it can decide which one to create. Call the factory, providing relevant information, and it will return an appropriate new object.

Have one factory for every type that has different implementations. The factory is often in a class of its own, and an instance of it is attached to something central.

Example

A new Loan must be created whenever a LoanableItem is handed over to a BookHolder. But there may be different subclasses of Loan, depending on the details of the period, and on different kinds of Items and Holders. Techniques, such as double-dispatching, can be used to distribute the decision across all the classes on which it depends. Instead, a more maintainable solution is to centralize the decision making and leave that item to make relevant queries of the other classes:

```
class LoanFactory         // there is one of these in every Library
{...
    Loan makeLoan (LoanableItem item, BookHolder holder)
```

```
{    xxx= item.variousEnquiries( ); yyy= holder.questions( );
     ... decide depending on xxx and yyy ...
     if (...) return new ShortLoan(item, holder);
     else if (...) return new StandardLoan(item, holder);
     else ....
```

Notice that the return type is declared as the supertype Loan, so the caller need not know anything about the implementing classes. When a new class of Loan is invented, we add it into the system *and* change the rules in the factory; but we need to change little else.

Benefit

The factory class acts as the central place in the design that knows about what implementations are available. This arrangement minimizes the number of places in the program that must be modified to be reused or to take account of additional implementations.

Variants

The factory can also act as the central point for constructing user menus—for example, of classes of Loan you can choose.

The LoanFactory may be a supertype, with different implementations providing different policies in different Libraries. See Pattern 16.18, Plug-Points and Plug-Ins.

Pattern 16.17   Observer

Whenever a change in state occurs, broadcast a generalized notification message to all those who have registered interest.

Intent

The goals are to keep one object up-to-date with the latest state of another and to allow many classes of Observer to observe the same Subject.

Considerations

It is often desirable to have one object continually kept up-to-date as another's state changes. Examples include GUI and other façades, replicated database entries, and cells in a spreadsheet.

A naïve scheme would invent purpose-designed messages for the subject to update the Observer whenever it changes (as part of its response to other roles it plays). This approach has the drawback that the two classes are coupled together, but we can apply role decoupling.

Strategy

The two classes—Subject and Observer—are related by Pattern 16.14, Two-Way Link. The association may be many-many. Once an Observer has registered with a Subject, any state changes cause the Subject to broadcast a notification to all its Observers. The notification must be appended to the code of any routine that might cause a change.

Pattern 16.15, Role Decoupling, is used to minimize the Subject's dependence on the Observer. All it knows about is a type that can receive the update messages (see Figure 16.10). Several Observers can watch one Subject at a time.

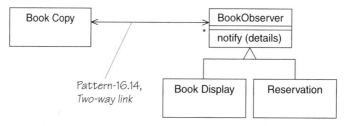

Figure 16.10   Using the Observer patterns.

Benefits

The Subjects can be designed without reference to how the Observers will work. In particular, the business core of a system can be designed independently of the user interface. New classes of Observer can be added without disturbing the Subject.

Variants

The notify message can contain more information or less information about the nature of the change and the new state. In some designs, it carries no further information at all, and the Observer must come back and ask for whatever details it is most interested in.

Pattern 16.18 Plug-Points and Plug-Ins

Variability in an object's behavior can be encapsulated in plug-ins.

Intent

The aim is to allow modular and extensible variety in an object's behavior.

Considerations

To provide different versions of the behavior of a class of objects, it is possible to write different subclasses. For example, a class of Report could have EmailReport and WebPageReport. But this doesn't work very well.

- You can't change an object's class during execution. This may be OK for some classes, but others may need to change their state.
- If you have more than one dimension of variability, you would need a subclass for all the combinations: LongEmailReport, ShortEmailReport, LongWebPageReport, and so on.

To get an object's behavior to change in different states, you could use a flag variable and a switch statement. The drawbacks are as follows.

- You must change the object's code to change the behavior.
- Many changes in behavior require a variation at many points in the code. It would be possible to get them out of sync.

Strategy

Move variation points into separate objects and have only one basic class of principal object (see Figure 16.11). Use Pattern 16.15, Role Decoupling, to keep the principal independent of the various plug-ins.

Benefits

- New plug-ins can be written without altering the principal.
- The plug-ins can be changed on-the-fly, representing modes or states [Gamma95].
- The pattern can be applied over as many variabilities as there are.

Variants

You can also use small "policy" plug-ins or equal-sized component "plug-togethers" (see Chapter 10, Components and Connectors).

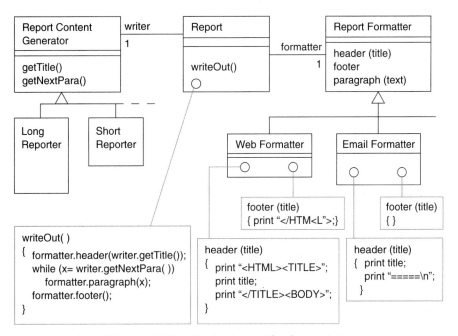

Figure 16.11   Designing with plug-points.

16.3   *Video Case Study: Component-Based Design*

In this study, we assume that there are several large components from which we wish to build. They may be third-party components or may exist from a previous piece of design.

   We make specifications of each component. Again, they may already exist, or we may build them from our understanding of the components. In dire cases, this means experimenting with them in testbeds; the process of formalizing the spec exposes the questions that need to be answered.

16.3.1   Rental Manager

Figure 16.12 shows the type model of the Rental Manager component. The Rental Manager knows just enough about renting to tell you how much it costs to rent an item, when it is due, and what payments have been made and which are outstanding.

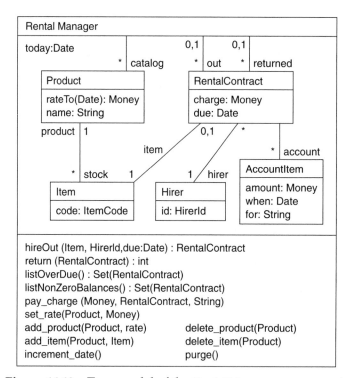

Figure 16.12   Type model of the Rental Manager component.

```
action Rental Manager:: hireOut(_item, _hirer, _due) : RentalContract
pre:      _item : catalog.stock & due>today
post:     out += result & result = RentalContract.new &
          result:: ( due=_due & hirer.code=_hirer & _item=item.code &
                   charge=_item.product.rateTo(due) &
                   account.–>size=1 &
                   account:: (charge = –amount
                          when = today & for="hireout"
          )           )
```

Notice that there is no payment recorded by this operation.

The initial item on the account is the charge for the hire to the agreed due date. If payment is made on the spot, it should be recorded separately.

```
return (_contract) : int
    pre: _contract::out
    post:out–=_contract & returned+=_contract &
        result =min(today – due, 0)

listOverDue() : Set(RentalContract)
    post: result = out[due<today]

listNonZeroBalances() : Set(RentalContract)
    post: result = returned[account.amount.–>sum <> 0] // only for returned items

pay_charge (amount, contract, why) // payments or charges, including fines
    post: contract.account+= AccountItem.new [amount, today, why]
```

16.3.2   Reservation Manager

Figure 16.13 shows the type model for Reservation Manager. The Reservation Manager is a database-based component set up to record the fact that a reservation is held for a particular title and that a particular copy is held for a reservation.

When a copy is returned, the wanted function should be used to find whether there is a reservation for its title; if there is, use hold to allocate the copy to the reservation. Use enquire(copy) to see whether a particular copy is being held.

Use delete(Reservation) when a reservation is canceled or out of date or to release a held copy.

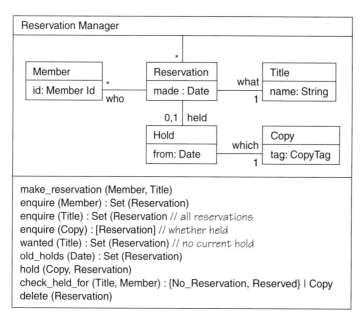

Figure 16.13   Type model of Reservation Manager.

16.3.3 Membership Manager

Figure 16.14 shows the type model of Membership Manager. Our architecture will use the Member::info field to store encoded historical statistics about the member: how many videos rented to date, how many returned overdue, and how many reservations not picked up.

External Reason is an identifier that we give to the Accounts Manager; when we retrieve the information about an account item, we must look up the details of the item elsewhere using the External Reason as a key.

The Membership Manager communicates with the outside world via an API over which can be transmitted keys and suitably encoded forms of the modeled types. There is a set of inquiry functions (not shown) for reading the database.

The designers will provide Java applets for displaying the following:

- List of Accounts or Members (with user facilities to select for further details)
- Member (with a pluggable routine for displaying the info field), with interactive facilities to edit name, address, and phone fields
- Account (with a pluggable routine for displaying External Reason as a hypertext link that can be queried further)

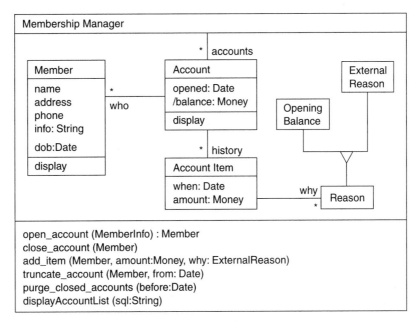

Figure 16.14 Type model of Membership Manager.

16.3.4 High-Level System Design

Here, the components are connected to form a design that meets the system spec. It's important to document some justification for believing that it does so properly. As a high-level design, only the overall scheme of interactions is decided; the detailed coding will be left until coding.

Two major activities must be accomplished to bolt the given components together to make the specified system.

- Decide how to represent the information—the state of the system.
- Decide how to implement each operation.

In terms of the general architecture, the system we have been specifying will be broken into several systems: one for each Store plus a head office (HQ) system (see Figure 16.15). In each store, there will be several Application (App) components: one for each Desk and one for each of the Manager components specified earlier, which will be driven by the user interfaces. We don't yet know exactly how the HQ system will talk to the Store systems, nor exactly what the communications between the Application and the Managers are.

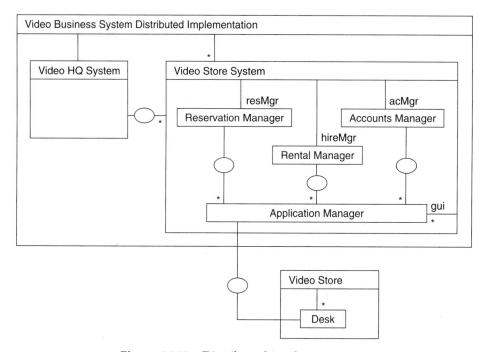

Figure 16.15   Distributed implementation.

We must relate the representation of state in the system specification to the representation in this architecture. We can do this in two steps. First, we split the system into stores (see Figure 16.16). Then we map from the refined design to the spec. We are given the following:

- The spec of Video Business System (VBS)
- The spec of a Video Store System (VSS)—like the VBS except that it deals only with a single Store
- A model of the proposed implementation (VBS-DI)

Does the VBS-DI correctly implement the VBS? We split the question into two parts:

1. Can the state of the VBS-DI represent the state of the VBS?
   - Yes. The set of stores for the business is represented as the set of stores in each VSS; the set of titles for the business is represented in the set of titles in the HQ system. Because we also keep a list in each store, we should provide a way of keeping them equal. This will entail a new set of actions between HQ and the Stores.
   - Other objects are partitioned between the store's systems accordingly.

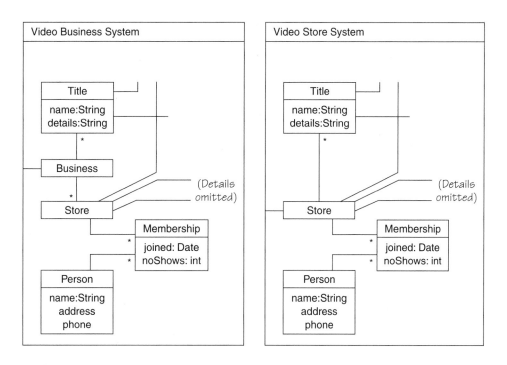

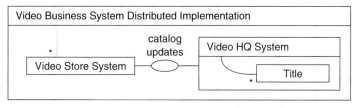

Figure 16.16   Separating store systems and business systems
in the architecture.

2. Can each action specified for the VBS be performed by the VBS-DI? We don't
   yet have a set of opspecs for the VBS-DI, but if we duplicate each VBS spec by
   one for the Store system, it should be easy to see that the functionality is the
   same. The main difference is that we now acknowledge that the customer
   talks directly to the Shop as opposed to the Business as a whole. (That is not
   entirely obvious. For example, telephone reservations could be handled cen-
   trally.) So the store parameter of each action is now self.

We can show the relationships among the state components pictorially (see Figure 16.17). Because the VBS is a spec of its implementation, we should be able to
replicate the VBS model in the implementation and show how its links are all
redundant. The invariants that relate the implementation and specification models are called retrievals.

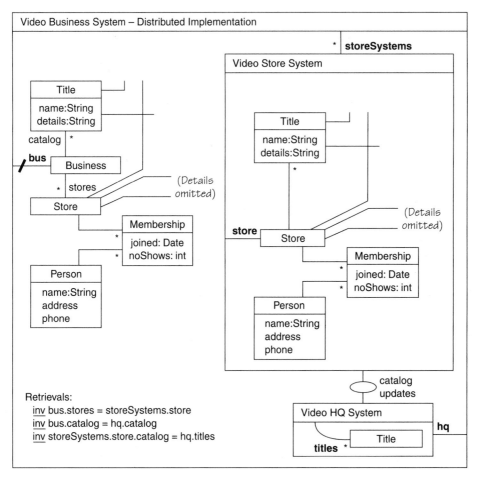

Figure 16.17   Retrievals of distributed architecture to specification.

The next step is to partition the store system between the Manager components. Again, it will help to put them all into one box and show the retrieval (see Figure 16.18). The hope is that the VSS component implementation (VSS-CI) can be shown to be a satisfactory implementation of the VSS. (We're highlighting certain parts of it here.)

We can first document the retrievals, showing how everything hanging from store is actually represented in the rest (details omitted here). Then we show how an interaction between the components realizes the abstract action specs.

We must show how each operation breaks down into a sequence of operations on the components. This can be illustrated using an interaction diagram (see Figure 16.19).

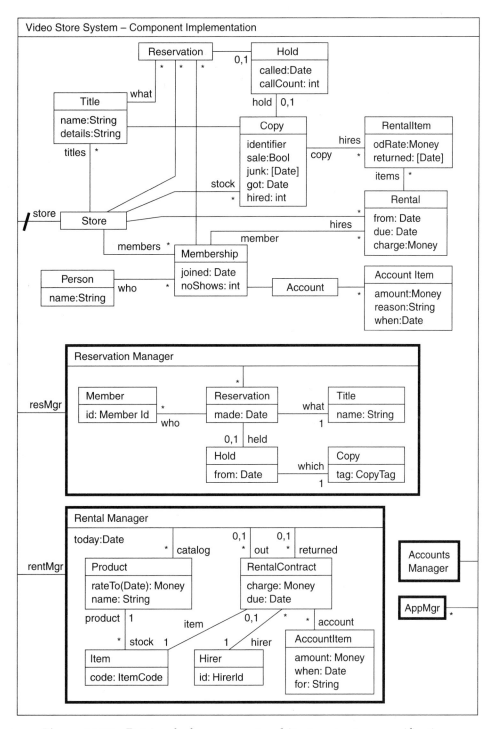

Figure 16.18   Retrieval of component architecture to store specification.

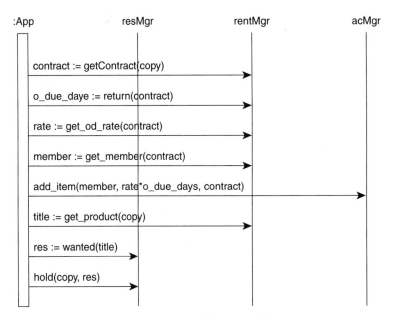

Figure 16.19   Interaction diagram of components.

16.3.5   Detailed Design

Further work is required for those components that are used in the design but not yet implemented—not purchased or adapted from previous projects. Just as we had a specification of the whole system and broke it into successive pieces, so each component can be broken into subcomponents, which in turn are specified and implemented, until we get down to units that are directly implementable in program code.

Appendix A Object Constraint Language

The Object Constraint Language (OCL), a standard part of UML 1.1, is a specification language used in conjunction with UML models. It is an expression-based, side-effect-free language that eschews mathematical symbols ($\forall$, $\exists$, and so on) for textual equivalents (forAll, exists). It uses a syntax more usual in object-oriented languages: $\forall$ x: T, p(x) becomes T->forAll (x | x.p).

OCL Summary

OCL uses a Smalltalk-based "block" syntax to allow you to define some kinds of functions conveniently and inline, but it does not provide corresponding type rules for this based on generic types. For our discussion here, we treat blocks as first-class functions and use the syntax (T1 X T2 X T3 -> T) for such a function. This is purely a syntactic convenience; functions can be modeled as objects. Any function f (a,b): c can be described as an object with a single method eval (a, b): c. Thus,

    aCollection -> select (x | p(x))   *-- returns those elements for which p(x) is true*

can be typed as follows:

    Collection(T):: select (T -> Boolean): Collection(T)
    -- select takes a block parameter that maps each element to a Boolean; select
      returns another collection of T

Most collection functions on Collection(T) use blocks that are Predicate(T) to do selection; Comparator(T) to do sorting; and Converter(T, T1) to do a general mapping from the collection elements.

    Predicate(T) = T->Boolean
    Comparator(T) = T X T -> Boolean
    Converter(T,T1) = T -> T1

Collection types include sets (no duplicates), bags (duplicates), and sequences (duplicates, ordered). In the following description, explanations in italics indicate where we use Catalysis semantics or extensions or alternative syntax. Functions on collections also apply to sets, sequences, and bags.

Collection

Expression	Description
Collection(T)	Collections whose members all belong to type T. In the following expressions, c, c2: Collection; e: T; P: T -> Boolean; func: T ->Object.
c->size	Number of elements in the collection; for a bag or sequence, duplicates are counted as separate items.
c->sum	Sum of elements in the collection. Elements must be numbers *or have a + operation defined with the appropriate properties (described as a "provided" clause on the framework).*
c->count(e)	The number of times that e is in c.
c->isEmpty	Same as (c->size = 0).
c->notEmpty	Same as (not c->isEmpty).
c->asSet	A set corresponding to the collection (duplicates are dropped, sequencing is lost).
c->asSequence	A sequence corresponding to the collection. *More useful:* c->sortedBy (Comparator(T)).
c->asBag	A bag corresponding to the collection.
c = c2	A standard "same object" test on c and c2. The uniqueness constraints on collections are Set: no two sets have the same elements; Bag: no two bags have the same elements in the same counts; Sequence: no two sequences have the same elements in the same order. This is a specification ploy to simplify things. When dealing with mutable collections in a typical programming language, you would more likely use c.equals (c2), where equals does the comparison appropriate to that collection type.
c->includes(e)	Boolean; c->exists (x | x = e). *Catalysis alternative,* e: c.
c->excludes(e)	Boolean; not c->includes(e).
c->includesAll(c2)	Boolean; c includes all the elements in c2. *Catalysis alternative,* c2->subsetOf(c)
c->including(e)	The collection that includes all of c as well as e. *Catalysis alternative,* c + e.
c->excluding(e)	The collection that includes all of c except e. *Catalysis alternative,* c − e.
c->exists(x | P)	Boolean; there is at least one element in c, named x, for which predicate P is true. *Catalysis alternative,* c [x | P] <> 0.
c->exists(P)	c->exists(self | P). *Catalysis alternative,* c [P] <> 0.
c->forAll(x | P)	Boolean; for every element in c, named x, predicate P is true. *In Catalysis, we use the context operator, "::", to mean for every element of this set, and write* x: c :: P.
c->forAll(P)	Same as c->forAll(self | P). *Catalysis alternative,* c :: P.
c->select(x | P)	The collection of those elements in c for which P is true. *Catalysis alternative,* c [x | P].
c->select(P)	Same as c->select(self | P). *Catalysis alternative,* c [P].
c->reject(x | P)	c->select(x | not P). *Catalysis alternative,* c [x | not P].
c->reject(P)	c->reject(self | P). *Catalysis alternative,* c [not P].
c->collect(x | E)	The bag obtained by applying E to each element of c, named x.
c->collect(E)	Same as c->collect(self | E).
c.attribute	The collection(of type of c) consisting of the attribute of each element of c.
c->iterate(x; a = E | E2)	The object obtained by applying E2 to each element of c, named x, where a is initialized to the value of the expression E.

Sequence

Expression	Description
Seq(T)	Sequence of elements of type T. In these expressions, s: Seq(T); e, x, y, z: T, i,j: Integer.
s->union (c)	The sequence obtained by appending c to s. *Catalysis alternative,* s + c.
s->append (e)	The sequence obtained by appending e to s. *Catalysis alternative,* s + e.
s->prepend (e)	The sequence obtained by prepending e to s. result = Seq { e, s }.
s->at (i)	The ith element of the sequence.
s->first	s->first = s->at(1).
s->last	s->last = s->at(s->size).
s->subSequence (i, j)	The sequence from positions i to j, inclusive (element positions start at 1). *In Catalysis you can define more convenient functions as extensions.*
Seq { x, y, z, x }	The sequence containing x, y, z, x, in that order.

Bag

Expression	Description
Bag(T)	Collection of elements of type T, with duplicates. In the following, b: Bag (T); e, x, y, z: T.
b->union (c)	The bag with all elements from b and c. *Catalysis alternative,* b + c.
b->intersection (c)	The bag with elements common to both b and c. *Catalysis alternative,* b * c.
Bag { x, y, z, x }	The bag containing two occurrences of x, one occurrence of y, and one occurrence of z.

Set

Expression	Description
Set(T)	The type of unordered collections of objects of type T with no duplicates. In the following, c: Collection; s1, s2: Set (T); x, y, z: T.
s1->union (c)	The set with all elements from s1 and c. *Catalysis alternative,* s1 + c.
s1->intersection(c)	The set with elements common to both s1 and c. *Catalysis alternative,* s1 * c.
s1->symmetric Difference (s2)	The set containing all the elements that are in s1 or in s2 but not in both. *Catalysis alternative,* s1 − s2.
Set { x, y, z }	The set containing x, y, z.

Object (Called OclAny)

Expression	Description
OclAny	The type that includes all others. In the following, x, y : OclAny, T is an OCL type.
x = y	x and y are the same object.
x <> y	not (x = y).
x.oclType	The type of x.
x.isKindOf (T)	True if T is a supertype (transitive) of the type of x. *Types coerce to sets, so the Catalysis alternative is* x : T.
x.isTypeOf (T)	True if T is equal to the type of x. *Don't use this one.*
x.asType (T)	Results in x, but of type T. Undefined if T is not the actual type of x or one of its subtypes.

OclType: A Metatype

Expression	Description
T: OclType	T is an OCL type.
T.new	The set of new instances of type T; also T*new. Not defined in OCL.
T.allInstances	All the instances of type T. *In Catalysis a type is a set, so this is not used.*

Boolean

Expression	Description
Boolean	Expressions yielding true, false (or unknown). In the following, b, b2: Boolean; e1, e2: Object.
b and b2, b or b2, b xor b2, not b	The standard operators. If any part of a Boolean expression fully determines the result, then it does not matter if some other parts of that expression have unknown or undefined results. *Catalysis alternatives:* b & b2, b I b2.
b implies b2	True if b is false or if b is true and b2 is true. *Catalysis alternative,* b ==> b2.
if b then e1 else e2 endif	If b is true the result is the value of e1; otherwise, the result is the value of e2.

String

Expression	Description
String	A sequence of ASCII characters. In the following, s, s2: String; l,u: Integer.
s = s2	s and s2 have the same characters in the same order.
s.size	The number of characters in s.
s.concat(s2)	The concatenation of s and s2.
s.substring(l, u)	The string from positions l to u, inclusive (positions start at 1).
s.toUpper	The value of s with all characters converted to uppercase characters.
s.toLower	The value of s with all characters converted to lowercase characters.

Real Numbers

Expression	Description
Real	Real numbers. In the following, r, r2: Real.
r = r2	r and r2 have the same value.
< > >= <=	Usual meaning for numbers.
+ −* /	Usual meaning for numbers.
r.abs	The absolute value of r. (result >= 0) and (result − r = 0).
r.floor	The largest integer, which is less than or equal to r. (result <= r) and (result + 1 > r).
r.ceiling	The smallest integer, which is greater than or equal to r. (result >= r) and (result −1 < r).
r.min(r2)	The minimum of r and r2. result = if r <= r2 then r else r2 endif.
r. max(r2)	The maximum of r and r2. result = if r >= r2 then r else r2 endif.

Integers

Expression	Description
Integer	Integers. In the following, i, i2: Integer.
i div i2	integer division. result * i2 <= i and result * (i2 + 1) > i.
i mod i2	i modulo i2. result = i − (i.div(i2) * i2).

OCL in Catalysis

In OCL the built-in objects are immutable and have fixed relations with other objects. In Catalysis we model all these relations as attributes or parameterized attributes. Thus, a < b is syntactical sugar for a.<(b), or a.isLessThan(b). Because Catalysis also offers package scope, this could also be described as a top-level query within a package: isLessThan (a, b).

We treat types as sets, so we can use type expressions such as Performer = Dancer + Singer. Note that this is different from inheriting from a common supertype Performer: In the former, Dancer and Singer are not defined in terms of Performer; instead, Performer is a type defined in terms of Dancer and Singer.

Catalysis collections are generic types in a template package that is predefined for basic UML. All collections are immutable; the many collection functions return other collections. A later section, Extending OCL, shows how extensions are readily accommodated in Catalysis.

In Catalysis, navigating through a collection yields a like collection: Bag->Bag, Sequence->Sequence, and so on. The asSet, asSeq, and asBag operators (or asType (T) equivalents) provide conversions. Thus, the following yields a bag of last names containing as many (possibly duplicated) entries as joe has friends.

    joe.friends ->asBag.lastName

OCL does not provide a simple means to refer to the creation of a new object in a postcondition; Catalysis provides Type*new and the more conventional Type.new.

The Choice of "->"

We have found the OCL "->" symbol counterintuitive to use and to teach to others. Popular languages such as C and C++ use -> to mean "dereference," that is, to move through a level of indirection. In contrast, OCL uses it to mean *do not move through a level of indirection.*

joe.cars	-- the set of Joe's cars
joe.cars.size	-- navigate through the set, collecting each car's size into the result
joe.cars -> size	-- do **not** navigate through; just give the size of the set

It would be more consistent to have the "." operator have the same meaning for collections and noncollection types and to use -> to apply to each element in the collection. In particular, Catalysis frameworks could be used to define the meaning of -> as no more than syntactic sugar for the following:

```
package Collections (X);
type Sequence(T)
    map ( T->X ) : Sequence(X)          -- sequence resulting from applying block to
                                           each element
    inv length = length(map(f)) & i: [0...length] map(f) [i] = f (self [i])
```

Now, c->a is just syntactic sugar for c.map (e I e.a).

Now, writing joe.cars -> size translates into joe.cars.map (e I e.size).

Extending OCL in Catalysis

OCL provides a fixed set of basic types and operations on numbers, sets, sequences, and so on. No such set will suffice for real applications unless they can be extended; many common constraints would be awkward if limited to the OCL set. The Catalysis semantics of packages lets us extend these basic types and operations without requiring any change to OCL. Thus, Catalysis sequences could support something like this:

```
Sequence(T):: shortestInitialSubsequence ( Predicate(Sequence(T)) )
```

This statement evaluates to the shortest initial subsequence that satisfies the test argument, assuming that such a subsequence exists.

A user-defined package can introduce additional convenient terms on existing OCL types as needed, without the need to modify the predefined OCL package in any way. According to the Catalysis package rules, they can even continue to use existing packages (see Figure A.1). Here are some expressions you might find useful as extensions to OCL:

```
Set(T)::
    any (Pred): T              -- returns any element that satisfies Pred
    one (Pred): Boolean        -- Boolean; exactly one element satisfies Pred
    theOne (Pred): T           -- returns the single element that satisfies Pred
```

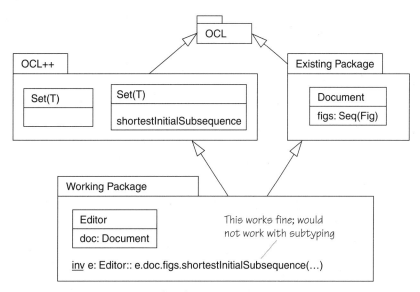

Figure A.1   Using Catalysis extension to customize OCL.

```
Map(A,B)::              -- a mapping from A to B
    domain             -- standard definitions of domain
    range              -- . . . and range
    value (A)          -- the corresponding B
    keys (B)           -- the set of A's that are mapped to this B
```

You will probably find Time, Date, DateRange, and Duration to be useful types. In reality, we would write these as frameworks on any total-ordered type (T, Range(T), and Delta(T)). For more details, see www.catalysis.org.

Defining Basic Types Using OCL

There are no "primitives" in Catalysis, only a set of basic object types that are defined in standard packages. Using exactly the same mechanisms, you can define your own basic types and packages of basic types suitable for your problem domain (see Figure A.2). Remember to add uniqueness constraints, which help define the meaning of object identity for your object type. There are frameworks, algebraic in nature, that capture even these basic recurring patterns.

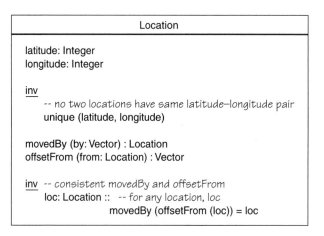

Figure A.2 Examples of defining basic types.

Appendix B UML Perspective

The Unified Modeling Language (UML) 1.0 was defined by a consortium of companies between 1996 and 1997 and was submitted for standardization by the OMG. The companies who cosubmitted the proposal were Rational, HP, TI, Microsoft, ICON Computing, Unisys, and MCI Systemhouse. UML 1.1 was standardized in September 1997.

Both Catalysis authors were involved in helping shape UML, which incorporated several Catalysis ideas. One author's company, ICON Computing, was a cosubmitter in defining and submitting the UML standard to the OMG.

This section briefly discusses UML and explains how we have used it in Catalysis, including some of the extensions or interpretation we have found useful or necessary, such as parameterized attributes, frameworks, and use cases. There are systematic approaches to using Catalysis with existing CASE tools (refer to www.catalysis.org).

Type versus Class

UML 0.8 did not distinguish type from class; 1.0 recognizes the distinction, thanks in part to Catalysis input. The standard UML box can have a <<class>> stereotype to indicate an implementation class, or can have a <<type>> for an implementation-free specification.

Combining Operation Specs

UML does not define multiple specifications for an operation. Catalysis permits two forms of combining multiple specifications: a conformant anding of the specs, for use with subtyping; and the join mechanism, in which one spec can impose additional preconditions to those defined in another view.

Frameworks

Catalysis depicts a framework application using the UML symbol for a pattern. The UML pattern notation has no defined semantics. Catalysis has a strong semantic foundation for frameworks; it is based on package imports and substitution. In addition to defining design patterns and domain-specific modeling patterns, frameworks can be used to define (and extend) the meaning of modeling constructs themselves. Type, associations, subtype—all these can be defined as frameworks, as can new constructs for workflow, event propagation, and property couplings.

Subjective Models of Containment

Catalysis gives a clear meaning to the containment of one type within another using state types. It is unclear in UML whether a given class diagram is defining intrinsic properties of the classes (what a theoretician might call axioms) or defining properties that happen to be true in the context of the containing type (theorems, based on constraints specific to the container).

const versus {frozen}

Catalysis uses an explicit const annotation to describe attributes that always refer to the same object. UML uses {frozen} and "composition" in sometimes unclear ways.

Stereotypes

UML provides the stereotype mechanism for extensibility. It has several weaknesses:

- There is no way to define the meaning of a stereotype and no mechanism for grouping stereotypes that can be meaningfully used together.
- A stereotype is attached to a single element; it cannot be used for a multi-way pattern.
- Only one stereotype can be attached to an element. UML permits a stereotype to be defined as a combination of several others. This arrangement causes problems with combinatorial explosion as well as lack of semantics.

Catalysis uses model frameworks for extensibility; stereotypes are only one special (and limited) syntax for applying a framework.

Attributes versus Operations

UML treats attributes on a <<type>> as abstract but does not permit attributes to take parameters; instead, you can use an operation that has been marked as read-only. Catalysis encourages a slightly different way of thinking about an object: Some things are abstractions of its state, and others are abstractions of its behaviors. Attributes, parameterized attributes, and invariants all help to define the model of state; operation specifications define the behaviors. There are no preconditions and postconditions on attributes, because they represent state; there can be conditional invariants on an attribute, and there can be syntactic shortcuts for expressing them, but they are not pre- and postconditions:

inv Man::   married ==> wife <> null

In Catalysis an attribute does not imply an access method; you would have to explicitly add one (or use a framework as a shortcut).

Sets and Flat Sets

Catalysis makes a distinction between sets and flat sets. By default, traversing a "*" association yields a flat set; further traversals also yield flat sets rather than sets of sets. However, you can always explicitly annotate a different type if needed; so you can, when needed, deal with sets of sets; UML/OCL does not permit this.

Primitives and Values

UML provides a set of primitive types as "values." There are no primitives in Catalysis; every type can be defined in Catalysis itself and we do not force a distinction between object and value. Programming "call-by-value" is easily accommodated by using a "copy" framework: A call by value means the same as to make a copy and call by reference to the copy.

Attribute, Role, and State

UML has three distinct constructs that remain largely unrelated to one another: an attribute, a role in an association, and a state in a state chart. For example, a pre- and postcondition pair cannot refer to the name of a state. In Catalysis these three constructs are closely related. An association defines a pair of inverse attributes that are drawn differently; a state defines a Boolean attribute, and the structure of states in a state chart defines invariants on those attributes. Transitions on a state diagram are thus no more than a graphical depiction of action specifications. This approach provides a simpler core set of constructs with different presentations. Actions on UML state transitions are imperative and appear unrelated to pre- and postspecification of operations.

Packages

A UML package is used primarily as a namespace mechanism; elements in one package can refer to elements in another by using package-qualified names. There are no strong semantics associated with import; instead, a general "dependency" relationship can be defined between packages. In Catalysis, packages and imports are fundamental to the structuring of any model, separation of business, specification, and implementation. We do not support arbitrary references across packages.

Packages can be nested in UML and Catalysis. In UML, the containing package automatically imports (transitively) its constituent packages. In Catalysis we much prefer to use the proven scoping rules of programming languages (or predicate calculus or lambda calculus). For example, a Java inner class can access members of its container and "sees" the changes in their values; a Smalltalk block can access variables in its scope and its containing class. A Catalysis nested package automatically imports its container package. If you import a container package and rename one of its types, that renaming effectively applies to all its contained packages that became visible to you only as a result of the import. This provides the intuitive behavior you would expect with frameworks: A container package can have a type parameter, T, and all its nested packages can refer to that type T.

In addition, Catalysis packages let you "say more" about a type, attribute, operation, and so on imported from another package. You can separate viewpoints and then rejoin them in an importing package downstream using well-defined join rules.

Type System

The Catalysis type system treats types as sets and correspondingly provides type expressions such as HotelGuest * Passenger:, which is the intersection of the two sets with both sets of properties.

Parameterized Types

UML has a specific notation for parameterized types: a type box with a syntactical place for its parameters. The semantics of such types are not defined within UML. We support this notation in Catalysis; its semantics are entirely defined in terms of frameworks.

Activity Diagrams

UML has an activity diagram; it is given semantics roughly like that of a state diagram but is not integrated to the other models. This is unfortunate, because the activity diagram is offered as *the* UML mechanism for modeling business processes when enhanced with diagramming constructs such as *swimlanes*.

There is a way in Catalysis to integrate the traditional business-process notations, including organization charting and process and activity flow and decomposition; we have not published it as part of this book.

Use Cases

The use case has become widely used in object methods; unfortunately, it is at least as widely misunderstood and misused. Catalysis provides the framework of joint actions and refinement as a way to clearly separate the specification of any action from the lower-level protocol that might realize that action—whether or not it involves a user. Catalysis lets you factor out common parts of use cases as effects, define exception paths via refinement, and describe rules that affect multiple use cases as dynamic invariants.

Components

UML offers one notation to define the interface of a component (the "lollipop" notation). Catalysis recognizes that component technology is about the connecting together of encapsulated units. The types of these connections will vary; a given component architecture will define its own types. You can define a component architecture using frameworks and then use those frameworks to compose components as diverse as workflow, event-property-method connections, and traditional objects.

Components in Catalysis need not be built using object technology. The concept of a type model and operation spec can be applied equally to a Java, C++, COBOL, or assembler implementations—and therefore to legacy systems—thanks to refinement.

Collaboration

In Catalysis, a collaboration is defined as a set of related actions between objects. UML provides one definition for collaboration and then uses the term *collaboration diagram* to depict a sequence of messages that result from a particular triggering request to an object. We considered the term *use case diagram* but have not seen that used consistently for anything except the actor-level context diagram of a system.

Joint Actions

A Catalysis joint action corresponds to a use case; we prefer to separate the specification of the net effect of a joint action—its postcondition—from the interaction sequence (one of many possible) that realizes it. A joint action is an abstraction of that detailed interaction, just as an operation invocation is an abstraction of a language-specific call-return convention. We depict occurrences of joint actions on an interaction diagram; we have not found any way to show this in UML.

We are uncomfortable with the treatment of use cases as objects and have found much confusion among practitioners about what this means. Just because there are commonality and variation across use cases does not mean that they should be modeled as objects; to do so confuses the separation of actions (interactions that cause changes of state) and attributes (the states that affect, and are affected by, actions). In Catalysis, what is modeled as an action at one level of abstraction (for example, buy_product) can easily be reified into a model object in a refinement (for example, place_order and deliver and pay actions revolving around an order model object).

We have found many use case practitioners confused about the definition of use case: What is its level of granularity? Does a use case always correspond to a unit of meaningful business interaction for an actor? What if two use cases share common parts, but that part does not form a meaningful unit of business interaction: can it still be modeled as a use case and "used" by the other two? In Catalysis we recommend a distinction between the action, or use case, and the *effects* of that action: it is easy to factor out effects that are common across two actions.

Exceptions

Catalysis provides explicit support for specifying exceptions, for composing specifications of an action with such exceptions, and for refining abstract actions with exceptions down to the level of operation invocation sequences and language-specific exception mechanisms.

Capturing Rules

Catalysis static invariants (this constraint between these attributes is always true) and dynamic invariants (any action that causes such-and-such must also cause so-and-so) let us succinctly capture most business rules.

Events

The UML definition, even of an "event" is very limiting:

> *UML: ". . . constraint on state."*

Events are fundamentally about changes of state, not about constraints on state.

Enumeration Types

UML/OCL has an enumeration type and a separate concept of "class attributes." In Catalysis we use shared attributes on a type, with an invariant, to provide enumeration types.

There are other important points to make regarding both UML and the Rational Unified Process. For details, see www.catalysis.org.

Appendix C Catalysis Support Tools, Services, and Experiences

Catalysis enables a high level of automated tool support for modeling and design based on frameworks, type specification, and refinement. Good Catalysis tools should go far beyond mere drawings on a database with some generation of documentation. Moreover, the use of standard notations and the clear relationship between artifacts mean that you can also use currently popular object-modeling UML tools on a Catalysis process by simply following simple usage guidelines.

There are several organizations that currently offer services (training, mentoring, and consulting) to support projects adopting Catalysis, including the authors' companies.

For the most current information on tools and service options for your Catalysis projects, and to stay in touch with other Catalysis projects and users, visit www.catalyis.org.

Notes

Following is a short chapter-by-chapter account of other published work that is relevant to each topic and has, in some way, influenced our work. All these works are listed in the References. Many of them are good supplementary or follow-up reading. Another good place to find follow-up reading is at www.catalysis.org.

Part I: Overview

Catalysis has been influenced by many sources, including both authors' prior work and existing OO methods. Some well-known work on object-oriented analysis and design methods are listed here. Fusion [Colman93] was one of the first methods that had a clear process and separation of concerns along with a strong foundation in formal methods. Syntropy [Cook94] made a clear distinction between essential, system, and software design models and had strong semantics for the authors' state chart-centric behavior models; their work on viewpoints was very insightful, although it was not made central to their approach. The OORAM approach [Reen95] pioneered role-centric and collaboration-based modeling and developed ideas of composition and abstraction based on it.

The work of Grady Booch [Booch91, Booch96] and the OMT book [Rumbaugh91] were influential and became market leaders; they brought, respectively, a pragmatic description of design, and a good information-centered object-modeling approach and state charts. The use case approach of Jacobsen et al. [Jacobsen92] first drew attention to the glaring lack of focus on user tasks in OO methods; [Jacobsen94] is a more readable account of the main ideas. ROOM [Selic94] offers an architecture-centric approach to modeling using executable state charts and makes a component-port-connector model central to the approach.

de Champeaux and Lea [de Champeaux93] provide a wealth of insights into the subtleties of good object-oriented design. The Shlaer–Mellor approach in [Shlaer88] and [Shlaer92], an early object-modeling approach, was focused on a normalized data model and executable communicating state-machine models for analysis and a translation-driven approach to architectural design. A comparison of OO methods is in [D'Souza93]. Martin Fowler [Fowler98] provides a good review of the UML notation, and the OMG Web site provides reference material [UML].

Chapter 1   A Tour of Catalysis

Earlier writeups and presentations on the Catalysis method include [D'Souza95, 96a, 96b].

Part II: Modeling with Objects

The useful separation of static, dynamic, and interactive modeling of objects has been recognized in formal approaches for some time, although it has not been exploited in mainstream OO methods. Among OO methods, the idea was used in Fusion [Col93] and in a less obvious way in Syntropy [Cook94].

Chapter 2   Static Models: Object Attributes and Invariants

The basic idea of modeling an abstraction of state regardless of concrete data implementation has pristine lineage, including the likes of formal methods such as Z [Spivey86] and VDM [Jones86], as well as more recent OO methods such as Syntropy and Fusion. Parameterized attributes are a simple variation of the many kinds of functions and relations that are predefined in Z or that can be user-defined in VDM; these variations can always be explicitly defined in Catalysis in a generic package.

The observation that a formal model is only a collection of symbols and could equally represent a physical world or software—and the need for a separate dictionary that maps the formal model to the things it represents—is well known to model theorists. The ideas are very well described in [Jackson96].

Logic that can cope with an undefined value—three-valued logic—comes from [Cheng91]. Flat sets were used to navigate object models in [D'Souza94], defined in [Wills97], and subsequently taken up by OCL.

Chapter 3   Behavior Models: Object Types and Operations

The concept of type as object behavior, regardless of implementation, is well known to those working in semantics of OO languages [America90] and in formal approaches such as [Wills91]. Using pre- and postconditions to specify an operation in terms of an abstract model of state goes back a long way, to work by Hoare and Dijsktra [Hoare94]. More current usage in the context of OO methods includes Fusion and Syntropy and, in OO languages, Eiffel [Meyer88]. Permitting and composing multiple specs for an action is based on [Wills91].

Our interpretation of a static type model of a component as being what the component needs to know about the world and happenings around it, and the way we relate a software system to a refinement of a business model, are fundamental to traceability from business to code.

Using snapshots to illustrate actions, conceptualizing the type model as a generalization of legal snapshots, treating attribute types and associations as defining invariants, the metaphor of the "film strip," and the relation between state charts, action specs, and snapshots are described in [D'Souza94].

The idea of joint actions between stateful objects was inspired by the work done in Disco [Kurki-Suonio90]. These authors describe how joint actions provide powerful abstractions, provide the first precise semantics for state charts in the context of object modeling, and show how entire object behavior models might be refined.

Using invariants to factor common static rules that apply to all pre/post conditions comes from formal methods such as Z and VDM. Our use of "derived specifications" is a simplified approach to what formalists might call "theorems" [Gries96]. Effect invariants—the idea that a dynamic constraint can apply to all actions—is related to a more powerful formula of temporal logic [Manna92]; temporal logic can sometimes greatly simplify a difficult specification, and we have used the more-general mechanisms on occasion.

The two fundamentally different ways of writing multiple specs (pre/post and pre=>post) were inspired by the work of D. Jackson [Jackson95]. He points out the importance of having specs from different views that, when composed, do not do so "monotonically"; we realized we could support both styles with a simple convention on how the specs should be written, while using a uniform rule about composition.

The idea of subtypes as subsets based on external behavior, independent of implementation, independent of classes, and with specs that simply extend (without overriding) is common in type theories, such as POOL [America90].

State types are discussed in D'Souza [D'Souza94]. Our use of a predicate to "classify" an object provides some convenient modeling capabilities.

Introducing convenience state modeling elements to simplify a specification is well known in formal methods; an analogous technique is used frequently by good OO designers in their designs and code. D. Jackson [Jackson95] makes a strong case for allowing different viewpoints to use different models of the state information; our use of packages carries this a step further.

Factoring common postconditions is done routinely in Z using schema composition. Our separation of actions and effects is meant to distinguish these convenience functions from the actual operations that must be supported. We allow "gray-box" specifications, in which certain aspects of the internal behavior, such as call sequences, can be exposed as a part of the specs. In the OO world, related work was done by Helm et al. [Helm90].

Quoting action specs is described in [Wills91] and elsewhere. The distinction between spec types and design types has long been known in formal methods; our highlighting it, and factoring effects to specification types, is somewhat unique among OO and CBD methods.

An excellent treatise on the use of state charts as a primary specification vehicle with objects is [Cook94].

The subjective model of containment is unique to our approach. It is related to the idea of subject-oriented programming [Harrison93], which is focused more in composing OO implementations.

A discussion of types and classes in programming languages is in [D'Souza97]. Specification aspects of classes and types is discussed in [Wills95b] and [D'Souza96b].

Using type models to precisely document the interface between a superclass and its subclasses is explained in [D'Souza96a].

Chapter 4   Interaction Models: Use Cases, Actions, and Collaborations

The idea of a joint action as an abstraction of many possible interaction protocols was inspired by the work of Disco [Kurki-Suonio90]. We treat localized actions as a degenerate case of joint actions. Clarifying the meaning of *parameters* (and the corresponding rules and documentation for refinement) in the context of objects, and the treatment of use cases, we believe to be unique to our approach. Traditional use cases are described by Jacobsen in [Jacobsen92].

Specifying concurrent actions using rely and guarantee is based on the work of Cliff Jones [Jones93].

Practical guidelines on how to deal with concurrency in a design—covering issues of interference (safety) and cooperation (liveness)—and higher-level concurrency design constructs are included in [Lea96].

Treating collaborations as first-class design entities has been done by Rom Casselman and, more informally, in the work of [Wirfs-Brock90]. OORAM [Reenskaug95] was the first OO method to make this a central way of thinking. The OORAM method is based almost exclusively on the idea of role models; it is closely related to collaborations, with an added element of implied object-identity constraints on the diagrams. Using collaborations as a scoping construct for invariants, distinguishing the internal and external actions for each collaboration it plays a role in, is unique to our approach.

The Ph.D. thesis of D. Beringer [Beringer97] generalizes the concept of scenarios; in that context, it has a good discussion of refinement (action and object refinement), good ideas about the systematic depiction of scenario types, and a brief, insightful, discussion of the need for more-effective state abstraction.

Chapter 5   Effective Documentation

Our overall approach to clear interwoven documentation, rather than the production of either pictures or formal mathematics, is based on Knuth's ideas in *Literate Programming* [Knuth84] and on the style espoused by Z. Permitting multiple appearances of an element on multiple drawings, clearly separating models of business from software specifications and from their internal implementations, would appear to be plain common sense; yet is not spelled out often enough. The high value we place on clear vocabulary and precise definintions of terms comes from project experience. Structuring documentation around package structure, and the emphasis on small fragments of models interleaved with explanatory prose, has not been emphasized in popular methods.

Part III: Factoring Models and Designs

The importance of careful factoring and abstracting away details underlies all good OO programs. Popular methods do not provide well-defined support for composition, and for factoring medium- to large-grained units.

Chapter 6   Abstraction, Refinement, and Testing

Almost every method, from the most dense and formal ones to those based on the most loosely defined sketches and drawings, stakes a claim to being "abstract." The formal ones have a precise idea of what kinds of things are omitted in the abstraction and exactly what it means to correctly implement that abstraction; they also share our idea of a conformance relation with a justification. Refinement is a well-established technique in the formal methods community. The ideas of protocol refinement and data reification (model or state refinement) have been separately but quite thoroughly worked out elsewhere.

Model and operation refinement ideas go back to VDM and Z and to the work of Hoare and Dijkstra [Hoare94]. Joint actions and state chart refinement are addressed thoroughly in Disco and ADJ; Syntropy [Cook94] has an excellent account of a subtyping-based refinement with state charts. Using specifications for testing and debugging implementations has been long practiced by good software developers; [Meyer88] has a good account of it and a programming language that directly supports some of it.

Refinement and subtyping in OO implementations are discussed in several recent works, including those by [D'Souza96b], [Utting92], [Wills93, 96a, 97a], and [Mikhajlova97]. A highly formal approach, suitable for very high integrity systems, is described by Kevin Lano [Lano95].

Doug Lea defines interaction protocols for open object systems, and their refinement rules, in [Lea95].

Michael Jackson and Pamela Zave [Jackson96a] clearly point out the difference between effects and operations; their framework is not one of refinement. Rather, it is centered on how to structure and compose abstract state changing actions (using Z) and finer-grained protocols (using state machines or other mechanisms) to be confident about the results. Many of those ideas fit into the rules for documenting a refinement.

The co-author's book [Wills91] has a good account of refinement based on model and operation abstraction and subtyping. The need for collaborations as first-class entities and collaboration refinements beyond subtyping are described in [D'Souza96a].

We believe the basic forms of refinement to OO methods and the strong link to systematic testing are part of our contribution.

Chapter 7   Using Packages

Packages as groupings for pieces of models, designs, or specs, in the sense we use in Catalysis, go back to the idea of mathematical theories and are exemplified by the specification language of Larch [Guttag90] and Mural's specification tool [Mural91]. The idea of extending type information in theory extensions comes from them, as does the definition of the language semantics from the ground up. [Wills91] describes how these theories, which he calls "capsules," can be used to separate specifications from code and to provide disciplined forms of class inheritance, method overrides, and code updates.

The more straightforward ideas of packages for grouping classes can be found in Eiffel's "clusters" [Meyer88], Booch's "categories" [Booch96], and Wirfs-Brock's "subsystems" [Wirfs-Brock90].

Treating all development artifacts as a part of a package would seem to be common sense, yet surprisingly few projects practice it and surprisingly few methods require it. Knuth's Web is based on strongly integrating code and documentation but does not address modeling or specification.

Java packages are clearly documented in [Gosling96]. Ways to use them to separate interfaces, collaborations, and classes, based on Catalysis techniques, are described in [D'Souza96a].

Our treatment of packages as units of version control, configuration management, and builds is similar to Sun's Forest project [Jordon97], which scales Java packages to very large-scale software development. The idea of being able to say more about any imported modeling element is supported in code in a limited way by the team-working product Envy for Smalltalk; it allows different aspects of the same implementation class to be defined in different "applications." It is commonly used in formal methods based on traits or theories [Guttag90]. The ideas behind this are discussed in [Wills91] and [Wills96b].

Chapter 8   Composing Models and Specifications

Composition is an age-old idea in software specification and development; any method must have clear rules about the outcome of combining designs, specifications, or code. Popular OO methods do not address this issue in a meaningful way. Exceptions are Disco's composition of entire models [Kurth90], Syntropy's subtyping and viewpoints [Cook94], and OORAM's role-model synthesis [Reenskang95]. Related work in non-OO approaches are plentiful: Z, Unity, and so on.

Our rules for intersecting types are based on well-known rules of conformance [Liskov91, Meyer88]; those for composing separate views in a nonmonotonic way were influenced by the work of D. Jackson [Jackson95] and Z [Spivey86].

Few OO approaches seriously support the specification of exceptions; yet exceptions often form the most complicated part of a complex specification and its implementation. Our approach to describing exceptions is based on the work on Assertion Definition Language [ADL], adapted to fit with our need to compose multiple specifications that can include exception conditions. Our integration of exceptions with use cases and action refinement we believe to be unique.

Chapter 9   Model Frameworks and Template Packages

The ideas of frameworks are akin to how Larch defines the importing of traits with renaming [Guttag90] and are related to the work in FOOPS [Goguen90]. Some of the earliest OO work related to our collaborations comes from Helm et al. [Helm90].

Our initial ideas of frameworks as generic collaborations in Catalysis were written up in [D'Souza95a]. Broader use of model templates using packages in Catalysis is described in [Wills96b].

The confusion between frameworks, generics, and subtypes is present even in the UML [UML].

The ideas of a framework at the level of OO implementation are well described in Taligent [Taligent94] and Johnson [Johnson92]. An excellent example of using the framework-like facility of C++ templates is in the Standard Template Library [Saini96]. At the level of design patterns, the historic GOF book [Gamma95] provides plenty of motivation for a specification construct like frameworks. Martin Fowler's book *Analysis Patterns* [Fowler97] elevates that need to a domain-specific level. Shlaer and Mellor [Shlaer92] use an idea akin to frameworks in their approach to recursive design, although they do not generalize it beyond that.

Framework provisions—constraints on properties an acceptable substitution must have when applying the framework—are used in Larch, FOOP, and even in well-documented implementations of the STL [STL96].

Using frameworks to define the meaning of the very modeling constructs themselves—and even to define and encapsulate known inference rules—is very similar to the approach in Larch [Guttag90]. Their application to Catalysis modeling constructs, UML stereotype-based extension, and new modeling constructs and notations is described in [D'Souza97a].

Frameworks seem quite related to some of the ideas of aspect-oriented programming [Gregor97], but we are not sure how. In particular, we would compose the models from multiple framework applications in which they would use an "aspect-weaver" program to combine implementation code.

A package might define a set of relevant object types with their states and interactions, but it also explicitly defines (or imports) the very rules that are used to make deductions about things. This arrangement can be useful in "agent-based" models; an economic simulation of a market might explicitly model the theory each company has of its competitors' actions, including the inference rules it uses. With good tool support, you might then do simulations and explore differ-ent hypotheses within a package.

Part IV: Implementation by Assembly

Many books have been written about good object-oriented design and implemen-tation. Component-based development and assembly have only very recently become hot topics. Component and connector technology, effective pluggable design, and a coherent architecture together enable implementation by assembly.

Chapter 10   Components and Connectors

Szyperski [Szyperski97] has several clear definitions of component technology, and we adapted several definitions from that book.

Using components and connectors to define architectural styles was intro-duced in [Allen94] and elaborated in [Shaw96]. Component connectors appear in a number of patterns in [PLoP]. Our definition of them in terms of actions appeared in [Wills97a].

Among current component technologies, CORBA technology is described at the OMG Web site [CORBA]; COM at Microsoft's Web site [COM]; and JavaBeans at the JavaBeans Web site [EJB].

The approach to treating entire systems and subsystems as objects is something we have been practicing for many years.

Chapter 11   Reuse and Pluggable Design: Frameworks in Code

A book by [Wong93] gives a clear account of pluggable designs. The idea can be traced back through the development of the Smalltalk class library. [D'Souza96a] describes documenting the interface of up-calls and down-calls using type mod-els. [Gamma95] has an excellent discussion of decoupling patterns, as does [PLoP].

Chapter 12   Architecture

Some of the early work on systematic description of software architecture was done by Shaw and Garlan [Shaw96b]. A good description of the breadth of issues involved in software architecture, which we have used and adapted, is in [Bass98]. Our informal definition of architecture was coined in frustration by D'Souza (we believe).

Architecture Description Languages (ADLs) have been receiving much study recently. Important work includes the ABLE project (with the language WRIGHT) [Able] and Rapide [Luckham95].

ROOM [Selic94] is one of the few OO methods that can be said to be based on an architecture definition (graphical) language. Shlaer and Mellor [Shlaer92] have long advocated a translation-based approach to architecture: You define the translation patterns and rules and generate the design from the analysis models.

Doug Lea's work [Lea95] addresses several architectural issues that arise in the building of object-oriented systems. And [Gamma95] is important in bringing pragmatic and proven design patterns to their rightful place in software architecture. Our use of frameworks for components, and connectors, and for other patterns and rules that describe architecture, provide additional expressiveness.

Part V: How to Apply Catalysis

Like the rest of this book, the processes and techniques have evolved from practical application and from the process definitions of many others. Catalysis emphasizes the systematic use of package structure, separation of package artifacts from the process and routes that populate those artifacts, refinement from business models to code, frameworks at all levels, precise use cases accompanied by clear supporting type models, and multiple views that can be composed.

Chapter 13   Process Overview

Good general project guidelines can be found in [Cockburn98] and [Goldberg95]. RAD is discussed in [McConnell97] and DSDM (an excellent RAD approach) is discussed in [Stapleton97].

Chapter 14   How to Build a Business Model

Modeling of business processes is often based on a flow-like notation. Examples include the activity diagram of UML [UML], role-activity diagrams [Holt83], the process flow (and related relationship and organization structure) of Rummler and Brache [Rummler90], and functions and information in IDEF0 [IDEF093]. These would need a semantic connection to our other, more-precise modeling techniques.

Martin Fowler and Craig Larman have each written good books on patterns for modeling [Fowler97, Larman98].

Chapter 15   How to Specify a Component

The vanilla process is like that followed by many authors such as [Cook94] and [Colman94]. The use case focus is related to Jackson's [Jackson92], although our emphasis on refinement is different.

Chapter 16   How to Implement a Component

Some good guidelines for design are in [Reil97], [Gamma95], and [Taligent94].

Glossary

abstract class   A class that defines a partial implementation for a set of objects.

abstraction   (1) An abstraction (noun) is a description of something that omits some details that are not relevant to the purpose of the abstraction; the converse of *refinement*. Types, collaborations, and action specs are different kinds of abstraction.   (2) Abstract (verb) means to create an abstraction; also called *generalize, specify,* and sometimes *analyze.*

action occurrence   A related set of changes of states in a group of objects between two specific points in time. An action occurrence may abstract an entire series of interactions and smaller changes.

action spec   A specification of an action type. An action spec characterizes the effects of the occurrences on the states of the participating objects (for example, with a postcondition).

Actions can be joint (use cases): They abstract multiple interactions and specific protocols for information exchange and describe the net effect on all participants and the summary of information exchanged.

Actions can also be localized, in which case they are also called *operations.* An operation is a one-sided specification of an action focused entirely on a single object and how it responds to a request, without regard to the initiator of that request.

action type   The set of action occurrences that conform to a given action spec. A particular action occurrence may belong to many action types.

architectural style   An architectural style (or *type*) defines a consistent set of architectural elements, patterns, rules for using them, and stereotype or other notational shorthand for expressing their use, all within a package.

architecture (system)   The architecture of a system consists of the structure(s) of its parts (including design-time, test-time, and runtime hardware and software parts), the nature and relevant externally visible properties of those parts (modules with interfaces, hardware units, and objects), and the relationships and constraints between them (there are a great many possibly interesting such relationships).

architecture   The set of design decisions and rules about any system (or smaller component) that keeps its implementors and maintainers from exercising needless creativity. Every refinement can have such architectural rules.

architecture implementation(s)   The way each category of connector works internally, including the protocol of interactions between ports. Component or object-oriented frameworks are effective ways to *implement* an architecture.

association   A pair of attributes that are inverses of each other, usually drawn as a line connecting two types.

attribute   A named property of an object whose value describes information about the object. An attribute's value is itself the identity of an object. In software, an attribute can represent stored or computable information. An attribute is part of a model used to help describe its object's behavior and need not be implemented directly by a designer.

class   (1) A language-specific construct defining the implementation template for a set of objects, the types it implements, and the other classes or types it uses in its implementation (including by class inheritance).   (2) An implementation concept that defines the stored data and associated procedures for manipulating instances of the class; the implementation construct can be mapped to OO languages and to procedural and even assembly language.

collaboration   A set of related actions between typed objects playing defined roles in the collaboration; these actions are defined in terms of a common type model of the objects involved. A collaboration is frequently a refinement of a single abstract action or a design to maintain an invariant between some objects.

collaboration spec   A collaboration is specified by the list of actions between the collaborators, an optional list of actions considered "outside" the collaboration, action specs, static and effect invariants that may apply to either set of actions, and an optional sequence constraint on the set of actions.

component (general)   A coherent package of software artifacts that can be independently developed and delivered as a unit and that can be composed, unchanged, with other components to build something larger.

component (in code)   A coherent package of software implementation that (a) has explicit and well-specified interfaces for the services it provides; (b) has explicit and well-specified interfaces for services it expects from others; and (c) can be composed with other components, perhaps customizing some of their properties, without modifying the components themselves. As a consequence of these properties, a component can be independently developed, delivered, and deployed as a unit.

component architecture type, or style   The categories of connector that are permitted between components, what each of them does, and the rules and constraints on their use. Some (unary) connector types can even be used to define standard infrastructure services that will always be provided by the environment.

component-based design   The mind-set, science, and art of building with and for components and ensuring that the result of plugging components together has the expected effect.

component-based development (CBD)   An approach to software development in which all artifacts—from executable code to interface specifications, architectures, and business models, and scaling from complete applications and systems down to individual components—can be built by assembling, adapting, and "wiring" together existing components into a variety of different configurations.

component instance   The object, set of objects, or predetermined configuration of such a set of objects that is the runtime manifestation of a component when composed within a particular application.

component spec   A specification of the external behavior of a component, covering the services provided and required and the underlying component technology.

components   Units of software that can be plugged in to a wide variety of others. They range in scale from small user-interface widgets to large transaction-processing applications.

conformance   One behavioral description conforms to another if (and only if) any objects that behave as described by one are also behaving as described by the other (given a mapping between the two descriptions). A *conformance* is a relationship between the two descriptions, accompanied by a *justification* that includes the mapping between them and rationale for choices made. Refinement and conformance form the basis of traceability and document the answer to the question, Why is this design done thus?

connectors   The connections between ports that build a collection of components into a software product (or larger component). A connector imposes role-specific constraints on the ports that it connects and can be refined to particular interaction protocols that implement the joint action.

convenience attribute   A redundant attribute (possibly parameterized) that is introduced to simplify the specification of actions or invariants—for example, age defined as well as birthday.

dialect   A package that contains a useful and agreed-on set of mutually consistent stereotypes, together defining a particular "dialect" of the modeling language. All modeling work is done in the context of selected dialect(s).

dictionary   The collected set of definitions of modeling constructs; the definitions must include not only the formal modeling and specification bits (relating the formal names and symbols to each other) but also the (usually informal) glossary of descriptions that relate the symbols and names to things in the problem domain. Dictionary definitions are scoped according to package scope rules.

dynamic invariant   *See* effect invariant.

effect   A convenience postcondition introduced (and named) to factor parts of postconditions that are common across more than one action. Unlike ordinary predicates, an effect can contain the special postcondition operator @pre.

equality   A generic relation on a type, in which the relation must satisfy certain mathematical properties; defined as a standard framework.

framework application   An import of a framework with substitutions; usually depicted graphically using a UML "pattern" symbol, with labeled lines for the type substitutions and text annotations for finer-grained substitutions (attributes, actions, and so on).

framework, model   A template package; a package that is designed to be imported with substitutions: It "unfolds" to provide a version of its contents that is specialized based on the substitutions made. (Note that our usage of *framework* is somewhat broader than its traditional usage as a collection of collaborating abstract classes.)

   A framework can abstract the description of a generic type, a family of mutually dependent types, a collaboration, a refinement pattern, the modeling constructs themselves, and even a bundle of fundamental generic properties (associative, commutative, and so on). Frameworks are themselves built on other frameworks; at the most basic level, the structure of frameworks represents the basis for the organization of all models.

implementation   Program code that conforms to an abstraction; requires no further refinement (strictly speaking, it still goes through compilation and so on).

import, extension   An extension import is a relation between packages whereby all names and definitions exported by the imported package are accessible in the importer, together with any new elements and added statements about the imported elements that the importer may introduce. A package exports all introduced elements as well as all elements accessible via extension imports. Import by extension is the default rule for import.

import, usage   A usage import is a relation between packages whereby all names and definitions exported by the imported package are accessible in the importer, together with any new elements and added statements about the imported elements that the importer may introduce. However, elements accessible only via usage imports are not exported by a package.

invariant effect   A transition rule that applies to the postcondition of every action in the range of the invariant; by writing a conditional (eff1 ==> eff2), you can impose the rule selectively on those actions that have effect eff1—for example, "all operations that alter x must also notify y."

object   Any identifiable individual or thing. It may be a concrete, touchable thing, such as a car; or an abstract concept, such as a meeting, relationship, number, or a computer system. Objects have individual identities, characteristic behaviors, and (perhaps mutable) states. In software, an object can be represented by a combination of stored state and executable code.

object behavior   The effects of an object on the outcomes of the actions it takes part in and their effects on it.

package   A named container for a unit of development work. All development artifacts—including types, classes, compiled code, refinements, diagrams, documentation, change requests, code patches, architectural rules and patterns, tests, and other packages—are in a package. A package is treated as a unit for versioning, configuration management, reuse, dependency tracking, and so on. It also provides a scope for unique names of its elements.

package, nested   A package whose name is itself scoped within a containing package. The contained package implicitly imports its container.

package, virtual   A named package that informally denotes (as opposed to actually containing) a set of terms and definitions that you want to refer to from other packages. A virtual package can be "virtually" imported by a "real" package.

parameterized attribute   An attribute with parameters such as priceOf(Product). Its value is a function from a list of parameters to an object identity. Unlike an operation, it is used only as an ancillary part of a behavioral description and need not be implemented directly. A partial parameterized attribute has a precondition.

ports   The exposed interfaces that define the "plugs" and "sockets" of components: Those places at which the component offers access to its services and from which it accesses services of others. A plug can be coupled with any socket of a compatible type using a suitable connector.

provisions   A set of prerequisites associated with a framework; any elements substituted when applying this framework must meet the prerequisites in order for the framework to be applicable. Provisions are analogous to design-time preconditions.

quoted actions   A postcondition can refer to another action by naming it within brackets: [[action(...)]]. This is called quoting, and it means that the effect specified for that action is a part of this postcondition. If written as [[->action(...)]], then the action must actually be invoked as part of the postcondition; if further prefixed with <u>sent</u>, it indicates that an asynchronous invocation must be made.

redundant specs   A specification (including invariants and pre- and postconditions) that is implied by other parts of the model but is included for emphasis or clarity. Such specs are prefixed with a "/".

refinement   (1) A refinement (noun) is a more-detailed description that conforms to another (its abstraction). Everything said about the abstraction holds, perhaps in a somewhat different form, in the refinement.   (2) *Refinement*, or *refinement of*, is also used to mean the relationship between the abstract and detailed descriptions rather than to only the detailed description itself.   (3) Refine (verb) is to create a refinement; also called *design, implement*, or *specialize*.

retrieval   A function that determines the value of an abstract attribute from the stored implementation data (or otherwise detailed attributes); used with a conformance to show how the attributes map to the abstraction, as a prerequisite to showing how the behavior specifications are also met. Also called an *abstraction function*.

Reuse Law 1   Don't reuse implementation code unless you also intend to reuse the specification. Otherwise, you have no reason to believe that a revised version of the implementation won't break your code.

Reuse Lemmas   (1) If you reuse a specification, try a component-based approach: implement against the interface and defer binding to the implementation.   (2) Reuse of specifications leads to reuse of implementations. In particular, whenever you can implement standardized interfaces, whether domain-specific or for infrastructure services, you enable the reuse of all other implementations that follow those standards.   (3) Successful reuse needs thorough interface specifications.   (4) If you can "componentize" your problem domain descriptions themselves and reuse domain models, you greatly enhance your position to reuse interface specifications and implementations downstream.

scenario   A prototypical trace of interactions, showing a set of action occurrences starting from a known initial state. Usually described as narrative steps, with accompanying interaction diagrams, and accompanying snapshots of an evolving state.

sequence expression   A textual representation of temporal composition of actions; some can be translated into an equivalent state chart.

snapshot   A depiction (usually as a drawing) of a set of objects and the values of some of their attributes at a particular point in time.

specification type versus design type   A *specification type* is one that is introduced as a part of the type model of another type to help structure its attributes and effects in terms closer to the problem domain. The behaviors of the spec type are not themselves of external interest, and it may never be implemented directly.   A *design type*, in contrast, is one that participates directly in actions; its behaviors are of primary importance, and it is not just a means to factor the specification of some other type.

state   A Boolean attribute that is drawn on a state chart. The structure of the states defines invariants on those attributes (such as mutually exclusive states, inclusive states, or orthogonal states); additionally, you should write explicit invariants relating the state attributes to other attributes in the type model.

state chart   A graphical description of a set of states and transitions.

state transition   A partial specification of an action drawn as a directed edge on a state chart. The initial and final states are part of the pre- and postcondition in the spec, and additional pre/post specs are written textually on the transition.

state type   A set of objects defined by a predicate: Unlike a true type, objects can move into and out of it during their lives. The predicate is defined within a parent true type; for example, caterpillar is a state within lepidopter.

static invariant   A predicate that forms part of a type model and that should hold true on every permitted snapshot—specifically, before and after every action in the model. Some static invariants are written in text; other common ones, such as attribute types and associations as inverse attributes, have built-in notations.

static model A set of attributes, together with an invariant, constitutes the static part of a type model. The invariant says which combinations of attribute values make sense at any one time and includes constraints on the existence, ranges, types, and combinations of individual attributes.

stereotype A shorthand syntax for applying a framework; a stereotype is used by referring to its name as «name», attached to any model element. Frameworks provide an extensibility mechanism to the modeling language; stereotypes provide a syntax for using this mechanism.

subclass A class that inherits some of its implementation from its superclass(es).

subtype A type whose members form a subset of its supertype; all the specifications of the supertype are true of the subtype, which may add further specifications. (Note that we use *subclass* to mean inheritance of implementation.)

testing The activity of uncovering defects in an implementation by comparing its behavior against that of its specification under a given set of runtime stimuli (the *test cases* or *test data*). Any refinement can have corresponding tests.

traceability The ability to relate elements in a detailed description with the elements in an abstraction that motivate their presence and vice versa; the ability to relate implementation elements to requirements.

type A set of objects that conforms to a given type spec throughout their lives.

type constant A named member of the type—for example, 7 is a type constant of Integer. Type constants can be globally referred to by type_name.member_name.

type expression An expression denoting a type using set-like operators—for example, Women + Men.

type intersection A combination of two specifications, each of which must be fully observed (without restricting the other) by an object that belongs to the resulting type. The designer must guarantee each postcondition whenever its precondition is met regardless of the other's pre/post condition.

Type intersection—or subtyping—happens when a component or object must satisfy different clients. Each specification must be satisfied independently of the other. A type specification defines a set of instances: the objects that satisfy the spec. Subtyping is about forming the intersection of two sets: those objects that happen to satisfy both specifications.

type join A combination of two views of the same type; each view may impose its own restrictions on what the designer of the type must achieve (conjoining postconditions) or what a client must ensure (conjoining preconditions).

Joining happens when two views of the same type are presented in different places; they might be in the same package or imported from different ones. Joining is about building the text and drawings of a specification from various partial descriptions.

type spec A description of object behavior. It typically consists of a collection of action specs and a static model of attributes that help describe the effects of those actions. A type spec makes no statement about implementation.

unfolding   Depicting the results of an import, possibly including substitutions, in the context of the importing package with the appropriate elements substituted.

use case   A joint action with multiple participant objects that represent a meaningful business task, usually written in a structured narrative style. Like any joint action, a use case can be refined into a finer-grained sequence of actions. Traditionally, the refined sequence is described as a part of the use case itself; we recommend it be treated as a refinement even if the presentation be as a single template.

Bibliography

[Able] The ABLE Project. See: http://www.cs.cmu.edu/~able/.

[ADL] Assertion Definition Language. See: http://adl.opengroup.org/.

[Allen94] Allen, R., and D. Garlan. 1994. *Formal Connectors*. Carnegie-Mellon CMU-CS-94-115 Technical Report, March.

[America90] America, P. 1990. Parallel Object-Oriented Language with Inheritance and Subtyping. In *OOPSLA Proceedings '90*.

[Bass98] Bass, L., P. Clements, and R. Kazman. 1998. *Software Architecture in Practice*. Reading, Mass.: Addison Wesley Longman.

[Beringer97] Beringer, D. 1997. Scenario Modelling: Modelling Global Behaviour with Scenarios in Object-Oriented Analysis. Ph.D. thesis, Swiss Federal Institute of Technology, Lausanne. See also: http://lglwww.epfl.ch/Team/DBR/Thesis.html.

[Booch95] Booch, G. 1995. *Object-Oriented Analysis and Design with Applications, Second Edition*. Menlo Park, CA: Benjamin Cummings.

[Booch91] Booch, G. 1991. *Object-Oriented Design with Applications*. Menlo Park, CA: Addison-Wesley.

[Cheng84] Cheng, J. H., H. Barringer, and C. B. Jones. 1984. A logic covering undefinedness in program proofs. *Acta Informatica*, 21: 251–269.

[Cockburn98] Cockburn, A. 1998. *Surviving Object-Oriented Projects: A Manager's Guide*. Reading, Mass.: Addison Wesley Longman.

[Coleman93] Coleman, D., et al. 1993. *Object-Oriented Development: The Fusion Method*. Englewood Cliffs, N.J.: Prentice Hall.

[COM] The COM and COM+ Models. See: www.microsoft.com.

[Cook94] Cook, S., and J. Daniels. 1994. *Designing Object Systems: Object-Oriented Modeling with Syntrophy*. Englewood Cliffs, N.J.: Prentice Hall.

[CORBA] Common Object Request Broker Architecture. See: www.omg.org.

[de Champeaux93] de Champeaux, D., et al. 1993. *Object-Oriented System Development*. Reading, Mass.: Addison Wesley Longman.

[D'Souza93] D'Souza, D. 1993. A Comparison of OO Methods. *In OOPSLA Proceedings '93*. http://www.iconcomp.com/papers/comp/index.htm.

[D'Souza94] D'Souza, D. 1994. OMT Model Integration. Report on Object-Oriented Analysis and Design, September. See also URL: http://www.iconcomp.com/papers/omt4-model-integr/OMT4ModelIntegration.frm.html.

[D'Souza95a] D'Souza, D., and A. Wills. 1995. Catalysis: Practical rigor and refinement. In *Fusion in Real World*, edited by Coleman, D., et al. Englewood Cliffs, N.J.: Prentice Hall.

[D'Souza95b] D'Souza, D., and A. Wills. 1995. OOA/D and Corba/IDL: A Common Base. See: http://www.iconcomp.com/papers/omg-ooa-d/OMG-OOA-D-rfi.frm.html.

[D'Souza96a] D'Souza, D. 1996. Advanced Modeling and Design for Java Systems Using Catalysis. In *OOPSLA Proceedings '96*. See also: http://www.iconcomp.com/papers/modeling-design-for-java/index.htm.

[D'Souza96b] D'Souza, D. 1996. Interfaces, subtypes, and frameworks. *Journal of OO Programming*, 9(7). See also: http://www.iconcomp.com/papers/inter-frameworks/Col2.frm.html.

[D'Souza97a] D'Souza, D., and A. Wills. 1997. Types and classes—A language independent view. *Journal of OO Programming*, 10(1). See also: http://www.iconcomp.com/papers/Types-and-Classes/Col5.frm.html.

[D'Souza97b] D'Souza, D. 1997. Meaningful UML <<extensions>> using Catalysis. See: http://www.iconcomp.com/papers/stereotypes-and-extensions/stereotype-fworks.pdf.

[D'Souza98] D'Souza, D. 1998. Interfaces, collaborations, refinements, and frameworks in Catalysis. *Software Development*, March; *Journal of OO Programming*, May. See also: http://www.iconcomp.com/papers/catalysis-overview/catalysis-overview.pdf.

[EJB] Enterprise JavaBeans. See: www.javasoft.com.

[Embley91] Embley, D., et al. 1991. *Object-Oriented Systems Analysis: A Model-Driven Approach*. Englewood Cliffs, N.J.: Prentice Hall.

[Fowler97] Fowler, M. 1997. *Analysis Patterns: Reusable Object Models*. Reading, Mass.: Addison Wesley Longman.

[Fowler98] Fowler, M., and K. Scott. 1998. *UML Distilled: Applying the Standard Object Modeling Language*. Reading, Mass.: Addison Wesley Longman.

[Gamma95] Gamma, E., et al. 1995. *Design Patterns: Elements of Reusable Object-Oriented Software*. Reading, Mass.: Addison Wesley Longman.

[Goguen90] Goguen, J. A. and D. Wolfram. 1990. On Types and FOOPS. *Proceedings of Conference on Database Semantics*, July.

[Goldberg95] Goldberg, A., and K. S. Rubin. 1995. *Succeeding with Objects: Decision Frameworks for Project Management*. Reading, Mass.: Addison Wesley Longman.

[Gosling96] Gosling, J., et al. 1996. *The Java Language Specification*. Reading, Mass.: Addison Wesley Longman.

[Gregor97] Gregor, K. 1997. Aspect-Oriented Programming. See: http://www.parc.xerox.com/spl/projects/aop/.

[Gries95] Gries, D., and F. B. Schneider, Eds. 1995. *First-Order Logic and Automated Theorem Proving*, 2d ed. New York: Springer-Verlag.

[Guttag90] In Horning, J. J., and J. Guttag, 1990. Larch in five easy pieces, Digital SRC Research Report 5.

[Harrison93] Harrison, W., and H. Osher. 1993. Subject-Oriented Programming (A Critique of Pure Objects). In *OOPSLA Proceedings '93*.

[Helm90] Helm, Richard, I. M. Holland, and D. Gangopadhyay. 1990. Contracts: Specifying behavioral compositions in object-oriented systems. In *Proceedings of OOPSLA/ECOOP '90—Conference on Object-Oriented Programming Systems, Languages, and Application*, October, pp. 169–180.

[Holt83] Holt, A. W., H. R. Ramsey, and J. D. Grimes. 1983. Coordination system technology as the basis for a programming environment. *Electrical Communication*, 57(4).

[IDEF0] Integration Definition for Function Modeling. 1993 (Dec. 21). FIPS Publication No. 183, Computer Systems Laboratory, National Institute of Standards and Technology, Gaithersburg, MD.

[Jacobson92] Jacobson, I., et al. 1992. *Object-Oriented Software Engineering*. New York: ACM Press.

[Jacobson94] Jacobson, I. 1994. *The Object Advantage*. Reading, Mass.: Addison Wesley Longman.

[JacksonD95] Jackson, D. 1995. Structuring Z Specifications with Views. In *ACM Transactions on Software Engineering and Methodology*, October, pp. 365–389.

[JacksonM95] Jackson, M. 1995. Designations. In *Software Requirements and Specification: A Lexicon of Practice, Principles, and Prejudices*. Reading, Mass.: Addison Wesley Longman.

[Jackson96] Jackson, M., with Pamela Zave. 1996. Where do operations come from? A multiparadigm specification technique. *IEEE Transactions on Software Engineering*, 22(7):508–528.

[Johnson91] Johnson, R., and V. Russo. 1991. Reusing Object-Oriented Designs. University of Illinois, TR UMCDCS 91-1696.

[Jones86] Jones, C. B. 1986. *Systematic Software Development Using VDM*. Englewood Cliffs, N.J.: Prentice Hall.

[Jones93] Jones, C. B. 1993. An Object-Based Design Method for Concurrent Programs. Manchester University, TR UMCS-92-12-1.

[Jordan97] Jordan, M., and M. Van De Vanter. 1997. Modular System Building with Java Packages. In *Proceedings Eighth Conference on Software Engineering Environments*, pp. 155-163. Cottbus, Germany, 8–9 April.

[Knuth84] Knuth, D. 1984. Literate Programming. *The Computer Journal*, 27(2): 97–111.

[Kurki-Suonio90] Kurki-Suonio, R., et al. 1990. Object-Oriented Specification of Reactive Systems. In *Proceedings of the International Conference of Software Engineering*.

[Lano95] Lano, K. 1995. *Formal Object-Oriented Development*. New York: Springer.

[Larman97] Larman, C. 1997. *Applying UML and Patterns: An Approach to Object-Oriented Analysis and Design*. Englewood Cliffs, N.J.: Prentice Hall.

[Lea95] Lea, D., and J. Marlowe. 1995. PSL: Protocols and Pragmatics for Open Systems. In *Proceedings ECOOP '95* .

[Lea97] Lea, D. 1997. *Concurrent Programming in Java: Design Principles and Patterns*. Reading, Mass.: Addison Wesley Longman.

[Liskov91] Liskov, B., and J. Wing. 1991. Type conformance. In *Proceedings ECOOP '91*. New York: Springer.

[Logic91] See, for example, Jones, C. B., et al. 1991. *MURAL: A Formal Development Support System*. New York: Springer.

[Luckham95] Luckham, D. C., J. J. Kenney, L. M. Augustin, J. Vera, D. Bryan, and W. Mann. 1995. Specification and analysis of system architecture using Rapide. *IEEE Transactions on Software Engineering*, 21(4).

[Manna92] Manna, Z., and A. Pnueli. *The Temporal Logic of Reactive and Concurrent Systems: Specification*. New York: Springer-Verlag.

[Martin95] Martin, R. 1995. *Designing Object-Oriented Applications Using the Booch Method*. Englewood Cliffs, N.J.: Prentice Hall.

[McConnell96] McConnell, S. 1996. *Rapid Development: Taming Wild Software Schedules*. Redmond, Wash.: Microsoft Press.

[Meyer88] Meyer, B. 1988. *Object-Oriented Software Construction*. Englewood Cliffs, N.J.: Prentice Hall.

[Mikhajlova97] Mikhajlova, A., and E. Sekerinski. 1997. Class Refinement and Interface Refinement in Object-Oriented Programs. See: http://ece.eng.mcmaster.ca/faculty/sekerinski/classinterfaceref/fme97.ps.gz.

[Mural91] Jones. C.B., et al. 1991. *MURAL: A Formal Development Support System*. New York: Springer.

[Nerson94] Nerson, J., and K. Walden. 1994. *Seamless Object-Oriented Architecture: Analysis and Design of Reliable Systems*. Englewood Cliffs, N.J.: Prentice Hall.

[Odell92] Odell, J. J., with J. Martin. 1991. *Object-Oriented Analysis and Design*. Englewood Cliffs, N.J.: Prentice Hall.

[PLoP] 1995–1998. *Pattern Languages of Program Design* conference series. Reading, Mass.: Addison Wesley Longman.

[Reenskaug95] Reenskaug, T., P. Wold, and O. A. Lehne. 1995. *Working with Objects: The OOram Software Engineering Method*. Greenwich, CT: Manning Publications.

[Reil96] Reil, A. J. 1996. *Object-Oriented Design Heuristics*. Reading, Mass.: Addison Wesley Longman.

[Rumbaugh91] Rumbaugh, J., et al. 1991. *Object-Oriented Modeling and Design*. Englewood Cliffs, N.J.: Prentice Hall.

[Rummler90] Rummler, G. A., and A. P. Brache. 1990. *Improving Performance—How to Manage the White-Space on the Organization Chart*. San Francisco: Jossey-Bass.

[Saini96] Saini, A., and D. Musser. 1996. *STL Tutorial and Reference Guide: C++ Programming with the Standard Template Library*. Reading, Mass.: Addison Wesley Longman.

[Selic94] Selic, B., et al. 1994. *Real-Time Object-Oriented Modeling*. New York: John Wiley and Sons.

[Shaw96a] Shaw, M., and D. Garlan. 1996. *Software Architecture: Perspectives on an Emerging Discipline*. Englewood Cliffs, N.J.: Prentice Hall.

[Shaw96b] Shaw, M., and D. Garlan. 1996. Formulations and Formalisms in Software Architecture. In *Computer Science Today: Recent Trends and Developments*, pp. 307–323, Jan van Leeuwen, Ed. New York: Springer-Verlag.

[Shlaer88] Shlaer, S., and S. Mellor. 1988. *Object-Oriented Systems Analysis: Modeling the World of Data*. Englewood Cliffs, N.J.: Prentice Hall.

[Shlaer92] Shlaer, S., and S. Mellor. 1992. *Object Life Cycles: Modeling the World in States*. Englewood Cliffs, N.J.: Prentice Hall.

[STL96] Standard Template Library, Programmer's Guide. See: http://www.sgi.com/Technology/STL/.

[Spivey92] Spivey, J. M. 1992. *The Z Notation*. Englewood Cliffs, N.J.: Prentice Hall.

[Stapleton97] Stapleton, J. 1997. *DSDM: Dynamic Systems Development Method*. Reading, Mass.: Addison Wesley Longman.

[Szyperski98] Szyperski, C. 1998. *Component Software: Beyond Object-Oriented Programming*. Reading, Mass.: Addison Wesley Longman.

[Taligent94] Taligent, Inc. 1994. *Taligent's Guide to Designing Programs: Well-Managed Object-Oriented Design in C++*. Reading, Mass.: Addison Wesley Longman.

[UML] UML specs, OMG Web site. See: http://www.omg.org.

[Utting92] Utting, M. 1992. An Object-Oriented Refinement Calculus with Modular Reasoning, Ph.D. thesis, University of New South Wales, Kensington, Australia. See also: http://www.cs.waikato.ac.nz/~marku/phd.ps.gz.

[Wills91] Wills, A. C. 1991. Application of Formal Methods to OO Programming. Ph.D. thesis. See: http://www.trireme.com/catalysis/fresco/specific.pdf.

[Wills93] Wills, A. 1993. Refinement in Fresco. In *Case Studies in OO Refinement*, K. Lano, Ed. Englewood Cliffs, N.J.: Prentice Hall. See also: http://www.trireme.com/fresco/refinement.pdf.

[Wills95a] Wills, A. C. 1995. Abstract Realism. In *Object Expert*. See: http://www.trireme.com/trireme/papers/20absreal/.

[Wills95b] Wills, A. C. 1995. Conform or die. In *Object Expert*. See: http://www.trireme.com/catalysis/3conform.pdf.

[Wills96a] Wills, A. C. 1996. Tricks with traits. In *Object Expert*. See: http://www.trieme.com.

[Wills96b] Wills, A. C. 1996. Frameworks and component-based development. In *Proceedings of OO Information Systems.*

[Wills97a] Wills, A. C., and D. D'Souza. 1997. Models and code: The connection. In *Handbook of Object Technology*. See: http://www.trireme.com/catalysis/refinement2.pdf.

[Wills97–98] Wills, A. C. 1997, 1998. Components: Principles and Process. Paper presented at Unicom Seminar (London, 1997) and OT98 (Oxford, 1998). See also: http://www.trireme.com/catalysis/cbdppt/.

[Wirfs-Brock90] Wirfs-Brock, R., B. Wilkerson, and L. Wiener. 1990. *Designing Object-Oriented Software*. Englewood Cliffs, N.J.: Prentice Hall.

[Wong93] Wong, W. 1993. *Plug and Play Programming*. New York: M&T.

Index ════════════════════════════

specifying effects abstractly, 125–126
Factoring of code, framework *vs.* traditional
approach to reuse, 461–463, 464
Factory
and decoupling, 265
to localize creation of new objects, 474
Factory class, 675
Factory-floor schedulers, and application
architecture, 520, 525
Factory objects, 31
Facts and rules, in package, 290
Failover behaviors, and Enterprise JavaBean
tier, 498
Failover mechanism, 496
Failure conditions, 333
Failure indications, guaranteed, 334, 335
False & b operator, 68
Family trees, and recursive composite pattern,
567
Fan-out, and component architectures, 414
Fault Management, in BluePhone, 302
Feature appearance, in package, 291
Features, in dictionary, 291
Federated architecture, 442–443
Federated schemes, benefits of, 407–408
Federation, benefits of, 443
Filled arrow, for property connector, 418
"Film strip" metaphor, 707
Final class, 146
findCustomer action, in requirements spec, 432
findOrderdispatches action, 440
findProduct action, in requirements spec, 432
Fine-grained actions, 157, 181, 300, 592
Fine-grained use cases, 167
Flag variables, 678
Flat files, 501
and objects, 501
Flat sets, 91
and Catalysis, 699
and object model navigation, 706
"Flat" state diagrams, 126
Flexibility, 154
constraints, 276
and decoupling, 25–29, 277
with federated scheme, 407
improvements in, 278
and partitioning components, 639

and two-way links, 670
Flowcharts, and recursive composite pattern,
567
FOOP
contributions from, 711
and framework provisions, 711
generic parameters of, 148
Footnotes, in narrative of package, 291
Foreign keys, 437
Forest project (Sun), 710
Formal definitions, 291
Formal descriptions, 68–70
purpose of, 70
Formal diagrams, in packages, 291
Formal functional requirements models, 17
Formalism, and life expectancy of product, 514
Formalization
and state charts, 605
and vocabulary, 602
Formalized model, 569–570
and dictionary, 706
of video case study, 570
Formalized refined use case specs, for video
business, 577–579
Formal justification, 272
Formally defined types, and dictionary, 76
Formal notation, 189
Formal postconditions, and system action
specification, 600
Formal preconditions, and system action
specification, 600
Forté, 408, 649
Forwarding
explicit, 477
and polymorphism, 473
Forward slash (/)
for derived attributes, 72
for postconditions, 576
Fountain, and spiral model, 513
Fowler, Martin, 705, 711, 713
Frames, in artificial intelligence subculture, 274
Framework applications, 342
defined, 344
unfolding, 351
Framework models, generic, 444
Framework provisions, 711